The Best Book of Microsoft Word for Windows

RELATED TITLES

The Best Book of Microsoft® Word 5
Kate Miller Barnes

The First Book of PFS®: First Publisher™
Karen Brown and Robert Bixby
(forthcoming)

The First Book of Ami
Judi N. Fernandez and Ruth Ashley
(forthcoming)

The First Book of Microsoft® Word 5
Brent Heslop and David Angell

The First Book of Q & A
Brent Heslop and David Angell
(forthcoming)

The Best Book of Microsoft® Word for the Macintosh®
Rob Krumm

The First Book of PC Tools™ Deluxe
Gordon McComb

The Best Book of Harvard Graphics
John P. Mueller
(forthcoming)

The Best Book of Peachtree Complete® III
Neil Salkind and Linda Flanders

The Best Book of: DOS
Alan Simpson

The Best Book of: Lotus® 1-2-3®, Third Edition, Release 2.2
Alan Simpson

Understanding Microsoft® Word 4 for the Macintosh®
Richard Swadley

The Best Book of Microsoft® Windows 3
Carl Townsend
(forthcoming)

The First Book of The Norton Utilities
Joseph Wikert
(forthcoming)

The Best Book of Microsoft® Works 2.0 for the PC, Second Edition
Ruth K. Witkin

The Best Book of Professional® Write and File
Douglas Wolf and Joe Kraynak

For the retailer nearest you, or to order directly from the publisher, call 800-257-5755. International orders telephone 609-461-6500.

The Best Book of
Microsoft Word for Windows

Richard K. Swadley

HOWARD W. SAMS & COMPANY
A Division of Macmillan, Inc.
11711 North College, Suite 141, Carmel, IN 46032 USA

© 1990 by Richard Swadley

FIRST EDITION
FIRST PRINTING—1990

All rights reserved. No part of this book shall be reproduced, stored in a retrieval system, or transmitted by any means, electronic, mechanical, photocopying, recording, or otherwise, without written permission from the publisher. No patent liability is assumed with respect to the use of the information contained herein. Although every precaution has been taken in the preparation of this book, the publisher and author assume no responsibility for errors or omissions. Neither is any liability assumed for damages resulting from the use of the information contained herein.

International Standard Book Number: 0-672-48468-4
Library of Congress Catalog Card Number: 90-60977

Acquisitions Editor: *James S. Hill*
Development Editor: *Scott Arant*
Manuscript Editor: *Don MacLaren*
Production Coordinator: *Becky Imel*
Cover Art: *DGS & D Advertising, Inc.*
Cover Photography: *Cassell Productions, Inc.*
Indexer: *Hilary Adams*
Technical Reviewer: *Peter Shirley*
Production: *Brad Chinn, Sally Copenhaver, Denny Hager, Bill Hurley, Jodi Jensen, Lori Lyons, Jennifer Matthews, Dennis Sheehan, Bruce Steed, Mary Beth Wakefield, Nora Westlake*

Printed in the United States of America

In memory of Don Hageman, whose love and wisdom enriched the lives of his family. The best people that we will become is the result of being guided by his hand. We owe him more than can be said in these simple words. He lives in our memory—with love, the family.

Overview

***Part 1* The Basics, 1**
1. Introducing Word for Windows, 3
2. Creating Documents, 51
3. Editing Your Documents, 89
4. Formatting Your Document, 129
5. Formatting Paragraphs, 147
6. Formatting Characters, 187
7. Formatting Complex Documents, 209
8. Printing Essentials, 239

***Part 2* Adding and Polishing Word, 273**
9. Running Heads and Feet, 275
10. Checking Spelling and Using the Thesaurus and Hyphenation, 301
11. Using Word's Tables and Math Features, 327
12. Using Word's Glossary, 363
13. Using Style Sheets, 379
14. Using Annotations and Revisions, 395
15. Working With Files, 415

***Part 3* Advanced Word, 437**
16. Using Form Letters, 439
17. Using the Outlining Feature, 465
18. Adding Tables of Contents, Indexes, or Footnotes, 485

19. Customizing Word and Using Macros, 511
20. Working with Pictures, 537

Appendix A **Installing Word for Windows, 559**
Appendix B **Keyboard Commands, 567**

Contents

Introduction······xxiii

PART ONE

The Basics······1
1. Introducing Word for Windows······3
Starting Word······4
    Starting Word from the DOS System Prompt······4
    Starting Word from within Windows······6
The Word Screen······6
    The Document Window······8

The Control Menu	12
The Menu Bar	14
The Different Views of Word	14
Using the Keyboard	19
The Enter Key	23
The Spacebar	24
The Caps Lock Key	24
The Shift Key	25
The Tab Key	25
The Function Keys	25
The Direction Keys and the Numeric Keypad	25
The Backspace Key	26
Using the Mouse	27
Accessing Menus and Choosing Commands	28
Choosing Commands with the Keyboard	28
Choosing Commands with the Mouse	29
Choosing Subcommands in a Dialog Box	30
Exploring the Menus	30
Short Menus vs. Full Menus	31
The Document Control Menu	31
The File Menu	32
The Edit Menu	32
The Insert Menu	34
The Format Menu	34
The Utilities Menu	34
The Macro Menu	35
The Window Menu	35
The Help Menu	35
The View Menu	36
Using Windows	40
Activating a Window	41
Closing a Window	41
Changing a Window's Size	41
Splitting a Window	43
Getting Help	44
Quitting Word	46
Review	47

2. Creating Documents — 51

Introduction to Word Processing — 52
    Basic Concepts of Word Processing and Tips for Using It — 52

Entering Text — 54
    Typing Some Text — 54
    Creating Paragraphs — 55
    Creating Letterheads and Salutations — 57

Moving Around Your Screen — 57
    Using the Mouse to Navigate Your Documents — 58
    Using the Keyboard to Navigate Your Documents — 59
    Using the Go To Command — 60
    Clearing Your Screen — 61
    Some Final Thoughts on Entering Text — 63

Introducing Files and File Names — 64

Saving Your Documents — 66
    Saving to an Existing Document — 71
    Saving Files As Backups — 72
    Saving Documents Automatically — 72
    Saving Documents to a Different File, Disk Drive, or Directory — 73
    Saving Documents with Different File Formats — 75
    Some Final Tips on Saving — 77

Retrieving Your Document — 78
    Opening a Recently Opened Document — 79
    Navigating Through and Choosing Different Directories — 81

Typing and Printing Your First Letter — 82
    Remember to Save Your Work! — 84
    Printing Your First Letter — 85

Review — 87

3. Editing Your Documents — 89

Selecting Text Before You Edit — 89
    Selecting Text with a Mouse — 90
    Selecting Text with the Keyboard — 91
    Extending Your Selection — 91

Editing Text	93
Remember the Backspace Key	93
Typing vs. Replacing	94
Using the Edit Menu	94
Cut, Copy, and Paste	95
Practice Inserting and Deleting Text	97
Deleting Text with Cut	98
Block Editing	100
Moving Text Around with Cut and Paste	101
Copying Text from One Document to Another	104
Using Move to and Copy to: The Clipboard Exception	106
Undoing Your Commands	110
Searching and Replacing Text	111
Using the Search Command	111
Using Go To for Searching	114
Using the Replace Command	116
Some Final Thoughts about Searching and Replacing Text	122
Editing in Windows	122
Review	125
4. Formatting Your Document	**129**
Introduction to Formatting	130
Introducing the Format Menu	131
Using the Document Command	133
The Document Window Control Buttons	135
Setting Margins	135
Using the Ruler to Change Margins	136
Using Print Preview to Change Margins	138
Using the Document Command to Change Margins	139
Changing Page Layout with Line and Page Breaks	143
Setting Line Breaks	143
Setting Page Breaks	143
Widow Control	144
Review	145

5. Formatting Paragraphs — 147
Introduction to Formatting Paragraphs — 147
Using the Ruler — 148
    The Different Views of the Ruler — 149
    What the Ruler Contains — 150
    How to Use the Ruler — 153
Setting Alignment — 154
Setting Spacing — 157
Setting Indentation — 161
    Using the Mouse to Set Indents — 162
    Using the Keyboard to Set Indents — 163
    Using the Paragraph Command to Set Indents — 164
    Indenting Shortcuts — 166
    Creating Hanging Indents — 167
Setting Tabs — 169
    Setting Tabs with the Ruler and Mouse — 170
    Setting Tabs with Keys — 170
    Setting Tabs with the Tabs Command — 171
Using the Paragraph Command — 176
    Paragraph Spacing from the Paragraph Dialog Box — 178
    Check Boxes for Aligning Paragraphs — 180
    Setting Borders — 182
Review — 184

6. Formatting Characters — 187
Introducing Character Formatting — 187
    Common Word Typography — 187
    Types of Character Formatting — 189
    What You See Is What You Print — 189
Applying Character Formatting — 190
    Using the Ribbon and Mouse — 191
    Using the Keys — 194
    Using the Character Command — 194
A Designing Exercise — 203
Review — 206

The Best Book of Word for Windows

7.	**Formatting Complex Documents**	**209**
	Using the Section Command	209
	Creating a Section	212
	Creating Multicolumn Text	215
	Setting Line Numbers	222
	Using the Position Command	224
	Deleting the Absolute Positioning	228
	Working with Bound Documents	228
	Using Page View	232
	Working in Page View	233
	The Page View Screen	233
	Selecting and Editing Text in Page View	234
	Navigating Around Page View	235
	Review	236
8.	**Printing Essentials**	**239**
	Introduction to Printing with Word	239
	The Basics of Setting Up Your Printer	241
	Setting Up Printing Capability	242
	Installing Your Printer Driver	242
	Connecting Your Printer to Your Computer	244
	Choosing Another Printer	247
	Deleting a Printer	248
	Using the Printer Setup Command	248
	Orientation	250
	Using the Print Command	252
	Word's Printing Options	253
	Printing the Entire Working Document	256
	Printing Specific Pages of Your Document	257
	Printing Selected Text Only	257
	Printing Multiple Copies	258
	Printing from Find on the File Menu	258
	Working While You Print	260
	Printing Hidden Text	262
	The Paper Feed Option	263
	Using the Include Option	264
	Canceling Printing	265

Printing Problems	266
Using Print Preview	267
Review	271

P A R T

Adding and Polishing Word — 273

9. Running Heads and Feet — 275

Creating a Header or Footer	276
Entering Text in a Header	278
Formatting a Header	279
Adding Page Numbers, Times, and Dates to Headers	281
Using the Icon Bar	281
Using Insert Page Numbers	284
Formatting Page Numbers	285
Deleting Page Numbers	287
Positioning Headers and Footers	287
Vertical Positioning: Adding Space Above or Below a Header	288
Horizontal Positioning: Headers and Footers in the Margins Area	289
Creating Different Headers and Footers by Section	290
Creating Headers and Footers on Facing Pages	292
The First Page Option	294
The Link To Previous Button	206
Deleting Headers and Footers	296
Storing Headers in the Glossary	297
Review	299

10. Checking Spelling and Using the Thesaurus and Hyphenation — 301

Using a Spelling Checker	302
Word's Dictionaries	303

Checking Spelling with the Main Dictionary	303
Touring the Initial Spelling Dialog Box	306
Touring the Second Spelling Box	307
Correcting Misspelled Words	307
Using Word's Suggestions for Correcting Words	310
Correcting Repeated Misspellings	310
Continuing and Stopping the Spelling Check	311
Checking Single Words and Sections	311
Building and Working with User Dictionaries	311
Adding Personal Terms to a User Dictionary	313
Deleting and Revising Words in a User Dictionary	314
Saving New User Dictionaries	314
Using the Thesaurus	315
Using Hyphenation	317
The Hyphenate Command	318
Which Hyphen Type	321
Using the Hyphenate Command	323
Undoing Hyphenation	324
Review	325
11. Using Word's Tables and Math Features	**327**
Introducing Tables	327
Creating Tables	329
Inserting Text	331
Changing Existing Text to a Table	332
Editing Tables	336
Making Your Selection First	336
Inserting and Deleting Rows and Columns	337
Cutting, Copying, and Pasting Tables	341
Formatting Tables	341
Resizing Rows, Columns, and Cells	343
Building a Table with a Consistent Height	344
Formatting with Decimals	345
Adding Borders	348
Aligning and Positioning Tables	348
Sorting Tables	348
Creating Side-by-Side Paragraphs	351

	Doing Math	351
	Doing Math in Columns	352
	Setting Up a Spreadsheet in a Table	353
	Doing Mathematical Formulas	357
	Review	360

12. Using Word's Glossary — 363
Introducing Glossaries — 363
    Understanding How Word's Glossary Works — 364
Creating and Inserting Glossary Entries — 365
    Inserting a Glossary Entry in Text — 367
    Inserting Entries with the Keyboard — 368
Deleting Glossary Entries — 369
Printing the Glossary — 370
Review — 370

13. Using Style Sheets — 373
Introducing Style Sheets — 373
    Understanding the Basics — 375
    Automatic Styles — 377
    Defining Styles — 379
Using and Applying Styles — 384
    Method 1—Using the Ruler and Mouse to Apply a Style — 386
    Method 2—Using the Format Styles Command to Apply Styles — 387
    Method 3—Using the Style Key to Apply a Style — 388
Editing Styles — 388
    Deleting a Style — 389
    Changing a Style Name — 389
    Changing the Formatting of the Style — 390
    Merging Styles — 391
Printing Style Sheets — 392
Review — 393

14. Using Annotations and Revisions — 395
Creating and Using Annotations — 396
    Opening and Closing Annotation Panes — 399

Navigating Between Annotations Marks	399
Moving Between Annotation Marks and Annotation Panes	401
Reading Annotations	402
Editing Annotations	403
Moving Annotation Text	403
Deleting Annotations	403
Locking and Unlocking Documents	404
Printing Annotations	404
Creating and Using Revision Marks	405
Turning Off Revision-Marking	408
Searching for, Accepting, and Removing Revision Marks	409
Comparing Two Different Versions of a Document	412
Review	413
15. Working with Files	**415**
File Handling and Management	416
Using a Hard Disk	417
Introducing Document Retrieval	418
Using and Updating the Summary Sheet	421
Searching for Documents	422
Loading a Document	428
Opening and Printing Multiple Documents	428
Deleting Documents	430
Using Document Templates	430
Creating Document Templates	431
Editing in a Template	433
Changing Styles in a Template	434
Customizing Keys and Menus	434
Review	435

PART three

Advanced Word — 437

16. Using Form Letters — 439
- Introducing Form Letters — 439
- Preparing Documents for Merging — 440
  - Creating the Main Document — 440
  - Creating the Data Document — 444
- Printing Form Letters — 447
- Fill-In Form Letters — 450
- Creating Mailing Labels — 454
  - Creating the Data Document for Mailing Labels — 454
  - Using Label Templates for Printing — 456
- Review — 462

17. Using the Outlining Feature — 465
- Introducing the Outline View — 465
- Creating an Outline — 470
- Collapsing and Expanding the Outline — 473
- Reorganizing Your Outline — 475
- Numbering and Renumbering Your Outlines — 478
  - Automatic Numbering — 478
  - Manual Numbering — 480
- Printing Outlines — 482
- Review — 482

18. Adding Tables of Contents, Indexes, or Footnotes — 485
- Adding Tables of Contents — 485
  - Creating Tables of Contents — 486
  - Creating Tables of Items — 493

Creating Indexes		496
Cross-References and Multiple-Level Index Entries		499
Compiling and Inserting the Index		502
Deleting and Saving Indexes		503
Creating Footnotes		503
Editing Footnotes		505
Deleting Footnotes		506
How and Where a Footnote Appears		506
Using Bookmarks		506
Creating a Bookmark		507
Jumping to a Bookmark		508
Editing and Deleting Bookmarks		508
Review		509
19.	**Customizing Word and Using Macros**	**511**
Preferences to Suit You		511
Reviewing the Customize Command		513
Introducing Macros		516
Using and Running Word's Supplied Macros		516
Creating New Macros		518
Planning and Recording a Macro		519
Running and Testing Your Macros		523
Editing a Macro		524
Renaming Your Macro		525
Assigning Your Macro to a Menu		527
Deleting a Macro		529
Customizing Existing Menus and Keys		529
The Assign To Key Command		531
Review		533
20.	**Working with Pictures**	**537**
Working with Pictures		537
Pasting and Inserting Pictures in Your Documents		538
Inserting Blank Picture Frames or TIFF Graphic Files		542
Changing the Size of a Picture		544
Cropping and Scaling a Picture with a Mouse		544

	Using Format Picture to Crop or Scale	546
	Drawing Borders Around Your Pictures	548
Positioning Pictures		549
Adding Captions		551
Deleting Pictures		552
Using Paste Link		554
Linking with Spreadsheets		556
Review		557

Appendixes

A.	**Installing Word for Windows**	559
B.	**Keyboard Commands**	567

Index   577

Introduction

At the beginning of 1990, Microsoft released the latest version of its best-selling word processor—Word for Windows. More than "just another word processor" for cranking out simple letters and memos, this powerful "document processor" can handle almost any type of document task you throw at it. Developed to run under Microsoft's Windows operating environment, or without it, Word for Windows offers many powerful features not found in other products. Here is a list of just some of the things that you can do with Word for Windows, as well as the related chapters where you will find the step-by-step instructions:

- Mix text, pictures, graphics, charts, and tables of information quickly and easily. You can even position the text, pictures, and tables anywhere in your document as objects and then flow text around them. (See Chapter 7 for creating complex documents and Chapter 20 for working with pictures.)
- Use five different "views" to look at your documents. Among these options is Page View, which allows you to see exactly how your pages will look before they are printed. You can also use Word's Print Preview feature to take a "sneak peek" at your document's overall structure and page layout. (See Chapter 8 for more information on using Page View and Print Preview.)
- Organize and rearrange the elements of documents with another of Word's five views—Outline View. Particularly handy for long and complex documents, you can easily rearrange the structure of a document by moving the document's individual headings with a few keystrokes or clicks of the mouse. It's also useful for quickly navigating your way around a complex document. (See Chapter 17 for working with Outline View.)

- Create document templates that allow you to produce routine documents that you can modify to suit your needs. With document templates, you can also customize Word's menus and key assignments to reflect your own working methods. (See Chapter 15 for creating document templates and Chapter 19 for customizing Word.)

- Create tables of information and side-by-side paragraphs quickly and easily. You tell Word about the dimensions of a table (columns, rows, height of table, and so on) and then insert or delete information without worrying about adjusting the table's alignment. You can even create a simple "electronic spreadsheet" to tabulate the numbers placed in a table. (See Chapter 11 on using Word's table feature.)

- Globally format your documents at the document level (e.g., setting margins); at the paragraph level (e.g., setting line spacing, alignment, tabs); at the section level (setting the number of columns in a complex document); or at the lowest document level, the individual character. You can change fonts, the size of fonts, or even the spacing between characters. To simplify formatting, you can use Word's styles feature to capture the "look" of a paragraph or of an entire document. Word's flexibility allows you to apply those "looks" as style sheets for new documents. (Chapters 4–7 discuss the different levels of formatting while Chapter 13 discusses creating and using style sheets.)

- Use Word's glossary to store text or graphics you commonly use and to quickly retrieve and insert them into your documents. (Word's glossary is discussed in Chapter 12.)

- Use some of Word's standard utilities—Spelling, Thesaurus, and Hyphenation—to add further polish to your documents. (All three utilities are discussed in Chapter 10.)

- Insert "fields of instructions" into your documents that direct Word to insert special elements, such as tables of contents, indexes, graphics, and whole files of information. (See Chapter 18 for creating tables of contents and indexes.)

- Create form mailings with Word's print merge feature. (See Chapter 16.)

- Add footnotes with a few keystrokes or clicks of the mouse. (See Chapter 18 for more information on creating footnotes.)

- Allow reviewers to add annotations to a document. Use Word's revision features to mark and "redline" changes to a document, or to compare two versions of the same document. (See Chapter 14.)

Introduction

- Use Word's powerful document retrieval feature to quickly search and find particular documents by author, date, subject, title, key words, or any text that you specify in summary sheets defining each document. (See Chapter 15.)
- Create and edit macros which automate a sequence of tasks. You can assign these macros to specific menus or keys for quick access. (See Chapter 19 on creating macros.)
- Create mathematical and scientific equations. (See Chapter 11 for using Word's table and math features.)
- Add numbers to pages or to individual document lines. (See Chapter 9 for adding page numbers in a header or footer.)
- Open documents created in different file formats, including: WordPerfect, DOS Word, WordStar, MultiMate Advantage, and Word for the Macintosh in Rich Text Format. (See Chapter 2 for opening documents.)
- Import text from spreadsheets, such as Microsoft Excel or Lotus 1-2-3, and create direct links to quickly update the information. (See Chapter 20 for linking information from spreadsheets.)

Who This Book Is For

Word for Windows is designed to create almost any type of document. You can easily create letters, memos, reports, newsletters, and more. Although all major features of this rich word processing program are introduced, this book is for beginning to intermediate users of Word for Windows. No knowledge of computers, or prior experience with Word for Windows or other word processing programs, is required to use this book.

Once you have mastered many of Word's powerful features, you'll find this book serves as a handy reference to the procedures required to complete the tasks for which you use your computer. If you're just starting out, please feel comfortable and let this book be your guide.

Where do you begin? If you are new to Word for Windows, please read the first three chapters in Part 1, The Basics. These chapters discuss the fundamentals of word processing, starting Word for Windows, and preparations for your first document. The remaining chapters in Part 1 start you creating, editing, formatting, and printing simple letters and memos to more complex documents, such as newsletters. If you are a more experienced Word user, you might want to jump to the section that you wish to review first or just use the Quick Guide (on inside front cover) to navigate your way around this book. Parts 2 and 3 cover most of the advanced and specialized features of Word. Each chapter in these sections can stand alone and will guide you in easy-to-follow stepped lists that show you how to accomplish your specific tasks.

Features of This Book

This book offers several features and design elements to help you master Word easily and to find information quickly. These features include:

- Step-by-step instructions for creating documents that range from simple letters and memos to complex newsletters and reference reports. Hands-on examples reinforce your knowledge while providing sample documents that you can modify to suit your own needs.
- Chapter summaries to help you remember important techniques and procedures.
- Quick Guide inside the covers to provide instant reference to the most common word processing operations.
- Margin notes that provide tips, hints, and reminders.
- Contents listings at the beginning of each chapter for easy reference.

How to Use This Book

- Text that you are to type at the keyboard is set off from the instructions in bold monospace like this:

    `Using Word for Windows is fun.`

    Enter the text exactly as shown, including spaces and special characters. Menu selections and commands you can choose with a mouse are also printed in boldface.
- Many keys are listed by name: Enter, Shift, Esc (for Escape), and F10 (the function key) are examples.
- Some commands require that you hold down one or more keys while you press another key. Such combination keypresses are

indicated by the plus (+) sign. Don't type the plus, however. For example:

Shift+F10

means hold down the Shift key while pressing the F10 key once, and

Ctrl+Shift+F10

means hold down both the Ctrl and Shift keys while pressing the F10 key once. If a key combination is given in parentheses, don't press the parenthesis characters.

- If you are to press more than one key in succession (pressing each key and releasing), the sequence of keys will be separated by a comma. For example:

  Alt,F

  means press and release the Alt key and then the F key, and

  Alt,F,P

  means press and release the Alt key, press and release the F key, and press and release the P key. Don't type the commas.

- Most Word for Windows commands appear on the screen with a key command letter underlined (for example, File). When they *first* appear in text, these commands will appear with the letter underlined. Thereafter, they will appear without the underline (File). In numbered instructions, however, the key command letter will be underlined.

- Numbered instructions will include both mouse instructions and related keypresses, each in bold. Following each instruction, a description of what's happening on the screen will appear as well. For example:

  1. Choose the **Exit** command from the File menu: **Alt,F,X**. Word asks if you wish to save the changes to the current document.

- DOS and Windows' file names are shown in all capital letters. For example:

  WIN.INI

- Word uses three ellipsis points after some of its command names to indicate you will have additional options with that command. *Preferences...* is an example. This book does not reproduce the ellipses.

Acknowledgements

Many thanks to those people who made this book possible: including Scott Arant, Marie Butler-Knight, and my editor, Don MacLaren, who always makes a book better. Also thanks to Microsoft's Tanya VanDam and Peter Shirley of P & S Enterprises for help in reviewing the manuscript for accuracy. And of course, thanks to Janet and Cameron whose tireless patience and love is much appreciated.

Trademarks

All terms mentioned in this book that are known to be trademarks or service marks are listed below. In addition, terms suspected of being trademarks or service marks have been appropriately capitalized. Howard W. Sams & Company cannot attest to the accuracy of this information. Use of a term in this book should not be regarded as affecting the validity of any trademark or service mark.

EPSON is a registered trademark of Seiko Epson Corporation.

IBM and IBM AT are registered trademarks and PS/2 is a trademark of International Business Machines Corporation.

Lotus and 1-2-3 are registered trademarks of Lotus Development Corporation.

Macintosh is a registered trademark of Macintosh Library, Inc., licensed by Apple Computer, Inc.

Microsoft and MS-DOS are registered trademarks and Microsoft Excel is a trademark of Microsoft Corporation.

PART

The Basics

O N E

Introducing Word for Windows

In this chapter:

- Starting Word
- The Word Screen
- The Different Views of Word
- Using the Keyboard
- Using the Mouse
- Accessing Menus and Choosing Commands
- Exploring the Menus
- Using Windows
- Getting Help
- Quitting Word

This chapter discusses how to start Word and introduces the Word screen. You will learn the basics of working with Word, including how to access menus and give commands with both the keyboard and the mouse. In addition, you will learn about the Help function. If you are a novice to Word and Windows, study this chapter carefully before continuing with the remainder of this book.

Starting Word

> Your computer system may have Windows already installed on your hard drive. To determine this, type **win** at the system prompt (or **win386** if you are using Windows on a 80386 microprocessor-based system).

When you start Word, you are transferring control of the computer to Word from DOS or from Windows. Before starting Word, you should refer to Appendix A to make a complete set of backups of your original Word disks and to be sure Word is properly installed on your hard disk.

Word will start from the DOS, or system, prompt (usually a C> or D>) or from within Windows itself. To decide whether your computer system already has Windows installed on your hard drive, at the DOS prompt type **win** for 80286-based computer systems or **win386** for 80386-based systems. If your hard drive is partitioned into more than one drive (e.g., drives C and D), you may need to switch to the drive where Windows is installed (e.g., type **D:** at the C>) before typing **win** at the system prompt. Windows will boot if it is installed. If Windows is installed, and you have installed Word on the same drive, then you can start Word from within Windows as well. Based on your computer's configuration, start Word by one of the two following options.

Starting Word from the DOS System Prompt

To start Word from the system prompt, you have several options, as detailed in Table 1.1. For example, you can start Word and open a new, untitled document by typing **winword** and pressing **Enter**. Or, you can start Word and open the last file that you worked on by including a *switch* (a slash followed by the letter l—**winword/l**). To open a specific file, enter **winword** followed by the exact name of the file (**winword letter**). If the file name includes an extension, remember to type it as well (**winword letter.doc**). Always press the Enter key after typing the document's name in order to execute the winword start sequence.

1—Introducing Word for Windows

Table 1.1 Options for Starting Word at the System Prompt

At the System Prompt, Type	Action
winword	Starts Word and opens a new, untitled document.
winword file name	Starts Word and opens the file specified by file name. Remember to include any file name extension (e.g., .doc). You can also specify more than one file name by separating the names with spaces (e.g., winword chap1.doc chap2.doc). Word will open the files in the order that you specified and place them in *stacked* windows. The last file you specify becomes the active window. See Chapter 15 for more details.
winword/l	Starts Word and opens the last file that you worked on.
winword/m macro name	Starts Word and immediately runs the specified macro. Like files, you can specify more than one macro and Word will run them in the sequence that you typed them. You can even open macros and documents at the same time. Word will open the selected documents first and then run the macros.
winword/t	Starts Word and runs the Word tutorial.
winword/n	Starts Word with no document.

Before you type winword, you may need to change to the directory where you installed the Word program files. The DOS change directory (cd\) command changes to a specified directory (e.g., cd\winword). If you called your directory something other than winword, type that name instead.

1. Turn on your computer. If you are asked to respond to date and time prompts, you can type your answers and press Enter after each response. Or, you can simply press Enter at each prompt.

   The C> prompt appears. Your drive may be D, E, or F.

2. Type **winword** and press **Enter**. If your system has Windows 386 installed on your hard disk, the computer will instruct you to type:

   The Word screen soon appears.

   win386 winword

5

The Basics

You may also use one of the start options from Table 1.1.

Starting Word from within Windows

Using Windows with Word allows you to switch rapidly between multiple applications and share information among them easily. You should have installed Word on your hard drive as detailed in Appendix A. If you need additional information for installing Windows itself on your hard drive, refer to your Windows user's manual.

1. Turn on your computer. Respond to the date and time requests by DOS (if necessary) and press Enter after each request.

   The C> (or D>, E>, or F>) prompt appears.

2. Type **win** at the C> prompt and press **Enter**. If you have Windows 386 installed, type **win386**.

   The MS-DOS Executive soon appears.

3. Select the drive where Word for Windows, or winword, is installed. If your hard disk is partitioned into more than one drive (e.g., C and D), you may have to switch to the appropriate drive (see Figure 1.1).

   The screen lists all the available directories for the selected drive.

4. Select the directory where the file WINWORD.EXE. resides.

   The selected drive lists all the available files in a window (see Figure 1.2).

5. Use the down arrow key to scroll the list of files. Select the file named WINWORD.EXE. With a mouse, you select a file in Windows by clicking to highlight it. Double-click the file to select and open it simultaneously. Without a mouse, you select a file with the up and down arrow keys

   In a few moments, the Word for Windows screen appears.

1—Introducing Word for Windows

and press **Enter**. (We'll discuss using the mouse and the keyboard in Windows shortly.)

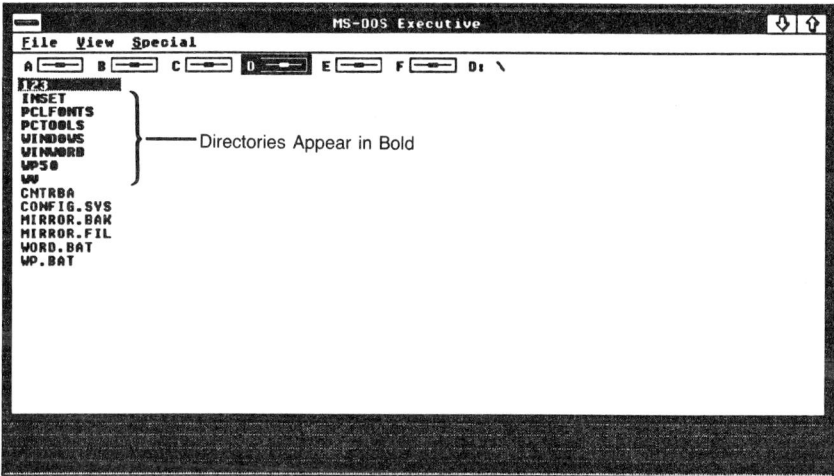

Figure 1.1 All directories are listed in a window for the selected drive.

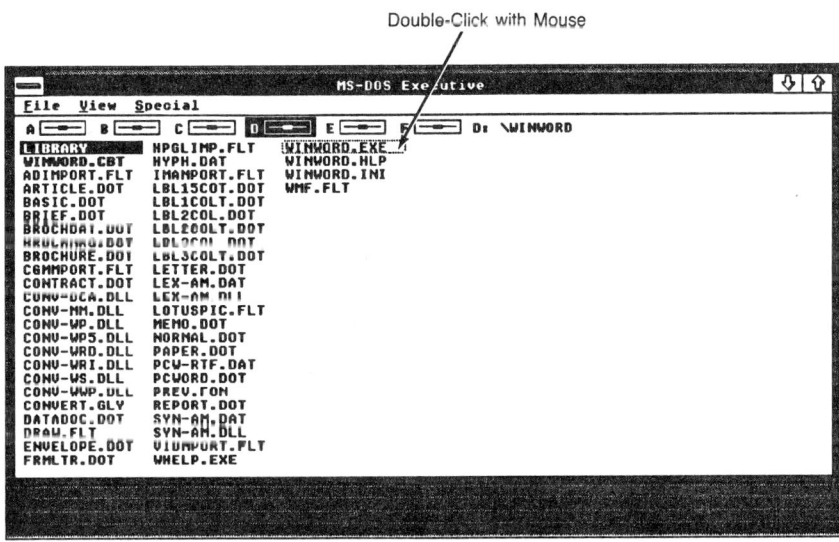

Figure 1.2 All files are listed in a window for the selected directory.

7

The Basics

The Word Screen

Once you start Word, its initial screen appears. The screen consists of three distinct parts: a large, empty *document window,* a *Control menu box,* and the *Control menu bar.*

The Document Window

The document window, shown in Figure 1.3, is the largest area on the screen. Sometimes called the *work area,* it is where you will do all your creative word processing. You'll enter and edit text, format it, and print the result. You will learn about the specifics of word processing in Chapter 2. This section focuses on the window and its characteristics.

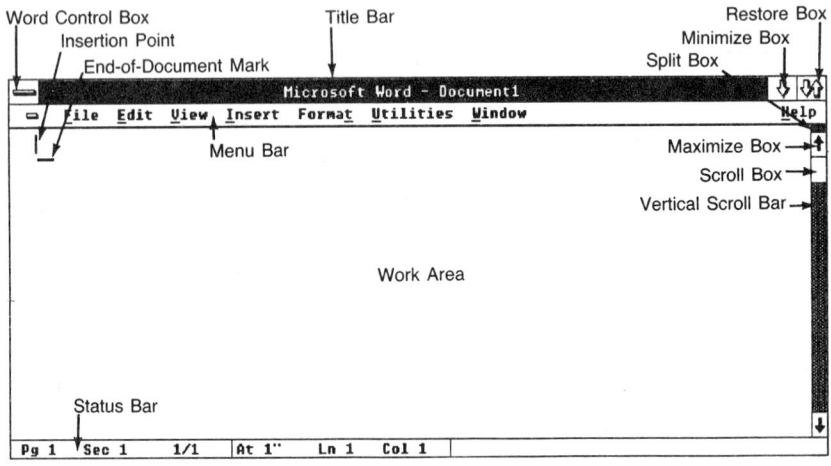

Figure 1.3 The initial Word screen appears as Microsoft Word—Document1.

You can change the speed of the blinker by opening the Control Panel via the Control.Exe file within Windows or by choosing Run and the same option from the Word Control menu after Word has loaded. The slower option seems less distracting.

The first characteristic of the document window that will draw your attention is the blinking vertical bar. It is also called the *insertion point* since its function is to point to the position on your screen where the next typed character will appear (or disappear if you press Backspace or Delete).

If you have installed a mouse with your system, the second characteristic that you will notice is the *I-beam pointer.* Don't confuse the insertion point with this pointer, which represents the location of the mouse. As you move the mouse within the document window, this pointer looks like an I-beam, but if you move the pointer to the menu bar, it becomes an arrow. The primary operation of the I-beam pointer within the document window is to locate the insertion point. Move it to the position you want the next character to appear, click once, and the blinking insertion point will appear there. When you begin with a blank screen, you can't actually reposition the insertion point until you type some text or move down a blank page by pressing Enter. Once you begin to enter text, however, you will quickly learn the value of moving the insertion point for the purpose of editing, formatting, or just correcting typos. If you have been working with computers for awhile, you will liken the combination of the insertion point and the movement of the I-beam pointer to a cursor. Window's users will notice the highlighted rectangle from the MS-DOS Executive screen as a true cursor. The insertion point and I-beam are not exactly the same as a cursor. To keep things simple, we'll refer to the cursor only when on a Window's opening screen. All other times within Word, we'll refer to the insertion point.

One last note about the mouse pointer: It can take as many as fifteen distinctive shapes, as depicted in Table 1.2. You'll see many of these shapes as you work through this book. For now, it's important for you to know how to use the mouse to move the pointer around the screen, what an insertion point is, and how to move it with the I-beam pointer.

Table 1.2 The Different "Looks" of a Pointer

The Pointer	Description	Function
I	I-beam	Moves insertion point in text and in picture frame. Used to select text when editing and formatting.
↖	Left arrow	Points to menu bar and selects commands and options. Also, it appears in scroll bars to move through your documents and as sizing arrow when you have a picture selected (drag sizing handles to scale or crop a picture).

(continued)

Table 1.2 *(continued)*

The Pointer	Description	Function
	Right arrow	Appears at the far left of your document window in an invisible selection area. It's used to select large blocks of text (line, paragraph, or whole document) and is about the same size as the visible vertical scroll bar on the right. Only the direction of the arrow changes.
	Down arrow	Appears when selecting columns of text in Word's *table* feature.
	Hour glass	Always appears while Word is executing last command.
	Cross-hair	In Print Preview, it's used to reposition items on a page.
	Split box	Appears when pointer is over the split box on the vertical scroll bar or when you choose Control Split.
	Split style	Appears when pointer is over the style name area split line.
	Vertical border	Appears when pointer is over the top or bottom edge of a window. Used to change the size of a window vertically.
	Horizontal border	Appears when pointer is over the left or right edge of a window. Used to change the size of a window horizontally.
	Diagonal border	Appears when pointer is in the bottom left or right corner of a window. Changes the size of a window diagonally.

The Pointer	Description	Function
✥	Move window	Appears after you've chosen Control Move command to reposition window. Also appears after you've chosen Control Size to resize window by dragging border.
✥	Heading	In Outline View, appears when pointer is positioned on a heading's icon.
↔	Left-right	In Outline View, appears when pointer is used to move a heading left or right within the outline.
↕	Up-down	In Outline View, appears when pointer is used to move a heading up or down (promote/demote) in an outline.

If you don't have a mouse installed with your system you still need to navigate through the document window. To do this, use the arrow keys to move the insertion point around. By pressing these keys you can move the insertion point up, down, left, and right.

The next item of note in the window is a dark horizontal line that appears just below the blinking insertion point. This line is referred to as the *end-of-document* mark because its function is to indicate the end of your current document. As you enter text, the end-of-document mark moves down your screen accordingly.

The document window contains many of the same components as other windows. If you're new to Windows applications, you'll learn about the key operations among these through the remainder of this chapter. At the top of all document windows is the *title bar*, which indicates the name of the application and/or file in which you are currently working. Since this is your first Word document, the name will appear as "Microsoft Word—Document1." Once you give

The Restore box returns a window to the size it was before you selected the Minimize or Maximize option.

The Basics

the file or document a name (discussed in Chapter 2), the name will replace the Document1 signature. If you have a mouse, you can use the *Minimize arrow box* to decrease the Document file window to a small icon on the Windows screen and the *Maximize arrow box* to increase the window to full-screen size. For those of you without a mouse, use the Minimize and Maximize commands on the pull-down Control menu. Later in this chapter, we'll look at minimizing and maximizing in more detail.

For you who have Windows, the MS-DOS Executive screen contains most of the components of the opening Word screen, including a Control menu box, menu bar, Maximize and Minimize boxes, and a work area.

The *scroll bar* at the right side of Figure 1.3 (it can also appear at the bottom) only appears if the vertical (or horizontal) scroll bar options are turned on via the Utilities Customize dialog box. When you first start Word, the vertical scroll bar is selected; the horizontal scroll bar is not. If you have a mouse, you can use the scroll bars to move the text in a window up and down and/or left or right.

The Control Menu

To access the Document Control menu, press Alt + Hyphen (-). To access the Word Control menu, press Alt + Spacebar. If you have a mouse installed, point and click on the appropriate control box.

The Control menu is accessed via the Control menu box in the title bar. Each window in Word actually contains two Control menu boxes. The box in the upper left corner of the title bar is for the Word (or application) Control menu. The box in the upper left corner of the menu bar itself is slightly smaller and is for the Document (or file) Control menu. The Control menu boxes are used to access their respective Control menus and function in a similar fashion. You can use the Word Control menu to move a window, change its size, restore a window to its previous size or location, and quit Word. The primary difference between the two is that the Word Control menu affects the Word application; the Document Control menu only affects the current active document.

To access a pull-down Control menu, you can either use the keyboard or the mouse. To use the keyboard, press the **Alt** key and then the **Hyphen (-)**. This keypress will access the Document Control menu as depicted in Figure 1.4. To access the Word Control menu, press the **Alt** key and then the **Spacebar** (Figure 1.5). To use the mouse, position the pointer over the appropriate control box and click the mouse button once.

1—Introducing Word for Windows

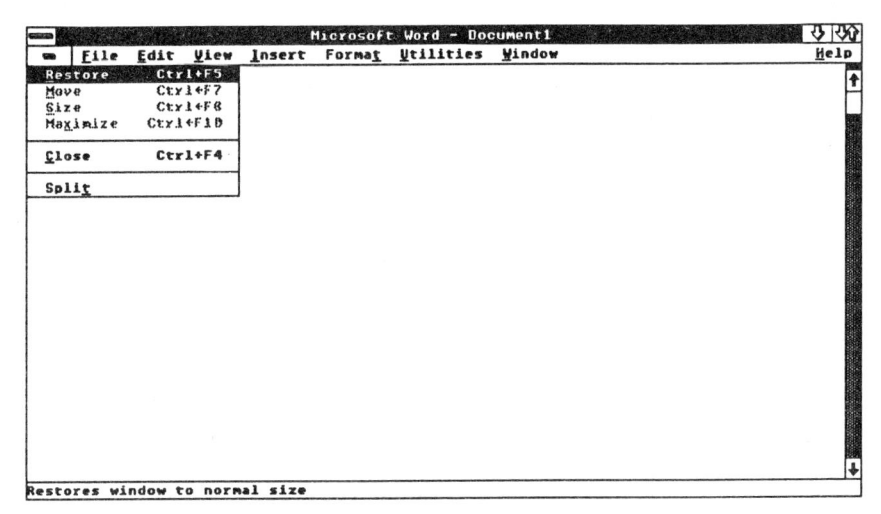

Figure 1.4 The Document Control menu.

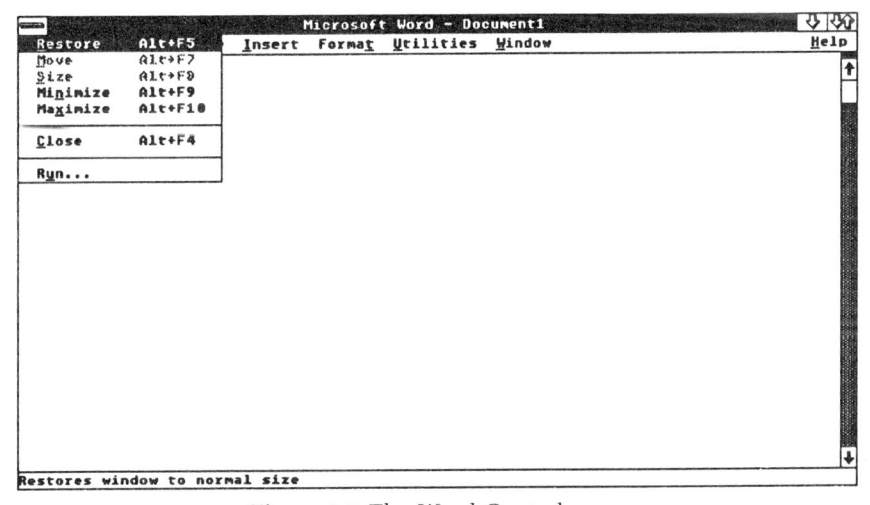

Figure 1.5 The Word Control menu.

Accessing a particular command in a pull-down menu is also accomplished with either the keyboard or a mouse. You can use the mouse to scroll through a menu by pointing to select and then clicking to execute. With the keyboard, use the up and down arrow keys to scroll the Control menu, and then type the letter underlined within a command or menu name to select it. To close a menu without selecting any command, either press the **Esc** key or click outside the pull-down menu with the mouse.

13

The Menu Bar

Running across the top of the document screen is the area commonly referred to as the menu bar, from which you use the keyboard or mouse to "pull-down" a list of available commands. The menu items (for example, on the Document Control menu: File, Edit, View, Insert, Format, Utilities, Macro, Window, Help) correspond to a separate list of commands. To view the list of commands in a particular menu item, use the keyboard in a method similar to that used to access a Control menu. First, press the Alt key and then press the underlined letter of the menu name to select it. For example, to access the File menu, press **Alt+F** and the pull-down menu shown in Figure 1.6 appears. Or, position your mouse pointer directly over the desired menu item and press the mouse button once. In either case, a window will drop down and display the commands available. To close a window, press the Esc key or click outside the window with the mouse. We'll explore accessing menus and choosing commands a little later in this chapter.

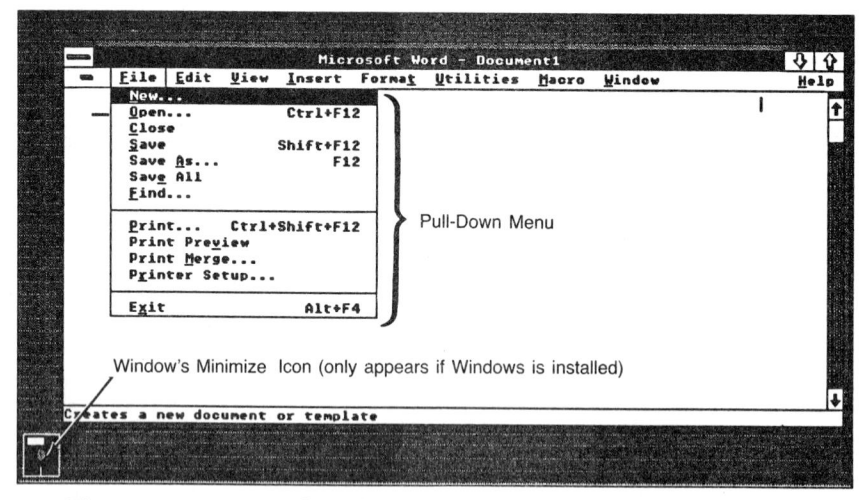

Figure 1.6 To access the File menu with the keyboard, press Alt+F.

The Different Views of Word

A significant feature of Word for Windows is that you can look at a document in several ways. When you first start Word, you are in the *Normal Editing View,* sometimes referred to as *Galley View.* Galley

View displays a "What You See Is What You Get" (WYSIWYG) look at your documents, including text and paragraph formatting, along with accurate page breaks. However, in Normal Editing View, you will not see all the possible formatting options, such as headers or footers; page numbers; or features of a complex document, such as multiple snaking columns and absolutely positioned paragraphs with text-wrap. To solve the need to look at a document's structure before you print it out, you can choose one of Word's optional views, *Page View* or *Print Preview*.

Word offers you five options for viewing your documents as described in Table 1.3. We have borrowed documents from the Sampler disk provided by Microsoft for each of these views in Figures 1.7 through 1.11 to give you an idea how they might appear. As we proceed through the book, we'll be exploring each of the views in detail. If you can't wait, however, press **Alt,V** to access the View menu. Then choose the desired view from the pull-down menu by scrolling the menu with the down arrow key and pressing Enter. The one exception is Print Preview, which is found on the File menu. If you have a mouse, click open the View menu (or File menu) and then click the desired view.

Table 1.3 The Five Views of Word for Windows

View	Description
Normal Editing View	Also called Galley View, this view is where you likely will spend most of your time entering and formatting original text. You can work with more than one document at a time in Normal Editing View. Most formatting tasks are available but not all of the formatting results will appear in Normal Editing View. For example, page and line numbers, headers and footers, multiple snaking columns, footnotes, text flowing around absolutely positioned paragraphs, tables, and graphics are not visible in Normal Editing View.

(continued)

Table 1.3 *(continued)*

View	Description
Page View	In Page View, you get a look at exactly how your document will appear when printed. Since the document window can only show a portion of the document in full size, you may need to scroll the document to view it in its entirety. All editing and formatting commands are available to you in Page View in order to make any last minute changes before you print the document. Depending on the amount of memory on your computer system, and the complexity of your document, Normal Editing View generally provides a faster display speed than Page View.
Print Preview	Found on the File menu, Print Preview shows a full page or two of all elements of your document on a reduced scale. All formatting elements of the document's structure are included (multiple columns, page or line numbers, headers or footers, footnotes, positioned paragraphs, tables, or graphics). No editing or formatting is possible in Print Preview but you can reposition certain elements, such as margins or positioned paragraphs.
Draft View	The fastest of the five views, *Draft View* changes the text to the system font and removes most of the formatting and all of the graphics from the display. The formatting appears as underlining (frames for graphics). The advantage of this view is that most formatting elements require additional computation time and by eliminating these elements, the display and printing speed is enhanced.
Outline View	*Outline View* is useful for creating outlines of your documents, or more specifically, for showing the structure of your document by highlighting the headings at a specific level. You can rearrange your heading levels and thus change the structure of your documents topics quickly and easily in Outline View.

1—Introducing Word for Windows

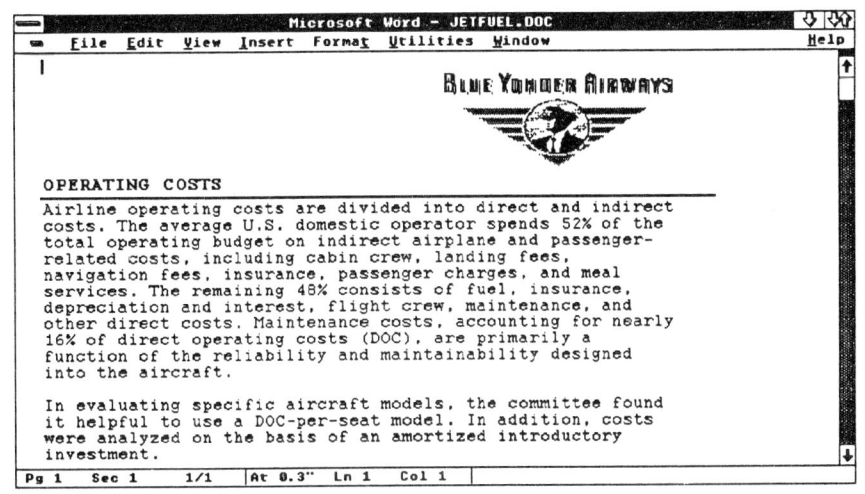

Figure 1.7 Sample document in Normal Editing View.

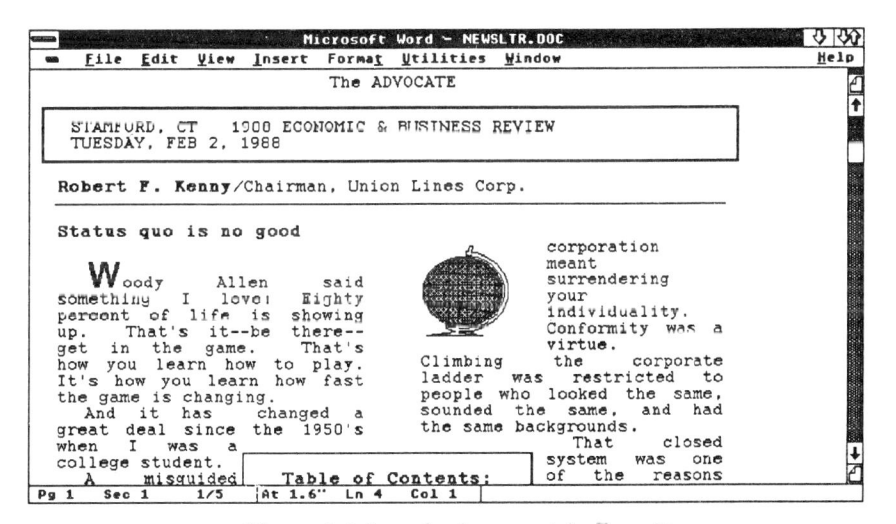

Figure 1.8 Sample document in Page View.

17

The Basics

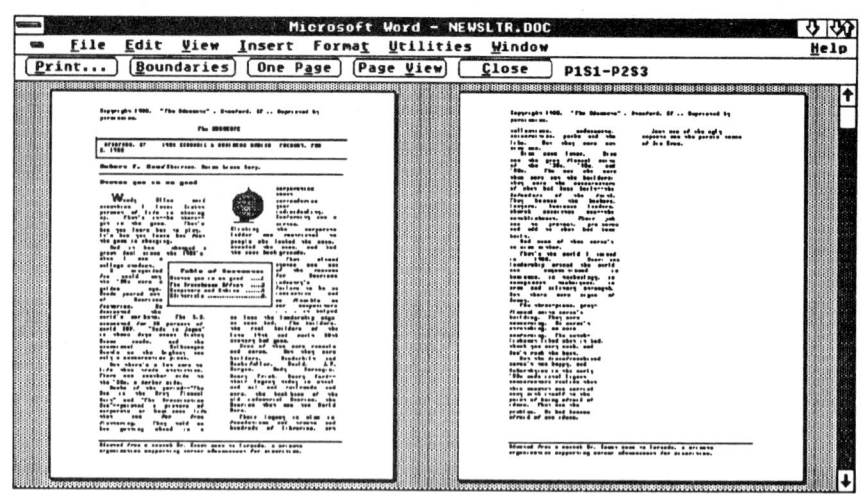

Figure 1.9 Sample document in Print Preview.

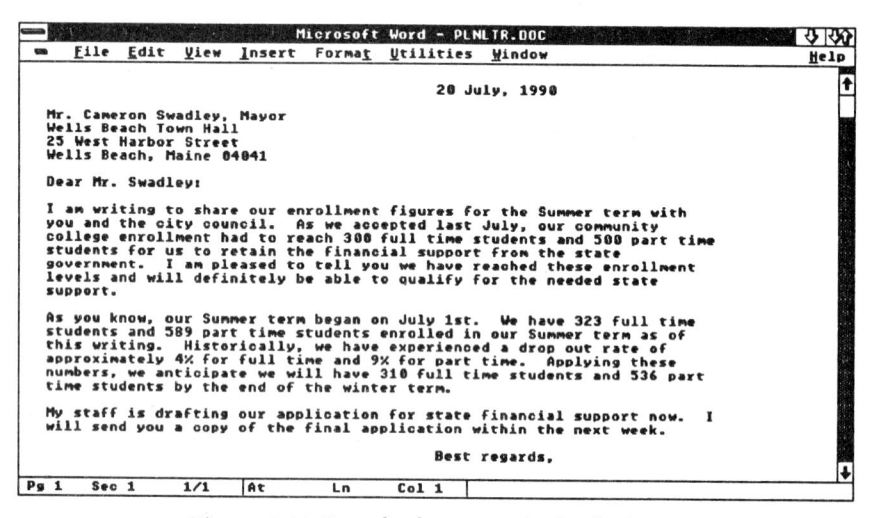

Figure 1.10 Sample document in Draft View.

1—Introducing Word for Windows

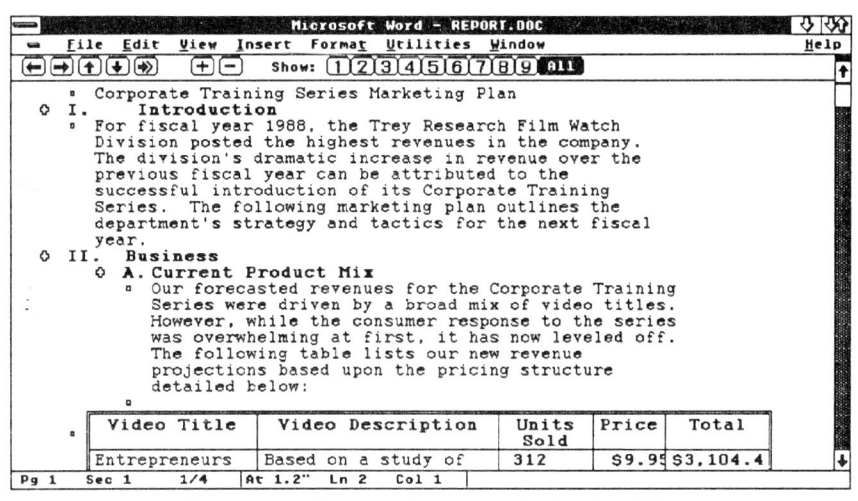

Figure 1.11 Sample document in Outline View.

Using the Keyboard

A computer performs three primary functions: It accepts data in the form of letters, numbers, special characters, and so on; performs an operation on the data; and outputs the resulting information. On your personal computer, or PC, you input the data via the keyboard (Figure 1.12).

Since the original IBM PC keyboard was designed, the PC itself and all the PC-compatible computers have evolved, and so has the keyboard. To use Word, it doesn't matter whether you have the original keyboard (Figure 1.13), the keyboard first introduced with the IBM PC AT's (Figure 1.14), or the new enhanced keyboard currently shipped with most IBM PS/2 computers (Figure 1.15). All of the keyboards use the standard QWERTY format (the leftmost six letters in the top row spell QWERTY). All the keyboards also have many keys common to the standard typewriter. Located in the center of the keyboard, you will find the keys used to "print" characters on your screen much as a typewriter does—with a single keystroke.

19

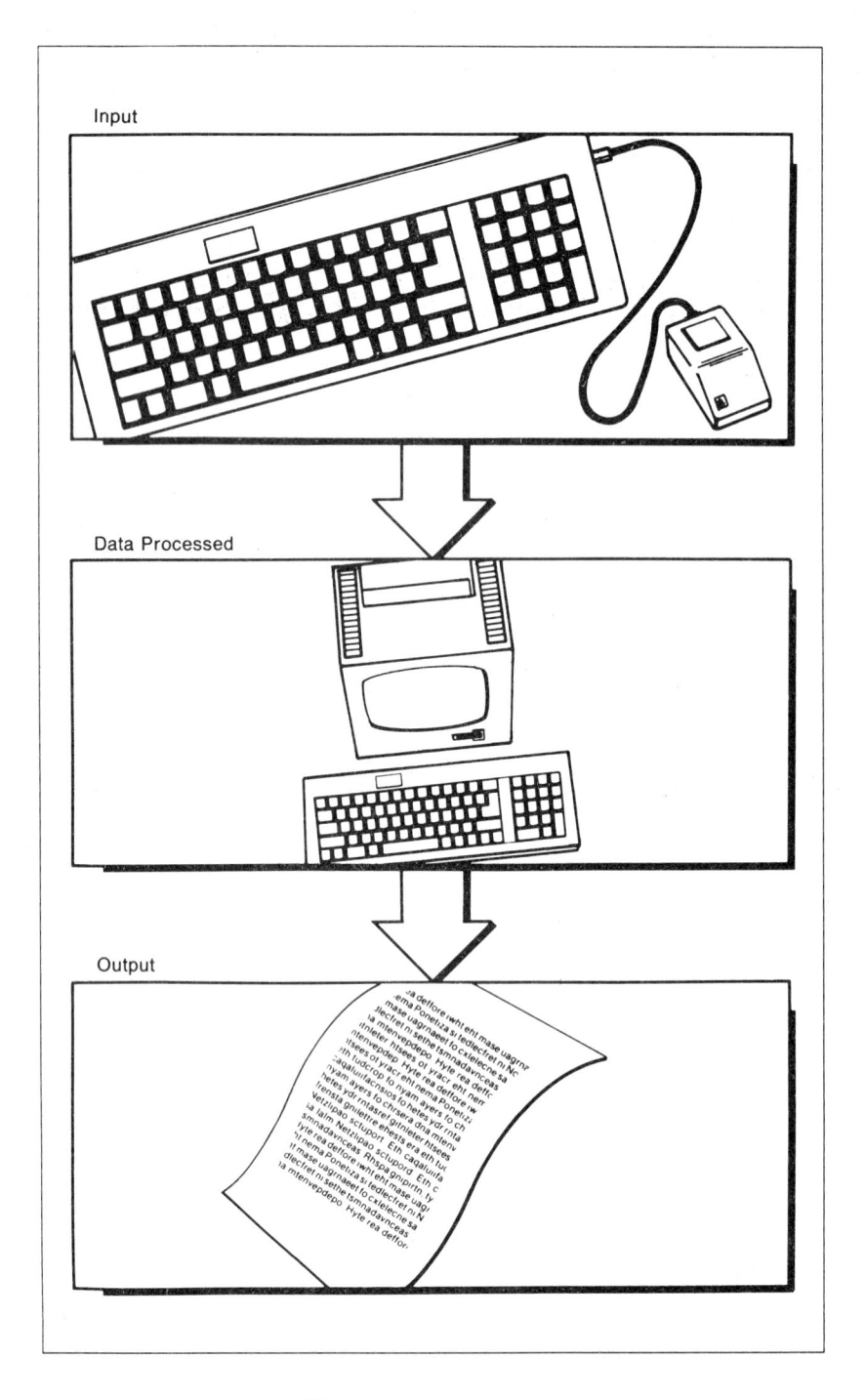

Figure 1.12 Processing data.

1—Introducing Word for Windows

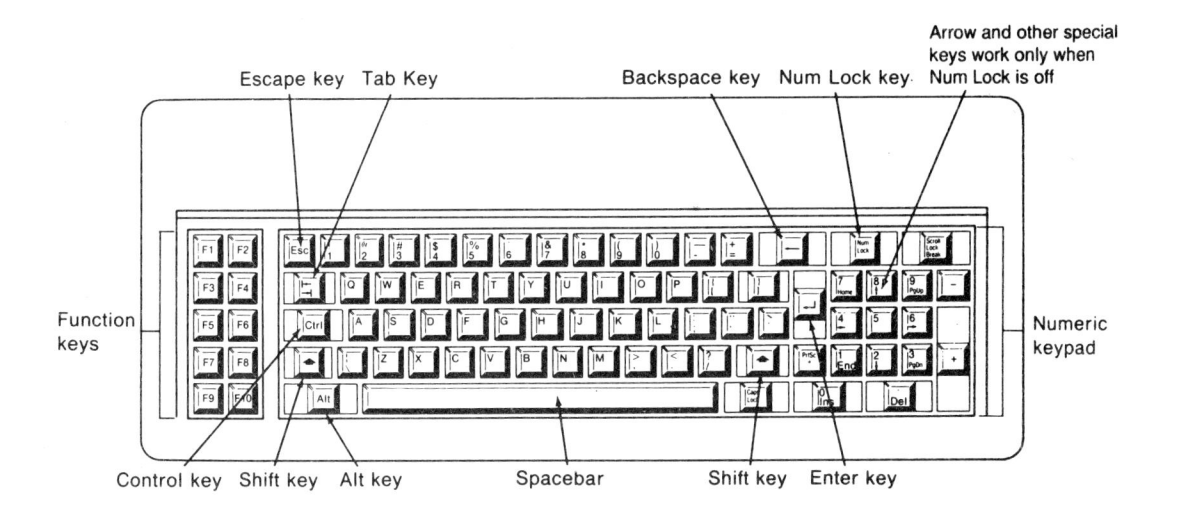

Figure 1.13 The original IBM PC keyboard.

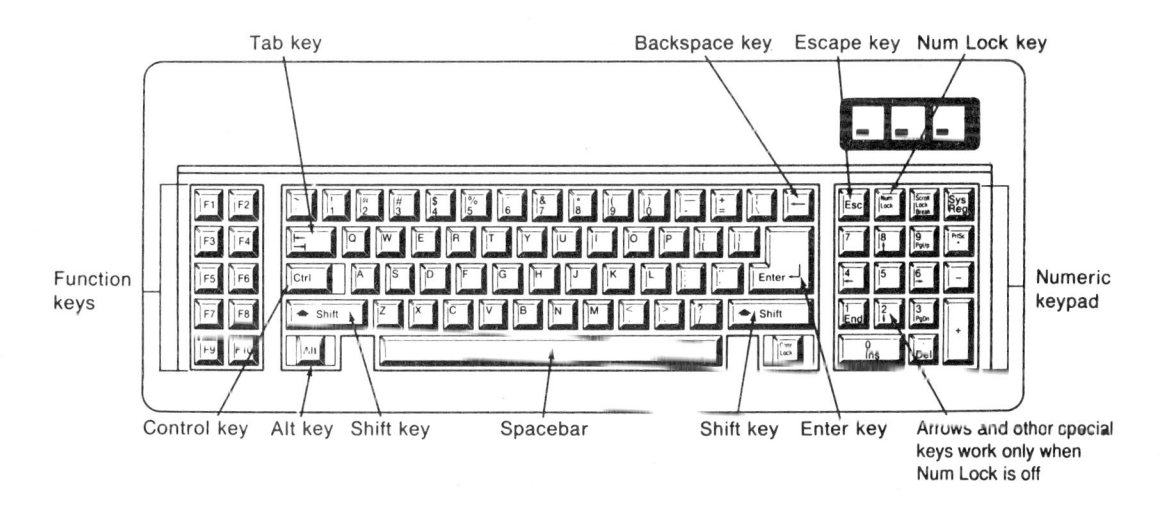

Figure 1.14 The IBM PC AT keyboard.

21

The Basics

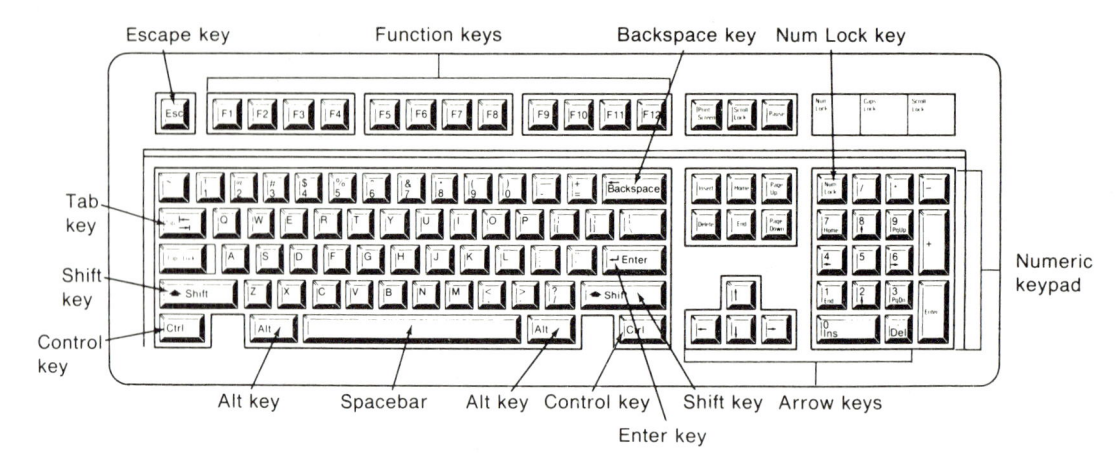

Figure 1.15 The new, enhanced keyboard.

The keyboard also includes a built-in function, called "auto-repeat." Because of auto-repeat, if you hold down one key, the corresponding character will print on your screen repeatedly, until you release the key.

If you have used a typewriter before, yet are new to computing, the keyboard is the one component of your system that will seem like an old friend. Aside from the standard QWERTY keys though, you will notice several special-purpose keys not common to the typewriter. Such keys, listed in Table 1.4, include Enter, Alt, Ctrl, Esc, and the *function keys* located along the top row or left side of the keyboard (depending upon which type of keyboard is connected to your system). Since you'll be using these keys throughout the remainder of this book, use Table 1.4 and the summaries that follow as an introduction. It's important that you master the use of these keys early.

Table 1.4 The Special Keys of Your Keyboard

Key	Name	Function
Enter	Enter	Acts as a "carriage return," consequently, sometimes called "Return."
Caps Lock	Caps Lock	Locks your keyboard in uppercase mode. Pressing Shift while in the Caps Lock mode produces a lowercase character.
Shift	Shift	One on each side of the keyboard, used to print uppercase letters and punctuation characters. May be marked with an up arrow, rather than "Shift."

1—Introducing Word for Windows

Key	Name	Function
Tab	Tab	Moves your insertion point left to right, stopping at 1/2" default intervals.
Esc	Esc	The Escape key. Used to toggle between commands and the document screen.
Alt	Alt	The Alternate key. Used in combination with other keys to perform a certain function or to access the menu bar and select commands.
Ctrl	Ctrl	The Control key. Used with other keys to perform a certain function.
Backspace	Backspace	Moves the insertion point one character space right to left, erasing characters in its path.
Delete	Del	The Delete key. Used to erase one character to the right of the insertion point and move existing text to the left.
Insert	Ins	The Insert key. Used to toggle the keyboard between insert and normal text mode.
(arrow keys)	Arrow keys (on enhanced keyboards)	Sometimes called direction keys, these move the insertion point up, down, left, and right.
(numeric keypad)	Function keys	Labeled F1–F10 or F12. Used with other keys to perform a specific function or command.
	Numeric keypad arrow keys	Used to navigate through your document as long as you haven't pressed the Num Lock key.
Home	Home	Takes you to the beginning of the current line.
End	End	Takes you to the end of the current line.
Page Up	PgUp	Takes you up one window.
Page Down	PgDn	Takes you down one window.

The Enter Key

Located on the right side of the keyboard, the Enter key is one of the most important keys that you will be using. It is used in one of two

23

communication operations: to end paragraphs in word processing or to confirm a selection from a dialog box or menu in lieu of clicking with the mouse.

Word uses a *word-wrap* feature that automatically wraps text around the end of one line down to the next line. So you should only press the Enter key when you wish to end a line, such as for ending a paragraph. Word has a special feature that inserts a hidden paragraph marker (¶) into the text each time that you press Enter. If you wish to see the paragraph markers, turn on the Paragraph Marks option in the View Preferences menu (a default setting). Don't worry about paragraph marks just yet, we will get to them in the next chapter. For those of you who are experienced with windows, the keyboard strokes to turn on Paragraph Marks are Alt,V,E to open the appropriate menu and then Alt,P to check the Paragraph Marks box.

In general, the Enter key tells the computer that you are finished with a command and you are trying to communicate with it. The Enter key must be pressed to send your data to the computer. When you press the Enter key, the insertion point acts as a carriage return and moves to the next line. The insertion point will flash on and off to signal that the computer is ready for more input at that position.

Finally, the Enter key might be labeled as "Return" or with a backward arrow (↵). To keep things simple, we'll refer to it as the Enter key from now on.

The Spacebar

When you press the Spacebar, the long bar at the bottom of the keyboard, a blank space is entered on the screen. If you press the Spacebar while the insertion point resides within a word, all characters to the right of the insertion point are moved one space to the right.

The Caps Lock Key

When you press Caps Lock, the status bar at the bottom of the screen shows "CAPS" as a reminder.

The Caps Lock key, once pressed, locks your keyboard into uppercase mode. This keypress, however, only affects the twenty-six letters of the alphabet. You use the Shift key to generate the symbols on the number keys and all other uppercase characters. Pressing the Caps Lock key repeatedly will toggle the keyboard from lowercase to uppercase and back. Unlike on a typewriter, you cannot use the Shift key to turn off the Caps Lock mode. You must press the Caps Lock key again to return to lowercase mode.

The Shift Key

The Shift key operates in Word as it does on a standard typewriter. Pressing the Shift key together with another key produces the uppercase character. With the Caps Lock key on, pressing the Shift key produces lowercase characters.

In Word, however, the Shift key provides additional versatility. For example, the Shift key can also operate as a special function key. When pressed in combination with the Alt, Ctrl, or one of the ten (or twelve) function keys, a number of shortcuts and special functions are possible. For example, with twelve function keys, you can press Shift+F12 executes the *Save* command listed in the File menu without your having to open the Save dialog box first.

The Tab Key

You will find the Tab key useful for moving from one option to another within a Word dialog box.

When you press the Tab key, the insertion point moves left to right across your screen, stopping at 1/2" intervals. You can change the default value of 1/2" by using the Ruler (detailed in Chapter 5). The Tab key is useful for setting text in columns.

The Function Keys

Your keyboard comes equipped with either ten or twelve function keys (F1–F10 or F12), located either on the left side (on IBM PC and XT keyboards) or on the top row (on PC/AT and PS/2 keyboards). You use the function keys in combination with Shift, Alt, or Ctrl to produce a special action or operation. These actions may provide a quicker method to complete a complex task. For a complete listing of the special actions of the function keys, refer to Appendix B.

The Direction Keys and the Numeric Keypad

On enhanced keyboards, you can use the direction keys (identified by the left, right, up, and down arrows) to navigate through your Word documents. If you are not in the Numerical (Num) Lock mode, you can also use the keys on the numeric keypad as direction keys. For

The Basics

You cannot use the keypad for numeric entry and directional movement at the same time. Use the Num Lock key to toggle between modes.

example, the number 8 key on the numeric keypad can substitute for the up arrow key.

Use the Num Lock mode with the numeric keypad for typing numbers, which is useful for making entries on a spreadsheet. Use the Num Lock key to toggle back and forth between the numeric mode and the directional-command mode of the arrow keys. When you use the Num Lock mode, the message "NUM" appears on the lower right side of the status bar (if you've selected the Status Bar option from the View Menu). Pressing Num Lock a second time returns your keyboard to directional mode.

The direction keys also include four additional keys worthy of note: Home, End, Page Up, and Page Down. These keys are used to move quickly to different points of your document, either by pressing them alone or in combination with other keys. For example, pressing Home moves the insertion point to the beginning of the current line, while pressing the Ctrl+Home combination moves the insertion point to the beginning of the document. Likewise, pressing End moves the insertion point to the end of the current line and Ctrl+End moves it to the end of the document. As might be expected, pressing Page Up and Page Down moves the insertion point either up one entire window or down one entire window. For a complete review of all the combinations of moving around your document with the direction keys, refer to Appendix B.

The Backspace Key

Some keyboards will also have a Delete key. This keypress produces a different result than using Backspace does. Pressing Delete will remove one character at a time to the right of the insertion point. As you press Delete, any existing text after the insertion point also moves right to left, while the insertion point retains its position.

Put away your correction fluid, eraser, scissors, and paste! A simple keystroke easily accomplishes error correction in Word for Windows.

The Backspace key is located in the upper right corner of the keyboard. When you press it, the insertion point will move one space back, erasing the character in its path. If you continue to hold down the key, the insertion point will scroll back to the previous line, moving from right to left until it reaches the home position of the active window. So, to correct a typing error, simply press the Backspace to the point where the error occurred, type the correction, and then retype the remaining characters. If you don't wish to retype text beyond the correction, use the arrow keys or the mouse to move the pointer to the character just to the right of the error, press the Backspace to remove the offending character, and then type the correction. When the correction is complete, use the arrow keys or the mouse to move the insertion point back to its original position. What happens to the spacing? Don't worry. Word automatically spaces your text according to the format you have selected. We will discuss more editing features in Chapter 3. For now, use the Backspace key to correct those typos.

Using the Mouse

Microsoft's Word for Windows is a visually oriented application that works very well with a mouse. The mouse is a pointing device introduced to increase the user's productivity by eliminating the need for unnecessary keystrokes. An arrow (the pointer) on your screen corresponds to the movement of the desktop mouse (which usually contains both a left and right button, e.g., the Microsoft Mouse). The mouse allows the user to make selections from the screen by positioning the pointer and pressing a single button (often the left button in Word for Windows). The selections are generally formed as text or as graphic objects known as *icons*.

Operating the mouse requires free movement on a flat surface of approximately 6" in all directions. The pointer on the screen cannot be moved off the screen, no matter how far you move the mouse. The screen movement of the mouse corresponds to the movement of the small rubber ball on the bottom of the mouse. If you have trouble positioning the mouse pointer on your screen because the free surface for the mouse is limited, lift the unit to another point on the surface area. The position of the pointer will not change until the ball is further displaced.

If you have been working with a mouse for awhile, its use has probably become second nature. If you are just beginning, you'll soon discover the efficiency of the mouse. As you read this book, you'll find equivalent instructions for the mouse as well as the keyboard. Here's a summary of how to perform the mouse instructions:

- Moving the pointer—Use the screen as the reference point for the pointer. Remember, the mouse can be lifted and put down again, allowing free movement of the unit.
- Pointing—When pointing the arrow at an icon, position the tip of the arrow directly over the icon.
- Dragging—While pointing at an icon, press the mouse button and continue to hold it down without releasing. *Dragging* is often used in Word for selecting text that you wish to copy, cut, or paste. Dragging with the left button pressed will select a character at a time, while dragging with the right button pressed will select a word at a time. From the Windows desktop, you can also drag to change the location of an object.
- Clicking—Pressing the mouse button and releasing it is called *clicking*. You can click to select a location, menus, a command from a pull-down menu, or to activate an icon. Clicking is the mouse operation that you will use most often.

- Double-clicking—Similar to clicking, the mouse button is rapidly pressed and released twice. *Double-click* to select an icon and choose a command in a single sequence.

It should be mentioned that there are different versions of mice that can be connected to your computer either via a serial port or an expansion card (called a *bus mouse)*. On IBM PS/2s, a special mouse port exists for *serial mice*. Serial and bus mice work the same way. Which type of mouse you choose will depend on whether your computer system has more serial ports or more expansion slots available. Generally, the serial mouse is preferred since it doesn't require an expansion card and thus is less expensive. Mice can be purchased from a variety of sources. Microsoft conveniently makes all types of mice, and it is a good alternative for choosing a mouse that is 100% compatible with both Word and Windows.

Finally, to use a mouse with your system, you must first properly install it. The mouse will come with a mouse driver program that must be installed via the DEVICE statement in your DOS CONFIG.SYS file. The documentation that came with your mouse should guide you through the installation procedure.

Accessing Menus and Choosing Commands

We have briefly touched upon the methods for accessing menus and choosing commands during our discussion of the Control menu. This section discusses both the keyboard and mouse methods. Either method will work just fine, but it is important that you master one or both methods in order to learn how to use Word itself.

Choosing Commands with the Keyboard

The first step to access any menu in Word is to press the Alt key. Pressing Alt will activate the menu bar and give you access to any of the menus. When the menu bar is activated, the Document Control box will be highlighted. To select a specific menu, press Alt and type the letter underlined in the menu name. For example, to access the File menu, press Alt and then the letter F. As you'll recall, to access the Document Control menu itself, press Alt and then the Hyphen key. To access the Word Control menu, press Alt, Spacebar.

Once a pull-down menu appears on your screen, you can choose a command by using the down and up arrow keys to move the highlighting down and up the menu to select the command. Then press Enter to execute the command. If you change your mind, and wish to close a menu, simply press the Esc key. Pressing Esc will close the menu and deactivate the menu bar. If you press the Alt key, you can close the current menu, but the menu bar will still be active to allow you to access another menu.

Once you press the Alt key, you can also use the left and right arrow keys to move from one menu (either an open menu or a closed one) to another. This is a real time saver if, for example, you have opened one menu by mistake and wish to open another window without first closing the original selection. Simply press the appropriate left or right arrow key and the menus open and close as you move across the menu bar. Remember though, you can always close an open menu by pressing the Esc key. Practice opening and closing pull-down menus from the menu bar and using the arrow keys to navigate around the menus quickly.

As you become more familiar with Word and all the associated menus, you will notice that many menu commands will list a keyboard shortcut command on the right side of the menu window. For example, the shortcut to exit Word is Alt+F4. In Chapter 19 you'll learn how to customize any menu with any keyboard shortcut to fit your particular needs. For a complete review of the default keyboard shortcuts, refer to Appendix B.

Choosing Commands with the Mouse

You can also use the numeric keypad for moving around in a document, selecting portions of text, and executing a few commands. For example, Ctrl+5(Numpad) selects the entire document. Remember that before you carry out a command by pressing Enter or clicking with the mouse, you can cancel the command by pressing the Esc key.

Opening menus and choosing commands with the mouse is simple. To access any menu, point to the desired selection and click the mouse button once. The selected pull-down menu will appear on your screen. To choose a specific command, you can use the pointer to drag up and down a particular menu. When the desired command is highlighted, click the command to execute it. Once a pull-down menu has been opened, you can use the mouse to drag across alternate menus to display their contents without closing the current menu first. To close a menu, point to any unused part of the screen outside the open menu and click the mouse button once.

Choosing Subcommands in a Dialog Box

You will notice that many commands within menus are followed by three periods, for example, *New...* in the File menu. This indicates that a *dialog box* will appear once the command is selected and opened. Depending on the specific command, you will need to respond to one or more boxes before the command will be executed. A dialog box may consist of more than one "field" or box option. To navigate from one field to another you can use either the mouse or the keyboard. To use the mouse, click inside the text box area to position the insertion point, and then click inside a *list box* to select it. If you wish to use the keyboard instead of the mouse, press the Alt key followed by the underlined letter representing the field you are choosing. Move from one position in a dialog box to another by pressing the Tab key (press Shift+Tab to move to the previous option). Some other commonly used keys for dialog box selections include:

- Spacebar—Use as a toggle to turn a check box on or off.
- Enter—Chooses the selected command button.
- Tab—Moves through the dialog box one option at a time.
- Shift+Tab—Moves to the previous option.
- Up and down arrow keys—Use to scroll through a list box one selection at a time.
- Esc—Closes a dialog box without implementing any changes. Note that this use may not apply to some dialog boxes.

Mastering how to move through and select options in a dialog box is an important task. You'll learn about several of the dialog boxes later in this book. Take time to learn some of the mouse methods as well as the keyboard methods.

Exploring the Menus

You should now know how to access menus and choose commands with either the keyboard or mouse. Let's take a quick tour of all the menus available in Word for Windows.

Word provides four sets of commands within each menu item. The two basic sets, called *Short menus* and *Full menus*, each present two subsets of options. These subsets generally depend upon whether a document is open or not when you choose the basic set. Beyond these four sets, however, the menus may also be affected by the location of the insertion point. For example, the commands available on the menus will be different if the insertion point is located inside a document window, as opposed to an annotations window. To help you get acquainted with the primary commands available, we'll look at how to switch in and out of Short and Full menu modes.

Short Menus vs. Full Menus

Whichever mode (Full or Short menus) you end your current work session in will be the mode in which Word begins your next session.

Word is initially loaded in the Short menus mode. Short menus offer the most common commands that you will need to run Word at first. In fact, Microsoft recommends beginners use this mode to learn the basic commands needed to produce simple documents, such as letters and memos.

Once you begin to master Word, you will probably want to switch to Full menus mode, which displays all the available commands and options of Word. To switch to Full menus, open the View menu and select the *Full Menus* command at the bottom of the menu with the mouse, or enter

Alt,V,M

from the keyboard (see Figure 1.16). Now when you open each of the menus along the menu bar you'll notice that many of them list additional commands. The number of options depends on whether a document is open or not and where the insertion point resides. If you wished to switch back to Short menus, you'd return to the View menu (Alt+V) and select the *Short Menus* command. In other words, you can toggle between Short and Full menus. The Short and Full menus for either an open or closed document are depicted in Figure 1.17. Before you go on, take a look at your screen in Full menus mode. Since we will be discussing all the features of Word, from this point on you should be in the Full Menus mode.

The Document Control Menu

If you have a mouse installed, you can also double-click on the Document Control menu box itself to close the current document file.

The Document Control menu was discussed earlier (access from the keyboard by typing Alt and then the Hyphen key or by pressing F10+down arrow). In general, use this menu to change the size of your current document window, to split the window into two parts, or to close the current document window itself. More detail will be provided on altering the size of windows in the "Using Windows" section of this chapter.

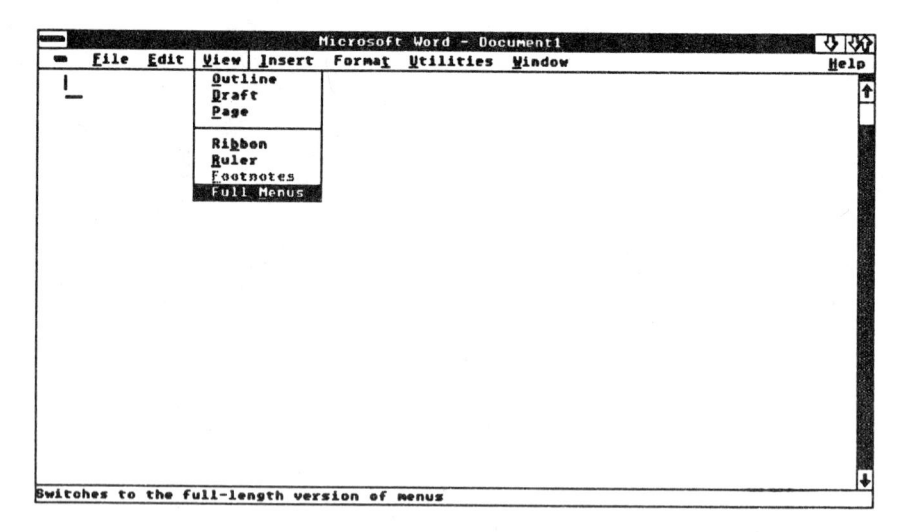

Figure 1.16 The Full menus option in the View menu.

The File Menu

You'll use this menu extensively in this book. It provides you with the commands and tools for creating new files, saving those files, and printing them out as hard copy. Among these tools in Full Menus mode is the Print Preview feature. Print Preview allows you to take a look at the layout of your finished documents in reduced form before you print them out. You can't edit while in Print Preview, however. For that purpose, you must use the Page View mode, which you access through the View menu.

The File menu also offers the *Exit* command, which you use when you want to exit Word and return to the Windows Executive screen (or to return to DOS if Windows is not installed). With a mouse, you can double-click the Word Control box itself to exit Word.

The Edit Menu

The Edit menu contains the tools that you need to add or delete files or modify your text. You can even move text in and out of files. The changes are accomplished with the *Cut, Copy,* and *Paste* commands. If you wish to "undo" the last editing or typing change, you will find the distinctly titled *Undo Typing* command here.

The Edit menu also includes the search and replace function, the commands for creating headers and footers, and the Command Glossary, in which you can store frequently used words or phrases for quick retrieval. Also included, is the *Table* command, which makes creating complicated tables a breeze.

The Insert Menu

The Insert menu is another "workhorse" utility menu. As its name implies, you use this menu to insert many items into your document, including a page, column, or section break; a footnote reference mark; an open footnote pane; the contents of a file; a page number; a table; an index entry; an annotation reference and subsequent pane; and a picture stored in memory. This menu also contains the commands necessary to compile and insert a table of contents and an index.

The Format Menu

The Format menu is the menu for that little bit of design creativity in everyone. Format has many commands for determining the appearance of your documents, including those for changing the size and position of individual characters or blocks of text; indenting text; creating columns; choosing single or double spacing; and determining text position, such as left-justified or centered. Other Format menu commands enable you to choose the style of text, with such options available as italics, boldface, and underlining. You can also create style sheets to minimize the time necessary to format your documents manually (detailed in Chapter 13).

In Word, formatting your documents begins at four distinct levels: at the Character level, Paragraph level, Section level (for complex documents, such as multiple columns and absolutely positioned paragraphs), and the Document level. All the formatting options are discussed in detail in Chapters 4 through 7.

The Utilities Menu

In this menu you find the commands necessary for using Word's spell checker, thesaurus, and other utilities. In addition, you'll find the commands for sorting text, activating Word's Hyphenate utility, and calculating numbers. Here, too, is the *Customize* command, which allows you to adjust some of Word's operations to better fit your work habits.

The Basics

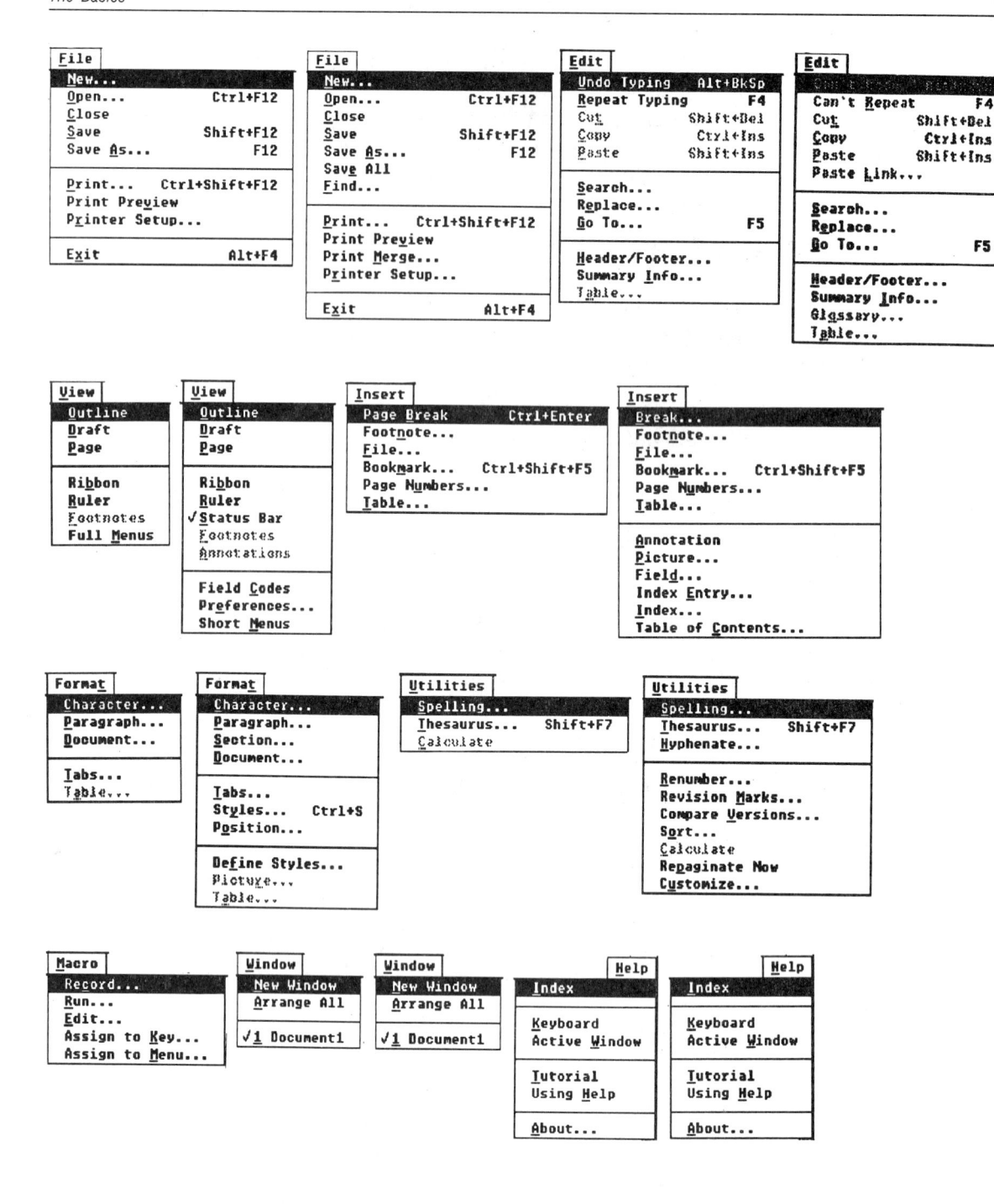

```
File
 New...
 Open...         Ctrl+F12
 Close
 Save            Shift+F12
 Save As...          F12

 Print...   Ctrl+Shift+F12
 Print Preview
 Printer Setup...

 Exit             Alt+F4
```

```
File
 New...
 Open...         Ctrl+F12
 Close
 Save            Shift+F12
 Save As...          F12
 Save All
 Find...

 Print...   Ctrl+Shift+F12
 Print Preview
 Print Merge...
 Printer Setup...

 Exit             Alt+F4
```

```
Edit
 Undo Typing    Alt+BkSp
 Repeat Typing        F4
 Cut            Shift+Del
 Copy            Ctrl+Ins
 Paste          Shift+Ins

 Search...
 Replace...
 Go To...             F5

 Header/Footer...
 Summary Info...
 Table...
```

```
Edit
 Can't Undo
 Can't Repeat         F4
 Cut            Shift+Del
 Copy            Ctrl+Ins
 Paste          Shift+Ins
 Paste Link...

 Search...
 Replace...
 Go To...             F5

 Header/Footer...
 Summary Info...
 Glossary...
 Table...
```

```
View
 Outline
 Draft
 Page

 Ribbon
 Ruler
 Footnotes
 Full Menus
```

```
View
 Outline
 Draft
 Page

 Ribbon
 Ruler
 √Status Bar
 Footnotes
 Annotations

 Field Codes
 Preferences...
 Short Menus
```

```
Insert
 Page Break     Ctrl+Enter
 Footnote...
 File...
 Bookmark...  Ctrl+Shift+F5
 Page Numbers...
 Table...
```

```
Insert
 Break...
 Footnote...
 File...
 Bookmark...  Ctrl+Shift+F5
 Page Numbers...
 Table...

 Annotation
 Picture...
 Field...
 Index Entry...
 Index...
 Table of Contents...
```

```
Format
 Character...
 Paragraph...
 Document...

 Tabs...
 Table...
```

```
Format
 Character...
 Paragraph...
 Section...
 Document...

 Tabs...
 Styles...       Ctrl+S
 Position...

 Define Styles...
 Picture...
 Table...
```

```
Utilities
 Spelling...
 Thesaurus...    Shift+F7
 Calculate
```

```
Utilities
 Spelling...
 Thesaurus...    Shift+F7
 Hyphenate...

 Renumber...
 Revision Marks...
 Compare Versions...
 Sort...
 Calculate
 Repaginate Now
 Customize...
```

```
Macro
 Record...
 Run...
 Edit...
 Assign to Key...
 Assign to Menu...
```

```
Window
 New Window
 Arrange All
 √1 Document1
```

```
Window
 New Window
 Arrange All
 √1 Document1
```

```
Help
 Index

 Keyboard
 Active Window

 Tutorial
 Using Help

 About...
```

```
Help
 Index

 Keyboard
 Active Window

 Tutorial
 Using Help

 About...
```

Figure 1.17 Word offers both Short and Full menus. The menus vary depending on whether a document is closed or open.

The Macro Menu

Word has a feature that allows you to create a set of instructions, called a *macro,* to automate a particular task. Word has supplied a variety of macros for you. You can also create your own macros to fit your needs. We'll explore macros in Chapter 19. For a sneak peak at the preset macros provided by Word, choose the *Run* command from the Macro menu, by pressing Alt,M,R, and then select the *Show All* option by pressing Alt+A.

The Window Menu

This menu opens additional windows on your screen, a feature that enables you to look at the same document in two places (you can also use the *Split* command from the Control menu to do this) or to look at more than one document at a time. You can open up to nine windows at a time (depending upon your PC-Word configuration), although only one window (the window in the forefront) can be active. Each time you open a window with the current document displayed on your screen, a version of the window will be displayed in the Window menu and on the title bar of your current document itself.

Two additional commands on the Window menu provide quick access to additional documents or to different windows of the same document. *Arrange All* places all open windows in nonoverlapping positions on your screen, while the last item in your menu is a list of documents that can be opened for quick access.

The Help Menu

"Context-sensitive" help is available if you press F1 from anywhere.

Word provides a very intensive "on-line" help facility in order to assist you in learning all about the Word program itself. Word's Help facility may be accessed in several ways, which we'll discuss in detail shortly. One method is to use the Help menu and all its related commands: *Index, Active Keyboard, Window, Using Help, Tutorial, and About.* In general, the Help facility contains information about all the commands and the steps necessary to use them. The Help facility can also be used as "context-sensitive" as well. In other words, you can get help about your current situation (i.e., depending on which command you select or which dialog box or message is active).

The Help facility is one long file that you can access at any time. To give you an idea, the *Index* option will list the highest level of the Help table of contents. If you wish to temporarily suspend your work, you can choose Word's Tutorial to get some hands-on training. As you progress through this book, you should test the Help facility and make use of its information.

The View Menu

This is the menu that you use when changing from the default Normal Editing View to one of Word's additional ways of looking at your document. You can select from the Outline, Draft, or Page Views, as discussed earlier. The View menu also provides access to some nifty features of Word, including the Ribbon, the Ruler, and the Status Bar. Selecting one of these options produces that formatting and editing tool on your screen. Use the *Ribbon* to set different fonts, font styles, and font sizes. The *Ruler* is useful for a variety of formats, including margins, indents, spacing, and tabs. The *Status Bar* gives you the status of your document. We'll be using each of these elements in this book.

You also use the View menu to create Annotations and Footnotes, as discussed in Chapters 14 and 18, respectively. Changing from Full menus to Short menus? Choose the View menu. One command, *Preferences,* allows you to change the display among other Word operations. A particularly helpful feature, selected via the Preferences dialog box, is the ability to see formatting elements, such as paragraph marks, table gridlines, text boundaries, and hidden text.

The Status Bar

When you first start Word, the Status Bar should be selected by default. When you select the Status Bar command from the View menu (by typing Alt,V,S), a status bar appears at the bottom of the document window (see Figure 1.18). It provides messages from Word and status information on the current document (see Table 1.5). Word delivers three general types of messages:

- As an additional help feature, Word always gives a brief description of the action performed by a selected command from an active menu. You can use this feature to brief yourself on all Word commands. If you need more detail, however, choose the Help facility by selecting the command and pressing F1 (if you are using a mouse, press Shift+F1 and then click with the mouse).

- A prompting message appears when Word needs additional information to complete a command. This is often the case when the command includes additional dialog boxes.

1—Introducing Word for Windows

- Word provides the status of a command as it is executing it. It also informs you when the task is completed.

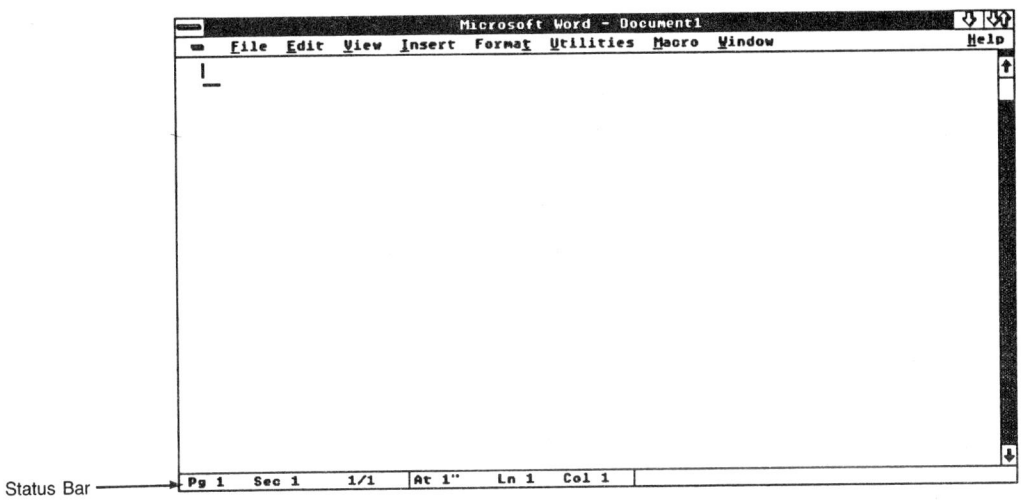

Figure 1.18 Word's status bar appears at the bottom of the document window.

Table 1.5 Status Bar

Item	Description	Function
Pg. 2	page status	Prints the page number of the currently displayed page of your document.
Sec. 3	section status	Prints the section number of the currently displayed page of your document.
4/12	total pages	Displays the page number of the currently displayed page as well as the total number of pages.
At 1.5"	insertion point location	Displays the current position of the insertion point in the active window.
Ln 6	insertion point location by line	Displays the current position of the insertion point in the active window.
Col 2	insertion point location by column	The column where the insertion point is located in the active document window.
REC	macro recorder	Appears when the macro recorder is on.

(continued)

The Basics

Table 1.5 *(continued)*

Item	Description	Function
EXT	extend selection	Appears when the extend selection is on.
COL	column selection	Appears when the column selection is on.
OVR	overtype mode	Appears when the Insert key is pressed and the keyboard is in overtype editing mode.
MRK	mark revision	Appears when the mark revisions option is selected.
CAPS	Caps Lock mode	Appears when the Caps Lock key is pressed and the keyboard is in Caps Lock mode. Mode affects the alphabetic keys only.
NUM	Num Lock mode	Appears when the Num Lock key is pressed and the keyboard is in Num Lock mode instead of directional mode. Mode affects the numeric keypad's arrow keys only.

The status bar provides general information regarding the current document, including the location of the insertion point. For example, it can tell you the page number of the currently displayed page as well as the section number. A great feature for writers is the status of the current displayed page relative to the total number of pages (e.g., 6/20 for page 6 of a 20-page document).

To help your editing, the status bar also gives the location of the insertion point, relative to the top edge of the page, or the specific line number (e.g., At 1.75" or Ln 8). The status bar also prompts you regarding keyboard mode. For example, if you press the Caps Lock, Num Lock, or Insert keys, a corresponding indicator appears on the status bar.

The Ruler

With Word's Ruler you can specify formatting features for your documents quickly and easily. You can establish format for such features as paragraph indents, paragraph alignment, line spacing, and tab settings.

The Ruler does not automatically appear on your screen the first time you start Word. To turn on the Ruler from the keyboard, press **Alt,V,R** and it will appear at the top of your document, as shown in

Figure 1.19. You can also press **Ctrl+Shift+F10** to turn on the Ruler and activate it at the same time (it must be active before you can use the keyboard to set tab stops and indents). With a mouse, click the View menu open, select the Ruler command, and click the mouse button once. To turn the Ruler off, select the Ruler command again or press Alt,V,R a second time. Typing Ctrl+Shift+F10 a second time will deactivate the Ruler, but it doesn't turn it off.

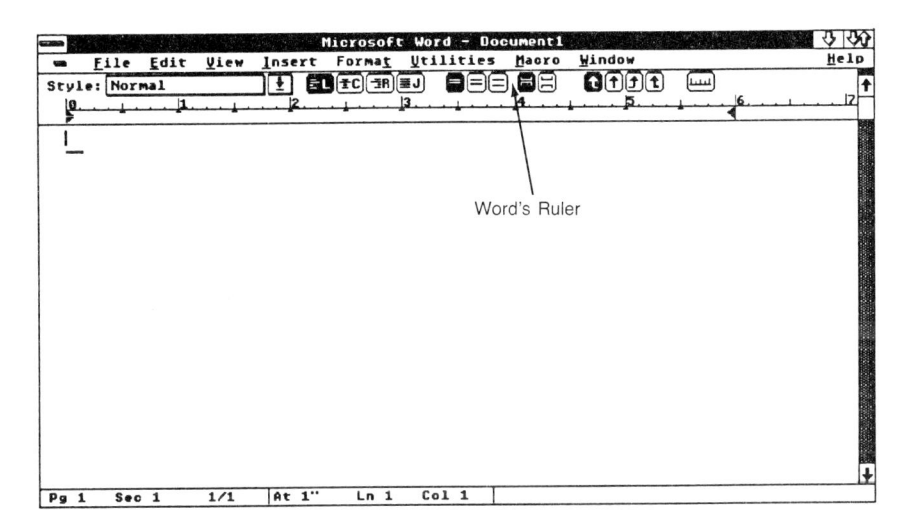

Figure 1.19 Word's Ruler appears at the top of the document window.

The Ruler is available in three views: Paragraph View, Column View, and Margin View. For formatting standard paragraphs, you work in the Ruler's Paragraph View. If you are working in a table, you can switch to Column View. And, if you wish to use the Ruler to change the margins of your document, you click the Ruler View icon (located on the far right side of the Ruler) to change to Margin View. Unfortunately, the latter two options require a mouse; neither Column View nor Margin View can be accessed from the keyboard.

Chapter 5 discusses all of the Ruler's features. For now, it's important to know of the Ruler's existence and how to turn it on or off with the keyboard or mouse.

The Ribbon

The Ribbon is another graphic formatting tool that shows the character formatting of the current selected text. To turn on the Ribbon from the keyboard, press **Alt,V,B** and the Ribbon appears at the top of the document window, as shown in Figure 1.20. If you have a mouse, click open the View menu and then click the Ribbon command. As with the Ruler, to turn off the Ribbon, simply select the command again.

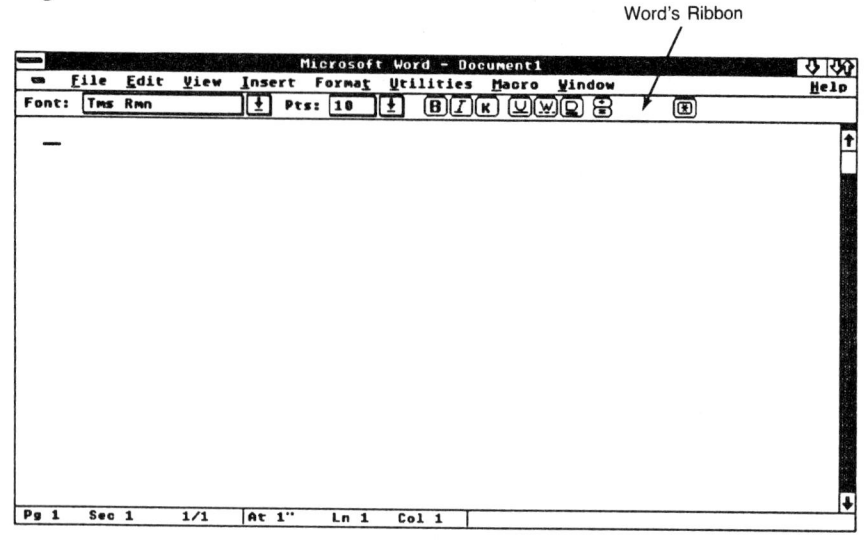

Figure 1.20 Word's Ribbon appears at the top of the Document window just above the Ruler if it is open.

The Ribbon lets you choose different fonts and font sizes from a list box. If a choice is not listed, you can type in the desired choice. To change character formatting using the Ribbon, simply point and click an icon with the mouse, or type the Ctrl key in combination with the letter representing the desired formatting selection. For example, to activate the Font box, first press Ctrl+F. Then, press Alt+down arrow to highlight the desired font. Finally, press Enter to apply the selected font. You can format font styles just as easily with the Crtl key. For example, to select boldface, you would enter Ctrl+B. In Chapter 6, we'll investigate the Ribbon in greater detail.

Using Windows

This section introduces the most important features of windows. You will use windows to view and work on different portions of your documents. Each window comes equipped with a Control menu, which we have previously discussed. Each window can only contain one document or macro at a time, but you can use the *split* feature to view

1—Introducing Word for Windows

and work on different portions of the same document in different windows. In Chapter 3 you'll learn how to manage multiple windows and to use them as you edit your documents.

Activating a Window

When you first start using Word, the document window is the active window (identified by the highlighted title bar). If you were to create a second window on your screen, by choosing New Window or a specific file from the Window menu, the new window becomes the active window. To make the original window active again, either press **Ctrl+F6** until the window you want is activated or click anywhere inside a visible window with the mouse. Of course, when you select a file from the Window menu, it will be opened inside an active window.

Closing a Window

If the Word document window is expanded to maximum size, Word will not respond to double-clicking the Control menu box to close the window.

To close a window, simply double-click the Control menu box with the mouse or press the appropriate keys from the keyboard. If you wish to close the document window, press **Alt,Hyphen,C**. To close the Word window, press **Alt,Spacebar,C**. Closing the document window only closes the current document but you remain within Word. Using the Word Control box (the larger of the two) causes you to exit Word and returns you to the Windows MS-DOS Executive screen (if you are using Windows).

Changing a Window's Size

Word allows you to change the size of its windows using either the keyboard or the mouse. Both methods require that you move the borders that surround a window. The following introduces both methods.

- Mouse method—First choose the window that you wish to change. Press **Alt,-,S** for the current document window and **Alt,Spacebar,S** for the Word application window). The pointer will change to a four-headed arrow. Move it to the border that you wish to change (left, right, top, or bottom). Drag the pointer to the new position for the border and release the mouse button. As an alternative, simply move the pointer to the border (or a corner of the border) that you wish to change

The Basics

and drag with the mouse. This method doesn't require that you first select the window with the keyboard.

- Keyboard Method—First select the window that you wish to change by choosing the *Size* command from the control box. Press **Alt,-,S** for the document window and **Alt,Spacebar,S** for the Word window. You can also select the windows using the function keys: **Ctrl+F8** selects the document window and **Alt+F8** selects the Word window. Once you've selected the Size command, the pointer changes to a four-headed arrow. Next, dictate which border you wish to change by pressing the corresponding arrow key. Once you've selected a key, the pointer becomes two-headed and appears at the bottom or the lower right corner of the window. Press the direction keys in order to move the border in the direction you want it to move. Once you're satisfied with the position of the window, press the Enter key to finalize your choice. As a tip, you can press two arrow keys in succession to move two borders at once. For example, press the left arrow key and then the down arrow key.

Maximizing and Minimizing Windows

Word also allows you to expand or shrink a window to fit the entire screen or just a portion of it. This function is accomplished with the *Maximize* and *Minimize* commands, respectively.

Some applications, such as Word, will fill the entire screen when first started. This is the maximum-sized position. If you were to minimize Word, it would be reduced to an icon on the Windows MS-DOS Executive desktop. This feature may be useful if you wish to "put away" an application until you need it. When you do, simply maximize it or choose the *Restore* command. It's important to note that you can shrink the Word application itself to an icon, but you can't shrink an individual document to an icon. To check, open both control boxes and you will notice that the Minimize command on the Document Control menu is absent. If you wish to minimize the size of a document window so that you can view more than one document window at a time, simply adjust the size of the window by moving the borders as discussed above. To shrink the Word application itself to an icon, use one of the following three methods:

- Choose the Minimize command from the Word Application Control box: **Alt,Spacebar,N**.
- Choose the Minimize command by pressing the Minimize function key: **Alt,F9**.

- With the mouse, click the Minimize box as depicted by a down arrow in the upper right corner of the Word application document window.

OK, so now your window has been reduced to either an icon or simply shrunk to a smaller size by moving the window borders. You can expand the window to its maximum size by using the Maximize command. To do this, complete one of the following:

- Choose the Maximize command from the appropriate control box. Choose **Alt,-,X** to maximize the current document window or **Alt,Spacebar,X** to maximize the Word window (from the icon level).
- Choose the Maximize function by pressing the Maximize function key. Choose **Ctrl+F10** for the document window and **Alt+F10** for the Word window.
- With the mouse, you can click the Maximize box as depicted by an up arrow in the upper right corner of the document window.

Finally, as we've hinted, you can use the Restore command from the control box to restore the window to its previous size. If the previous size was full screen, then selecting Restore will maximize the window. Both the Word and Document Control boxes have Restore commands available. To Restore either a Word window or a document window, click the Restore box (the up arrow box changes to a box with both an up and down arrow as the Restore box). To use the keyboard, press **Ctrl+F5** or **Alt,-,R** to restore a document window, and press **Alt+F5** or **Alt,Spacebar,R** to restore the Word window.

Splitting a Window

You can also double-click the split box to add (and split the document in two equal parts) or remove the split box. This is one of Word's "hot spots."

Word also allows you to split a window by using the *split box*, the small black rectangle located at the top of the vertical scroll, or the Control Split command: Alt,-,T. You use a split window to view the same document in two parts.

To divide a window, you use either the mouse or the keyboard. Let's review the mouse procedure first. Position the pointer on the split box and drag it down the vertical scroll bar to the desired division point. Upon releasing the mouse button, the window will be split into two windows, called *panes*, similar to Figure 1.21. In Chapter 3, you will see that any editing you do in one pane automatically occurs in the second pane. To move from one pane to another, click inside the second pane. It is important to note that both of the split panes represent the same document, complete with individual scroll bars. The scroll bars enable you to move up and down a document to view different portions of the same document at the same time. To close the split with the mouse, drag the split box back to the border or simply double-click the split box.

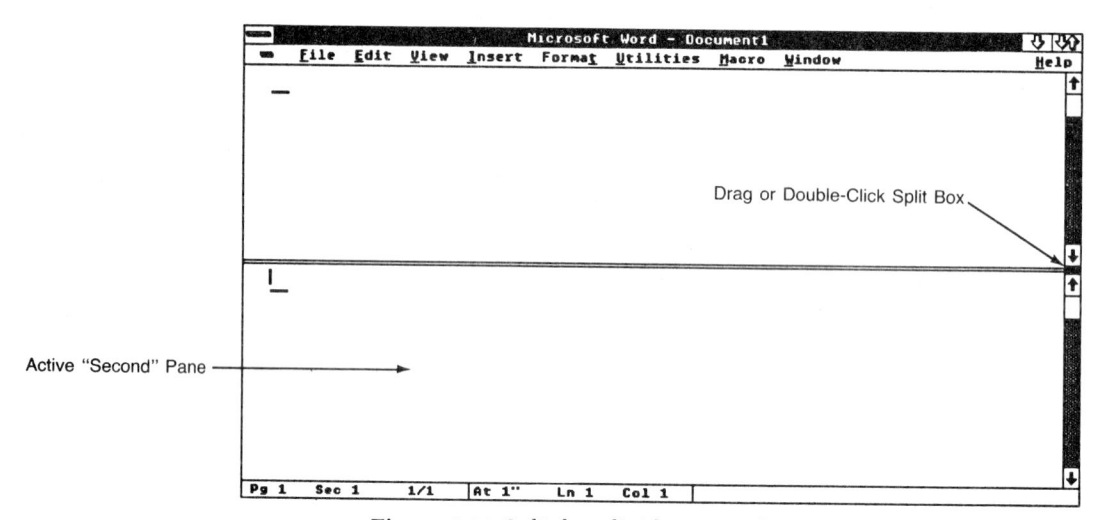

Figure 1.21 Split bar divides a window into two parts.

To split a window with the keyboard, choose the **Split** command from the Control menu: **Alt,-,T**. When the window is first split, it consists of two equal parts. To change the position of the split, use the up and down arrow keys to position the split bar. Once the split bar is in the desired position, press **Enter** to set the split. To close the split, choose the Split command a second time (Alt,-,T), use the up or down arrow key until the split box moves into the border area, and then press Enter.

Getting Help

Many programs today offer a Help utility, and Word is no exception. Think of the Word Help utility as an "on-line" tutor, available at any time to provide additional information about a particular feature or command. Word provides many ways to get help. You can access "context-sensitive" help by pressing the F1 key for help with a specific task, or you can press **Shift+F1** and then use the mouse to click the command or area on the screen for feature-specific help. For example, if you highlight the Save command from the File menu (don't execute it yet), and then press Shift+F1, your screen will look like Figure 1.22.

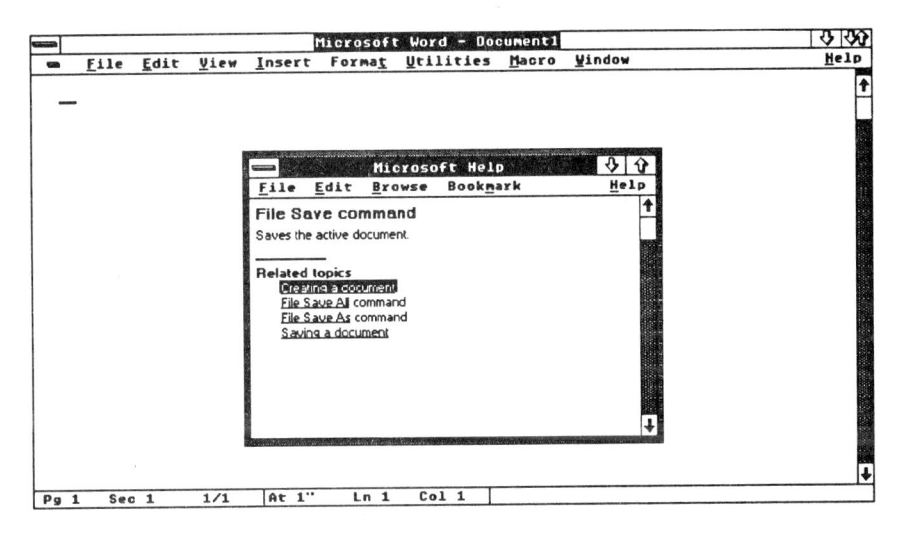

Figure 1.22 Use Word's Help facility for context-sensitive help.

You can also access the Help Menu by pressing **Alt,H**. The Help menu includes several command options: Index, Keyboard, Active Window, Tutorial, Using Help, and About. These commands are summarized as follows:

- Index—Provides an index of all of the help operations within Word.
- Keyboard—Displays the highest level of keyboard topics in an open Help dialog box.
- Active Window—Displays the topic on the current view in an open Help dialog box.
- Tutorial—This command starts Word's "on-line" tutorial. Highly recommended for beginners as well as a great refresher for old pros.
- Using Help—Discusses how to use the Help function in an open Help dialog box.
- About—In a dialog box, this command simply displays some information about the Word version, such as the version number, copyright notice, and memory and disk space available.

The Basics

If you don't know where to begin using the Help feature (other than choosing the Tutorial), we suggest that you first select the Index command. Choosing Index allows you to learn about the many features of Word, including the Help dialog window itself (see Figure 1.23). Once you choose Index, the initial Help screen lists words and phrases that are underlined. Use the underlined words, called *jump terms,* as cross references between related topics. If you use the arrow keys or mouse to highlight a jump term, and then press the Enter key or click with the mouse, the Help facility will move to the selected topic. Use the commands on the Browse menu to help you navigate from one topic to another. For example, the *Backtrack* command, F9, moves you back to the original topic so you can toggle quickly between topics using the jump terms and the Backtrack command. The remaining commands on the Browse menu are self-explanatory and easy to use. If you wish to study the information found in one of the Help windows, you should choose the *Print* option on the Help window's File menu. This command works just like a standard Print command.

Finally, to leave Help, use the control box to close the window as you would with any window or simply press the Esc key.

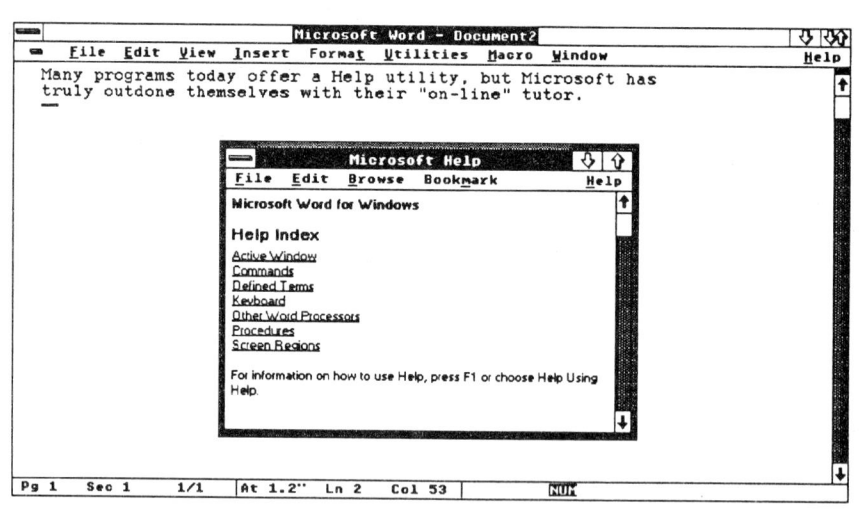

Figure 1.23 Use the Index command from the Help menu to select a topic for additional information.

Quitting Word

To leave a Word session, you can either close the Control menu (Word or the MS-DOS Executive Control menu), or choose the Exit

1—Introducing Word for Windows

command from the File menu. The steps are easy, but it is important to use the proper method. Don't simply turn off your computer.

1. Choose the **Exit** command from the File menu with the mouse, or press **Alt,F,X**. You can also close the Control menu by pressing **Alt,Spacebar,C**.

    If you entered text, a dialog box appears and asks whether you want to save the document. (Saving documents is discussed in Chapter 2). If you didn't enter any text, step 2 doesn't apply, and you will be returned to the Window's MS-DOS Executive screen or to the DOS prompt.

2. Since you are not ready to save anything just yet, click **No** or press **Enter**.

    If you closed the Window's Control menu, you are asked to confirm that you wish to quit Windows. If you don't plan to quit Windows, step 3 doesn't apply.

3. Click **OK** or press **Enter** to confirm that you wish to quit Windows, if necessary.

    You will be returned to DOS. Note that the next time you start Word, it will appear exactly as you last left it. All Word settings are recorded in the WINWORD.INI file when you quit.

Review

In this chapter you learned:

1. You can start Word for Windows from the DOS system prompt or from within Windows itself. To start from DOS, type winword. (Keep in mind that you may need to change to the directory where the Word files reside on your hard disk.) You can also start Word with some variations—for example, you can open a specific file or multiple files, run a macro, or open files and run macros in combination.

2. To start Word from within Windows, select the drive and directory that contains the WINWORD.EXE file, select the file, and press Enter.

The Basics

3. The Word screen primarily consists of three parts: the menu bar running across the top of the screen, a control menu box, and a large empty document window area.

4. The document window, or work area, is where you will type, edit, and format your word processing documents.

5. The insertion point is the blinking vertical line that first appears in the upper left corner of the document window. Its job is to point to the current position on the screen where the next typed character will appear.

6. The pointer can take many shapes, depending on where it is located on the screen and in what mode you are running. It represents the location of the mouse and is used to move the insertion point. You can also use the arrow keys to freely move the pointer around the screen.

7. An end mark is a thick, short horizontal line that indicates the end of your document.

8. Word offers you several ways of looking at your document. When you first start Word, you are in Normal Editing View. Using the View menu, you can change to Draft, Outline, or Page View. To see the overall structure of your document before you print it out, choose Print Preview from the File menu.

9. Word offers several tools to help make formatting easy. Two of these tools are graphical, the Ribbon and the Ruler. The Ribbon is used to format characters. The Ruler can help format paragraphs and set margins, but it requires use of a mouse.

10. In addition to the control box, the Word menu bar is represented by the following menu items: File, Edit, View, Insert, Format, Utilities, Macro, Window, and Help. Each menu item corresponds to a separate list of commands available in a pull-down list.

11. You can use the mouse to select commands from the menu items on the menu bar, or you can enter an equivalent command directly from the keyboard. The keyboard method uses the Alt key in combination with other keys represented by underlined letters in menus and commands. These commands are generally executed in successive keystrokes (one key is not necessarily held down while the second key is pressed). Some commands can also be selected if you use the Ctrl key in combination with the function keys (F1–F12) in a single keypress.

12. You can also use the numeric keypad in directional mode to move the insertion point around your screen and to highlight command selections from an active menu.
13. Word offers both Short and Full menus. The commands available on the menus vary depending on whether a document is currently open or not. The location of the insertion point can also affect the available commands to you (e.g., whether it resides inside a document pane or an annotations pane).
14. Word allows you to use windows in a variety of ways. You can enlarge (maximize), shrink (minimize), relocate (move), and even split windows. By splitting windows, you can look at two parts of the same document at once.
15. Getting help with Word is easy. You can choose Help to learn more about a particular command or feature. To use the Help feature, either access the Help menu or press F1 or Shift+F1 (for mice) to access context-sensitive help. You can even use the Help tutorial as a hands-on electronic manual to learn how to master Word at your leisure.
16. To leave a Word session, choose Exit from the File menu or close the Word Control menu. If you close the Document Control monu, you will only leave the current document, but remain in Word.

Chapter TWO

Creating Documents

In this chapter:

- Introduction to Word Processing
- Entering Text
- Moving Around Your Screen
- Introducing Files and File Names
- Saving Your Documents
- Retrieving Your Document
- Typing and Printing Your First Letter

Word processing is a favorite tool for use with a microcomputer. It helps you improve your writing by increasing your productivity or by improving your creativity. Professional writers have a passion for it. Many businesspeople wonder how they ever managed to be productive without it. Students discover the rewards and flexibility of word processing while preparing homework, reports, and term papers. Enough drum beating. In this chapter, you'll learn to enter text and create your first document. You will also learn how to save a document, make copies of a document, store your documents in files, and retrieve existing documents from those same files.

Introduction to Word Processing

Word processing is the manipulation of text on your screen before you print it. Word processing enables you to make corrections, deletions, and modifications to your text without the need for erasures or cutting and pasting. This is the beauty of word processing: It allows you to concentrate on writing creatively without worrying about misspellings. Revising a draft is simple. So, instead of "getting it right the first time," you can easily revisit your work to modify it. In fact, the task of writing doesn't have to be one of drudgery—it can even be fun!

A number of commercial word processing software packages are available today, including Microsoft Word for Windows. Some of the original text processors were "dedicated" for the sole purpose of processing words, but with Word, as with most contemporary word processing programs, you have the flexibility to do much more than simply process words. While word processing features vary from one software package to another, most of them allow you to complete three common functions. The first function is full-screen editing. The second is the ability to format the printing of your documents. This feature includes such tasks as setting margins, justifying lines (left, right, and center), and calculating page breaks ("pagination"). The third function is the ability to move a section of text from one area to another. This powerful feature enables writers to modify their work without the need for cutting and pasting.

Basic Concepts of Word Processing and Tips for Using It

When you first use word processing, your screen typically includes a work area, an empty area with a flashing insertion point appearing in the upper left corner of the screen. This is where you will begin to type all your text. All text placed in the work area is stored in the central memory (RAM) area of the computer. The information stored in RAM is volatile and may be lost if you accidentally turn the computer's power off (or if you are unfortunate enough to have lightning strike your power line before saving your changes).

Word processing gives you the ability to store your work on magnetic media, such as a floppy disk, for later use or modification. Saved to a disk in this way, the information will remain there until you change the information or erase it; it is no longer volatile.

Saving your documents is a fundamental procedure in word processing. Later in this chapter you'll learn all the steps necessary to store a document on your diskette or hard disk. But for now, be advised: Save your work often! During a work session, save your work about every 15 minutes. This method ensures that you will never lose more than 15 minutes of work at a time in the case of some unforeseen disaster (remember the lightning?). Don't stuff the envelope. Save your work.

A document is saved as a word processing *file*. A file is the basic storage unit of the computer and is sometimes used synonymously with the term "document." You always wanted to know why we refer to your letters as documents. In fact, many IBM-compatible word processors will recognize a word processing file as a document in its DOS directory when the document is saved, and then automatically attach a file name extension to it such as .DOC, for document.

The first time you save a document, you create a file for it. Then you may want to create a backup for the file. Having done this, you can edit the work on the backup while leaving the original version of your work intact in case you decide later that you prefer the original to the edited version.

Using a word processor like Word is like using a typewriter—but easier. Certain details of using a typewriter are avoided with word processing. For example, you don't need to hit a carriage return when you reach the end of a line because the word processor will automatically word-wrap and drop down to the next line for you. In other words, the computer will not break words in two, leaving a portion of the word on the previous line and another portion on the new line. The only time you use a carriage return is when you wish to start a new paragraph. Further, you don't need to worry about line spacing or indenting or about resetting margins. With Word, you don't even need to worry about spelling (Word includes a spelling checker to help you check your work). The editing and formatting features of Word relieve you of attending to such details. With a typewriter, most of the formatting must be set before you start typing a document. If you do decide to change margins or the spacing, for example, the material you previously typed must be retyped. On the other hand, Word can do it for you automatically with a few simple keystrokes or clicks of the mouse.

Some people believe the "learning curve" for a new technology, such as a word processor, is too long and cannot be made up in terms of speed and productivity. But, increasing the speed and ease of your work is only a fraction of the benefit of using a word processor. The quality of your work actually should improve as you can focus on the creative aspects of the work and not on the mechanics of completing the work. To top it off, working with a word processor—and computers in general—can be quite addictive. As soon as you discover the power of using a word processor, and the simplicity of learning how

The Basics

to use Word in particular, you will discover that the effort you make learning to use a word processor is very small compared to the benefits you derive from its features.

Entering Text

The purpose of using a word processor is to make the writing process as simple as possible. For its part, Microsoft has provided a tool that is very easy to use in Word. In fact, the beauty of word processing is that you can just begin to type without formatting first. You can format later.

This section provides tips about entering text. From now on, you will be using the Full Menus mode so select that option from the View menu. If you haven't yet started Word and the initial screen is not displayed, read the beginning of Chapter 1 first. If you have jumped ahead and your screen is already filled with text, close all active windows, open the File menu, and select the New command. Use the mouse, or from the keyboard press **Alt,F,N**. From the New dialog box, accept the default option for creating a new document based on the Normal style by clicking **OK** or pressing **Enter** (creating new documents based on a particular document template will be discussed later in this chapter). Choosing New will open another window with an empty document labeled "Microsoft Word—Document2."

Typing Some Text

Entering text with a word processor should be simple. You don't need to worry about your text's appearance or accuracy. To fix a typo, simply use the Backspace key to erase the error and then retype the text. In Chapter 3, you will learn more complete methods of editing and correcting mistakes. For now, the Backspace key will do. The insertion point will be blinking at the top left of your screen, marking where the next typed character will appear. As you begin to enter the sample text, the insertion point will move from left to right until the text reaches the end of the line and word-wraps to the next line as you continue entering text. Type the following text and do not press the Enter key when you reach the end of the first line:

```
Word processing is easy and fun with Microsoft Word. I am sure that
I will soon master this program.
```

This text will fit nicely on two lines on your screen and demonstrates a few points. First, conveniently, Word has made several default settings on the Ruler for you. Word's Ruler is the horizontal line measure which is located in the View menu. If you open the View menu and select the Ruler command, the Ruler will be displayed at the top of your document window. In Chapter 5, you will explore all the Ruler's features for formatting your documents. Don't worry about its contents now; just be aware of its existence and that your text will appear on your screen following the default format values. For example, your text will be formatted as left-justified (text appears flush left and ragged on the right) and single spaced.

Creating Paragraphs

In Word, a paragraph is technically just a line, a graphic, or group of lines that appear together and are followed by a trailing paragraph mark. This is not exactly grammatically correct, but rather a visual understanding of Word. With the word-wrap feature, it is not necessary to press Enter at the end of each line as you continue to type. However, if you want to start a new paragraph, you press the Enter key to create the necessary carriage return. Pressing Enter inserts the invisible paragraph mark in your document at the point where the carriage return is to occur. To view this, and other formatting symbols, you can select the Preferences command from the View menu by pressing Alt,V,E or using the mouse. The Preferences dialog box will appear as shown in Figure 2.1. The first time you start Word, all the hidden formatting symbols that appear in the left column in Preferences are turned off by default. Turn on any of these options by pressing the corresponding underlined letter in the command, or click the appropriate box with the mouse. To turn on all options in the left column, choose the Show All * option. If you wish to choose one of these options, do so now and then click OK or press Enter to register the change. You can, of course, toggle back and forth between the Preference options by choosing them a second time to turn the option off. You'll explore how the Preference options are useful in later chapters. To give you an idea how these options might affect the appearance of a standard document, see Figure 2.2.

The paragraph symbol is considered a part of the paragraph. It marks the end of the last word and the last sentence of the paragraph. In fact, Word treats the symbol as a character itself and considers it a delimiter for the beginning sentence of the next paragraph. More important, the paragraph symbol carries a paragraph's formatting.

The Basics

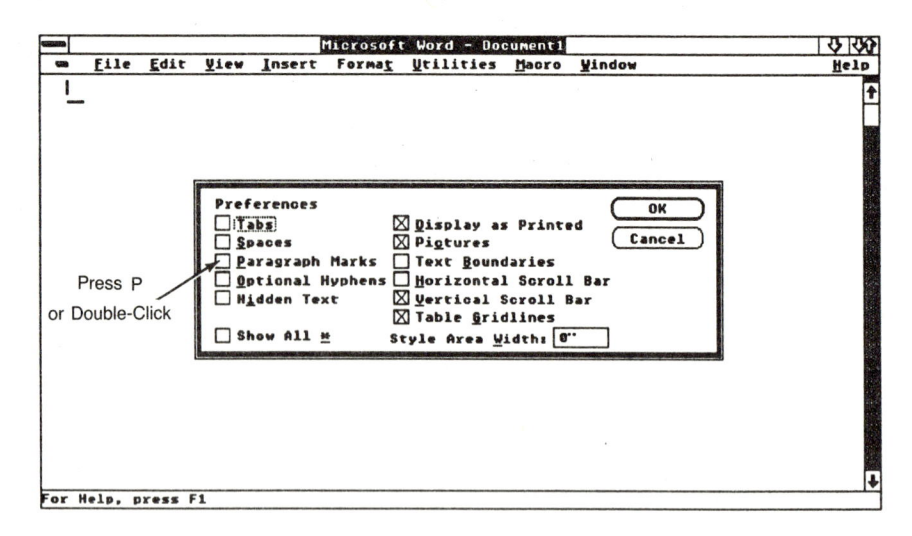

Figure 2.1 Use Preferences to turn on and off the paragraph symbol.

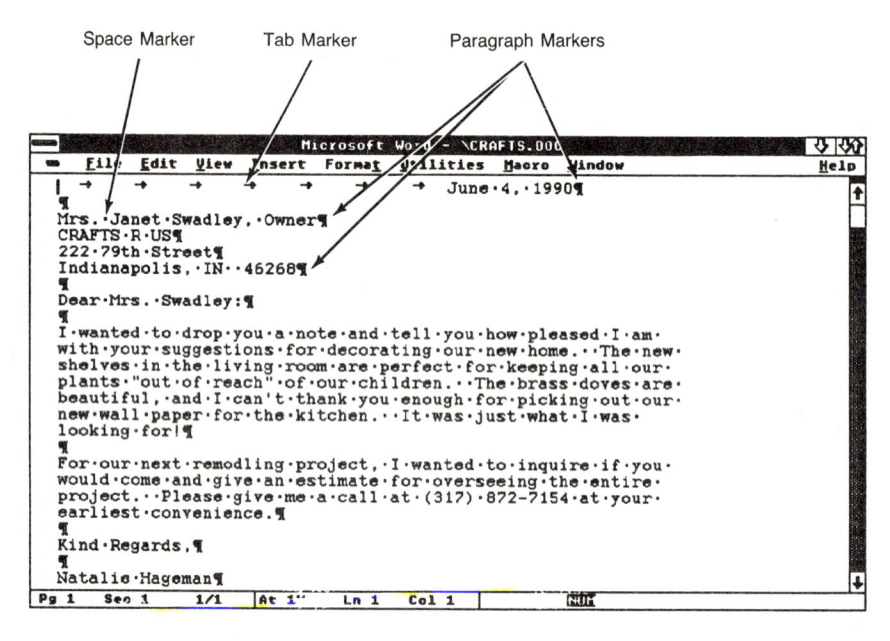

Figure 2.2 A standard document with all the Preference options selected.

When you first create a paragraph, the symbol carries the formatting of the default Normal style. Later in this book, you'll learn about applying a different style to your paragraphs.

During an editing session, you may decide to go back and delete some text within a group of paragraphs or to change the formatting with a margin change. Word will automatically reset the flow of text during your editing session. One important point to remember: If you delete a paragraph symbol, the formatting of that paragraph is removed. The remaining contents of that paragraph (text without the trailing paragraph symbol) become a part of the following paragraph and take on its formatting style.

Creating Letterheads and Salutations

When you create letterheads and salutations, you must somehow create line breaks in your text. You could simply press Enter at the end of each line, but Word would insert the paragraph symbol. An alternate method is to perform a Shift+Enter keypress, called a *Newline*, which instructs Word to break the line without creating a new paragraph. The advantage of Newline is that you only have to format the text once; some of Word's formatting commands pertain to an entire paragraph, so when you set a new line with Enter you must format it. Beginners, though, may wish to stay with the Enter key to create a letterhead or salutation.

Moving Around Your Screen

Most monitor screens are not designed to show you a "what you see is what you get" page of text, unless your document contains very few lines of text. Word can give you a hand here, because you'll remember that Print Preview will show you the structure of your pages in reduced form while Page View will show you exactly how your text will look in portions that will fit on your screen. When you type more text than the screen will hold, the new lines appear at the bottom as the old text scrolls upward and out of view (see Figure 2.3). The old text is not lost. To review the text, either use the mouse or the keyboard to scroll your document as detailed in the next three sections.

Using the Mouse to Navigate Your Documents

Select Word's Print Preview command from the File menu to get a more accurate WYSIWYG view. Print Preview is discussed in Chapter 8.

To review the text from the beginning (top-down) use the vertical scroll bar on the right of your screen by positioning the pointer on the scroll box or scroll arrow and dragging or clicking with the mouse in the direction you wish your document to scroll. You can also navigate horizontally by using the horizontal scroll box that is located at the bottom of your screen.

Even though your entire document may not appear on your screen, the document will print in its entirety, regardless of the location of your pointer.

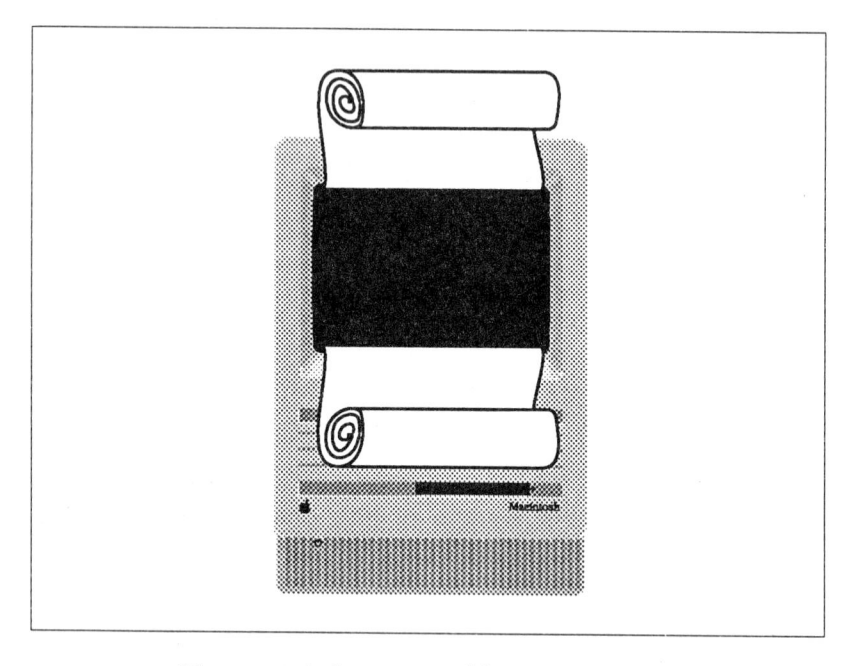

Figure 2.3 A document is like a vertical scroll.

To move into the left margin, use both the mouse and the keyboard. Move the scroll box to the left end of the horizontal scroll bar with the mouse, press the Shift key and then the left arrow key as desired.

You can also use the mouse to move through your document in a variety of other ways. Obviously, you can point and click in your document to move the insertion point, but you can also scroll through your document window without moving the insertion point itself. Using the scroll bar as discussed above is one example of this. For additional ways to scroll your document without moving the insertion point, refer to Table 2.1.

Table 2.1. Scrolling Your Document with the Mouse

Mouse Action	Resulting Scroll
Click up or down scroll arrow	Moves through document line by line
Click above or below scroll box (vertical scroll bar)	Moves through document screen by screen
Click right or left arrow scroll bars	Moves right or left by character
Drag vertical scroll box	Moves to a relative point of document length
Drag horizontal scroll box	Moves to a relative point of document width

Using the Keyboard to Navigate Your Documents

You can move the insertion point and easily scroll your document using the keys of your keyboard or the *Go To* command on the Edit menu. This section details the movement of the insertion point with the arrow keys and the numeric keypad. The next section discusses the versatile Go To command.

Do not be tempted to use the Enter key to scroll down your document. Pressing Enter will simply place additional blank lines in your document.

When you scroll with keys, you use the arrow keys and the keys on the numeric keypad, including the location-control keys of Home, Page Up, Page Down, and End. These keys can "extend" the movement of the insertion point. For example, to move to the beginning of your document, press Ctrl+Home. Table 2.2 lists additional ways to scroll through your document.

Table 2.2 Scrolling Your Document with Keys

Key Action	Result
Right arrow	Moves to next character
Left arrow	Moves back one character
Up arrow	Moves up one line
Down arrow	Moves down one line
Home	Moves to the beginning of the line
Home+down arrow	Moves to the bottom of the page
Home+up arrow	Moves to the top of the page
End	End of line

(continued)

The Basics

Table 2.2 *(continued)*

Key Action	Result
Page Down	Moves to next screen
Page Up	Moves to previous screen
Ctrl + Page Down	Moves to bottom of window
Ctrl + Page Up	Moves to top of window
Ctrl + right arrow	Next word
Ctrl + left arrow	Previous word
Ctrl + down arrow	Next paragraph
Ctrl + up arrow	Previous paragraph
Ctrl + Home	Moves to beginning of document
Ctrl + End	Moves to end of document

Please note that once you have repositioned the insertion point with either the arrow keys or the mouse, do not be tempted to use the space bar to move from left to right unless you want to move the text to the right. Conversely, using Delete to move from right to left will erase any character in the path.

If you use the arrow keys on the numeric keypad, remember to use the Num Lock key to switch to directional mode. If you press Num Lock and NUM appears in the status bar, when you press the arrow keys the numbers will be typed instead of the insertion point being moved. To switch to directional mode, press Num Lock a second time.

Using the Go To Command

To jump quickly from one point in your document to another, you can use the Go To command found on the Edit menu. To use this command, press Alt,E,G and then select your destination by typing the desired page number (see Figure 2.4). Once selected, click OK with the mouse or press Enter. For Word to use the Go To command effectively, you should select the default Background Repagination option (found on the Customize dialog box of the Utilities menu). If you don't select it, your document won't be divided into proper pages, although you can choose the *Repaginate Now* command to bring your pagination up to date if the Background Repagination option is turned off.

2—Creating Documents

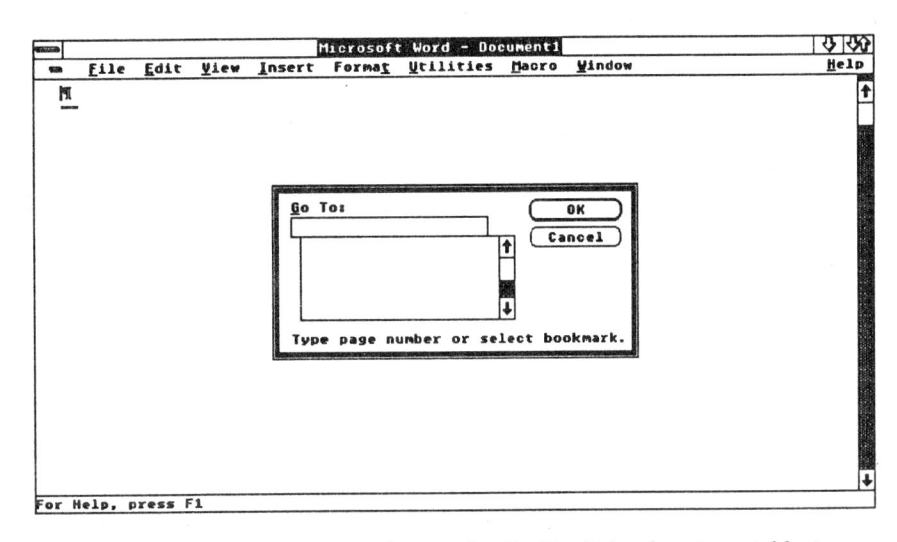

Figure 2.4 Enter the page number in the Go To dialog box to quickly jump from page to page.

The Go To command can also be accessed using the F5 function key. Pressing F5 places the command in the status bar at the bottom of your screen. Enter the destination by typing the page number, and then press Enter.

Clearing Your Screen

If you wish to clear your screen and start with a fresh page, one method you could use would be to hit the Backspace key repeatedly until all the characters are erased. A better, much faster method is to use the New command from the File menu as the following instruction details. But be sure to close all unneeded windows before using the New command. The windows take up valuable memory and keep Windows working overtime.

Caution Save any valuable documents before closing the windows because the documents might otherwise be lost.

1. Choose the **New** command from the File menu or type **Alt,F,N**.

    The New dialog box appears (see Figure 2.5). The New Document option, based on Normal style, is selected by default.

The Basics

2. If you wish to fill in the summary information regarding the new document, click **Summary** or type **S** now. If you don't, go on to step 3.

   Choosing the Summary option produces the dialog box in Figure 2.6. The advantage of adding summary data is that you will be able to use the Find command (discussed in Chapter 15) more effectively. Once you have added the Summary information, click **OK** or press **Enter**.

3. Accept both default values for New Document and Normal style by clicking **OK** or pressing **Enter**.

   Your new document appears as Document2, 3, and so on, depending upon how many new documents you have opened during the current session.

Chapter 3 demonstrates another method for clearing your screen. If you can't wait, you can drag the mouse pointer to select all the text and then press the Delete key. Presto! All the selected text will be erased!

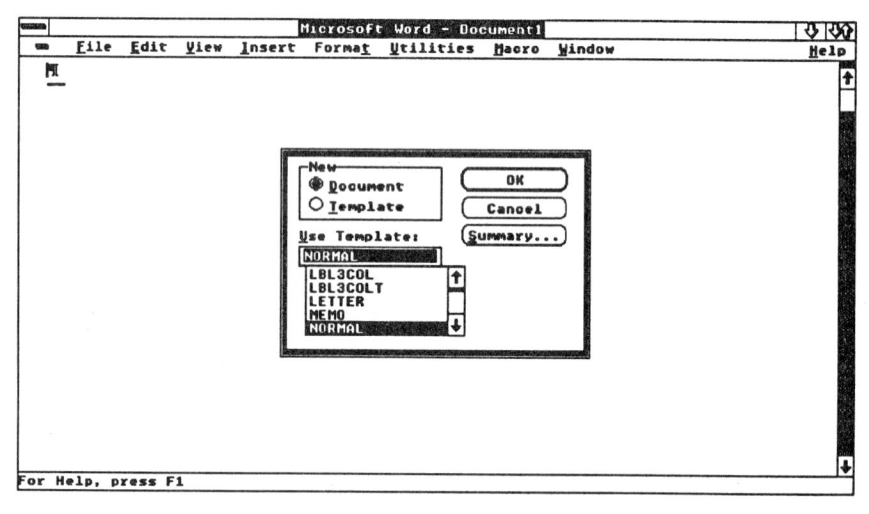

Figure 2.5 Choose the New command from the File menu to get a clean page.

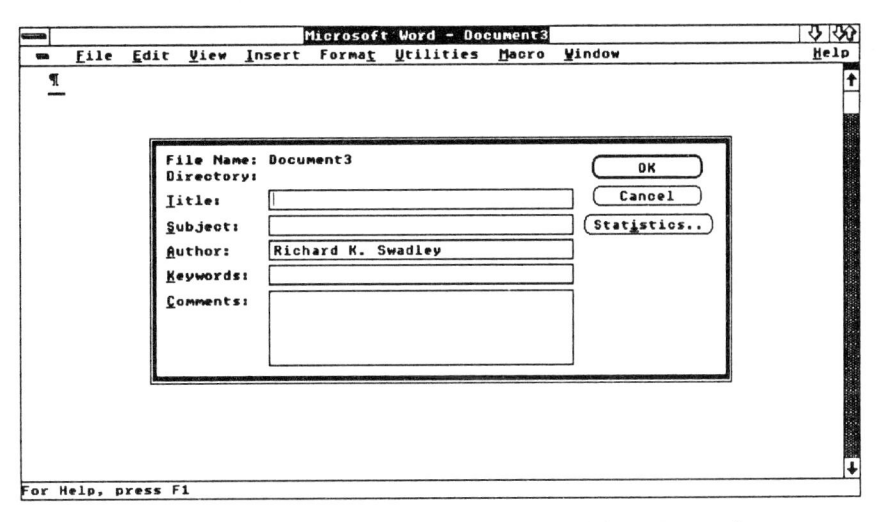

Figure 2.6 Adding summary information will benefit you later.

Some Final Thoughts on Entering Text

Finally, some reminders and a tip before you begin the serious word processing:

- Do your writing first and worry about the editing and formatting later. You can get bogged down worrying about these while your writing becomes secondary. You'll learn about editing and formatting in chapters that follow.
- Second, you will be typing and thinking, typing and thinking. Time will pass. Remember to save your material often (see the next section).
- Remember, on a word processor like Word, 1 is not l and 0 is not O. Typists might be tempted to substitute the letters l and O for the numerals 1 and 0, or visa versa. However, a computer is not so forgiving. Be precise.
- Insert mode vs. typeover mode—this is not a boxing match, but a choice of how to insert text into your documents. With insert mode, everything you type is entered at the location of the insertion point. If the insertion point is between existing text segments, the text is pushed to the right and wraps around to

63

The Basics

the next line as it reaches the right margin. If you press the Insert key to turn on *typeover* mode, then anything that you type replaces existing text as the insertion point moves right to left. You toggle between insert mode and typeover mode by pressing the Insert key. If the status bar is present at the bottom of your screen, turning on typeover mode will display the symbol, OVR.

- Remember, to cancel many commands and close menus before they are executed, press the Esc key.

- Here's an advanced tip from an old word processing hand: Use Word's search-and-replace capability to substitute a common word or abbreviation for long phrases whose repeated typing would slow you down. Later, while cleaning up the document, use the search-and-replace procedure to change all occurrences of the phrase throughout the document. This way, you only type it once. Of course, you must remember to do the search and replace. (It wouldn't do to turn in a report in which the phrase, "People's Republic of China" is represented by "PORK"! This procedure is detailed in Chapter 3, and in Chapter 12 you'll learn to use the glossary feature to insert commonly used phrases in your documents.

Introducing Files and File Names

As we have discussed, any program or collection of data used by the computer is stored in a file. Word stores information, such as letters, memos, names, and addresses as data files (sometimes called text files). When you are ready to store your documents as data files on a diskette or your hard disk, you will be required to give the file a name. When naming such files, you must obey certain rules that are enforced by the operating system of your computer, such as DOS. If you don't follow the rules, your computer will provide a message like:

```
Not a valid filename
```

If you get this message, then you know you have broken one of the rules for properly naming a file. Since naming files is a basic skill that you must acquire early, let's review some rules and helpful suggestions.

- All file names consist of two parts; a base file name and an extension. The base file name may consist of a total of eight characters, or as few as one. The extension always begins with a period (.) followed by as many as three additional characters.
- Most characters are allowed in the base file name with a few exceptions. Blank spaces are not allowed. It's best to use the letters of the alphabet, numbers, hyphens, or underscores. A period (which Word supplies) separates the base file name from the extension. Never use the following characters in a file name:

    ". / \ [ ] : * <> + ; , ?

- If you don't give your documents a file name extension, Word will automatically apply the .DOC (for document) extension for you. When you learn how to use Word's backup option for saving files, you will notice that Word will apply the .BAK extension as an identifier that the file is a backup copy of another file.
- If you don't want Word to add a file name extension for you, enter a period after the file name. For example, if you name a file:

    SAMPLE.

    Word will not add the three-character DOC extension to the end of the name.
- These would be legal file names:

    CHAP1
    INVOICE
    1LETTER.DOC
    LEDGER.DAT
    MYLETTER.DOC

    These are illegal file names:

    CHAP 1 (contains a space)
    LETTER.1.DOC (contains two periods)
    FIRSTLETTER.DOC (contains too many characters)

- Use meaningful file names that describe the contents of the file. This is especially important when you are ready to retrieve a file from storage on a diskette or hard disk. For example, instead of first.doc for your first-quarter sales report, you might enter 1stQ-90.DAT for a name.

65

The Basics

- Some file name extensions are reserved for special programs. .EXE, .COM, and .BAT are among those that are reserved.

Now that you have an understanding of the rules for naming files, let's review the steps necessary for creating document files and the need for naming them.

Saving Your Documents

The short-cut Shift+F12 keypress sidesteps the File menu and executes the Save command instantly.

As a task, saving your documents is second in importance only to the process of creating them in the first place. If you fail to save your documents, you will lose them when you turn off the computer. This applies to saving a new document during your first work session or to saving new material to an existing document or to a different directory or second disk drive. Following is a list of Save options available with Word:

- Saving Your New Document—The steps that follow describe the first time you attempt to save your current document. The document will be untitled until you name it during the save operation. Saving a document involves copying the information currently residing in RAM to a more permanent storage location, such as a floppy diskette or a hard disk. Until you change or erase it, the file remains as you stored it.

- Saving to an Existing Document—Each time you edit or modify an existing document, you will probably want to save this new version as well. You do not need to give this document a name since you are simply updating the same document. Remember, though, unless you save the new information, only the previous version will remain safely stored on your diskette or hard disk.

- Saving Files as Backups—Use this method to save a new version of a document while retaining the old version. This method uses the Create Backup option.

- Saving to Second Disk Drive—Use this method when you need to store your document files on a data disk. This is the method that you will follow as you read this book. Because your documents take up a lot of space, use this method to keep your hard disk free from clutter. Although many hard disks have tons of space, you might want to save that space for the

2—Creating Documents

applications themselves. When you need to retrieve an existing file, place the data disk into the designated disk drive and you're ready to go.

- Saving to a Different File or Directory—This method also allows you to save an existing file with a different name while leaving the old file intact. Similar to using the Create Backup option.
- Saving Automatically—Word provides a feature that will automatically save the changes to your document for you at regular intervals. This feature doesn't replace the standard Save procedure, however.
- Saving to a Different File Format—Allows you to save a document in a file format other than the standard Word file format. You can also save the document as a document template.

To move around the Save dialog box, press Alt followed by the letter of the edit field. For example, to move to the directory field, press Alt + D. Use the arrow keys to scroll a particular edit field.

1. Open the File menu with the mouse and select the **Save** command or press **Alt,F,S** from the keyboard.

The Save dialog box appears (see Figure 2.7). If you have saved this document before, the dialog box will not appear and, in a few seconds, the command will be executed.

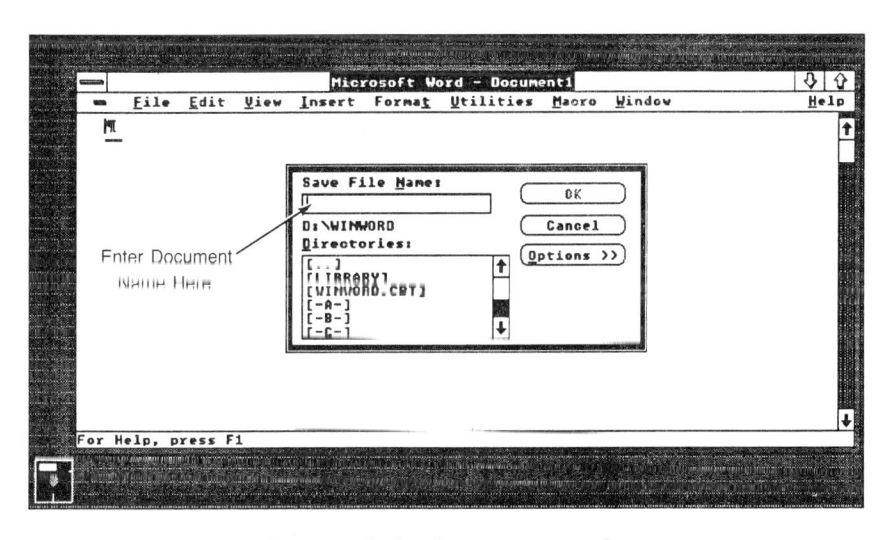

Figure 2.7 The Save dialog box requires a document name.

The Basics

2. The dialog box will show an empty File Name and the name of the current directory, such as: D:\WINWORD in Figure 2.7. The first time you save a file, you must give the document a name. Choose a name characteristic of the document, such as RESUME.DOC or REJECT.LTR to identify it. Remember the base name must be from one to eight characters followed by an optional period and one- to three-character extension (see the previous section on naming files). Type the desired file name and choose the drive and directory where you want the file stored. Then, click **OK** or press **Enter**.

3. If you turned off the Prompt for Summary Info option, then Word accepts your name when you click **OK** or press

Word accepts your file name if it's valid, and displays the Summary Info dialog box as shown in Figure 2.8. If you don't wish to use Word's file retrieval system, you can turn off the Prompt for Summary Info option on the Utilities Customize dialog box by pressing **Alt,U,U,O**.

It's that simple! When you click OK or press Enter, the Save command is executed and you are soon

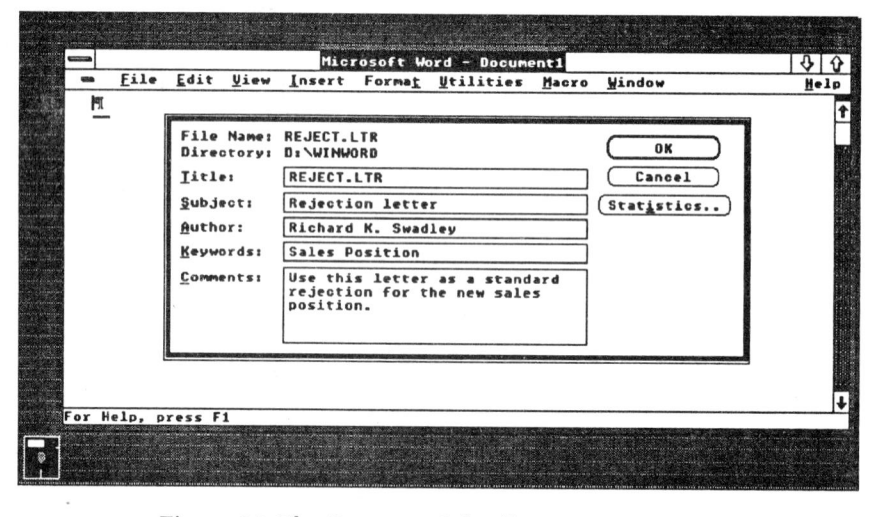

Figure 2.8 The Summary Info allows you to use Word's file retrieval system.

Enter, and you are returned to the current document. However, if you wish to use Word's retrieval system to help you find files later, fill out the Summary Info fields: Directory, Title, Subject, Author, Keywords, and Comments. Use Table 2.3 as a guide. Note that to move from field to field, use the Tab key and then the arrow keys to scroll any field boxes. When finished with the Summary, Click **OK** or press **Enter**.

returned to the current document window. The title bar will now bear your chosen file name instead of Document1. One other note: As the command executes, Word will display the number of characters in the file in the lower left corner of the status bar.

Table 2.3 Summary Information Sheet Fields

Field Name	Description
File Name	This is the DOS name that you have provided the current active document. To change this name, you must perform a *Save As* command, which is discussed shortly.
Directory	This is the directory where the current active document is located. To change this directory, you must use the Save As command.
Title	You can type a more descriptive name for the document (up to 255 characters, including spaces).
Subject	You can type a description (up to 255 characters long) of the document's contents.
Author	The name of the person who created the document (up to 255 characters long). You can change this name if you wish.
Keywords	Type a list of words, or phrases, that will help you identify this document. Use general topics, such as a product or customer name. Keywords may be up to 255 characters long, including spaces between the words.
Comments	Type any additional information about the document that you may wish to save (up to 255 characters long). For example, *this letter discusses our new sales discount structure for dealers.*

Using the Summary Information

Word also provides a related Statistics panel for each of your documents. From the Summary Info dialog box, click the Statistics button or press Alt,E,I.

To help you recall a document in a variety of ways, Word provides the Summary Info Prompt. The first time you save a document, the Summary Info dialog box will appear (see Figure 2.8). You can edit the information in any of the fields at any time (for a description of the fields, see Table 2.3). Use the Tab key to move from one edit field to another. In the Comments edit box, use Ctrl+Home and Ctrl+End to go to the beginning or the end of the comment, just like working inside a standard document window. If you have already filled in the Summary Info for an existing document, Word will not display the Summary dialog box automatically. The Summary Information dialog box is a default option that can be turned off via the Utilities Customize dialog box.

Your Document's Vital Statistics

You can stop the save procedure at any time before you click the Save command itself. To do this, choose Cancel or Esc instead of Save.

You can easily keep track of some important statistics regarding the current active document by viewing the Statistics dialog box. This dialog box will provide such information as the date and by whom a document was last updated. It also includes the number of pages, words, and characters of the current active document. Keep in mind that the statistics are sensitive to the last time a particular operation was completed. However, the Update option on the Statistics dialog box provides a method to immediately update the document's statistics, including any new words added during a current editing session. To get a peek at your current document's statistics, you can choose the Summary Info command from the Edit menu by pressing Alt,E,I or use your mouse. Once selected, the Summary Info dialog box appears just like it does when you save your documents (assuming this option is on by default). From the Summary Info dialog box, choose the Statistics button with the mouse or press Alt+I and a Statistics panel like that in Figure 2.9 will appear on your screen. Obviously, you can view the statistics of your document at any time during a save operation by choosing the Statistics button just prior to clicking OK or pressing Enter.

When you are finished with the Statistics panel, click OK or press Enter. You will soon be returned to the Summary Info dialog box. One last note. Unlike the Summary information, you cannot edit the information in the Statistics panel. It's for viewing purposes only.

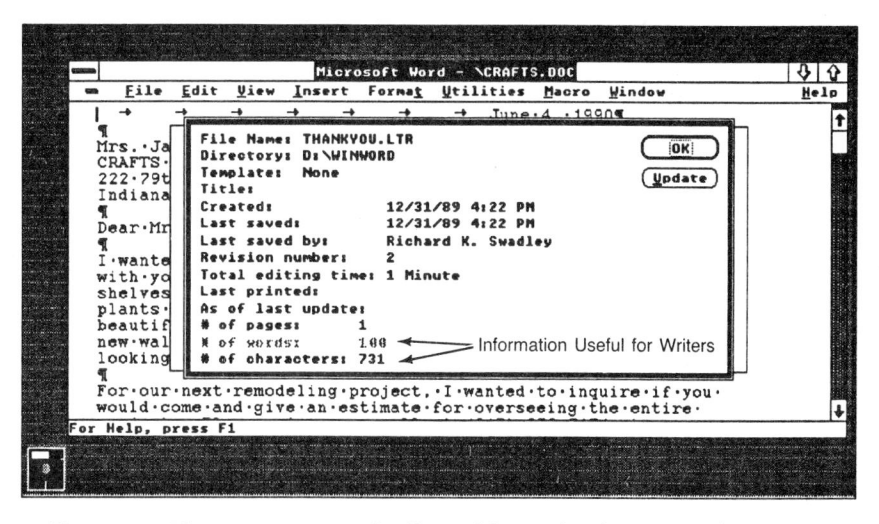

Figure 2.9 The Statistics panel offers additional information about your current document.

Saving to an Existing Document

Each time you edit your documents or change them in some way, you must save the document or the new information will be lost. As we have stated, it is a good idea to set up standard time intervals for saving your new material during the current work session. The common suggestion is once every 10 to 15 minutes. To save the new edited version of your existing document, simply choose the Save command by pressing Alt,F,S and click OK or press Enter. If you have filled in the Summary Info, you won't need to do so a second time. Of course, you can change the information by choosing the Summary button from the Save dialog box *before* you press Enter or click OK.

Keep in mind that when you save the changes made during the current work session, the original version of your document file will be replaced with the new edited version. Therefore, if you wish to save the original version, you must save the new version with a different file name, to a different location, or use the Create Backup option (discussed next).

Saving Files As Backups

Sometimes you may wish to save a new edited version of your current document without replacing the original version. To do this, you can choose the Create Backup option from the Save As dialog box. When you turn on the Create Backup option, Word will save the current active document using the same file name as the previous file, except it will add the three-letter extension .BAK to indicate the file is a backup of the new file. For example, the file named SAMPLE.DOC might be named SAMPLE.BAK to represent two similar, but different, documents. To turn on the Create Backup option, you must first choose the Options button from the Save As dialog box with the mouse or press Alt+I from the keyboard. You can also press the Tab key to move the highlight through the dialog box until the Options button itself is highlighted. When the Options button is selected, press Enter or click with the mouse and the Save As dialog box will be extended to show the additional save options, as shown in Figure 2.10. Then, to choose the Create Backup option, click inside the box with the mouse or press Alt+B from the keyboard. Select the Create Backup box a second time to turn off this option.

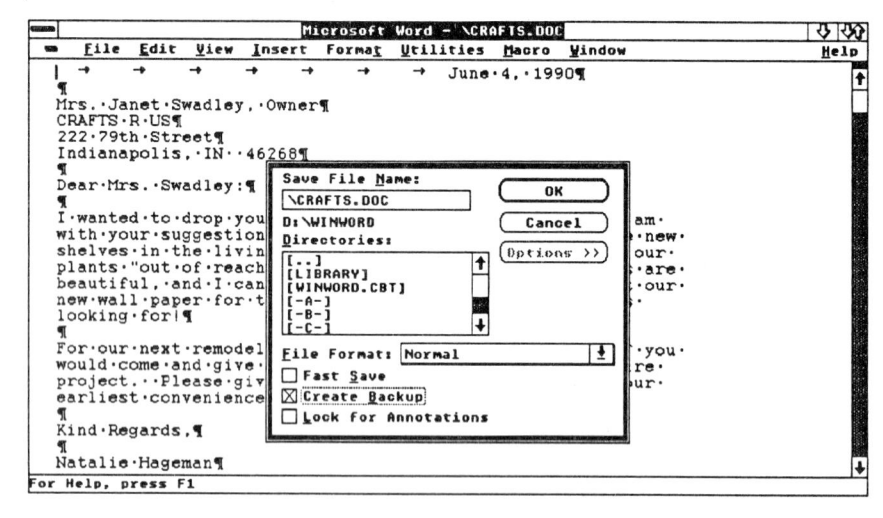

Figure 2.10 Choose the Options button to view additional save options.

Saving Documents Automatically

We have stated more than once that it is a good idea to save your work often in case of a power failure or some other unforeseen disaster. However, saving is sometimes the very last thing you remember to do. For those of you who need extra reminders, Word provides the Autosave Frequency option.

From the Customize command on the Utilities menu, you will find the Autosave Frequency option in the upper right corner. At default, the Never option is selected. However, to provide you with on-screen "reminders" to save your documents, you can choose a frequency time interval of low, medium, or high. The time intervals depend on the amount of editing and formatting changes that you have made to the current document. An approximate range might be 30-60 minutes for a low setting, 20-45 minutes for a medium setting, and 10-30 minutes for a high setting. For beginners, it might be best to choose a high setting until you can trust yourself to save your work without reminders. Simply ask yourself, "How much work am I willing to lose?"

To choose a particular setting, click with the mouse or press Alt,U,U to open the dialog box, and then Alt and the key representing the underlined letter of the frequency. To turn off the Autosave option, you must choose the Never option.

Saving Documents to a Different File, Disk Drive, or Directory

Sometimes you may wish to save your current document with a different file name or to a different directory or disk drive entirely. The advantage of saving your document to a different location is that you can retain the previous version of the same document without using a different file name. Another advantage is that you can use this method to store your document files as data files on a diskette that you can take along with you. For example, you may have created a directory for monthly sales reports on a disk in drive A. Each month you create a new sales report as JAN.DAT, FEB.DAT, MARCH.DAT, and so on. When it's time to save the next monthly sales report, you can choose the Save As command, and then select the appropriate directory from the Directories list box. The available number of disk drives will be represented as well. Click on the drive or directory where you want your document stored or press Alt+D to activate the Directories list box and then use the up and down arrow keys to scroll the box. If you select (highlight) a different drive other than the current one, click on that drive with the mouse or press Enter, and the available number of directories for that drive will be selected (see Figure 2.11).

As you select a directory or a drive from the Directories list box, you'll notice that the highlighted drive and/or directory will be listed

The Basics

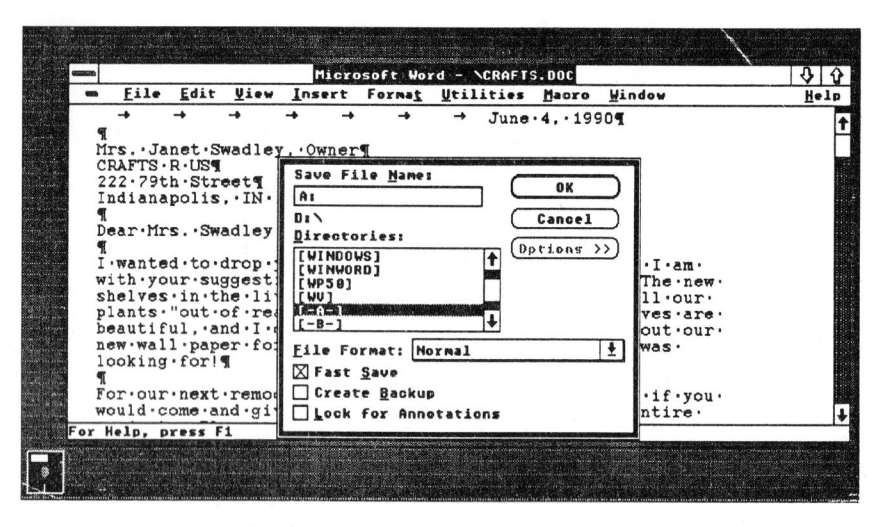

Figure 2.11 Highlight the drive and then press Enter or click the name of the drive to view the available directories for that drive.

in the Directory field just below the Save File Name edit box. As you scroll through the available directories and drives in the Directories list box, the Directory field above it changes accordingly.

For example, to save the monthly sales report for April, first select the drive and directory, if any, where you wish to store the document. Enter the name of the file, such as APRIL.DAT, in the Save File Name edit box. Figure 2.12 shows where such a file might be saved in a directory named REPORT on a disk in drive A. If you need

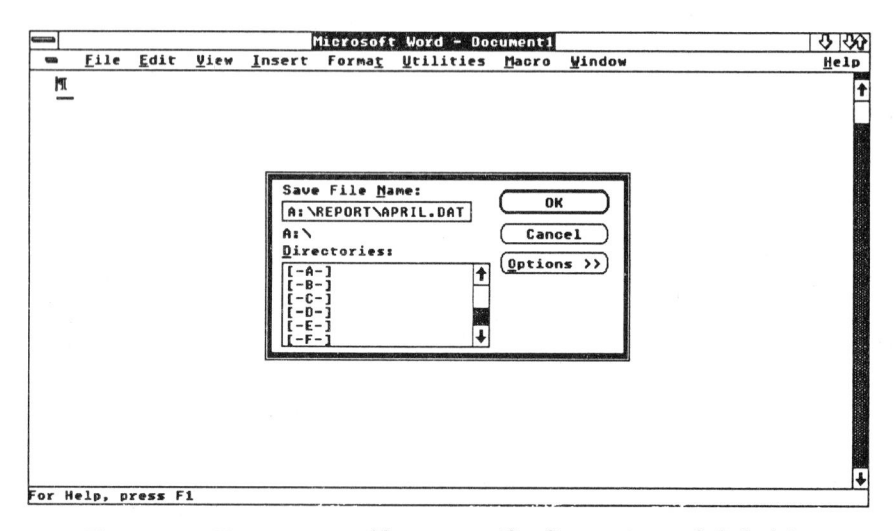

Figure 2.12 You can save files to specific directories and disk drives.

additional help with understanding how directories and files work, refer to Chapter 15 to learn the basics of file management. When you are comfortable with the concepts, you can return to this chapter.

Saving Documents with Different File Formats

Word allows you to save the text of your documents in a format that can be used with other word processors. For example, you might want to share your documents with someone who uses Microsoft Word for DOS or Word for the Macintosh.

The Word default file format is called Normal. To view the available format options, you must choose the Options button from the Save As dialog box. The available options for saving a document depend upon which options you selected during the installation procedure. These are all the options available to you:

DCA/RFT (Format for DisplayWrite and DisplayWriter)
Document Template
Microsoft Windows Write
Microsoft Word for DOS (i.e., Word 5)
Microsoft Works for DOS (the word processing files)
MultiMate (Versions 3.3 and 3.6)
MultiMate Advantage II
Normal (default Word for Windows setting)
RTF (Rich Text Formatting, used by some applications, including Word for the Macintosh)
Text Only (creates an ASCII file without Word formatting, except text, tabs, and paragraph marks)
Text Only With Breaks (same as Text Only but also includes all carriage returns for line breaks)
Text (PC-8)
Text (PC-8) with Breaks
WordPerfect (Versions 4.1, 4.2, 5.0)
WordStar (Versions 3.3, 3.4, 4.0)

It is important to note that merely saving a file in a format other than one compatible with the desired word processor may not be enough to transfer a file. Some systems offer additional incompatibilities. If you are transferring a file from Word for Windows to Word on the Macintosh using the RTF file format, for example, you must also transfer your files electronically using a modem or special

75

cable to load your files into the RAM of the desired system. This problem is especially true if the IBM system uses 5 1/4" disks instead of the micro floppy 3 1/2" diskettes required by the Macintosh.

Despite all this discussion, the procedure for saving your document in a different file format is actually a simple process. To save the document in an ASCII Text Only format, complete the following steps.

1. Open the File menu and choose the **Save** command or press **Alt,F,S**. Give the document a name if you have yet to do so. You may also change the name of the new document if you want to have one copy of the document in normal format and the other in ASCII format. The Save dialog box appears.

2. Use the mouse to click the **Options** button on the right side of the dialog box or press **Alt+O**. An extended view of the Save dialog box appears with the default Normal listed in the File Format edit box.

3. Select the format from the File Format field. Use the mouse to point and click, or you can use the down and up arrow keys to scroll the available options that you specified during the installation procedure. As you scroll, these options will appear one-by-one in the File Format edit box. To get a better look, press **Alt+F+down arrow** and a window will appear listing the available file formats. For example, select **Text Only** in order to choose ASCII.

4. To execute the Save option, click **OK** or press **Enter**. Word will display a message that asks you to confirm the loss of formatting.

5. Press **Y** or **Enter**. In a few seconds, the Save command will be complete and the document appears on your screen in an ASCII format (all the text appears, without any special characters or paragraph formatting). The ASCII format is commonly used for transferring one document from one program to another.

For a more complete discussion on sharing files with other programs, refer to your user's manual. All of the options for saving files, however, are encompassed in the steps just listed.

Some Final Tips on Saving

Here are a few tips to bear in mind about saving your documents:

- You can use the document file name previously given to a file by using the Save command. When you use this procedure, however, the contents of the new file always will replace the contents of the existing file. So using this method will erase any original work that you might wish at a later date you had retained. It might be better to give a new document a new file name, say RESUME1, while the original draft remains unchanged under the name of RESUME. This method requires the use of the Save As command instead of Save. You can, of course, use the Create Backup option previously discussed or simply save the document to a different directory.

- Word offers the command feature, *Fast Save.* You find this option in the Save or Save As dialog box when you choose the Options button to extend the dialog view. Fast Save can be used to save a document much more quickly since it only saves the current changes to the file instead of saving the entire file all over again. Using Fast Save, however, causes your documents to grow in size and consume more valuable memory because it retains all the changes as they accumulate. Eventually, you will need a normal Save to consolidate all changes. Since you only save a few seconds with Fast Save, a normal Save will save memory and headaches.

- Word offers the Lock For Annotations as an option under the File Format edit box. This option allows you and/or others to annotate a document or to prevent others from providing annotations. Only the author of the document can turn on or off this option. To choose the Lock For Annotations option, choose the option by pressing Alt+O from the Save dialog box, and then click the Lock For Annotations box with the mouse or press Alt+L from the keyboard.

- Choose the *Save All* command from the File menu to save all the work you have done during the current session. The work might include creating or changing documents, templates, macros, glossaries, customized menus, and key assignments.

The Basics

- To save a document that is larger than the amount of space available on a particular disk, choose a different disk drive where a disk with sufficient disk space resides or remove the full disk and insert a data disk containing sufficient space.

- Save your work often. If you are working on an incomplete document, save the portions of it that are finished as a safeguard against accidental erasure. This point can't be stressed enough!

Retrieving Your Document

Once you have saved your documents on a diskette or hard disk, the documents will remain there until you erase or change them, even if you turn off the computer. This provides a big advantage over the typewriter since it's not necessary to retype your document the next time that you wish to use or modify it. Now that your documents are stored, suppose that you do turn off your computer or that you wish to work on a stored document other than the one that appears on your screen. To retrieve such a document from storage, you can use the *Open* command from the File menu. In Word, the process of retrieving a stored file is called *opening documents* and is completed as follows:

1. From the File menu, choose **Open** with the mouse or press **Alt,F,O**.

   The Open dialog box appears (see Figure 2.13).

*If you don't see the file name in the directory that you want, select a different directory in the Directories list box, and then click **OK** or press **Enter** to see a list of available files for that new directory.*

2. Type the name of the document that you wish to open in the Open File Name edit box (or select the desired file from the Files field to highlight it in the File Name edit box—the easier method).

   The edit box is currently highlighted and lists *.DOC to represent all the documents available under the current directory with a document extension (e.g., \WINWORD might be the current directory listed).

3. You may also select a file from another directory by typing the other directory before the desired file name:

   C:\REPORTS\SALESJ90.DOC

   where C: is the drive in which the file is stored,

   As you type, the desired file name appears in the File Name edit box.

REPORTS is the name of the directory, and SALESJ90.DOC is the name of the document for the sales report of January, 1990. Remember to include the proper file name extension (.DOC) and separate elements by the backslash (\). The name must be exact or Word won't be able to find it.

4. Once the correct file name appears in the edit box, click **OK** or press **Enter** to open the file.

The selected file is retrieved from storage on your hard disk or diskette and appears in the document window.

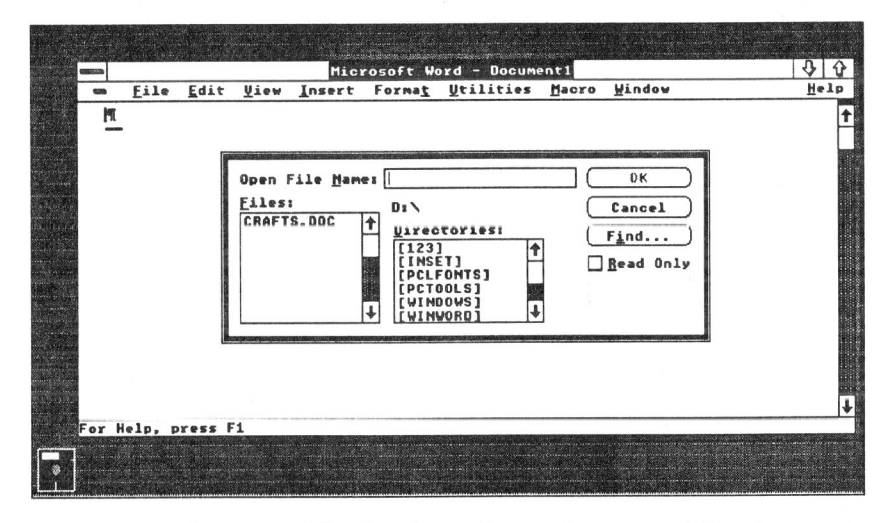

Figure 2.13 The Open dialog box is used to retrieve any existing document from a specified directory.

Tip: To retrieve any file created in a different file format (e.g., WordPerfect), first rename the file and give the .DOC extension. You can then use Word's conversion feature to open the file.

Opening a Recently Opened Document

Once your document is opened and appears in the active document window, you can edit, format, or print the document just as if you created it for the first time. Further, if you close the document, and it

The Basics

remains one of the last four documents that you worked on, it will appear as one of the documents listed at the bottom of the File menu (see Figure 2.14). To open any document file listed in the File menu, point and double-click with the mouse or press **Alt,F,number of the file**. The selected file will then appear in an active document window. Not to be outdone, the Window menu will also list documents opened during the current work session, but only during the *current* work session. Each time you open a document from the File or Window menu, the document will appear as the active window replacing any previous active window. If you didn't close the previous document window, it will remain on the desktop but its window will not be active and probably not visible. To see two windows at the same time, choose the Arrange All command from the Windows menu and your screen will split so you can view several windows at one time (see Figure 2.15). Remember though, only one window will remain active at a time. To switch between an active and inactive window, simply click anywhere inside the desired window, or choose the number of the document from the Window menu to make that window active.

You should close each document window prior to opening a new document unless you plan to switch between the two documents. Leaving several document windows open takes up precious memory space and slows down your computer's operation.

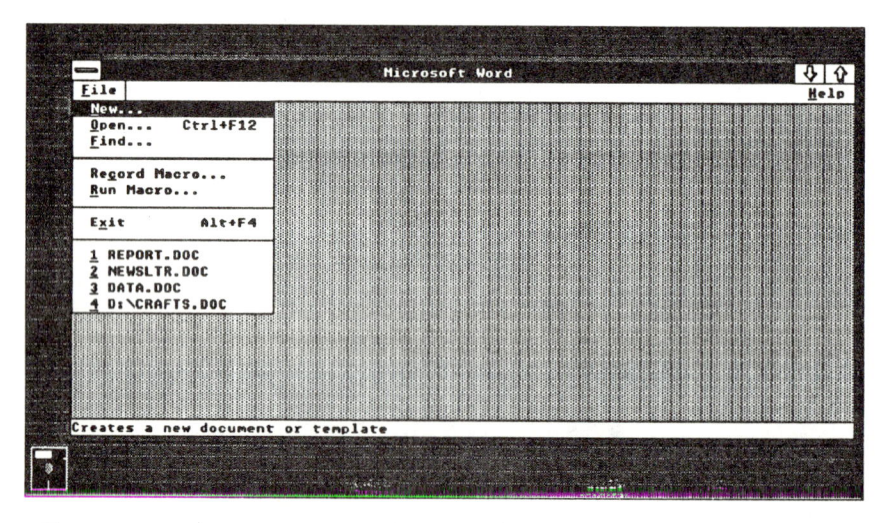

Figure 2.14 Documents opened and closed during the current work session are listed in the File menu.

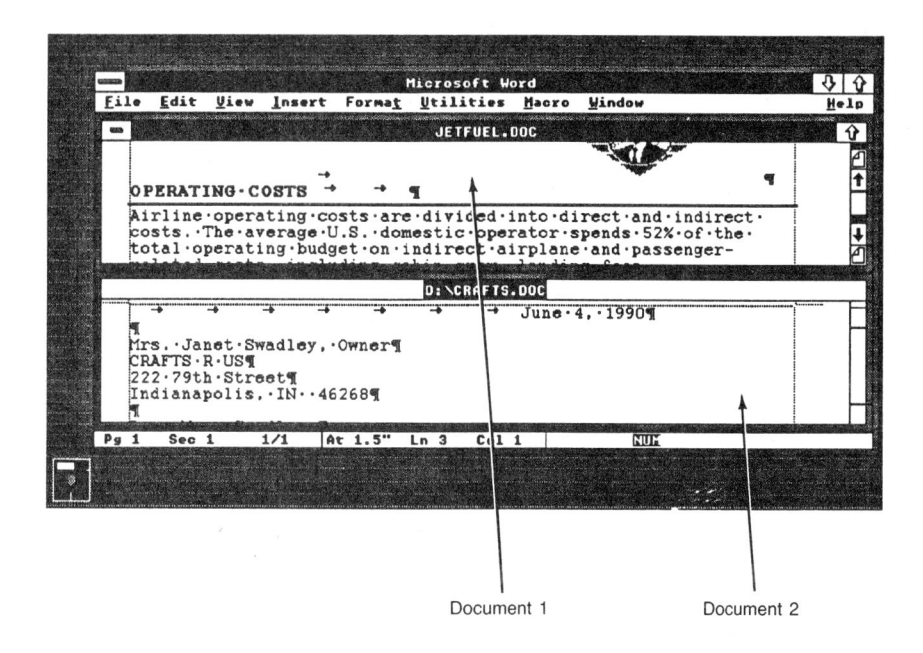

Figure 2.15 Choose the Arrange All command to view more than one open document window at a time.

Navigating Through and Choosing Different Directories

We need to make some important points about navigating in the Open dialog box window. The list of files for the selected directory is stored in a window, complete with a vertical scroll bar. You use the scroll bar to move through a long list of files stored in the current directory that appears in the Directories list window. To change from one directory to another, click the desired directory or drive with the mouse, or press Alt+D and then press Enter. The files for that directory will then be listed in the Files window. To change directories in order to open a file, complete the following steps:

1. Choose the desired directory by clicking with the mouse or pressing **Alt+D**.

   The selected directory or drive is highlighted.

81

2. Press **Enter** to see the list of available files for the selected directory or double-click with the mouse.

The available files for the selected directory appear in the Files window. Note that the first file in the window now appears in the File Name edit box.

3. Activate the Files window by clicking with the mouse or pressing **Alt+F**. If you use the mouse, you can simply double-click the desired file and it will be opened in one step. From the keyboard, press the up and down arrow keys to highlight the available files in the Name edit box.

Highlighted files appear in the Name edit box as you scroll with the up and down arrow keys.

4. If you didn't double-click the desired file with the mouse, press **Enter** or click **OK**.

The selected file is opened in an active document window.

We have covered the basics of saving and opening files here. In Chapter 15, we'll discuss Word's document-retrieval system further, including using the Find command and how to delete unwanted files. Now you'll get some hands-on experience by typing and printing your first letter.

Typing and Printing Your First Letter

If your screen is messy from entering text, you need to erase that text first. It's best to close all open windows, and choose the New command from the File menu (accept Word's default Normal style and press Enter when the dialog boxes appear until a new document screen appears). Do that now and you'll get a clean page. Since you're not ready to save any documents, ignore your desire and any warnings to do so.

With the insertion point in the top left corner of the screen, type the letter in Figure 2.16 exactly as it appears. Don't alter the default settings for spacing and so on; they will serve well until you explore editing and formatting changes in Chapters 3 through 7. Use the Backspace key to correct typos and to edit your document. Remember, you can use the mouse pointer or the arrow keys to reposition the insertion point, then backspace to erase any offending characters and enter the correct text. Complete the following steps using Figure 2.16 as a guide.

- Type the date on the first line. The insertion point should be located on line 1. You can check by looking at the status bar. If the insertion point is not on line 1, you can position it with the mouse or press the arrow keys or Ctrl+Home. Type:

  August 15, 1990

  and then press **Enter** three times. Pressing Enter the second and third time will insert the proper number of blank lines between the date and inside address.

- Type the inside address in the upper left corner of the screen as shown. At the end of each line, simply press Enter. This keypress technically creates each line as an individual paragraph and is appropriate for most situations. If you are not crazy about this idea, you can enter a **Shift+Enter** to execute a Newline. When you're ready, type:

  Mr. Alan Foster
  District #2 Sales Consultant
  25 Madison Ave.
  New York, NY 10173

- Press **Enter** once to insert a blank line and then type the salutation:

  Dear Mr. Foster:

  Again, press **Enter** twice to insert a blank line prior to the body of the letter.

- Your date, address, and salutation are set. Now type the letter, without concerning yourself with carriage returns—the word processor's word-wrap feature will break words for you. All you need to remember is to hit the Enter key for a new paragraph. If you forget and press Enter before you are ready to begin a new paragraph, simply press the Backspace key to return the insertion point to the end of the previous line. Ready? Now complete the body of the letter in Figure 2.16. Stop when you get to the closing.

- The final step is to complete the closing of the letter. Allow two blank lines prior to the complimentary close and insert three or four blank lines to allow room for the actual signature.

- Congrats! You have just typed your first letter with Word.

The Basics

```
August 15, 1990

Mr. Alan Foster
District #2 Sales Consultant
25 Madison Ave.
New York, NY  10173

Dear Mr. Foster:

Congratulations!  You have just been recommended by the
senior management of your firm, Scented Soaps Limitied, to
attend the sales management seminar to be held in Chicago,
Il, at the Ritz Carlton hotel on the 1st, 2nd, and 3rd of
October.

You were chosen from among 55 field consultants nationwide
for the opportunity to advance into the ranks of sales
management.  For three days, you will be exposed to the most
intensive classroom presentation of successful management
techniques and practices employed by the parent firm, Very
Big Brands, Inc.  Upon completion, you will be ready to step
into the role of East Coast Sales Manager.

On the 30th of this month, we will be forwarding a complete
itinerary of the seminar for your review.  If you have any
questions, please contact our seminar hostess, Ms. Bonnie
Summers, at (312) 723-4000.

We look forward to meeting you in Chicago!


Sincerely,



Cameron A. Davis
Director of Training


Enclosure.
```

Figure 2.16 Drafting Your First Letter

Remember to Save Your Work!

Now that you have written your first Word document, you'll need to save your work. Choose the **Save** command from the File menu to open the Save dialog box (**Alt,F,S**). Since this is your first time to save this document, give it an appropriate name, such as FOSTER.LTR. When you're ready, click **OK** or press **Enter**. If necessary, enter any summary information and then click **OK** or press **Enter** a second time. Soon, you will be returned to your document window with FOSTER.LTR now appearing in the title bar.

Printing Your First Letter

Be sure you have properly installed your printer driver during the Word setup installation procedure. See Appendix A.

The next step is to print your letter. Complete the following steps to get some practice with the printer. You should have the printer properly connected and configured to your computer system and turned on, the appropriate printer driver file present in your Windows directory on your hard disk (you can check via the Control Panel), and the printer paper properly in position and ready for printing. If you haven't installed your printer yet, please turn to Appendix A to review the setup procedure before continuing.

Many printers require that the online or select switch be turned off when the automatic line-feed or form-feed mode is in operation. Make sure your select switch is in the ready mode (depressed) when you are ready to print.

1. Turn on the printer. Most printers must be set in an *on-line* position, indicating to the computer that they are ready to accept instructions to begin the printing process. On many IBM compatible printers, this switch is labeled "Select." Depress this switch, as well as the Power switch.

   The lights for the Power button and possibly a Ready or Select button are on, indicating that the printer is ready. If no paper is in the printer, the paper-error or a similar light will be on.

2. Choose the **Print** command from the File menu or press **Alt,F,P** from the keyboard.

   The Print dialog box, shown in Figure 2.17, appears.

3. The Print dialog box provides you the opportunity to print additional information at the same time. It also gives you the standard printing options of printing a draft version and choosing the number of copies and the destination where printing should begin. Since you only want to print the current document with the standard print options in place, press the **Enter** key or click **OK**.

   A message appears in the status bar (if it's visible) indicating the progress of the printing and telling you the total number of characters in the document upon completion.

The Basics

To stop the printing, press the Esc key.

4. In a few seconds, the printer should begin to print your letter. If printing doesn't start after a minute or so, make sure the Select button is depressed. If it's in the Off position, turn it On and printing should start.

If the printer is not properly connected, your screen displays a message to indicate that it tried to communicate with the printer but the printer was not ready.

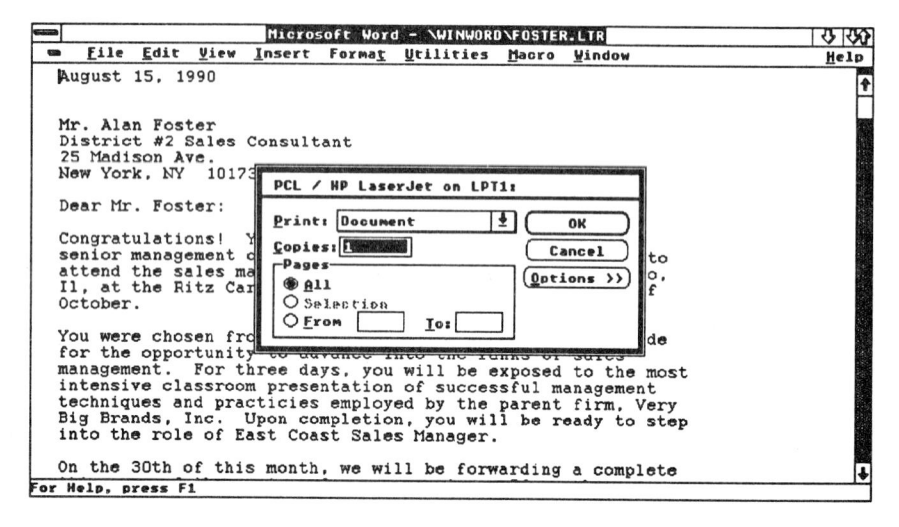

Figure 2.17 The Print dialog box offers several options.

    Congratulations! You have just learned how to create, save, and print your first letter with Word for Windows. If you're a beginner, these first two chapters may prove to be your biggest step. You might not think so, but it's all downhill from now. Sit back and take a deserved break before going on to Chapter 3. Remember to quit Word the proper way with the Exit command from the File menu (if necessary, review the end of Chapter 1). If you forgot to save any documents, Word will remind you to do so if you use this method. Don't just turn off the computer; start making the Exit command a habit right now.

Review

In this chapter you learned:

1. You don't need to worry about how your text looks when you first begin to type. With Word's editing and formatting tools, you can fix it later. Creating the text remains your first priority.
2. To start a new paragraph, press the Enter key. To break a line without starting a new paragraph, enter the Newline keypress, Shift+Enter.
3. Use a nonbreaking space to avoid an undesirable word-wrap. (The parts of a date [October 5] are a good example.) To enter the space, press Ctrl+Shift+Spacebar between the characters or words that you don't want to split.
4. Choosing the Save command will always replace the contents of the existing file. To save the current document and retain the existing file, use the Save As command and give the current document a new name or store it on a separate data disk or directory. You can also use the Create Backup option to save the previous document while saving the current document with the same name. Only the file name extensions will be different (i.e., DOC or BAK).
5. Retrieving a document file from the data disk or hard disk is an easy task. First, choose the Open command from the File menu. From the Open dialog box, select the directory where the file is stored (or disk drive where the data disk is inserted) from the Directories list window. Finally, select the file from the available directory (files appear in the Files window) and click OK or press Enter. Also, you can just type the exact name of the file, including the directory path where the file is located in the Name File edit box before clicking OK to execute the Open command.
6. A document is saved as a file. When saving a file, you must give it a file name. The file name consists of a base (from one to eight characters) and an optional extension (a period, followed by from one to three characters). Use the alphabet characters, numerals, and a few select special characters, such as the hyphen or underscore when naming files. Some special characters are not allowed, however.

7. If you don't add a file name extension to your file, Word will apply the standard document extension (.DOC) for you.

8. To clear your screen quickly, choose the New command from the File menu. The New command opens a clean document in a new active window.

9. To create and print your first letter, type it in the document window, correct any typos with the Backspace key, and choose Print from the File menu.

10. Moving around your screen with Word is a snap. You can either use a mouse to point and click to move the insertion point, or use the arrow keys and the numeric keypad to move around your screen. If you have a mouse, you can also use the vertical and horizontal scroll bars to drag to approximate areas of a document. Once the Repaginate Now command has been executed (or if Background Repagination is on), you can also use the Go To command to seek a particular page in a long document.

T H R E E

Editing Your Documents

In This Chapter:

- Selecting Text Before You Edit
- Editing Text
- Using the Edit Menu
- Block Editing
- Undoing Your Commands
- Searching and Replacing Text
- Editing in Windows

This chapter introduces Word's editing tools, including the Edit menu. You will learn how to cut, copy, move, and paste text and how to search for old text and replace it with new text. And, you'll find that you can "undo" an edit if you change your mind. Finally, you'll cover the technique of editing documents more than one window at a time. This is an important chapter, so jump right in now.

Selecting Text Before You Edit

Editing with Word is a two-step process. First you select the text that you wish to change in some way and then you choose a command from the Edit menu to execute the change. You can select a single character, a single line, a paragraph, a block of text, or an entire document. Word allows you to select text using the mouse or the key-

The Basics

board. With the help of a special feature called the *Clipboard,* a temporary holding place in memory, you can move text or graphics in and out of a single document or from one document to another, but you must first select it. So, you'll begin with learning methods for selecting text of your choice.

Selecting Text with a Mouse

In general, you select text by positioning the insertion point at the beginning of the text that you wish to edit and then dragging through the text by moving the mouse while continuing to hold the mouse button down. As you drag through the text with the I-beam, the text will appear in white letters on a black background (color monitors will highlight the text in the color you select). When you release the button, the text is selected. To cancel the selection, click the mouse button anywhere within the document window.

The left mouse button itself also offers a quick method for selecting an entire word or sentence. To select an entire word, position the insertion point anywhere inside that word and double-click the left mouse button. If you hold down the Ctrl key and then click the left button once, the entire sentence will be selected.

The location of the selection bar is different in Page View or Print Preview.

You can also select text by using the hidden *selection bar.* As you recall, the document window first appears in Normal Editing View the first time you start Word. In Normal Editing View, the selection bar is located in a column on the left side of the screen. When you move the I-beam to the left edge, it changes to a pointer heading up on a *diagonal,* from left to right. (If it points horizontally to the left, it is outside the invisible selection bar area.) You can use this selection bar to select single or multiple lines, single or multiple paragraphs, or an entire document. To select a single line, position the pointer in the selection bar next to the desired line and click the left mouse button once. To select multiple lines, hold down the left button and drag up or down as desired. For a single paragraph, place the pointer in the selection bar anywhere next to the paragraph, and then press the left mouse button once and then the right mouse button once. For multiple paragraphs, double-click the left mouse button instead of clicking, but also hold down the button on the second click and drag the pointer up or down as desired. Finally, to quickly select the entire document, hold down the Ctrl key while clicking the left button in the selection bar once. Remember that you must use the *left* side of the screen, *not* the scroll bar on the right side of the screen. The invisible selection bar on the left is for selecting text while the visible scroll bar on the right is for moving vertically through your document.

Selecting Text with the Keyboard

If you don't have a mouse installed on your system, or you just prefer to leave your hands on the keyboard, you can also use the keys to effectively select text in a document. To do this, first move the insertion point to the beginning of the text that you wish to select with the arrow keys. Next, hold down the Ctrl and the Shift keys while pressing the arrow keys again to move the insertion point to the end of the text that you are selecting. To cancel your selection, simply press any arrow key by itself.

Extending Your Selection

Word provides another method for selecting text rapidly, the *extend selection* or F8 key. Pressing F8 places Word in the extend mode to allow you to select parts of your document in accumulating pieces. For example, the first time you press F8 you simply turn on the extend mode. If you have the status bar visible, EXT will appear. The second time you press F8, Word will select the first whole word following the location of the insertion point. Press F8 a third time, and Word selects an entire sentence. Continue to press F8 and Word will select the paragraph where the insertion point resides, the section (if your document is divided into sections), and finally the whole document. Once you have selected all the text that you wish, you must turn off the extend mode by pressing the Esc key. Once you turn off the extend mode, you can deselect your text by simply pressing any arrow key.

You don't need to use the F8 key as the sole keypress for selecting text. You can use the extend mode in combination with the arrow keys, or the mouse, to select individual characters or large amounts of text rapidly. For example, to select individual characters at the location of the insertion point, you press F8 and then the left or right arrow keys. Remember to press F8 to turn off the extend mode when you have finished.

As you have already seen, Word offers a variety of methods for selecting text with the mouse or keyboard. You'll find some methods more suitable than others. Table 3.1 lists the various options for selecting text. You should practice all of them so that you can determine which methods you are most comfortable with. When you get bored with that method, you'll want to try something different Finally, note that selecting text within tables and columns requires special methods. We'll discuss columns and tables in Chapter 11.

Table 3.1 Editing Selection Options

Selection	Mouse Method	Keyboard Method
Selecting a single character	Drag across text character	(1) Ctrl+Shift+left arrow or Ctrl+Shift+right arrow or (2) Press F8 and left arrow or right arrow
Selecting a single word	(1) Drag across word (2) Double-click left button anywhere on the word (also selects trailing spaces).	Press F8 twice in front of or on word.
Selecting a single line	(1) Drag across line or (2) Click once in selection bar next to line.	
Selecting a paragraph	(1) Drag across paragraph, or (2) Double-click left button twice in selection bar anywhere next to paragraph followed by one click of right button.	Press F8 four times.
Selecting a sentence	Drag across sentence	Press F8 three times while on line.
Selecting a block of text	(1) Drag across text, or (2) Click insertion point at beginning, press F8, move pointer to end and click left mouse button.	
Selecting an entire page	Drag from the top of the page to the bottom	

Selection	Mouse Method	Keyboard Method
Selecting an entire document	(1) Drag from the beginning of the document to the horizontal scroll bar. From the scroll bar, Word will scroll, selecting one line at a time until you reach the end of the document. (2) Hold down the Ctrl key while clicking anywhere in the selection bar.	(1) Press F8 five or six times (six if more than one section), or (2) Press Ctrl+5 (on numeric keyboard), or (3) Press Ctrl+Home followed by Ctrl+Shift+End or vise versa.
Selecting a graphic	(1) Drag over graphic (2) Click inside it.	

Editing Text

Editing your documents is a less formal process than saving or printing them. The facility of editing your work gives word processing a distinct advantage over the common typewriter. You know that you can create your documents without worrying about making mistakes; word processing allows you to "fix it later." Word offers many tools that allow you to just fix it. The simplest of these is the Backspace key.

Remember the Backspace Key

The Backspace key is located just above the Enter key. Press it once and the insertion point moves one character space backward, erasing any character in its path. Be careful when pressing the key: Like all keys, it features the auto-repeat function and will continue to erase characters if you continue to hold it down.

Correcting simple typos is the primary function of the Backspace key. Use the arrow keys or the mouse to move the insertion point to the point of the error, and then use the Backspace key to erase it. You can then type the correction or insert additional text.

Remember, the Backspace key is not the same as the key labeled Delete. Delete removes characters to the right of the insertion point but leaves the insertion point stationary, while the Backspace key moves the insertion point from right to left, erasing characters in its path. One tip about using the Delete key, though: You can use it to erase sentences, large blocks of text, or the entire screen. To do this, you select text with the mouse or the keys (see Table 3.1), press Delete, and the block will be erased. (Note: Shortly, you will learn that the Cut command from the Edit menu can do the same delete procedure. The primary difference is that Delete will not place the selected text in the Clipboard as does the execution of the Cut command.) Pressing Backspace will not remove the text (unless the Typing Replaces Selection option, which we discuss next, is turned on in the Utilities Customize box). Only the Delete key erases the text from your screen in this situation.

Typing vs. Replacing

When you first start Word, when you select text and then type new text, that new text is inserted at the beginning of the selected text. If you press the Delete key, the selected text is erased. Word provides you an additional option, however, of replacing existing text with any keystroke. To do this, choose the **Customize** command from the Utilities menu in Full menus (**Alt,U,U**) and turn on the **Typing Replaces Selection** option. Once this option is turned on, any selected text is automatically replaced when you press a key.

Using the Edit Menu

While you can get by with the simplest tools—selecting text with the mouse or keys and using the Backspace key, for maximum efficiency you should use all the available tools. The Edit menu provides alternate methods for block editing and erasing or inserting text or graphics into your documents. Many of the commands in the Edit menu have shortcut key combinations that you can use in lieu of using the mouse.

Cut, Copy, and Paste

The primary editing tools in the Edit menu are Cut, Copy, and Paste. These commands are common among graphical-based word processing software so experienced users will probably find their use old hat. New users must first learn to use the Clipboard, where you move text or graphics by using either the Cut or the Copy command. The Clipboard can only hold one item (text or graphic) at a time. If you place new text in the Clipboard, it replaces whatever is stored there. After you place text in the Clipboard, you can use the Paste command to insert it into any document. Text in the Clipboard remains intact until you execute either the Cut or Copy command again.

To view the contents of the Clipboard, you use the Run command on the Word Control menu. The procedure for displaying the contents of the Clipboard is as follows:

1. Choose **Run** from the Word Control menu or press **Alt,Spacebar,U**.

   The Word Control menu appears.

2. Choose the **Clipboard** command by pressing **Alt,C** and then **Enter** (it's selected by default).

   The Clipboard program dialog box appears (Figure 3.1).

3. Click **OK** or press **Enter**.

   The last-entered contents of the Clipboard appear in a window (Figure 3.2).

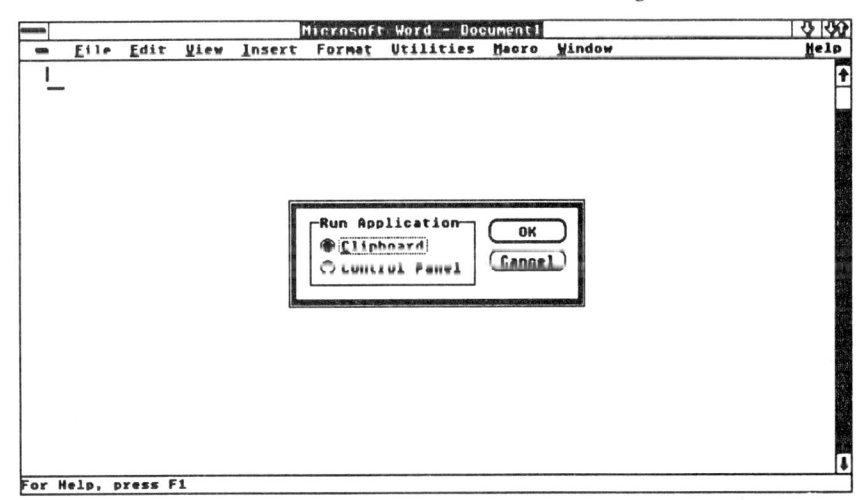

Figure 3.1 Choose the Run command for the Clipboard program.

The Basics

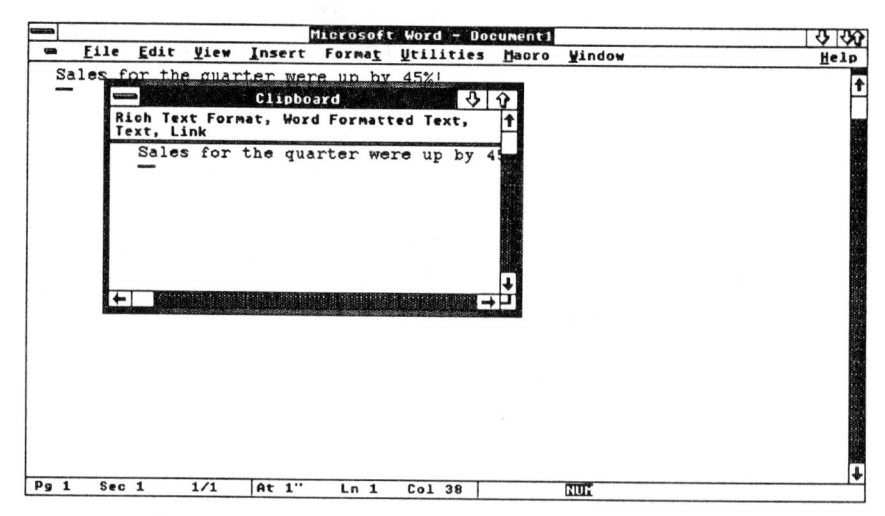

Figure 3.2 The current contents of the Clipboard appear in an active window.

    The Clipboard window has vertical and horizontal scroll bars for moving through the window to display any text that is not visible. You can't edit in this window, but you can use the contents from the Clipboard in another work session by saving the material when you leave the current session. If you used the Clipboard to store a large amount of text, when you leave the current session Word will ask if you want to save the contents of the Clipboard. If you do, click yes or press Enter.

    Once you are finished viewing the contents of the Clipboard, you can close the window by choosing the Close command from the Control menu or pressing Alt,Spacebar,C. You can also keep the Clipboard program running by activating a document window with either the Alt,Tab keypress or clicking anywhere inside the document window with the mouse. You also have the option of reducing the Clipboard to an icon for easy access. Closing the Clipboard window will not erase the contents of the Clipboard while you are still working in Word. Keeping the Clipboard running simply allows you a faster way of viewing its contents, but it will slow down Word.

    In the sections that follow, you'll explore Word's editing tools. For practice, retrieve the FOSTER.LTR file you saved in Chapter 2 and load it as the current working document. If you failed to save the document, type the letter now. It is reprinted as Figure 3.3 (in 10-pt. Tms Rmn font—the default selection) for your convenience.

```
August 15, 1990

Mr. Alan Foster
District #2 Sales Consultant
25 Madison Ave.
New York, NY  10173

Dear Mr. Foster:

Congratulations!  You have just been recommended by the
senior management of your firm, Scented Soaps Limited, to
attend the sales management seminar to be held in Chicago,
Il, at the Ritz Carlton hotel on the 1st, 2nd, and 3rd of
October.

You were chosen from among 55 field consultants nationwide
for the opportunity to advance into the ranks of sales
management.  For three days, you will be exposed to the most
intensive classroom presentation of successful management
techniques and practices employed by the parent firm, Very
Big Brands, Inc.  Upon completion, you will be ready to step
into the role of East Coast Sales Manager.

On the 30th of this month, we will be forwarding a complete
itinerary of the seminar for your review.  If you have any
questions, please contact our seminar hostess, Ms. Bonnie
Summers, at (312) 723-4000.

We look forward to meeting you in Chicago!


Sincerely,



Cameron A. Davis
Director of Training


Enclosure.
```

Figure 3.3 The FOSTER.LTR

Practice Inserting and Deleting Text

Now suppose you want to make the phrase "sales management seminar" in the first paragraph a little more descriptive by inserting "training" after "management." To do this, move the insertion point

The Basics

Remember that you can use the arrow keys to move your insertion point around your document prior to selecting text.

to the third line of the first paragraph just in front of the s in seminar. Now type the word "training" and then press the Spacebar once to insert a space between words.

The next edit that you might make is to delete the "and practices" from the second paragraph. Once again, use the mouse or keys to position the pointer. In this case, you are going to select the phrase first with either the mouse or the keys. To use the mouse, click before the word to set an anchor and then drag across the phrase to select it (Figure 3.4). If you are using the keys, remember to turn off the extend selection mode by pressing **Esc**. Now position the insertion point in front of the phrase, press **F8** and then the **right arrow key** to select the phrase. Then, to delete the phrase, including any spaces between words, press the **Delete** key or choose the **Cut** command from the Edit menu. When completed, your edited letter will look like Figure 3.5.

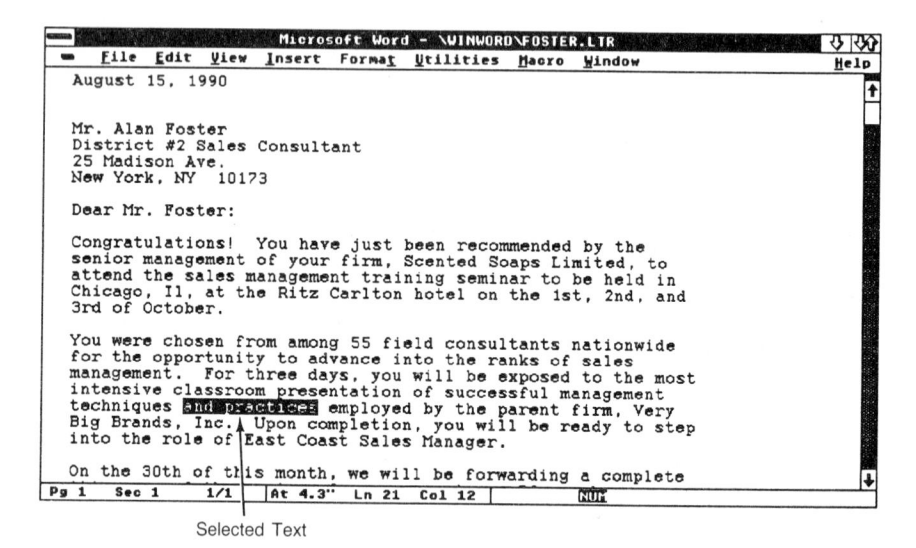

Figure 3.4 Select text by dragging with the mouse or using F8 and the arrow keys.

Deleting Text with Cut

When you erase text with the Cut command, the text is placed in the Clipboard. For practice, erase the entire second paragraph of the FOSTER.LTR document by completing the following steps.

1. Move the insertion point to the beginning of the text that you wish to cut and click the

The insertion point should be anchored in front of the word You.

98

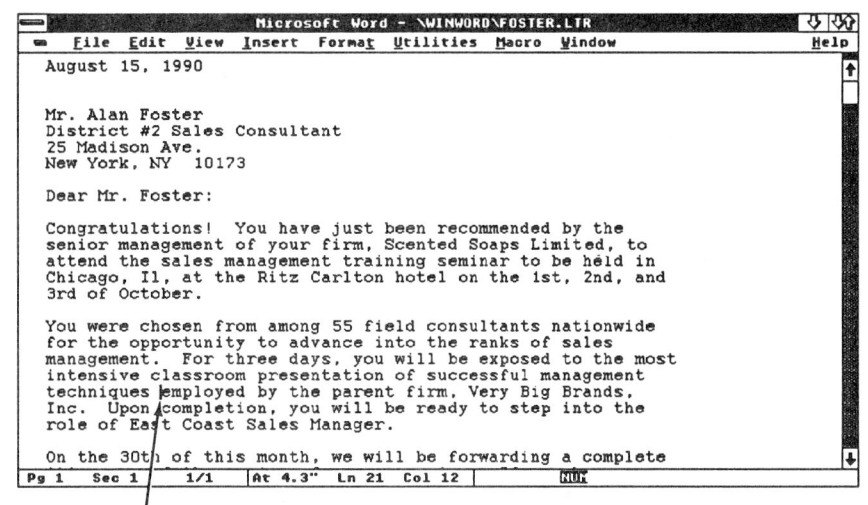

3—Editing Your Documents

```
┌──────────────────────────────────────────────────────────────┐
│ ▬           Microsoft Word - \WINWORD\FOSTER.LTR        ⇩ ⇩⇧ │
│  ▬   File  Edit  View  Insert  Format  Utilities  Macro  Window   Help │
│ August 15, 1990                                              ↑│
│                                                               │
│ Mr. Alan Foster                                               │
│ District #2 Sales Consultant                                  │
│ 25 Madison Ave.                                               │
│ New York, NY  10173                                           │
│                                                               │
│ Dear Mr. Foster:                                              │
│                                                               │
│ Congratulations! You have just been recommended by the        │
│ senior management of your firm, Scented Soaps Limited, to     │
│ attend the sales management training seminar to be held in    │
│ Chicago, Il, at the Ritz Carlton hotel on the 1st, 2nd, and   │
│ 3rd of October.                                               │
│                                                               │
│ You were chosen from among 55 field consultants nationwide    │
│ for the opportunity to advance into the ranks of sales        │
│ management.  For three days, you will be exposed to the most  │
│ intensive classroom presentation of successful management     │
│ techniques employed by the parent firm, Very Big Brands,      │
│ Inc.  Upon completion, you will be ready to step into the     │
│ role of East Coast Sales Manager.                             │
│                                                               │
│ On the 30th of this month, we will be forwarding a complete  ↓│
│ Pg 1   Sec 1 /   1/1   At 4.3"  Ln 21  Col 12        NUM      │
└──────────────────────────────────────────────────────────────┘
         Text Is Removed
```

Figure 3.5 Your edited document.

mouse once to anchor or use the arrow keys. In this example, move the insertion point until it resides at the beginning of the second paragraph (in front of the letter Y).

2. Select the paragraph by dragging across it or double-clicking the left button in the selection bar anywhere inside the paragraph. Or, press **F8** four times.

   The paragraph is highlighted, as in Figure 3.6.

3. Choose the **Cut** command from the Edit menu by pressing **Alt,E,T** or type the shortcut **Shift+Delete** command.

   The text is deleted and the rest of the document automatically reformatted with the correct spacing as in Figure 3.7.

You now know how to perform simple editing tasks. You have learned how to select text and how to insert and delete text by using the Delete key and the Cut command. Word offers still more editing tools, however. In the next section, you'll explore how to edit entire blocks of text by using the Copy and Paste commands from the Edit menu.

99

The Basics

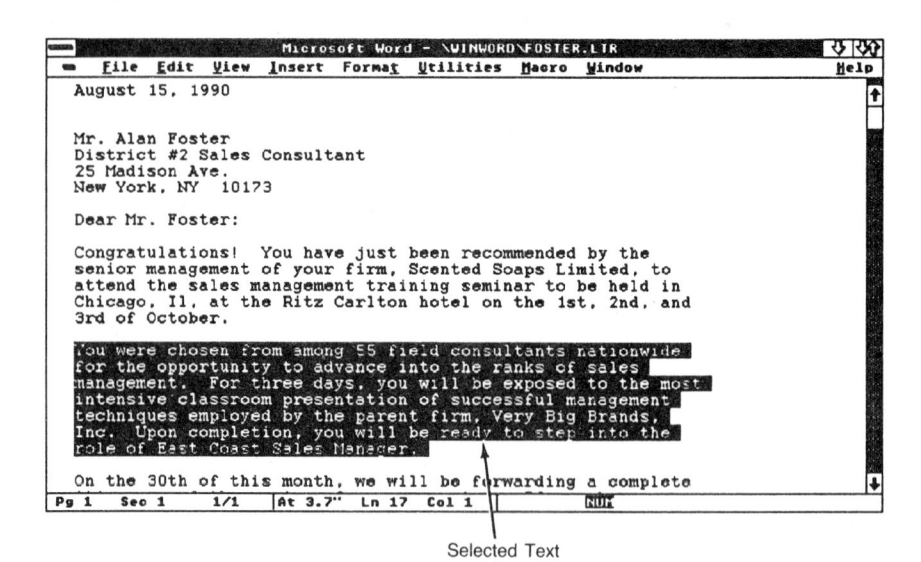

Figure 3.6 Selecting an Entire Paragraph.

Figure 3.7 Your document following execution of the Cut command.

Block Editing

Your first draft of a document need not be your last. You can use a great number of methods to change, add, or delete text. Sometimes you can improve your prose by moving entire "blocks" of text around, rearranging paragraphs, or deleting them entirely. In this section, you'll learn the methods of *block editing*, also called "cut and paste." In this procedure, you first designate the area of text that you wish to move, cut the text from the document, and paste the designated text into the document in its new location. Cutting and pasting blocks of text provides you with an advanced editing tool. For a temporary storage place, you can move the text into the Clipboard, where it remains intact until you have cut, moved, or copied more text or until you leave Word and turn off the computer. The Clipboard provides a limited amount of storage, but if the text that you wish to cut, copy, or move is too large, the system will alert you. In this case, you can move the desired text in stages until all the text is moved.

To perform a block edit, first designate the text by selecting it. Then, choose whether to cut, copy, or move the text to the Clipboard. Finally, if you wish, paste the selected text in its new location, either in the working document or in a separate document. In the next two sections, you'll practice block editing a sample memo using the Cut, Copy, and Paste commands.

Moving Text Around with Cut and Paste

Use the Edit menu to cut and paste a new document. The first step is to clear your screen. Choose the Close command from the File menu to put away the document window that now appears on your screen. Word now gives you the option of saving your last edited changes to the FOSTER.LTR document. Since the original is stored safely on your disk, choose **No**. Then, choose **New** from the File menu to get a fresh and clean document window. When the New dialog box appears, accept the default option and press **Enter** or click **OK**. With a clean document page, type the following memo:

```
                         MEMO

     TO: All Managers
   FROM: Sam Davis, Sr. Vice President
   DATE: November 8, 1990
SUBJECT: Organizational Planning Meeting

On December 1, 1990, the Davis Toy Company will conduct an
organizational planning meeting for the coming year. Each
manager will be expected to provide a 15-minute follow-up
presentation for his or her department. Each presentation
should include sales forecasting and cost control measures
for the department.
```

The Basics

> The meeting will be held at 9:00 A.M. in the west board room. A group from the Season's Consulting Company will present a new business plan for expansion into children's sportswear for the 1991 selling season. Attendees and their respective presentations will include:
>
> * Tom Willis-Marketing and Sales
> * Brenda Smith-Manufacturing
> * Ron Hageman-Distribution
>
> Attendance is mandatory. I look forward to a very successful meeting!

To get your feet wet with block editing, you'll rearrange the order of attendees by moving Tom Willis to the bottom of the list. To do this, complete the following steps:

1. Move the insertion point to the beginning of the text that you wish to select. The I-beam should be positioned just left of the first character—the asterisk before the word Tom. Select the line by dragging across it or press **Ctrl** and click the left mouse button next to the line in the selection bar. From the keyboard, press **F8** three times to select, followed by the **Esc** key to turn off extend selection mode.

   The selected text is highlighted.

2. Now that you have selected your text, you can cut it or copy it from the working document. Since you want to move it, choose **Cut** from the Edit menu with the **Alt,E,T** keypress or type

   The selected text disappears from your document and is stored in the Clipboard while the gap left can be easily removed by pressing the Delete key once.

3—Editing Your Documents

Shift+Delete.

3. You are ready to paste the selected text into its new location. Use the mouse (or arrow keys) to place the insertion point where you want the text block to appear. In this case, at the bottom of the attendee list. Use the Enter key to properly position the insertion with the proper spacing between lines. Choose **Paste** from the Edit menu or press **Alt,E,P**, or type **Shift-Insert**.

Your text is copied from the Clipboard to its new location as shown in Figure 3.8.

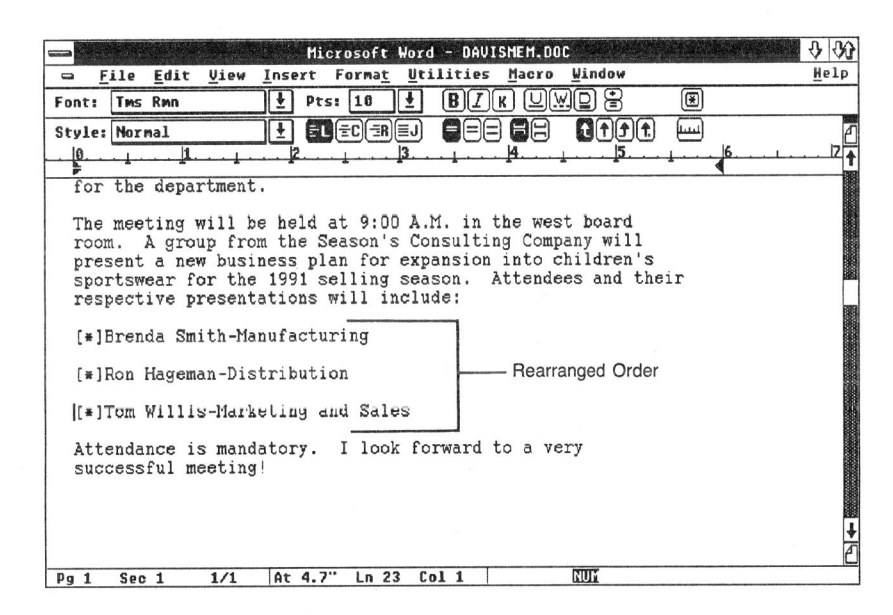

Figure 3.8 A sample edited memo.

Practice cutting and pasting your document. As an exercise, cut and paste your document until it looks like the one in Figure 3.9. As a hint, move the block of text that begins with the second sentence to

103

a position just below the attendee list. Use the Delete key to remove any unnecessary hard returns (leaves blank spaces) that fill the gaps between the remaining lines.

```
      TO:  All Managers
    FROM:  Sam Davis, Sr. Vice-President
    DATE:  November 8, 1990
 SUBJECT:  Organizational Planning Meeting

On December 1, 1990, the Davis Toy Company will conduct an
organizational planning meeting for the coming year.

The meeting will be held at 9:00 A.M. in the west board
room.  A group from the Season's Consulting Company will
present a new business plan for expansion into children's
sportswear for the 1991 selling season.  Attendees and their
respective presentations will include:

Tom Willis-Marketing and Sales

Brenda Smith-Manufacturing

Ron Hageman-Distribution

Each manager will be expected to provide a 15-minute follow-
up presentation for his or her department.  Each
presentation should include sales forecasting and cost
control measures for the department.  Attendance is
mandatory.  I look forward to a very successful meeting!
```

Figure 3.9 Revising your memo with cut and paste is easy.

Copying Text from One Document to Another

Using the Copy command to copy and move a block of text to another document is much the same as moving text with the Cut command in the previous example. The one difference is that the Cut command erases text from your current document, while the Copy command only duplicates the text, leaving the original text intact. Choosing Copy will place a duplicate of the selected text into the Clipboard where it remains until a new selection is copied or cut to the Clipboard. To see just how this works, you can copy a text block from your current document to the Clipboard, open a new document win-

3—Editing Your Documents

dow, and then move the text block to the new document, as in the following steps.

1. Select the text that you wish to copy. In this exercise, select the memo's entire heading by dragging across thetext.

    The selected text appears, as in Figure 3.10.

2. Choose the **Copy** command from the Edit menu by pressing **Alt,E,C** or enter **Ctrl + Ins**.

    A duplicate of the text is copied into the Clipboard. You may click anywhere in the document or press one of the arrow keys to turn off the highlighting once the Copy command is executed.

3. Open the document in which you wish to move the text. In this example, you choose a brand new document. Choose **New** from the File menu with the **Alt,F,N** keypress and accept the default New document options by clicking **OK** or press **Enter**. You have the option of closing any existing windows since the copied text is stored safely in the Clipboard (until you replace it or turn off your PC). You can use this method to move text into any existing document prior to quitting Word.

    A new blank document window appears on your screen.

4. The last step is to choose the location in your document where you want the stored text to appear. Since you are beginning a new document here, select **Paste** from the Edit menu by pressing **Alt,E,P** or press **Shift + Ins**.

    The text stored in the Clipboard appears in your document window, as illustrated in Figure 3.11

105

The Basics

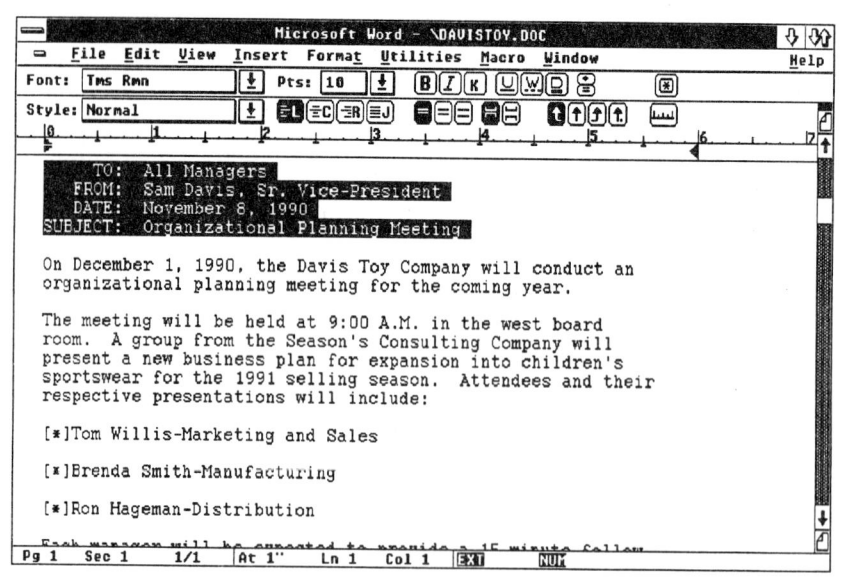

```
┌─────────────────── Microsoft Word - \DAVISTOY.DOC ───────────────┐
│  File  Edit  View  Insert  Format  Utilities  Macro  Window  Help│
│ Font: Tms Rmn      ↕  Pts: 10  ↕  B I K U W R ⚙        ⊠         │
│ Style: Normal      ↕  ≡L ≡C ≡R ≡J ═ ═ ═ ═  ↑ ↑ ↑ ↑  ⌶             │
│ 0....|....1....|....2....|....3....|....4....|....5....|....6....│
│                                                                   │
│       TO:    All Managers                                         │
│       FROM:  Sam Davis, Sr. Vice-President                        │
│       DATE:  November 8, 1990                                     │
│       SUBJECT: Organizational Planning Meeting                    │
│                                                                   │
│    On December 1, 1990, the Davis Toy Company will conduct an    │
│    organizational planning meeting for the coming year.           │
│                                                                   │
│    The meeting will be held at 9:00 A.M. in the west board       │
│    room.  A group from the Season's Consulting Company will      │
│    present a new business plan for expansion into children's     │
│    sportswear for the 1991 selling season.  Attendees and their  │
│    respective presentations will include:                         │
│                                                                   │
│    [*]Tom Willis-Marketing and Sales                              │
│                                                                   │
│    [*]Brenda Smith-Manufacturing                                  │
│                                                                   │
│    [*]Ron Hageman-Distribution                                    │
│                                                                   │
│ Pg 1  Sec 1    1/1   At 1"  Ln 1  Col 1  EXT     NUM              │
└───────────────────────────────────────────────────────────────────┘
```

Figure 3.10 Copying a block of text.

Practice using the block editing features of moving text with Cut, Copy, and Paste from the Edit menu. You'll find that these powerful editing tools in Word are simple to master.

Using Move to and Copy to: The Clipboard Exception

If you find yourself in a memory bind, Word offers faster, perhaps more efficient methods for moving and copying text: *Move to* and *Copy to*. These methods move or copy text without putting the text in the Clipboard first and are useful when memory is running low or you don't want to remove the contents from the Clipboard by using another Cut or Copy command. Both commands work like their Edit menu cousins.

As an exercise, save any document that you wish to save, and then get a clean page or new document on your screen. Type the following text and then complete the steps that follow.

> This is my testimony. My son is now 6 years old. He has enrolled in first grade and wishes to learn how to read and write. I have consented to let him practice his alphabet on my prize possession, my personal computer. With Word for Windows, he will quickly fall in love with computers as I did at a much older age.

3—Editing Your Documents

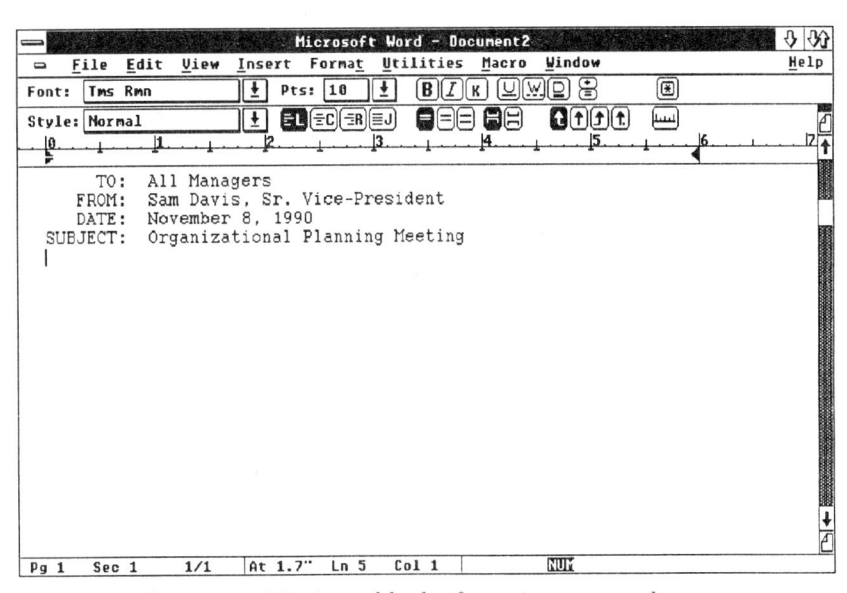

Figure 3.11 Moving a block of text into a new document.

To cancel a Move to command prior to its completion, press the Esc key.

1. Select the text that you wish to move. In this example, select the first sentence.

    The first sentence is highlighted.

2. To use the Move to method, press the Move key, **F2**.

    Unlike Cut, the text does not disappear from your screen, nor is it placed in the Clipboard. The text simply remains highlighted (see Figure 3.12). In addition, the box in the lower left corner of the status bar (if it's on) displays "Move to where?" in place of a page number and section number.

3. Move the blinking vertical insertion point to the location where you wish to move the selected text, and click the mouse once to anchor the insertion point (or use the arrow keys). In this case, move it to the end of the paragraph. Please note that you cannot move the insertion point anywhere inside the current selection.

    The anchored insertion point changes to a blinking *dotted* vertical line.

107

The Basics

4. Once the new location has been selected, press the **Enter** key.

The selected text moves to the new location in one single move (Figure 3.13).

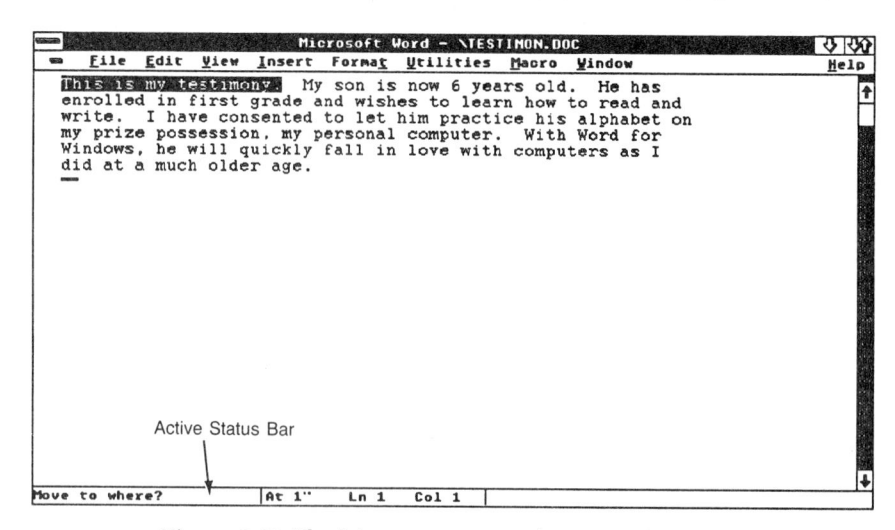

Figure 3.12 The Move to command stores selected text without the Clipboard.

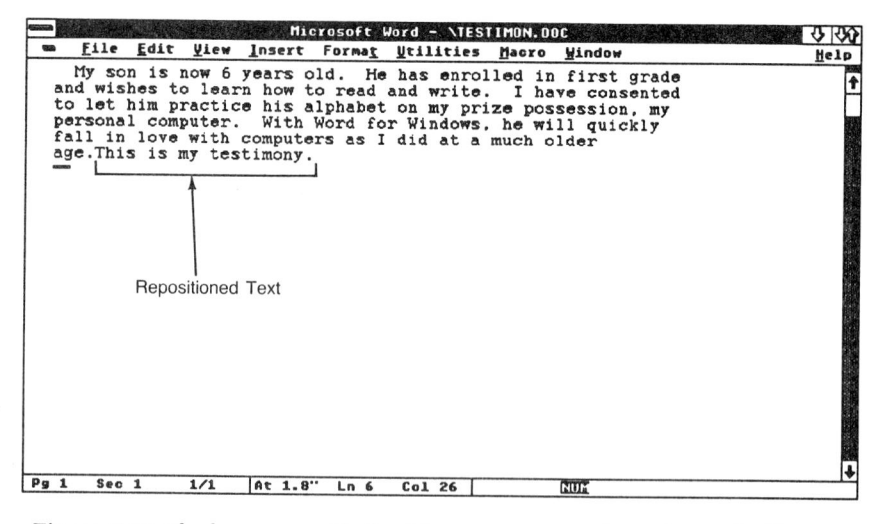

Figure 3.13 Block moves with the Move to command are fast and efficient.

Using the Copy to command is similar to using the Move to command. The Copy to command makes a duplicate of the selected text and places that duplicated text in the location that you select by moving the insertion point. However, you cannot use the Copy To

3—Editing Your Documents

command to make multiple copies without executing the entire procedure again. As with Move to, Copy to does not use the Clipboard, so using it maintains the current contents of the Clipboard. For practice, we can make a copy of the first sentence of our sample text and move it to the end of the paragraph. To do this, complete the following:

1. Select the text. In this example, select the first sentence as before.

   The first sentence appears highlighted.

2. Next, enter the Copy to command by pressing **Shift-F2**.

   The text stays put and remains highlighted, but a copy is made in a hidden buffer of memory not related to the Clipboard. As with the Move to command, the lower left box of the status bar now displays "Copy to where?"

3. Use the mouse or the arrow keys to move the insertion point to the new location. In this case, move the insertion point to the end of the paragraph.

   As with the Move to command, the anchored insertion point changes to a blinking dotted vertical line.

4. Press **Enter** to complete the Copy to command.

   The selected text is now duplicated and displayed, as in Figure 3.14.

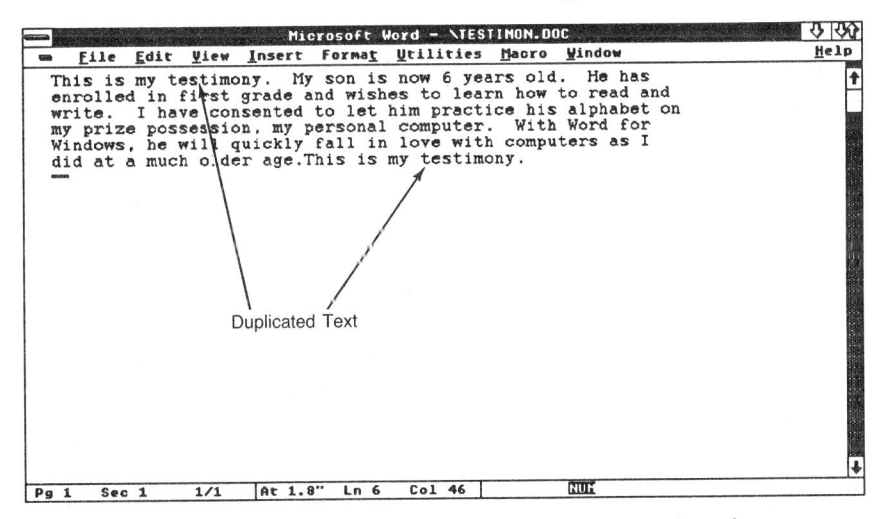

Figure 3.14 The Copy to command duplicates your selected text.

The Basics

One more option is available to you using the Move to or Copy to keys. You don't necessarily need to select text before you choose either F2 or Shift+F2 to activate the Move to or Copy to commands. In this case, Word will assume that you wish to paste text at the current insertion point location. For example, if you press F2 to turn on the Move To command, and then select text, the selected text will appear underlined with a dotted line. Once you have selected the text to move, press Enter and the text moves to the location of the insertion point.

Tip: For those of you who have a mouse, you can simulate a Move to or Copy to command by selecting the text and using the Ctrl key with the mouse right button. For example, to perform a Move to, first select the text and then point to the place in the document where the text is to be moved. Don't click the left mouse button to move the insertion point. Rather, hold down the **Ctrl** key and press the right button instead of the left button and your text will move to its new location. Similarly, to perform a Copy to simply select the text as before, point to the position where the text is to appear, and then hold down **Ctrl**+**Shift** while clicking the right mouse button. Remember, in both cases, use the right mouse button instead of the left mouse button.

Undoing Your Commands

Many word processing packages feature the ability to undo the last command. Word is no exception. Word will remember the last action that you performed, including typing, editing, deleting, and even most formatting. The *Undo* command is found on the Edit menu (press Alt,E,U) and is considered "action sensitive." In other words, if your last action was typing, pulling down the Edit menu would display the command as Undo Typing. If your last command was to erase a word with Delete or with the Cut command, the command would be displayed as Undo Cut. A Paste would result in an Undo Paste and a Format command would produce an Undo Formatting, and so on. Not all actions can be reversed, however. In this case, Word displays a dimmed "Can't Undo." You'll find, however, that there are alternate ways of undoing commands. For example, choosing the Save As command produces a dialog box; to Undo this command, and others like it, choose the Cancel button.

An additional feature of the Undo command is that it will let you continue to change your mind. After the Undo command is invoked, you can use the Undo Undo command to revise your action. Your reversed action will be reversed again! As a shortcut, the Undo key combination, Alt+Backspace, lets you toggle back and forth between undoing and redoing the last action or command. If a command or action can't be undone, you will see something like, "Can't Undo" and "Can't Repeat" listed as dim characters at the top of the Edit menu.

Searching and Replacing Text

One of the most powerful editing tools is the ability to search for and replace text. The Word *search and replace* feature enables you to search for every occurrence of a series of up to 256 characters in your text. This standard word processing feature is accomplished in Word with the *Search* and *Replace* commands found in the Edit menu. These commands are not only useful for searching and/or replacing text, but formatting within a document as well. This section details searching for and replacing text or formatting within a document. To use Word's retrieval system to search among documents, refer to Chapter 15.

Using the Search Command

Suppose you want to review a document to determine if you have used one of your pet phrases a little too often. Or perhaps when you reach the end of a long document you "just know" that you've been incorrectly spelling a name. The Search command allows you to search a document for a word or a group of words and to find every occurrence of such text. Once you have found each occurrence, you can type in a correction or change.

Word doesn't actually search for words; it searches for a series of characters or codes strung together in a sequence that matches a sequence you have specified. Using the Search command is simple, but there a few important points to remember. A normal (default) search is not limited to exact matches of character strings. Word can search for up to 256 characters in any particular "field." Since many character strings may appear similar, a search can produce undesirable results. For example, searching for the word "it" will produce every single occurrence of the exact character string (including leading spaces) as well as any character string that includes the same letter sequence in a larger string, such as "itself" or "limit." To limit your search, you can choose from two options that will help you find exactly what you want. The first is *Whole Word*. With the Whole Word option on, a search for the word *ball* will flag only ball and not

The Basics

any related string or derivation of the word, like balloon or snowball. The second option is *Match Upper/Lowercase.* This option will specify your search to look for any words that are capitalized or not, as you specify. If you search for the word *Christmas,* without clicking on this option, Word will search for any form of the characters, such as christmas, CHRISTMAS, or christMAS. To search only for Christmas, click on the case option.

Finally, Word gives you the option of searching forward to the end of the document (Search Direction: Down) or backward to the beginning of the document (Search Direction: Up). You can also search through a portion of text if you wish. If you don't start at the beginning of the document for a forward search or at the end for a backward search, Word will give you the opportunity to do so via a dialog box for continuing the search.

To search for text, complete the following steps.

You can cancel a search by clicking Cancel with the mouse or you can press Tab until Cancel is highlighted and then press Enter. You can also press the Esc key to cancel the search and close the window.

1. To search a complete document, it's best to move your insertion point to the beginning or end of the document, although Word will give you the option of continuing the search from the opposite end if you don't.

2. To begin a search, choose the **Search** command from the Edit menu or press **Alt,E,S**.

   The Search dialog box is displayed, as in Figure 3.15.

3. In the *Search For* text box, enter the word or phrase for which you wish to search (up to 256 characters). The text remains in the Search For text box until you enter a different text string in your next search session. Do not click OK or press Enter just yet.

   If your string exceeds 38 characters, the text will scroll back to the left in the Search For box window.

4. Choose any search options, such as Whole Word or the case option, by clicking in the appropriate box or by pressing **Alt** and the W or M.

   Choosing a search option places an X in the selected box.

5. Choose the direction that you wish the search to go through your document: Up or Down.

6. Click **OK** or press **Enter**.

Use the Repeat Search key (Shift + F4) to repeat the last search of text. This feature allows you to find multiple occurrences of the same text quickly.

7. After the first occurrence of the text string is found, the search procedure is over. If you wish to continue the search through the remainder of the document, you must execute the Edit Search command again. When you choose the Search command, you will notice that the text in the Search For edit box is the same as you last left it. Thus, to find the next occurrence, simply choose **OK** from the Search dialog box. As a tip, you can also use the shortcut, **Repeat Search**, by pressing **Shift + F4** to execute the last search as many times as you like.

If your insertion point is at the beginning of the document, the Down option is on by default.

Word will search your document for the nearest occurrence of the text string listed in the Search For text box. If you didn't start your search at the beginning or end of your document, Word will provide a dialog box that gives you the opportunity to do so when it reaches the opposite end of the document (see Figure 3.16). When a string is found, it will be highlighted on your screen.

Each time you execute a search, the last occurrence of the text string found will remain highlighted. At this point, you can use your editing tools to change the text if you so desire.

Figure 3.15 The Search dialog box.

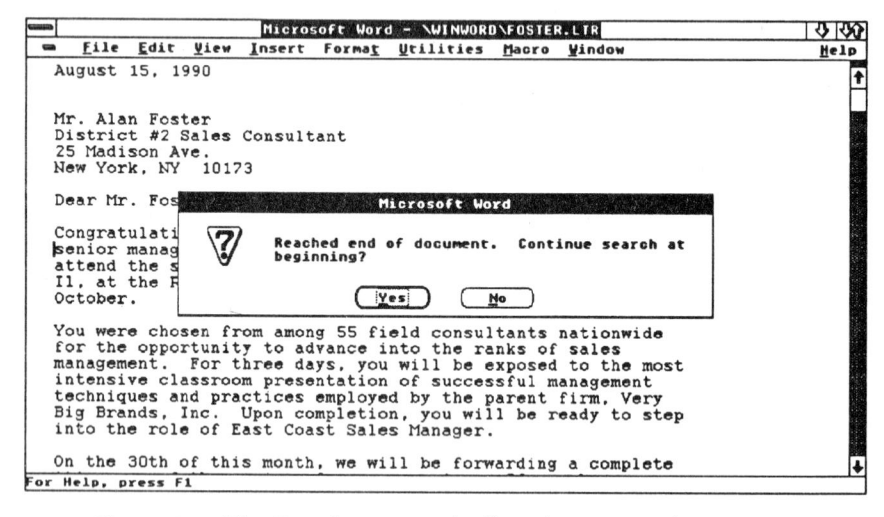

Figure 3.16 The Search command offers the option of continuing the search automatically.

Using Go To for Searching

You can use the Go To command on the Edit menu to search for specific page breaks, section marks, line numbers, footnotes, or annotations. As an example, if you choose the Go To option from the Edit menu (Alt,E,G) then a Go To dialog box appears as shown in Figure 3.17. From the Go To dialog box, you can move your insertion point to the next occurrence of a specified item, such as a page number or a bookmark (if any exists—bookmarks are covered in Chapter 18). A handier method is to use the Go To function key, F5. Pressing F5 produces a Go To prompt in a visible status bar as shown in Figure 3.18. Whether the Go To dialog box or the Go To prompt appears, you must enter an appropriate destination for the Go To, such as a valid page number or an existing bookmark.

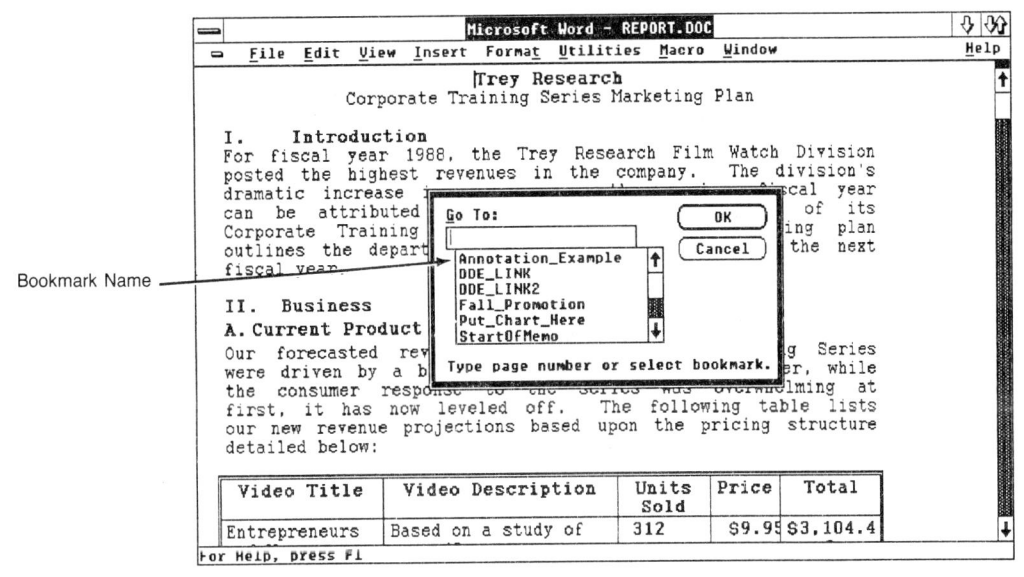

Figure 3.17 The Go To dialog box.

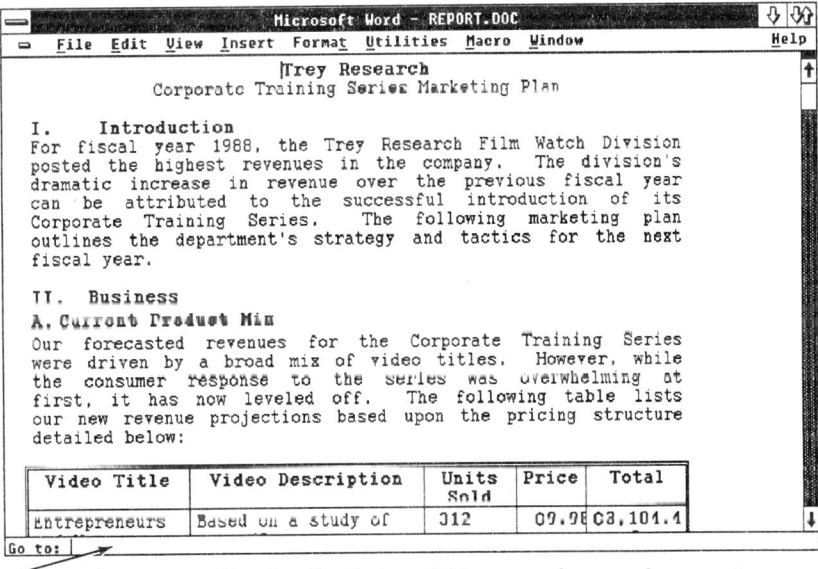

Figure 3.18 Use the Go To key (F5) to search your document for a specified item.

The Basics

Using the Replace Command

Searching for the occurrence of text is handy, but replacing that text with new text is a powerful editing feature. The Replace command is a natural extension of the Search command and works much the same way. Like Search, the Replace command lets you find the places in your text where a particular set of characters occurs but it also gives you the option of changing them automatically.

To begin replacing text or formatting, or perform a combination of replacing and formatting, move the insertion point to the beginning of the document so that you don't inadvertently miss a change. Although Word gives you the option of continuing the search at any point in your document, it's easier to start at the beginning than it is to backtrack.

The same searching options are available in the Replace dialog box as were available with the Find command. You have the option of searching for a Whole Word or for a word by its case. If you don't care about searches that might find characters embedded in other words, leave the Whole Word option off. Without the Match Upper/Lowercase box selected, Word will find all instances of the selected character string regardless of capitalization.

Replacing text with the Confirm option off allows you to choose the Edit Undo command to reverse all changes. If the Confirm option is selected, only the last change will be reversed.

The Replace dialog box does offer some options not available with the Search command. The Replace option enables you to replace all occurrences of text automatically by turning off the *Confirm Changes* button or one at a time by clicking the box on. If you change them one at a time, Word will find the text, wait for you to change it by choosing Yes, No, or Cancel, and then move on to the next occurrence to begin again until all occurrences have been found. If you choose Cancel, the Edit Replace command is stopped, but all changes made up to that point are left intact. Obviously, the automatic route is much faster, but it doesn't allow you to change your mind.

The following steps show you how to execute a search and replace. First, as practice, save any document that you wish to save and then clear your screen with the New command. Enter the following text as an exercise and then perform the necessary steps. Type the text just as it appears; it contains some intentional typos in order to make a couple of points.

Before I decided to buy my International Business Machine PS/2 computer, I considered a number of options. Did I want to buy a computer that may not be compatible with the 5 1/4" disk drive type computers owned by my co-workers? Perhaps our company needed some new blood and the International Business Machine PS/2 might just be the ticket. From the

3—Editing Your Documents

moment I laid my hands on the keyboard, I fell in love. The new Microsoft Word for Windows software was simple to use, and the machine itself was a dream. All I needed to do was to convince my boss, ddf, and I would show this company what the meaning of the word "productivity" was all about.

Use the Tab key to move around the Replace dialog box or click with the mouse.

1. Move the insertion point to the beginning of the document.

    The blinking insertion point appears in the upper left corner of the text.

2. Choose the **Replace** command from the Edit menu or enter **Alt,E,E** from the keyboard.

    The Replace dialog box appears on your screen (refer to Figure 3.19).

3. In the Search For box, type the string of text (a word or phrase) that you wish to change. The string can include up to 256 characters. For this example, enter

    International Business Machine.

    The box holds 38 characters before it begins to scroll back to the left.

    The phrase *International Business Machine* appears in the Search For window.

4. Next, click in the **Replace With** box or press the **Tab** key to move the insertion point, and then enter the string of text that you wish to change the original text to. The new text will take on any formatting characteristics of the old text, including correct capitalization (at the beginning of a sentence, for example). In this example, enter

    IBM.

    Just like the Search For box, you can enter up to 256 characters, but only 38 will appear at a time. *IBM* will appear in the Replace With window, as in Figure 3.19.

5. Before you begin the search, click on the **Whole Word** option and the **Match Upper/Lowercase** option. These options shorten most searches.

    Both boxes display an X. To turn off the selection, click the box again.

117

The Basics

6. The next step is to decide whether you want to confirm each change. Do this by turning on the Confirm box which is on by default. For practice, change them one at a time instead of all at once automatically.

   The Confirm box will also display an X.

7. The final step is to begin the search. Click **OK** or press **Enter**. If you had turned off the Confirm option, *International Business Machines* would have been replaced with *IBM* instantly. In this case, though, you will need to replace them one at a time by clicking **Yes** or pressing **Enter** to confirm each highlighted change.

   When the first occurrence is found, Word highlights the word or phrase to be changed and waits for you to confirm the change.

8. If you want to continue to the next occurrence without making a change, select **No**. If you wish to make a change, click the **Yes** button or press **Enter**. At each occurrence, you will make this decision. For practice, click the **Yes** button until all changes are indeed made.

   IBM text replaces the old text. Your document should look like Figure 3.20.

You may have noticed that one typo remains to be fixed. In the last sentence, you will find a reference to the boss's name *ddf*. Practice the Replace command by replacing this string with a proper name, such as Dr. David Finkelstein. Remember that when you work with long names or strings, it is handy to use abbreviations as a temporary substitute to save time (especially if the long string is repeated frequently). When the document is complete, use the Replace command to edit out the abbreviations and insert the appropriate text in one swift stroke by turning off the Confirm option.

Note on Searching and Replacing Formatting

As you've seen, you can use Word's search and replace feature to find and change specific formatting or any combination of text and format-

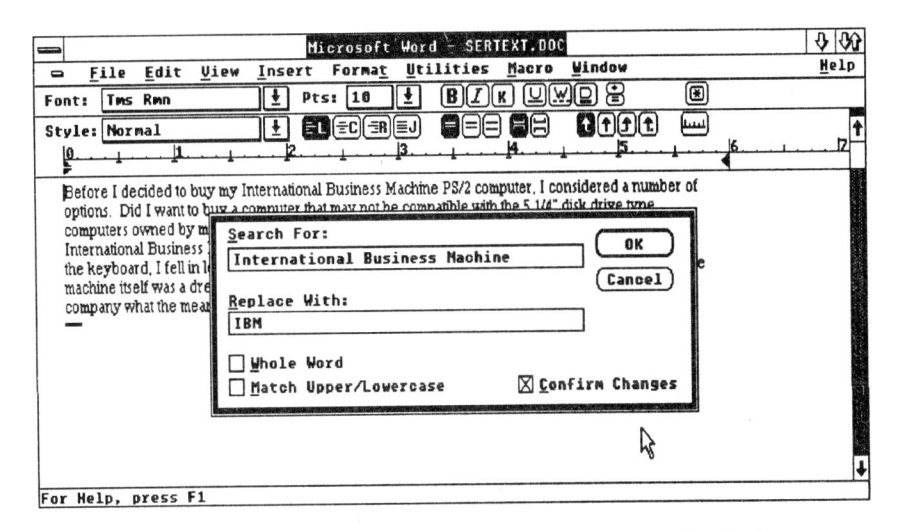

Figure 3.19 Enter the new text in the Replace With edit box.

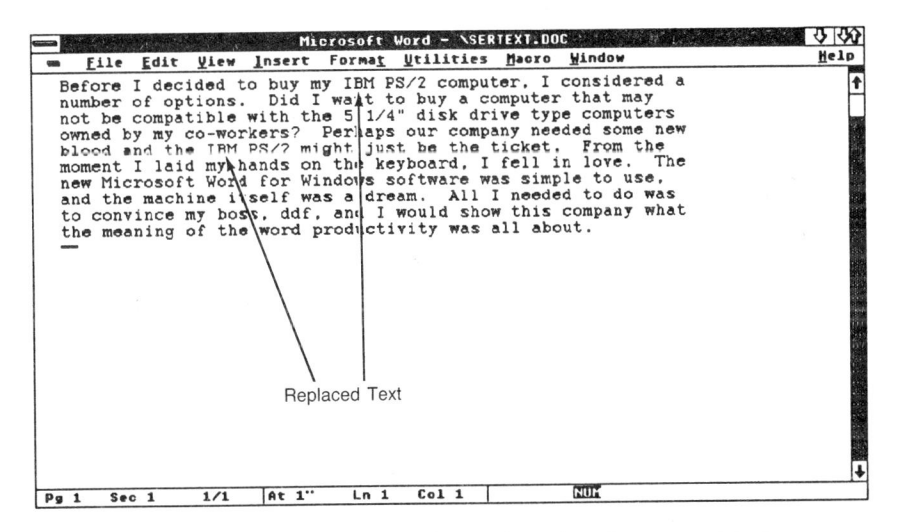

Figure 3.20 A successful search and replace completed.

ting. You can even search for a certain style by specifying it in the Search For and Replace With edit boxes with the keys that apply the character or paragraph formatting. You cannot use the Ribbon or the Ruler to specify the formatting characters. You must use the keys detailed in Table 3.2. Please note that there are some restrictions and in addition, the following paragraph formatting keys are not available in either the Search or Replace dialog boxes: Ctrl+G, Ctrl+N, Ctrl+M, Ctrl+S, and Ctrl+T.

The Basics

Table 3.2 Character and Paragraph Formatting for Search and Replace

Press These Keys	For This Format	Restriction
Character Formatting:		
Ctrl + B	Bold	
Crl + D	Double underline	
Ctrl + I	Italic	
Ctrl + U	Underline	
Ctrl + W	Word underline	
Ctrl + K	Small caps	
Ctrl + H	Hidden text	
Ctrl + Spacebar	Blank characters	Removes character formatting.
Ctrl + F and Ctrl + Shift + F	Font	Continue to press in order to display fonts used in document.
Ctrl + = (equal sign)	Subscript	3 points below text baseline only
Ctrl + + (plus sign)	Superscript	3 points above text baseline only
Ctrl + P and Ctrl + Shift + P	Point size	Each press displays next or previous point size in document from 4 to 127 points in 1/2-point increments.
Ctrl + Z	Delete strikethru text in mark revision mode	Search only.
Ctrl + N	New text in marks revision mode	Search only.
Paragraph Formatting:		
Ctrl + 1	Single-space lines	
Ctrl + 2	Double-space lines	
Ctrl + 5	1 1/2-space lines	
Ctrl + C	Centered text lines	
Ctrl + L	Left-aligned text lines	
Ctrl + J	Justified text lines	
Ctrl + R	Right-aligned text lines	
Ctrl + O	Open space before paragraph	

The Basics

4. In the Replace With edit box, type ^c to instruct Word to insert the contents of the Clipboard.

   The special characters appear in the Replace With box.

5. Click **OK** or press **Enter** to complete the search and replace.

Some Final Thoughts about Searching and Replacing Text

As with the Search command, you have the option of cancelling the Replace command. You can click the Cancel button, press the Tab key until the Cancel option is highlighted and then press Enter, or simply press the Esc key. Keep in mind, though, any changes that you have made with the Replace command prior to choosing Cancel will still be applied. If you change your mind, use the Edit Undo command to reverse the last change executed with the Replace command (or all of them if you had turned off the Confirm option).

You can find and change text contained in headers, footers, and footnotes as long as the window containing the header, footer, or footnote is active and open.

Finally, you can use the Search and Replace commands to search for, and then replace, special characters, such as blank spaces (any combination of spaces, tabs, newline characters, carriage returns, page breaks, or section breaks in a string), question marks, or paragraph marks. To do this, you must type the character combinations shown in Table 3.3 in the Search For box or the Replace With box.

Editing in Windows

You were introduced to windows in Chapter 1. If you have been working with your Microsoft Windows for awhile, you know that mastering the flexibility of windows is a must. One of the best features of window flexibility is that you can open as many as nine windows at once. You can use this feature to look at several different documents or view different parts of the same document.

For practice with this unique feature, type the letter in Figure 3.21 in a new document window. Then split the window in two parts by dragging the split bar down the vertical scroll or choose the **Split** command from the document control box or press **Alt,-,T**. The split

Press These Keys	For This Format	Restriction
Ctrl+E	Close space after paragraph	
Ctrl+X	Deletes paragraph formatting	
Styles:		
^ystyle-name	To search for specific style.	Don't insert space between y and style name.

If you combine both character and paragraph formatting, Word will find all text with the specified character formatting as long as it appears within the paragraphs specified by paragraph formatting. The character formatting is only applied to the specific text found, while the paragraph formatting is applied to the entire paragraph.

Note on Searching and Replacing Large Amounts of Text

Suppose you wish to search for and replace text that is greater than the 256-character limit. To do this, you copy the large block of text or a graphic to the Clipboard, select it, and then use the ^c key combination in the Replace With box to paste the contents of the Clipboard into your document. You cannot use the ^c key combination in the Search For box, however. The following steps highlight this procedure.

1. Copy the desired block of text or graphic to the Clipboard. Remember, to copy a block of text, select the text first and then choose **Ctrl+Ins** or the **Copy** command from the Edit menu.

    The highlighted text or graphic is copied to the clipboard when you execute a Copy command. The text remains highlighted until you click somewhere with the mouse or press an arrow key.

2. Choose the **Replace** command from the Edit menu with the mouse or press **Alt,E,E**.

    The Replace dialog box appears.

3. Type the text that you wish to change in the Search For edit box.

    The text appears as you type.

121

3—Editing Your Documents

Table 3.3 Special Character Codes for Searches

To Search for or Replace	Enter This Code
An unspecified character	?
Question mark	^?
White space	^w
Nonbreaking space	^s
Tab mark	^t
ASCII value	6### (### is ASCII value for any decimal in character set—e.g., ^1 to find a picture)
Paragraph mark	^p
End-of-line mark	^n
Optional hyphen	^-
Nonbreaking hyphen	^—
Section mark	^d
Caret or circumflex	^^
Formula character	^\

*Remember, to change from one window to another, click inside the desired window, or press **Ctrl** + **F6** and **Ctrl** + **Shift** + **F6** to move back and forth between the next and previous document windows. To change from one pane to another, press **F6** and **Shift** + **F6**.*

bar is the black box that appears at the top of the scroll bar, just above the arrow icon. The result will look like Figure 3.22.

Once your window is split into two windows, you can scroll each window independently to look at different parts of the same document. For example, you can use the top window to look at the beginning of the document and the bottom window to look at the end of the document (Figure 3.23). This feature is handy for those documents that won't fit on a single screen, and most of them won't. One important point to keep in mind regarding windows: Even if you have more than one window open, only one window can be active at a time. Any corrections or changes that you make in that active window will be applied to all windows of the same document, though.

Perhaps the best feature of windows is that you can use all the editing tools as if you were working in a single window. For example, you can use the Cut, Copy, and Paste commands to move or cut text from a part of the document in one window and then paste it into another part of the document in a second window. You can even use the Copy to (Shift + F2) and Move to (F2) methods for quickly moving text between windows. Remember that the Copy to method moves a duplicate of selected text to the second window, while the Move to method moves the selected text itself, deleting it from the first window.

Additionally, you can move selected portions of text across windows representing different documents. To do this, open one docu-

123

The Basics

```
                SMITH & TUBBS
               101 Alabama Ave.
               Chicago, IL  60612


                                              May 5, 1990

Mrs. Jean Burke:

    It's been more than six months since you charged a
purchase at Smith & Tubbs, and we can't help worrying that
we've done something to offend you.  We wanted to assure you
that everyone at Smith & Tubbs is ready to serve you.

    If you have encountered some problems in the past, we
like to know.  It is our sincere desire to meet the needs of
our customers in every way.  We welcome any suggestions from
our customers and friends here at Smith & Tubbs.

    Please complete the enclosed reply card and help
improve our service.  We will give your comments immediate
attention.  Thank you in advance, and we look forward to
seeing you again.


                                              Sincerely,



                                              Mr. Richard Stewart
                                              Customer Relations
```

Figure 3.21 Sample document for splitting.

```
================= Microsoft Word - \SMIT&TUB.DOC =================
   File  Edit  View  Insert  Format  Utilities  Macro  Window                Help
                   SMITH & TUBBS
                  101 Alabama Ave.
                  Chicago, IL  60612

                                              May 5, 1990          Pane 1
Mrs. Jean Burke:

    It's been more than six months since you charged a
purchase at Smith & Tubbs, and we can't help worrying that
we've done something to offend you.  We wanted to assure you
----------------------------------------------------------
that everyone at Smith & Tubbs is ready to serve you.

    If you have encountered some problems in the past, we
like to know.  It is our sincere desire to meet the needs of
our customers in every way.  We welcome any suggestions from
our customers and friends here at Smith & Tubbs.           Pane 2

    Please complete the enclosed reply card and help
improve our service.  We will give your comments immediate
attention.  Thank you in advance, and we look forward to
seeing you again.

 Pg 1   Sec 1    1/1    At 3"   Ln 13  Col 1
```

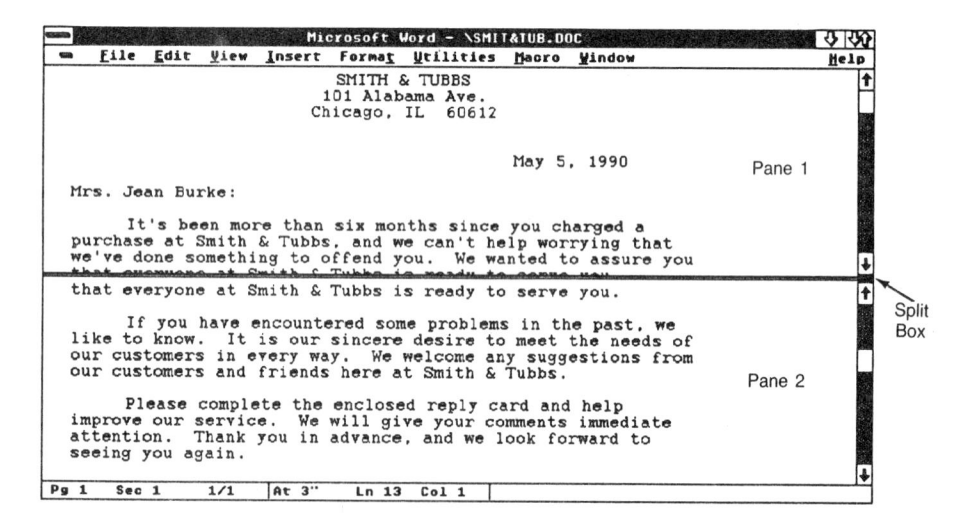

Split Box

Figure 3.22 Sample document split into two parts by dragging the split bar.

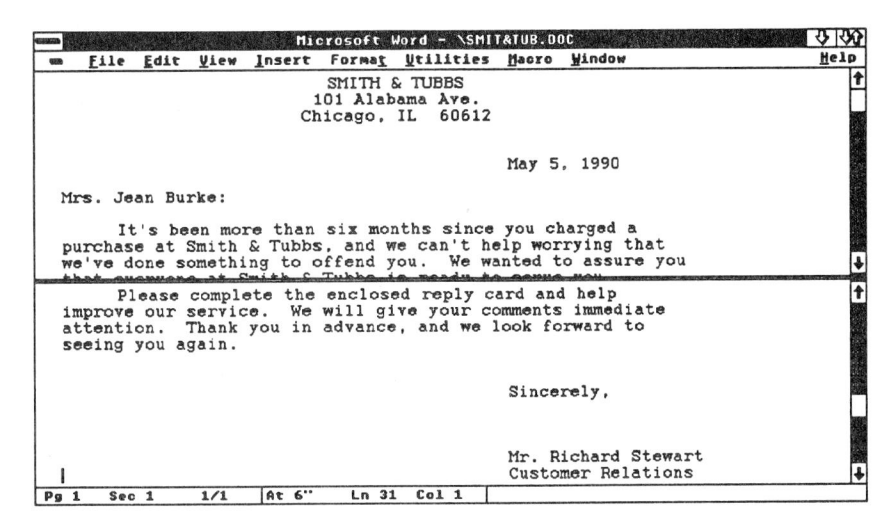

Figure 3.23 Use the scroll bars in each window to view parts of the same document.

ment, shrink it with the Control Size and Move commands, and open a second document with the Open command. Shrink the second document and reposition both documents until you can see them clearly. Use the scroll bars or arrow keys to view various portions of the documents and use the Cut, Copy, and Paste commands to interchange text. As you master using windows in your work you'll find that the options are almost limitless.

Review

In this chapter you learned:

1. Before you can use any of Word's editing tools, you must select the text that you wish to change. In general, you select text by dragging across it with the mouse or by clicking/double-clicking the mouse next to the text in the selection bar or using the Shift key in combination with the arrow keys. You can also use the Extend Selection key, F8, to quickly select pieces of text.
2. The simplest editing tool is the Backspace key. Pressing Backspace moves the insertion point one character space backward, erasing any character in its path.

3. To erase large blocks of text quickly, select the text and then either press the Delete key or choose the Cut command from the Edit menu. The Cut command places the deleted material in the Clipboard, a temporary holding place, while the delete method does not.

4. When you first start Word, the Typing Replaces Selection option is turned off in the Utilities Customize dialog box. Turning this option on is a handy way to change large selections of text with a single keystroke.

5. The Edit menu offers the primary editing tools: Cut, Copy, and Paste. To use these commands, select the text first and then choose Cut to erase it or Copy to make a copy of the selected text and store it in the Clipboard. Once the text is stored in the Clipboard, you can choose Paste to insert a copy of the text at the current location of the insertion point.

6. Block editing involves moving sections of text around your document or rearranging or deleting paragraphs. This procedure is sometimes referred to as "cut and paste."

7. The Clipboard is a temporary storage area that is useful when you are relocating blocks of text or moving text or graphics from third-party software packages (for example, a chart from Microsoft Excel) into your documents. Each time you execute another Cut or Copy command, the contents of the Clipboard change according to your last Cut or Copy selection. When you turn off the computer, the content of the Clipboard is erased.

8. To save the Clipboard contents during the current work session and still move blocks of text, use the Copy to and Move to methods. The Move to method requires the F2 function keypress, and the Copy to method requires the Shift+F2 keypress.

9. Change your mind? Word remembers many of your last actions performed at the keyboard or with the mouse. You can use the Undo command from the Edit menu to negate your last typing, editing, deleting, or formatting commands. Change your mind again? Choose the Repeat option.

10. Word enables you to search through a document for a particular word or phrase with the Search command. A cousin of Search, the Replace command lets you search for text and/or format and replace them.

11. The Go To command allows you to specify a page number or an existing bookmark to move the insertion point. You can also use the Go To key, F5.

12. Editing in windows is a simple task. You can use the Control box Split command to divide an existing document in order to view two parts of the same document via two window panes. The important point to remember is that any editing you do in one window pane of the document is also automatically done in the second pane.

13. To switch between panes use the F6 and Shift+F6 keys. To switch between two document windows, use Ctrl+F6 and (Shift+Ctrl+F6). You can also click with a mouse anywhere inside a visible window to make that window active.

F O U R

chapter

Formatting Your Document

In this chapter:

- Introduction to Formatting
- Introducing the Format Menu
- Using the Document Command
- Setting Margins
- Changing Page Layout with Line and Page Breaks

Having created your text and edited out all the mistakes, you now have the opportunity to design your text's appearance. Design is important because first impressions can be lasting. Designing, or formatting, your text does not just mean making your letters look pretty. Your document should be informative, professional looking, and useful. And yes, it can even be pretty. This section introduces the concept of designing your documents, called in Word *formatting*. The implementation of your design determines the effectiveness of the words you've created and pushed together to form a meaningful and communicative document. This chapter introduces you to the basic concepts of formatting text and shows you how to set formatting changes that affect your entire document, including setting margins and setting line and page breaks.

Introduction to Formatting

Word's formatting options are detailed at four basic levels: Character, Paragraph, Section, and Document. Beyond these, Word offers the special formatting options of reviewing and modifying the formatting of styles, tables, pictures, and the absolute position of objects, such as text and pictures. We'll explore all of these options as we progress through this book. For now, we'll concentrate on the four basic levels.

When you begin to create a document, you might start with a general idea and then move to particular sentences and words to explain the idea. Formatting with Word is a similar process. You can begin formatting with the general and move to the more particular. At the most general formatting level, called Document formatting, you would specify formatting changes that would affect the entire document. A common general formatting decision is establishing the document's margins. At the most particular level, or Character formatting, you can specify the appearance of the individual character, such as boldface or italicized text. For an overview of all the formatting options at the four levels, refer to Figure 4.1. As the figure illustrates, you might think of formatting as either a "top-down" or "bottom-up" process, in which you begin at one end of the spectrum and move to the other end.

Keep one point in mind when beginning to format your document. Some formatting options are interrelated and may affect other formatting options. A clear example is that of changing the margins at the Document level which, in turn, affects every subsequent paragraph of the entire document. With this thought in mind, you might wish to begin with the more general aspects of formatting before moving to the more specific. This is the approach that we'll take in this book.

The basic appearance of your document is controlled by the formatting options that you choose from each of the four basic formatting levels. In this chapter we'll look at the most general level, Document formatting. In Chapters 5 and 6, we move from the general to the specific as we examine Paragraph formatting followed by Character formatting. Section formatting will be reserved for Chapter 7, where we discuss creating complex documents with multiple columns.

Type of Formatting	Options	Notes
Document	Margins Page size Default tab stops Footnote placement Window control	Affects entire document
Section	Section start Line numbering Number of columns Vertical alignment Page numbering	For complex documents
Paragraph	Alignment Line spacing Indentations Paragraph spacing Page-break control Tab settings Borders Line numbering Style names	Also see the Ruler
Character	Font Style Size Color Small caps Spacing Subscript Superscript	Also see the Ribbon

(General ↕ Specific)

Figure 4.1 The formatting spectrum.

Introducing the Format Menu

If you choose the Format menu (Alt,t) in Short menus mode, only the Character, Paragraph, and Document options are available (including tab stop setting and alignment and table formatting). In Full Menus mode, Section formatting is available to you, as well as Styles, Picture, and Position formatting options. For now, let's list the basic formatting levels along with their characteristics:

- *Character formatting* is the lowest (most particular) level of formatting options. You can change the style and size of characters and the spacing between them. The style of a font refers to text enhancements or attributes, such as boldface, underlining, or italics. You can adjust the spacing between individual characters, and create subscripts and superscripts of characters, which are especially handy for math and the sciences.

- *Paragraph formatting* is the next level. Remember that Word recognizes a paragraph as a string of characters delimited by the paragraph symbol, caused by pressing the Enter key. You want the character strings that you enter to take shape as meaningful lines of text, organized into paragraphs, and designed with a readable layout. In Chapter 5, you'll learn many of the paragraph-formatting options that enable you to create documents that do just that. You will learn how to set the alignment of your paragraphs, such as left-justified or centered text, and to set the spacing of your paragraphs. You will also learn about indenting paragraphs and setting tabs. In addition, paragraph formatting offers some unusual options, such as drawing borders around paragraphs and creating special paragragh placement, such as printing two related columns of text side by side. In the second part of this book, you'll explore how to store paragraph-formatting information as a style sheet in order to apply that style to paragraphs that you create in new documents. Styles and how to use the Style command found in the Format menu are discussed in detail in Chapter 13.

- *Section formatting* refers to a collection of paragraphs that you must control when designing special documents, such as a newsletter that uses several columns of text and graphics. You'll use section formatting to control many of the larger design elements, such as headings to be placed at the top of a document, specialized columns to be on the right side, footnotes at page bottoms, and so on. Chapter 7 introduces the advanced formatting features available with the Section command.

- *Document formatting* is the most general level, and it is the focus of the rest of this chapter. Document formatting refers to all pages and sections—an entire document. A good example of this is setting margins, page size, and footnote placement. Document formatting is accomplished with the Document command from the Format menu.

  Document formatting is also available with the Print Preview option found in the File menu. Print Preview provides additional methods for formatting margins, setting printing options, and more important, taking a "sneak peek" at your

4—Formatting Your Document

documents before you print. Page View allows you to move quickly from Print Preview to complete unfinished edits or additional formatting changes.

Using the Document Command

Layout and design contribute greatly to a document's readability and its consequent ability to communicate. Document formatting is "global" in that its parameters affect the page layout of the entire document. Document formatting is accomplished with the Document command, which is found on the Format menu. This section reviews the use of the Document command and its associated Document dialog box for setting margins, changing the width of the type area, changing the default tab stops, reviewing widow control, and formatting footnotes.

To examine the elements of the Document dialog box, shown in Figure 4.2, first choose the **Document** command from the Format menu (**Alt,T,D**). The elements of the dialog box can be divided into the following sections:

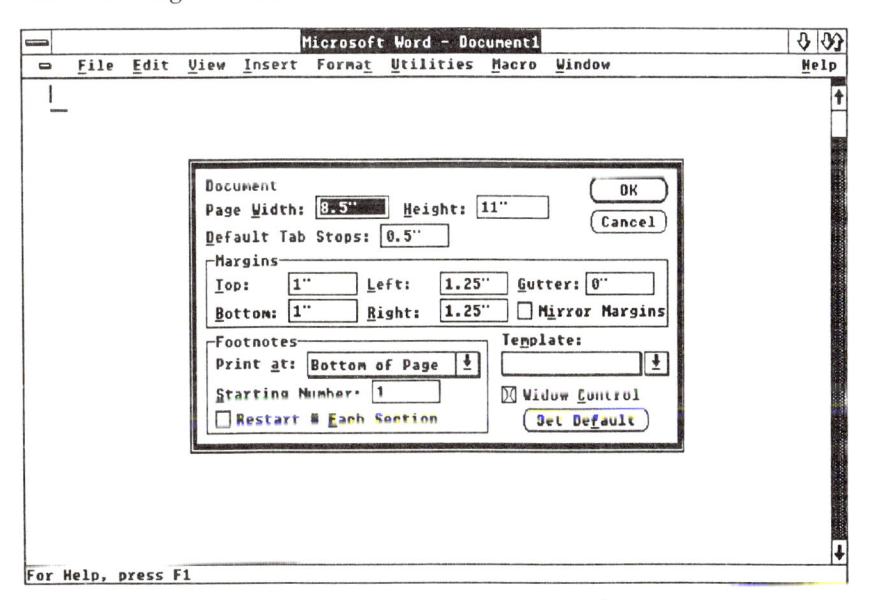

Figure 4.2 The Document dialog box.

- Setting margins—Margins exist on the left, right, top, and bottom of your document. The Word default settings are 1 1/4"

133

for the left and right margins and 1″ for the top and bottom margins. Setting your margins to different dimensions involves changing the defaults, as you'll see shortly. Don't confuse indentation with the margin. An indentation or a tab provides greater white space and gives an appearance of a larger margin. The extra space is still a part of the print area.

In the margins section of the dialog box, you will also notice the options of setting a gutter or mirrored margins. Both are used when creating documents that will be bound and consequently require binding margins. Since these options are generally used with more complex documents, we'll save our discussion of these gems until Chapter 7.

- Formatting footnotes—The footnote option is useful for numbering your footnotes and for specifying their location: at the bottom of the page, at the side of the text, or at the end of a document or section. This section is used for formatting your footnotes only. To learn how to create a footnote, see Chapter 18.

- Setting paper size—Word enables you to specify the size of paper you have in your printer. The default settings are 8 1/2″ for the Width and 11″ for the Height: a standard US business-letter size. The paper size affects the size of the available text area of your document. For example, the width of the text area equals the Page Width minus both the left and right margins. Similarly, the height of the text area equals the Page Height minus the top and bottom margins. Thus, using Word's default settings, the amount of text area available is 6″ wide and 9″ high.

It should be noted that the size of your document text area will affect the appearance of your document. Similar to setting the paper size, you can also affect the appearance of your document with the "orientation" of your document—whether the text is printed horizontally or vertically across the page. The orientation of the printing can be established or changed using the Setup option from the Printer Setup dialog box found on the File menu. You will notice that the option for setting the paper size also depends on the type of printer you have installed. We'll review printing your documents in Chapter 8.

- Default tab stops—When you press the Tab key, the insertion point moves to the default tab stop (1/2″). To change the default value during a work session, enter the desired value in the Tabs Stops edit box. When you leave Word, any changes you've made to the default tabs (or, generally, in the Document dialog box) are negated, as Word reverts to the original default values. To make your changes the new default values, click the Set Default button. One last point to keep in mind regarding the page layout of your document: Tab stop measurements begin at the left and right margin.

- Widow control for formatting page layout—Located at the bottom right corner of the Document dialog box is a check box to control widows and orphans.
- Document templates—Use this section to format your document according to a particular *document template,* which can contain text, styles, graphics, or glossary items that you may wish to insert into your document. Using a template can save you formatting time, since you will have done much of the formatting work. We'll discuss how to create, modify, and save document templates in Chapter 15. If you can't wait, you can use the mouse to pull down the list of available document templates provided by Word in the Template window or press Alt,M. Select the desired template from the list and it will appear on your screen.

The Document Window Control Buttons

The Document dialog box contains three control buttons: OK, Cancel, and Set Default. Choosing OK is the same as pressing Enter. Any selections you've made in the dialog box will be immediately executed, and the window will close. If you choose Cancel, the window is also closed, but any changes made in the dialog box are reversed to the default settings. Choosing Set Default will change the default settings to the new values that you have selected. These changes will not only affect the current work session, but will be in place the next time you start Word. Keep in mind that, after selecting Set Default, these changes will be in place even if you choose Cancel. Choosing Cancel will not reverse any selections made with a Set Default selection. Choosing Set Default will not close the window. You must choose Cancel or OK to close the window.

Setting Margins

When you look at a document, one of the first things that you notice is the placement of that document on a page. Is the document neat?

The Basics

Are the paragraphs properly aligned? Is the document attractive, and most important, is it readable? Does the appearance of the document achieve its primary goal—communication?

In general, the margin is the white space between the edge of the paper and the text area that you create. While Word enables you to set the four primary margins—left, right, top, and bottom—it has preset default margin settings of 1 1/4" for left and right and 1" for the top and bottom.

Word provides you with three different methods of changing these default settings:

- Using Margin View with the Ruler (left and right margins only, and only if you have a mouse installed)
- Using the Print Preview feature
- Using the Document command

Each method offers a different look and certain advantages. These methods are explored in the three sets of step-by-step instructions that follow. Try each method to determine which meets your needs best.

Using the Ruler to Change Margins

You must have a mouse installed with your system in order to use the Ruler to change your margins. If you do not, select one of the alternative methods for changing margins: using Print Preview or the Document command. Next, type the letter in Figure 4.3 exactly as it appears. To be sure that the document will fit on a single page, be careful not to insert too many blank lines between paragraphs. In this and the next two sets of steps you will change the left and right margins of the letter from the default setting of 1 1/4" to 2".

If your insertion point is inside a table, you will be in Column View. Move the insertion point outside the table when you wish to choose Margin View.	1. If you haven't already, choose **Ruler** from the View menu by pressing **Alt,V̄,R**.	The Ruler appears at the top of your document window with the default Paragraph View setting.
	2. Click the **Ruler View icon** located at the right of the Ruler.	The scale of the Ruler changes from Paragraph View to Margin View format. In Margin View, the Ruler shows the left edge of your screen with a 1. The 0 point of the ruler is now aligned

4—Formatting Your Document

3. To change your margins, drag the left and/or right margin brackets across the Ruler. For this example, drag each margin to a length of 2" from the edges of the page. (On the Ruler, approximately 2 for the left margin and 6 1/2 for the right margin.)

with the left edge of the page.

After the left and right margins are changed to 2" your document should look like Figure 4.4.

```
                    BETTER BOOKS, INC.
                       4 Main Street
                     New York, NY 10010

April 10, 19--

Mrs. Bee Taylor
RR#3
Remington, IN 47993

Dear Mrs. Taylor:

Thank you so much for ordering Cal Smith's An Introduction
to Maintaining Your Car's Motor.  As you may know, this book
has been a classic for the past 10 years and has set a
standard for good auto maintenance.

Sadly, the requested title is no longer in print, and I am
returning your check for $14.95.  But to satisfy your
request, I would like to suggest an alternative publication
that is just hot off the press, Burnadette Simpson's Guide
to Mastering Your Car.  The new Simpson book is a complete
introduction to car maintenance and engine troubleshooting.
We cover all American made models since 1979 as well as many
leading imports.

If you would like a copy of Guide to Mastering Your Car,
please complete the enclosed postage paid reply card and I
will be happy to send it to you immediately.  We are
offering this complete guide for only $24.95 through the end
of May ( a $5.00 savings!).

Sincerely,


Kathy Shoemaker
Customer Order Department
```

Figure 4.3 Sample letter with default 1 1/4" left and right margins.

The Basics

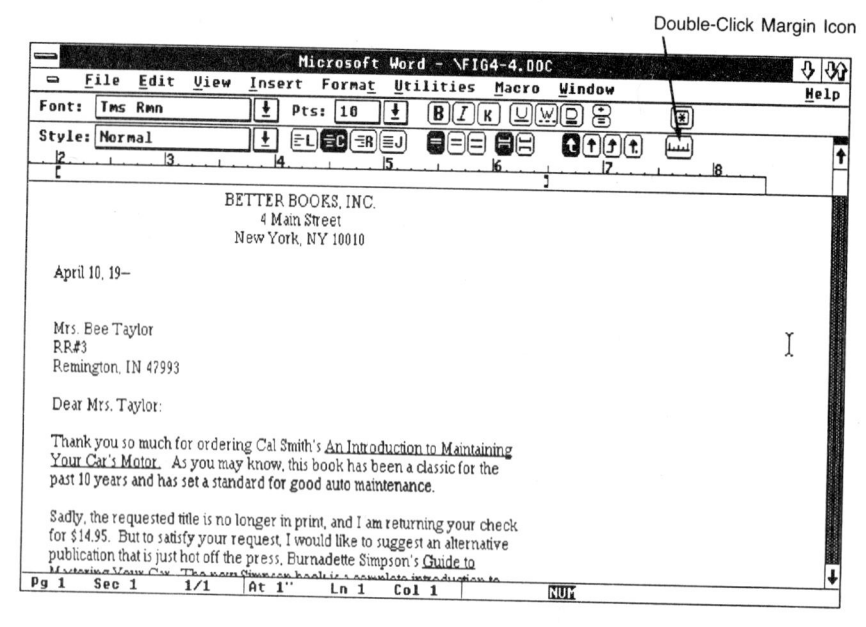

Figure 4.4 Sample letter with 2" left and right margins.

Using Print Preview to Change Margins

Print Preview is a command found in the File menu. Chapter 8 explores the Print Preview option in detail, but the next set of steps will show you how to use this handy formatting tool to change your margins.

Print Preview shows you exactly how your document will look on a page, including the margins, before you print it out with your printer. Even the margin boundaries themselves are depicted graphically so that you can get a good idea of how your document will look. To see this, review the Sample letter from Figure 4.3. In this exercise, however, you'll use the Print Preview feature to change your margin settings.

1. With your document on your screen, choose **Print Preview** from the File menu by pressing **Alt,F,V**. Again, the Sample letter is your document.

    The Print Preview dialog window appears on your screen. See Figure 4.5.

2. Next, click the **Boundaries** button or press **B**.

    The margin boundary lines appear across your document to indicate the boundaries.

138

4—Formatting Your Document

3. To change any of the margins, drag the margin boundary handles, which are labeled in Figure 4.6. To drag the handles, position the pointer over the black square on the margin line. The pointer changes to a cross-hair. In this example, drag the left margin to a size of 2" and the right margin to a size of 1". If you don't have a mouse, press the **Tab** until the boundary handle that you wish to move is selected and then use the arrow keys to move the handle. This example provides a nice inside margin (called a *gutter*) for a document that is to be bound and printed on one side only.

4. Once you're satisfied with the position of the margin boundaries, click anywhere outside the page or press the **Tab** key a second time.

Be sure that your pointer depicts a cross-hair before you begin to drag or move the boundary handles. As you move the handles, the dotted boundary lines move in the direction desired and the size of the margin is depicted in the top of the window.

Word automatically adjusts your new margins along with the alignment and spacing of your text and any headers or footers, and so on. Figure 4.7 shows the results.

Using the Document Command to Change Margins

In the previous sections, you explored setting margins using the Ruler and the Print Preview command. You can also use the Document command found on the Format menu to set the margins.

You can use the Document command to set the margins at any time. Since the margins determine how much space is allowed for the printed text area, though, they affect the page layout of your documents and so you may want to set the margins for the document before you begin. But don't worry if you're not sure how you want to format your document, because Word's flexibility allows you to test a variety of options throughout the writing process. But planning certainly helps. Choosing the right margins, the right font, and so on, will reduce the time required to format your document. It is the creation of the writing itself that is most important. Editing can remove

139

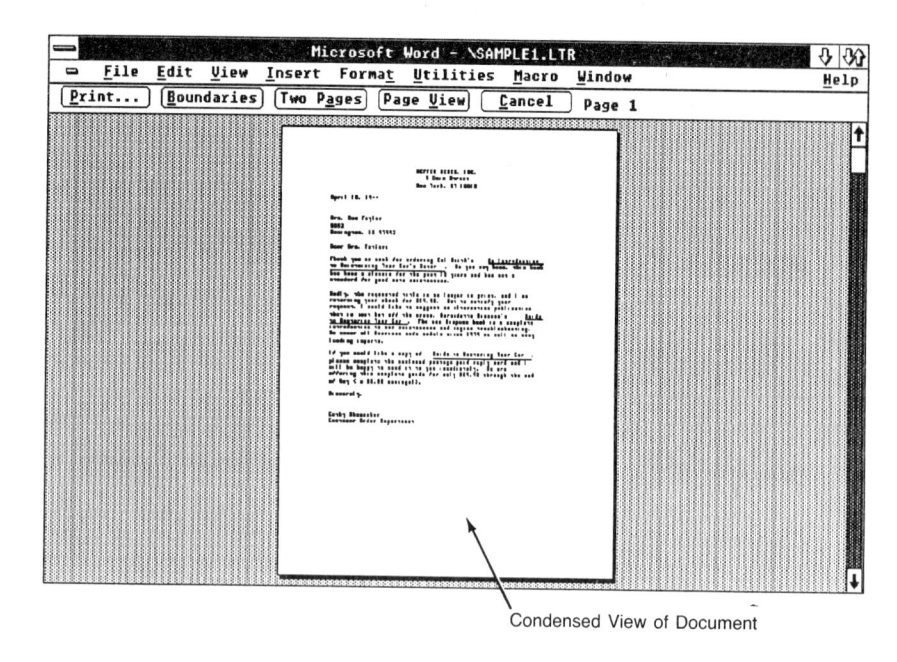

Figure 4.5 Choose Print Preview to see how your document will look when printed.

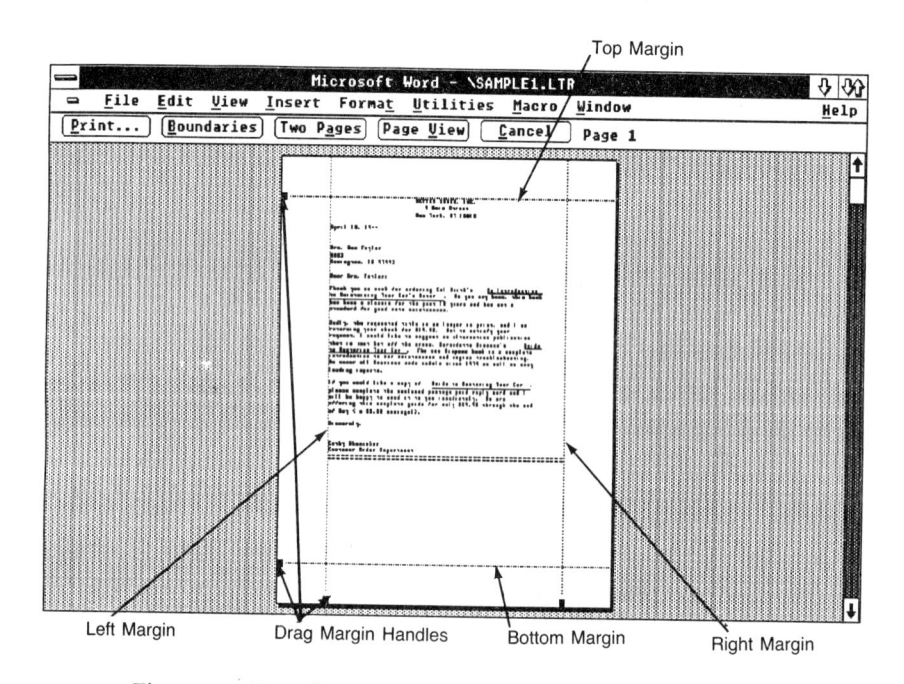

Figure 4.6 Drag the margin boundary handles to change the size of your margins.

4—*Formatting Your Document*

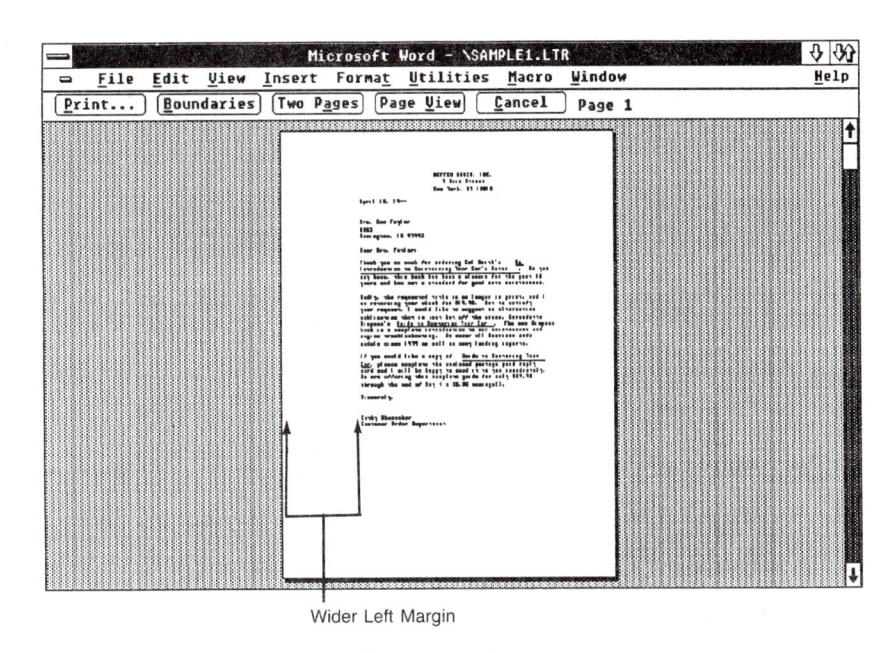

Wider Left Margin

Figure 4.7 Clicking outside the page automatically adjusts your margins and text.

errors and organize your text. Formatting establishes the page layout and design that gets the message across most effectively. To get an idea of the page layout for your document, you might create a worksheet similar to the one in Figure 4.8. As you can see, we have provided the standard default values for margins using a standard US business-letter size.

To use the Document command to set a margin, complete the following steps.

1. Choose the **Document** command from the Format menu (Alt,F,D).

    The Document dialog box appears (see Figure 4.2).

2. The default settings for your document appear in the Margins edit boxes for Top, Bottom, Left, and Right. The first value for the Top margin is highlighted (1"). Enter the value that you wish to set for the Top margin or accept the

    As you enter the new margin value, it replaces the existing default value.

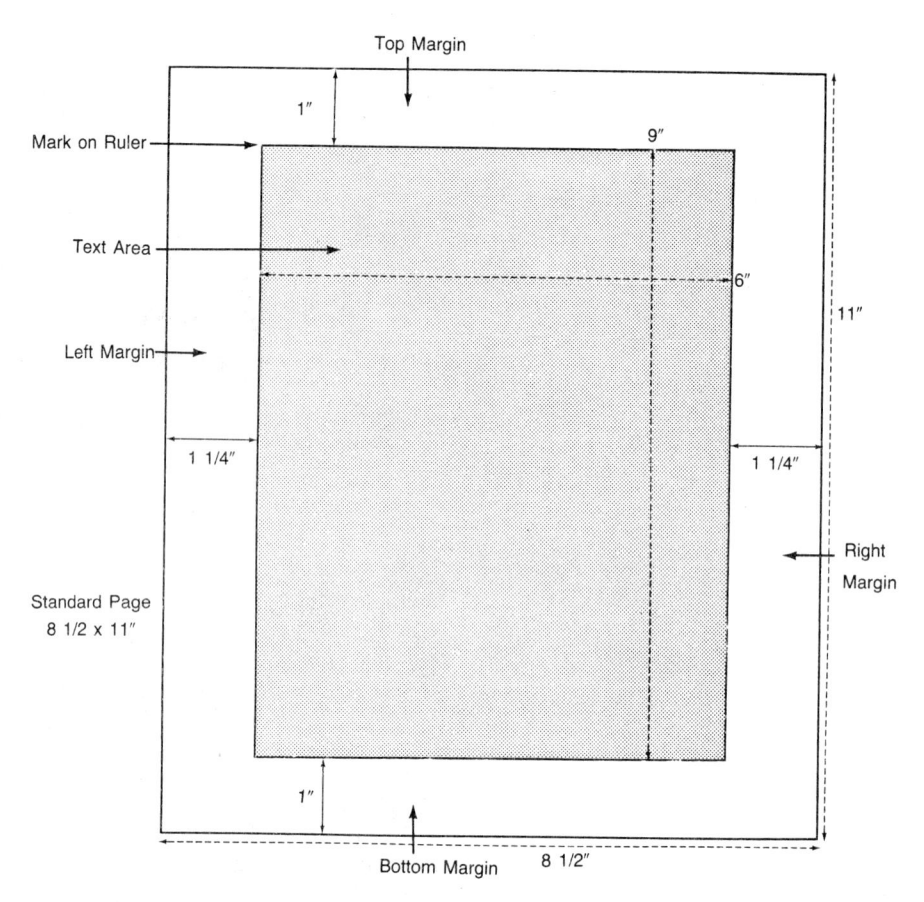

Figure 4.8 The page layout of a document using Word's default settings.

default and move to another margin by clicking the appropriate box or pressing the Tab key. Change any margin you wish. Values can be entered in numbers (including decimals) with or without a unit of measure (in, or ", for inches, cm for centimeters, or pi for picas).

3. Click **OK** or press **Enter**. Your new margins are set (for this document only), and you are returned to the document window. The default settings are restored when you begin a new document.

If you want to substitute your newly defined margins for the defaults, click the *Set Default* button or press **Alt,F** instead of OK. These settings are then stored in files called WINWORD.INI and NORMAL.DOT in your WINWORD directory. The next time you start Word, these new settings will automatically apply to your document unless you restore the original default settings by deleting these files or entering the original margin settings and clicking Set Default a second time. The latter option might be better if you plan on changing other default values in Word that you wish not to change.

The previous sections described how to change margins using three different methods for standard documents. If you wish to set margins for more complex documents, such as documents that will be bound together, or perhaps creating side-by-side paragraphs, refer to Chapter 7.

Changing Page Layout with Line and Page Breaks

As we have stated, the margin sizes affect the size of the text area of your document. The appearance of the text area itself can also be controlled using line and page breaks. These breaks can either be set automatically by Word or manually by you. Let's review the options available to you.

Setting Line Breaks

When you press the Enter key, Word will break the line, insert a paragraph marker, and create a new paragraph. Remember, if you press Shift+Enter, Word will break the line but create a "newline" instead of a paragraph. The line will be represented by a character instead of the paragraph marker to indicate a newline. To see these formatting characters, turn on the Paragraph Markers option in the Preferences dialog box: Alt,E,P. Thus, to create line breaks, either press Enter or Shift+Enter. Keep in mind that the Shift+Enter method will create a newline that takes on the formatting characteristics of the previous paragraph.

Setting Page Breaks

When you create a document that is more than a single page, the document must be divided into individual pages and separated by page breaks. There are two kinds of page breaks: soft and hard.

Soft Page Breaks

When you first start Word, a long document is automatically created with *soft page breaks*. A soft page break appears on your screen as a dotted horizontal line. It is removed by Word as necessary when new page breaks are required due to editing and formatting changes. Soft page breaks appear for the first time when the length of a document causes a break to a second page. A soft page break always appears at the end of a full page before text flows into the next page. The command that tells Word to automatically insert soft page breaks is the Background Repagination option found in Preferences. If this option is turned off, you can also choose the Repaginate Now command on the Utilities menu to divide your document into pages and highlight the soft page breaks as necessary.

You can also see how your document is going to be divided with soft page breaks by choosing the Print Preview or Page View command. Soft page breaks will also be effected when the document is printed. It is a good idea to make all necessary editing and formatting changes prior to using one of these options to see exactly how your pages will look when printed.

Hard Page Breaks

Sometimes it might be necessary to insert a page break into your document other than at the bottom of a page. To do this, you use a *hard page break*. These breaks will not change with the execution of the Repaginate Now command nor as a result of editing and formatting changes to your document. Hard page breaks must be moved or removed by you.

To set a hard page break, position the insertion point where you want the break to occur, and then press **Ctrl+Enter**. You can also select the Insert Break command from the Insert menu (press **Alt,I,B**) in Full menus (see Figure 4.9). To remove a hard page break, delete the page break character or drag the page break off the page in Print Preview mode. To move the page break, use Print Preview Boundaries to reposition the break.

Widow Control

The Widow Control box helps determine how many lines of text are printed on a single page. When you first start Word, this option is on by default, represented by an X in the box. In this condition, a single line can never be separated from the rest of its paragraph, eliminating both widows and orphans from your document. A *widow* occurs when the last line of a paragraph is printed at the top of a page while

4—Formatting Your Document

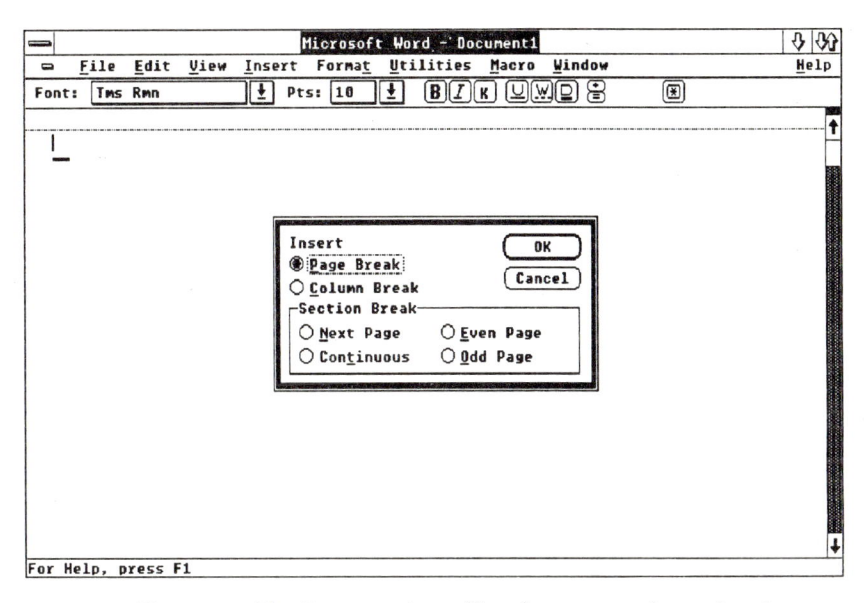

Figure 4.9 The Insert option offers four types of page breaks.

the rest of the paragraph is printed at the bottom of the preceding page. An *orphan* occurs when the first line of a paragraph appears at the bottom of the page, while the remainder of the paragraph is printed at the top of the next page. If you click the Widow Control box (or press **Alt,C**) to remove the X, Word will print as many lines on a single page as possible, regardless of how page breaks affect individual paragraphs. When do you turn off widow control? In the event that you wish all of the pages of your document to have the same number of lines, e.g., a legal document.

Review

In this chapter you learned:

1. Word's formatting options are detailed at four levels, from the general to the specific: Document, Section, Paragraph, and Character.
2. Character formatting is the lowest formatting level, and involves the point size and font of a character. Changing the style of a font, such as to boldface or italic, is also character formatting.

The Basics

3. Paragraph formatting involves setting the alignment of paragraphs, the line spacing, indentations, and tabs. You can also draw borders around paragraphs as well as absolutely positioned text.

4. Section formatting refers to a collection of paragraphs that you control when designing special documents, such as a newsletter with multiple columns.

5. Document formatting affects all pages and sections of a document. Some key document-formatting elements include: setting margins, paper size (in your printer), the placement of footnotes, and the default tab stops.

6. Document formatting is accomplished via the Format Document command.

7. The preset default margin settings for the left and right margins are 1 1/4"; the top and bottom default margins are set at 1" each.

8. There are three ways to change margin settings: using Margin View (left and right only) with the Ruler, using the Print Preview feature, and using the Document command.

9. To use the Ruler to change the left and right margins, you must have a mouse installed.

10. To change the default settings for margins or tabs, choose the Set Default command button on the Format Document dialog box.

11. Long documents in Word are automatically created with soft page breaks. You can insert hard page breaks with Ctrl+Enter or the Insert Break command.

12. Widow control is a Word option that is selected by default on the Format Document dialog box. With it turned on, Word prevents the creation of widows and orphans within your document.

F I V E

chapter

Formatting Paragraphs

In this chapter:

- Introduction to Formatting Paragraphs
- Using the Ruler
- Setting Alignment
- Setting Spacing
- Setting Indentation
- Setting Tabs
- Using the Paragraph Command
- Setting Borders

Now that you have a good idea of the page layout of your document, and how to set the margins at the Document level, the next step is to format the individual paragraphs of your text. This chapter covers all the tools necessary to format paragraphs, including: alignment or justification of text, line and paragraph spacing, indentation, setting tabs, and even drawing borders around paragraphs to highlight the text. We will cover a lot of ground in this important chapter, so let's get started.

Introduction to Formatting Paragraphs

In this chapter, we will show you how to apply Word's formatting features to paragraphs using both the Ruler and the *Paragraph* command. In general, the Ruler is handy for beginners since you can always have it appear on the screen as you work through your document. The Paragraph command, however, provides a little more accuracy and includes some options not found on the Ruler (e.g., formatting borders around your text).

Word also provides another method for formatting your text: use of a style sheet. We'll explore style sheets in Chapter 13.

Recall that as soon as you press the Enter key you create a new paragraph that takes on the formatting characteristics of the previous paragraph. Many simple documents may only require one or two types of formats. You'll learn, however, that you can also apply different formats to individual paragraphs in more complex documents.

One cue to keep in mind is that of the paragraph marker. When you press Enter the paragraph marker is inserted at the end of the paragraph and acts as a delimiter where the paragraph's formatting is stored. You can display the paragraph markers by turning on this option in the Preferences dialog box. Now, if you were to delete the paragraph marker, the formatting for that paragraph would be deleted and it would take on the formatting of the following paragraph. If you are just beginning to use Word, it might be a good idea to turn on the paragraph markers option so that you don't accidentally delete a marker when cutting and pasting text. To access this option, choose the Preferences command from the View menu by pressing **Alt,V,E** and then choose the Paragraph Marker option: **P**.

Finally, Word's default settings for paragraph formats are:

- Alignment—Flush left
- Line spacing—Single spaced
- Indentation—No first-line, left, or right indents

We will explore how to change all of these default settings to customize your document. To begin, let's jump right in to paragraph formatting by reviewing how to use Word's handy Ruler. If you prefer to use the Paragraph command to format your paragraphs, you can skip to that section. You'll find, however, that you can do most of the formatting you want with the Ruler.

Using the Ruler

Word's Ruler feature is normally hidden from view, but you can make it visible at the top of your document if you choose the Ruler command from the View menu by pressing **Alt,V,R**. Shown in Figure 5.1, the Ruler's scale is initially divided into inches and can be changed into other units of measure using the Customize command from the Utilities menu (i.e., you can select Centimeters, Points, or Picas from the Unit of Measure option). This author was weaned on the inch as the standard unit of measure, so this book's examples stay with this option.

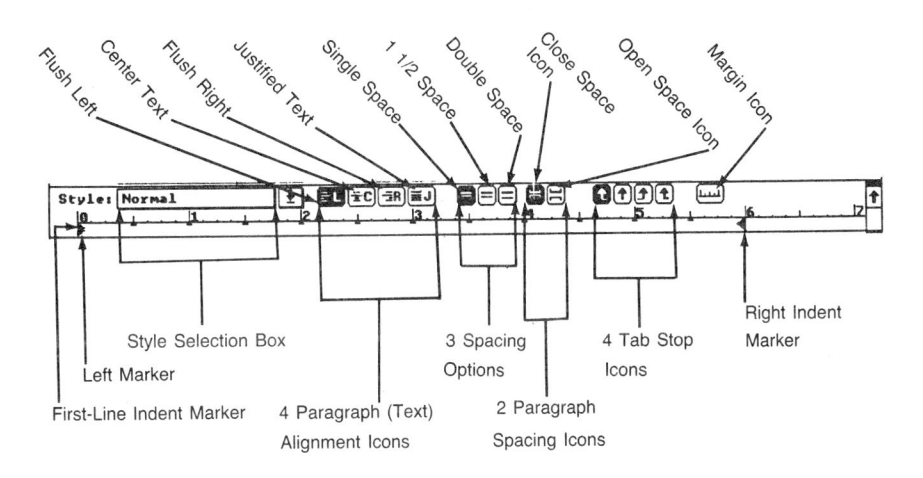

Figure 5.1 The Ruler command from the View menu displays the Ruler.

You can use the Ruler as a shortcut to complete many of the formatting tasks, such as setting and changing the spacing between lines of text, setting and using tabs, setting and aligning paragraph indents, or creating and applying styles. If you have a mouse installed with your system, you can also use the Ruler to set margins and to set column widths in tables. In Chapter 4, you learned how to set margins using the Ruler. The Ruler will also show which formatting options are in effect for the paragraph where the insertion point resides. Since the formatting applied to a paragraph represents the format for the whole paragraph, you can quickly see what effect a format change has on your text. Further, if you are only using one type of format for all of your paragraphs, then the Ruler is a good "snapshot" of the formatting for your entire document.

The Different Views of the Ruler

In Word for Windows, the Ruler actually consists of three separate looks, or views. The view that you will probably use most often is

Paragraph View, the default view of the Ruler when you first start Word. In other words, if you haven't created a document yet, then the flush-left alignment icon, the single-space icon, and so on, will appear blackened.

Later in this book, we'll see how to create a table using Word's Table command. When you are working inside a table (the insertion point resides inside a table), you can switch to *Column View* so that you can set column widths. Remember, though, this option is only available to you if you have a mouse because you must be able to click the Ruler View icon located on the right side of the Ruler. Similarly, you can switch to the Ruler's third view, Margin View. In Chapter 4, you learned that Margin View is used to change the margins for your entire document. Just like Column View, you must click the Ruler View icon to switch from Paragraph View to Margin View.

What the Ruler Contains

The Ruler contains several icons, some of which may appear grey if, for example, you have selected more than one paragraph with a multiple of paragraph formats. In Figure 5.1, you'll notice that the icons are represented in groups. With the Ruler in normal Paragraph View, for example, you can find the grouping of three icons that represent the spacing options: single, one-and-a-half, and double spacing.

In Paragraph View, the left edge of the Ruler begins at the 0" (zero) mark. This mark represents the first position of the text area at the left margin, a point that is 1 1/4" from the left edge of the paper in the default setting. If you change the left margin, the zero point would reflect the new distance from the left edge of the paper (e.g., a 2" margin would be 3 1/4" from the left edge of the paper). Word always positions the first-line and left indent markers with the zero point on the Ruler. These markers look like blackened triangles.

On the right side of the Ruler, you will notice a third blackened triangle, which is the right indent marker. Using Word's default setting, the right indent marker would appear at the 6" position on the Ruler, and marks the right edge of your text area. Thus, the width of your text area is 6 inches. One point to keep in mind: Although the first-line, left, and right indent markers are positioned at the left edge and right edge of your text area initially, they are not the source of your left and right margins. Later, you'll learn how you can reposition these indent markers to indent individual paragraphs. The margins themselves remain intact, however, unless you change the margin settings using the methods described in Chapter 4 (using the Document command, Print Preview, or Margin View with the Ruler). Only the position of the indents would change relative to the settings of the margins.

Finally, you will also notice that the Ruler is divided by 1/8" marks in its default setting (if you switched to another unit of measure, such as centimeters, the Ruler would appear different). You will use these marks to set indents, tabs, and the like that correspond to the text area of your document page. Later in this chapter, you'll learn how to use the Paragraph command to set more precise positions along the Ruler.

Table 5.1 summarizes the formatting options available on the Ruler. If you have a mouse installed, you can use Table 5.1 to select and execute a formatting option. If you don't have a mouse, you must first activate the Ruler from the keyboard (**Ctrl+Shift+F10**) and use the left and right arrow keys to make your selections from the Ruler (setting tabs, indents, and horizontal scrolling). In the next section, we'll explore how to use the Ruler with a mouse and from the keyboard.

Table 5.1 Text Paragraph Formatting Options with the Ruler and a Mouse

Icons	Description/Usage	To Select Option
▶◀	The indent markers are used to determine how far from the margins to begin printing the text. Useful for formatting individual paragraphs, the markers are represented by three triangular markers, two small ones on the left and one larger one on the right side of the ruler. The top left triangular marker is the first-line indent marker, and the bottom left is the left indent marker.	Drag marker icon to desired position to create the appropriate indentation for both the left and right sides of your document. To create a hanging indent, drag the left indent marker independently from left first indent marker to the left of the first-line indent by holding down Shift while dragging. As you drag, the bottom left corner will display the number of inches of the indentation. A hanging indent will display a negative indent. **Note for Keyboard method:** Press Ctrl+Shift+F10 to activate ruler mode. Use the left and right arrow keys to position the ruler cursor. Then, press L, F, or R (left, first, right) to select the type of indent and press Enter to apply the indent and turn off ruler mode.

(continued)

The Basics

Table 5.1 *(continued)*

Icons	Description/Usage	To Select Option
Normal	The style selection box displays the style selected for a particular paragraph. You can apply the standard default style, Normal, or create and redefine new styles based on selected paragraphs.	Select a style by clicking style selection box and typing the name of the desired style or by selecting style name from drop down list. **Note for Keyboard method:** Press Ctrl+S, type or select the name of the style, and press Enter.
	These icons set tab stops other than the default value of 1/2" used with the Tab key. In addition, the default value is flush left. You can change this value to centered tabs, flush right tabs, or decimal tabs as depicted by the up arrow followed by a decimal point.	Click the desired Tab icon, and then drag to the desired location on the Ruler and release. **Note for Keyboard method:** Press Ctrl+Shift+F10 to activate ruler mode. Press right or left arrow to move ruler cursor. Press the appropriate key (1 = Left, 2 = Center, 3 = Right, 4 = Decimal) to select the type of tab stop. Press Ins to set the tab stop. For more information, see "Setting Tabs" later in this chapter.
	Align text flush left, centered, flush right, or justified. You can align individual paragraphs or the entire document.	To begin entire document with a particular alignment, click the desired icon before you begin to enter text. You can, however, simply select the text, and then click the appropriate icon. This feature allows you to mix and match the alignment of individual paragraphs easily. The default value is flush left. Ctrl+C will produce centered text alignment.
	You can set the line spacing for the entire document or individual paragraphs or sections. Single spacing is the default or automatic selection. One-and-a-half spacing and double spacing are the other options. In terms of points, single spacing represents 12 points, one-and-a-half represents 18 points, and double, 24 points.	Simply click the desired icon. You can change the spacing from within a document by selecting the text and then clicking the appropriate spacing icon. **Note for Keyboard method:** Press the Ctrl key in combination with the appropriate key (i.e., Ctrl+1 = single space, Ctrl+5 = one-and-a-half space, Ctrl+2 = double space).
	The icon on the left is the close-space icon. This option will remove open space before a	Simply click the desired icon or press Ctrl+E for close space and Ctrl+O for open space.

5—Formatting Paragraphs

Icons	Description/Usage	To Select Option
	selected paragraph. The open-space icon, just right of the close-space icon, adds 12 points before the selected paragraphs.	
▭	The Ruler View icon is used to switch between Paragraph View, Margin View, or Column View on the Ruler. The default view is Paragraph View and shows the column boundaries, tabs, and indents. Use Margin View to change the margins of your document. Column View is only available when you selected a table or the insertion point is within a table. Use Column View to see the boundaries of columns in a table and adjust those boundaries.	To choose one Ruler View over another, click this icon. Continue to click the Ruler View icon to toggle between view options. Note that in Paragraph View, the zero mark is on the left margin while in Margin View, the zero mark is on the left edge of the page (the left margin would be set at the default 1 1/4" mark). The 1" mark will be at the left edge of your screen in Margin View.

How to Use the Ruler

To use the Ruler, you must first determine if a mouse is installed with your system (an easy observation). With a mouse, you either click an icon selection in the area beneath the Ruler or drag a symbol across the Ruler itself (e.g., setting indent markers). Clicking an icon is the simplest method for setting any formatting option and it is commonly used for setting paragraph or text alignment and line spacing. Some options, such as setting tab stop options within a paragraph, require a two-step process. First, you click the type of tab stop icon, and then point and click on the Ruler at the location where you want the tab stop to appear.

Suppose you don't have a mouse installed. You can still use the Ruler to format your paragraphs, using all options except setting page margins and column width in tables. Some format options are simply selected using the Ctrl key in combination with other keys. For example, to select paragraph alignment, you press Ctrl+L, Ctrl+R, Ctrl+C, or Ctrl+J for left flush, right flush, center alignment, or justified alignment, respectively. Similarly, you can select line spacing by choosing Ctrl+1 for single space, Ctrl+2 for double space, and Ctrl+5 for one-and-a-half spacing. To choose a paragraph spacing

153

The Basics

*If you don't have a mouse, press **Ctrl+Shift+F10** to activate ruler mode.*

option, enter either Ctrl+E or Ctrl+O to choose space before the paragraph or open one line of space (12 points) before a paragraph.

Some Ruler format options, however, require additional steps. To set paragraph indents or to set and delete tab stops, you must first place your Ruler in *ruler mode* by pressing **Ctrl+Shift+F10**. In ruler mode, an additional rule appears below the Ruler and features a black block, or ruler cursor (see Figure 5.2).

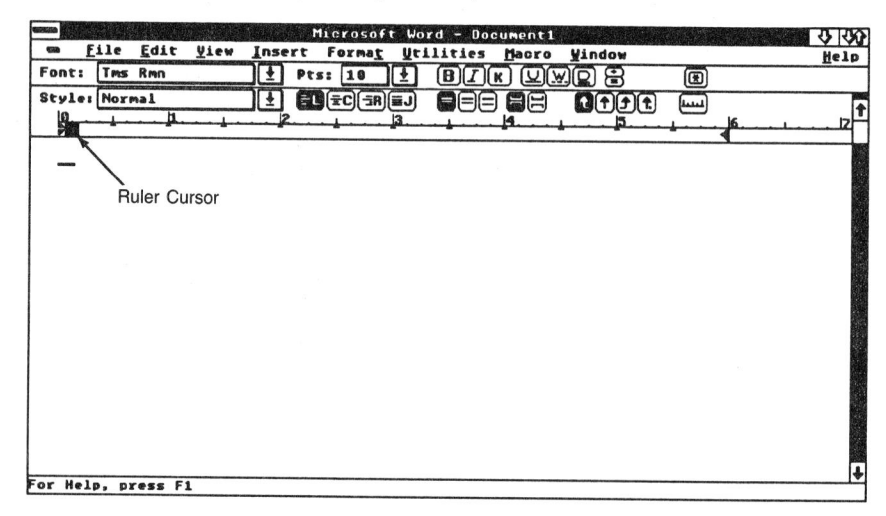

Figure 5.2 In ruler mode, a black cursor is moved via the left and right arrow keys to position indents and tab stops.

To use ruler mode, use the left and right arrow keys to position the cursor on the ruler where you want to set a tab stop or paragraph indent. Then, select the appropriate key for the type of indent or tab that you want to set. Finally, press Enter to set the indents and turn off ruler mode, or press Ins to set the tab stops. In either case, to turn ruler mode off and cancel any settings selected, you press the Esc key. Use Table 5.1 as a reference for the steps necessary to select formatting options with either the mouse or the keyboard.

Setting Alignment

You will probably want most documents formatted with left-aligned justification ("flush left"). Word automatically displays your document with the text flush left and the right side of the document ragged.

Word provides the options of full justification, flush right alignment, or centered justification. In full justification, both left and right margins appear even, meaning each line prints out approximately the same length, except perhaps for the last line in a particular paragraph, which may be shorter. The word processor accomplishes this task by inserting irregular spaces within a text line. This can be a little distracting depending on how many spaces are needed to justify a line.

In flush right alignment, the right margin appears even while the text on the left may appear a little uneven. With flush right text, the insertion point actually positions itself on the right margin and then, as you type, enters the text right to left. This author has never found a good reason to use right justification, but I have seen some interesting designs that do use it.

Finally, there is the centered justification option, in which justification works outward, so not all line lengths appear equal. This option is useful for centering all kinds of text on your document, such as headings, titles, company logos, and so on.

To change the alignment of your text, you display the Ruler and choose the appropriate icon or press the appropriate Ctrl-key combination (i.e., Ctrl+L, Ctrl+C, Ctrl+R, Ctrl+J). There are three methods of changing the alignment of the text:

- Before you begin to type—choose the alignment you wish. Simply click the desired icon from the Ruler (or press the Ctrl key in combination with the appropriate key), and begin to type. From the location of the insertion point, your text will be justified as designated on the Ruler.

- Changing alignment anywhere in an existing document—by first selecting text with the mouse unit (or holding down the Shift key while pressing the arrow keys) and then clicking the appropriate icon on the Ruler to change the justification of the selected paragraph (or pressing the appropriate Ctrl-key combination). Any paragraph not included in your selection maintains the original alignment. If you wish to change all the existing text, you must select it all and then click the appropriate icon to register the change. By selecting text first and then changing alignment with a click of the mouse, you can present different types of alignment in a single document. Remember, you can use either the keyboard or the mouse when selecting text and types of alignment from the Ruler.

- Changing alignment of an entire paragraph—without selecting the text. Place the insertion point anywhere inside the paragraph and then click the desired alignment icon on the Ruler (or use the Ctrl-key combination method). Remember that

The Basics

Word recognizes a paragraph by a string of characters or sentences typed together until it reads the insertion of the paragraph marker.

Once you have changed the alignment, any text entered beyond the location of the insertion point will demonstrate the new alignment until you either change the alignment again or move the insertion point to another location within the document. Once the insertion point is moved, it will reflect the formatting characteristics of the previous line or paragraph. You can, of course, toggle between alignment settings by clicking the appropriate alignment icons again and again.

To get a little practice, let's examine a sample document again. Refer to the document that we have called Sample Letter in Figure 5.3. Enter this document and then use the following steps to center justify the company name at the top of the letter. These same general steps can be used to change alignment of any existing text.

1. If you haven't already, open the Ruler by choosing the **Ruler** command from the View menu.

    The Ruler appears at the top of your document window.

2. Select the text that you wish to center. In this example, either use the mouse or hold down the Shift key and use the arrow keys to select:

    Your selected text is highlighted on your screen, as in Figure 5.4.

    SMITH & COMPANY
    "A Complete Marketing Group"

    located at the top of the document.

3. Choose your desired alignment icon from among four on the Ruler. In this case, for centered justification, click the Centered icon or press **Ctrl+C**.

    The selected text is automatically center justified and appropriately spaced, as in Figure 5.5.

Your choice of alignment is a matter of preference and style. Centering text is used frequently for designing key elements (such as headings) in memos, flyers, reports, and letters. Many publications, particularly books, tend to use full justification, but that may seem a

```
SMITH & COMPANY
"A Complete Marketing Group"

August 24, 1990

Mr. Bill Smart
Baker's Computers, Inc.
200 South Street
Indianapolis, IN  46268

Dear Mr. Smart:

Your name was recently given to me by Teri Lewis as the head
of the newly formed educational division of Baker's
Computers, Inc.  Congratulations!  It appears that you've
got a rather challenging, yet rewarding, task ahead of you.

As you prepare to tackle this elusive marketplace, let me
introduce you to one of Chicago's finest advertising/direct
marketing agencies in the U.S. today.  We have successfully
directed a similar situation, when we helped Best Software
enter the college market.

We would welcome the opportunity to discuss further your
needs and our abilities.  I will call you on Monday, August
30th, to schedule an appointment.  In the meantime, please
find enclosed a copy of some samples and a brochure about
Smith & Company.

Thanks for your consideration.  I look forward to speaking
with you soon.

Kind regards,

SMITH & COMPANY


Raymond J. Beeks
Account Executive
```

Figure 5.3 Sample Letter—SMITH & COMPANY.

bit unnatural for your letters, for which flush left alignment is standard. Some people believe that the full justification makes their letters look more modern. Figures 5.6 and 5.7 present the same letter using both flush left alignment and full justification. See which appearance you prefer.

Setting Spacing

Most applications require single spacing. While Word offers the three spacing options on the Ruler, the default setting is single spacing. Just like changing the alignment, you can change the spacing of your documents by:

The Basics

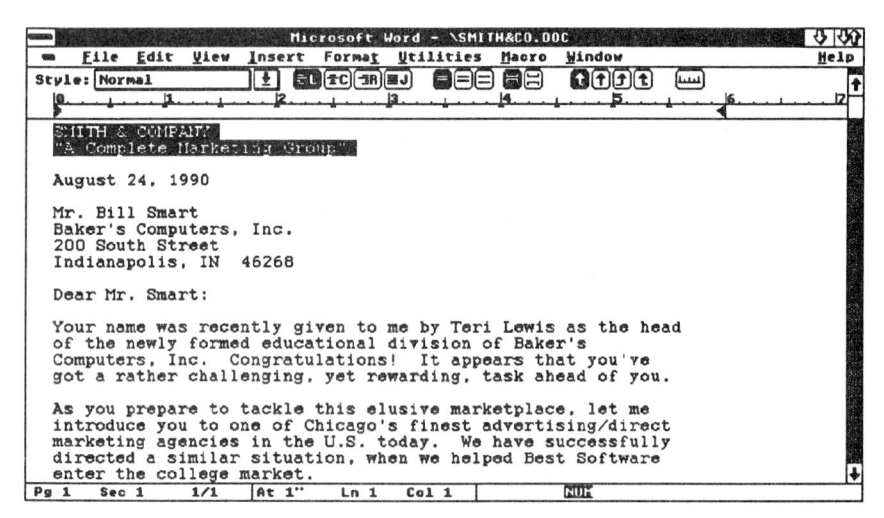

Figure 5.4 Select text you wish to center.

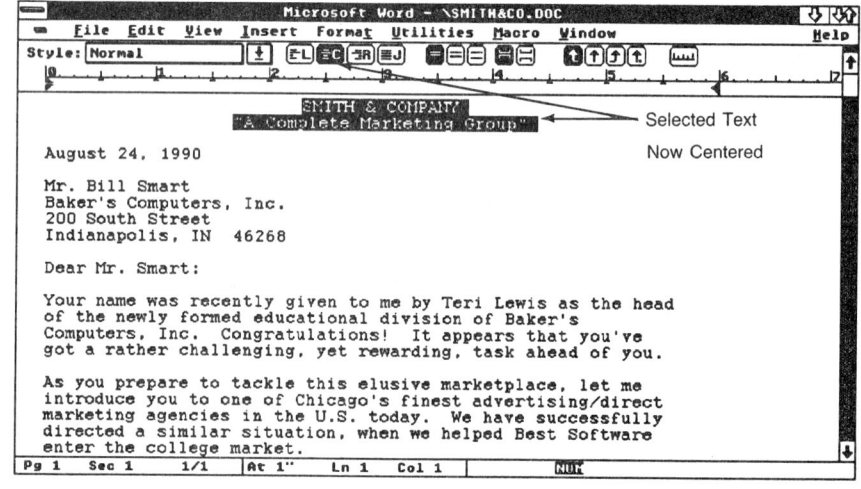

Figure 5.5 Click the centered icon from the Ruler for center justification.

- Clicking the desired spacing icon from the Ruler before you begin to type (or pressing the appropriate Ctrl-key combination).
- Selecting text from an existing document and then clicking the desired icon from the Ruler (or Ctrl-key combination).
- Changing the spacing of an entire paragraph by placing the insertion point anywhere within the paragraph and then clicking the desired icon on the Ruler (or Ctrl-key combination). Note that, unlike changing the alignment,

```
                    SMITH & COMPANY
                "A Complete Marketing Group"

August 24, 1990

Mr. Bill Smart
Baker's Computers, Inc.
200 South Street
Indianapolis, IN  46268

Dear Mr. Smart:

Your name was recently given to me by Teri Lewis as the head
of the newly formed educational division of Baker's
Computers, Inc.  Congratulations!  It appears that you've
got a rather challenging, yet rewarding, task ahead of you.

As you prepare to tackle this elusive marketplace, let me
introduce you to one of Chicago's finest advertising/direct
marketing agencies in the U.S. today.  We have successfully
directed a similar situation, when we helped Best Software
enter the college market.

We would welcome the opportunity to discuss further your
needs and our abilities.  I will call you on Monday, August
30th, to schedule an appointment.  In the meantime, please
find enclosed a copy of some samples and a brochure about
Smith & Company.

Thanks for your consideration.  I look forward to speaking
with you soon.

Kind regards,

SMITH & COMPANY


Raymond J. Beeks
Account Executive
```

Figure 5.6 Sample letter with flush left alignment.

changing the spacing with this method will also change the spacing of the previous line. Remember, you can also select the paragraph text by placing the insertion point anywhere inside the paragraph.

As you might expect, you can mix spacing options within a document. If you haven't typed any text, choose your spacing icon from the Ruler (by clicking or using the Ctrl-key combination with the appropriate key), and then toggle among the spacing options. If you wish to change previously entered text from one spacing to another, you must first highlight, or select, the text. Then use the mouse to click the desired icon or press the appropriate Ctrl-key combination

The Basics

```
              SMITH & COMPANY
          "A Complete Marketing Group"

August 24, 1990

Mr. Bill Smart
Baker's Computers, Inc.
200 South Street
Indianapolis, IN  46268

Dear Mr. Smart:

Your name was recently given to me by Teri Lewis as the head
of  the  newly  formed  educational  division  of  Baker's
Computers,  Inc.   Congratulations!   It appears that you've
got a rather challenging, yet rewarding, task ahead of you.

As  you  prepare  to  tackle  this  elusive marketplace, let me
introduce you to one of Chicago's finest advertising/direct
marketing agencies in the U.S. today.  We have successfully
directed  a  similar  situation,  when  we helped Best Software
enter the college market.

We  would  welcome  the  opportunity  to  discuss further your
needs  and  our  abilities.   I  will call you on Monday, August
30th,  to  schedule  an  appointment.   In the meantime, please
find  enclosed  a  copy  of  some  samples  and a brochure about
Smith & Company.

Thanks  for  your  consideration.   I  look forward to speaking
with you soon.

Kind regards,

SMITH & COMPANY



Raymond J. Beeks
Account Executive
```

Figure 5.7 Sample letter with full justification.

to change the selected text. Remember, only the selected text will change spacing; text surrounding the highlighted area will remain as originally spaced. If, however, you were to insert new text into a paragraph or within the highlighted area, the new text would appear with the new spacing format as well.

Changing the spacing is as simple as changing the alignment. You should practice changing the spacing of one of your sample documents; such spacing changes are not permanent unless you save them. Try all three spacing styles out if you wish. The following steps enable you to change the spacing.

1. Choose **Ruler** from the View menu.   The Ruler appears.

5—Formatting Paragraphs

If you remember the Ctrl-key shortcuts for changing the line spacing, alignment, and the like, you don't need to activate the Ruler to use this method. Simply select the text that you wish to change, if necessary, and then press the appropriate Ctrl-key combination.

2. If you haven't entered any text, click the desired spacing icon or press the appropriate Ctrl-key combination shortcut (Ctrl+1 for single space, Ctrl+2 for double space, and Ctrl+5 for one-and-a-half space). If you are changing the spacing within an existing document, go on to step 3.

3. Select the appropriate text and then click the desired spacing icon or type the Ctrl-key combination shortcut.

New text from the position of the insertion point will be entered using the spacing selected. Existing text is unaffected unless your insertion point is within a paragraph.

The selected paragraph changes to the appropriate setting.

Setting Indentation

Indentation is an option that writers use to begin new paragraphs. In this book's examples, the documents appear with extra space between new paragraphs, a style favored in many business letters and reports. To indent is perhaps a little more personalized and informal.

Don't confuse indentation with a margin setting. The margin is the space from the edge of the paper to the text area. An indentation is the distance from the edge of the margin itself to the point where you begin to enter a paragraph's first line of text. An indentation should be about 1/4" to 1/2". On a typewriter, a 1/2" margin is about five spaces.

You can use a paragraph indent to control the width of a paragraph within the boundaries of the text area as set forth by the page margins set in the Document command dialog box. With this in mind, you can use indents to change the width of individual paragraphs, while the width of the overall text area as specified by the margins remains the same. As long as you understand the difference between indents and margins, you can think of indents as a way of making temporary margins of individual paragraphs.

Word provides three types of indents: the left indent, the right indent, and a first-line indent. The left indent is the distance from the left margin to the left boundary of the paragraph. The right indent is the distance from the right margin to the right boundary of the paragraph. The first-line indent is the distance from the left indent to the

161

left boundary of the first line of the paragraph. Initially, the left indent and the first-line indent appear aligned with the left edge of your text column (beneath the zero mark on the Ruler in Paragraph View), while the right indent is aligned with the right edge of your text column area. You can use the indent markers on the Ruler to change the width of one or more paragraphs as you wish.

To set indentation with Word, you can use one of three methods. You can use the Ruler with the mouse, the keyboard method, or the Paragraph command. Let's review all three methods.

Using the Mouse to Set Indents

Setting indents is automatic and always affects your selected paragraphs. This method utilizes the *left indent marker, first-line indent marker,* and *right indent marker* located on the Ruler. (For a quick review, refer to Table 5.1.) As an example, you can automatically set Word to indent the first line of every paragraph by dragging the first-line indent marker (the top triangle icon located just under the 0 in the default Paragraph View on the Ruler) to a desired location on the Ruler. If, for example, you dragged the first-line indent icon to the 1/2" mark on the Ruler, every time you started a new paragraph by pressing the Enter key, the first line would automatically be indented the 1/2".

In addition to using the first-line indent marker, you might wish to indent entire paragraphs of text. You might wish to indent from the left the return address of a business letter. Or you might want to indent from left and right an example or a long quotation. To do this, you move the left indent marker and the right indent marker (the triangle located just below the 6 on the Ruler in Paragraph View) to the indent you choose. For example, to set indentation at 1" from both the left and right margins, you would drag each marker in 1" on the Ruler. One point to keep in mind: When you drag the left indent, the first-line indent marker will move the same distance. If you wish to only move the left indent, hold down the Shift key while dragging the left indent (this method is often used to create a hanging indent as we will discuss shortly).

Remember that if you set the indentation markers at the beginning of your document, the formatting of indents will affect your entire document. You can, however, change the indents for any given paragraph at any time. If you change the indents on an existing document, only the paragraph and any new text that you type from the point of the insertion point will be affected by the new formatting. Paragraphs appearing before or after the reformatted text adhere to the original formatting options. If you wish to change the formatting of

5—Formatting Paragraphs

any of those paragraphs, click anywhere inside the paragraph(s) and then drag the indent markers as before.

To set indentation with the mouse, use the following general steps.

1. If you haven't already, choose **Ruler** from the View menu.

   The Ruler appears at the top of your document window.

2. If you wish to indent existing text, first select the text, otherwise go on to step 3.

   Any text that you select appears highlighted.

3. Drag the left, right, or first-line indent markers to the desired position. If you wish to drag the left indent marker only, hold down the Shift key while you drag.

   If you selected text in step 2, then that text will move to the indent as specified. Any new text added to this paragraph will also align with the indent.

Using the Keyboard to Set Indents

To use keys to set indents is similar to using the mouse. You have the choice of selecting existing paragraphs that you wish to indent, or to start new paragraphs at the location of the indents that you specify. In either case, however, you must first activate the ruler mode. To use the keys, complete the following steps.

To turn off the ruler mode, cancel any formatting selections, and return to the document window, press the Esc key.

1. Turn on the Ruler from the View menu and activate the ruler mode. You can do this in one easy step by pressing **Ctrl + Shift + F10**.

   The Ruler appears and is active.

2. If you so desire, select any paragraph(s) that you wish to indent. Otherwise, go on to step 3.

   Selected text will appear highlighted.

3. Use the right and left arrow keys to move the cursor to the position on the Ruler where you want the indent to occur.

   The black rectangular ruler cursor moves as you press the right arrow key.

4. Press the appropriate key to move the indent marker to the location of the ruler

   If you choose L, then both the left indent and first-line indent marker will move.

163

cursor. Press L for left indent, R for right indent, or F for first indent.

Using the Paragraph Command to Set Indents

A third option to set indentation involves using the *Paragraph* command. This option is also automatic and affects your current paragraph(s) selected and any new paragraphs you type after, as with setting your indents with the Ruler. We are getting a little ahead of ourselves as we will discuss the Paragraph command in detail shortly. However, using the Paragraph command option enables you to provide a little finer measurement when setting your indents than using the Ruler does. As an example, look at Figure 5.8 which uses the default 0" settings for all indents. Figure 5.9 shows the result of selecting the second paragraph and applying 1" left and right indents. Practice using this option by completing the following steps.

1. Select any paragraphs that you wish to indent. If you don't wish to select a paragraph, go on to the next step. From our example in Figure 5.8, we selected the second paragraph.	Selected paragraph(s) are highlighted.
2. Choose the **Paragraph** command from the Format menu, or type **Alt,T,P**.	The Paragraph window appears on your screen (see Figure 5.10).
3. Click the insertion point inside the desired box in the Indents section (either From Left, From Right, or First Line). You can also use the Tab key to highlight a specific area or press the Alt key in combination with the letter representing your command.	Any values previously entered or set with the indent markers on the Ruler for the current selection appear in the appropriate boxes. If no indents have been set, 0" will show in the boxes.
4. Type in the desired size for the indents where appropriate. Do not type *inch*, but you can type " as	The size in inches (") appears as you type. Word automatically inserts the abbreviation for inch as " the

the unit of measure. To produce the finished sample in Figure 5.9, enter 1 in the From Left and From Right Indents edit boxes.

5. Click **OK** or press **Enter**.

next time you open the window.

Word automatically sets the indents for you on the paragraph where the insertion point resides. From that point forward, all new paragraphs default to this formatting option. However, any existing text retains its previous paragraph formats.

June 5, 1990

Dr. Edward Blue
The Blue Dental Clinic
505 Blackhawk Road
Hatchet Hill, ND 90012

Dear Dr. Blue:

This month I completed a two-year course of study as a dental assistant at the Professional Careers Institute. Dr. Fielding, head instructor, suggested I apply to you for a position as an apprentice dental assistant.

As you will see from my enclosed resume, I have taken courses in nearly every aspect of dental hygiene. I have participated in a work study program with Dr. Kyle Longfellow in Hightstown during the past 12 months.

My education and my work experience has helped me develop an ability to deal with the public. Moreover, I have been able to display a compassionate trust with concerned patients- a valuable asset for a dental assistant.

I would very much like to put my skills to work for The Blue Dental Clinic. I am available for an interview Monday through Friday during business hours. You can reach me at (414)666-2341.

Sincerely,

Barb Dale

Figure 5.8 Sample document with no indents.

The Basics

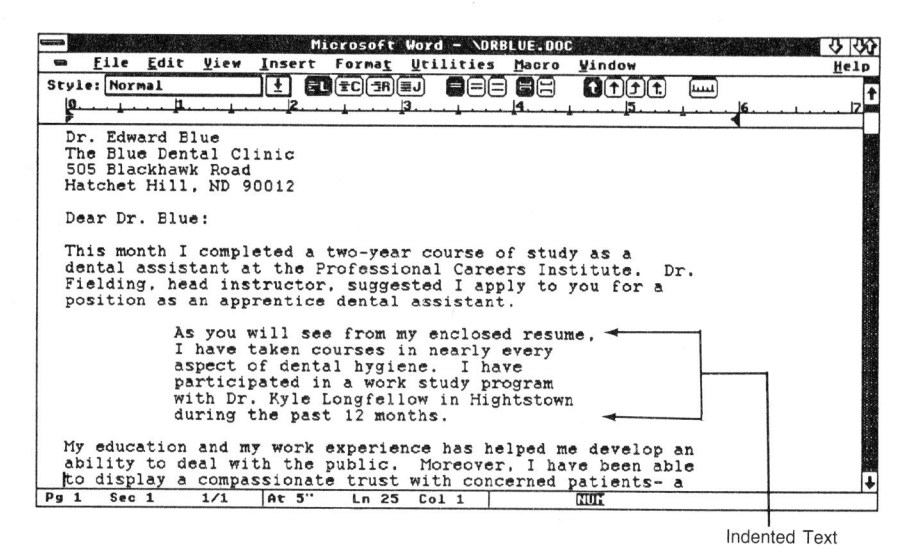

[screenshot of Microsoft Word document showing letter to Dr. Edward Blue with indented paragraph, annotated "Indented Text"]

Figure 5.9 Second paragraph features 1" left and right indents.

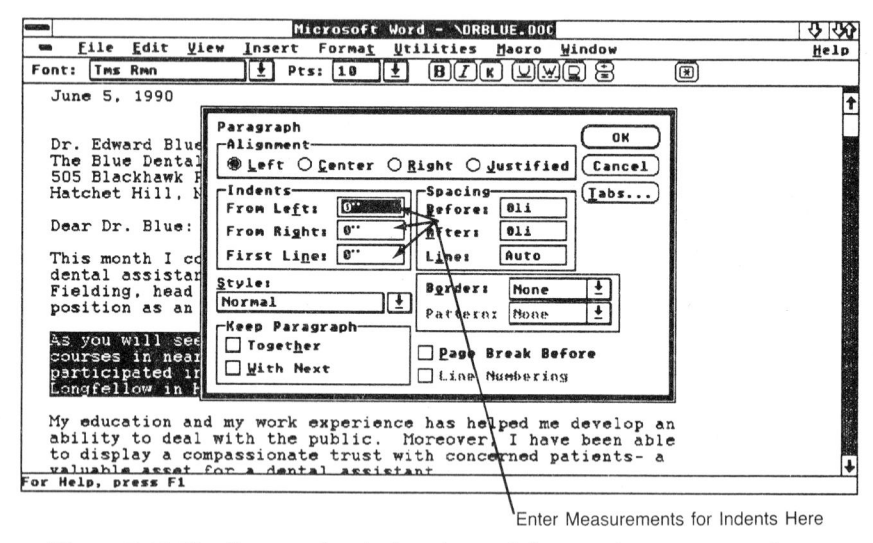

[screenshot of Microsoft Word Paragraph dialog box over the letter, annotated "Enter Measurements for Indents Here"]

Figure 5.10 The Paragraph window is used for creating precise indents.

Indenting Shortcuts

Word offers a keyboard shortcut to indent paragraphs by default by simply pressing the Ctrl key in combination with another key. For

166

example, every time you press **Ctrl+N** the left indent will move to the next default tab stop, usually about 1/2". Of course, you can change the default tab stop, and we'll explore that a little later in this chapter. If you continue to press Ctrl+N, Word will continue to move the left indent marker (as well as the first-line indent marker, but it retains any offset distance that you may have set) to the next tab stop. To move the left indent marker backward a tab stop at a time, press **Ctrl+M**. If you wish to move the left indent marker without moving the first-line indent marker, press **Ctrl+T**. Similarly, to move back to the previous tab stop without moving the first-line indent marker, press **Ctrl+G**.

When do you use these shortcuts? A common use is to provide a "nested" look of your paragraphs to emphasize the text from the rest of your document. The following shows an example of a nested paragraph in the body of a memo:

> The sales for 1989 were below the 1988 levels in several store locations. The new store in Manhattan has been open for two months, yet the initial orders for inventory have yet to be placed. To get sales back on track, please put a business plan in effect that includes expanding distribution, cost control of inventory, and monthly sales promotions.
>
>> Please note that new accounts must be approved by the home office. It has come to my attention that too many bad credit reports are being overlooked.
>
> I trust that each of the department heads will complete their sales forecasts for the forthcoming year by no later than the 15th of this month. For further questions, please contact me for additional information regarding your budgets and the new business plan. Good Luck!

Creating Hanging Indents

A *hanging indent* describes the appearance of a paragraph whose first line is not indented while the remaining lines are. A hanging indent gives the "appearance" that the first line is actually printed to the left of the left margin. A typical example of a hanging indent is that of a bulleted or numbered list. Sometimes you may want the text to "hang out" from the first line to provide visual explanation. To illustrate, enter the following text:

SUCCESSFUL SALES PRESENTATIONS: The key to a successful presentation is to always be prepared. Know your product and you'll become more relaxed and able to handle any questions that may arise. Anticipate what the audience might ask. Be confident and earn the audience's trust from the start.

Next, we are going to give an impression of a side-by-side paragraph, but instead, we will insert a hanging indent of 2 1/2" to highlight the text following the first line. (To follow our example, use a clean page with the Ruler showing and the zero mark on the Ruler at the top left of your screen.) In reality, the first line of text is given a negative indentation value or one less than the left indentation. For our example, we'll leave the first-line indent marker at the default 0" mark and set the left indentation at 2 1/2" on the Ruler. This example would give you a 2 1/2" hanging indent. Select the text that you just entered, and then create the hanging indent. To do this, you hold down the Shift key while dragging the left indent marker to the 2 1/2" mark on the Ruler. You can move it a little further on the Ruler to get the text to align properly. When finished, your text should look something like Figure 5.11.

As previously noted, hanging indents are particularly useful for creating numbered or bulleted lists. The number or bullet actually appears to disguise the hanging appearance. As with the previous example, use the left indent to properly position the text following the bullet or number. Some examples might be:

* The new head of the sales department will be interviewing candidates for the inside sales position.
2. After you finish the cherry sauce, place the duck in the oven at 400 degrees for 2 hours.

If you wanted to create a hanging indent with the first line extending into the margin, you could set the first-line indent marker at a negative number, say −1/2" and set the left indent at 0.

To create a hanging indent, you can either use the Ruler or the Paragraph command. The easier method is to use the Ruler to drag the left indent marker to the right of the first-line indent marker. Remember, you must hold down the Shift key while dragging the left indent marker or the first-line indent marker will move the same distance. A more precise method is to choose the Paragraph command from the Format menu, and then enter the appropriate size of the hanging indent desired in the First-Line Indent edit box. For example, you might wish to create a hanging indent for the first line of text that

5—Formatting Paragraphs

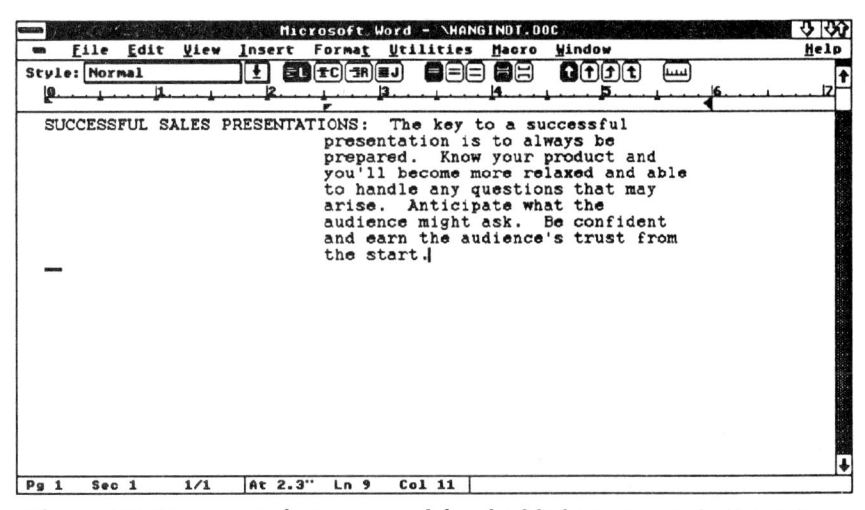

```
┌─────────────────────────────────────────────────────────────┐
│                    Microsoft Word - \HANGINDT.DOC           │
│   File  Edit  View  Insert  Format  Utilities  Macro  Window        Help
│ Style: Normal                                               │
│ 0........1.........2.........3........4.........5........6........17
│    SUCCESSFUL SALES PRESENTATIONS:  The key to a successful │
│                        presentation is to always be         │
│                        prepared.  Know your product and     │
│                        you'll become more relaxed and able  │
│                        to handle any questions that may     │
│                        arise.  Anticipate what the          │
│                        audience might ask.  Be confident    │
│                        and earn the audience's trust from   │
│                        the start.                           │
│                                                             │
│ Pg 1  Sec 1    1/1    At 2.3"  Ln 9   Col 11                │
└─────────────────────────────────────────────────────────────┘
```

Figure 5.11 Hanging indents are useful to highlight text or in bulleted lists.

exists to the left of the left indent. In this case, you could enter a negative value (e.g., −.5″) for the first-line indent and a positive value for the left indent (e.g., 1″).

Tip: If you change to a hanging indent with a negative value (or any value) for the first-line indent marker, in order to change the indentation again you must enter another value. Simply erasing the old value does not register a change. You must enter a 0 if you want a default value again.

Setting Tabs

Tabs can be useful for more than just setting a first line indentation at the beginning of every paragraph. Tabs are an efficient formatting tool for working with text arranged in simple columns, but if you're planning to create complex tables, you should wait for Chapter 11 and our discussion of Word's Table command.

By default, the Tab key can only move 1/2″. But Word offers two more flexible options for setting tabs: Using either the Ruler or the Document command from the Format menu. Once you set a tab stop with either method, the insertion point moves to that tab stop location each time you press the Tab key. In other words, creating a custom tab stop overrides any previous default tab stops.

Setting Tabs with the Ruler and Mouse

The Ruler offers four types of tabs: left, centered, right, and decimal. Located just left of the Ruler View icon, you will find the arrow icons that represent the tab options. When setting tabs, the text at the location of the tab stop is aligned according to the type of tab set icon selected.

- Left tab—Left side of text aligns to tab stop. New text appears to the right as you enter text.
- Right tab—Right side of text aligns to tab stop. New text appears to the left as you enter text.
- Center tab—Text is centered at the location of the tab stop. New text appears to the left and right as you enter it.
- Decimal tab—If text includes a decimal point, the point itself aligns to tab stop; otherwise, the right side of text aligns to tab stop.

Setting a tab with the Ruler and a mouse is simple. If you are inserting a tab stop within existing text, select that paragraph (or those paragraphs) first. Next, select the icon that represents the type of tab desired by pointing with the mouse and clicking once. Next, drag the icon to the position on the Ruler where you want the tab stop to appear and release the mouse button. To delete a tab, simply drag the icon off the Ruler and release.

Note that setting a tab with the Ruler will reformat any Tab keypress made previously within the paragraph in which the insertion point is located. Any existing paragraph that follows the insertion point, however, will retain its original tab formatting.

Setting Tabs with Keys

If you don't have a mouse installed, you can still set tabs easily using the keyboard. Just as before, you first select any desired text to which you wish to apply a tab stop. If you don't select text, the tab stop will exist for new text. To set tab stops with the keys, complete the following steps.

1. Select the paragraph(s) where you want to enter a tab stop.   Selected text will be highlighted.

2. Activate the Ruler and the ruler mode by pressing **Ctrl+Shift+F10**.

   The Ruler appears at the top of the document window. In one easy step, the ruler mode is active.

3. Press the right or left arrow key until the ruler cursor stops where you want to insert the tab stop.

   The black cursor moves left to right as you press the right arrow key.

4. Press the appropriate key to select the desired type of tab stop: 1 = left, 2 = Center, 3 = right, 4 = decimal.

5. Press **Ins** to insert the tab stop at the location of the ruler cursor.

   The tab stop arrow will appear on the Ruler.

6. Repeat steps 3 and 4 to add additional tab stops.

   Each time you press Ins, the tab stop arrow icon will appear on the Ruler at the location of the cursor.

7. When you've finished inserting all the tab stops, press **Enter** to set the tab stops and return to the document window.

   The tab stops are applied to the paragraphs you selected.

Setting Tabs with the Tabs Command

Setting a tab with the *Tabs* command is just as easy as it is with the Ruler, but it may offer a greater degree of accuracy. The Tabs command is found on the Format menu. To open the Tab dialog box, choose this command from the Format menu or press **Alt,T,T** and the dialog box appears as shown in Figure 5.12.

The Tabs dialog includes three primary areas:

- Tab Position—The Tab Position lists all current tab stops for all the paragraphs selected in a list window below the Tab Position edit box. If you haven't applied any custom tab stops, or selected any text, this Tab Position list box will be empty. You add tab stops by entering the measurement (a numeric value that may include a decimal point) where the tab stop is

The Basics

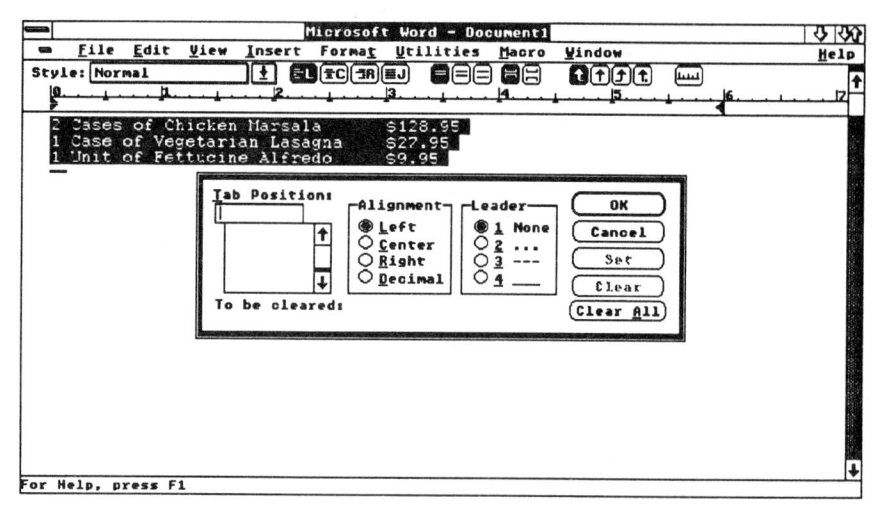

Figure 5.12 The Tabs dialog box.

to occur along the Ruler in the Tab Position edit box and then clicking the Set button. Once these tab stops have been added, they will appear in the list window below the Tab Position edit box. As you scroll from one tab position to another (moving the highlight), any alignment applied to that tab stop will also be listed in the dialog box.

If you select a tab alignment format icon from the Ruler and then double-click the location on the Ruler where you want the tab stop to appear, Word will open the Tab dialog box. This is another one of Word's "hot spots."

- Alignment—The Alignment box offers four types of standard formats: Left, Center, Right, and Decimal. Once you select a tab stop position, you can select one of these types of alignments (for the tab stop position highlighted) by clicking the appropriate selection. If you don't have a mouse, use the Tab key to highlight the Left alignment option and then press the up or down arrow keys to make your selection. Just like setting the tab position above, you must select the Set button to apply the alignment format to the selected tab stop position.

- Leader—The Leader option allows you to fill the tab character space with periods, hyphens, or underlines. Of course, you can leave this character space with the default blank character.

On the right side of the Tab dialog are five selection buttons (see Figure 5.12). The Set button is used to insert the measurement that you type in the Position edit box where you want the tab stop to occur. When you choose Set, the tab stop is given the alignment and leader options that you may have checked. If you wish to change these options, highlight the tab stop in the Position list window, enter the new alignment and/or leader options and click Set again. The tab stop selections that you make in the Tab dialog box are not applied to your text until you choose OK or press Enter. If you neglect to press Set, you can still set the tab stop positions to selected paragraphs if you simply choose OK. If you choose Cancel, all tab stop options that you may have set prior to choosing OK are canceled. Any previous tab stops that have been set, either default or custom, will remain unless you select the paragraphs where the tab stops occur and then choose the Clear All button in the Tab dialog box. Finally, pressing the Clear button will place the measurement of the tab stops one at a time in the To be cleared edit list at the bottom of the Tab dialog window. The tab stop positions are cleared one-by-one each time you choose OK until all tabs are removed from the To be cleared list.

You can use the Tabs command to format new text as you create it, or you can use it to select existing text and then apply the Tab format in order to align the text correctly in relation to the tab stop. For practice, enter the following simple table. Use the Tab key to create a column of white character space between the two columns. Press the Tab key only once and don't worry about the spacing. Type:

```
2 Cases of Chicken Marsala $128.95
1 Case of Vegetarian Lasagna $27.95
1 Unit of Fettucine Alfredo $9.95
```

Now, select the entire table and then choose the Tabs command by pressing **Alt,T,T**. Notice that the Tab Position edit box lists appear empty since we haven't added any custom tab stops yet. The only tab stop so far is the default 1/2" tab. Next, enter the measurement where you want the tab stop to occur. For our example, enter **3** in the Tab Position edit box. The next step is to choose the type of alignment. Select **Decimal**. To apply the decimal tab stop at 3", choose the **Set** button. Click **OK** or press **Enter** to close the Tab dialog window and apply the tab stop to the selected paragraphs, as shown in Figure 5.13.

All tab stops can be applied to your existing paragraphs or to new text by using the steps discussed in the previous example. As a handy reference, use the following numbered steps to add tab stop positions to your documents. Figure 5.14 provides a letter for you to duplicate for use in a practice exercise.

1. Select the text or paragraph where you want the tab set formatting to occur. If you are beginning a new paragraph, you can set the tab stops and the formatting

The Basics

```
┌─────────────────── Microsoft Word - Document1 ──────────────┬──┐
│  File  Edit  View  Insert  Format  Utilities  Macro  Window │Help│
│ Style: Normal                                               │    │
│ 0......1......2......3......4......5......6......7          │    │
│  2 Cases of Chicken Marsala   $128.95                       │    │
│  1 Case of Vegetarian Lasagna  $27.95                       │    │
│  1 Unit of Fettucine Alfredo    $9.95                       │    │
│                                                             │    │
│                                                             │    │
│                                                             │    │
│ Pg 1  Sec 1   1/1   At 1.3"  Ln 3  Col 34          NUM      │    │
└─────────────────────────────────────────────────────────────┴────┘
```

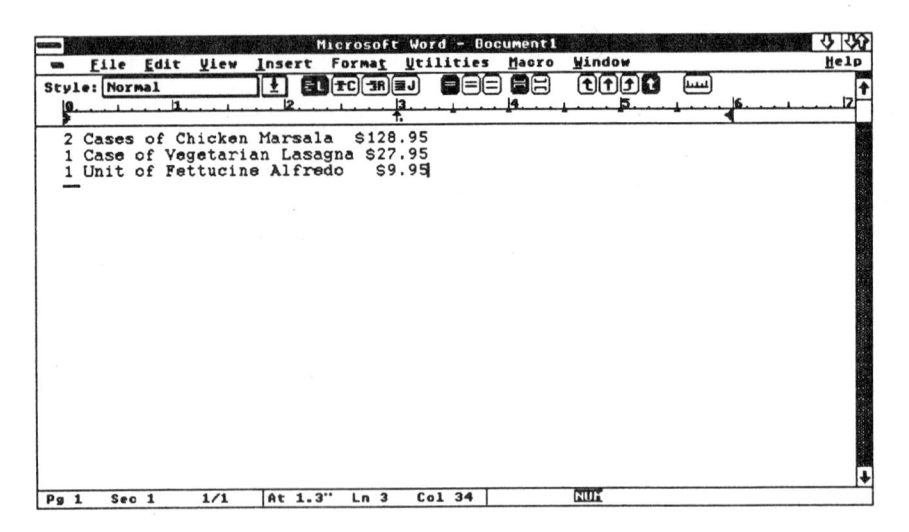

Figure 5.13 Paragraphs aligned to a decimal tab stop.

will apply to the current paragraph and any subsequent paragraphs until you reformat. Any existing paragraphs retain their current formatting unless you change it.

2. Choose the **Tabs** command from the Format menu. Or enter the **Alt,T,T** command from the keyboard.

   The Tab dialog window appears on your screen, as in Figure 5.12.

3. Enter the measurement in the Position edit box where you want the tab stop to occur. The measurement must be entered numerically and will correlate to the position on the Ruler.

   The measurement that you enter appears highlighted.

4. Choose the alignment type for the highlighted tab that appears in the Position list window. Choose either Left, Center, Right, or Decimal.

   The selected alignment is checked.

5. If you wish to add a leader to fill the tab character's space, click either periods, hyphens,

   Any selection you make applies to the highlighted tab position.

5—Formatting Paragraphs

```
            WHOLESALE HARDWARE SUPPLIES, INC.
                     1900 Summit Street
                     Chicago, Il 60025


March 3, 1989


Mr. Sam Swadley
Hometown Hardware
1 Monroe Street
Indianapolis, IN  46269

Dear Mr. Swadley:

Thank you for your interest in WHOLESALE HARDWARE supplies and
equipment.  We are happy to supply you with the information you
requested.

The following prices are quoted per unit:

              6 foot display rack       $100.00
              AAA counter display         50.00
              AAA aisle rack              75.00

In case you have any further questions, please don't hesitate to give
me a call.  I can be reached Monday through Friday, 8:00 A.M. to 5:00
P.M., at (317) 872-7155.


Sincerely yours,
```

Figure 5.14 Sample letter that uses tabs to align a paragraph.

or underline characters. The default selection is a blank character space.

0. Choose **Set** to apply the tab stop position at the measurement highlighted.

Any alignment and/or leader option is also applied to that position. If you wish to add more than one tab stop, you must choose Set each time. It is important to press Set each time, or the previous tab stop location will be lost. If you are only adding one tab stop, you can simply press Enter to apply the tab stop and close the Tab window in one easy step. In doing this, you can skip the next step.

7. Choose **OK** or press **Enter**. The Tab dialog window is closed, and the tab stop selections are applied to any selected paragraphs.

Using the Paragraph Command

Many of the formatting options available through the Ruler are also available with the Paragraph command. The Paragraph command, with all its options, offers even greater flexibility than the Ruler.

To access the Paragraph command, you choose it from the Format menu or enter **Alt,T,P** from the keyboard (or use another one of Word's hot spots on the Ruler—i.e., double-click on an empty area on the Ruler). Invoking the Paragraph command produces a master dialog box, shown in Figure 5.15, for formatting your paragraphs.

The Paragraph dialog box can be divided into six distinct formatting areas.

- Paragraph Alignment—Word provides the four standard types of alignment: Left, Center, Right, and Justified. The default value is flush left. The important point to remember is that these alignment formatting options will align your lines of text with the indents of your paragraphs and not the margins (although these distances may in fact be the same). Thus, choosing Left alignment will align the lines of the selected paragraphs (or new paragraphs from the point of the insertion point) at the left indent. Similarly, choosing Right alignment

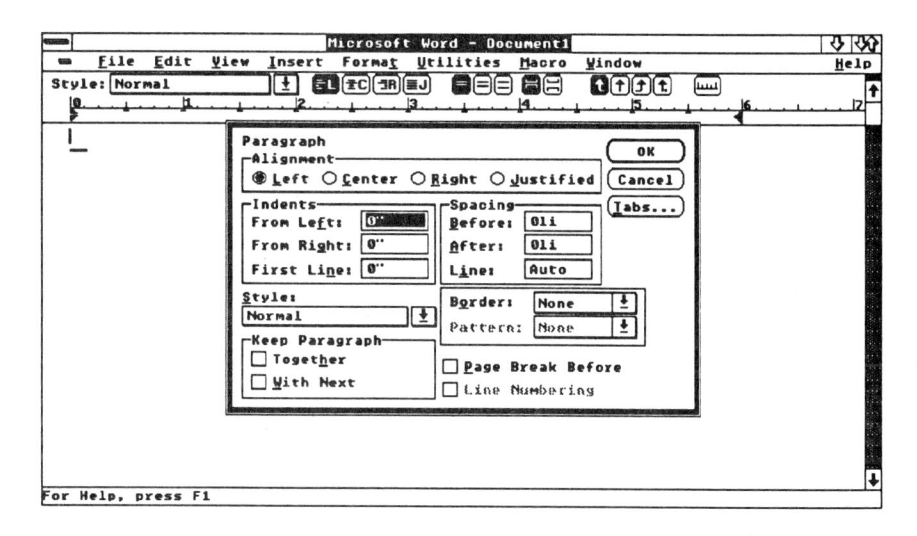

Figure 5.15 The Paragraph dialog box is the control panel for formatting your paragraphs.

aligns the lines of text with the right indent while Center alignment centers the lines of text between the left and right indents. Justified alignment will also align the text between the left and right indents, but adds spaces to stretch your text between the indents to fill the lines evenly.

- Setting Indents—Just below the alignment options on the left side the dialog box, are the From Left, From Right, and First Line indent options. You can set indents with either the indent icons on the Ruler or the Paragraph command. Further details and the necessary steps were given in the earlier "Setting Indentation" section.

- Setting Spacing—Located in the middle of the Paragraph dialog box. You can set line spacing with the Ruler icons, but using this command provides a greater degree of accuracy, as well as more spacing options. You'll learn more about paragraph spacing shortly.

- Choosing Styles—In the middle of the Paragraph dialog box is pull-down window that enables you to select a style and apply it to a selected paragraph(s). Later in Chapter 13, we'll discuss how to apply styles to selected paragraphs to make your formatting tasks simpler.

- Setting Borders—The Border formatting option is next to the Style section in the middle of the dialog box. You can use the Border's pull-down window to draw a variety of boxes and borders around your selected paragraphs. You can even place a border around a table (including an individual or a group of cells in a table, which is discussed in Chapter 11) or a picture. The procedures for placing a border around these different objects are slightly different. The one step that each procedure has in common, though, is that the object must first be selected before you can add a border to it. In this chapter, we'll focus attention on drawing borders around selected paragraphs.

- Check boxes for controlling paragraph positioning—These four check boxes, located at the bottom of the Paragraph dialog box, are used to control the paragraph positioning relative to each other and to their position on a page. Two options are under the Keep Paragraph heading, and the two options on the right are entitled Page Break Before and Line Numbering. These options are discussed in detail shortly.

If changes are made in the paragraph dialog box, clicking the Tabs button is a way of accepting the changes.

On the top right corner of the dialog box are two buttons that you are keenly aware of by now: the OK and Cancel buttons. The OK button immediately implements the selections you've made in the dialog box and closes the dialog window, while the Cancel button turns off selections, closes the dialog window, and returns you to the document window. A third button, Tabs, closes the Paragraph dialog window and immediately opens the Tab dialog box, described in the previous section, "Setting Tabs."

Paragraph Spacing from the Paragraph Dialog Box

You've learned how to set line spacing using the Ruler options of single, double, or one-and-a-half spacing. The Paragraph dialog box provides additional control over the spacing of your paragraphs.

To access the Paragraph spacing box, choose the Paragraph command from the Format menu, type **Alt,T,P** from the keyboard, or double-click one of the open areas on the Ruler. The Spacing section in the Paragraph dialog window provides three boxes: a Before box, an After box, and a Line box. When you first start Word, the default value listed in the Line box is *auto* (automatic line spacing), which sets the value as the default height of the current font of the paragraph style. This value is also automatically adjusted to the tallest character in the line. As an example, suppose the font you have selected is listed as 12 point. In this case, a single line is generally equivalent to 12 points of vertical spacing. In other words, from the descender (or tail) of a lowercase character in one line is 12 points of vertical space to the descender of the text in the next line. If your text for this font is using the double-space option, the default value is 24 points. Keep in mind that line spacing will vary with the size of the font(s) (or superscript, formulas, and so on) used in the line. As an example, the 12-pt New York font (even with the auto line spacing option on) is actually a bit larger than 12 points. You can see this if you apply absolute (12-pt) line spacing to a paragraph.

With the Ruler, you are limited to single, double, or one-and-a-half spacing. With the Paragraph spacing dialog box, though, your options are nearly unlimited. To change the vertical space for all lines in a paragraph, simply enter another value in the line box. The value can be entered in one of three ways. You can enter the actual value of points, for example, 24 pt (the measurement unit *pt* for point is mandatory) for double spacing. Or you can enter a value followed by the delimiter *li* (for line), where each li represents a single line (or 12 points). For example, to triple space, enter the value 3 li. If you enter a positive decimal value, line spacing is set to a minimum height but will automatically adjust to the tallest character in the line above the minimum height. If you enter a negative decimal value, line spacing is set to a specified height that will not adjust. In this case, characters exceeding the specified height would overlap each other during printing (on the screen they are cut off).

The third option is to use a unit of measure in inches (in) or centimeters (cm). To return to the default value of automatic line spacing as set by the current font of the paragraph style, enter either 0, 1 li, or auto. Note that when you use automatic spacing the distance of the spacing field is calculated from the ascender, or height, of the tallest character to the ascender of the tallest character in the next line.

Use the Before and After options to add space above and below the edges, respectively, set by the line spacing of the paragraph. These options are handy when you wish to provide blank lines or space before or after a paragraph (to set off text). One point to keep in mind: These paragraph spacing options only affect the first line of the selected paragraph while line spacing options affect all lines of the selected paragraph. The default value for the paragraph options is 0 li (lines). If you add white space, it is added to any space created by the line spacing setting (or the line spacing icons on the Ruler). As with the Line box, enter the values in pt (points), li (lines), or 0 (for auto) for the default value. Note that the Before option is ignored when the paragraph falls naturally at the top of a new page, unless you have inserted a manual page break prior to the Before paragraph format.

Following are detailed steps for setting the amount of space for all lines in a paragraph using the Spacing format option:

Choosing the auto option becomes helpful when you are using extremely small (4 pt.) or large (48 pt.) fonts.

The Basics

1. Select the paragraph to apply the spacing option to by placing the insertion point anywhere inside the paragraph.

2. Open the Paragraph dialog box by choosing the **Paragraph** command from the Format menu or typing **Alt,T,P** or double-clicking any open area on the Ruler.

   The Paragraph command appears, as shown in Figure 5.15.

3. Move to the **Line** option in the Spacing box by clicking with the mouse or pressing **Alt,I**. Enter the desired spacing value in the Line box. Remember, auto represents single spacing for the current default font of the paragraph style. Enter a value in points (e.g., 12 pt for single or 24 pt for double) or as a number of lines (e.g., 3 li for triple space). You may also enter another unit of measure, such as in, cm, or pi (e.g., 0.167 in equals 1 line at 6 lines per inch).

   The value in the box replaces any existing value. A positive value provides minimum line spacing and a negative value provides fixed line spacing.

4. If desired, enter a value and measurement unit for adding vertical space before the paragraph in the Before box or space following the paragraph in the After box.

   The value you've entered appears.

5. Click **OK** to execute the format change or simply press **Enter**.

   If you click OK, you'll be returned to your document with the new spacing set.

Check Boxes for Aligning Paragraphs

The four check boxes at the bottom of the Paragraph dialog box enable you to align your paragraphs relative to each other or to the page. Select a check box by clicking in it or using the Tab key to first

5—Formatting Paragraphs

highlight the section and then pressing the corresponding underlined letter. For example, to choose the **Together** option in the Keep Paragraph section, press the **Tab** key until the command is highlighted with a dotted rectangle. Then simply press the **h** key to select its corresponding check box. To cancel a selection, click inside the box a second time (or enter the corresponding letter key again). The check box options include:

- Keep Lines Together—Keeps an entire paragraph on a single page, and it prevents any lines of that paragraph from being separated by a page break. It is preferable not to break at the last line of a paragraph and place it at the top of a page (referred to as a "widow") or to place a paragraph's first line at the bottom of a page (referred to as an "orphan") with the rest of the paragraph following the page break. Don't use this option to prevent either widows or orphans, however. Instead, choose the Document command from the Format menu and use the Widow control option, which is set at default. Finally, as a word of caution, do not overuse this option along with the Keep With Next Paragraph option or you may end up with too much white space on your document and very little text on your pages.

- With Next ¶—Keeps two related paragraphs together on a single page. With this option, you can prevent a page break between a heading or graphic and following text, for example. In the case of starting a new page, Word could actually break in the midst of either paragraph, but not between the paragraphs.

    Perhaps the best example of this option's use is in preventing a page break in the middle of a table that you created by pressing the Enter key at the end of each line (and thus created several paragraphs in Word's interpretation). To keep the entire table together, select all lines of the table except the last one. (The paragraph keeps its format to its end, plus the line that follows it. But if you select the last line, Word will link the next paragraph to the table). Then select the Keep With Next ¶ option and click OK. If the table is too large for the current page, the entire table will be moved to the next page. Remember, though, that tables are better created with newlines than with paragraphs.

- Page Break Before—Adds an automatic page break before the selected paragraph. Thus this option is used to force a page break in a long document. To set, click the Page Break Before option and then click OK (or press Enter). It is a good idea to

181

use the Print Preview option to review any page breaks before printing out your document.
- Line Numbering—Applies only if you turned on the Line numbering option in the Section dialog box, otherwise it appears dimmed or grey. Chapter 7 discusses the Section dialog box. You can use this option to turn off the line numbering feature in a paragraph where you don't want line numbers to appear. Line numbers, when activated, only appear in Print Preview and when you print your document.

Setting Borders

Word allows you to add borders to paragraphs, pictures, tables, or even to a single cell or group of cells in a table. This feature is called *Border* and is found on the Paragraph dialog box (Alt,T,P) under that name in the right center of the window (see Figure 5.15). A border is useful for framing text and pictures to enhance the readability of your document.

The Border option gives you several choices within two pull-down menus labeled "Border" and "Pattern." The default selection for no border is listed as None. From the Border menu, you can draw a border as either a plain box or a shadowed box (choose Box). Instead of an entire box, you can place a vertical bar to the left of a paragraph (select Bar) or a horizontal border on top or bottom of the paragraph (select Above and/or Below). If you have a Postscript printer, you can even print a border around an entire document. The one exception is for pictures where a border must be an entire box that surrounds the picture. In other words, you can't place a single vertical or horizontal border next to a picture, you must enclose it with an entire box.

Word also offers different line styles, or *patterns*, to make your borders. The default is a single line, but you can also use a thick line, a double line, or a shadow line. Choose your pattern from the Pattern pull-down menu.

Let's review the steps to add borders to a selected paragraph. The process for adding borders to tables or pictures are slightly different. See Chapters 11 and 20 for complete discussions on creating tables and using graphics.

1. Select the paragraph that you want to border by placing the insertion point anywhere inside the paragraph. You

may also highlight the
   paragraph using the usual
   methods.
2. Choose the **Paragraph**
   command from the Format
   menu or enter **Alt,T,P**.

   The Paragraph window
   appears.

3. Choose the placement of the
   border by pressing **Alt,O**.
   Select from Box, Bar, Above,
   or Below. None (meaning no
   border) is the default. Use the
   mouse to open the pull-down
   menu or highlight the Border
   option with the **Tab** key and
   use the down arrow key to
   scroll the border type
   options.

   As you scroll with the arrow
   keys, the border types are
   highlighted.

4. Choose the Pattern or style
   for the border type that you
   selected in step 3. Click the
   Pattern pull-down window
   open or press **Alt+E** and
   then scroll the options with
   the down arrow key. Choose
   from single, thick, double, or
   shadow style.

   The pattern you select
   appears in the Pattern
   window.

5. Click **OK** or press **Enter**.

   You return to your document
   with the border drawn
   around your selected
   paragraph.

To delete a border, select the paragraph(s) where the border exists, and then choose the option None from the Border pull-down menu.

   The border you draw will comply with the formatting options applicable to the current paragraph. Of particular interest in this regard is the width of the border. The border will extend from the left indent to the right indent, not just the length of the text itself. If your text is centered, and does not extend to the margins, for example, the border may appear with extra white space evenly balanced on each side of the text. To reduce the amount of white space around the text itself, you must reformat the indents.

   Practice using the border options on your documents. Try out all of the line patterns and border positions. Experiment with paragraphs that use a special indentation, and then readjust the left and right indents to give the border a better fit. Be sure to examine the effect of adding borders to more than one paragraph. Figure 5.16 shows some of the possibilities.

```
                    Minutes of the Meeting of the
                    COMPANY IMPROVEMENTS COMMITTEE
                    The Bennie Johnson Company, Inc.
                         February 13, 1990


Presiding:   Cam Stewart

Present:     Jay Baker
             Gary Hageman
             Kathleen Smith
             Stephanie Kramer

Absent:      John Wolf

The weekly meeting of the Company Improvements Committee of
the Bennie Johnson Company was called to order at 9 A.M. in
the west conference room by Mr. Stewart.  The minutes of the
meeting of February 6 were read by Ms. Smith and approved.

The main discussion was the concern of new employee policies
and the purchase of new equipment.  Among the proposals
were:

     *Mr. Hageman presented a plan to eliminate coffee
     breaks for clerical positions and to reduce the
     clerical work staff by three positions in the
     sales department.  By incorporating job sharing
     through part-time staff, the plan was approved by
     a majority vote.

     *Ms. Smith presented a request for one new copier
     and two replacement computers for the marketing
     department.  Due to a lack of capital expenditure
     finances, Ms. Smith's request was not approved.

The meeting was adjourned at 11:15 A.M.

                              Respectfully submitted,


                              Judy Davis, Secretary
```

Figure 5.16 Sample document illustrating border positions and patterns.

Review

In this chapter you learned:

1. You can apply Word's formatting features to paragraphs using both the Ruler and the Format Paragraph command.
2. Word's default settings for paragraph formats are: flush left alignment; single spacing; and no first-line, left, or right indents.

3. To access the Ruler, choose it from the View menu by pressing Alt,V,R. The Ruler is a shortcut to complete many paragraph formatting tasks, including setting and changing line spacing, setting and using tabs, indenting paragraphs, and applying styles.

4. You can use either the mouse or the keyboard to access the formatting options available on the Ruler. If you have a mouse, you can select most options by pointing and clicking. If you wish to use the keyboard, press Ctrl+Shift+F10 to activate the Ruler. Once activated, use the left and right arrow keys to make your selections.

5. Word provides four options of text alignment: full justification, flush left, flush right, and centered justification.

6. You can change the spacing or the alignment of text either before you type new text or on existing text. To change the spacing or the alignment of existing text, you must first select the text.

7. You can set indents by moving the left indent marker, the right indent marker, and the first-line indent marker on the Ruler. You can also set more precise indents with the Indent section of the Format Paragraph command.

8. The easiest way to create a hanging indent is to drag the left indent marker on the Ruler to the right of the first-line indent marker. To do this, hold down the Shift key while you drag the left indent marker.

9. The Tab key is preset to tab in 1/2" increments. For more flexibility, use the Tabs command on the Format menu to set tab stops. You can choose from four types of tab formats: left, centered, right, and decimal.

10. You can use the Borders option from the Paragraph dialog box to apply borders around individual paragraphs in order to draw attention to your text. You may choose from several line styles.

11. The Paragraph command provides nearly unlimited spacing options. For example, you can triple space your document by entering 3 li in the spacing edit box. You can even add space above and below the edges of line spacing set for the paragraph. You can also use the Paragraph command to control the alignment of paragraphs relative to each other. If, for example, you want to prevent a page break in the middle of a table, the Paragraph command option, Keep With Next, is your answer.

SIX

chapter

Formatting Characters

In this chapter:

- Introducing Character Formatting
- Applying Character Formatting
- A Designing Exercise

In this chapter we'll look at the methods for formatting individual characters. You'll learn about different families of fonts and how to change their size. You'll also learn how to change the style of a character, such as boldfacing, and how to change the spacing between individual characters. Finally, we'll investigate subscripting and superscripting characters.

Introducing Character Formatting

This section introduces how to format text at Word's lowest level, the individual character. You'll learn about font style, size, and spacing and how to change fonts. Character formatting options apply to individual characters, whole words, or entire sections of text.

Common Word Typography

Before beginning a discussion of character formatting, let's review some common terms of typography as defined by Microsoft Word.

The Basics

Word's default character format is a Times Roman (Tms Rmn), 10-point Plain. *Times Roman* is the font (or typeface) name. In true typography, the *font* is defined as a collection of type of one size, character configuration, and face. *Face* refers to style elements such as bold and italic. Thus, a 10-point Times Roman type and an 18-point Times Roman type would be considered different fonts. Similarly, the 10-point Times Roman Plain is considered a different font from the 10-point Times Roman Bold. In Word though, all of these fonts would be considered the same font, Times Roman, regardless of size or style, because Word considers a font to be a set of unique characters. The set includes all of the letters of the alphabet, numerals, special characters, and symbols.

Your printer must be able to produce the Times Roman font. If your printer can't produce it, Word will substitute the nearest format that can be produced. You may, of course, choose a font that your printer can produce. Later you'll learn how to change to other font character sets that are installed with your printer driver. Such character sets might include Helvetica, Courier, and Times, to name a few. Further, you can add to the special appearance of a font by adding a character enhancement or style, such as bold, italic, underline, and so on. Once again, with Word, these enhancements are part of the same font family.

Font size is also important. Word's default size is 10 points. A *point (pt)* is a printer's measure for 1/12 of a pica, which, in turn, is 1/6 of an inch. So, you can determine that there are 72 points to an inch.

Finally, it is important to note that the font size is also affected by the individual character itself. For example, some letters have strokes that appear above the body of the character (such as the lowercase letter h) and others, below (such as the lowercase g). In typography terms, the extending strokes are called ascender and descender, respectively, and the body of the character is referred to as the *x-height* (Figure 6.1). It appears that the letter a is the same height as the letter c (although some x-heights may also vary from one font to another), but that the letter d is taller due to its ascender. The size of the font is not measured by the x-height, but rather is measured from the top of the tallest ascender to the bottom of the lowest descender in the font family.

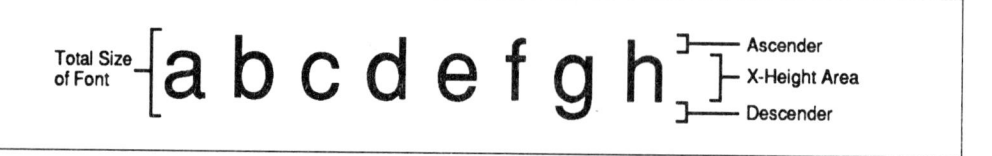

Figure 6.1 Font size is measured from the top of ascender to the bottom of descender.

Types of Character Formatting

Word provides five general types of character formatting. We have touched upon these types in the last section. However, for a quick reference, the types of formats and how to change them are summarized here:

- Fonts—A family of letters, numbers, and symbols in a distinctive design. Changing fonts alters your text's basic appearance.
- Style or Attribute—In Word, style is often referred to as "emphasis." The style or attribute of a character is what makes that character stand out from the rest of the text. For example, boldface characters appear darker and thicker than normal characters. Other styles include italic, which slants characters to the right; underline, which prints a line under the character; and so on.
- Size—You can change the size of a character by specifying its height. The measurement for setting the height is points (remember, the default size is 10 pts). Word will print your documents in the size that you select unless the size is unavailable on your printer. In that case, Word uses the available size closest to the one you have selected.
- Font Spacing—Also called *kerning*, Word allows you to adjust the amount of space between individual characters. Often used for text that uses mixed fonts where the characters don't line up particularly well.
- Font Position—This formatting option refers to the position of characters relative to the line. Specifically, we will discuss how to print characters above (superscript) and below (subscript) the line of surrounding characters.

In addition to these types of character formats, Word provides a sixth option—formatting the characters of your document in one of eight specific colors. This is useful if you have a color printer or plotter. For more information on formatting characters in color, see "Changing Color" later in this chapter.

What You See Is What You Print

Character formatting affects each letter, number, or symbol of your documents. You can format one character at a time or an entire document. One important consideration though is how the characters of your document will look on your screen as you work. Word provides two options for seeing how character formatting will look on your screen. Both options are related to the type of hardware, specifically, the printer's ability to print formats as specified by the installed printer driver (for more information on installing printer drivers, see Chapter 7).

One option is to show on the screen all character formats that you choose, even if your printer cannot print the character formats. In this situation, Word disregards the printer driver information as it displays your text on the screen. However, when it's time to print your document, only the character formats that your printer can handle will be printed. The second option is to display on your screen only the character formats that your printer can print. In other words, your display will show you the character format of the text exactly as it will look when the document is printed. If you wish to choose this option, you should turn on the *Display As Printed* option, located on the View Preferences dialog box. To do this, use your mouse to click the appropriate box, or press **Alt,V,E** to open the Preferences dialog box and then press **Alt,D** to select the option. To execute the command and close the dialog box, click **OK** or press **Enter**.

Applying Character Formatting

When you change the format of a character, you can either select the text first and then choose a specific formatting option (e.g., font type or style), or you can choose an option first and then begin to type new text that adheres to that format. To actually apply character formatting, Word provides three general methods:

- Formatting with the ribbon and mouse
- Formatting with the character-formatting keys
- Formatting with the character command

In the sections that follow, we'll explore each of the above methods in detail. Regardless of which method you use, you still have the option of either formatting existing text or formatting new text. If you wish to format existing text, you must first select that text before choosing any character format. For new text, simply choose the desired format and begin to type. Any format that you choose will be applied to the new characters from the location of the insertion point. Any characters that appear before the insertion point, however, will retain their original character formats unless you first select them and then apply a new character format.

Now that you understand the basics of character formatting, let's turn our attention to the three methods for applying character formats.

Using the Ribbon and Mouse

The easiest character-formatting option for beginners to use is Word's Ribbon feature. You can use the Ribbon as a shortcut to complete many of the character-formatting tasks: choosing fonts, point sizes, style or emphasis of characters, and setting superscripting and subscripting. It's not necessary to have a mouse installed with your system in order to use the Ribbon, but it makes its use simpler. The Ribbon is not only handy, but it's also useful for viewing the current formatting choices that you have selected. In this regard, the use of the Ribbon is very similar to that of the Ruler in paragraph formatting. Select the Ribbon option from the View menu (**Alt,V,B**) and the Ribbon will be displayed at the top of your document window, as shown in Figure 6.2.

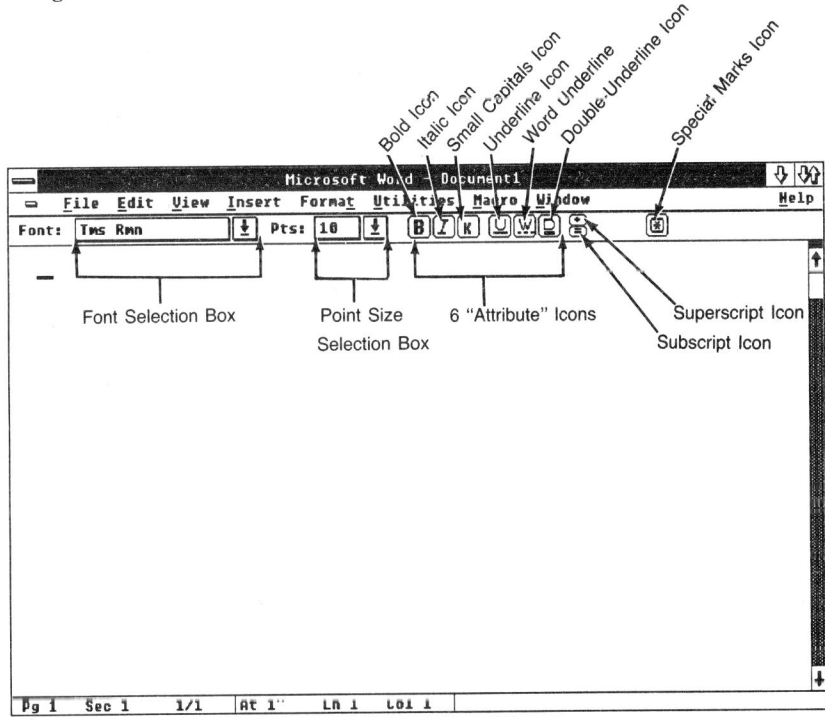

Figure 6.2 The Ribbon is used to format **characters**.

The Basics

From Figure 6.2, you can see that the Ribbon contains several icons. To use the Ribbon, simply click the appropriate icon. Table 6.1 summarizes the formatting options available on the Ribbon and also gives the keystrokes needed to select them.

Table 6.1 Character-Formatting Options

Format Option	Description/Usage	To Select Option
`Helvetica`	Depicts the font slected from fonts available with your printer are listed in pull-down window.	Type font name in Font edit box or select from pull-down window.
`14`	Depicts the size of the font selected. Only the size of fonts available with your printer are listed in pull-down window.	Type the size of font desired in Pts: edit box, or select size option from pull-down window.
B	Depicts boldface. Use to apply bold to or remove bold from existing text or use for new text that you type.	Click icon or press Ctrl+B.
I	Depicts italics. Use to apply italic to or remove italic from existing text, or use for new text that you type.	Click icon or press Ctrl+I.
K	Depicts small capitals. Use to apply or remove small capitals from existing text, or use for new text that you type.	Click icon or press Ctrl+K.
U	Depicts underlining. Use to apply or remove underlining from existing text, or use for new text that you type. This option is for individual characters.	Click icon or press Ctrl+U.
W	Depicts word underlining. Use to apply or remove word underlining from existing text, or use for new text that you type.	Click icon or press Ctrl+W.

Format Option	Description/Usage	To Select Option
▣	Depicts double-underlining. Use to apply or remove double underlining from existing text, or use for new text that you type.	Click icon or press Ctrl+Shift++.
⊕	Depicts superscript. Use to apply or remove superscript format for existing text, or use for new text that you type. Option only raises character 3 pts from text baseline.	Click icon or press Ctrl++.
⊖	Depicts subscript. Use to apply or remove subscript format for existing text, or use for new text that you type. Option only lowers character 3 pts from text baseline.	Click icon or press Ctrl+=.
⊞	Depicts Word formatting marks. Use to turn on or off Show All option in View Preferences dialog box.	Click icon.

The Ribbon is a visual look at what character formats are applied at the location of the insertion point. When you select text, some parts of the Ribbon may appear dimmed or grey if the selection consists of mixed character formats. Once you select text, you can easily switch between character formats by clicking different icons or making the necessary keystrokes.

Although you can simply change style attributes of characters by clicking icons, choosing a font or font size is a two-step process. For example, to choose a font:

1. Click **the arrow** in the font box. You can also complete this step from the keyboard by pressing **Ctrl+F** to activate the Fonts box on the Ribbon.
2. Choose the **name** of the font from the pull-down window. From the keyboard, type a font name or use Alt+down arrow to select the font name from the pull-down window and press

The Basics

Enter. Note: You can also press the Tab key to apply the font selected and move on to the points box without closing the window.

The process for choosing a point size is similar to that of choosing a font.

1. Click **the arrow** in the Pts box, or press **Ctrl+P** to activate the Pts box itself.
2. Click the **size** of font that you wish to apply with the mouse from the pull-down window. From the keyboard, type a font size or use Alt+down arrow to select the font size from the pull-down window and press Enter. Note: Press the Tab key prior to pressing Enter to apply the size and move to the font box without closing the window.

Using the Keys

As a shortcut, Word provides character-formatting keys to complete many of the format selections in lieu of using the Character command or the Ribbon. These shortcut keys use the Ctrl key in combination with another key. For example, to apply or remove boldface from existing text or for new text that you type, you would press Ctrl+B. These formatting keys are listed in Table 6.1, along with their Ribbon counterparts.

Using the Character Command

The options discussed thus far for formatting characters primarily required selecting text and then choosing a formatting command with either the Ribbon or using a Ctrl-key combination. Although these options are handy, Word offers a method for providing greater control and flexibility with character formatting—the *Character Command*.

If you double-click on the Ribbon, you will access one of Word's hot spots and open the Character command dialog window.

The Character command is located on the Format menu. You can access this command by dragging down the Format menu or by typing a **Alt,T,C** from the keyboard. Similar to the Paragraph command, the Character command will produce a dialog box, shown in Figure 6.3, from which you make your formatting selections.

Many of the formatting options available on the Character dialog box are also available through the Ribbon and formatting keys. You can change a character's font type and size and add style enhancements such as boldface, for instance. There are some formatting fea-

6—Formatting Characters

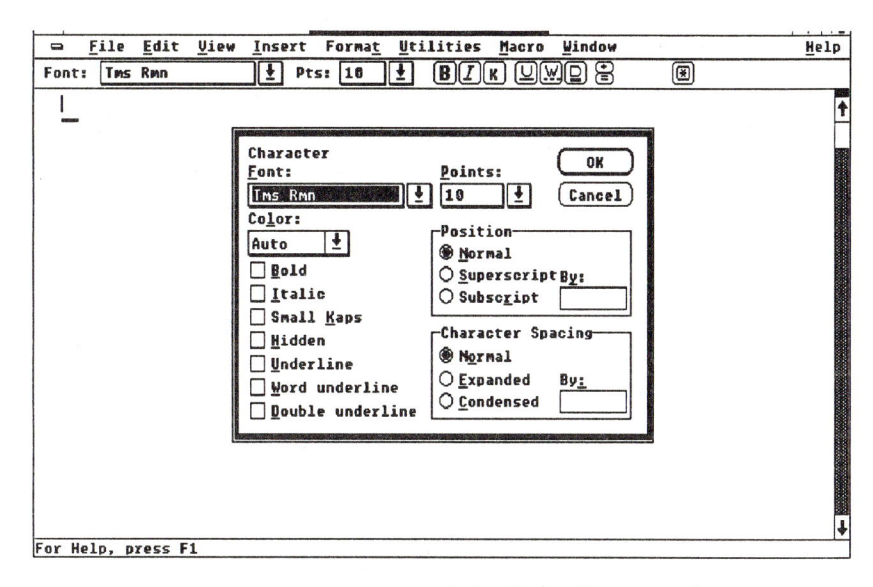

Figure 6.3 The Character dialog box offers several character-formatting options.

tures, however, that you cannot accomplish with the Ribbon or the formatting keys. These features involve changing the spacing of characters relative to each other, providing more superscripting and subscripting options, choosing a hidden text format, and specifying additional colors of type (for printers equipped to handle color).

You could divide the Character dialog box (see Figure 6.3) into six categories: Font, Points, Color, Style or Emphasis check boxes, Position (superscripting and subscripting), and Character Spacing. When you open the Character dialog box, the boxes of current formatting selections are checked. To change a selection, click the appropriate empty box (or use the Alt key in combination with the appropriate underlined letter). To cancel the selection, click or choose a checked box again. If you select text before you open the Character dialog box, all style selections previously made will appear in the check boxes. However, if you select text that has conflicting character formats (e.g., more than one font type), then the boxes will be shaded rather than checked. In this situation, to remove a style you must first click the box to select it (the shading will disappear, leaving a checked box), and then click it a second time to remove the style (the check is removed).

Similar to the Paragraph command, the Character dialog window produces the usual control buttons: OK and Cancel. Click the OK button when you want to execute the formatting change immediately and be returned to the current document window. Click the Cancel button to cancel the current formatting session before you click OK.

105

The sections that follow describe the many character formatting options available with the Character dialog box. Practice the steps along the way. If you have been experimenting with the previous methods for character formatting, you'll be able to determine which method works best for you. In addition, you'll also learn some new character formatting options that are unavailable with the Ribbon or the formatting keys.

Changing Fonts

The Font edit box is in the upper left corner of the Character dialog box. If you press the down arrow on the right side of this box, a window will drop down and display all the fonts installed on your printer. If your printer's number of available fonts is greater than will fit in the visible portion of the window, use the scroll bars or the down arrow key to continue to scroll the window.

Selecting a font type is an important consideration. It is a matter of preference and it's very subjective. The beauty of Word is that you can create your text and edit out imperfections, leaving the formatting for last. You might want to experiment with different format types, styles, and sizes to produce that perfect-looking document. As a suggestion, keep this in mind: Less is more. A document too cluttered with character or paragraph formatting is difficult to read, inhibiting the document's ability to communicate.

To choose or change a font type with the Character command, complete the following steps. If you have yet to begin typing, the font type you choose will be your text font until you change it. If you wish to change the font of existing text, you must first select the text before choosing the Character command. In either case, any text that you enter from the location of the insertion point onward will use the new formatted font. Existing text that is not selected retains the old font.

1. If you are changing the font of existing text, first select the text. Otherwise, go on to step 2.

    The text is highlighted.

2. Choose the **Character** command from the Format menu or type **Alt,T,C**.

    The Character dialog box appears.

3. Click anywhere on the Font box to display the available fonts or press **Alt+F**. Select the font that you want by highlighting with the mouse or using the down arrow key from the keyboard.

    The selected font is displayed in the Font window box.

6—Formatting Characters

4. Click **OK** or press **Enter**.

The format selection is executed and you are returned to the document window.

Tip: It's no secret that writers change their minds frequently. If you just changed the format and decide the new one is not for you, try the shortcut keypress **Ctrl+Spacebar** to remove all but the default character formatting.

Changing the Size of a Font

Postscript printer font sizes go up to 48 pts, but the printers will accept up to 120 pts. To use the larger sizes, enter the value manually.

Changing the size of a font is similar to changing the font itself. On the Character dialog box, located just right of the Font window, is the Points window box. The Points box displays the type size currently in use. If you are using the default Times Roman font, 10 points (the default value) will be displayed. When you first choose another font, all the available size options installed on your printer for that font can be displayed by pointing anywhere on the Points dialog box with the mouse, or by pressing **Alt+P**. If your printer driver contains more sizes than the Points box can hold, use the scroll bar or down arrow key to scroll the list of sizes. To change the size of a font with the Character command, complete the following:

1. Select the text whose size you wish to change. If you are just beginning to type, go on to step 2.

   The selected text is highlighted.

2. Choose the **Character** command from the Format menu or type **Alt+T+C**.

   The Character dialog box is displayed.

3. All current available size options for your font type are listed in the Points box. Choose the desired size from the Points box or enter the size in the window. If you enter a size that is not available with the font, Word will construct that size by scaling to the closest value.

   The current size value was listed in the Points box. Your new selection now replaces it.

4. Click **OK** or press **Enter** to implement the format change immediately and close the window. Clicking **Cancel** will

cancel any selections made during the current session.

Word actually allows you any font size available with your printer as long as your printer is capable of scaling fonts. If you choose a size that isn't installed on your printer, Word will use the nearest font size. While many of the fonts when scaled still provide a clean, crisp look (e.g., Times and Helvetica), some scaled fonts appear rough, with uneven edges. If you are using a Laser printer, your scaled fonts may look fine because laser printers often smooth some of the roughness.

You have learned that changing from one font size or font type to another is simple. Use either the Ribbon or the Character command; whichever method best suits your needs. Keep in mind that you can change from one size to another whether you change font types or not.

Finally, Word always puts the name of the current font and font size in the Ribbon and the Font and Points edit boxes on the Character dialog window. These format settings apply to the current selection where the insertion point resides. As a reference to some possible font selections and font sizes for those selections, refer to Figure 6.4. Note, however, that these samples were printed with a laser printer. Your printer might provide a slightly different look.

Changing Styles or Emphasis

You have learned that you can change the emphasis of a character's appearance by choosing the appropriate icon from the Ribbon or typing the formatting Ctrl-key combination. You can also change the style of your text by using the list of check box options running down the left side of the Character dialog window. Most style selections are

This is 10 pt Times Roman, Plain
The sub-zero parka is one of our warmest parkas, suitable for severe conditions because of its rugged and extremely warm triple-layer construction. You won't find a warmer parka anywhere on the market today.

This is 12 pt Times Roman with a variety of styles.
The sub-zero parka is one of our **warmest parkas**, suitable for <u>severe conditions</u> because of its rugged and <u>extremely warm</u> triple-layer contruction. You won't find a *warmer* parka anywhere on the market today.

Figure 6.4 Sample fonts and sizes provide a different look and feel.

This is 18 pt Modern, Plain
The sub-zero parka is one of our warmest parkas, suitable for severe conditions because of its rugged and extremely warm triple-layer construction. You won't find a warmer parka anywhere on the market today.

This is 24 pt Roman, Plain
The sub-zero parka is one of our warmest parkas, suitable for severe conditions because of its rugged and extremely warm triple-layer construction. You won't find a warmer parka anywhere on the market today.

This is Script, Plain
The sub-zero parka is one of our warmest parkas, suitable for severe conditions because of its rugged and extremely warm triple-layer construction. You won't find a warmer parka anywhere on

Figure 6.4 (continued)

The Basics

available on the Ribbon just as they are on the Character dialog window. These options include Bold, Italic, Small Kaps, Underline, Word Underline, and Double Underline. One option, however, not found on the Ribbon is the Hidden Text option. The basic style options (such as bold and italic) are rather straightforward. Click one of these options and the style will be added to your character format. It is the capitalization style (Small Kaps) and the Hidden style that require further explanation.

The Small Kaps option will format the selected text in all caps (changes all lowercase letters to uppercase letters) but in a smaller font size than the current size. Small caps are commonly used for such abbreviations as A.M. or P.M.

The Hidden Text option is dependent upon the status of the Hidden Text box located in the Preferences dialog box (the Preferences command is found on the View menu). When the HiddenText box is checked, characters formatted as Hidden are displayed with a dotted underline. If the Hidden Text box is turned off, characters formatted in the Style box as Hidden are not displayed.

Click the appropriate box (or use Alt and the appropriate corresponding letter key) to add a style to your font. These styles can be added to your font to enhance its appearance and you can mix or add styles to a font. To remove a style, click the checked box a second time. If the boxes are shaded, you need to click each box twice to remove character styles.

Be cautious about choosing too many styles. Choosing too many will begin to clutter your document. Keep it simple. Also, some of the format styles you could choose will change the spacing of your document. Some of the style options require more space and thus force your document down as Word allows for the additional character formatting required.

To use the Ribbon to add styles to your fonts, follow the procedures discussed in the previous sections. To use the Character command, complete the following steps.

When spell checking, Word treats lowercase characters changed with Small Caps as lowercase still.

To spell check hidden text, first turn on the Hidden Text option in the View Preferences dialog box.

1. Select text if desired.
2. Choose the **Character** command or type **Alt,T,C**. — The Character dialog box appears.
3. Click your selected style box from the list of options on the left side of the dialog box. You can choose more than one style at a time. — An X will appear in the selected style box.
4. Click **OK** or press **Enter**. — The style is added to your font.

200

Choosing Color

The Color option displays the current color of your text. The default option is automatic, or auto, and appears in the Color edit box within the Character dialog box. The auto option will display your text using the default color of your monitor's display. If you have a color monitor, you can display your text using eight different colors. If you have a color printer or plotter, you can also print your text using any of the color options that are available with your printer or plotter.

To choose a different color, first select the Character command by pressing **Alt+T+C**, and then open the Color box with the mouse or by pressing **Alt+L**. A pull-down window will display eight color options: Black (the default), Blue, Cyan, Green, Magenta, Red, Yellow, and White. To choose another color than black, drag down to the one you want and click **OK** or press **Enter**. You may also simply type the name of the color desired in the Color edit box instead of selecting that color from the list. Either way, you can choose any color you desire even if you don't use a color printer. The alternate color options will not be displayed, but saved as a formatting option. If you print out your document with a printer capable of printing in additional colors, your document will be printed in the color selected.

Creating Subscripts and Superscripts

Two special types of character formatting—subscripts and superscripts—are often needed, especially by scientists and mathematicians. These formatting types require characters that will print above and below a line. For example, a scientist might want to use a subscript to properly print the formula for water, or H_2O. Similarly, many mathematical equations require superscripting, such as $x^2 + y^2 = z^2$. To format characters with either a subscript or superscript, use the following steps.

Tip: To eliminate extra line spacing or overlapping of characters, reduce the size of the superscript or subscript characters.

1. Choose the text characters that you wish to appear above the line (superscript) or below the line (subscript).

    The selected text is highlighted.

2. Choose the **Character** command from the Format menu or enter **Alt+T+C** from the keyboard.

    The Character command dialog box appears.

3. If you want a superscript, click the **Superscript** box or

    Both the superscript and subscript options display a

The Basics

press **Alt+S**. If you want a subscript, click the **Subscript** box or press **Alt+R**.

default value of 3 points. Note: This is the only value that can be achieved with the superscript and subscript options on the Ribbon.

4. If you want the positions greater than 3 points removed from the text line, enter the value in the By edit box. You can enter a value in positive decimal measurements between 0 and 63.5 points in .5-point increments.

5. Click **OK** or press **Enter**.

Your selected text will be automatically raised or lowered.

As previously discussed, Word also allows you to use the Ribbon icons or the keyboard shortcuts for formatting superscripts and subscripts. To use the keyboard shortcut for superscripting, first select the text and then press **Ctrl+Shift++**. Be sure to use the plus key on the main keyboard. Similarly, to format a subscript, enter **Ctrl++**. Note that these two keypresses will also decrease the font size of the selected text in addition to applying super- or subscript formatting. This feature helps maintain line spacing.

Changing Font Spacing

When selecting a font, you should know something about the amount of space it occupies. Some fonts are *proportional,* meaning that the width of the individual characters can vary. Other fonts are *nonproportional,* or *monospace,* in that each of their characters are assigned the same amount of space. Most typewriters today use nonproportional spacing. Among basic fonts, some printers offer two that are nonproportional: Courier and Monaco. Other fonts (e.g., Chicago, Geneva, Helvetica, New York, Times, Times Roman) are proportional.

This section discusses how Word lets you manually control the horizontal spacing between characters, called kerning. In addition, Word also lets you control the vertical spacing between lines, known as *leading.* The height of a font is always determined by the distance of the tallest ascender to the lowest descender, plus a single buffer point to prevent any overlapping. To control the spacing between lines, you change the size of fonts between lines.

Examine the Spacing section located in the bottom right side of the Character dialog box (Figure 6.3). The Spacing box offers three

6—Formatting Characters

selections for horizontal spacing: Normal, Condensed, and Expanded. The Normal spacing option is the default setting and it should be an acceptable setting for most of your character format designs. Use the Condensed option, however, if you decide to reduce the space between two characters (up to 1.75 points). If you want to increase the space between two characters (up to about 14 points), use the Expanded option. The Condensed format is set with a default value of 1.5 points, while the Expanded format is set with a default value of 3 points. Use the empty edit box, defined with By, to enter your own space setting for either the Condensed or Expanded options. Condensed will accept avalue from 0 to 1.75 points, while Expanded will accept a value from 0 to 14 points. The values can be entered in increments of 0.25 points.

To change the character spacing, complete the following steps.

1. Select the text for which you wish to change the spacing.

   The selected text is highlighted.

2. Choose the **Character** command from the Format menu or enter **Alt+T+C**.

   The Character dialog box appears.

3. Click the desired spacing option from the Character Spacing dialog box. Click **Condensed** (or press **Alt+C**) to reduce or **Expanded** (or press **Alt+E**) to increase the spacing. Choose Normal to return to the default spacing settings.

   The spacing option is checked.

4. Enter the spacing value in the By edit box. Move to this box by clicking with the mouse or press **Alt+:** (colon).

   The value, in points, appears in the edit box.

5. Click **OK** or press **Enter**.

   The spacing of the selected text is reformatted, and you are returned to the document window.

A Designing Exercise

It's time to practice some of these techniques by formatting a sample document. If you missed a formatting technique, simply refer to the

203

The Basics

appropriate section and follow the necessary steps. For this exercise, you're going to format a sample resume. Feel free to modify it to suit your own needs. Your goal is to enter the text that follows, and then format the text so that it will look something like Figure 6.5. Of course, if your printer cannot print the specific fonts used in the sample, your resume will look slightly different. Begin by entering the following text. Don't worry about formatting. We'll get to that later. If you make any errors, use Word's editing tools to help you correct the mistakes. Type:

Carey Polnick
2500 Northridge Way
Lafayette, IN 47904
(317)-463-2486

Career Objective:
To obtain a position as an executive secretary with an opportunity for advancement in a large corporation.

Work Experience:
June 1987 to present-Secretary, The Hall Corporation, 24 East Street, Lafayette, Indiana. Responsible for general running of the office of a private firm. Duties include typing, answering telephones, filing, etc.
October 1985 to June 1987-Receptionist, Dr. Mark Mathews, 202 Center Street, Williamsport, Indiana.
January 1984 to Oct. 1985-Clerk and Receptionist, Craig's Pharmacy, 10 Main Street, Williamsport, Indiana. Also served as the second-shift Assistant Manager.

Education:
Ivy Secretarial School, Lafayette, Indiana: September 1986-May 1987. Courses in typing, filing, wordprocessing, and bookkeeping.

Special Skills:
Typing-80 W.P.M.
Shorthand-120 W.P.M.
Languages-Spanish

References:
Mr. Miles Thompson, President   Pastor John Smith
The Hall Corporation   Eastside Christian Church
24 East Street   206 Highland Avenue
Lafayette, IN 47918   Williamsport, IN 47993
(317)-828-5550   (317)-762-3233

6—Formatting Characters

Once you have completed typing in the text above, check for typos and make any corrections necessary. Now, let's use some of the formatting techniques that we have learned in the last two chapters. Complete the following:

Format Task	Do This
Center address.	Select the entire address and then click the **Center** icon on the Ruler or press **Ctrl+C**.
Change the font and font size of the address.	If necessary, select the address again and then choose the font and font size desired from either the Ribbon or the Character dialog window. For our example, choose 14 pt, Roman Bold. You must choose the font, point size, and the emphasis (boldface) separately and while the text is highlighted.
Add border under the phone number in address.	Select the phone number only, and then choose the **Character** command. Move to the Border option and select the **Beneath** option with a **Thick** pattern.
Double underline headings and add boldface.	Select each heading (i.e., Career Objective, Work Experience, Education, Special Skills, and References) one at a time and click the **bold** option on the Ruler or press **Ctrl+B**. Then, while the headings are still selected, click the **Double-underline** option or press **Ctrl+D**.
Add spacing after headings.	Just as above, select each heading and then click the **Open Spacing** icon on the Ruler or press **Ctrl+O**. In this case, however, also select the first line following the heading so that Word will add space after the heading and before the beginning of the line that follows the heading. This assumes that you added a blank line following the text. If you didn't, position the insertion point at the end of each heading and press **Enter** once.

(continued)

Format Task	Do This
Use hanging indents to align information under work experience.	Select the section of text that begins with "June 1987" and ends with "filing, etc." Now create a hanging indent using the Ruler. For example, if you have a mouse, hold down the **Shift** key while you drag the left indent to the right to approximately the 1.55" mark. You can also use the Paragraph command to get a precise measurement. Do the same for all three chronological dates of the work history. Remember to choose only each individual paragraph separately. You might have to fudge a little in order to get the hanging indents to align evenly with all three paragraphs.
Apply Small Kaps format.	Select the "W.P.M." text and then choose the small caps option from the Ruler or press **Ctrl+K**. Note: Some laser printers cannot print this format.
Tab References section at the bottom.	If you didn't press the Tab key to evenly space the addresses at the bottom of the résumé, you might try to select the text and then apply a single tab setting. Of course, you'll still be required to press the Tab key to space the addresses properly.

If you followed our suggestions, your finished text should look something like Figure 6.5. You may need to fudge with the number of blank lines or your margins in order to get the document to fit on a single page. In this exercise, you practiced centering text, selecting different fonts and font sizes. You applied boldface, used the small caps option, and created hanging indents. You even applied a border. For practice, create your own résumé, using all of the formatting techniques at your disposal.

Carey Polnick
2500 Northridge Way
Lafayette, IN 47904
(317)-463-2486

Career Objective:

To obtain a position as an executive secretary with an opportunity for advancement in a large corporation.

Work Experience:

June 1987 to present- Secretary, The Hall Corporation, 24 East Street, Lafayette, Indiana. Responsible for general running of the office of a private firm. Duties include typing, answering telephones, filing, etc.

October 1985 to June 1987- Receptionist, Dr. Mark Mathews, 202 Center Street, Williamsport, Indiana.

January 1984 to Oct. 1985- Clerk and Receptionist, Craig's Pharmacy, 10 Main Street, Williamsport, Indiana. Also served as the second shift Assistant Manager

Education:

Ivy Secretarial School, Lafayette, Indiana- September 1986- May 1987. Courses in typing, filing, wordprocessing, and bookkeeping.

Special Skills:

Typing--80 W.P.M.
Shorthand--120 W.P.M.
Languages--Spanish

References:

Mr. Miles Thompson, President   Pastor John Smith
The Hall Corporation   Eastside Christian Church
24 East Street   206 Highland Avenue
Lafayette, IN 47918   Williamsport, IN 47993
(317)-463-2486   (317)-762-3233

Figure 6.5 A sample résumé using paragraph and character formats.

Review

In this chapter you learned:

1. You can format text at Word's lowest level, the individual character, including choosing font style and size and spacing.
2. In Word, a font contains different sizes of type (e.g., 10-point Times Roman and 18-point Times Roman).
3. Word provides five general types of character formatting: fonts, style, size, font spacing, and font position.
4. You can tell Word to show you how the font characters will look even if your printer cannot print them, or you can tell Word to display only the character formats that your printer can print. This latter option is accomplished by choosing the Display As Printed option on View Preferences.
5. To actually apply character formatting, you can use one of three methods: using the Ribbon and mouse, using the character formatting keys, using the Character command.
6. If you have a mouse installed, you will find that the Ribbon is the easiest method for beginners to learn how to do character formatting. You can choose fonts, point sizes, emphasis of characters (e.g., bold), and set subscripting and superscripting with the Ribbon.
7. The Character command offers greater control and flexibility of character formatting. These features are not available on the Ribbon or through formatting keys: changing the spacing of characters relative to each other, choosing a hidden text format, and specifying additional colors of type for printers equipped to handle color.
8. You can change the font type or size before or after you type text. If you wish to change the font type of existing text, you must first select it before choosing the Character command.
9. Some fonts are proportional and some are nonproportional. Nonproportional means that the width of the individual characters can vary from one another.

S E V E N

chapter

Formatting Complex Documents

In this chapter:

- Using the Section Command
- Using The Position Command
- Working With Bound Documents
- Using Page View

You have now learned many of the basic word processing steps required to create documents with Word: how to create and enter text, how to edit text, and how to format that text at the document, paragraph, and character level. This chapter shows you how to format more complex documents. To do this, you'll learn to use the Insert Break command to create sections and the Format Section command to format documents divided into sections. You will also learn about Word's ability to absolutely position text or pictures using the Position command and to set margins for documents that are to be bound. Finally, you'll learn more about Page View, which allows you to examine your pages and to make last-minute changes before you begin to print your documents.

Using the Section Command

The example documents illustrated thus far have generally been one-page letters or résumés requiring simple formatting techniques that you could easily accomplish with Paragraph or Character formatting.

The Basics

Suppose, however, you want to format a more complex document, one divided into sections, each of which contains special elements, such as graphics or multicolumn layouts, that require specific formatting details. Good examples might include a newsletter that contains several columns of text or a long business report that runs several pages. Further, different sections might require a different set of format options and styles, such as page numbers, header or footer positions, footnote positions, or even special page breaks to make new sections begin at the tops of new pages. A typical example is a business plan (or a book) that consists of a title page, an outline, a summary, the detailed report, and some appendix material. It is common to begin each section of a business plan at the top of a new page. Some sections of the business plan, such as the financial report, are generally formatted with a specific style. With Word's *Section* command, you can easily format sections individually so that each section's unique formatting requirements are addressed.

The Section command provides you with the ability to control the formatting and thus the page layout of individual divisions of your document. A section can be any size: a single line, a single page, or an entire document. If you don't divide your document into sections, your entire document uses the current formatting setting as if it were one section. By dividing your document into sections, however, you can control the page layout of those sections, including page numbering, page breaks, multicolumn layout, and layout of headers and footers. The Section command also provides some additional formatting features, such as formatting your footnotes as endnotes, vertically aligning your text between top and bottom margins, and line numbering.

Before you learn how to format individual sections of a document, an examination of the elements of the Section command is in order. Choose the **Section** command option by dragging the Format menu or typing **Alt,T,S**. The Section dialog window is depicted in Figure 7.1.

The Section dialog window can be divided into five functional areas:

- Columns—From the Columns section you can control the number of columns (Number edit box) and the amount of space between each column (Spacing edit box). The number of columns must be a positive integer and limited to the page layout of your document. The amount of space between each column must be a positive decimal measurement. The last option in the Columns section is Line Between. When selected, this option prints a vertical line between columns as long as there are two or more columns within the current section.

7—Formatting Complex Documents

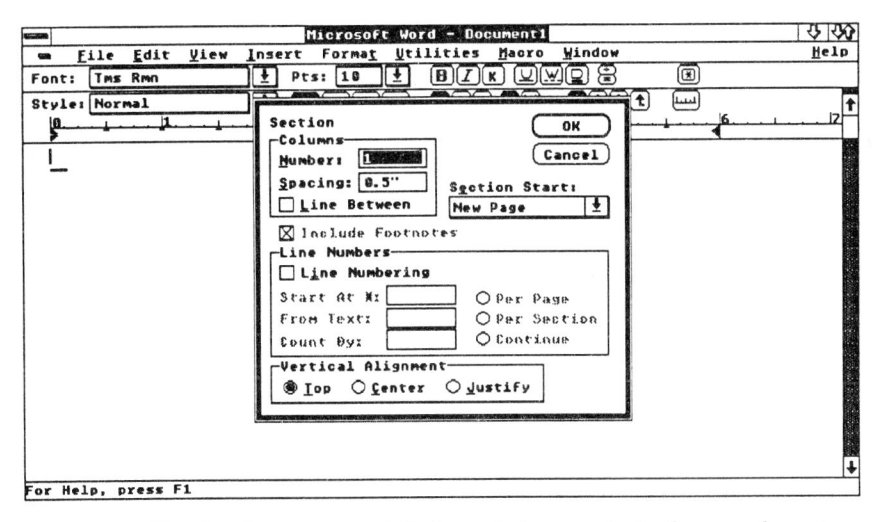

Figure 7.1 The Section command dialog window controls the page layout of individual sections.

- Starting Sections—Identified by the Section Start edit window located just to the right of the Columns section. The Start option lets you specify where to begin a new section (e.g., at the top of a new page or on the same page) and how to begin a section (e.g., mixing columns on a single page). Note that many of the options in this section correspond to the same Section Break options located on the Insert command dialog window. For example, New Page is the same format option as Next Page from the Insert command. Likewise, No Break is the same as Continuous, and Even Page and Odd Page are the same as their counterpart commands found on the Insert command. All of these commands will be discussed in more detail shortly.

- Footnotes—When you check the Include Footnotes box at the center of the window and then select End of Section for footnote position in the Document dialog box, endnotes are printed at the conclusion of the current section. If you don't check the box, footnotes appear at the end of the entire document.

- Line Numbers—The default of the Line Numbering option is off, but you can specify line numbers to appear at the left of individual lines of your current section. Line Numbering can also be turned off for a specific paragraph via the Format Paragraph command. In Normal Editing View or Page View, line numbers will not print on your screen although they will appear on your printed document. In Print Preview mode you can see how the final product will look before you print it out.

211

- Vertical Alignment—The Vertical Alignment options of Top, Center, and Justify are used along with the top and bottom margins to align the text of the current section. These options are available to you regardless of which Start option is selected.

In addition to these functional areas, the Section dialog box also includes the OK and Cancel command key buttons. The OK button executes your formatting command selections immediately and returns you to the document window, while the Cancel button lets you change your mind before any changes are set.

Creating a Section

When you think of a section, think of a document within a document. Just as each individual chapter in a book represents a section, each section represents a related document. In books, some formatting settings remain the same, such as the margins (which you can set with the Document command), but other formats may differ, such as how you paginate each chapter or section. The front matter, including the table of contents and perhaps a preface or foreword, is generally numbered with roman numerals, for instance. The first chapter usually begins arabic numbering.

When you decide that you want to divide your document into sections, the first step is to determine where to begin a new section and insert a *section break mark*. Move the insertion point to the location where the new section is to start and then complete the following steps:

1.	Choose the **Break** command from the Insert menu or press **Alt,I,B**.	The Insert dialog box appears.
2.	Word provides four types of section breaks. For example, to start a section at the top of a new page, select Next Page (**Alt+N**). If you wish to create a complex document with multiple columns on a single page, choose Continuous (**Alt+T**).	The type of section break is highlighted.

3. Click **OK** or press **Enter**.

You are returned to the document window. The insertion point now resides in the new section. Notice that upon execution of the Insert command, Word produces a double dotted line (the section mark) at the location of the insertion point, as shown in Figure 7.2.

Section Mark   Section 1   Section 2

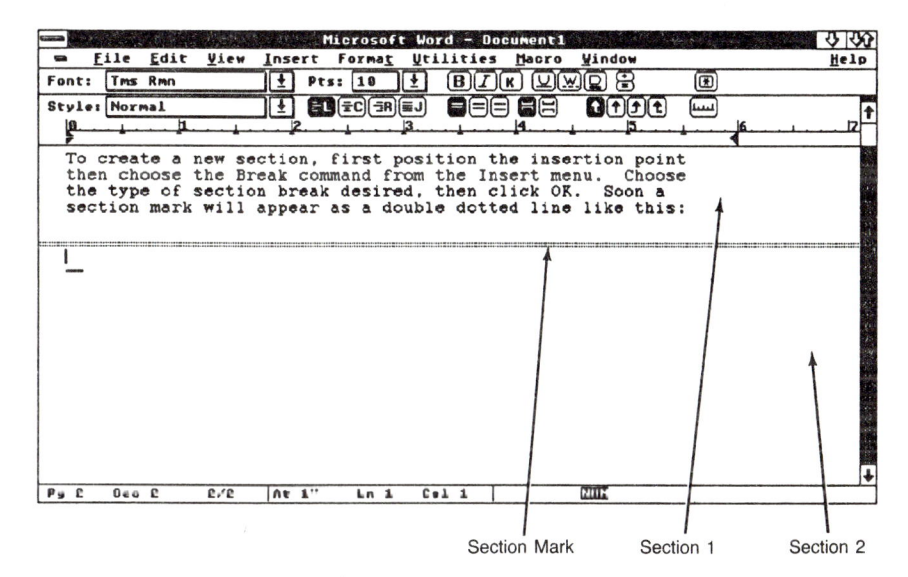

Figure 7.2 A section mark is indicated by a double dotted line.

When you create a new section, the insertion point will always drop below the section mark. The next typed character will be entered in that new section. When you insert a section mark, you'll notice that the status bar (if you turned it on via Preferences) in the lower left corner now displays the current section number for the top line displayed as well as the current page number (e.g., P1 S1 for page 1, section 1).

If you've created a new section, but then changed your mind, you can remove the section mark by choosing **Undo Insertion** from the Edit menu as long as you haven't typed new text or given a new command. If you have already entered text or given a command, move the insertion point to the selection bar on the left side of your screen (the arrow will point to the right), click once to select the section mark (the double dotted line will be highlighted), and then press the **Delete** key to erase the section mark.

When you first create a section, Word will treat the section with the same formatting selections applied to the previous section. You can change the format of the new section, however, by positioning the insertion point anywhere inside that section and choosing the Section command from the Format menu in order to reformat. You can also reformat two sections simultaneously by first selecting portions of sections above and then below the section mark and making your formatting changes within the Section Command dialog box. Any reformatting choices you make will then apply to both of the selected sections.

Where a Section Starts

When you create a new section with the Insert Break command, you need to tell Word where to start the new section. By default, Word has the Page Break option selected. Since you wish to insert a section break instead of a page break, use the mouse and select a section start option or use the Alt key in combination with the appropriate underlined letter. The type of section starts that you may select include the following:

- Next Page—Starts printing a new section following the page break.
- Continuous—Starts the new section on the same page as the previous section. Select this option if you want to vary the number of columns on a single page. For example, if you wish to print the first section on the page with one column and the remainder of the page with two columns, as shown in Figure 7.3, divide the page in two sections with Continuous.

  Using Continuous, you can easily mix the number of columns within your document. You can start with one column, switch to two columns in a second section, change the number of columns in the third section, and so on. Word will even balance the column widths from one section to another to provide a uniform look. Some common uses include newspapers, magazines, or newsletters in which you mix text and graphics.
- Even Page and Odd Page—Use these to start a new section at the top of a new page, with one proviso: the new section will begin at the next even- or odd-numbered page, sometimes

leaving a blank page inserted between the previous section and the new section.

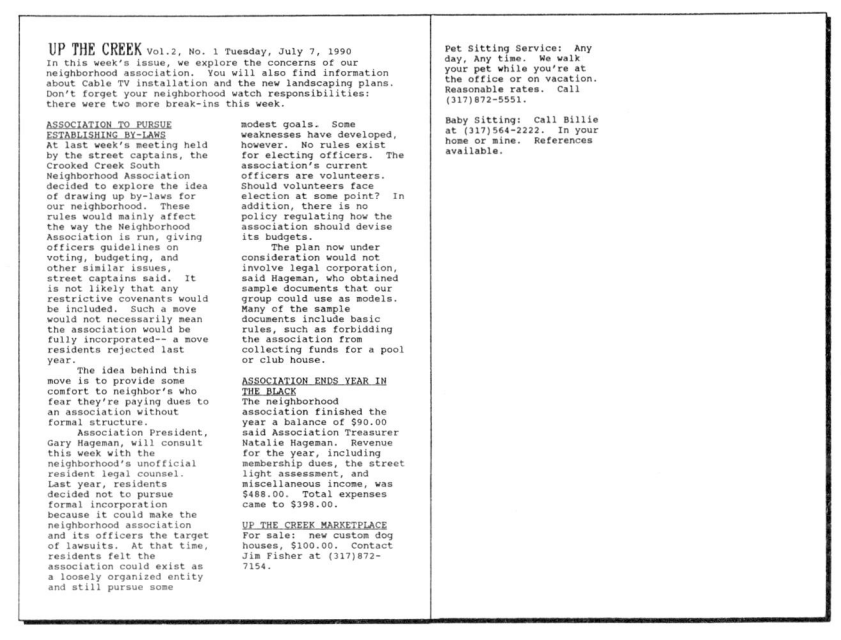

Figure 7.3 The Continuous option formats documents with varying numbers of columns per page.

Finally, you will notice that all of the types of section starts listed in the Insert Break dialog box have corresponding commands listed in the Section command dialog box. For example, Continuous in the Insert Break window is the same format option as No Break found on the Section dialog window. This compatibility of commands allows you to easily change the type of section start with the Section command once the break itself is created with the Insert Break command.

Creating Multicolumn Text

To this point, all of the discussion and the example documents have been formatted in a single column. You are certainly familiar with newspaper and magazine multicolumn formats, however. Their columns flow naturally from the bottom of one column to the top of the next column. This type of column formatting is sometimes referred to as *snaking* columns. To create snaking columns, Word provides the

The Basics

Columns option in the Section dialog box. You specify the number of columns in the Number edit box. The default value is 1 when you first start using Word. To indicate the amount of space between columns (sometimes the term "columns gutter" is used to describe this space), enter the desired amount in the Spacing edit box. For example, to create a document with two columns and a 1/2" space between them, enter 2 in the Number edit box and leave 0.5" (the default value) in the Spacing edit box. Then click **OK** (or press **Enter**) to return to Normal Editing View and a two-column section.

When you are creating snake columns, clicking OK returns you to the previous view. In Normal Editing View, your text appears as a single narrow column instead of the number of columns that you specified in the Number edit box. You won't be able to see all the columns until you print your text unless you switch to Page View. You can also see the effect of columnar formatting with Print Preview before you print it out.

For some practice with this, get a clean page, and then complete the following steps to set a two-column format with a .5" distance between columns. Then type the sample glossary in Figure 7.4. Note that the heading is centered in a separate section followed by a Continuous (or No Break) option from the Insert Break dialog box prior to the second section (Figure 7.5). This creates a single page with two different columnar formats: The first section contains one column

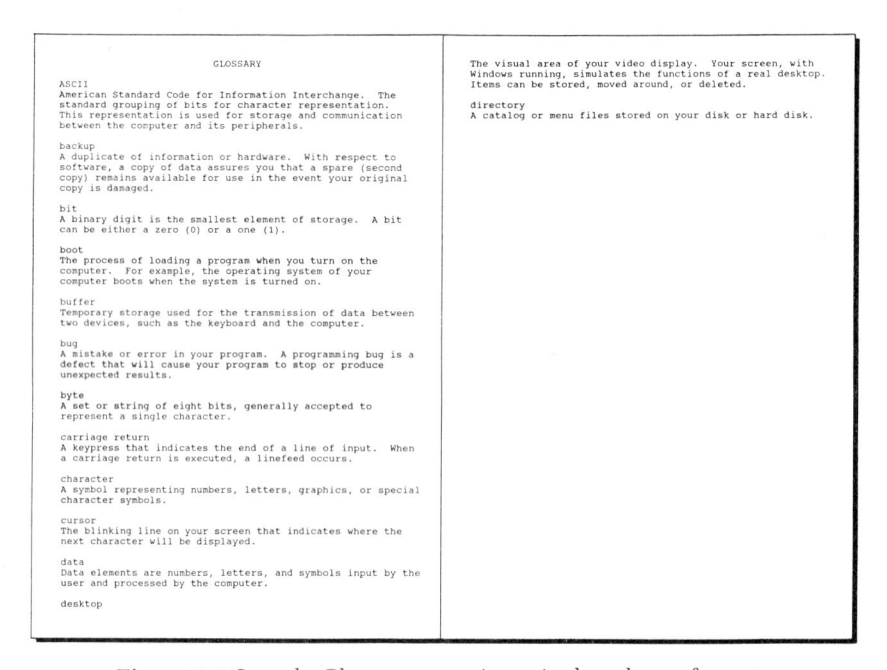

Figure 7.4 Sample Glossary page in a single-column format.

(the heading), and in a moment the second section is reformatted with two columns. The Continuous or No Break option is required in order to force both formats onto the same page. Figure 7.6 illustrates how the same document will appear in two-column format and Figure 7.7 depicts the same document with three columns.

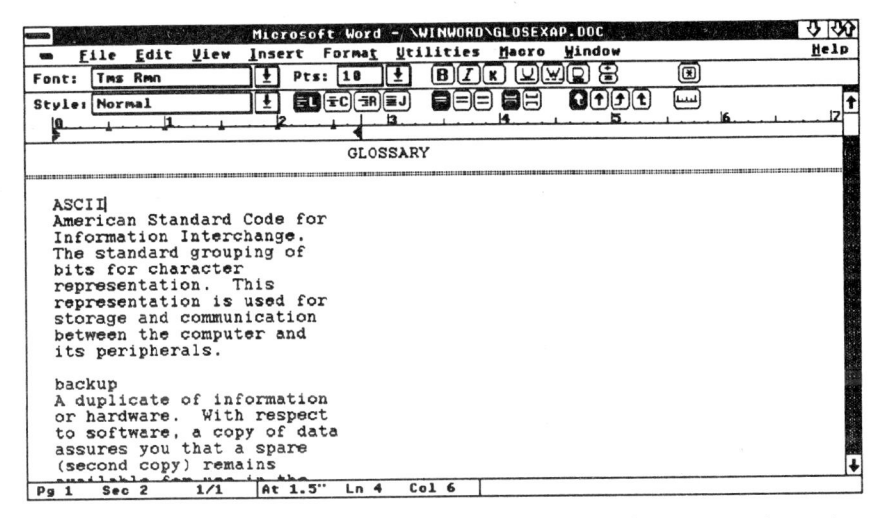

Figure 7.5 Text in snaking columns appears as a single narrow column in Normal Editing View.

Tip: Use left justification instead of full justification when creating text with multiple columns. Columnar formatting reduces the number of characters you can get on a single line, and left justification fits more characters per line than full justification.

To create the multiple column document in Figure 7.6, complete the following steps:

1. In the first section, type the Glossary heading and center it. Position the insertion point on a line following the heading and then choose the **Break** Command from the Insert menu (**Alt,I,B**).

    The Break dialog box opens.

2. Since we want to keep the sections on the same page, choose the **Continuous** option and then click **OK** or press **Enter**.

    The dialog box closes and you are returned to the document window with the insertion point at the beginning of section two.

The Basics

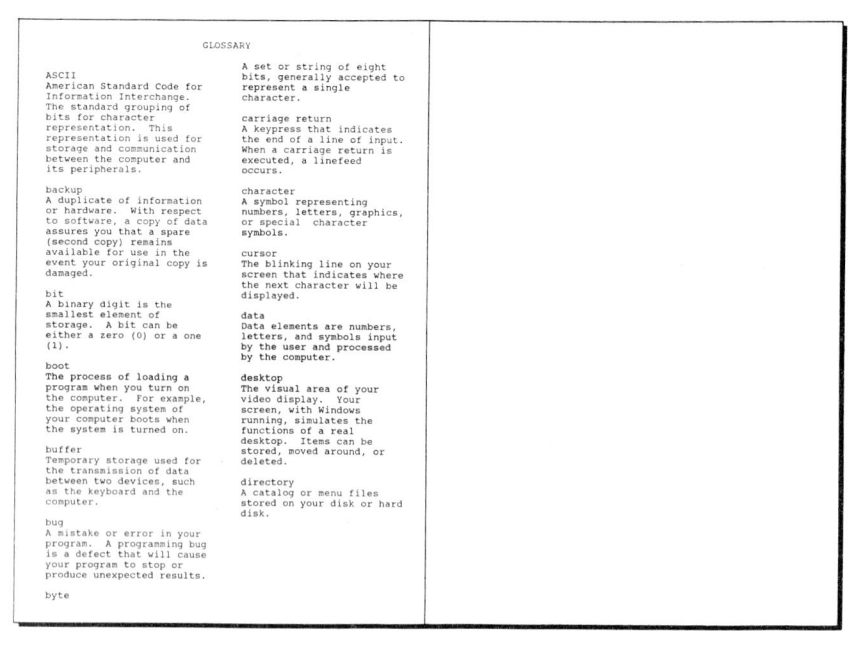

Figure 7.6 Sample Glossary page in a two-column format.

3. Choose the **Section** command from the Format menu (**Alt,T,S**).	The Section dialog box appears.
4. Enter **2** in the Number edit box. You can choose any number of columns that will fit on a single page. For a three-column format, you would enter 3, and so on.	The 2 replaces the default value 1, indicating that this section will be two columns.
5. Choose the amount of space between columns. For this example, the default value **0.5"** in the Spacing edit box will do just fine.	The desired value appears.
6. Click **OK** or press **Enter**.	You are returned to the document window.

7. Begin to enter text.

Text appears in a single narrow column in Normal Editing View, as in Figure 7.5. Notice that the default right edge of the text is delimited by the dotted vertical line on the Ruler at the 2 3/4" mark. The right margin has not changed, only the width of the specified column.

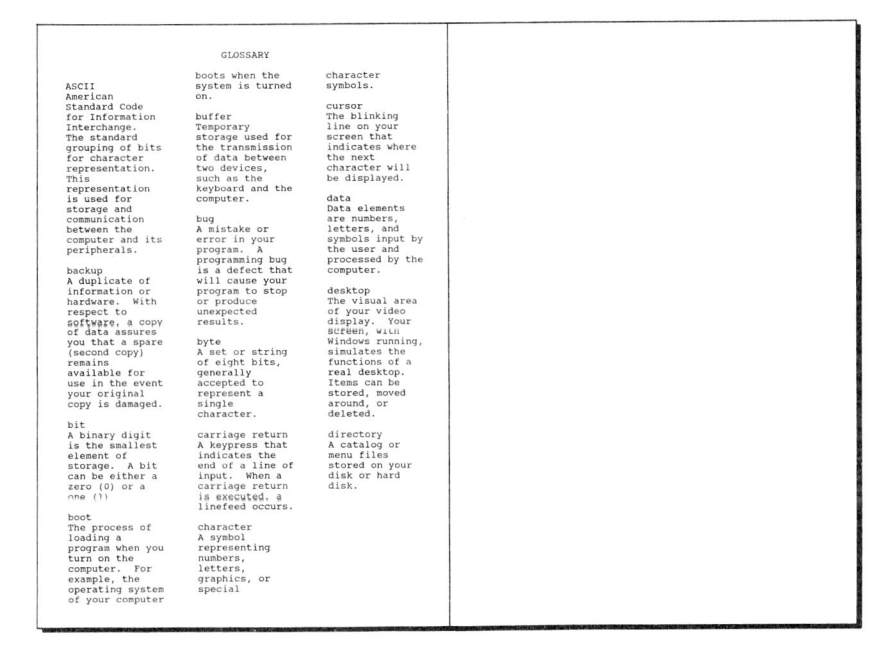

Figure 7.7 Sample Glossary page in three-column format.

As you can see, creating multicolumn snaking text is easy. You can change the number of columns either before you enter text, or you can position the insertion point in the current section and then change the number of columns after you've entered the text. Once you change the number of columns and click OK, the columnar formatting of the current section will change accordingly.

Keep the following two points in mind when you engage in multicolumn formatting:

- To insert a break in a multicolumn format where the new text starts at the top of a new column, you must insert a new section (Insert Break) and then choose the New Column option in the Section dialog box. This option only works if the new section contains the same number of columns as the preceding section.
- Use the No Break option in the Start section of the Section dialog box (or Continuous from the Insert Break dialog) to create more than one columnar format on the same page. You can mix the number of columnar formats by dividing your documents into separate sections. For example, you can start a document with one column for the heading, create a new section for a three-column formatting, and then create a third section for a single-column format. Remember to use the No Break (or Continuous) option to force all three formats onto the same page.

Creating a Newsletter

Now that you have an idea how to create multicolumn documents, let's try another example. Our goal is to create the sample newsletter shown in Figure 7.3. To start, get a clean page and then enter the following text. Don't worry about formatting just yet. You can always go back and add the character attributes later (i.e., boldface and underlining of text). Type:

```
UP THE CREEK Vol.2, No. 1 Tuesday, July 7, 1990
In this week's issue, we explore the concerns of our neighborhood
association. You will also find information about Cable TV
installation and the new landscaping plans. Don't forget your
neighborhood watch responsibilities: There were two more break-
ins this week.
```

The next step is to press Enter twice to insert two blank lines and then insert a new section. To do this, choose the **Break** command from the Insert menu or press **Alt,I,B** and then choose the Continuous option by pressing **T**. Once you have selected the option, choose **OK** or press **Enter** to insert the proper section break. Your screen should now show a double dotted line following the first section of material just typed. With the insertion point at the beginning of the second section, choose the **Section** command from the Format menu or press **Alt,T,S**. In the Columns edit box, enter **2** and accept the 0.5" default

Spacing value. Click **OK** or press **Enter**. You're now ready to enter the text for the second section. As you type in Normal Editing View, the text will appear in two snaking columns. Type:

ASSOCIATION TO PURSUE ESTABLISHING BY-LAWS
At last week's meeting held by the street captains, the Crooked Creek South Neighborhood Association decided to explore the idea of drawing up by-laws for our neighborhood. These rules would mainly affect the way the Neighborhood Association is run, giving officers guidelines on voting, budgeting, and other similar issues, street captains said. It is not likely that any restrictive covenants would be included. Such a move would not necessarily mean the association would be fully incorporated--a move residents rejected last year.

The idea behind this move is to provide some comfort to neighbors who fear they're paying dues to an association without formal structure.

Association President Gary Hageman will consult this week with the neighborhood's unofficial resident legal counsel. Last year, residents decided not to pursue formal incorporation because it could make the neighborhood association and its officers the target of lawsuits. At that time, residents felt the association could exist as a loosely organized entity and still pursue some modest goals. Some weaknesses have developed, however. No rules exist for electing officers. The association's current officers are volunteers. Should volunteers face election at some point? In addition, there is no policy regulating how the association should devise its budgets.

The plan now under consideration would not involve legal corporation, said Hageman, who obtained sample documents that our group could use as models. Many of the sample documents include basic rules, such as forbidding the association from collecting funds for a pool or club house.

ASSOCIATION ENDS YEAR IN THE BLACK
The neighborhood association finished the year with a balance of $90.00, said Association Treasurer Natalie Hageman. Revenue for the year, including membership dues, the street light assessment, and miscellaneous income, was $488.00. Total expenses came to $398.00.

UP THE CREEK MARKETPLACE
For sale: new custom dog houses, $100.00. Contact Jim Fisher at 872-7154.

Pet Sitting Service: Any day, any time. We walk your pet while you're at the office or on vacation. Reasonable rates. Call 872-5551.

The Basics

> Baby Sitting: Call Billie at 564-2222. In your home or mine. References available.

The final step is to complete the formatting of your document. Move the insertion point to the first section and select the UP THE CREEK heading. Choose a larger font size and boldface to highlight the text. Since the default font is 10-pt Times Roman, try **18**-pt Roman instead. Next, select each of the headings in the second section and choose the underline character option. To do this quickly, use the Ribbon. When you have finished polishing and editing your document, choose Page View to see exactly how it will look when printed. The result should look something like Figure 7.8.

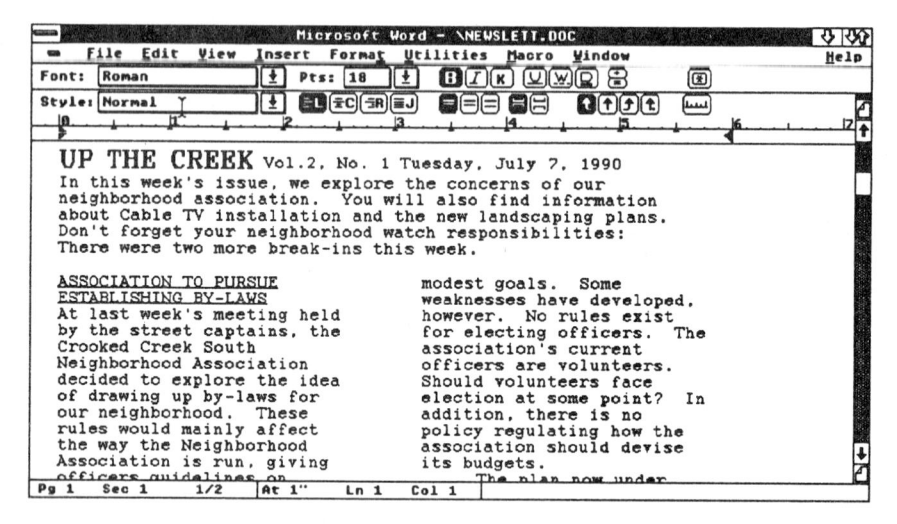

Figure 7.8 Sample newsletter in Page View.

Setting Line Numbers

Use the Line Numbers option to set a line number to the left of each individual line in a document. Some publishing requirements may require that you use the Line Number option, such as for technical or research papers. The legal profession commonly uses line numbers for easy reference. The line numbers will not appear on your screen in Normal Editing View, only on the document itself when printed.

But you can see line numbers in Page View or Print Preview prior to printing.

To turn on Line Number for the section where the insertion point resides, choose the **Section** command from the Format menu as before and then either click inside the **Line Numbering** box or press **Alt+I**. The Line Numbering option allows you to specify where the number will print on the page (From Text), when the line number will print (Per Page, Per Section, Continue, Count By) and at what positive integer the line numbering begins (Start At #). The default option has the Line Numbering option turned off so line numbers will not print on your document.

Specifying Where Lines Numbers Print

To control how close the line number prints to the actual text, use the From Text option. You can enter any positive decimal measurement that specifies the distance from the left margin and the rightmost digit of the line number. A typical distance is 1/4" (0.25").

Specifying When Line Numbers Print

Word provides four print options: Per Page, Per Section, Continue, and Count By. Unless you specify a different Start Number, Word will begin numbering with 1. Note that blank lines will be numbered too, unless they are created with spacing options in the Paragraph command.

The Per Page option begins numbering at the top of each page while the Per Section option starts numbering at the top of each section. If you want to number each line in a section continuously throughout the document, choose the Continuous option.

Finally, the Line Numbers option lets you decide whether to print all the line numbers or just a few. Using the Count By option, you can tell Word to skip a certain number of lines before printing the next number. For example, if you enter a 10 in the Count By box, Word will print a line number every 10th line.

Specifying the Starting Line Number

Generally, you will begin your line numbering with 1. If you wish to change the start number, however, simply click inside the Start At # edit box or press Alt+A, and then type the appropriate positive integer for the first line. Remember, unless you choose the Continuous option, Word will begin each new section or page with the same start number that appears in the Start At # edit box.

The Basics

Using the Position Command

Let's take a break from the Section command and turn our attention to one of Word's more powerful features, the ability to absolutely position text or pictures on a document page. This feature is accomplished with the *Position* command. Found on the Format menu (Alt,T,O), the Position command is an advanced document-design tool that you can use to place a block of text, a table, or a picture anywhere on a page and flow text around it. This feature gives you more desktop publishing capabilities when laying out such complex documents as brochures.

With the Position command, you absolutely position a paragraph consisting of a frame and the text or graphic that goes in that frame. You specify the frame's position on the page horizontally and vertically and its width via the Position dialog box (Figure 7.9). The frame's height is adjusted by Word depending upon the amount of text in the positioned paragraph. All other text on the page flows around the positioned object.

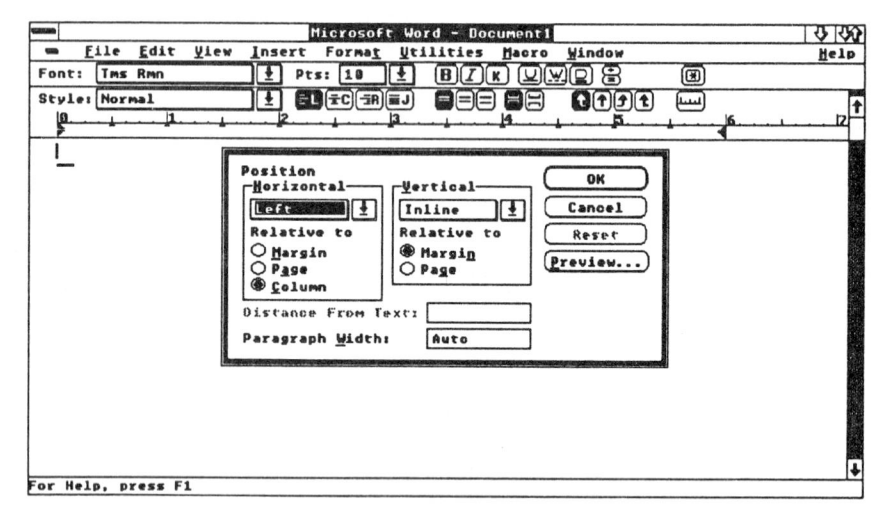

Figure 7.9 With the Position dialog box you tell Word where to position a paragraph, table, or picture.

The first step to position a paragraph or object is to format it as you want it to appear in your document. Select the object then and choose the **Position** command from the Format menu or press **Alt,T,O**. Setting the Horizontal and Vertical choices in the dialog box, shown in Figure 7.9, specifies where the object will be positioned.

224

7—Formatting Complex Documents

Both choices include a drop-down list and a Relative to heading, enabling you to specify horizontal and vertical positioning relative to a particular part of the page. The Horizontal options include Left, Center, Right, Inside, and Outside, relative to the Margin, Page, or Column. The Vertical options are In Line, Top, Center, and Bottom, relative to the Margin or Page. After you specify an object's relative position, you can also specify the alignment from one of these standard options, or you can type an absolute value in the edit bar at the top of each dropdown list.

Tip: Many laser printers cannot print anything that is positioned less than 3/8" from the edge of the paper.

At the bottom of the Position dialog box are two edit fields, Distance From Text and Paragraph Width. The Distance From Text specifies the amount of space from the frame around the object to the text that flows around it. This option appears dim or grey unless you first choose a Relative to option. If, for example, you select Margin with the standard default margin settings, the default value in the Distance From Text box will be approximately 1/8" or .13 in, of white space. To change this value, enter another positive decimal value in the Distance From Text edit bar. Keep in mind that Word must have at least 1" of white space between the frame and the left and right boundary text. Word maintains this parameter by considering both the horizontal position and the value in the Distance From Text edit box. If Word cannot maintain 1" of white space, it will not flow the remaining text around the positioned object.

Auto, the default value for Paragraph Width, is simply as wide as it is already formatted. If you are working in multiple columns, for example, the default value of the Paragraph Width is the width of the column. You can set the width of the paragraph to be either smaller or greater than the width of the column. In either case, Word will flow the text for you automatically.

Once you have positioned your paragraph or object, click **OK** or press **Enter** to apply it, and the dialog box will be closed and you are returned to your document. To see how your positioned object will look on the page, you can turn on Page View mode or switch to Print Preview. You can go directly from the Position dialog box to Print Preview by clicking the Preview button. The Cancel button closes the dialog without formatting the paragraph, while the Reset button allows you to return a positioned object to its previous format.

After you have positioned a paragraph or object, it will be surrounded with a frame that appears as dotted lines representing the boundaries of the positioned object. These boundaries are not visible in Normal Editing View. To view them, choose Print Preview from the File menu and then turn on the Boundaries option. You can also choose Page View and then select the boundaries option from the

The fonts and sizes for absolutely positioning text depend upon the fonts available with your printer.

225

The Basics

Preferences dialog box. Later in this chapter, you'll learn more about how to use Page View, while Chapter 8 provides more detail of the Print Preview options.

As an example of positioning paragraphs, Figure 7.10 shows a modification of the multicolumn newsletter from Figure 7.3. This document has two absolutely positioned paragraphs. First is the centered paragraph in all caps, ELECTION OF NEW OFFICERS TO BE HELD WEDNESDAY. You can enter this text anywhere on the first page of your document since you are going to absolutely position it. To simplify things, position the pointer at the top of the second section and then enter the text. Next, select the text and format it in 24-pt Times Roman Bold. Surround it with a shadow style border, which you access via the Borders dialog through the **Paragraph** command.

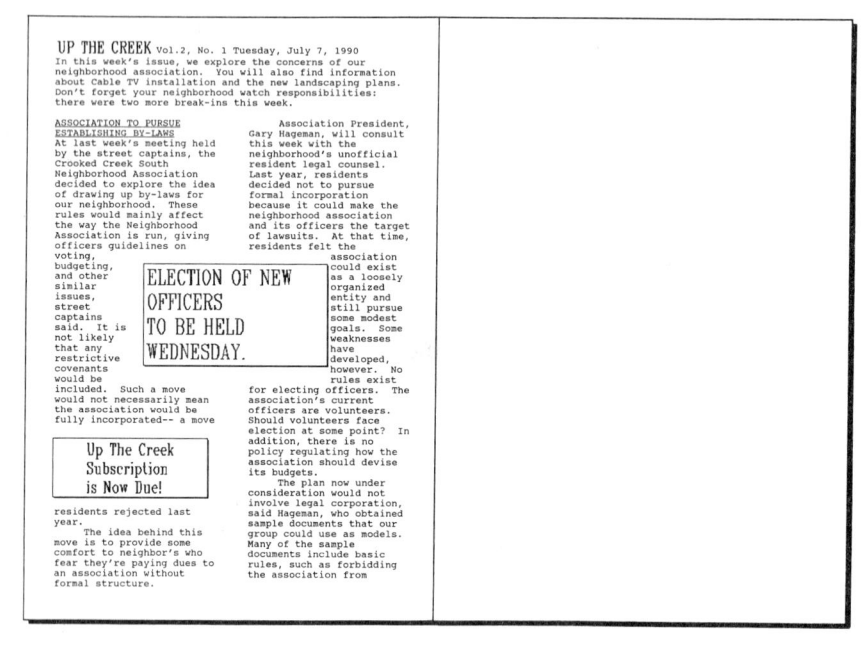

Figure 7.10 Multicolumn document with two absolutely positioned paragraphs.

(Note: If you have trouble with the border overlapping or hiding text in the larger font, insert additional space by placing the text on separate lines with the **Enter** keypress.) Next, choose the **Position** command from the Format menu or press **Alt,T,O**. To center the paragraph, set the Horizontal position to **Centered** and **Page** and the Vertical position to **Centered** and **Page**. Leave the Distance From Text option with the 0.13" default value. Set the Paragraph Width at **3"** now. The completed Position dialog for the centered paragraph is shown in Figure 7.11. To apply the absolute position, click **OK** or press **Enter**. Remember, to view how the positioned object will look prior to printing, switch to Page View mode.

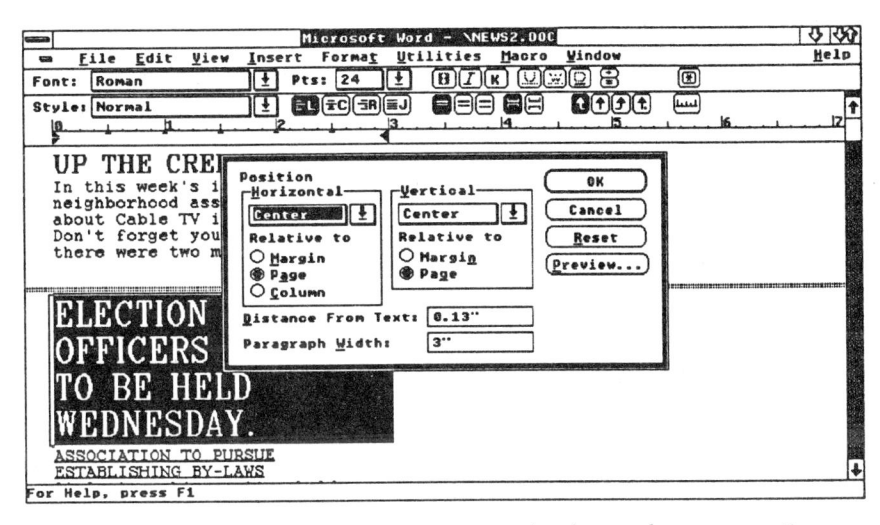

Figure 7.11 To absolutely center a paragraph, choose the center options relative to the page.

You absolutely position the second paragraph in much the same way. Enter the text and format it in 18-pt Times Roman Bold. Next, place a shadow border around it and then select the paragraph and choose the **Position** command. As shown in Figure 7.12, select **Left**

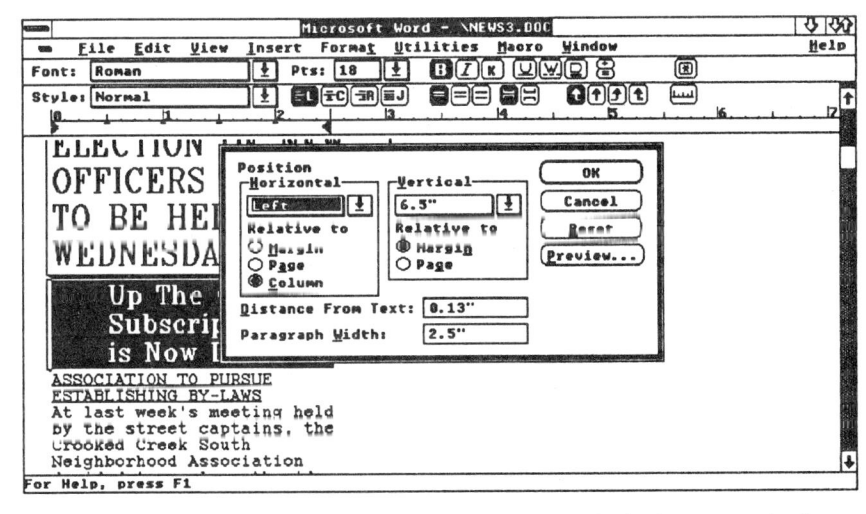

Figure 7.12 You can enter a value in the Vertical edit box instead of selecting the standard options.

The Basics

relative to **Column** for the Horizontal position, and enter **6.5"** in the Vertical edit box relative to the **Margin** for the Vertical position. Enter the Paragraph Width as **2.5"** and the Distance From Text as **.13"**. Click **OK** or press **Enter** to apply the absolute formatting, and you will be returned to your document. Choose Print Preview or Page View to see how your finished document will appear with your positioned paragraphs.

Deleting the Absolute Positioning

Once you format your objects with absolute positioning, it's just as easy to remove the positioning formats. First select the object and return the horizontal and vertical positions to their original settings. For example, select the object, choose Format Position to open the Position dialog box, and then reset the following options as needed:

Horizontal Position—Left
Vertical Position—Inline
Paragraph Width—Auto

Once you've selected the above formats, choose OK or press Enter and the paragraph will return to its previous positioning.

Working with Bound Documents

If your document will be bound, it's a good idea to plan the size and layout of the document in advance. For example, it is likely that you will need a little extra gutter (or gutter margin): additional space added to the right margin of even-numbered pages and the left margin of odd-numbered pages. The purpose of the gutter margin itself is to allow for additional space so the document can be bound in some way, such as with a three-hole punch and three-ring binder.

There are two general situations for formatting your document to accommodate additional spacing for binding. The first case is the easier to handle. For example, if your document is to be printed only on one side, simply create a larger left margin. Generally, an extra 1/2" of space will do just fine. To do this, adjust the left margin by creating a 1/2" gutter. Figure 7.13 illustrates a gutter margin of 1/2" while the following steps accomplish this task:

7—Formatting Complex Documents

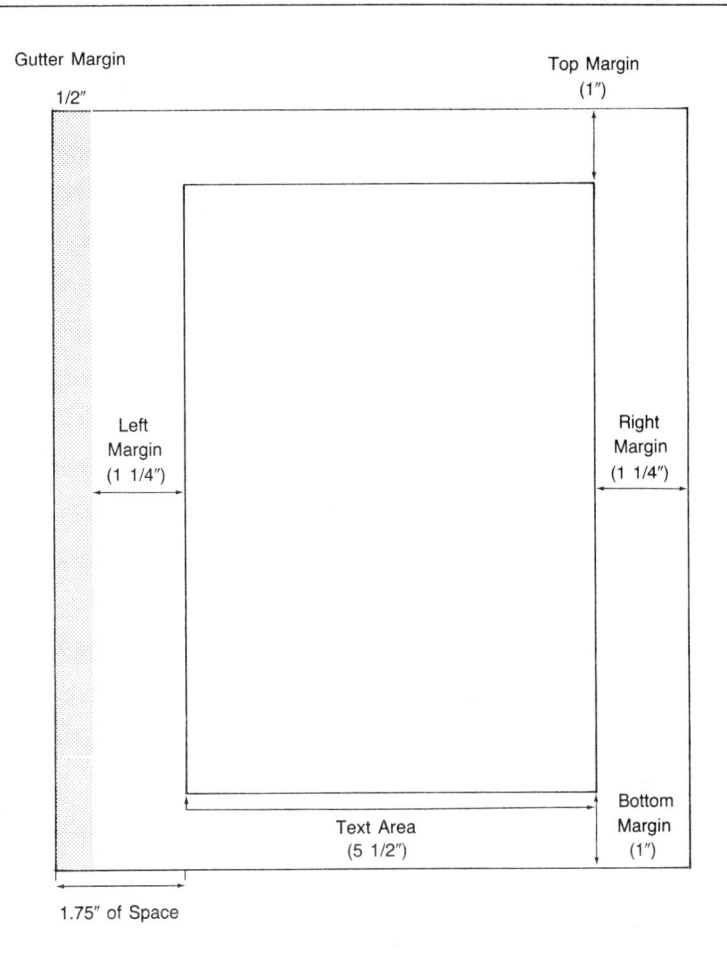

```
Gutter Margin                    Top Margin
   1/2"                             (1")

        ┌─────────────────────────────┐
        │                             │
        │                             │
        │                             │
   Left │                             │ Right
 Margin │                             │ Margin
(1 1/4")│                             │(1 1/4")
        │                             │
        │                             │
        │                             │
        │                             │  Bottom
        └─────────────────────────────┘ Margin
              Text Area                   (1")
              (5 1/2")

  1.75" of Space
```

Figure 7.13 The gutter margin of a document printed on one side.

1. Choose the **Document** command from the Format menu (**Alt,T,D**).	The Document command dialog box appears.
2. Move to the Gutter box (**Alt+G**) and enter the measurement for the amount of space to be added to the left margin. If for example, the Left margin value is 1.25", then entering a value of **.5"** in the Gutter edit box will create a total amount of 1.75" of space between the left edge of your paper and the text.	The space measurement you enter in the Gutter edit box replaces the 0" default value.

The Basics

3. Choose **OK** or press **Enter**.   The Document dialog window closes and the Gutter margin is now added to the left margin for your binding.

As you can see, adjusting the gutter for binding is no problem. Suppose, though, you need to print a document on both sides, creating facing pages with potentially different gutters. To do this, you can use the Mirror Margins option on the Document command to determine the margin sizes for both odd and even numbered pages so that the facing pages will use the same margin space. Obviously, if you set the size of both left and right margins to be the same, you would have no problem. This is not often the case, unfortunately.

Word uses the odd-numbered page as the "master page." Therefore, begin your page layout design for binding double-sided pages with page 1.

Strictly speaking, the gutter is the space between the left edge of your paper and the left margin on odd pages and the right edge and right margin on even pages. Your text may actually be indented from the left margin itself, giving an appearance of a larger left margin, and thus a larger gutter. It is clearer to use the terms *inside margins* and *outside margins*. These terms correspond to the margins that run along the inside edge of a page—which is next to the binding—and the outside of the page. The inside margin, then, always refers to the left margin of an odd-numbered page and the right margin of an even-numbered page. In fact, you will notice that when you choose the Mirror Margins option, the Left and Right Margins edit boxes will indeed change to read "Inside" and "Outside," respectively. Thus, to create binding space for pages that will be printed on both sides, use the following steps:

1. Choose the **Document** command from the Format menu or press **Alt,T,D**.   The Document dialog window appears once again.

2. Since you are printing on both sides of your pages, move to the Mirror Margins option by pressing **Alt+I**.   The Left and Right options now read Inside and Outside.

3. You have an option here. You can either move to the Gutter box and enter additional space, or the easier method is to simply move to the Inside margin edit box (**Alt+N**) and type the amount of space that you wish reserved for the binding. In

230

other words, if you wish to have a space of about 1 3/4" where an extra 1/2" is added for the binding to the default margin size, enter **1.75"** in the box.

4. Click **OK** or press **Enter**.

The dialog window is closed and your margin gutters are set for pages to be printed on both sides. Figure 7.14 illustrates such an example.

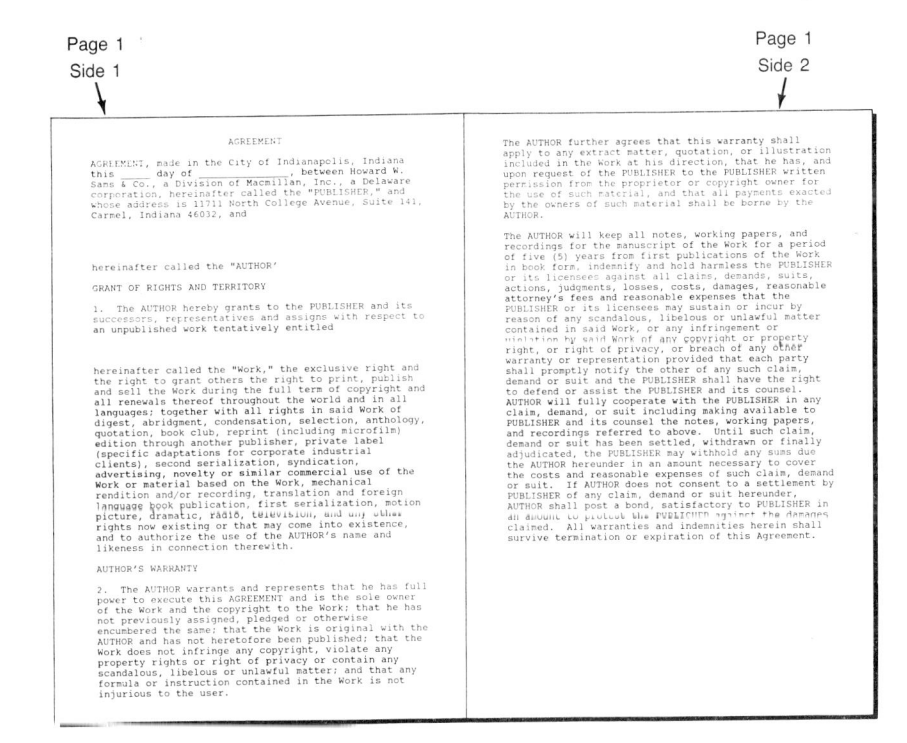

Figure 7.14 Even- and odd-numbered pages with mirrored margins.

As you learn more about Word's formatting functions, you will have additional elements that you might wish to add to your documents. You might add a header or footer, which requires additional space at the top or bottom margin, for example, or you might want to leave room for a particularly nifty graphic. The key is to plan ahead. With Word's formatting tools you can easily solve many of the problems that crop up, but some common sense and planning will save you a lot of time.

Using Page View

In Chapter 1 you were introduced to both Print Preview and Page View—two of Word's more enticing features. In Chapter 8, we'll discuss Print Preview in greater detail. Since Page View offers the ability to do last-minute editing and formatting on any type of document (simple or complex), and further, lets you see the exact result immediately, it is appropriate to explore this feature now.

Although Print Preview gives you an idea of the overall appearance of your documents before you print them out, you cannot edit or see any of the detail up close unless you choose the Page View option (or Page View button from Print Preview mode). Page View, like Print Preview, displays your document just as it will appear when printed. Page View is not a reduced version, but rather a full-sized view of your text as it appears on your screen and as it will appear when it's printed out. Thus, Page View will likely display only a portion of the document on the screen at any one time.

Similar in size to the standard Normal Editing View, Page View shows all the elements of your document that are unavailable in Normal Editing View, including page numbers, headers or footers, multi-column text, and pictures or graphics (see the example in Figure 7.8). Page View allows you to make last-minute editing and formatting changes in the document without returning to Normal Editing View. In other words, you can enter text, cut and paste, or reformat your document and get immediate visual feedback on exactly how your document will look before you print. Page View is your magic wand.

If you can do all the editing and formatting of text directly in Page View, why not just skip Normal Editing View altogether? Since Page View builds a final product exactly as it will look, it requires more time to finish the product than Normal Editing View does. So, use Normal Editing View when you need to work quickly. Use Print Preview to check the overall appearance of an entire document page. Once you are satisfied with the general page layout, switch to Page View to make the final adjustments or editing changes before you print your document.

To access Page View, you can first choose the Print Preview command and then click the Page View button. You can also go directly into Page View from Normal Editing View by choosing the Page View command from the Document menu or by typing Alt,V,P. In fact, the Page View command acts as a toggle between Page View and Normal Editing View. When you are working in Page View, the Page View command is checked inside the Document menu. To turn off Page View and return to Normal Editing View, choose Page View again (and the check mark will disappear).

Because Word remembers where it was last, if you choose Print Preview from Page View and then close or cancel the Print Preview command, you'll be returned to Page View. You can always double-check to see if you are in Page View by looking for the checkmark next to the command in the Document menu.

Working in Page View

Working in Page View is similar to, but slower than, working in Normal Editing View; all of the same commands are available. The difference is that when you make changes in Page View, you can see how these changes will affect the layout of your printed document. These features appear on screen in Page View, and not in Normal Editing View:

- Headers and Footers—Word moves the insertion point to the appropriate header or footer area instead of opening a header or footer pane. For more information on headers and footers, see Chapter 9.
- Line Numbers—Line numbers appear along the left side of the document.
- Multiple columns—Complex documents that use multiple columns appear in their snaking format rather than a single column.
- Footnotes—When you choose the Insert Footnote command, Word opens an appropriate area in the document (and moves the insertion point to that area) instead of opening a footnote pane. For more information on footnotes, see Chapter 18.
- Absolutely positioned paragraphs and pictures—Text will flow around the fixed position.

The Page View Screen

When working in Page View, you will notice some additional changes. For example, if you turn on the Text Boundaries option from the View Preferences dialog box, Word distinguishes individual text areas on the page by placing a dotted line around those areas. All the

The Basics

different areas on your page are considered to be separate text items, rather than a single column of text area delineated by the top, bottom, left, and right margins. To illustrate, refer to Figure 7.15 where the sample newsletter that we created previously now appears with boundary lines to separate the individual text areas. Remember, with the View Preferences Boundaries option active, all possible elements of a complex document, including headers and footers, absolutely positioned objects, tables, graphics, and so on, would be bordered. As we learn more about adding the elements just mentioned, remember to use Page View to give you a "visual" of how your document page is divided into separate text areas.

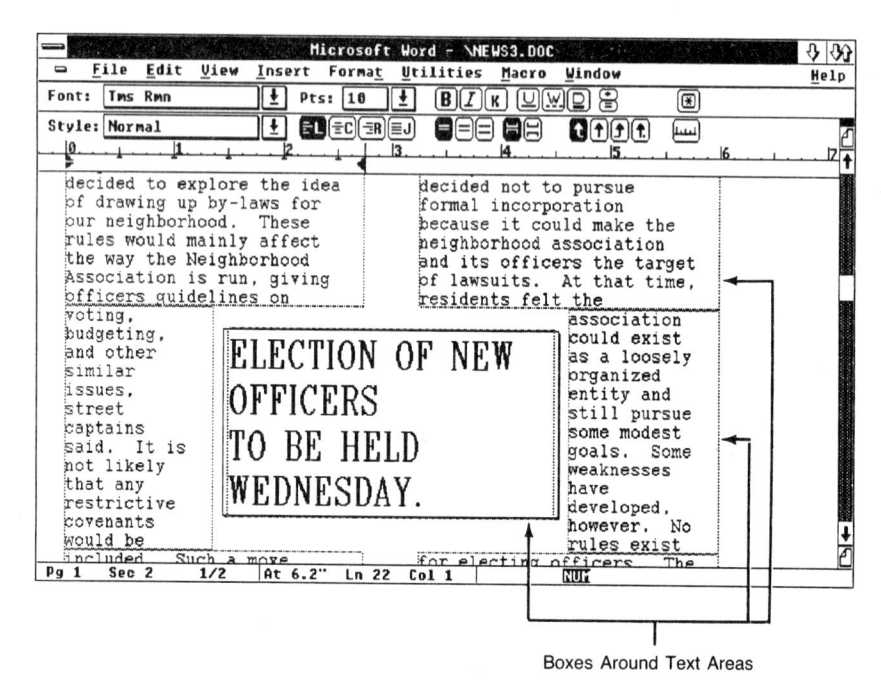

Figure 7.15 Page View allows you to view different elements of your document as separate text areas.

Selecting and Editing Text in Page View

Editing in Page View is just the same as editing in Normal Editing View. All of Word's editing tools are available to you in either. The

7—Formatting Complex Documents

primary difference between the two is that any changes that you make appear in Page View exactly as they will appear when the document is printed. There is one exception: If any editing or formatting changes cause the text to exceed the current page, you must choose the Repaginate Now option found on the Utilities menu. This command only repaginates through the current page so any page that you are currently looking at in Page View will reflect correct pagination through that page. If you want the document beyond that point to be correctly paginated, choose the Background Repagination option in the View Preferences command.

Another feature of Page View involves selecting text. Since all elements in your document are divided into individual areas, Word provides the Alt+up arrow key and Alt+down arrow key combinations to allow you to select the next or previous text areas on your document page. These keys are handy for moving quickly through the various elements on your page. If your document consists of multiple columns, you can use the Alt+left and right arrow keys to move from one column to another.

Finally, note that the Ruler in Page View now aligns its zero point with the left boundary of the current selected text area. This feature allows you to change the individual paragraph format settings (e.g., indents on documents that contain multiple-column documents).

Navigating Around Page View

When you first choose Page View, Word will display at the top of the window the main text area of the current paragraph, from the first line down. If your document has a header, that area will not appear since it is located above the top margin. To view the remaining areas of your document, you can use the mouse to click on the horizontal or vertical scroll bars (if active, of course). As you scroll down the vertical bar, you can bring into view a different page. The new page is separated by a shaded portion of the screen that depicts the edges of your document page instead of the horizontal dotted page breaks that you see in Normal Editing View. As you scroll vertically, the bottom edge of the current page disappears while the top edge of the next page comes into view. To move quickly up or down one entire page at a time, use Word's paging icons which are located at the top and bottom of the vertical scroll bar. Clicking one of these icons (they look like a page with one edge folded down) will move the insertion point to the beginning of that page.

Review

In this chapter you learned:

1. To create more complex documents, you may wish to divide your document into sections. With Word's Format Section command, you can easily format sections individually.

2. A section can be any size: a single line, a single page, or an entire document.

3. The Format Section command provides five distinct functions: With it, you can control the number of columns, specify the starting point of new sections, specify where footnotes will be printed, turn on line numbers for the current section, and set the vertical alignment of the current section.

4. To divide your document into sections, move the insertion point where you want the section break to appear, and then choose the Break command from the Insert menu. Word provides four types of section breaks: next page, even page, add page, and continuous.

5. A section mark appears on your screen as a double dotted line. To remove a section mark, move the insertion point to the selection bar on the left side of your screen, select the section mark, and then press the Delete key.

6. To create a section with multiple columns, use the Columns option in the Format Section dialog box. In Normal Editing View, your text appears as a single narrow column instead of the number of columns specified in the Number edit box. To see exactly how the columns will look, either print the document or choose Page View. You can also see the effect of columnar printing in Print Preview.

7. Line numbers are not visible on-screen in Normal Editing View. Only when a document is printed can you see them. Line numbers are common only for certain types of documents, such as those used by the legal profession.

8. The Format Position command is an advanced document-design tool that you can use to place a block of text, a table, or a picture anywhere on a page and flow text around it. In other words, this feature lets you absolutely position text or pictures on a document page.

9. The first step of using the Position command is to select the text or picture. Positioned objects are surrounded with a frame of dotted lines. Only visible in Print Preview (or in Page View with the Boundaries option turned on in View Preferences), these lines will not print when the document is printed.

10. To remove an absolute positioning format from an object, you must select the object and then return the horizontal and vertical positions to their original settings via the Format Position dialog box.

11. For documents that will be bound together, add a gutter to the margin. This is accomplished with the Format Document command's Gutter box option. If your document is printed on both sides, you use the Mirror Margins option on the Document command to determine the margin sizes for both odd- and even-numbered pages.

12. You can use Page View to complete any last-minute editing and formatting before you print out your documents. Since Page View builds a final product (including any pictures, absolutely positioned objects, etc.), it requires more time to finish the product than Normal Editing View does.

E I G H T

Chapter

Printing Essentials

In this chapter:

- Introduction to Printing with Word
- Setting Up Printing Capability
- Using the Printer Setup Command
- Using the Print Command
- Cancelling Printing
- Printing Problems
- Using Print Preview

In the typical writing process, you first create the text, edit that text using Word's surplus of editing features, and then format the text from the document level to the character level. This chapter discusses the last step in the writing process, printing. Once your computer system is properly connected to your printer, the printing process is a simple one.

Introduction to Printing with Word

After you begin to finalize your documents, you soon will want to print those documents as hard copy with a printer. In this chapter, you will learn about printing your documents, installing your printer to work with Word, changing among various printers, and using the print options available to you. To begin, let's look at those print options:

- Printing Documents—This option is probably the one you will use most often. Later in this chapter, you will learn how to print an entire document, a single page, a specific page range, or a block of pages. You can also choose a document template and print it while it is still active on the screen.
- Printing Style Sheets—Word enables you to print a copy of a style sheet so that you can use it as a reference to all the styles used for that document. Style Sheets are covered in Chapter 13.
- Printing Glossaries—You can print a list of glossary entries in alphabetical order in order to see all the glossary entries and their contents at once. Word's Glossary feature is discussed in Chapter 12.
- Printing Annotations—Similar to other printing options, you can print a list of all annotations attached to your document by others. For more information on using annotations, see Chapter 14.
- Printing Summary Information—To get accurate information concerning the date, time, and contents of your current document, after it has printed you can print the summary information sheet.
- Printing Key Assignments—If you customize your keyboard layout, it's a good idea to print out a hard copy of the new key assignments. This option lets you do just that. Customizing Word is discussed in Chapter 19.
- Printing Hidden Text—If you have text that is formatted as hidden, you can tell Word to print that text. Examples of hidden text might include the fields for index and table of contents entries. You will learn more about hidden text in Chapter 14.
- Printing Field Codes—Word provides you with the option of printing field codes instead of just field results. You use this feature to analyze unexpected printing results.

To learn about printing mailing labels, see Chapter 16.

As you can see, Word provides many print options. In this chapter, however, we'll focus on printing your documents (and related summary information sheets) and portions of your documents. We'll hold off on our discussion of the remaining options (style sheets, glossaries, annotations, key assignments, hidden text, and field codes) until later, although you'll find that the methods for printing any of the options are similar.

The Basics of Setting Up Your Printer

Now that we have whetted your interest, let's preview the steps to complete before you are ready to print. Although we'll discuss each step in detail shortly, an overview is important because people seem to have more trouble with their printers than any other feature of word processing. Once you understand the basics, you should be able to predict and/or troubleshoot most problems. We can summarize the basic steps as follows:

1. Install the *printer driver*—This step was generally accomplished when you first installed Word for Windows. During the Word setup procedure, Word asked if you would like to install the necessary printer drivers (a software file that provides correct printing instructions) so that your computer could communicate with your printer. If you completed this step, and selected your printer to work with Word (see step 2), then you can choose the Print command from the File menu, make your selections, and begin printing documents. You'll find Word's default settings suitable for most simple documents.

    Now, suppose you didn't install the printer driver during the setup procedure. Don't worry. You can still add the necessary printer driver file and thus complete this necessary step. In the sections that follow, we'll go over the necessary steps to install a printer (and the necessary printer driver) to your computer system.

2. Choosing a printer—Word allows you to install more than one printer driver at a time. This feature enables you to quickly switch between different printers. Once you decide on which printer to use mainly, however, you must connect that printer to your computer, and, most important, tell Word where that printer is connected to your computer system (i.e., at which port your printer cable is connected to your computer).

3. Checking the Printer Setup options—This step need not be taken in order to complete most simple printing requirements. Choosing the correct printer driver and printer port, as discussed in steps 1 and 2, are more important. However, if you decide to change certain default settings that affect the overall appearance of a document—such as the orientation, or direction, of printing—you'll need to use the File Printer Setup option.

The Basics

Unless you are planning to change printers or other setup procedures, you only have to complete the steps above once. If you are confident your printer is already installed properly with your computer (and you don't wish to modify your printer's setup options), you can skip to the section, "Using the Print Command." If you have not yet installed your printer, or you wish to set up your computer to work with a different printer, read the next two sections. If you thought you installed your printer properly and you still can't print your documents, you should review the following sections and the "Printing Problems" section.

Setting Up Printing Capability

Hundreds of printers will work with Word. If you plan to use a printer, be sure to read the printer user's manual thoroughly.

Installing Your Printer Driver

The first step of setting up your printer is to install the appropriate printer driver file. A printer driver file provides the instructions that your computer will need in order to communicate with the printer. The printer driver also contains the fonts that are available for that printer as well as any sheet feeder options.

Printer driver files are identified by the extension, DRV. When you install printer driver files, you copy those files to a specific directory on your hard disk. Then, when you are ready to select a printer driver file that matches your printer, you select the file by choosing the name of your printer from a dialog box. Your first step is to locate the directory and/or disk drive where the printer driver file is stored.

During setup procedures, when you installed Word, you were given the opportunity to install printer driver files. If you haven't installed any printer driver files, Word will "beep" and provide an error message indicating so when you try to print. If you have installed one or more printer driver files, those files will be listed in a dialog box along with a list of available fonts or font cartridges. Finally, if you wish to add a new printer driver file that you have not installed (copied to a specific directory on your hard disk), you will need to insert the Utilities diskette (or a separate "Printers" diskette)

8—Printing Essentials

containing that printer driver file into the disk drive and then choose that disk drive to access the file.

Now that you have an idea of the function and importance of printer driver files, you can use the following steps to install your printer driver:

1. Choose the **Run** command from the Word Control menu or press **Alt,Spacebar,U**.

   The Control menu appears.

2. Click the **Control Panel** option or press **P** from the keyboard. Then, click **OK** or press **Enter**.

   The Control Panel dialog window appears as shown in Figure 8.1.

3. To install a new printer, choose the **Add New Printer** option from the Installation menu. You can use the mouse or press **Alt,I,N** from the keyboard.

   Word provides a new dialog box requesting more information. Note that the A drive has been selected by default.

Microsoft will place printer driver files either on a Printers diskette or on the Utilities diskettes.

4. In the edit box, type the name of the disk drive and directory where the appropriate printer driver files are located. You must determine which drive, directory, and/or disk contains the proper .DRV file for the printer that you want to add. If the printer drivers (the .DRV files) are stored on a separate disk (generally a Utilities disk), you must insert that disk into drive A (or the drive specified in the edit box). Once you have specified the proper drive and/or directory and, if necessary, inserted the disk containing the .DRV files into the specified drive, select **OK** or press **Enter**.

   If you enter the wrong directory or drive, or you insert a disk that does not contain the printer driver files, Word will provide a message that indicates "printer files not found." If you enter the correct location, then Word provides yet another dialog box showing the printer driver files available on the directory or disk.

243

The Basics

5. Select the printer that you want to add, and choose the **Add** command or press **Alt+A**.

   Another dialog box will ask you to specify the drive or directory to which you want to copy the printer driver file.

6. This step gives you the opportunity to move the selected printer driver file. If the file is in a directory that is different from the directory or location where you normally store those files, choose **Yes** or press **Alt+Y**. If it is in the proper directory already, choose **No** or press **Alt+N**. If you try to move the file to a directory that doesn't already exist, Word will give you an error message.

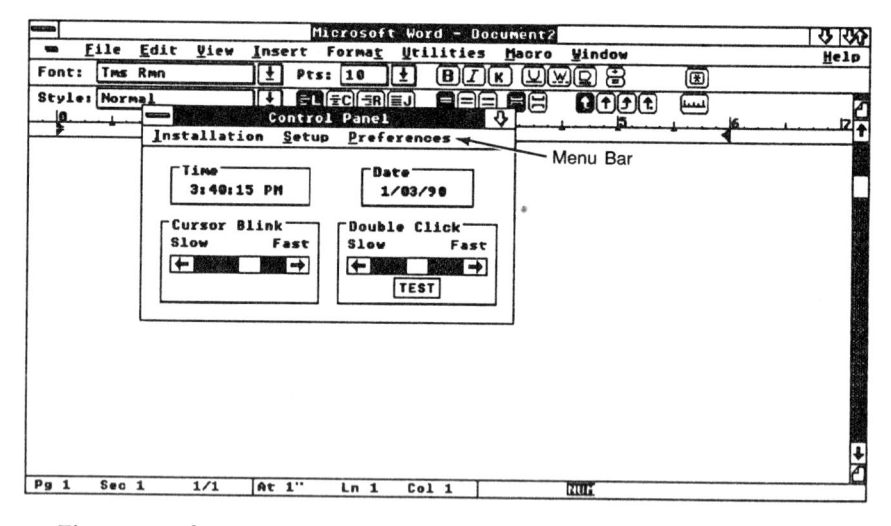

Figure 8.1 The Control Panel dialog window.

Connecting Your Printer to Your Computer

Now that you have installed your printer driver files, you must complete the next set of steps to tell the computer and Word at which

8—Printing Essentials

port on the back of the computer the printer is connected. You do this with the Connections command on the Setup menu as follows:

1. The Control Panel window must be activated first, if you closed it after step 6 above. If necessary, press **Alt,Spacebar,U**. Open the Setup menu from the Control Panel window and select the **Connections** command. Use the mouse or press **Alt,S,C**.

    The Setup Connections dialog window appears, as shown in Figure 8.2.

2. Select both your printer and the connection where the printer is hooked up to your computer, and then click **OK** or press **Enter**. For example, if you are using a Laser printer and it's connected to the LPT1 port, choose that printer and that port connection. If you are changing printers and the port that you wish to use is already assigned to another printer, you must first select the old printer and choose the NONE connection option. This step will free up the port so you can now connect the new printer.

    Once you click OK, the hard disk will copy the necessary information, and in a few moments, you are returned to the Control Panel window.

3. Choose the **Printer** command from the Setup menu with the mouse or press **Alt,S,P**. This option allows you to set a printer as the default printer you will use most of the time. You can, of course, return to the Setup menu and temporarily switch to a different printer. Once you're satisfied with the printer selection, click **OK** or press **Enter**.

    You are returned to the Setup menu again.

215

The Basics

4. This step is only necessary if you are using a serial printer (i.e., connected to a serial or COM port, instead of a parallel or LPT1 or such port). If you're using a serial printer, choose the **Communications** command from the Setup menu with the mouse or press **Alt,S,M**. If you are using a parallel printer, skip this step.

5. Select all necessary communications settings and enter the baud rate; use your printer's user's manual to provide the correct settings. When finished, choose **OK** or press **Enter** and your printer is ready to go!

The Communications dialog box appears.

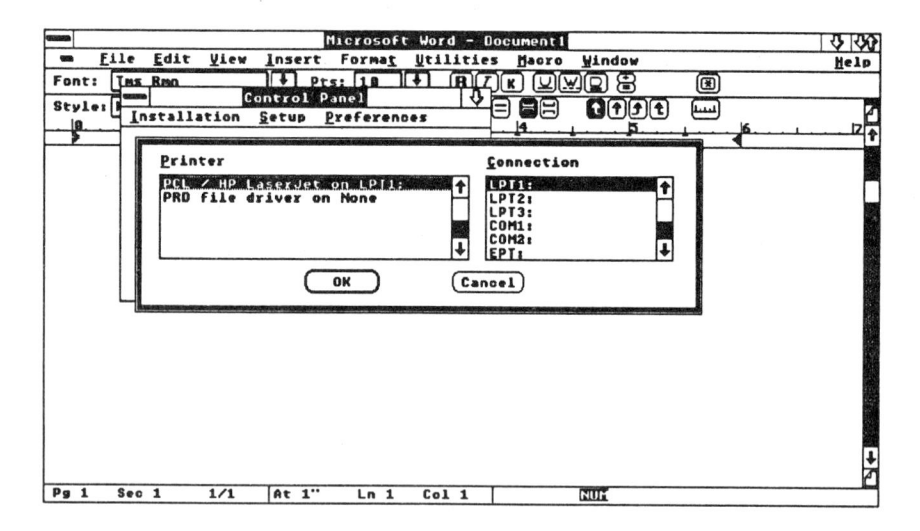

Figure 8.2 Use the Setup Connections command to properly connect your printer to the appropriate printer port.

Choosing Another Printer

Once you have copied the necessary printer driver files to a Window's directory on your hard disk, you can switch from one printer type to another. To do this, you pull down the File menu and select the **Printer Setup** command with the mouse or press **Alt,F,R**. Printer Setup tells the computer at which port your printer is connected, and which printer is available to you. As soon as you add printer driver files to a Word directory on your hard disk, Printer Setup communicates between Windows (and DOS) and your applications to let you know which resources are available. Thus, to change from one printer to another, do this:

If the printer type that you wish to change to doesn't appear in the Printer Setup window, you need to add it by installing the printer driver file in Windows as discussed previously.

1. Select **Printer Setup** from the Format menu or press **Alt,F,R**.

2. From the list of available printers, select the printer that you wish to use and then click **OK** or press **Enter**. Please note that if you select a laser printer, you may need to select a specific font cartridge as well.

The Printer Setup dialog appears as shown in Figure 8.3.

Clicking OK will return you to the document window. You have successfully changed printers. For further modification of printer output, you might need to change printing options via the Printer Setup option, which is described shortly.

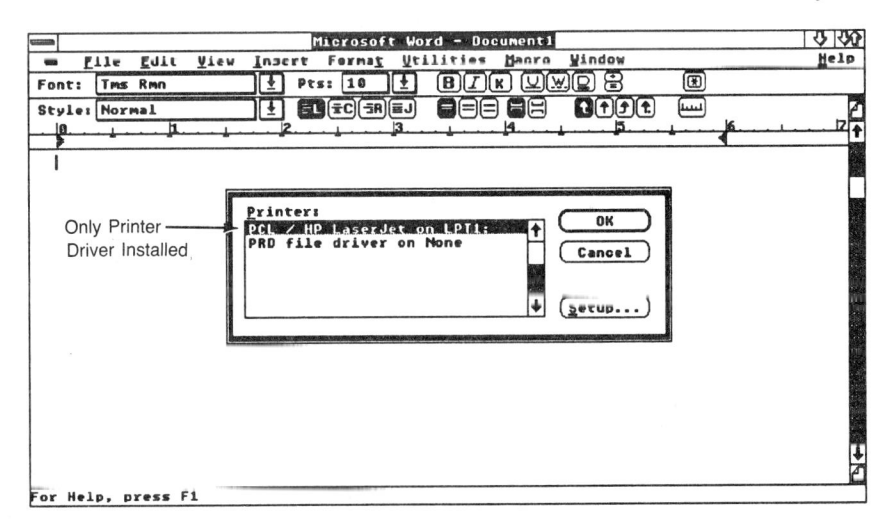

Figure 8.3 Use the Printer Setup command from the File menu to switch between printers.

The Basics

Remember, your computer only knows what you tell it: The printer that you are trying to send to must be connected to the appropriate printer port, turned on, properly loaded with paper, the select light turned on (if applicable), and the proper printer resource selected with the Printer Setup command. If you give your computer erroneous instructions, you'll get an error message and the printer won't be able to print your document.

Deleting a Printer

It's even easier to delete a printer than it is to add a new one. To do this, simply access the Control Panel by selecting the **Run** command from the Word Control Menu with the mouse or pressing **Alt,Spacebar,U**. From the Control Panel, open the Installation menu and choose the **Delete Printer** command. A dialog box will appear listing all the printers that you have installed. Select the one that you wish to remove and then choose **Delete**. Another dialog box will appear that shows the location (directory or drive) of the printer driver file that you have selected for deletion. Confirm your decision by choosing **Yes**.

One note about Windows and Word. If you delete a printer driver file that is used by more than one printer, the printer driver file is not removed, but the printer reference itself will be. This feature leaves the printer driver file intact for the other printer.

Using the Printer Setup Command

Use the Printer Setup command to choose printing options corresponding to the type of printer you are using. When you choose Printer Setup, you will see the Printer dialog window (Figure 8.3). This is the initial window that lists the printers that you have installed.

At the bottom of the initial window is the Setup option button. Click this option with the mouse or press **Alt+S** from the keyboard and you will get the Output Mode dialog window. Which Output Mode window appears depends upon the type of printer that you have currently selected. For example, Figure 8.4 shows the Output Mode window of an Epson LQ850 printer while Figure 8.5 shows the Output Mode window of a LaserJet Plus II. As you can see from the figures, the printing options will be specific to your printer. The specifications for many of these options, such as the type of paper for width and height, quality of printing, and graphics resolution, will depend on the information contained in the printer driver file for that specific printer. Although many of these options seem self-explanatory, you should consult your printer's user's manual for additional information.

Most versions of the Output Mode will contain the option for the direction of the printing—called *orientation*. This option is discussed next.

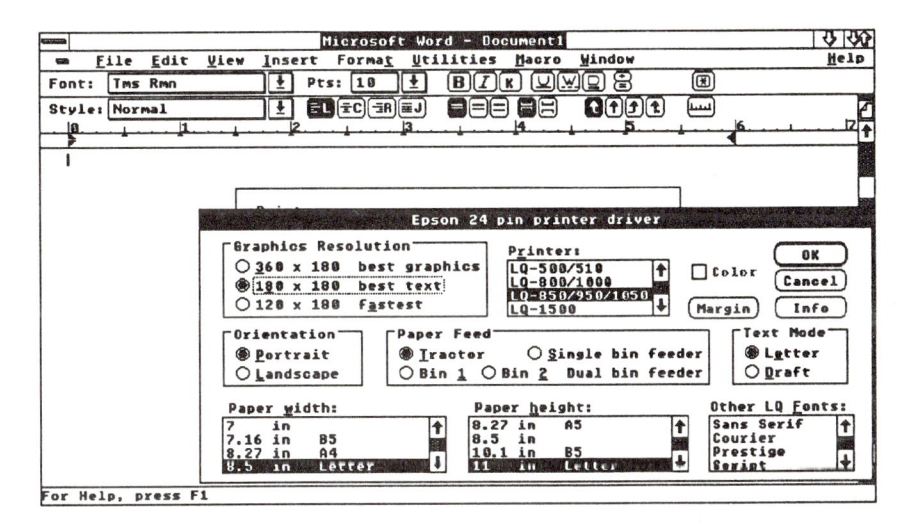

Figure 8.4 The Output Mode window of an Epson LQ850 Printer.

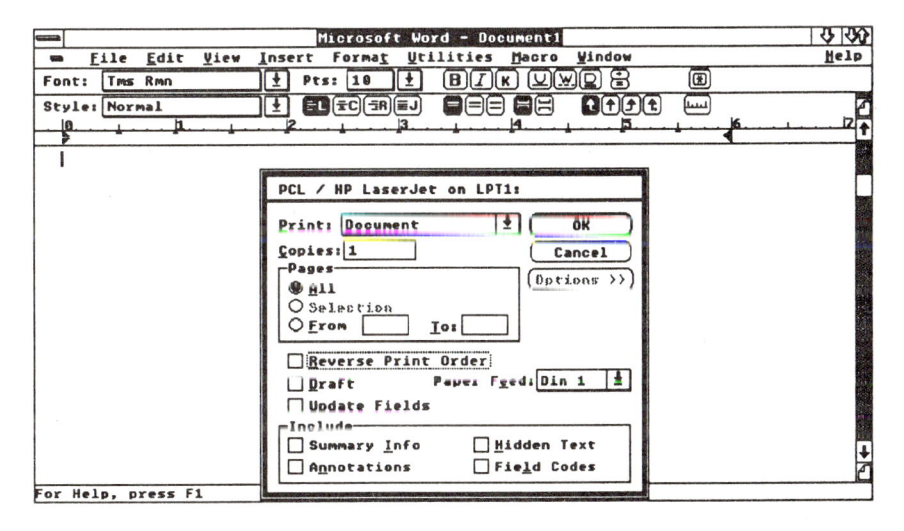

Figure 8.5 The Output Mode window of a LaserJet Plus II Printer.

Orientation

It is likely that most of your printing will be printed across the width of the page, which is Word's default value. But, you also have the option of printing lines of text sideways across the length of the page to accommodate "wide" page designs (you can do this with many types of printers). These two settings are referred to as *Portrait* for the default horizontal setting, and *Landscape* for the sideways page setting. When choosing between Portrait and Landscape printing, please note that the page height and width measurements listed in the Document dialog box of the Format menu must match the orientation of the printing.

You should also note that if you do change the orientation from a Portrait to a Landscape setting, while your margin settings will not need to be changed, the amount of text that "appears" across the page as you read it will increase, and so, you'll need to rotate your paper 90 degrees to read the document straight out of the printer. Only the orientation changes as the margins pertain to the edges of your paper. In other words, the left and right margins of a document that is printed in Landscape mode, will correspond to a page that is 11" wide instead of 8 1/2" wide on a standard US business-letter page (see Figure 8.6). To see how your documents will look in Landscape mode, complete the following steps:

1. Choose **Printer Setup** from the File menu or press **Alt,F,R**.

    The Printer Setup window appears.

2. Click the **Setup** button with the mouse or press **Alt+S**.

    The Output Mode window for your printer appears.

3. Select the **Landscape mode** option with the mouse or press **Alt+N**, and then click **OK** or press **Enter**.

    You are returned to the Printer Setup dialog window.

4. Click **OK** or press **Enter**.

    As a neat feature of Word, a dialog box will appear shortly that asks if you wish to change the current document size to fit on the new page size. Choose Yes and Word will update the format for you. If you choose

5. Choose **Yes** to update the current document size.

No, you must do this manually by choosing the Document command from the Format menu and changing the page size.

You are returned to the document window in Landscape Orientation. To return to Portrait, repeat steps 1–5, except select the Portrait option in step 3 (**Alt + R**) instead of the landscape option.

UP THE CREEK Vol.2, No. 1 Tuesday, July 7, 1990
In this week's issue, we explore the concerns of our neighborhood association. You will also find information about Cable TV installation and the new landscaping plans. Don't forget your neighborhood watch responsibilities: there were two more break-ins this week.

ASSOCIATION TO PURSUE ESTABLISHING BY-LAWS
At last week's meeting held by the street captains, the Crooked Creek South Neighborhood Association decided to explore the idea of drawing up by-laws for our neighborhood. These rules would mainly affect the way the Neighborhood Association is run, giving officers guidelines on voting, budgeting, and other similar issues, street captains said. It is not likely that any restrictive covenants would be included. Such a move would not necessarily mean the association would be fully incorporated-- a move residents rejected last year.
   The idea behind this move is to provide some comfort to neighbor's who fear they're paying dues to an association without formal structure.
   Association President, Gary Hageman, will consult this week with the neighborhood's unofficial resident legal counsel. Last year, residents decided not to pursue formal incorporation because it could make the neighborhood

ELECTION OF NEW OFFICERS TO BE HELD WEDNESDAY.

association and its officers the target of lawsuits. At that time, residents felt the association could exist as a loosely organized entity and still pursue some modest goals. Some weaknesses have developed, however. No rules exist for electing officers. The association's current officers are volunteers. Should volunteers face election at some point? In addition, there is no policy regulating how the association should devise its budgets.
   The plan now under consideration would not involve legal corporation, said Hageman, who obtained sample documents that our group could use as models. Many of the sample documents include basic rules, such as forbidding the association from collecting funds for a pool or club house.

ASSOCIATION ENDS YEAR IN THE BLACK
The neighborhood association finished the year a balance of $90.00 said Association Treasurer Natalie Hageman. Revenue for the year, including membership dues, the street light

Figure 8.6 The Landscape option is used to print text sideways on the page.

Choosing the Landscape option in the Printer Setup dialog box will not "appear" to change the orientation of your text on your screen in Normal Editing View before you print. To see the full effect of printing in Landscape mode, get an audition in Print Preview and then a closer look in Page View.

Using the Print Command

Choosing the Print command from the File menu, or typing Alt,F,P from the keyboard, produces a Print dialog box whose appearance depends upon whether you have selected the Options button to display all the printing options available to you. The initial printing dialog box is shown in Figure 8.7 and the expanded version is shown in Figure 8.8.

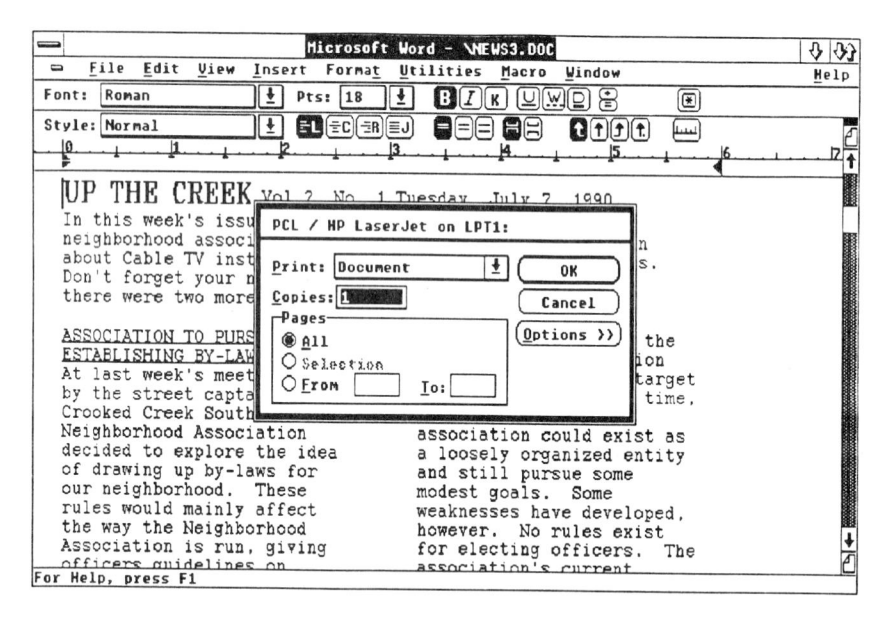

Figure 8.7 The initial Print dialog box.

When you are ready to print, choose the **Print** command, check over the current settings in the dialog box, make the changes you wish, and then click **OK** (or press the **Enter** key). In a moment, a message will appear in the status bar on your screen that printing is in process, and a moment later your printer should begin to print. Be patient, because it sometimes takes a few seconds for the files to be transferred from your computer to the printer before printing begins. If printing doesn't start and the status bar continues to display a message box that says printing is taking place, first check that the Select light is on. If it's turned off, printing won't start. Press it on and printing should begin almost immediately. Once printing does begin, you can cancel printing by pressing the Esc key.

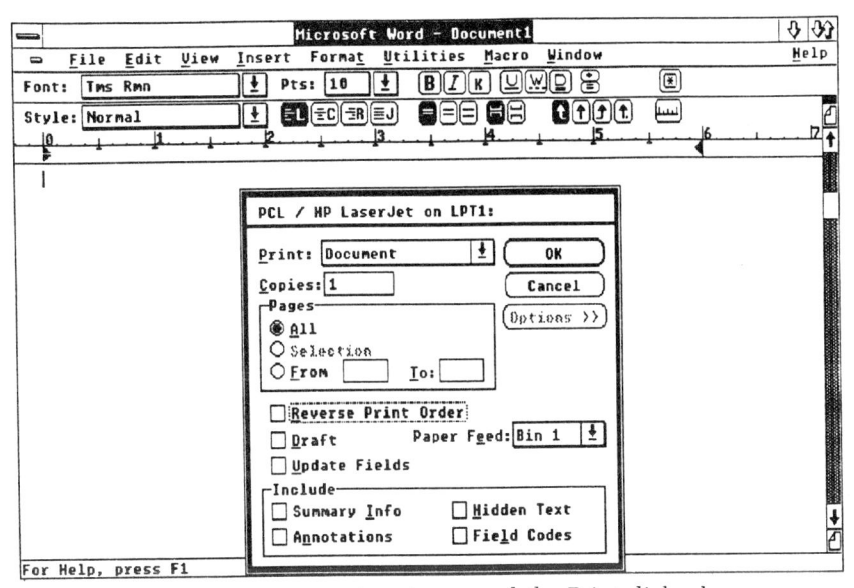

Figure 8.8 Choose options to expand the Print dialog box.

Many of the options that you set in the Print dialog box are standard regardless of which printer you are using. Some options are only available on certain printers.

Word's Printing Options

The currently selected printer and its connection are listed at the top of the Print dialog box. You can choose another printer and its connection via the Printer Setup command on the File menu. In Figure 8.7 you can see the rest of the initial Print dialog box features:

- Print—This pull-down window allows you to select from a list of "what to print" options. These options include: Document, Summary Info, Annotations, Styles, Glossary, and Key Assignments.

- Copies—This edit box allows you to specify how many times to print the document.

- Pages—The pages option allows you to specify exactly which pages to print. You can print an entire document (All), a portion of selected text (Selection), or a specific range of pages (From, To).

The Basics

At the right side of the Print dialog box are the OK button to begin printing, Cancel to close the dialog box without printing, and Options. Choosing the Options button will expand your Print dialog box (see Figure 8.8) to provide these additional printing options:

- Reverse Print Order—Prints your document in reverse order: The last page of your document prints first. This is a handy feature if you want your documents to be in the correct order when you retrieve them from the paper tray. Normally, you would retrieve a five-page document from the paper tray with page 5 on top, then page 4, and so on. With this option on, the pages would print in reverse order so that the top page is page 1. This convenient option does have one drawback. The printing is initially slower since Word must number the document pages all the way to the end before beginning to print.

- Draft—The fastest method of printing your documents. When you select the Draft option, Word does not print any specified character or paragraph formatting. If your printer is capable, character formatting is printed as underlining. Pictures will be displayed as empty box frames. Use Draft mode for a quick review of your text only. As an example of Draft printing the result of printing our previous newsletter is now shown in Figure 8.9. (Notice the lack of character formats and the empty frames.)

- Update Fields—Although some fields are updated automatically by the printing process, this option instructs Word to update all fields prior to printing your document.

- Paper Feed—Corresponds to the type of paper that you use with your printer and how that paper is fed into your printer. For more information, see "The Paper Feed Option," which is discussed shortly.

- Include—Allows you to print additional parts of your document at the same time, including: Summary Information, Annotations, Hidden Text, and Field Codes. For more information, see "Using the Include Option" a little later in this chapter.

If any of the print options appear dim or grey, they are not available with your current selected printer. Further, although Word remembers some options selected in the previous session (even if you turned the computer off), the printing options Page and Copies are exceptions. The Pages option always reverts back to All to indicate

> Vol.2, No. 1 Tuesday, July 7, 1990
>
> In this week's issue, we explore the concerns of our neighborhood association. You will also find information about Cable TV installation and the new landscaping plans. Don't forget your neighborhood watch responsibilities: there were two more break-ins this week.
>
> ASSOCIATION TO PURSUE ESTABLISHING BY-LAWS
>
> At last week's meeting held by the street captains, the Crooked Creek South Neighborhood Association decided to explore the idea of drawing up by-laws for our neighborhood. These rules would mainly affect the way the Neighborhood Association is run, giving officers guidelines on voting, budgeting, and other similar issues, street captains said. It is not likely that any restrictive covenants would be included. Such a move would not necessarily mean the association would be fully incorporated-- a move residents rejected last year.
>
> The idea behind this move is to provide some comfort to neighbor's who fear they're paying dues to an association without formal structure.
>
> Association President, Gary Hageman, will consult this week with the neighborhood's unofficial resident legal counsel. Last year, residents decided not to pursue formal incorporation because it could make the neighborhood association and its officers the target of lawsuits. At that time, residents felt the association could exist as a loosely organized entity and still pursue some modest goals. Some weaknesses have developed, however. No rules exist for electing officers. The association's current officers are volunteers. Should volunteers face election at some point? In addition, there is no policy regulating how the association should devise its budgets.
>
> The plan now under consideration would not involve legal corporation, said Hageman, who obtained sample documents that our group could use as models. Many of the sample documents include basic rules, such as forbidding the association from

(Empty Frames and Space)

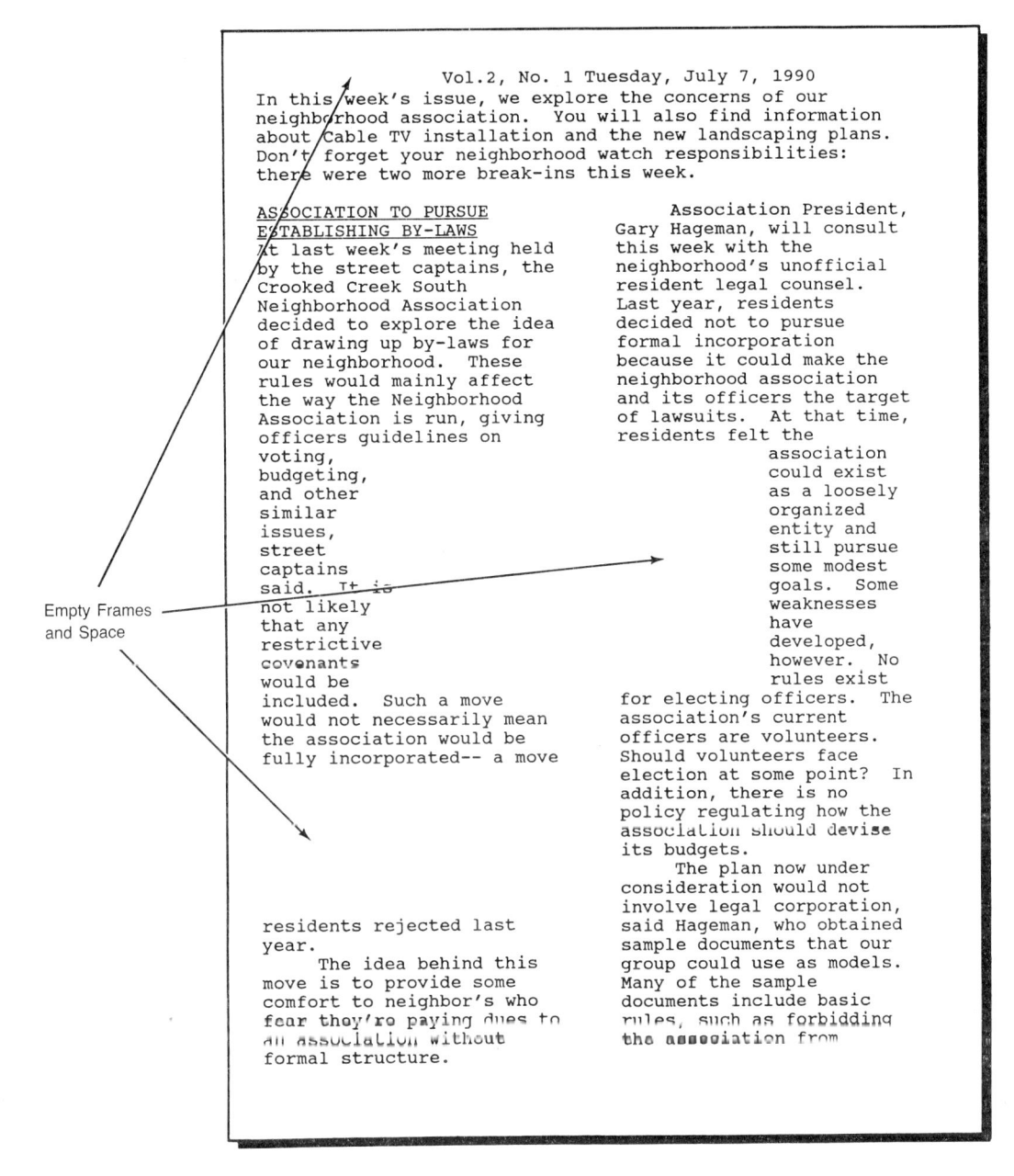

Figure 8.9 Sample text using the Draft Printing option.

that you want to print all pages of the document, and the Copies option always indicates that you want to print a single copy, or 1.

Printing the Entire Working Document

The first step to printing the working document is to make sure that the document that you are currently working on is the one that you wish to print and that it resides in the active window on your screen. Remember, you can open more than one window, and more than one document at a time, but it is only the "active" window, identified by the rules running through the title bar, that will print when you invoke the Print command. If no document appears on your screen, or the wrong document window is active, you must retrieve the appropriate document from the disk by using the Open command and make that file the active window. The steps to print the entire working document in the active window follow.

1. Check to see that the document on your screen is the one that you want to print. It must reside in the active window. If you have more than one window open, click the window that you want to print.

   The active window has horizontal rules running through the title bar.

2. Choose **Print** from the File menu or enter **Alt,F,P** from the keyboard.

   The Print dialog box appears. It will look something like either Figure 8.7 or 8.8 depending upon which printer you are using and whether you have clicked open the Options button.

If printing doesn't occur shortly, be sure the Select light is on. If not, press it and printing should soon begin. If your cables are not properly connected, or the wrong printer is selected with Printer Setup, the computer will display a dialog box that indicates that the printer is not found or is improperly connected.

3. Check the printer options in the Print dialog box. Since you want to print the entire document, the default All in the Print edit box will do just fine.

   The Copies option lists the default value of 1 to indicate that Word will print just one copy of the entire document. Many of the remaining options will be set according to the last print session and will remain the same until you change them.

4. If you are satisfied with all the Print options, click **OK** or press the **Enter** key.

   The status bar depicts a message indicating the status of printing. In a few seconds, the computer will send the file to your printer and printing will begin.

These steps print the entire document, but remember that you do have the option of printing only a portion of the document file.

Printing Specific Pages of Your Document

To print certain pages of your document, use the From and To edit boxes in the Pages section of the Print dialog box to specify a page range. First click the **From** option (**Alt + F**) and enter the page number where you wish the printing to begin. Then click the **To** option (**Alt + T**) and enter the page number where you want it to end. You must enter the page numbers in arabic numerals even if your document is numbered in a different format (e.g., roman numerals). Don't worry: Word will print the correct page numbers.

Finally, If you intend to print only a single page of the document, specify that page by entering the same value in both the From and To edit boxes.

Printing Selected Text Only

Word also gives you the option of printing just a portion of text within a document page. The selected portion can be a single character, a single word or paragraph, or a group of paragraphs. To do this, before you choose the Print command, you must use the mouse or keyboard to select the text that you want to print as if you were selecting text to perform any editing function. Once you've selected the text, the Selection option no longer will appear dim. Click this check box or press **Alt + S**, and click **OK** or press **Enter**. The following steps are used to print selected text.

1. Select the text that you wish to print with the mouse or use the Shift and arrow keys.

    Selected text appears as white letters on a black background.

2. Choose **Print** from the File menu or enter **Alt,F,P**. If you want to print all the selected text, do not change the default value in the Page Range section.

    The Print dialog box appears as before, except the Selection option is now available.

3. Click **Selection** or press **Alt + S**.

    The Selection option appears blackened.

The Basics

    4. Click **OK** or press **Enter**.　　The selected text prints after the file is transferred to the printer in the usual manner. If printing doesn't occur within a few seconds, check to see that both the power light and the Select light are turned on and that your paper is properly aligned. Your computer will alert you if it can't find the specified type of printer.

Printing Multiple Copies

The Copies option lets you print as many copies of a single page as you desire. The default value is one. If you want to print two copies, enter the value 2 in the Copy edit box. If you want to print multiple copies of a document, Word will print the entire document one copy at a time. To print more than one copy:

    1. Choose the **Print** command from the File menu or press **Alt,F,P**.　　The Print dialog box appears.

    2. Type the number of copies that you want to print in the Copies Edit field. If necessary, move to this field by clicking with the mouse or pressing **Alt+C**.　　The default value is 1. The new value will replace this value as you type.

    3. Click **OK** or press **Enter**.　　Shortly, printing will begin.

Printing from Find on the File Menu

Using the *Find* command, you can also use the Print option to print documents directly without opening the document first. If you need to print several unrelated documents, you can select each of them first by dragging across the file names or holding down the Shift key as you click in turn. Once you have highlighted all the files that you want to print, choose the Print option from the File Find dialog box, choose any additional print options as before, and then choose OK to start the printing. The document files themselves will be printed in the order that they appear in the File Find dialog box, from top to bottom. The procedure is as follows:

1. Choose the **Find** command from the File menu or press **Alt,F,F** from the keyboard.

    After choosing the Find command, Word will search for all the available files and then list them in a dialog box as shown in Figure 8.10.

2. From the list window, select the file or files that you wish to print.

    The selected file(s) is highlighted.

3. Choose the **Print** button or press **Alt+P**.

    You are switched from the Find dialog window to the File Print dialog box.

4. Select from any of the standard printing options available to you. Then, click **OK** or press **Enter** to begin printing.

    In a few moments, printing will begin. The status bar provides a message that printing is taking place.

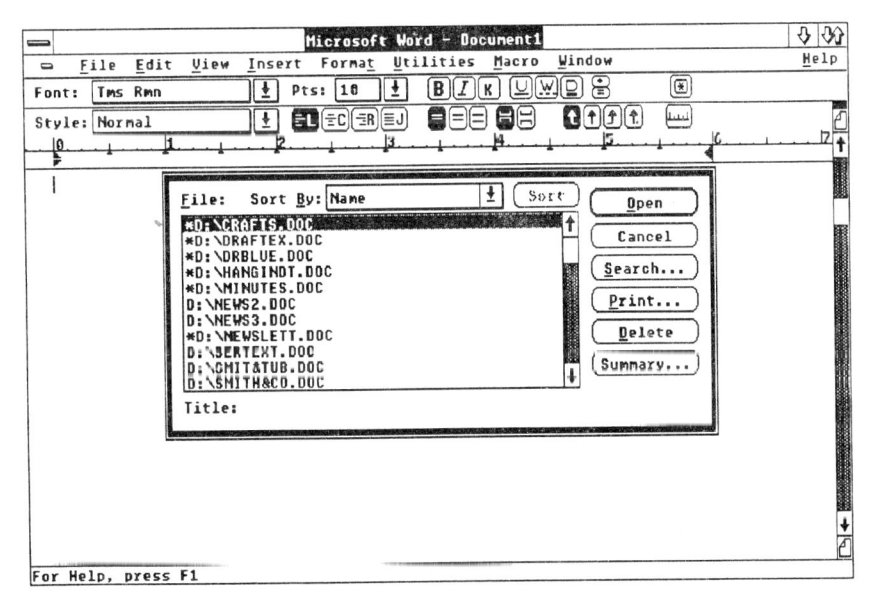

Figure 8.10 Choose the files that you wish to print from the File Find window.

Working While You Print

If you are using a full version of Windows (installed Windows on your hard disk) and not just a run-time version of Word for Windows, you can take advantage of Word's queued printing feature. Queued printing allows you to start the printing of one document while you work on another document. In other words, Windows will set aside some memory in a buffer to store the selected document(s) that you wish to print. This buffer is made available in Windows by the feature known as a *Windows Spooler*.

You can place more than one file in the buffer at a time. When you begin to print, the files in the buffer will print one after another in the order that you selected them. Think of each of the files stored in the buffer as "print jobs." Once you begin the process of queued printing, all of the print jobs will run until no more files are in the spooler's buffer. To cancel printing, at any time, simply press the Esc key, although any portion of a file, once started printing, will print until completed. Keep in mind that, depending upon your computer's memory, queued printing may make Word respond slower.

There are two ways to use Word's Spooler for queued printing. The first method is to set up Word so that every time you use the Print command, you access the Spooler for queued printing. Such a method requires that you first modify your WIN.INI file by setting the option:

    spooler=yes

The option above is completed in the Windows section of the WIN.INI file. For more information on modifying the WIN.INI file so that you can always print using queued printing, refer to your Window's user's manual.

Second, you can use queued printing only occasionally. In other words, if you just want to use queued printing for the current work session, just run the SPOOLER.EXE file from the MS-DOS Executive screen prior to giving the Print command in Word. This is the suggested method for beginners and requires these steps:

1. Start Word, if necessary. | A Word document window appears on your screen.

2. Press **Alt**+**Esc** to switch to the MS-DOS Executive screen. | The MS-DOS Executive screen appears.

3. You must now switch to the Windows directory to locate the SPOOLER.EXE file by using the Change Directory command found on the Special menu (i.e., enter **Windows**).

   The Windows directory appears.

4. Select the **SPOOLER.EXE** file and then choose the **Run** command from the File menu or simply double-click on the file name.

   A dialog box appears and asks if you want to minimize the Spooler window.

5. You don't, simply click **OK** or press **Enter**.

   The Spooler window appears as shown in Figure 8.11.

6. Now switch back to Word by pressing **Alt+Esc** again. Do not close the Spooler window before you switch or Spooler won't work.

   You are returned to your Word document window.

7. When ready, choose the **Print** command or enter **Alt,F,P** and print your documents in the usual way. Remember, you can use the **File Find** command to select more than one file at a time to print.

   Each file that you print will use queued printing until you quit the current work session and stop running the Spooler. You can also simply press **Esc** to cancel queued printing.

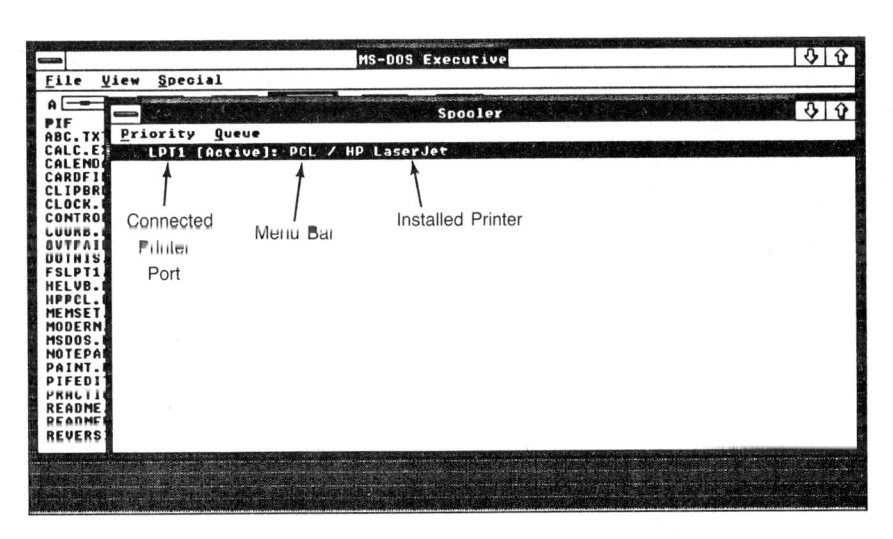

Figure 8.11 The Spooler window.

As we have stated, before you can use queued printing, you must first run the Spooler. Some of the elements of the Spooler's window in Figure 8.11 are worthy of note. For example, Port refers to the connection between your printer and your computer. A parallel printer is likely connected to a port named LPT1 and a serial printer is likely connected to a port named COM1. The Spooler window also offers a *Port Status,* which shows whether the printer is active or passive. Active means that the printer is ready to print or is printing. Paused means that you temporarily have stopped the print job. The Installed Printer shows the name of the printer that you installed with Windows.

The menu items, Priority and Queue contain some commands of interest as well. In the Priority menu, you'll find two commands, Low and High. Select *Low* when you want the Spooler to feed files to the printer "in-between" other jobs that the computer is doing. This option allows you to continue to work on other documents, such as editing and formatting. The *High* option simply takes over control of the computer's processor and completes the print jobs. To temporarily stop a print job, select the *Pause* command from the Queue menu. When you're ready to continue printing, select the *Resume* command. If you want to stop the printing of a particular file from the files listed in the Spooler window, select that file and then choose the *Terminate* command from the Queue menu.

To close the Spooler, choose the Exit command from the Priority menu, press Alt+F4, or select Close from the Control menu. Closing Spooler returns Windows to standard printing.

Printing Hidden Text

Word provides the option of printing text to which you applied the hidden text format. Word uses hidden text for special purposes: to create hidden characters to flag entries for tables of contents or indexes, or even referenced document fields, for example. In Chapter 14, you will also learn that Word uses hidden text for annotations or comments that reviewers can insert into your document. You can even leave messages in your documents for yourself by assigning the hidden text format. If you click the Hidden Text option (Alt+H) on the Print dialog box, any text that you assigned the hidden text format will print out on paper, even if the hidden text is not currently visible on your screen. If you do not check the Print Hidden Text option, the hidden text will not print (the default), even if you turn on the Preferences Hidden Text option to display the hidden text on your screen. As long as you have the Hidden Text option on the Print dialog box checked, however, the hidden text will print. You can turn off the display of hidden text on your screen by turning off the Hidden Text option in the Preferences dialog box. Finally, keep in mind that since hidden text would occupy additional space in your document, whether it is present or not will alter the pagination of your document as well.

The Paper Feed Option

Use the Paper Feed option to select the type of paper source that you will be using with your printer. The Paper Feed option may not be available to you if your printer doesn't include more than one paper resource option. For example, there are two basic types of paper for printing documents. One type is continuous, or fanfold, meaning the sheets of paper are connected end to end, with perforated edges between. Select the *Automatic (Auto)* option if your printer is using fanfold paper that feeds the printer automatically. The second type of paper is the single sheet that must be hand-fed into the printer or loaded with a sheet feeder. Select *Manual* if you are using individual sheets that you must insert into the printer one at a time. Each time you insert one page of paper, the printer will print, and then pause and wait for you to insert another page. If necessary, click the Continue button to begin printing on the next page of paper. The Manual option is handy for addressing and printing envelopes or for letterhead paper that does not come in a continuous form. If you are using a laser printer, your printing will all be done with sheet-fed paper that the printer loads automatically or that you insert manually. If you are using a printer that uses fanfold paper, you'll use the Automatic option, which sometimes allows printing to occur much faster. The speed of the printing and the type of paper it requires is solely dependent upon the printer itself. Please be sure to study your printer's user manuals to learn as much as you can regarding your printer's capabilities. Table 8.1 provides a list of common options.

Table 8.1 Paper Feed Printer Options

Option	Description
Manual	Printing stops at the end of each page. Word will pause and display a message that requires you to press Y to confirm that another sheet of paper has been inserted into the printer. Not all printers have this capability.
Auto	This is the automatic option that will print continuously until the end of the document is reached. Typically used with fanfold paper on tractor-fed printers or laser printers with automatic sheet feeders.
Bin 1	The printer gets paper from bin 1, usually, where most of the paper stock is located.
Bin 2	The second paper bin of the printer.
Bin 3	The third paper bin of the printer.
Mixed	The document is printed with the first page from bin 1 and the remaining pages from bin 2. This method is commonly used with letterheads in bin 1 and second sheets in bin 2.
Envelope	This option is available if the printer supports an envelope feeder. If not, choose the Manual option.

Using the Include Option

When you select the Option button to expand the Print dialog box, you'll notice the Include option located at the bottom of the window. The Include option allows you to print your document along with additional parts of your document that you may or may not have included. These parts include: Summary Info(rmation), Annotations, Hidden Text, and Field Codes. Depending upon which option(s) you select by clicking inside the appropriate box, or pressing the Alt-key combination, the part of the document selected will print according to a specific sequence. Keep in mind that you can print two of the options, Summary Information and Glossary, from the document itself. Table 8.2 summarizes the Include print options.

Table 8.2 The Include Print Options

Option	Description	Restrictions
Summary Info	After the document has printed, the summary information is printed on a separate sheet. If you also elected to print annotations, the summary information is printed after the annotations have printed.	You can only print this option when the selection in the Print field is Document.
Annotations	Prints the annotations after the document has printed. Since the annotations are hidden text, this option is automatically selected as well.	The Print field selection must be set on Document.
Hidden Text	This option will print all hidden text, such as annotations, and index and table of contents entries.	The Print selection must be set on Document, Annotations, or Glossary.
Field Codes	Choosing this option will print the result assigned to the field codes in your document.	The Print selection must be set on Document, Annotations, or Glossary.

Canceling Printing

Choosing the Print command starts the print process by producing the Print dialog box. Clicking OK or pressing Enter sends instructions and a file to your printer to begin printing of your document. At all times during the actual printing process, Word displays the printing status in the status bar. Word provides the option of canceling the

265

The Basics

printing by pressing the Esc key. Pressing Esc returns control of the screen to you, and the printing will stop at the conclusion of the queue. (Note: Printing won't stop immediately because your printer will finish whatever remains in its own memory.) If you haven't clicked OK or pressed Enter when the Print dialog box is displayed on your screen, you can also cancel the Print command by clicking the Cancel button in the dialog box.

Printing Problems

You have now learned to create, edit, and format your documents on your screen. The next step is to use your printer. If you followed the setup procedures to install your printer, and selected the appropriate commands from the Print dialog box, you should now be ready to start printing. If Word displays a message that your document is indeed printing, and yet nothing is happening, don't panic just yet. First, use the following checklist to see if you can fix your problem.

1. The first step is to check that your printer is plugged in and turned on.

2. If you received an error message, make sure that you have installed the printer driver required to run your printer (via the Control Panel Installation and Connection commands). Also, check to see that your printer is connected to the proper printer port. Use the Printer Setup command (on the File menu) to double-check that you have told Word which printer and port you have selected is correct. Be sure to write down any error message that is given. You may need it later to help solve your problem.

3. Double-check your setup via the Printer Setup option. Check that your computer paper is properly installed in your printer. Whether you are using fanfold sheets or single sheets that are hand-fed, make sure that you have indicated the correct type of paper. It should be noted that fanfold paper should fit snugly into the tractor feed and feed properly through the paper alert mechanism, which will signal when paper runs out.

4. Check to see that your printer cable is firmly attached to both your computer and your printer.

5. If your printer is turned on, be sure an On-Line (or similar signal, such as Ready, SEL for select, or Print On) light is turned on as well. If your printer has an Alert light, it must be off. If the On-Line light is off, pressing it on will often solve many printing problems.

6. If you just turned on your printer, it may require a few moments to warm up.

If you have checked each of the options above, and your printer still won't work, refer next to your printer's user's manual for advice. Then call either the printer's customer service number or the customer support number at Microsoft.

Using Print Preview

Use the Print Preview command from the File menu to examine your documents before you print them out. Print Preview allows you to view all the page layout elements of one or two pages in a reduced size, scaled according to the paper size you specify in the Printer Setup dialog box. The default setting is 8 1/2 x 11", the standard U.S. business-letter size. To get a sneak peek at the first one or two pages of your document, choose the Print Preview command. You should see something like Figure 8.12.

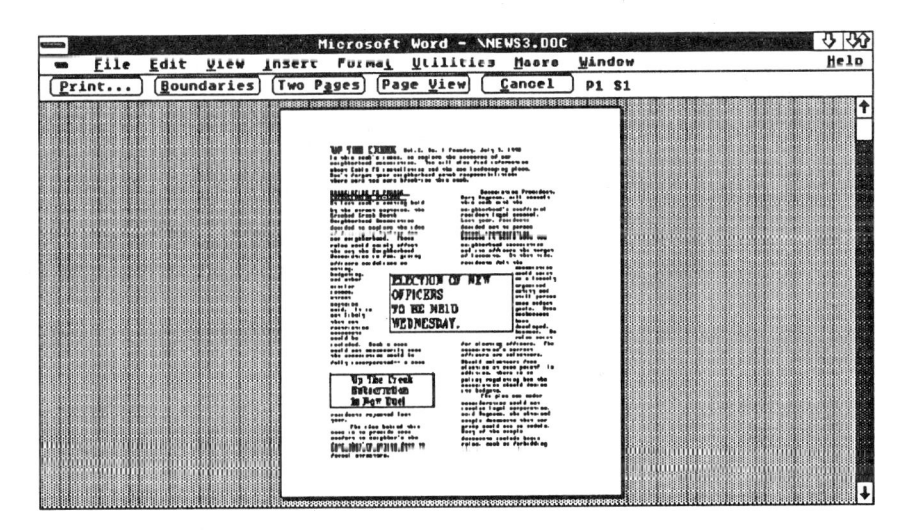

Figure 8.12 The Print Preview command offers a sneak peek at your documents.

You cannot edit the document while in Print Preview (Page View, discussed shortly, allows this), but you can use Print Preview to adjust the position of your margins (left, right, top, and bottom); to change the location of page breaks, positioned objects, and headers or footers; to display one or two pages of a document at a time; and to

The Basics

access the Print dialog box directly. It is important to remember that any changes made in Print Preview are automatically saved by Word and are reflected in the settings of other commands.

As you can see from Figure 8.12, the Print Preview command offers five command buttons at the top of the window. Running from left to right, they are: Print, Boundaries, the One Page/Two Pages display, Page View, and the Cancel button. These command buttons and their uses are summarized below:

- The Print button—Displays the Print dialog box. Printing has been discussed in detail in this chapter, but you should know that the Print dialog box enables you to print a few pages of a document by specifying a range (From, To) or to print the entire document by clicking OK. You'll notice that Word automatically proposes the number of pages to print in the From and To range edit boxes. As with printing any document, you can also choose the Options button and display other printing choices.

The Boundaries option is useful for adjusting the layout of your documents before you print. It lets you adjust the page layout by creating manual page breaks.

- The Boundaries button—Displays key elements in page layout of your document, including boundary lines for your margins, page breaks, headers or footers, and any positioned objects, as shown in Figure 8.13. The function of the Boundaries is to allow you to select the key elements and drag them to new locations. To do this, drag the automatic page break (light

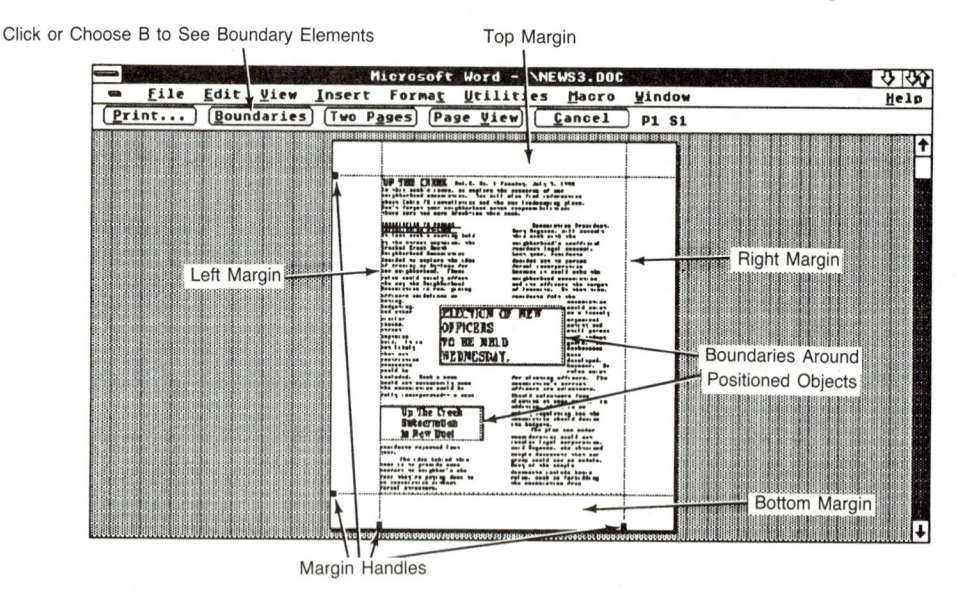

Figure 8.13 The Boundaries option depicts key elements of your document in its current settings.

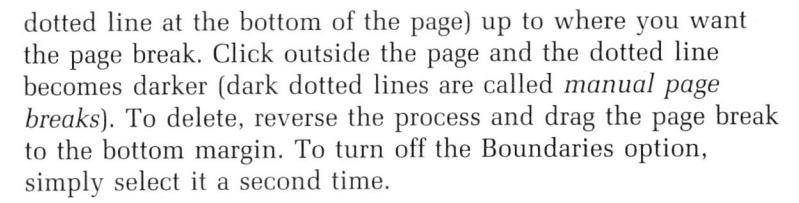

dotted line at the bottom of the page) up to where you want the page break. Click outside the page and the dotted line becomes darker (dark dotted lines are called *manual page breaks*). To delete, reverse the process and drag the page break to the bottom margin. To turn off the Boundaries option, simply select it a second time.

Tip: If you use the mouse and click anywhere in your document, the horizontal and vertical measurements are displayed. This is great for measuring graphics.

Chapter 4 demonstrated the steps to take to change the margins with Boundaries. For a review: To change any of the four margins (left, right, top, or bottom), activate the Boundaries button by clicking or press the letter B, and then drag the margin by its handle (the little black box) in the direction that you wish to move the margin. When the pointer is properly positioned over the margin handle, it will change to a cross-hair. As you press down on the mouse, the exact location of the margin is displayed at the top of the window. (Note: If you don't have a mouse, press Tab to select the appropriate margin handle and then use the arrow keys to move it). To see the effect of a margin alteration, once you move its location, click outside the page to update the screen or press the Tab key a second time. To change the location of other objects (page breaks, headers or footers, positioned text or pictures), you use the same procedure. Once the Boundaries option is activated and the guidelines are displayed, use the mouse (or Tab and arrow keys) with its cross-hair pointer to adjust the location of any of these elements. The positions of the elements are always displayed in a status box at the top of the window. Click outside the page to update the screen each time you make a change.

Tip: You can only change the vertical position of a header or footer by dragging within Print Preview (via the Boundaries option). Word won't let you drag the position of a header or footer beyond a set top or bottom margin (unless you set negative top margins). If you require more space, you must adjust the top and bottom margins first. To change the horizontal position of a header or footer in Print Preview, hold down the Shift key while dragging across. The effect will create an absolute top or bottom margin by using a negative value for the top or bottom margin.

Finally, note that changes made with the Boundaries option in Print Preview only affect the current section. If your document contains more than one section, you will need to change all the sections to incorporate a global look.

Select positioned objects either with the mouse or by pressing Tab or Shift+Tab. Once you have relocated the object, press Tab, Shift+Tab, or Ctrl+Tab to update the page layout.

The Basics

- The One Page/Two Pages button—Displays either one or two pages of your document at a time. Clicking the button or pressing the Alt-letter key alternates between choices. You can change which pages are displayed in a long document by using the scroll bar on the right side of the Print Preview window. If you are displaying facing pages, the related facing pages will scroll two at a time. Clicking the down arrow will display the next page or two pages. Similarly, clicking the up arrow will change the display back to the previous page or two pages. You can also use the PgUp and PgDn keys to scroll by entire pages. Finally, note that the right end of the icon bar shows the page number of the page or pages currently on display.

- The Page View button—Changes from Print Preview to Page View with a click of the mouse or pressing the V key. Page View shows how your document will look when printed but displays your document in portions that will fit on your screen. A neat feature of Page View is that it allows you to make last-minute editing changes since all the editing and formatting tools are available to you. Unlike Print Preview, this handy feature can be used just prior to printing. In fact, if your computer is loaded with lots of memory and speed, you might want to do all your work in Page View instead of Normal Editing View. We discussed the features of Page View in Chapter 7.

While you're in Print Preview mode, many of the menu commands are unavailable to you and appear dimmed, or grey, and you cannot open files or change windows.

- The Cancel button—As expected, you can choose the Cancel button to quit Print Preview and return to the previous view. It should be noted, however, that as soon as you make any boundary adjustments, the Cancel button changes to a Close button. Unlike Cancel, choosing Close will save any changes that you have made in Print Preview. You can also quit Print Preview by selecting the Esc key, the Close command from the Control Menu (Alt,-,C), or by choosing any one of the alternate views: select Page View or V; Outline View or Alt,V,O; Draft View or Alt,V,D. Except for choosing Cancel when it's available, all of these optional exit methods will save any changes you've made while in Print Preview before returning you to the previous active view.

Tip: If you click the Close button on the Print Preview window or the Esc key or the Control Close command, any changes made to your document will be saved by Word and made in your document as you are returned to the previous view.

8—Printing Essentials

Review

In this chapter you learned:

1. Before you can print your documents, you must install the correct printer driver for your printer during the setup procedure. You must also tell Word where your printer is connected to your computer system (i.e., which port on the back of your computer). This latter option enables you to connect more than one type of printer to your computer.

2. A printer driver file is identified by the extension, DRV. To install a new printer driver file, choose the Run command from the Word Control menu. Choose the Control Panel option and then select the Add New Printer command from the Installation menu. In the edit box, type the name of the disk drive and directory where the printer driver is located. Once you have added the printer driver, you must also tell Word where it's connected via the Connections command.

3. Use the File Printer Setup command to check printing options that correspond to the type of printer you are using and to determine whether the printer is set up to produce the results you expect.

4. Word provides the option of printing your documents using the Portrait or Landscape settings. Portrait prints across the width of a page while Landscape prints across the length to accommodate wide page designs.

5. To begin printing your documents, choose the Print command from the File menu. The standard options that can be printed include: Document, Summary Info, Annotations, Styles, Glossary, and Key Assignments.

6. The Copies option on File Print allows you to specify how many times to print the document.

7. Word allows you to print the entire document, or any part of the document, by using the From and To edit boxes located on the Print dialog box.

8. If you are working with a full version of Windows, you can use Word's queued printing to start the printing of one document while you work on another document. This option uses the Windows SPOOLER.EXE file.

9. When you wish to print your documents in addition to other elements (e.g., summary information, annotations, hidden text, or field codes), use the Include option found on the expanded Print dialog box (by choosing Option).

10. To cancel printing at any time, press the Esc key. Printing will stop when the printer is finished with whatever remains in its own memory (i.e., it prints out all documents in the queue).

11. Use the File Print Preview command to examine the structure of your documents before you print them out. You can see all the page layout elements of one or two pages in a reduced scale according to the paper size you specify in the Printer Setup dialog box.

12. You cannot edit the document in Print Preview, but you can adjust many of the key elements of the document, including the margins, location of page breaks, positioned objects, and headers or footers. If you need to edit the document, choose the Page View button and edit in that view.

13. In order to see all the key elements of your document in Print Preview, choose the Boundaries option.

PART TWO

Adding and Polishing Word

NINE

chapter

Running Heads and Feet

In this chapter:

- Creating a Header or Footer
- Formatting a Header
- Adding Page Numbers, Times, and Dates to Headers
- Positioning Headers and Footers
- Creating Different Headers and Footers by Section
- Deleting Headers and Footers
- Storing Headers in the Glossary

In this part of the book, you'll learn some more advanced features of Word, and you'll learn how to apply these features to give your documents more polish. This chapter treats running text that prints at the top (headers) or bottom (footers) of each page of your document.

You can use headers and footers in almost any document, from books and research papers to letters, in fact, most documents today use headers or footers. Generally, a header or footer provides additional information about the document, including page numbers and the time and date the document was created. It may also include information that describes the document in some way, such as a chapter or section title. Books commonly provide different information on facing pages, such as the chapter title on the left page and the section title on the right page.

This chapter introduces the commands you use to create a header or footer and how you enter and format the header/footer text and position it on your page. Finally, the last section of this chapter discusses how to delete a header or footer.

Since the procedure is essentially the same for setting up a header or a footer, our examples will focus on headers to simplify the discussion. Once you have mastered creating headers, you'll have no problem with footers. You'll learn, too, of special circumstances or commands applicable only to footers.

Creating a Header or Footer

The first step to creating a header or footer begins with the **Header/Footer** command located on the Edit menu. Click this option or press **Alt,E,H** and the Header/Footer window appears, as shown in Figure 9.1.

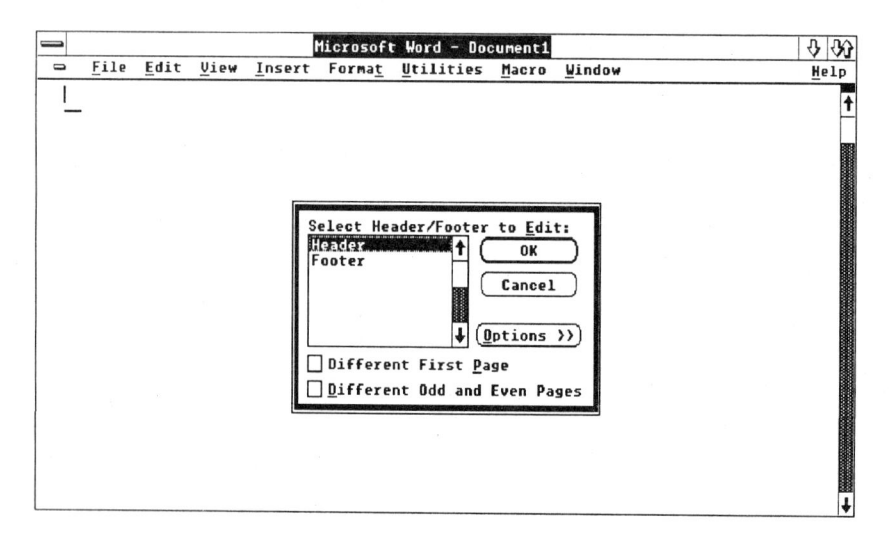

Figure 9.1 The Header/Footer window.

You can choose either Header or Footer, depending upon whether you want the running text to appear at the top or bottom of your document page. Make your choice by clicking with the mouse or pressing Tab to move the highlight and using the up and down arrow keys to select. By default, Header is selected. Once you have made your choice, click OK or press Enter. If you change your mind and wish to return to the document window, simply choose Cancel instead of OK. The third command button, Options, enlarges the header/footer window and will be discussed shortly.

Choose **Header** or **Footer**, press **Enter**, and a pane will appear at the bottom of your document window, as shown in Figures 9.2 and 9.3. One important point: If you are in Normal Editing View when you choose the Header/Footer command, the header/footer pane will appear with an icon bar that shows the name of the header/footer and has scroll bars (if turned on in the Preferences dialog box), and two button commands, Link To Previous (appears dim until you change your header or footer) and Close. This is the view shown in Figures 9.2 and 9.3. Just like any other empty window, it has a blinking insertion point in the upper left corner of the pane as well as an end mark. The icon bar of the header pane also includes three distinct icons, displayed left to right, for adding page numbers, dates, and times to your header. If you were previously in Page View, the insertion point will still jump to the beginning of the selected header or footer pane, but the icon bar and the rest of the command options will not be available to you. So, from this point on, you should begin from Normal Editing View.

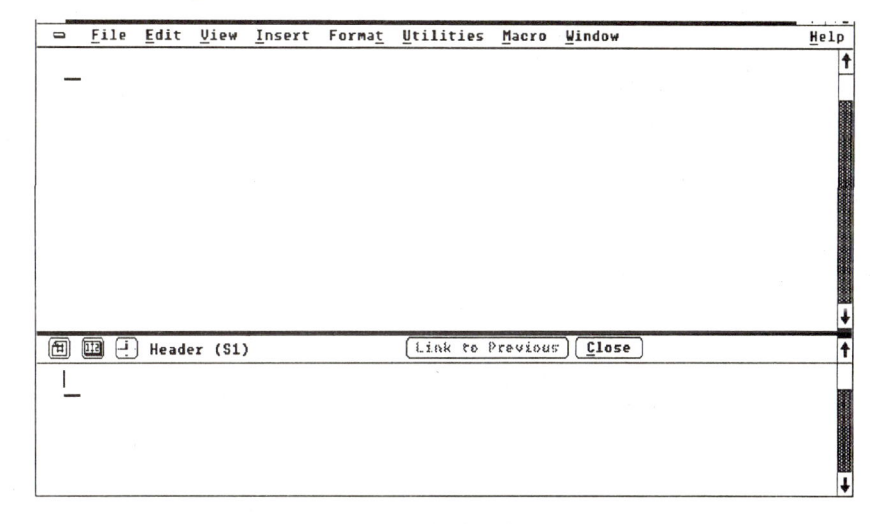

Figure 9.2 The header pane.

You can place any information you want in a header pane, such as text, page numbers, even pictures. You treat the header pane just like any document window; you can create, edit, and format text as you ordinarily would in Normal Editing View. Once your header is created, click the **Close** button shut and the header information is saved. If you don't have a mouse installed, activate the Header icon bar by pressing **Shift+F10** and then choose the desired command with the appropriate letter (e.g., C to choose Close). You won't be able

Adding and Polishing Word

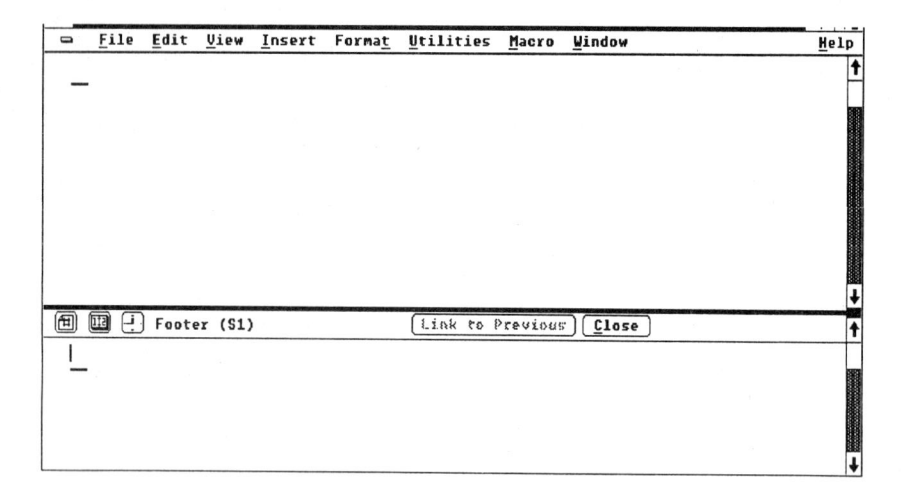

Figure 9.3 The footer pane.

to see the header in Normal Editing View, but you can use Print Preview and Page View to see how the header will appear.

Entering Text in a Header

Word will display your header text in the space occupied by the top margin. If your header text consists of several lines and would be too long to fit in the top margin (remember the default setting for the top margin is 1"), Word automatically expands the top margin to make room for the longer header (or moves the bottom margin up to make room for a footer). Once you've opened the header window, the next step to creating a header is to type the header text. Suppose, for example, you wanted to enter some descriptive text for a research paper entitled "Future Communications of Our Society." At the blinking insertion point in the header window, enter the phrase, as shown in Figure 9.4.

Most headers consist of a line or two of descriptive text and perhaps a page number or date. If you want your header to appear in multiple lines, allow the text to word-wrap or create a Newline by pressing Shift+Return or new paragraph by pressing Enter, just as you would in a standard document window. For example, Figure 9.5 shows what adding a line of text to the header in Figure 9.4 might look like. (Notice that Word doesn't add any white space above the header to allow for the second line of text.)

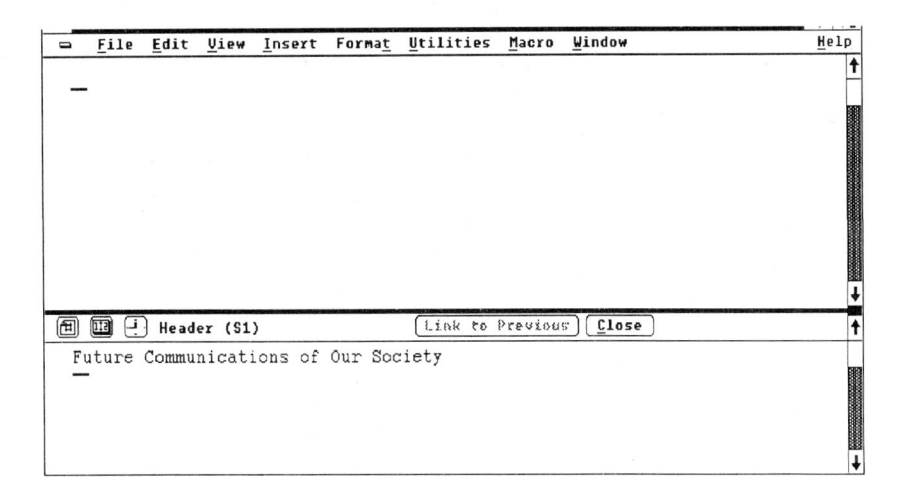

Figure 9.4 Type the header text in your header pane.

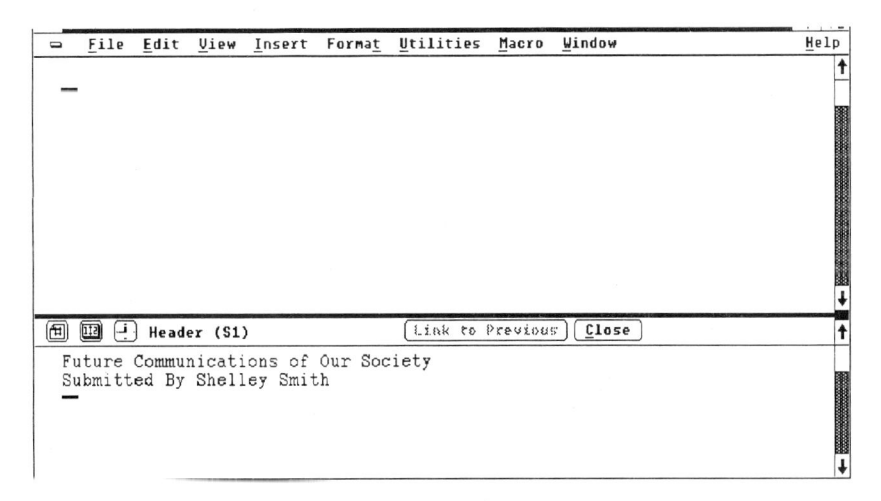

Figure 9.5 A header can be several lines long and space is automatically adjusted.

Formatting a Header

When you enter text in a header window, the text will appear left-aligned in the default type, 10-point Times Roman Plain. You can use Word's character and paragraph formatting options to change the text by selecting the text and then using the corresponding Character and Paragraph commands. You can even use the Paragraph command to add a special graphic touch to your headers by applying borders.

In addition to the Character and Paragraph commands, you can use the Ruler and its standard formatting options, such as aligning text (left, right, centered, full) and line spacing (single, one-and-a-half, double). For this, choose **Ruler** from the View menu while in Normal Editing View prior to opening the header/footer pane. The Ruler will appear at the top of your document window as shown in Figure 9.6. As long as the insertion point resides within the header pane, you'll notice that the Ruler now offers different settings. For example, the Ruler will contain a Header style box instead of the Normal style box associated with a standard document window. The header style itself, however, is based on the Normal style with two additional elements: a tab stop at the center of the Ruler (at the 3″ mark), and a right-aligned tab stop. As with the Ruler of the document window, you can redefine the header style itself or simply change the style of the text that you create in the header window.

To illustrate, we formatted the previous header by selecting the center icon with the header Ruler, and choosing a boldface 8-point Roman font from the Ribbon. We also added a border to the header by selecting the header text, choosing the Paragraph command, and clicking the Borders button. As you know, clicking the Border Box option places a border around the entire selected text. The revised header is depicted in Figure 9.7.

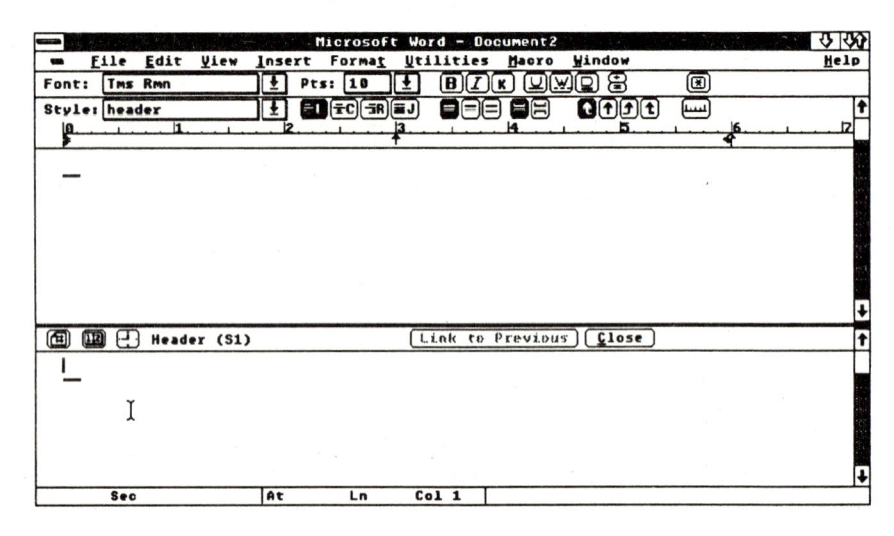

Figure 9.6 Format the text within a header using the Ribbon and Ruler.

> Future Communications of Our Society
> Submitted By Shelley Smith

Figure 9.7 The new formatted header text.

Adding Page Numbers, Times, and Dates to Headers

You can incorporate many elements in a header or footer. The most common element is a page number. To do this with Word, you have two options:

- Using the icon bar on the header/footer pane
- Using the *Insert Page Numbers* command

As you have learned, you can add and format text, as well as format the page number itself, but the Insert Page Number option limits you to inserting a page number at a specific location. So let's begin by investigating the icon bar options on the Header/Footer Pane.

Using the Icon Bar

You can use the icon bar on a header pane with either a mouse or directly from the keyboard. If you have a mouse, simply click the desired icon once. For example, to add a page number to a header, click the page-number icon in the icon bar once. The leftmost icon on the icon bar, it is identified by the numeral symbol (#). When you click the icon, the current page number appears at the location of the blinking insertion point. If you have not entered any text in the header pane, clicking the page-number icon places the page number in the upper left corner of the header pane. To change the location of the page number, you must move the insertion point. For example, to insert a page number in the center of the header, you can use the Spacebar to space over to the center of the pane or you can press the Tab key once. As you'll recall, the header Ruler is preset with a centered tab. Once you center the insertion point in the header pane, click the page-number icon and the page number that represents the current page will be displayed in the center of the header pane.

Don't have a mouse? Using the keyboard is just as handy. To use the keyboard, you must first activate the icon bar by pressing

Shift+F10. To choose an option from the icon bar, press a corresponding letter, such as P for page number or D for date. A complete list of the options is given in Table 9.1.

Table 9.1 Using the Icon Bar with Keys

Icon	Do This:
Page Number	Press Shift+F10 and then P
Date	Press Shift+F10 and then D
Time	Press Shift+F10 and then T
Link to Previous	Press Shift+F10 and then L
Close	Press Shift+F10 and then C

Remember, a nice feature of adding page numbers to a header is that you can insert additional text along with the page number, such as Page, or Page 1 of.... Sure, ho-hum page numbers are OK, but add a little spice and enter some descriptive text.

The header window also provides icons for adding the current date and time to your documents. This option is useful for tracking the current version of a document. Word uses the date and time as set by the Window's Control Panel accessory (determined by the System clock and modified by DATEFORMAT=entry in the WIN.INI file), which enables you to keep a running record of a document so that you can tell when you last modified it. To add the current time or date to your header, follow the procedure just described for adding page numbers. Move the insertion point where you want the current time or date to appear and click the appropriate icon once. The date icon is a page from a desk calendar with the numerals 1 and 2 printed on the front, and the time icon is a clock. Figure 9.8 depicts a header with all three elements added.

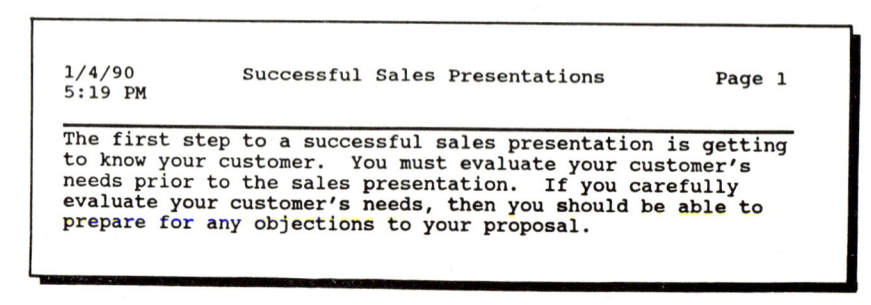

```
1/4/90              Successful Sales Presentations              Page 1
5:19 PM
```
```
The first step to a successful sales presentation is getting
to know your customer.  You must evaluate your customer's
needs prior to the sales presentation.  If you carefully
evaluate your customer's needs, then you should be able to
prepare for any objections to your proposal.
```

Figure 9.8 Header with page number, time, and date fields.

The date and time icons are updated every time you turn your computer on or off or open, close, or print a document. You can place them anywhere inside a header or footer, just like the page number. You can't edit portions of the time or date, since Word identifies each as a whole unit. If you attempt to erase a portion of one, the entire field will be deleted. These units are referred to as fields because they occupy a field of space. The time field will always be in the form H:M AM/PM and the date in the form M/D/YY.

You have learned how to create text in a header, format that text, and add page numbers, dates, and times to a header. For a quick review, refer to the following steps.

1. Choose **Header/Footer** from the Edit menu or press **Alt,E,H** from the keyboard.

    The header window appears.

2. Choose **Header** or **Footer** and then press **Enter** or Click **OK**.

    If the previous view was Normal Editing View, the header or footer pane appears at the bottom of the document window and the icon bar is visible.

3. To help formatting, select the **Ruler** and **Ribbon** options from the View menu.

    A header Ruler appears in the header window. Notice the center tab. (The left indent is set at the zero mark and the right indent at the 6" mark.) If you relocate the insertion point outside the header or footer pane, the options on the Ruler will change back to the document window selections.

4. Type the text of the header.

    Text appears at the location of the insertion point

5. Format the header text using the Ruler and Ribbon or the Paragraph and Character commands. For multiline entries, allow word-wrap or use a **Shift | Enter** for a Newline keypress. Use **Enter** to start a new paragraph.

6. To add a page number, date, or time to the header,

    Page numbers will represent the current page appearing on

position the insertion point where you want the element to appear, and click the corresponding icon on the icon bar. You may also use the keys by pressing **Shift+F10** to activate the icon bar and then pressing the appropriate key as listed in Table 9.1.

your screen. The time and date are controlled by the Control Panel. Time and date will change each time you start a new session.

7. When finished, click the **Close** button in the upper right corner of the header pane or use the keyboard method by pressing **Shift+F10,C**.

You return to your document window. The header will print on every page of your document. The header is not visible in Normal Editing View; to see it, choose either Print Preview or Page View.

Using Insert Page Numbers

All page numbers in Word are printed in headers or footers. You have just learned how to add page numbers using the icon bar within a header or footer pane. If you don't wish to add other elements to your header or footer other than a page number, Word provides a quicker method—the Insert Page Numbers command. To add only page numbers to a header or footer, complete the following steps:

1. Choose the **Insert Page Numbers** command from the Insert menu or press **Alt,I,U** from the keyboard.

   The Insert Page Numbers dialog window appears, as shown in Figure 9.9.

2. Now determine if you want the page number printed in a header or a footer. If you want it printed in a header, choose **Top** or press **Alt+T**. If you want the page number printed in a footer, choose **Bottom**, or press **Alt+B**.

   Your choice is highlighted.

3. Now select the horizontal position within the header or footer. Choose **Left** or press **Alt+L, Center** or press

   The horizontal position is highlighted.

Alt+C, or **Right** or press Alt+R.

4. Choose **OK** or press **Enter**. If an existing header or footer is contained in the current section, Word will ask if you want to replace it. If you do, choose **Yes**. If no header or footer previously existed, you are returned to the document window immediately.

Just like using the Header/Footer command from the Edit menu, using the Insert Page Numbers command will insert a page number "field" into your document at the point you specified. However, you can't add additional elements (e.g., text, time, or date) to the header or footer unless you use the Header/Footer command. In the next two sections, though, we will see how to format or erase the page number set with either method.

Formatting Page Numbers

When you set a page number in a header or footer, Word will begin the pagination with the numeral 1. However, Word provides the option of changing both the starting number and the format of the pagination itself. To format page numbers, choose the **Header/Footer**

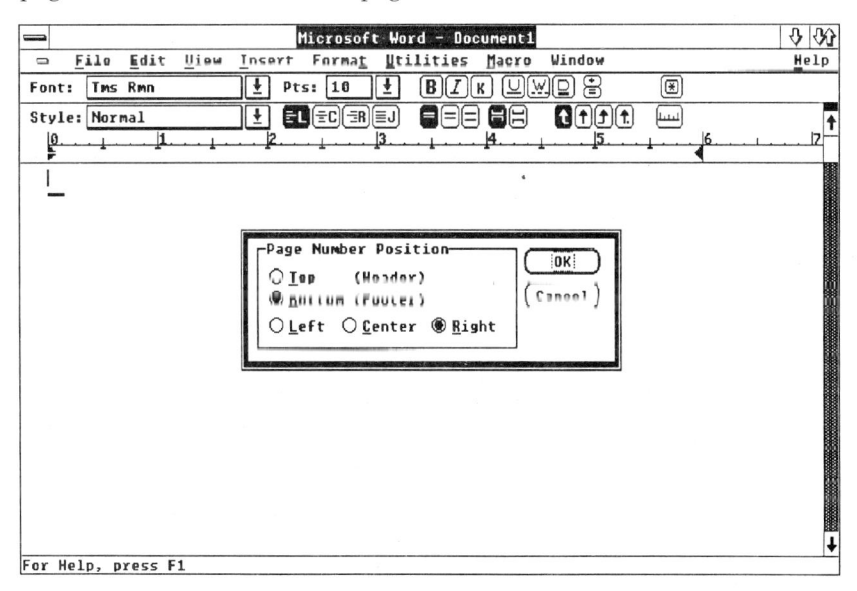

Figure 9.9 The Insert Page Numbers window.

Adding and Polishing Word

command from the Edit menu or press **Alt,E,H**. Clicking the **Options** button or pressing **Alt+O** produces the dialog box shown in Figure 9.10.

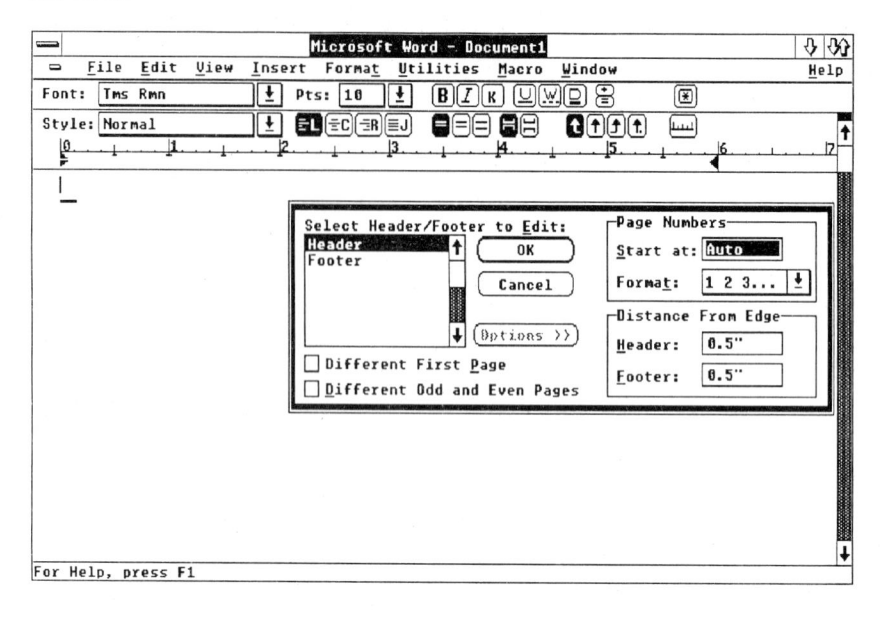

Figure 9.10 Clicking Options expands the Header/Footer window.

To change the number you want printed on the first page, simply click inside the **Start At** edit box in the Page Numbers section or press **Alt+S** and type the desired number. You will notice that the edit box displays Auto, which means that the header or footer will begin printing with the numeral 1 in the page-number field as defined by your printer. To replace this Auto value, enter a different starting number. Keep in mind that the starting number reflects pagination for the current section. If your document consists of only one section, then the pagination applies to the entire document. If your document consists of more than one section, then you have the option of beginning each new section with a new starting page number.

Below the Start At edit box is a pull-down window for applying a different page number format. Word provides five choices of formats that you can apply to the page numbers you select in the Start At edit box:

- 1 2 3... for arabic numerals
- a,b,c for lowercase alphabetic
- A,B,C for uppercase alphabetic

- i,ii,iii for lowercase roman numerals
- I,II,III for uppercase roman numerals

The default value is the standard arabic numerals (1 2 3...). To choose a different format, click open the pull-down menu with the mouse and select your choice, or press **Alt+T** and use the up and down arrow keys to scroll the choices in the Format window. Once you have made your selections, choose **OK** or press **Enter**.

Deleting Page Numbers

*To close a header or footer pane, press **F6**, or click inside the document pane, or click the **Close** button on the icon bar, or use the keys by pressing **Shift+F10** and then **C**.*

Once you have set page numbers in a header or footer, you can delete them if you change your mind. To do this, simply choose the **Header/Footer** command from the Edit menu or press **Alt,E,H**, and then choose **Header** or **Footer** from the list window and click **OK** or press **Enter**. The header or footer pane appears from which you can select the page-number field. The field will be represented by the starting page number and format that you selected in the expanded Header/Footer dialog window. Once the field is selected, press the **Delete** key and the page number is removed. When you close the header or footer pane you are returned to your document, which now has no page numbers.

Positioning Headers and Footers

You have seen how to format header text with the Character and Paragraph commands as well as the Ruler and Ribbon. You've also seen how to change the alignment of your header text simply by selecting the appropriate icons on the Ruler (left, right, centered, justified). In addition, we discussed how to change the starting number and format of page numbers in a header or footer. In this section, you'll learn to position headers and footers on your document page using Word's default options for vertical and horizontal positioning. You can adjust the vertical default position by adding white space above or below the header itself with the Distance From Edge section in the expanded Header/Footer window. And you can adjust the horizontal position by using the header Ruler to place the header in the left or right margins area. In addition, you can drag the header outline with Print Preview to alter the vertical and horizontal positioning of your headers.

Vertical Positioning: Adding Space Above or Below a Header

Use the Before edit box of the Paragraph command to add more space between your header and the top edge of the first paragraph on the page.

A standard header prints 1/2" from the top of the page. But you can adjust the vertical spacing of your headers by using the Header and Footer edit boxes in the Distance From Edge section of the expanded Header/Footer window. You can expand the Header/Footer window by choosing the Options button. When you do, the Distance From Edge section will show the standard default values. To change these, simply enter any new value you choose. For example, if you were to enter a value of 2 in the Header edit box, your header would appear 2" from the top of the document page. As a reference, use the following steps to change the vertical position of your headers or footers:

1. From the Edit menu, select **Header/Footer** or press **Alt,E,H**.

   The Header/Footer window appears.

2. Click **Options** or press **Alt+O**.

   The dialog window expands to the larger size.

3. Move to the appropriate Distance From Edge box. Choose **Header** or press **Alt+H** or choose **Footer** or press **Alt+F**.

   Presently, 0.5" is the default value for each.

4. Type in the new amount of white space you want from the edge of the paper.

   That value replaces the default.

5. Click **OK** or press **Enter**.

   The new distance is set.

6. Choose the **Close** button or press **Shift+F10,C** to close the header pane and return to the document window.

Caution: If you are using a laser printer, and the header or footer position is closer than 1/2" to the edge of the page, it is likely that the header or footer won't print.

Changing the Position of a Header with Print Preview

As you've learned, you can easily adjust elements on your document page by using the Print Preview command. To move a header or footer up or down the page, follow these steps:

1. Choose **Print Preview** from the File menu or press **Alt,F,V**.

    The Print Preview window appears.

2. Click the **Boundaries** button or press **B**.

    Word draws boundaries around the elements of the document page. The header appears with a dotted box drawn around it, as in Figure 9.11.

3. Place the pointer in the header area and it will change to a cross-hair. Drag the header up or down to reposition it. As you drag the header, the status window changes to indicate the distance of the header from the top of the page. If you don't have a mouse, press Tab until the object that you want to move is selected (the header). Then press the direction keys to move the header.

4. To register the change, click anywhere outside the document page or if you are using the keys, press Tab a second time.

    The pointer becomes an hourglass while Word formats all pages of your document. When the pointer returns to your control, the header box appears at its new location.

5. Click **Page View** or press **V**.

    Page View displays the header in its new position.

Horizontal Positioning: Headers and Footers in the Margins Area

Sometimes it's desirable to display your headers in the left or right margins. To position a header or footer in the margins, you must change the position of the left or right indent markers. To do this, choose the **Header/Footer** command from the Edit menu, select either **Header** or **Footer** from the list window, and then choose **OK** or press

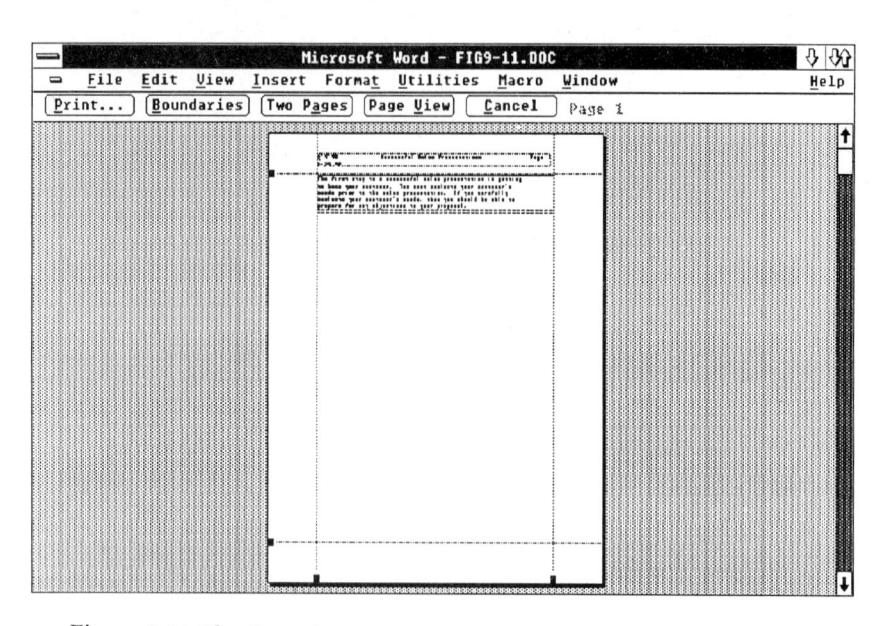

Figure 9.11 The Boundaries option draws a box around the header.

Enter to display the header (or footer) pane. Next, choose **Ruler** from the View menu. Be sure the insertion point resides inside the header window in order to display the Ruler as a header Ruler. Now, to position a header in the left margin, you create a negative left indent by dragging the left indent and the first-line indent marker to the left of the zero mark on the header Ruler while holding down the Shift key. To print a header in the right margin area, you first drag the right indent marker to the right of the default 6" mark on the Ruler and then drag the first-line indent and left indent markers right of the mark that represents your right margin. In Figure 9.12, the first-line indent mark is dragged to the left of the default mark (0 on the Normal Ruler) by -1" and the left indent to the -.5" mark to create a header that is displayed in the left margin.

Of course, you can use the Ruler to indent the header text anywhere inside the header window just like a standard document window. You use negative indents only when you want to place the headers in the margins.

Creating Different Headers and Footers by Section

When you create a header or footer, it prints on all subsequent pages of your document. You can vary the headers or footers of your docu-

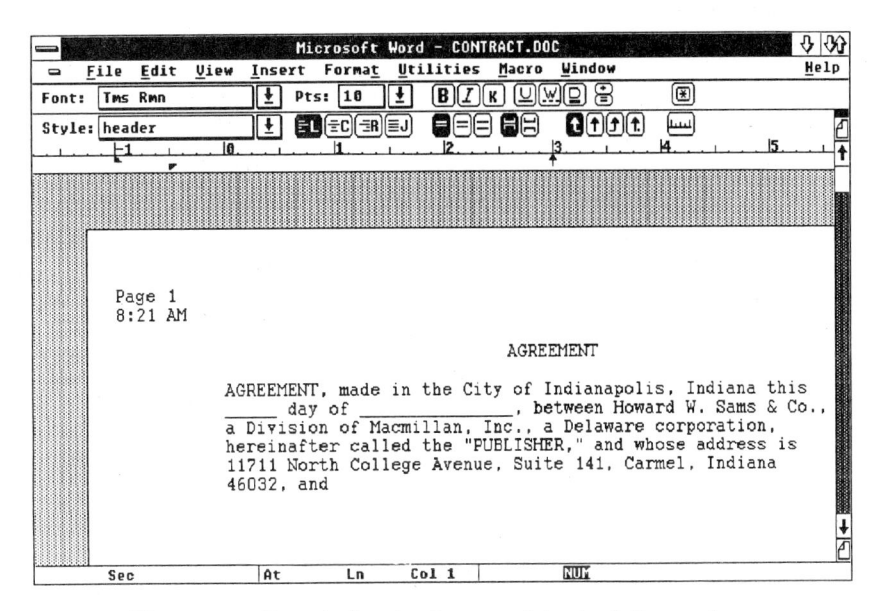

Figure 9.12 Sample header formatted in the left margin.

ment, however, by dividing the document into sections. Each section can have its own set of headers or footers. The advantage of dividing your document into sections is that you can control the type of header or whether one is to be printed. For example, you could give the individual chapters of a book different headers by making each chapter correspond to a different section. You can manipulate each chapter or section to print different headers on facing pages. You can use Word's Different First Page option to print a unique header or footer on the first page of a document or section. Or you can print nothing at all.

To divide the document into sections, you first position the insertion point to indicate where you want the section to begin. Next, choose the **Break** command from the **Insert** menu or press **Alt,I,B**. From the Insert dialog box that appears, select the type of section break (Next Page, Continuous, Odd Page, Even Page) and click **OK** or press **Enter** (for more information on sections, see Chapter 7). When you create a new section, the header and/or footer will carry the previous section's settings by default. Succeeding sections will carry the same header and/or footer, and their settings, as the current section.

To change the settings of a header, position the insertion point anywhere inside the desired section and then select the **Header/Footer** command from the Edit menu. In the header window, choose **Header** from the list window (or footer) and click **OK** or press **Enter**.

A header pane appears with the icon bar displaying the relevant section number next to the page number. If the insertion point resides in the second section, for example, the status bar and the icon bar will reflect the relevant page number and section number (S2 2/2).

Once you divide your document into sections, you can use all of the formatting options that are available to you in a header pane just like you were working in a standard document window. But remember that all sections of a document are linked until the link is broken. If you make changes to a current section, only that section is affected if you already have set up headers in other sections. If you want each section to print individual header information, you need to reformat each section individually. The most common occurrence of formatting individual sections with differing headers is with facing pages, such as in a book.

Creating Headers and Footers on Facing Pages

Books typically feature differing headers on the odd- and even-numbered pages (called "facing pages"). The position of the page number as well as the header text itself may vary. For example, the header on the even-numbered or left page might print the book title with the page number in the upper left corner, and the header on the odd-numbered or right page would display the chapter title with the page number in the upper right corner of the page. The headers just described are called *facing page headers*, and are shown in Figure 9.13.

To create facing page headers, you turn on the *Different Odd and Even Pages* option in the Edit menu's Header/Footer window. Choosing this command will change the options in the Select box window to: Even Header, Even Footer, Odd Header, Odd Footer. To create the facing page headers in Figure 9.13, complete the following set of steps.

1. Begin this step in Normal Editing View. Choose the **Header/Footer** command from the Edit menu or press **Alt,E,H**.	The Header/Footer dialog box appears.
2. Click the **Different Odd and Even Pages** option or press **Alt+D**.	The option appears with an X inside the box to indicate it has been turned on. To

9—Running Heads and Feet

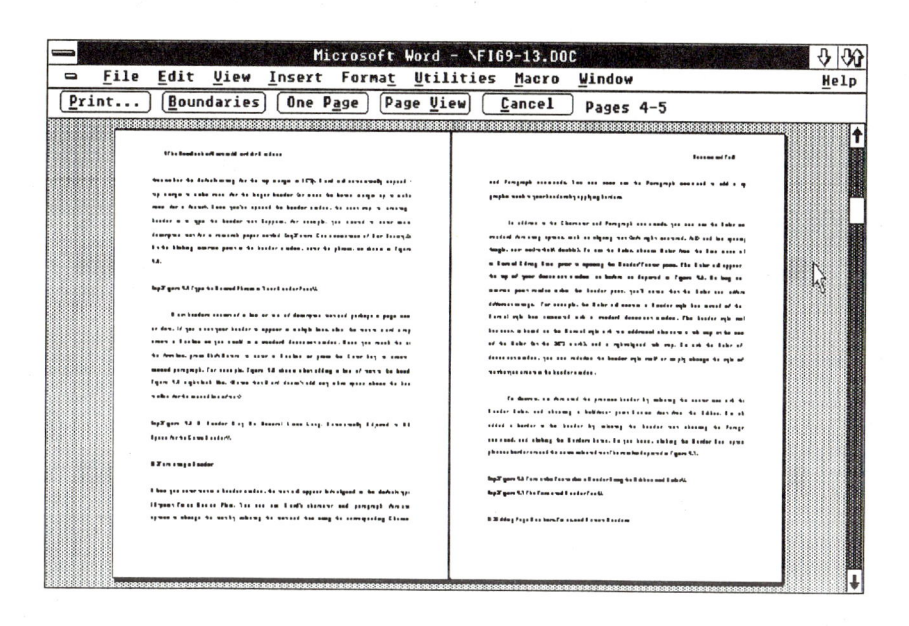

Figure 9.13 Facing page headers of a book.

3. Choose **Even Header** (or **Even Footer** if you're using footers instead of headers) and click **OK** or press **Enter**.

5. Enter the text that you want to appear on the left or even-numbered pages. Click the **Page Number (#)** icon to place it in the upper left corner of the header window and space over to enter the header text, or Book title, **The Best Book of Microsoft Word for Windows.**

deselect it, click it a second time. The list of options in the Select Edit box changes to: Even Header, Even Footer, Odd Header, Odd Footer.

The header pane appears with *Even Header* in the icon bar.

The page number appears at the location of the insertion point, followed by the book title (Figure 9.14).

Adding and Polishing Word

6. Choose **Header/Footer** from the Edit menu a second time. This time, however, choose **Odd Header** from the Select edit list window (or **Odd Footer** if you're using footers).	This time the header pane displays *Odd Header* in the icon bar. Note: It's not necessary to close the Even Header pane prior to choosing the Header/Footer command for the second time. The new odd header pane will simply replace the even header pane at the bottom of the document window.
7. Press **Tab** twice to position the header text on the right side of the page. Then enter the header text and Page Number icon for the right or odd-numbered pages. Enter **Running Heads and Feet**, and then click the **Page Number (#)** icon to place the page number at the location of the insertion point.	The chapter title appears, followed by the page number.
8. Click the header pane **Closed** or press **Shift+F10,C**.	

The First Page Option

Sometimes you'll want to customize the header or footer on the first page of a document or section. For example, you might want to grab the reader's attention with a letterhead. You might even wish to omit a header or footer from the first page altogether. Word lets you design the first page of a header separately by using the Different First Page option in the Edit Header/Footer window. The following set of steps highlight this option.

1. From Normal Editing View, choose the **Header/Footer** command from the Edit menu or press **Alt,E,H**.	The Header/Footer dialog window appears.
2. Click the **Different First Page** option or press **Alt+P**.	The option is checked.

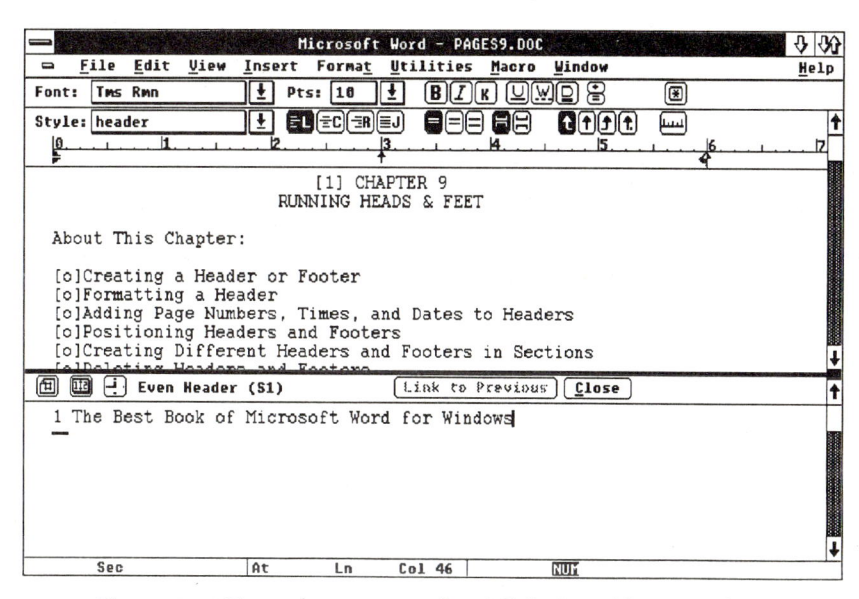

Figure 9.14 Enter the page number (click # or Alt+P) and text for even-numbered pages.

3. The Select Edit window now contains two additional commands, First Header and First Footer. Choose which you want and click **OK** or press **Enter**.

   The header window is displayed. First Header appears in the icon bar. See Figure 9.15.

4. Enter the text and format it as you want it to appear only on the first page of the section or document. If you don't want any text or page number to appear, leave the header window blank. Click **Close** or press **Shift+F10,C** to close the header window pane.

5. Choose **Header/Footer** from the Edit menu a second time.

   The header window appears.

6. Now select **Header** (or **Footer**)—by pressing the arrow key to highlight—and click **OK** or press **Enter**.

   The header pane appears.

Adding and Polishing Word

7. Type the text you want to appear in headers on all *other* pages in that section. When finished, click the header pane **Closed.**

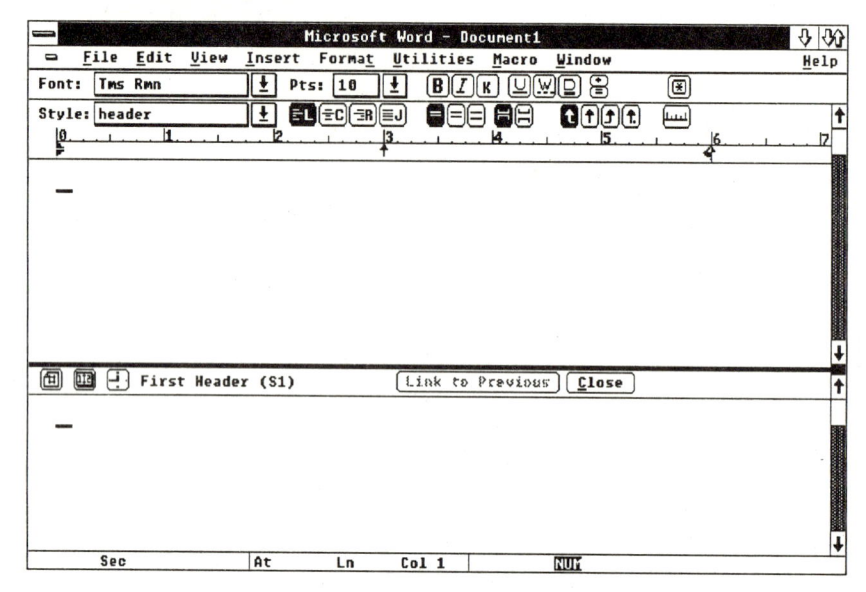

Figure 9.15 The first header pane offers two command options.

The Link To Previous Button

You can use the Link To Previous button to duplicate the same text and formats of a header (or footer) for the current header as on the previous section of your document. Clicking this button simply copies the header into the space of your current header window. If the previous section's header text and formats are identical, or you are in the first section of the document, then the Link To Previous button will appear dim. If you are using odd and even headers, Word will copy the previous section's odd header text.

Deleting Headers and Footers

Word makes it just as easy to change your mind and delete or erase headers and footers as it was to create them in the firstplace. To delete a header or footer, open the header or footer window, select all the text and header elements (such as page numbers), and press the Delete key. Once all the text and header elements are deleted, click the header window closed. However, if you have more than one header defined in a multisection document, you cannot delete a header by simply deleting the contents of a header window. In this case, you must replace all of the header text with a single space (to create a blank header). To do this quickly, use the Replace command discussed in Chapter 3.

Storing Headers in the Glossary

One feature of Word that has yet to be discussed is the *Glossary* command. Chapter 12 looks at this command in detail, but there is a feature of the Glossary command that is related to working with headers and footers. In particular, you can store the contents of a header or footer in Word's glossary, a time-saving device when you are formatting complex header or footer entries.

To add a header or footer to the glossary, you use Word's Cut, Copy, and Paste editing commands. The following steps highlight this procedure.

1. From Normal Editing View, choose **Header/Footer** from the Edit menu or press **Alt,E,H**.

   The header window appears.

2. Select **Header** and click **OK** or press **Enter**.

   The header window pane appears.

3. Using any of Word's selection commands, select the header text that you wish to copy to the glossary.

   The selected text is highlighted.

4. Select the **Copy** command from the Edit menu to place the selection in the Clipboard or press **Alt,E,C**.

   If you only want to create a glossary entry without saving the contents of the header window, you can also use the Cut command to move the contents to the Clipboard.

5. Choose **Glossary** from the Edit menu or press **Alt,E,O**.

   The glossary window (available only in full menus) appears.

297

Adding and Polishing Word

6. Choose **Paste** from the Edit menu to paste the header entry into the glossary or press **Alt,E,P**.

   The selected entry is depicted as Unnamed in the Name edit box. The entry is listed below the Name edit box itself.

7. Enter a descriptive name in the Name edit box that will represent your new glossary entry. Then, choose the context for the glossary entry as Template or press **Alt+T** or Global (**Alt+G**). Template is for a particular type of document while Global means for all documents.

8. Click **Define** or press **Alt+D** to record the new entry.

9. Click the glossary window **Closed** or press **Alt+C**.

Once your glossary entry is recorded with the *Define* command, you can easily insert the entry into a header window. To do this, open a standard empty header window and choose the Glossary command from the Edit menu. Once the Glossary dialog box appears, scroll down the glossary window until you find the entry that you wish to insert into your header window. The selected entry will be highlighted with white letters on a black background. Insert the entry into your empty header window by clicking the Insert button (Alt+I). When you close the glossary window, the header window will contain the new header entry. Close the header window.

Placing header entries in a glossary is a great time-saving feature. Suppose, for example, you wanted to create a set of headers that you commonly use, such as special letterheads, or headers that contain such complex text as mathematical or chemical equations. With these headers stored in the glossary, you have to create and format them only once. You can then quickly select and insert them into your header window panes.

One last note: The First Header, Odd Header, and Even Header commands (and corresponding footer commands) only appear on the Header Select edit menu in Normal Editing View (not Page View). In general, it is easier to add headers or footers in Normal Editing View so that you can specify the pages for which you created them. In addition, Page View does not offer the same ease of use with the time, date, and page-number icons as Normal Editing View.

Review

In this chapter you learned:

1. The running text that appears across the top of a page is called a header and the text that runs across the bottom is called a footer. Many documents use a header or footer to provide additional information about the document.

2. A header or footer can consist of multiple lines of text, including page numbers, time and date the document was created or printed, and text information that describes the document in some way.

3. You can create a header or footer by choosing the Header/Footer command found on the Edit menu.

4. You treat a header pane just like a standard document window. You can enter text and then edit and format the text any way you like.

5. You can see a header pane on your screen in Normal Editing View, Page View, or Print Preview. However, the icon bar of the header pane is only visible in Normal Editing View. Once the header pane is closed, the header itself is visible in Print Preview or Page View.

6. To format a header, open the header pane and then use Word's Character or Paragraph commands. You can even use the Ruler and Ribbon and their standard formatting options.

7. The header or footer panes include three basic elements on an icon bar: Page Number, Time, and Date. Choosing these icons inserts the respective fields into your header or footer at the location of the insertion point.

8. All page numbers in Word are inserted into a header or footer. If you don't wish to add elements other than page numbers to a header or footer, you can use the Insert Page Numbers command.

9. To delete page numbers, choose the Edit Header/Footer command, select either header or footer, select the page-number field from the header or footer pane, and then press the Delete key. Since page numbers are inserted via a page-number field, you must delete the field to remove them.

10. You can use Print Preview to change the position of a header. From Print Preview, click the Boundaries button and then drag the header vertically to reposition it. Always click outside the document page in Print Preview to register the change. To

reposition headers in the margin area, choose the Edit Header/Footer command and then use the header Ruler to create negative indents.

11. Use the Different First Page option found on the Edit Header/Footer window to omit headers from the first page of a section.

12. You can store header information as a glossary entry. Once stored in Word's glossary, use the Insert button in the Edit Glossary dialog box to insert it quickly.

TEN

Checking Spelling and Using the Thesaurus and Hyphenation

In this chapter:

- Using a Spelling Checker
- Checking Spelling with the Main Dictionary
- Building and Working with User Dictionaries
- Using the Thesaurus
- Using Hyphenation

You can use the spelling checker and Word's built-in hyphenation program, two of Word's commonly used utilities, to further polish your documents. Word's spelling checker is accessed via the Spelling command, and it works with other Word files, such as the main dictionary, to help you find and correct misspelled words. Although the main dictionary is handy, it is limited, just as a standard desktop dictionary is, to a specific set of entries. To solve this problem, Word enables you to create and customize your own dictionaries (called *user dictionaries*) to help you keep track of those special words, abbreviations, and so forth, that are particular to your business or field of interest.

If you need additional help, Word also provides a built-in thesaurus to look up synonyms for your most commonly used words. Just like the Spelling command, you will find the *Thesaurus* command on the Utilities menu.

Finally, Word accesses the built-in hyphenation program with a command on the Utilities menu: the *Hyphenate* command. The Hyphenate command allows you to control the appearance of docu-

Adding and Polishing Word

ments that might have a ragged right edge or ugly spacing due to Word's wrap-around feature. Hyphenate gives you control over when and where to hyphenate a word.

You will discover that the spelling checker, thesaurus, and hyphenation options are useful tools that will help you create better documents and also save you time. This chapter discusses these often overlooked, but always necessary tools.

Using a Spelling Checker

If nothing else about them is true, all people who use a computer and a word processing package are human. Humans tend to make mistakes, and we forget things—like how to correctly spell a word. Fortunately, the humans at Microsoft had enough wisdom to create a utility to help the human users of Word—the spelling checker.

A spelling checker is a program that helps you find and correct typing mistakes within your documents. It also helps you remember spellings that you have forgotten. A spelling checker works in much the same way you would to solve the same problems without the aid of a computer: it looks up unknown words in a dictionary. The best part of the spelling checker is that it is part of your program. You don't need to go looking for a dog-eared reference. You can quickly check the spelling of a single word or all the words in your entire document without leaving Word and starting a new application.

Word's Dictionaries

To use the spelling checker, you choose the *Spelling* command from the Utilities menu, which enables you to check the spellings of words in your text against the approximately 100,000 permanent entries stored in the program's *Main* dictionary. You also have the option of using two *supplemental* dictionaries. One of these is called STDUSER.DIC (standard user dictionary), and the other is called a "user dictionary." As you will learn, you can add new words to either supplemental dictionary, but only the user dictionary may be given a new name. The primary difference between the two supplemental dictionaries is that the standard dictionary can be used with any document while you will likely create a specific new user dictionary for a particular document.

When Word begins the spell check, it looks for the main dictionary file and loads it into memory. The Main dictionary file is located in the same directory as the Word program so there is no problem finding it. You will learn, however, that you can create new user dictionaries and store them in separate directories or on a separate disk just like any other document file. If you designate a user dictionary during a spell check that is not in the same directory as the Word program file, Word asks you to locate the file. We'll discuss how to access such a file shortly.

Checking Spelling with the Main Dictionary

When you use Word's spelling checker, every word in your document is compared against the entries in Word's Main dictionary file. To begin an actual spelling check of your document, first move the insertion point where in the document you want the spelling check to begin. For example, if you want to check the entire document, place the insertion point directly in front of the first character of the document. Although Word will provide a dialog box that lets you do the spell check from the beginning, regardless of where the insertion point is, it saves time if you move the insertion point to the beginning of the document prior to starting the spell check. The next step is to choose the Spelling command from the Utilities menu with the mouse or to press Alt,U,S as shown in Figure 10.1.

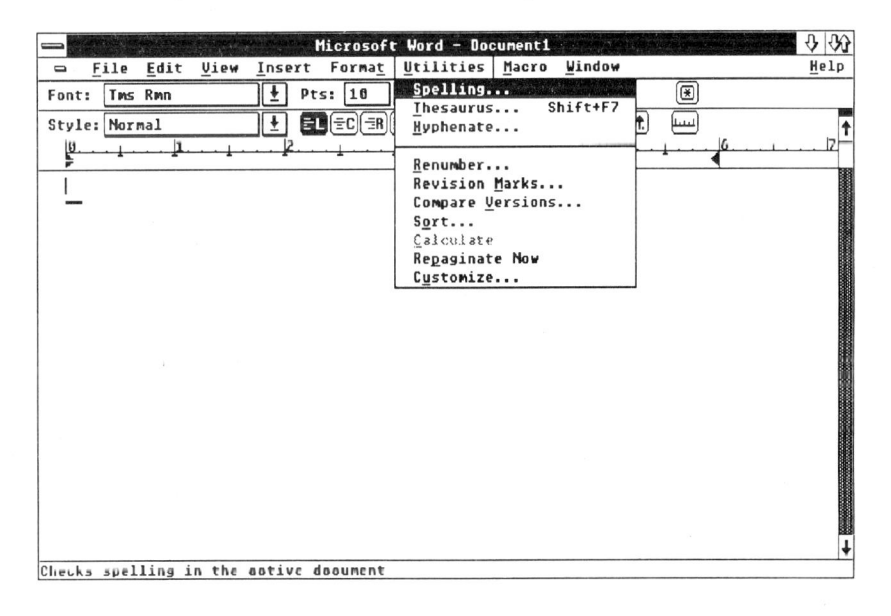

Figure 10.1 The Spelling command is located on the Utilities menu.

Shortly, Word loads the spelling checker file and opens the Spelling command window as shown in Figure 10.2. This is the first of two different Spelling command windows. The first dialog window allows you to spell check individual words in your document. If you click the Options button or press Alt+O, the first dialog box expands to allow you to select supplemental dictionaries, as shown in Figure 10.3.

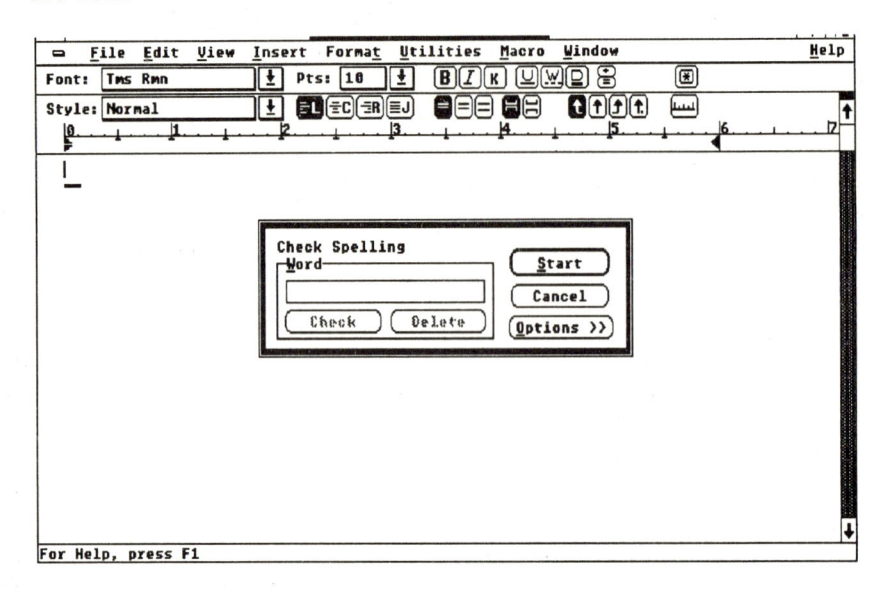

Figure 10.2 The first Spelling dialog window appears.

The second Spelling window only appears when Word can't match one of the words in your document with one of the words in any of the three active dictionary files (Main dictionary file, standard user dictionary file, and any user dictionary file that you select). The second Spelling window (see Figure 10.4) allows you to ask Word for suggestions of the unknown word, add such a word to one of the supplemental dictionaries, correct the word, or simply to leave the word alone.

When you choose the Spelling command, Word places the dialog box as the active window. However, Word assumes that you want to spell check the current document that appears behind the Spelling dialog box. The Spelling dialog box contains several spelling check options. You can check the spelling of an entire document, a section of text of any size, or even of a single word. (You can even use the spelling checker to suggest the spelling of an unknown word and then add that word to your user dictionary.) Before we list the steps necessary to complete a spell check, we'll take a quick tour of the com-

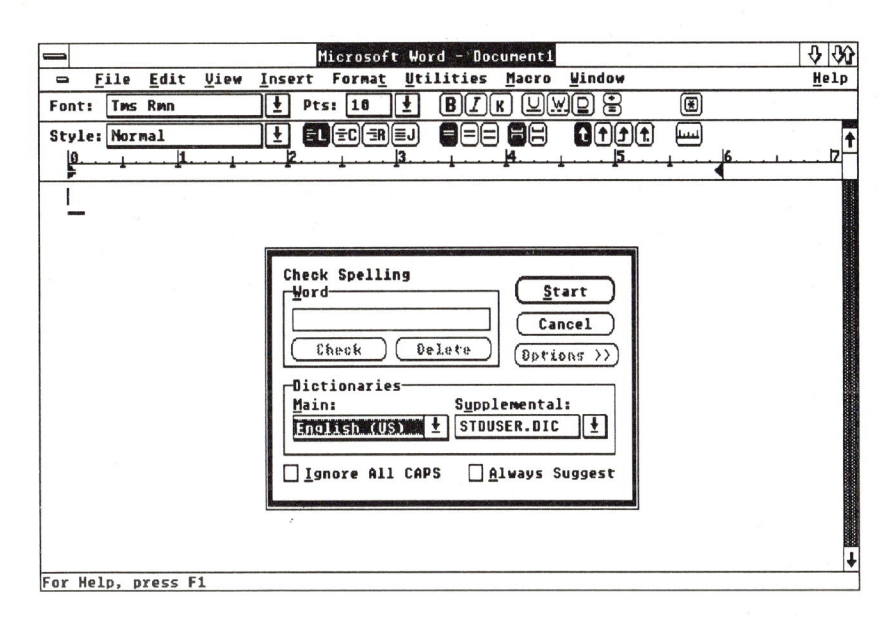

10—Checking Spelling and Using the Thesaurus and Hyphenation

Figure 10.3 The expanded Spelling window allows you to select optional dictionaries.

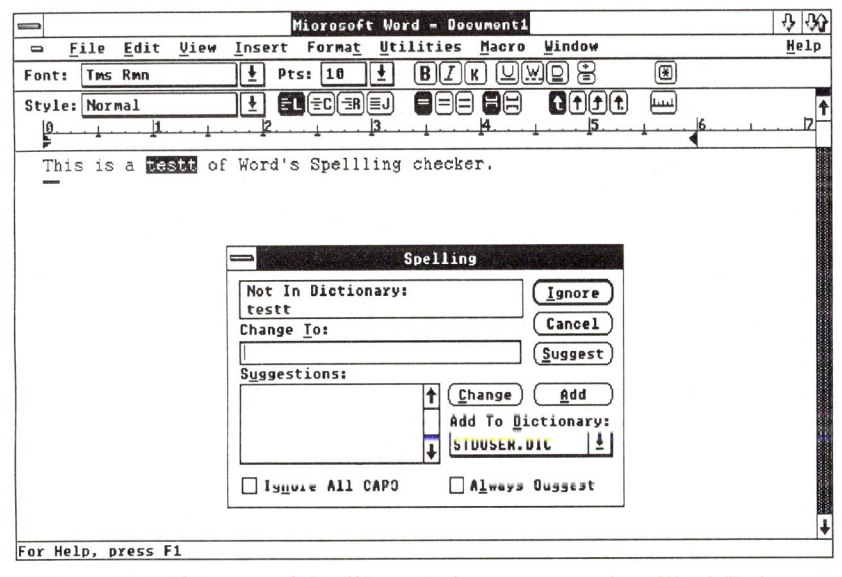

Figure 10.4 This second Spelling window appears when Word finds an unknown word.

mands and options found on the two Spelling dialog boxes that will appear. You should familiarize yourself with all of these options to help you master the spelling checker facility.

Touring the Initial Spelling Dialog Box

The initial Spelling dialog box looks just like any other window, complete with command buttons on the right side of the dialog box. The Start button begins the spell check process while the Cancel button is used to cancel a spelling check.

At the top left of the initial Spelling dialog box is a long edit window, Word, where you type the word whose spelling you wish to check. Once you type the word, choose the Check command button and Word will try to match that word against the entries in the active dictionaries (i.e., Main and any optional supplemental dictionary that you might choose). The Delete command button allows you to erase the word that appears in the Word edit box from the selected supplemental dictionary.

Choosing the Options button expands the Spelling dialog box (Figure 10.3) to show two pull-down menus that feature Word's dictionaries. The Main dictionary (of American English) is listed on the left. The *Supplemental* list box on the right can be selected for use prior to choosing Start for beginning the spell check process. A total of three active dictionaries can be open at one time (the Main dictionary file, the STDUSER.DIC file, and one optional user dictionary file), but the spell check can only be done with one supplemental dictionary along with the Main dictionary file. To select a specific dictionary, you can either use the mouse or an Alt+down arrow keypress to highlight a dictionary, or you can type the name of the dictionary in the appropriate edit box. Keep in mind that dictionary file names contain the extension, .DIC, which must be entered as a part of the name. If the dictionary file is located in a different directory, you can specify that directory by typing the pathname as well as the dictionary file name in the edit box (e.g., \dicfiles\legal.dic, where the legal dictionary file named legal.dic is stored in a directory named dicfiles). The Supplemental list box automatically lists the STDUSER.DIC file each time you issue the Spelling command. Later in this chapter you'll learn how to create additional customized user dictionaries that you can add to the Supplemental list. However, the Main dictionary file is the primary file Word uses to check your misspelled words. You can use the STDUSER.DIC file (or other user dictionary files) to begin to store your own entries for a personalized dictionary.

When you expand the Spelling dialog box, you'll notice two check box options labeled Ignore All Caps and Always Suggest. By default, both of these options are turned off. However, if you turn on the Ignore All Caps option, Word will do just what you expect it to do. In other words, during a spelling check, Word will not bother with any word that appears all in uppercase letters, such as an acronym or an individual's initials. If you turn off this option, a document that is filled with acronyms will require a great deal of time to spell check as Word will stop at each individual entry.

The Always Suggest option is used with Word's second Spelling dialog box to automatically suggest a list of words for correcting a mismatched word found during a spell check. As desirable as this feature sounds, the drawback is that it takes Word a long time to build such a list of words for every occurrence of a mismatched word. Leaving this option turned off allows you to use the Suggestion button (found on the second Spelling dialog window) to request help only when you need it.

Touring the Second Spelling Box

When Word finds a word that doesn't match any of the words in the active dictionaries, the unmatched word is highlighted and listed in the *Not In Dictionary* list box. At this point, you have three options: you can choose to leave the word alone by selecting Ignore, or you can ask Word to list alternative spellings of the word to correct it by choosing Suggest, or you can simply Cancel the spell check altogether (any corrections made prior to choosing Cancel will still apply). If you chose the Always Suggest option from the first Spelling window, when Word finds a word that it doesn't recognize, it will automatically suggest entries from the Main dictionary or the user dictionaries in the Suggestions list box. If more suggested entries are available than the list box holds, you can use the scroll box to scroll down the list until you find the correct word. If the Suggestions list box doesn't contain a proper correction for the misspelled word, you can type the correct word in the Change To edit box. Once the correct word appears in the Change To edit box, simply select the Change button. You can also use the Change To box to add or delete new entries in your user dictionaries.

In the lower right corner of the Spelling dialog box is a pull-down window labeled *Add To Dictionary*. When you wish to add a new word not presently listed in a supplemental user dictionary, you need to choose which of the two active user dictionaries to add it to, and then select the Add button command.

Correcting Misspelled Words

To begin correcting misspelled words, click the **Start Check** button on the Spelling dialog box or press **Alt+S**. Word begins comparing your words to the entries in the main dictionary (and any optional user dictionary that you select) and it stops at a word that it can't recognize. The unknown word is listed in the Not In Dictionary edit box of the second Spelling dialog window. At this point, you have several options. The first option is to correct the misspelled word by typing the correct spelling in the Change To edit box. Once you're satisfied that the correct spelling now appears in the Change To edit box, click the **Change** button or press **Alt+C**. This effects the change and causes Word to continue with the spelling check of your document.

When you edit the contents of the Change To box, you can position the pointer anywhere in the box and enter or delete characters just as if you were editing inside a typical document window. Like many boxes or windows, you can enter more characters—even several more words or a sentence or two—than the Change To box will display.

Now suppose the unknown word is spelled correctly, but Word's dictionary simply doesn't recognize it. A good example might be a person's name (e.g., author Swadley) or an address. In this case, simply click the Ignore button or press Alt+I and Word will leave the word as it appears. The Ignore option appeared in the window in place of the Start option once the spelling check began. If you select Ignore for a word, the spell check will not single out that word again during the current session; Word remembers the word as one you don't want to change. This handy feature lets you check such common occurrences as a person's name and address just one time. Word knows those words are not listed in its Main or any optional supplemental dictionaries (unless you add them), but it will pass on them just the same. As with Change, choosing Ignore will continue the check for other unknown words.

The basics of correcting a misspelled word with Word's spell checker are easily mastered. For practice, load one of your working documents, or create a new one, and then check your spelling using the following steps.

Use F7, the Spelling Key, to immediately begin spell checking a portion of selected text. This handy feature bypasses the initial Spelling dialog box. If you haven't selected any text, Word begins its check with the first word following the insertion point.

1. Place the insertion point at the beginning of your document.

A spell check begins with the first word following the insertion point. It's not necessary to place the insertion point at the beginning since Word provides you with an option of continuing the spell check if you haven't. However, it might save you some time.

10—Checking Spelling and Using the Thesaurus and Hyphenation

2. Choose **Spelling** from the Utilities menu or type **Alt+U+S** from the keyboard.

3. If you wish to use any optional user dictionaries during the spell check in addition to the Main dictionary, click the Options button (Alt+O) and make your selection from the Supplemental dictionaries pull-down window. (Use the arrow keys to highlight the desired dictionary name.) If you simply wish to use the standard Main dictionary, go on to step 4.

4. Click **Start** or press **Alt+S**. Word begins checking each word in your document against all the words in its Main Dictionary file (and any optional user dictionary file that you may have selected in step 3).

5. Click inside the **Change To** edit box or press **Alt+T** and enter the correct spelling of the word.

6. Once the word is spelled correctly, click **Change** or press **Alt+C**.

7. Word continues the spell check until it reaches the end of the document. If you didn't begin the spell check at the beginning, Word will provide the message: "Continue checking at beginning of document?" If you want to continue the spell check, click **OK** or press

The initial Spelling dialog box appears (see Figure 10.2).

If you choose Options, the initial spelling window appears as shown in Figure 10.3.

When Word finds a word that doesn't match any entries in its own file, the word is highlighted and listed in the Not In Dictionary edit field of the second Spelling dialog window. See Figure 10.4.

As the new word is entered inside the Change To box, the Change button becomes active and is no longer dim.

The word in the document is changed to the corrected word you entered into the Change To box.

309

Enter to do so, or choose
Cancel to return to the
document window.

Using Word's Suggestions for Correcting Words

Correcting all your misspelled words manually might become tedious. Further, you may be a good speller, but you probably aren't perfect. Unless you're a walking dictionary yourself, let Word's Main dictionary walk for you by suggesting alternative spellings for unknown words. When the spelling check identifies an unknown word, click the **Suggest** button or press **Alt+S**. In the Suggestions list box, Word will display all the words in the Main dictionary that are close to the word that you are trying to spell. If it can't find a word that is similar, it will tell you "No Suggestions" in a message box. Then, unfortunately, you're on your own—almost. Give it your best shot by typing the word in the Change To box the way you think it should be spelled. Click the **Change** button or press **Alt+C**. Then, double-check that word by choosing the **Spelling** command a second time and entering the unknown word in the Words edit window (a faster method is to choose the word and then press **F7**). Choose Check from the initial Spelling dialog window. If you guessed right, Word should let you know. If Word still says you're wrong, get out that dog-eared dictionary; Word's dictionary isn't perfect, either.

If, when you select the Suggest button, there are more alternative spellings than the box can hold, use the scroll bar on the right to go through the options. When a suggested word meets your needs, select it and then click the Change button to continue the check.

Finally, remember you can tell Word to automatically suggest words for every misspelled or unknown word by turning on the Always Suggest box (Alt+L) found on the Options portion of the initial Spelling window. If you leave Options off, you can choose when to ask Word for help by choosing the Suggest button or pressing Alt+S.

Correcting Repeated Misspellings

We are creatures of habit. If you misspelled a word once, it is likely that you will misspell the word again. Word helps you correct repeated misspellings with a single click of the Change button or press Alt+C. Once you correct a misspelled word, the corrected spelling automatically replaces every occurrence of that same misspelling throughout your document.

Continuing and Stopping the Spelling Check

You can start and stop a spell check at any point within a document. The spell check begins with the first word following the insertion point and continues to the end of the document. When it reaches the end of the document, an alert box asks, "Continue checking at beginning of document?" If you don't want to continue the check, choose the Cancel button.

You can also stop the spell check each time the speller stops at a word that it can't recognize. You can either choose Close from the Control box or choose the Cancel button. The next time you choose the Spelling command from the Utilities window, the spell check will again begin from the insertion point.

Checking Single Words and Sections

To select either a single word or a section of text for checking, first select the text you want to spell check and choose the **Spelling** command from the Utilities window or press **F7**. For a single word, choose **Check**. For a section of text, choose **Start**. If you select a single word, the spell checker will check that word against the entries in the Main dictionary, and if it doesn't recognize it, the word will be listed in the second Spelling window in the Not In Dictionary window. Just as before, to fix the unknown word, you can ask Word for suggestions, choose Ignore, or enter the corrected spelling in the Change To box. Once you've corrected the misspelled word, choose the **Change** button.

If you are just checking a single word, Word will return you immediately to the document window once you've made the change. If you selected a section of text, Word will continue to check each word until it reaches the end of the section. When the entire section has been checked, Word returns you to the document with the entire section still selected. The spell check will not continue checking the remainder of your document, as long as you first select a specific amount of text prior to choosing the Spelling command.

Building and Working with User Dictionaries

All dictionaries are limited, and Word's Main dictionary is no exception. Many words that the Main dictionary flags as incorrect, are, in fact, spelled correctly. Some of these flagged words may be common to your profession, such as standard abbreviations, that you will use frequently. Other terms may simply be words that are not stored in the Main dictionary file. Whichever, Word will stop and identify these words as unknown during a routine spell check, which can be an annoyance, indeed. Word offers a remedy for this potential headache in the form of user dictionaries. When you find yourself spell checking a word that you know is correct, but Word doesn't, you can add the word to your own dictionary. The next time Word's spell checker runs across the word, it will not stop because it can locate it now in one of your user dictionaries.

Because Word will automatically open the default STDUSER.DIC file as well as the Main dictionary file, you can easily add your new words to the STDUSER.DIC file. Once your words are stored in STDUSER.DIC, you don't need to worry about opening and closing any other dictionary file since STDUSR.DIC will always be open each time you choose the Spelling command. If you wish to personalize your user dictionary for the various types of documents you work on, Word lets you create additional user dictionaries that you can add to the Supplemental list box by opening a new user dictionary file. To create a new user dictionary file, complete the following steps:

1. Choose the **Spelling** command from the Utilities menu or press **Alt,U,S**.

   The initial Spelling window appears.

2. Select the **Options** command button or press **Alt+O**.

   The initial Spelling window expands to show the Supplemental list of available dictionaries. The STDUSER.DIC file is highlighted if it was the last user dictionary opened or if no other user dictionary exists.

3. To create a new user dictionary, type the name of that dictionary in the Supplemental edit box. The file name follows the rules for creating file names, but it uses .DIC for the extension. If you simply wish to open an existing user dictionary, select that dictionary from the pull-down menu.

   The name of the new or selected user dictionary is highlighted in the edit box window.

4. If you entered a new user dictionary file name, Word displays the message: "User dictionary not found. Create?" If you wish to create this new dictionary file, choose **Yes**.

As soon as you do, the new user dictionary file is created and you are returned to the document window. The next time you choose the Options command button from the Spelling dialog window, you will notice that the Supplemental list box now contains your new user dictionary as well as the STDUSER.DIC file.

Adding Personal Terms to a User Dictionary

Since Word's Main dictionary file cannot be altered, you need a method to create a new dictionary to which you can add and delete entries not currently recognized by Word as valid. Word lets you create your own "personalized" dictionary by simply adding words to the empty file identified as STDUSER.DIC or to a new user dictionary that you create (see the previous section). The method for adding words to any user dictionary is similar. When Word finds a mismatched word during a spell check, the second Spelling dialog window appears. The unknown word is listed in the Not in Dictionary window. Once you decide whether the word is properly spelled (correct it by using Change To), choose the supplemental dictionary where you wish to store that word with the **Add To Dictionary** command and then choose the **Add** command button. You cannot add words to the Main dictionary, but you can add them to STDUSER.DIC or any other user dictionary file that you've created. Remember, STDUSER.DIC is just like any other user dictionary file and contains no entries when you first begin working with the spell checker.

Adding a word to a user dictionary can begin from two points: during a current spell check or prior to starting the spell check. The steps necessary for adding a word to a dictionary are as follows:

1. If you haven't begun to spell check, choose the **Spelling** command or press **Alt,U,S**. If you are currently checking a document and wish to add a mismatched word, go on to step 3.

2. Enter the word that you wish to add to a user dictionary in the Word edit box, and then choose the **Check** command.

   If the word doesn't match any word in the Main dictionary file, the second Spelling window will appear with the word in the Not in Dictionary window.

3. Move to the **Add to Dictionary** pull-down window or press **Alt+D**, and select from the active dictionaries where you wish to store the new word.

   The selected dictionary will appear highlighted in the edit window.

4. Choose the **Add** command button or press **Alt+A**.

   The word in the Not in Dictionary window is added to the selected user dictionary.

Deleting and Revising Words in a User Dictionary

Delete user dictionaries like any other file: Use the Delete command from the MS-DOS Executive screen.

Occasionally you might wish to remove a word from a user dictionary. To do so, first select the dictionary from the Supplemental list box and then enter the word in the Word edit box. Then, choose **Delete** from the initial Spelling window to remove the word from the dictionary.

What if, instead of deleting a word, you wish to revise one? Perhaps you've added a word that was misspelled. To revise a word, follow the same procedure as when adding a word to the desired user dictionary. Of course, the original term, spelled incorrectly, remains in the user dictionary along with the revised term. To remove it, enter the original term in the Words edit box and delete it as just described. This procedure requires that you pay particular attention to the correct spelling of words added to a supplemental user dictionary. If you don't, you can fill a dictionary file with a lot of useless words.

Saving New User Dictionaries

Every time you add to or delete words from a user dictionary, Word automatically saves the changes to that dictionary. Unlike other files, you don't need to save it prior to leaving the current session.

Using the Thesaurus

Many a wordsmith uses synonyms for those words that always seem to be used over and over. To find a variety of word options, you can use the *Thesaurus* command found on the Utilities menu. Word's thesaurus not only serves to find a synonym for a selected word, but to provide you with the definitions of a list of possible synonyms for a particular word. The thesaurus is a versatile tool that will provide some additional flexibility to your writing. For example, to look up synonyms for a particular word in your document, or to simply type a word and to look up synonyms for that word, use the following steps:

1. To look up synonyms for a particular word, select the word by positioning the insertion point within the word itself or by placing the insertion point to the right of the word (i.e., between words), and then choose the **Thesaurus** command from the Utilities menu or press **Alt,U,T**. You can also use the shortcut keypress **Shift+F7** to open Word's thesaurus feature.

    The Thesaurus dialog window appears as shown in Figure 10.5.

2. The selected word now appears in the Look Up edit box. A list of synonyms for that selected word appears in the Synonyms list window.

    A list of definitions for the word in Look Up now appears in the Definitions list window.

3. Select a synonym from the Synonyms list window.

    Its definition appears in the Definitions list window. If necessary, scroll the list windows to read the synonyms and corresponding definitions.

4. If you decide to replace the selected word with one of the synonyms, select it from the list and then click the **Replace** command button or press **Alt+R**.

Adding and Polishing Word

To select a synonym from a list, move to **Synonyms** *or type* **Alt+Y** *and then use the up, down, right, or left arrow key. If you have a mouse, simply click on the synonym desired.*

The features of the thesaurus are not limited to words found in a specific document. You can also use it to find synonyms for any word at random. To do this, choose the **Thesaurus** command without first selecting a word (or select more than one word at a time) and then type the word for which you wish to find a synonym in the Look Up edit box. Choose the **Synonyms** command button or press **Alt+S** and the Synonyms list window will show a list of synonyms for your word (see Figure 10.6). If you type a new word in Look Up or choose a definition from the Definition list window, the list of synonyms changes to reflect the item you typed or the definition you selected.

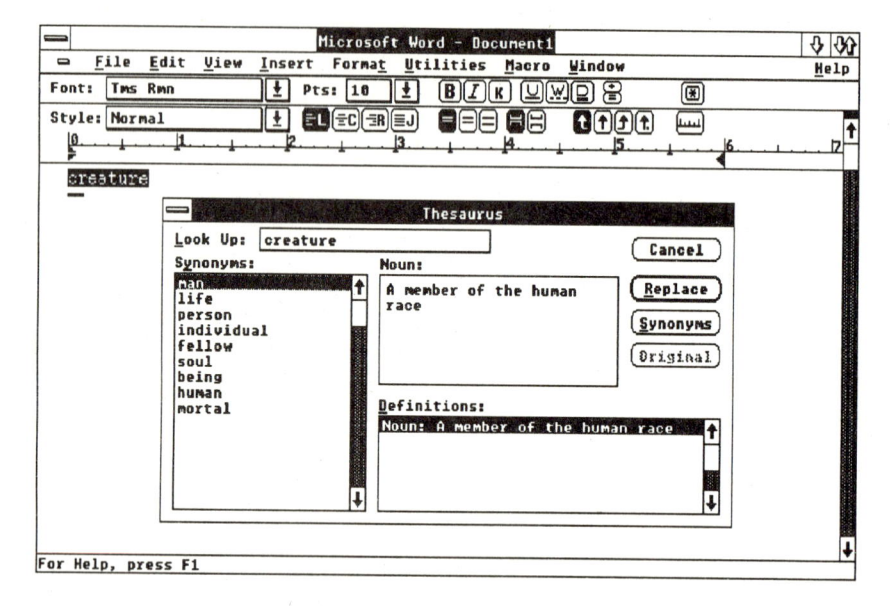

Figure 10.5 The Thesaurus window lists synonyms for a selected word.

The Thesaurus dialog window and related commands are very flexible. You can enter new words in Look Up or select an item from Definitions and then choose Synonyms to see a new list of synonyms. You can look up definitions for synonyms or look up synonyms for definitions. Simply select the appropriate item and choose the Synonyms button to change the lists of synonyms or definitions. With all this changing, it's nice that Word provides the Original command button to see a list of original synonyms that was displayed when the command was first selected. To cancel the Thesaurus, choose the Cancel button or the Close command from the window's control box.

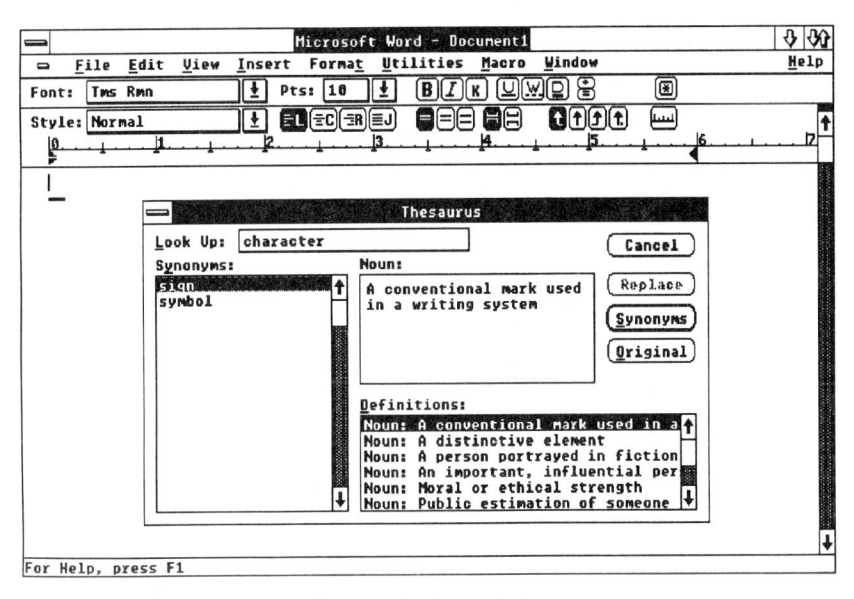

10—Checking Spelling and Using the Thesaurus and Hyphenation

Figure 10.6 Type any word in Look Up and choose Synonyms to show a list of synonyms and corresponding definitions.

Using Hyphenation

Hyphenation is used to clean out ugly spacing that can occur in a document. In most justified documents, Word will insert spaces in a line that appear to "stretch" that line until it reaches the margin. With hyphenation, you can avoid those unsightly spaces and in general create a more polished looking document. For example, consider the two samples of identical text depicted in Figures 10.7 and 10.8. Paragraph 1 uses full justification without hyphenation. Paragraph 2 also uses full justification, but it also uses hyphenation within some lines to produce a better-looking document. In particular, notice that by using hyphenation the extra spaces have been removed from several lines. Judge for yourself and then read on.

You can use hyphenation any time you are creating a document. Word won't automatically hyphenate your words as you enter the text, but you can easily hyphenate the document once it's finished. You can hyphenate a word at the end of the sentence as you type, but that process reduces your productivity. It's much easier to wait until you've finished creating and editing your document, and then hyphenate as you are formatting. You don't want unsightly spacing

317

```
Paragraph 1
Raising children is a mystery to me.  I suppose I am not
unlike many folks.  Children can be very frustrating and
require a great deal of patience.  Thankful as I am,
sometimes I wonder what it would be like to be a kid again
myself.  Perhaps, I haven't really grown up at all.  Yet
when my son tugs on my leg and wants to play, I know he
really needs me.  He needs me in ways that I cannot find a
substitute for the same love and satisfaction.  Of all the
miracles that could have happened to me, I believe the joy
of hearing my son call me "dad" is the best.
```

Figure 10.7 Full justification without hyphenation "stretches" lines to fit across the screen.

```
Paragraph 2
Raising children is a mystery to me.  I suppose I am not un-
like many folks.  Children can be very frustrating and re-
quire a great deal of patience.  Thankful as I am, sometimes
I wonder what it would be like to be a kid again myself.
Perhaps, I haven't really grown up at all.  Yet when my son
tugs on my leg and wants to play, I know he really needs me.
He needs me in ways that I cannot find a substitute for the
same love and satisfaction.  Of all the miracles that could
have happened to me, I believe the joy of hearing my son
call me "dad" is the best.
```

Figure 10.8 Hyphenation eliminates some of the extra spaces.

(probable with full justification) or badly ragged edges on the right or left margin (likely with right- or left-justified text) due to the wrap-around feature of Word.

The Hyphenate Command

The *Hyphenate* command is found on the Utilities menu. When you choose Hyphenate or press Alt,U,H, the command uses a built-in utility program to call upon the hyphenation file. The file came stored on your Utilities 1 disk (the same disk that stored your Main dictionary file). In order for the Hyphenate command to work, the hyphenation file must be present on the current Word directory (installed on your hard disk during the setup procedure).

You can hyphenate your entire document or just a portion of your text if you select it prior to choosing the Hyphenate command. Once you begin to use the Hyphenate command, Word will find the first word following the insertion point and then look for words that it can move to the end of the previous line. Word allows you to hyphenate your documents manually, semi-automatically, or fully automatically. Manually means that as you type your document and reach the end of a line, you insert a hyphen by pressing the Hyphen key (or some combination of the hyphen key for optional—Ctrl+Hyphen—or nonbreaking hyphens—Ctrl+Shift+Hyphen. If you hyphenate your documents semi-automatically, Word will stop at each word so you can confirm each hyphenation with an optional hyphen. Full automatic hyphenation means that Word automatically inserts optional hyphens at the end of a line where appropriate. Such automatic hyphenation is quicker than the other two methods, but it doesn't enable you to use your judgment about how your document should look. The basic operation of the Hyphenate dialog box (Figure 10.9) is similar to that of other Word dialog windows. That's one good reason to love Word for Windows, the operations are so uniform, even "user-friendly." Before we walk you through the steps of using the Hyphenate facility, let's investigate the commands found on the Hyphenate dialog window.

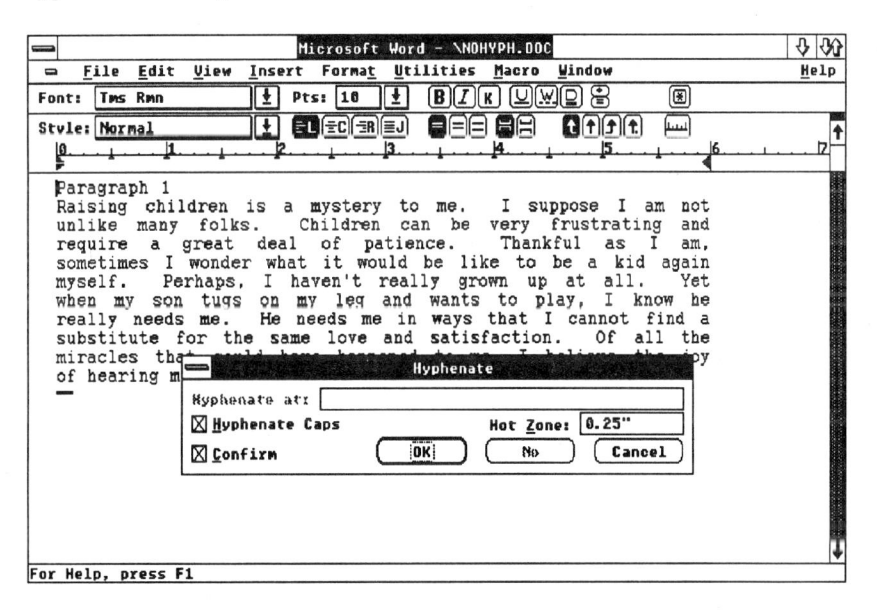

Figure 10.9 The Hyphenate command produces this dialog box.

The Hyphenate dialog box contains one large edit box (entitled appropriately, Hyphenate at) located at the top line of the window. During a hyphenation run, the Hyphenate at edit box will list words suggested for hyphenation. The words themselves are displayed in suggested syllables where hyphen breaks might occur. Word will also

319

highlight its preferred hyphen break, but you can easily change where to break a word by clicking on one of the other listed breaks or on another break not shown by Word. If you don't have a mouse, simply use the right and left arrow keys to reposition the hyphenation point. The last element you will notice is a dotted vertical line that runs in the suggested syllable break. This line indicates where the right margin would occur if the word were hyphenated as Word suggests. If you move the hyphenation point to the right of the line break, Word won't use it during the current situation unless you change the amount of text prior to the break and Word finds it appropriate to do so.

Below the Hyphenate edit box is a Hyphenate Caps check box. This option is selected by Word by default and treats all uppercase and lowercase words the same during the hyphenation process. This feature is great for long titles, but might be inappropriate for proper names. To turn off this option, click it once prior to starting the hyphenation process or press Alt+H.

In the lower left corner of the Hyphenate window is the Confirm check box entitled. Also selected by Word by default, this option allows you to use the Hyphenate command semi-automatically. In other words, each time Word finds a word to add an optional hyphen, the process pauses and lets you confirm each proposed hyphen before it's inserted. If you wish to hyphenate your document or selected text automatically without any review, simply turn this option off by clicking the box or pressing Alt+C.

On the right side of the Hyphenate dialog box you will find an edit box called Hot Zone. The Hot Zone is the length of space at the right margin that determines when a hyphenation will take place. Set at a 1/4" default value, the Hot Zone tells Word to hyphenate a word if the space left over at the end of a line is wider than the Hot-Zone measurement. In other words, if the space at the end of a line is greater than 1/4" (using the default measurement), the first word on the next line is hyphenated to eliminate some of the space on the previous line. Since you can change the width of the Hot Zone, keep the following two guidelines in mind:

- Less raggedness on the right requires a smaller Hot Zone. Generally, however, you will increase the number of optional hyphens.
- Increasing the size of the Hot Zone will produce less need for optional hyphens. However, you increase the chance for more raggedness and wasted space on the right side of your document.

Three control options are at the bottom of the Hyphenate window: OK, No, and Cancel. You will probably find these options self-explanatory. Before you choose the Hyphenate command, however, you must decide whether you want to hyphenate the entire document or a portion of selected text. If you choose the latter, select the text you've chosen prior to choosing the Hyphenate command. Then, to begin the hyphenate process, choose the Hyphenate command from Utilities and click OK or press Enter. Note that hyphenation always begins at the insertion point or at the beginning of the selected text. You should also note that the action of the OK button depends upon whether the Confirm option has been selected or not. If Confirm is on, Word stops when it finds the first word to be hyphenated and highlights it in the Hyphenate at edit box. A Yes button replaces the OK button at the bottom of the window. If you choose Yes, Word inserts a hyphen at the suggested hyphenation point and then displays the next word for hyphenation (if any). If the Confirm button is off, choosing OK starts the automatic hyphenation process, which will run to completion and then close the dialog box. If you choose No during the hyphenation process, Word skips to the next word that is available for hyphenation.

Finally, the Cancel button lets you change your mind about hyphenating. Choosing this button stops hyphenating and closes the window, but does not remove any hyphens that you may have already inserted. As an alternative to choosing Cancel, you can also press the Esc key or choose Close from the Control box. Choosing either of these latter methods will also retain any hyphens that may already have been inserted.

You've probably breezed into the Hyphenate command already. Before running through the necessary steps, you should explore the types of hyphens available to you.

Which Hyphen Type?

Word offers three types of hyphens: normal, nonbreaking, and optional. Each time you decide to hyphenate a word, you can choose among these. The appearance of these hyphens on your screen depends on the Optional Hyphens option on the Preferences command dialog box. If this option is turned off, all three hyphens will have the same appearance. If this option is turned on, the options will all look slightly different.

Normal Hyphens

The distinction of the normal hyphen is that it will always appear. This feature is great for words that you always want to print with a hyphen, regardless of the word's location within a line, such as:

It's time to say good-by to all your old friends.

If a normal hyphen appears at the end of the line, Word breaks the word after the hyphen. You can enter a normal hyphen manually from the keyboard by pressing the Hyphen key, which is located next to the equal sign (=). A normal hyphen at the end of a line might look like:

When I write, I like to get lost in a sound-
proof booth.

Nonbreaking Hyphens

The nonbreaking hyphen is also always visible. However, this option is used for hyphenated words or text that you *never* want to break, such as "sing-along" or "wrap-around" or perhaps a social security number: 357-84-8883. To enter a nonbreaking hyphen, hold down the Control key and the Shift key, and then press the Hyphen key simultaneously (Ctrl+Shift+-). Using a nonbreaking hyphen prevents Word's wrap-around feature from breaking hyphenated words and giving undesirable results.

Optional Hyphens

Optional hyphens are the third type of hyphen, and they differ from the normal and the nonbreaking hyphen because they do not show on your screen unless they appear at the end of a line. The optional hyphen is used for adjusting lines that don't look quite right due to the automatic word-wrap feature. The advantage of using optional hyphens is that the hyphen won't appear unless the word occurs at the end of a line. If you reformat your document, say, to change your margins, it's possible a hyphenated word made with optional hyphens will now appear at your line break. Likewise, if a line break once created an optional hyphen and the word no longer occurs at the end of the line, Word will remove the optional hyphen. Thus, you can use an optional hyphen to mark the location of a word break in the event that a word does appear at the end of a line. Because of the flexibility of the optional hyphen, Word uses this type of hyphen with the Hyphenate command. To create an optional hyphen manually, press the Ctrl key and the Hyphen key simultaneously.

Using the Hyphenate Command

Remember, you can insert manual hyphens (normal, nonbreaking, or optional) directly from the keyboard by pressing the correct key combinations at the end of a sentence.

You have a choice with the Hyphenate command: You can hyphenate a document semi-automatically by turning on the Confirm check box or let Word do it automatically by turning off the Confirm check box. If you wish to hyphenate your document manually, simply use the hyphenate key options as you enter your text. You also need to decide whether to hyphenate the whole document or just a part of it, which you indicate by selecting that part first. The following steps will guide your use of hyphenation.

1. Determine whether you want to hyphenate the entire document or a portion of it. If you want to hyphenate a section of text, select that text now. Otherwise, place the insertion point at the location where you want the hyphenation to begin.

   Selected text is highlighted.

2. Choose **Hyphenate** from the Utilities menu or press **Alt,U,H**.

   The Hyphenate dialog box appears.

3. Decide whether to use semi-automatic or automatic hyphenation. For automatic hyphenation, turn off the Confirm option or press **Alt+C**.

   The Confirm option is selected by default. If you turned it off for automatic hyphenation, its check box appears empty.

4. Decide whether to hyphenate capitalized words. This check box is on by default.

5. To start hyphenation, click the **OK** button or press **Enter**.

   This is called the "confirming hyphenation procedure." Word begins looking at each word in your document following the insertion point. When it finds a word to hyphenate, the word is listed in the Hyphenate at edit bar with the suggested word breaks. Note that the default OK

6. Confirm hyphenation by clicking **Yes** or pressing **Alt+Y** to accept Word's suggestion or click on any other possible breaks first. If you don't want to hyphenate the selected word, click **No** or press **Alt+N** to continue.

button will be displayed as Yes if the Confirm option is turned on. If the Confirm option is turned off, then Word hyphenates your document automatically and closes the dialog window. The remaining steps are then unnecessary.

Word now looks for the next possible word to break. When it is found, that word is listed in the Hyphenate at edit box.

7. After Word reaches the end of the document, an alert box asks you if you want to continue at the beginning of the document. Click **OK** or press **Enter** to continue or choose **Cancel** to stop. Note: If you started the hyphenation process at the beginning of the document, however, an "End of Document Reached" alert is displayed.

If you choose Cancel, Word closes the Hyphenate box for you. Any hyphen inserts made prior to choosing Cancel are still applied, however.

Undoing Hyphenation

You can manually "undo" hyphenation by selecting the hyphens and then pressing the Delete key. A quick method is to choose the Undo Hyphenation command from the Edit menu, but, as with all Undo commands, it is only available to you immediately after you've completed the hyphenation procedure. If you enter any other command, type new text, edit text, and so on, the Undo option is turned off and appears dim again.

You are not quite up the creek yet, however. To remove any optional hyphen, choose the Replace command from the Edit menu and complete the following steps.

10—Checking Spelling and Using the Thesaurus and Hyphenation

1. Choose **Replace** from the Edit menu or press **Alt,E,R**.

   The Replace dialog box appears.

2. Enter a **caret** (^) followed by a **Hyphen** in the Search For edit box (Figure 10.10).

   Do *not* enter anything in the Replace With edit box.

3. To delete all hyphens, first turn off the **Confirm** option or press **Alt+C** and then click **OK** or press **Enter**. If you want to delete some of the hyphens, leave the **Confirm** option turned on and then choose **OK**.

   If you left the Confirm option turned on, Word will stop at the location of each hyphen and let you decide whether to delete it.

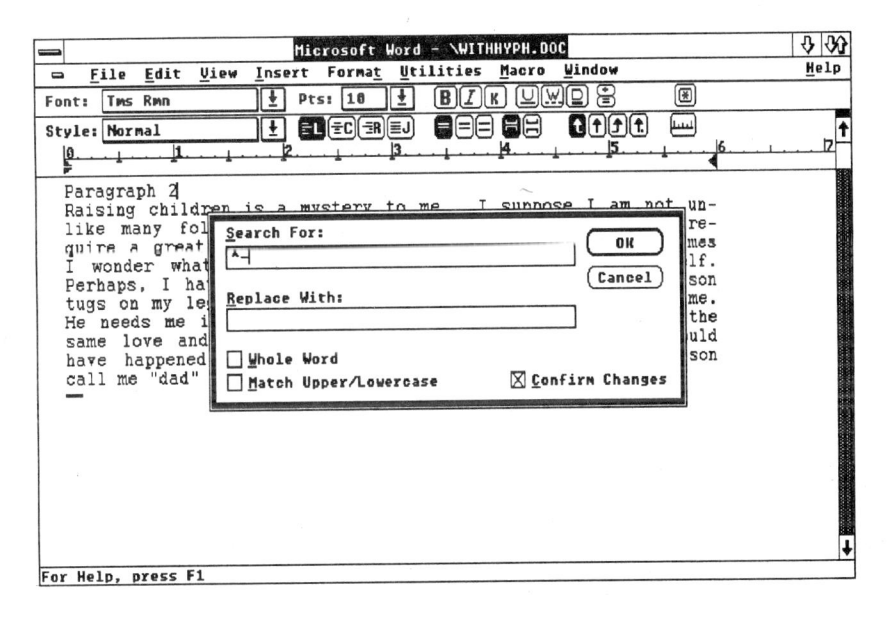

Figure 10.10 The caret followed by a hyphen removes hyphens from your documents.

Review

In this chapter you learned:

1. To access Word's built-in spelling checker, use the Spelling command from the Utilities menu.

2. Each time you issue the Spelling command, Word loads the Main dictionary file and the STDUSER.DIC file. Use the STDUSR.DIC file to store your own entries for a personalized dictionary.

3. When Word executes a spell check, it checks every word in your document against the words stored in the Main dictionary file, the STDUSER.DIC file, and one of any user dictionary files that are currently open. If Word finds a word it doesn't recognize, it stops and highlights the word as a potential misspelled word.

4. You can correct misspellings manually or you can let Word do some of the work. Word's Suggest button offers alternative spellings for words it doesn't recognize. You can check the spelling of an entire document or just a portion of it. To check a single word or a section of text, select the text and then choose the Spelling command.

5. Add words to the User 1 dictionary with the + button. You can save all your new words in the User 1 dictionary or rename the file using the Save As command to customize it.

6. You can create a variety of user dictionaries. To navigate in and out of dictionaries, use the standard Open and Close commands from the File menu while in the Spelling dialog box.

7. Use hyphenation to avoid unsightly spaces added by Word in justified documents.

8. To begin hyphenation, choose the Hyphenate command from the Utilities menu. You can hyphenate an entire document or a portion of selected text.

E L E V E N

Chapter

Using Word's Tables and Math Features

In this chapter:

- Introducing Tables
- Creating Tables
- Editing Tables
- Formatting Tables
- Creating Side-by-Side Paragraphs
- Doing Math

Microsoft has provided one of the best features for making life easier while working with a word processor—the tables feature. In this chapter, you'll learn how to create tables quickly without using tabs. You will learn how to create, edit, and format tables and how to use Word's Sort and Calculate commands to do basic mathematical calculations. You will find many uses for the tables feature, and some of the more common uses will be explored in this chapter, including tabular columns and side-by-side paragraphs.

Introducing Tables

One of the word processing tasks that seems to consume a great amount of time is the creation of tables. A table is a way of organizing text and/or numerical data in neatly defined rows and columns. For example, the following are examples of tables of information:

Table 11.1 Sales Salaries

Salesperson	**Number**	**Territory**	**Salary**
Tony Zabinski	161	Massachusetts	$28,400
Alice Smith	219	Indiana	$22,000
John Stein	108	California	$26,500
Bo Castle	222	New York	$25,300

Table 11.2 1989 Sales of Widgets (in 1000s)

Month	**Budget**	**Actual**	**Variance**
January	10	15	+5
February	12	10	(2)
March	15	12	(3)
April	8	10	+2
May	10	11	+1
June	10	12	+2
July	6	7	+1
August	5	2	(3)
September	12	15	+3
October	15	18	+3
November	20	18	(2)
December	22	25	+3

Without Word's tables feature, you would create such a table of information by pressing the Tab key at a series of tab stops. The information that you want in the table wouldn't fit or it would appear uneven, and adding or deleting any of the tabular material would throw the entire table out of alignment. To test this, type Table 11.1 and then change Indiana to North Dakota. The extra characters will push the alignment out of whack.

Fortunately, Word has come to the rescue with its brand new table feature. You can use Word's _Insert Table_ command to insert an empty table in your document. You then use the mouse or Tab key to move around the table, inserting your information, be it text or numerical data, without worrying about changing the alignments in the table. This is possible because Word's tables are made up of a series of individual _cells,_ similar to a spreadsheet. You can format each cell independently, or you can format all the cells the same way. Since each cell in a table is separate, Word allows you to enter text of any length in a cell. If a cell is not wide enough, Word wraps the text to the next line as if the cell were an independent little document. In other words, the cells in a Word table will expand and contract according to the amount of text that you enter. If you cause the cell you're working in to expand, the others will likewise expand.

Text or numerical data are not all you can enter into a table; you can even enter graphics, or a combination of text, numerical data, and graphics. The only thing you can't enter into a table is another table. You will find that creating tables with Word, even long tables of financial ledger data, is a snap. You can use Word's Utilities Sort command to arrange text alphabetically or your numerical data sequentially. Once your data is set in a table, you can even use the Utilities Calculate command to add, subtract, multiply, or divide groups of numbers.

Once you have mastered setting up and creating tables, you'll probably find a number of uses for tables that will make your work easier. An obvious use is to create tabular columns of information as just illustrated. A little later in this book, we will explore an example of side-by-side paragraphs. In Chapter 16, you'll learn to use the table feature to format data files (names and addresses) in order to create and merge form letters. Indeed, there are many uses for the table feature, so let's get started learning the basics.

Creating Tables

The first step to creating a table has generally been to determine how you want the table to look. How many columns and how many rows? How far apart do you space the columns? Determining the numbers of columns and rows is still the first step, except Word has just made the task seem simpler. To set up an empty table, you use the Insert Table command from the Insert menu. Get a clean document page and practice creating a table of data with the following steps.

1. Place the insertion point where you want to insert your empty table. For this example, use a blank document. Choose **New** from the File menu by pressing **Alt,F,N** and click **OK** or press **Enter**.

2. To view the cell boundaries of your table on the screen, turn on the **Table Gridlines** option found on the View

Preferences menu. You can leave this option off if you wish, but it's easier to see the dimensions of the table when it's turned on.

3. Choose **Table** from the Insert menu or press **Alt,I,T**.

   The Insert Table dialog box appears.

4. If necessary, move to the Number of Columns edit box by pressing **Alt + C**, and enter the number of columns you want in your table. The default value is set to 2 columns. Enter **4** for this example.

   As you enter a value in the Number of Columns edit box, notice that the width of each column is displayed in the Column Width box with the default value of Auto. The width of each column is determined by dividing the column width for the current section by the number of columns specified. Auto means that the column widths are divided evenly among the columns with space between the columns subtracted first.

5. Click in the **Number of Rows** edit box or press **Alt + R** or simply press the **Tab** key once to move the highlighting. The default value is set at 1 row. Again, enter a value of **4**.

   Figure 11.1 shows how the dialog window now looks.

6. Click **OK** or press **Enter**.

   An empty table with the number of columns and rows that you specified is inserted into your document at the location of the insertion point. If you turned on the Table Gridlines option, you'll be able to see the table outlined in a dotted gridline, as in Figure 11.2. The gridline will not print.

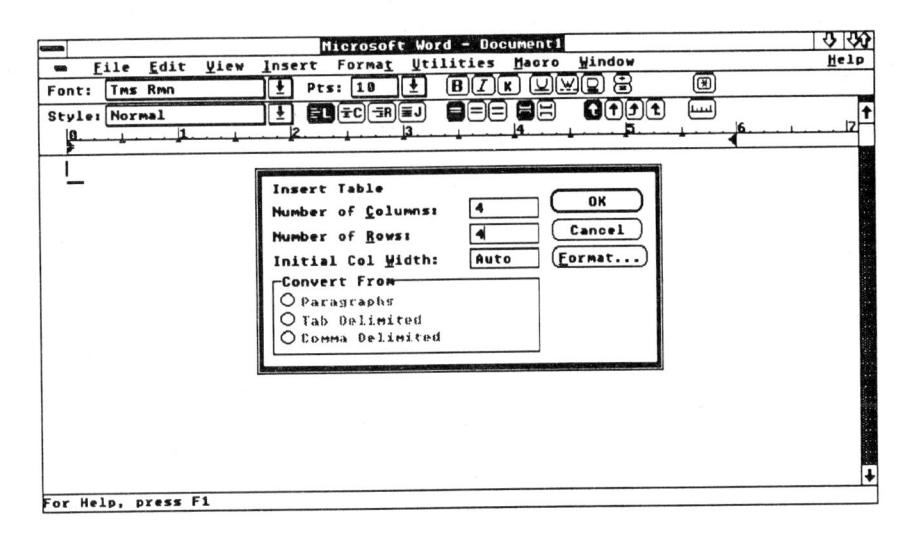

Figure 11.1 Specify the number of columns and rows for a table by choosing the Insert Table command.

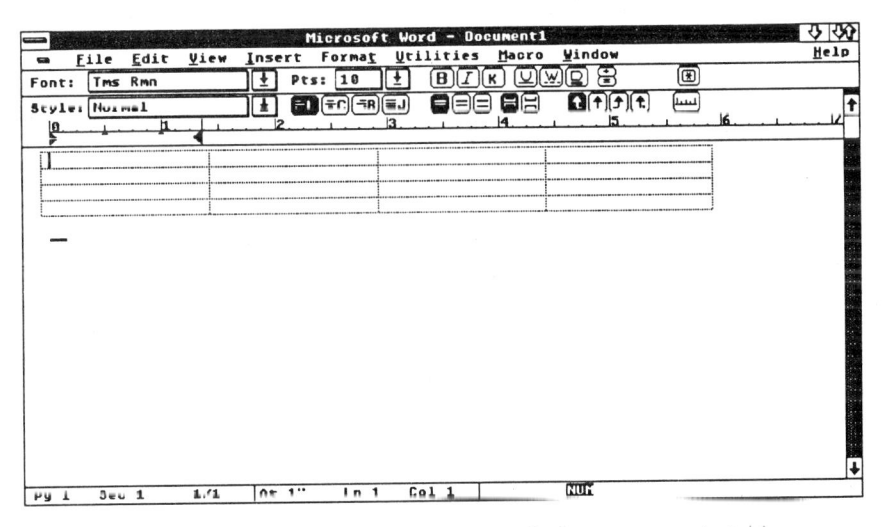

Figure 11.2 The Insert Table command places an empty table in your document.

Inserting Text

Inserting text in an empty table created with Word's table feature is a simple process. Click inside any cell, type the information you want there, and then move on to the next cell. You can move from one cell to another by clicking with the mouse or by pressing the Tab key. When you reach the end of a row, do not press the Enter key; instead, press the Tab key again or use the mouse. If you forget and press Enter, press the Backspace key to erase the paragraph mark before continuing with the Tab key (the cell will be increased in size to allow for the additional paragraph mark). If you reach the last cell on the last row and press Enter, Word will add an additional row. To delete the row quickly, select the entire row, including the paragraph mark, and then press Delete. For practice, use the next set of steps to create the table in Figure 11.3.

You can also use the arrow keys on your keyboard to move any direction, or you can use Shift + Tab to move to the previous cell in the table.

1. When you first insert an empty table into your document, the insertion point will appear in the cell in the upper left corner of the table. Type the text you want in this cell.

   If your text will not fit within the width of a single cell, Word will use its wrap-around feature to display the text on the next line without affecting the remaining cells. The other cells will expand or contract according to the amount of text that you enter.

2. To move to the next cell, or column, simply press the **Tab** key or click inside the desired cell with the mouse. You can also use the arrow keys to move through all elements of a cell and to the next cell.

   As you press Tab, the insertion point jumps from cell to cell, moving from left to right. Press Shift + Tab to move backward.

3. Continue moving from cell to cell by pressing the **Tab** key and entering the desired information. Do not press the Enter key when you reach the end of a row; continue using the Tab key.

   When you have finished entering the text into your table, the result will look like Figure 11.3.

Changing Existing Text to a Table

Word's tables feature enables you to select existing text and change it into a table. This feature is useful with material that you have separated by tabs or paragraphs, whose structure appears out of alignment

11—Using Word's Tables and Math Features

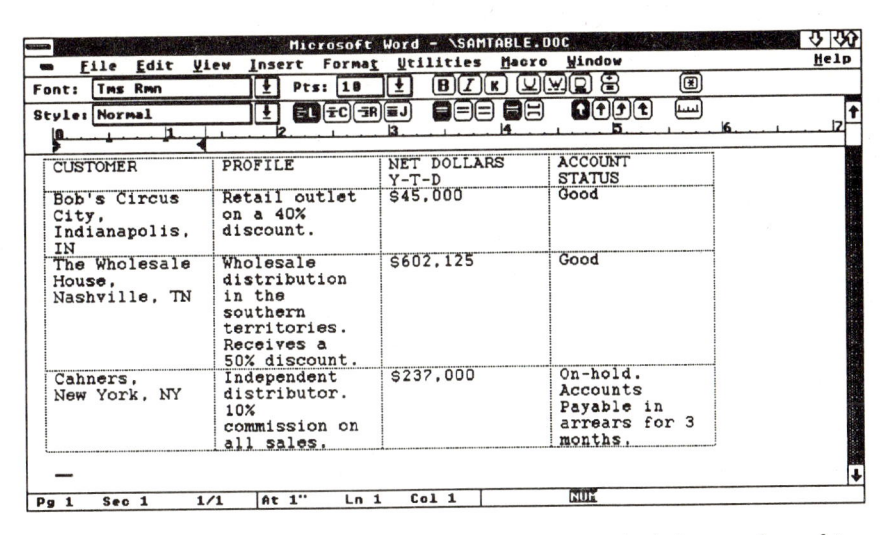

Figure 11.3 The completed table can mix text, numerical data, and graphics.

with the rest of your document or doesn't seem to flow with the presentation of the material. It might be better to place the material in a table for quick reference so the reader can refer to it later. For example, you can select text that you have already attempted to set in a table, but, because each column represents an inconsistent amount of text, the material appears out of alignment. As you have discovered, the cells of Word's tables feature can adjust to that problem. Another example might be information that you have arranged in individual paragraphs. If you select a set of paragraphs, Word can set up a table in which each paragraph is represented by a row. In this situation, Word will initially suggest a single column. However, you can specify any number of columns that seems appropriate. To illustrate, consider that the information in Figure 11.4 might appear within the body of a document. If you use Word's table feature to align that information in a table, the presentation would look much better, as Figure 11.5 shows. To change existing text into a table, simply select the text and then choose the Insert Tables command. Word will then ask you to specify the number of columns, but it will suggest 1 as a standard default. Use the following steps as a guide to converting existing material to a table.

1. Select the existing material that you wish to rearrange in a table. Be sure to select all the paragraphs that you intend to convert to a table.

   The selected material is highlighted.

333

Adding and Polishing Word

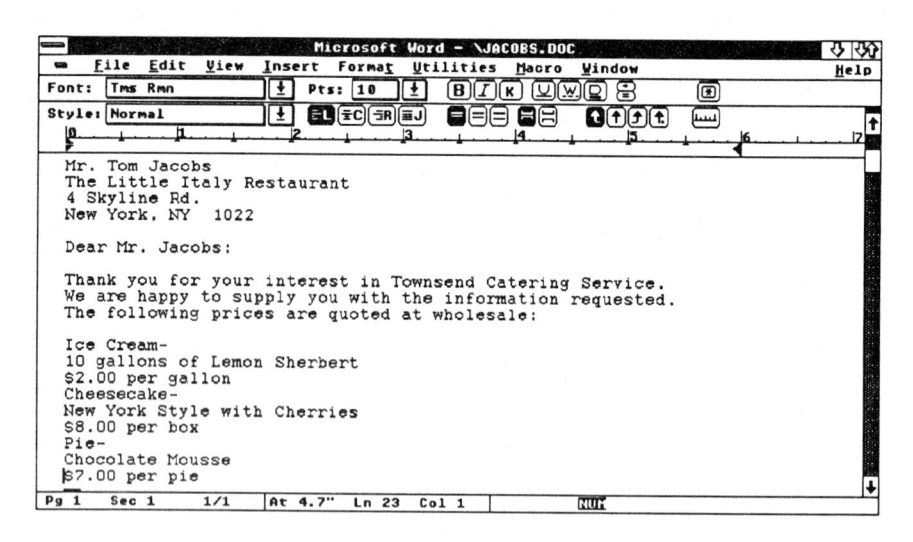

Figure 11.4 You can select this existing material to convert to a table.

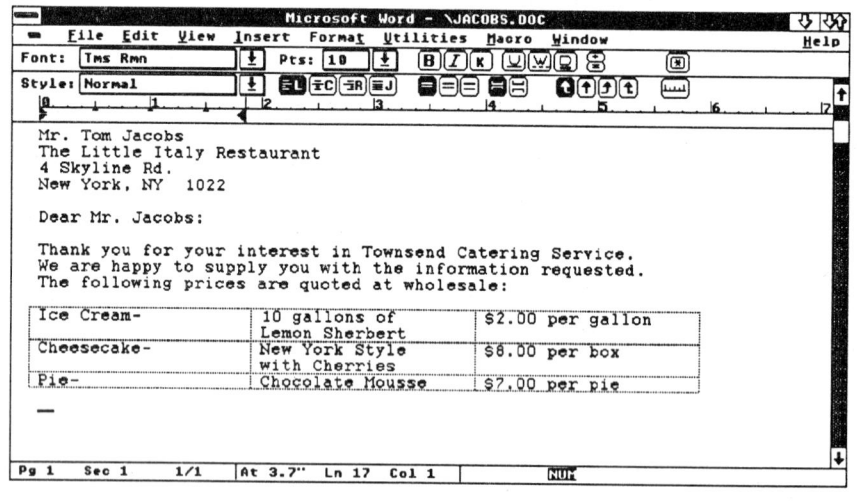

Figure 11.5 The material from Figure 11.4 rearranged in a table.

2. Choose the **Insert Table** command from the Utilities menu or press **Alt,I,T**.

The Insert Table dialog box appears. Word initially suggests that you arrange the text in a single column and specifies the number of rows, one for each paragraph.

334

11—Using Word's Tables and Math Features

3. Either accept Word's default values or enter the number of columns you want in the Number of Columns edit box. (Move to this section by pressing Alt+C.) For this example from Figure 11.5, select **3** columns.

   As you change the number of columns, Word automatically updates the number of rows (to 3).

4. If the material that you selected is separated by individual paragraphs, accept this delimiter in the Convert From edit box by pressing **Alt+P**. If you separated your selected items by commas or tabs, you need to choose the Comma Delimited or Tab Delimited option, respectively. For this example, click the **Paragraph** option or press **Alt+P**, if necessary.

   The number of columns is determined by the line that has the greatest number of commas or tabs (e.g., a table that has a line with 4 commas while the other lines have 3 commas will have 4 columns).

5. Click **OK** or press **Enter**.

   Word will convert your selected text to a table. The table will remain highlighted until you click outside the table on your screen.

6. If you don't like the appearance of your table (while the table is still highlighted) choose **Table to Text** from the Insert menu or press **Alt,I,T** to convert the selected table back to text. A dialog box, shown in Figure 11.6, appears. Click **OK** to return the table back to text. Note: If the text is no longer highlighted, you can also choose Undo Edit Table from the Edit menu before you type another command.

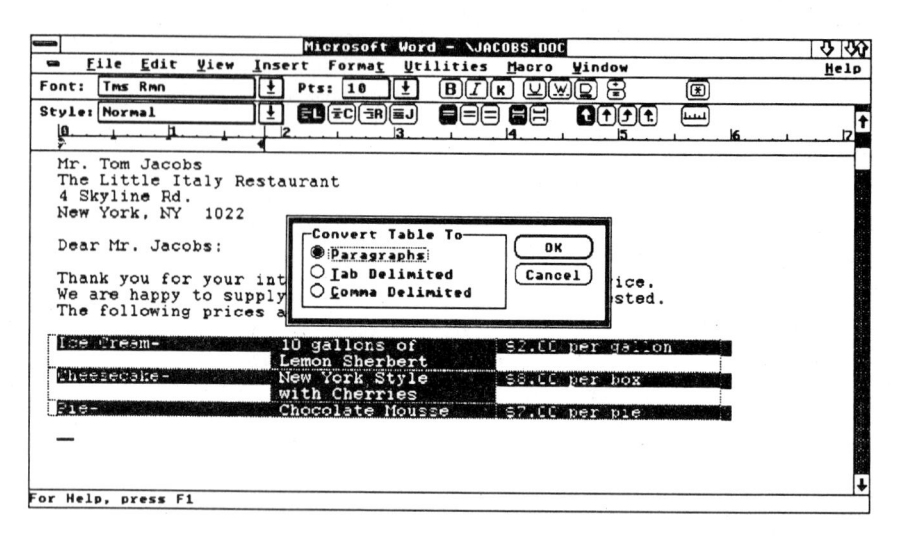

Figure 11.6 You can also convert your tables back and forth between text and table formats.

Editing Tables

Word allows you to edit tables just like any other document element. You can select any item in a cell and add or delete text, and the changes will not affect the other cells in the table. Further, Word lets you change the number of rows and columns in a table, and you can even alter the size of the rows or columns or cells. This section demonstrates the steps necessary to complete all these editing changes.

Making Your Selection First

You can select cells, rows, or columns in a table by clicking and dragging with the mouse.

Before you begin editing your tables, you must first select the part of the table that requires work. You can select text within a cell, a column, a row, or the entire table. The key to selecting a part of the table is to position the pointer until it changes shape. Depending upon where the pointer is placed, its shape will change. For example, if you want to add to, delete, or modify the contents of an individual cell, first select the cell by clicking inside it with the mouse or using the Tab key to reposition the insertion point. This method makes the pointer an I-beam. If you position the pointer at the beginning of the cell, its shape changes to an arrow pointing to the right. With the

11—Using Word's Tables and Math Features

pointer in this shape and position, click the mouse and the entire cell is selected. Double-click the mouse to select the entire row.

If you position the pointer directly on top of the end-of-cell mark (these marks looks like open bullets with four legs) within a gridline in the top row, visible when Table Gridlines from View Preferences is turned on, the pointer changes to a down arrow. Clicking the mouse while the down arrow is visible selects the corresponding column. To select the entire table, place the pointer in the first row of the leftmost column and click the right or left mouse button. Then, drag to the last cell of the last row of the table. To select the entire table with the keys, simply press Alt+5 on the numeric keypad (the Num Lock mode must be turned off). You can also select blocks of cells with the keys by first pressing Ctrl+Shift+F8 to turn on the Column Selection mode and then using the arrow keys to select the blocks of cells. Of course, you can use the customary method for selecting text with keys by using the Shift key in combination with the arrow keys or the Extend Selection key. Once any portion of the table is selected, to deselect it you just click outside that portion of the table.

Inserting and Deleting Rows and Columns

Now that you know how to select a row or column, the steps necessary to insert or delete rows and columns is a simple one. Since Word treats each row as a separate element within a table, you can vary the number of rows as well as the number of columns. The following steps illustrate how to add a row to Figure 11.5 in order to place column headings above the table body.

To add a row quickly to the end of a table, place the insertion point inside the last cell of the last row and press the Tab key

1. Everything begins with the position of the pointer. For this example of adding a row, place the pointer in the first column directly below the row on top of which you want to insert the new row. To add a new top row, place the pointer at the beginning of the first cell.

   Word always inserts rows above the current row. If you want to insert a new column, place the pointer to the left of the current column.

2. Choose **Table** from the Edit menu or press **Alt,E,A**.

   The Table dialog box, shown in Figure 11.7, appears.

3. If you are adding a row, you would click the Row option

or press Alt+R. If you are adding a column, you would click the Column option or enter Alt+C. For this example, click **Row** or press **Alt+R**.

4. Click **Insert** or press **Alt+I**.

   Word inserts an empty row, as in Figure 11.8, or an empty column.

5. The last step in this example is to enter the headings in the table. Click inside each cell (or use the Tab key to move the insertion point) and enter the appropriate heading. Your result should look like Figure 11.9.

Word not only enables you to add rows and columns to your table, but you can also add individual cells. To do this, select the number of cells that you want to insert. Your selection should be to the right of, or below where you want the new cells to appear. Then choose the Table command on the Edit menu or press Alt,E,A, and indicate to Word which way to adjust the table (horizontally or vertically) to accommodate the new cell. For example, to add a row, choose Row or press Alt+R and then choose Insert or press Alt+I. To

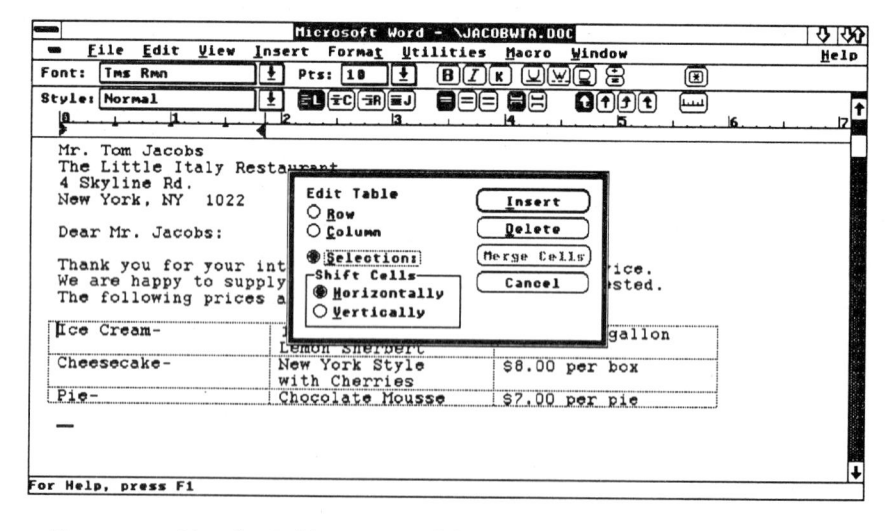

Figure 11.7 Use the Table command from the Edit menu to add or delete rows and columns.

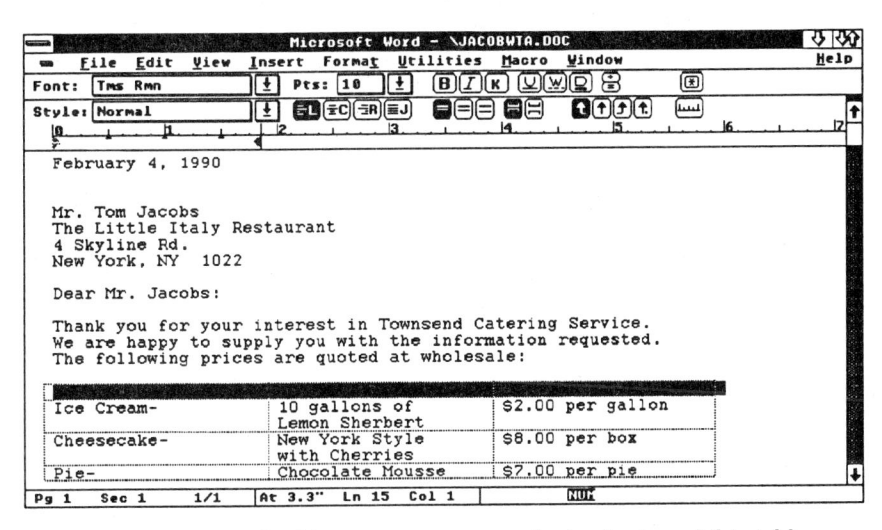

Figure 11.8 Word adds an empty row to the beginning of this table.

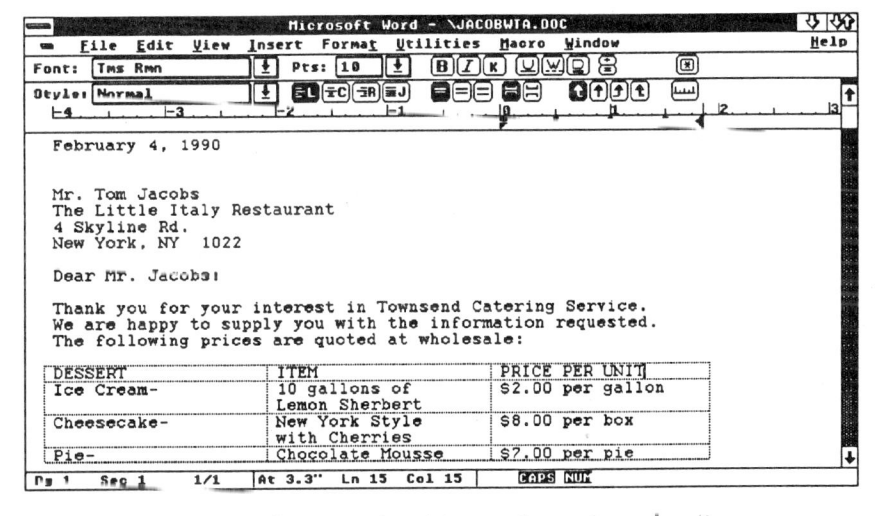

Figure 11.9 The sample table now has column headings.

add a column, choose Column or press Alt+C and choose Insert or press Alt+I.

To delete rows, columns, or cells from your table, select the cells and then choose the Table command from the Edit menu. Instead of choosing the Insert command, click the appropriate item (row or column or selection, though Word guesses automatically), and then click Delete or press Alt+D to erase the selected cell(s) from your table. Deleting a row or column erases the row or column in addition to the information contained in that element.

Finally, you'll notice the Merge Cells command button on the Edit Table dialog window. Choosing Merge Cells allows you to remove the boundaries and borders between selected adjoining rows of cells and to combine the contents of those cells. You may even select more than one row of adjoining cells to merge. As two or more rows are merged, Word inserts a separate paragraph mark for each former row of cells. Once you have merged cells in a table, the Merge Cells command changes to Split Cells. This command allows you to select previously merged cells and change them back to separate rows of cells.

Cutting, Copying, and Pasting Tables

Instead of using the Cut and Copy commands within a table, you can use the Shift+Del or Ctrl+Ins methods.

Since the content of each cell within a table created by Word is treated like any other paragraph, you can use the Cut, Copy, and Paste commands to move or erase a cell's contents. When you select a cell or cells, you can move the contents to an empty cell by choosing the Copy or Cut command, clicking in the new cell location, and choosing the Paste command. There are some restrictions on pasting into a table, though. First, you can only have one cell selected when you attempt to Paste normal text. You can Paste either text from a single cell, or normal text outside a table into a cell, but the selection cannot contain both normal text and cell text. Finally, the area you Paste to must have the same dimensions as the original selection of cells. You can also erase the contents of a cell by selecting the cell and choosing the Cut command. In both cases, choosing the Cut and Copy commands places a copy of the selected text into the Clipboard until you issue another Cut or Copy command or turn the computer off. Once the cell text is placed in the Clipboard, the cells of the table are left empty while the Clipboard contains the text from the table in the same structure as when it was selected. You cannot use the Cut command to erase a selected cell, row, or column itself—just the text within the cell(s). To delete these, you must use the Table command found on the Edit menu as discussed in the previous section. The one exception is that if you first select normal text from outside the table as well as table cells, then choosing the Cut command will remove both the contents of the cells as well as the cells themselves.

A cell contains an end-of-cell mark, which is not visible unless you turned on the Table Gridlines option in View Preferences. If you select the entire cell in order to move its contents to another location, the end-of-cell mark will move as well. The advantage of moving the end-of-cell mark is that you can click anywhere in your document outside the table and insert another table having the same dimensions as the selected cell or cells.

Formatting Tables

You can change the dimensions of a table by altering the size of individual rows, columns, or cells. You can even draw borders around any of these components to draw attention to a particular set of information or just to fancy it up.

Resizing Rows, Columns, and Cells

Once you have created your table, you might want to change its appearance by changing the size of the rows, columns, or cells. The beauty of Word's table feature is that you can have any combination of rows, columns, and cells in any size. Of course, this liberty can lead to some pretty awful-looking tables, too.

To adjust the width of a column or cell, you can use either the Ruler in Column View (when the insertion point resides inside a table) or the *Table* command on the Format menu (press Alt,T,A). The following steps adjust the width of a column or cell with the Format Table command. This exercise reduces the width of the cells in the previous example (see Figure 11.9).

To adjust the width of a column with the Ruler, choose Ruler View, select the columns (or cells) that you wish to change, click the ruler icon, and then move the column markers to the desired location (moving them left or right of the T marker that represents a column position).

1. Select the column or cell whose width you wish to change. If you have to, turn on the Table Gridlines option from View Preferences so that you see the gridlines. In this example, you'll change the width of the columns of the entire table by selecting it.

    The selected item is highlighted.

2. Choose the **Table** command from the Format menu (**Alt,T,A**).

    The Format Table dialog box, as in Figure 11.10, appears. (You cannot choose the Format Table command unless you first selected a table cell or column. The command will appear inactive otherwise.)

3. Select the **Width of Columns** edit box or press **Alt+W**. To change the current value,

    The box now has a value of 1 inch.

Adding and Polishing Word

type a new value. For this example, enter 1" or 1 in.

4. Notice the Apply To option. To change the entire column in which you have selected cells, click the **Whole Table** option or press **Alt+O**. Otherwise, only the selected cells will be changed.

5. Click **OK** or press **Enter**.

The width of the selected cells or column is changed as you have specified. The text in each column is word-wrapped and reformatted to fit the size of the cell. This example is shown in Figure 11.11 with columns of 1 inch instead of 2 inches wide. Note: You may need to adjust existing text to fit into shorter cells as we did with the word, Cheesecake (adding a hyphen).

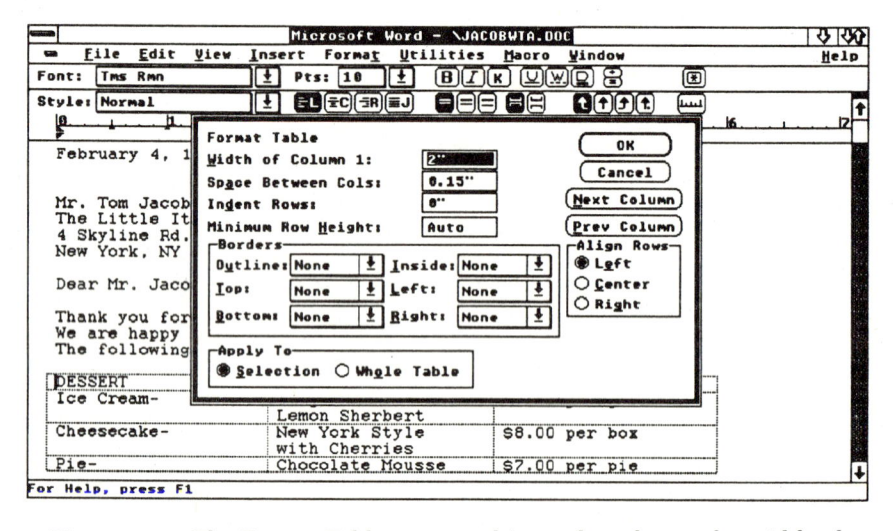

Figure 11.10 The Format Table command is used to change the width of selected cells or columns.

342

11—Using Word's Tables and Math Features

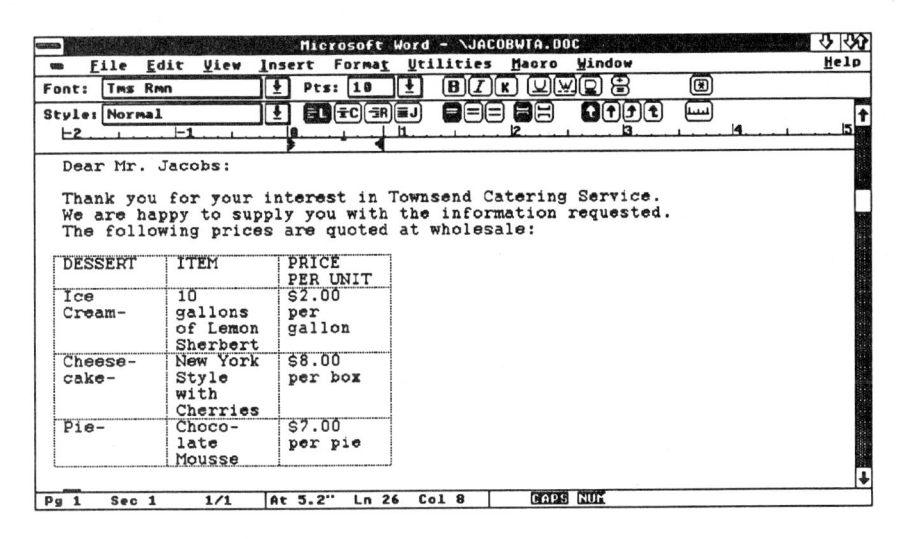

Figure 11.11 The sample table now has narrower columns.

Building a Table with a Consistent Height

On the Format Table command, you can choose the Next Column and Previous Column command buttons to select the next or previous column of cells for formatting without first closing the dialog window.

When Word builds a table, the cells may have text of varying height. To ensure consistency, you can set a minimum height requirement for all fonts in a particular row, or for the entire table. To do this, once again you use the Format Table command.

Changing the height of a row is just as easy as changing the width. First you select the row or rows and then choose the Format Table command. From the Format Table dialog box, you click the Minimum Row Height or press Alt+H. The default setting is Auto, which means the minimum height of a row is adjusted automatically depending on the height of the tallest cell within that row (actually it depends on the height of the tallest font within that row). Enter the positive decimal measurement for the minimum height of the row in either inches or points. For example, if you wish to change the minimum height requirement to 14 points (.19") or 18 points (.25"), simply enter the desired value and then click OK or press Enter.

Note: You can fix the row height absolutely by typing in a negative number for Minimum Row Height. When you type text beyond the fixed length of the cell, the text will be truncated and all cells in the table will look uniform.

Formatting with Decimals

Since tables often depict financial data, you should know how to format a table with decimals. To do this, you format the cells containing decimals with a decimal tab stop. Decimal tabs are treated specially in table cells. You do not need to type a tab character in each cell in order to align text with the tab stop. First you need to set up the table in Figure 11.12, which contains five columns and four rows. If you need help, refer back to the steps for creating an empty table and inserting the text in that table. Then complete the next set of steps.

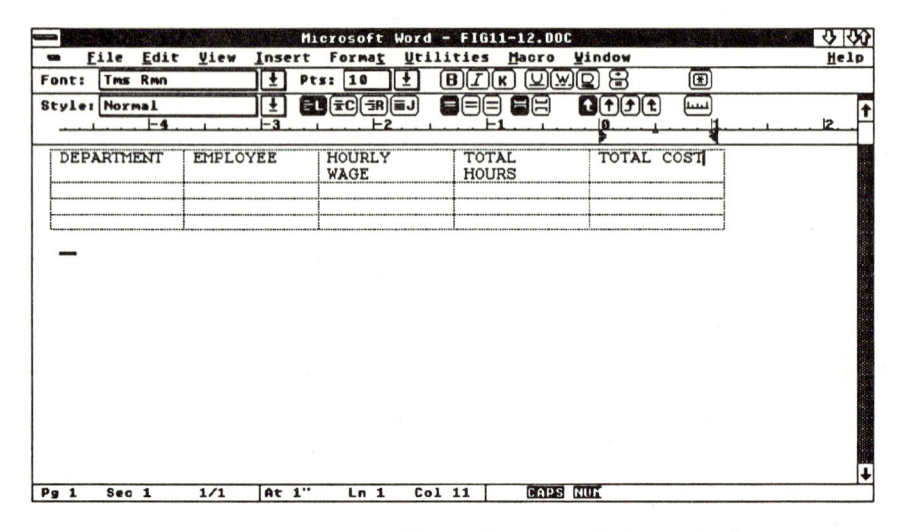

Figure 11.12 Setting your table's columns with decimal tab stops.

You can use all types of tabs in table cells. To insert a tab character, press Ctrl + Tab. Remember, pressing Tab simply moves the insertion point to the next cell in the table.

1. Select the column to which you want to add decimal tab stops. In this example, first select the Hourly Wage column.

2. If you haven't already, choose the **Ruler** from the View menu and then click the **ruler** icon (on the Ruler's far right) until the Ruler is in either the Paragraph or Column mode, although this author recommends Paragraph View for setting tabs.

The options on the ruler are active (do not appear grey). You can toggle between the paragraph ruler mode and the column mode by clicking the ruler view icon.

3. Click the **decimal** icon (fourth from the right) to select it. Then position the pointer on the Ruler where you want the decimal tab stop to be set and click the mouse button once. Note: If you don't have a mouse, you can use the usual methods for setting tabs with the keys. To do this, press **Ctrl+Shift+F10** to activate the Ruler, press the appropriate arrow key to position the Ruler cursor, press **4** to select decimal tab stop, and then **Ins** to set it. For this example, position the insertion point on the 1/2" mark on the Ruler in Paragraph View. In Paragraph View, the zero point on the Ruler aligns with the left boundary of the cell containing the insertion point.

   When you click the mouse, the icon depicting the decimal icon is left on the Ruler. Note that the entire column is now set with a decimal tab stop.

4. Complete steps 1-3 for each column that contains decimal numbers you want to align. For this example, add the decimal tab stop to the TOTAL HOURS and TOTAL COST columns.

   Your completed table should look like Figure 11.13.

Adding Borders

As you work with Word's table feature, you need to remember that the hidden gridlines will not appear when you print the document. You can simulate these gridlines, however, by adding borders to your tables. You are not limited to borders that outline every cell, though. You can add a border to one cell or add a border that separates a cell or group of cells horizontally or vertically. To do this, you select the cell or group of cells that you wish to add the border to and then

Adding and Polishing Word

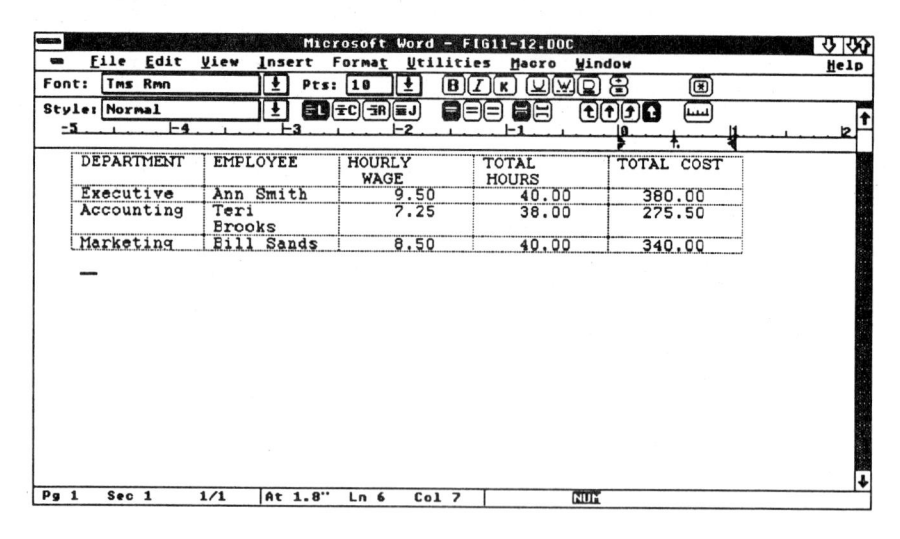

```
                Microsoft Word - FIG11-12.DOC
  File  Edit  View  Insert  Format  Utilities  Macro  Window        Help
Font: Tms Rmn        Pts: 10      B I K U W
Style: Normal

DEPARTMENT   EMPLOYEE    HOURLY    TOTAL     TOTAL COST
                        WAGE       HOURS
Executive    Ann Smith    9.50     40.00      380.00
Accounting   Teri         7.25     38.00      275.50
             Brooks
Marketing    Bill Sands   8.50     40.00      340.00

Pg 1  Sec 1  1/1  At 1.8"  Ln 6  Col 7           NUM
```

Figure 11.13 Completed table with decimal tab stops.

choose the Table command from the Format menu. The following set of steps uses the table in Figure 11.13 to demonstrate this procedure.

1. Select the cell or cells that you wish to add the border to. For this example, place the insertion point anywhere inside the table. Don't select the entire table just yet.

2. Choose **Table** from the Format menu or press **Alt,T,A**. If the Table command is dim, the insertion point is located outside the table.

   The Format Table dialog box appears.

3. Move to the Borders section of the dialog window. Since we want to draw a border around the entire table, choose the **Outline** option or press **Alt+U**. Select a pattern from among Single, Thick, Double, or Shadow. For our example, select **Single** (a 1-point line) using the mouse or simply press the **down**

   The Single pattern appears in the Outline edit window instead of the default None. Notice that the Top, Bottom, Left, and Right options automatically appear with the Single pattern as well since you selected the Outline option.

346

11—Using Word's Tables and Math Features

arrow key once to highlight it.

4. Next, move to the Inside edit window by pressing **Alt+I** and select a pattern to draw a border between all selected cells. Once again, for our example, select **Single** (press the **down arrow** once).

   The Single pattern appears in the Inside edit window instead of the default None.

5. The Selection option is set as the default in the Apply To section of the dialog window. This option is used for set borders around a block of cells or between all selected cells. If you wanted to set custom borders around cells or to set lines horizontally and vertically between selected cells you'd use the Selection option. For this example, choose **Whole Table** or press **Alt+O**.

To turn off the borders, select the cell(s), choose the Format Table command, select None as the appropriate pattern. Click OK to apply the None selection, exit to the document, and you'll have deleted the borders.

6. Click **OK** or press **Enter**.

   Your borders are applied and you are returned to the document window. Notice that single-line borders have now replaced the dotted gridlines. To see how your final product will look, choose Print Preview or Page View. Once printed, the table will look like Figure 11.14.

The steps above highlight how to apply a border to your table. You can easily modify a border's location. For example, you can select a portion of the table and draw a border only along the top of the selected cells by choosing the Top option. Similarly, you can choose to draw a border along the bottom edge of selected cells with the Bottom option. The Inside option can be used alone as well to draw a border between all selected cells while the Left and Right options place borders on the left and right edges of selected cells. You can use any of these options together or by themselves to customize your tables.

347

DEPARTMENT	EMPLOYEE	HOURLY WAGE	TOTAL HOURS	TOTAL COST
Executive	Ann Smith	9.50	40.00	380.00
Accounting	Teri Brooks	7.25	38.00	275.50
Marketing	Bill Sands	8.50	40.00	340.00

Figure 11.14 Sample table with single-line borders around every cell.

Aligning and Positioning Tables

You can tell Word how to align your table's position relative to the page margins. To do this, select the Format Table command and then move to the Align Rows section or press Alt+L. If you click the Left option, Word aligns the selected rows of your table with the left margin of your document. Choose Right to align the selected rows with the right margin or Center to center the selected rows between margins. If you wish to indent selected rows, simply enter a positive (or negative for absolute positioning) decimal measurement for the distance between the left margin and the left edge of the selected rows.

For more absolute positioning of your tables on a document page, select the table and then choose the Format Position command. As you recall, you can absolutely position an object horizontally and vertically on a page using the Position command. For a complete review on this command, refer to Chapter 7 on creating complex documents.

Sorting Tables

You can use the Utilities *Sort* command to sort the rows and columns of your tables. Word uses the Sort command to sort alphabetically in ascending or descending order (from A to Z or Z to A), or numerically from the lowest number to the highest number and vice versa. In addition to sorting rows in a table, you can use Word's sort command to sort whole paragraphs or items in a list separated by commas or tabs. In this section, we'll only concern ourselves with sorting tables. Although the principle for sorting standard text is similar, refer to your user's manual for further details.

The first step to sorting rows or columns in a table is to select the text area that you wish to sort; otherwise, Word's Sort command will sort every paragraph in your document in ascending order! To get some practice using the Sort command, sort the following table.

Department	Employee	Hourly Wage	Total Hours	Total Cost
Executive	Ann Smith	9.50	40.00	380.00
Accounting	Teri Brooks	7.25	38.00	275.50
Marketing	Bill Sands	8.50	40.00	340.00

1. The first step is to select the column that you wish to sort. Word sorts tables by rows. You can choose to sort an entire table by the leftmost character in each row or you can choose to sort by a particular column. For this example, you'll sort by the Total Cost column. Since you don't want to include the actual heading row in your sort, select the three cells beneath the heading in that column.

2. Choose **Sort** from the Utilities menu or press **Alt,U,O**.

   The Sort dialog box appears on your screen as shown in Figure 11.15.

3. Choose the options for sorting as desired. For our example, choose **Ascending** for Sort Order and then move the Key Type box or press **Alt+K** and select **Numeric** (press **down arrow** once) to specify the type of data being sorted. In other words, only numbers are used as sort items while letters are ignored.

4. Choose **OK** or press **Enter**.

   Word produces your sorted table as shown in Figure 11.16. Note: If you selected the Sort Column Only option,

Adding and Polishing Word

only the values in the selected column are sorted and not the associated rows of data pertaining to the selected column. Turn this option off to sort all rows of data for the selected column.

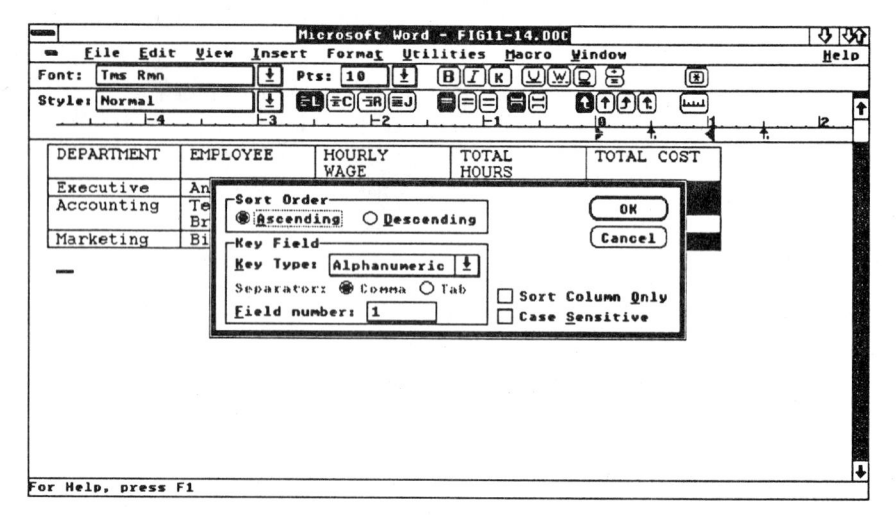

Figure 11.15 The Sort command allows you to sort tables, whole paragraphs, or items in a list.

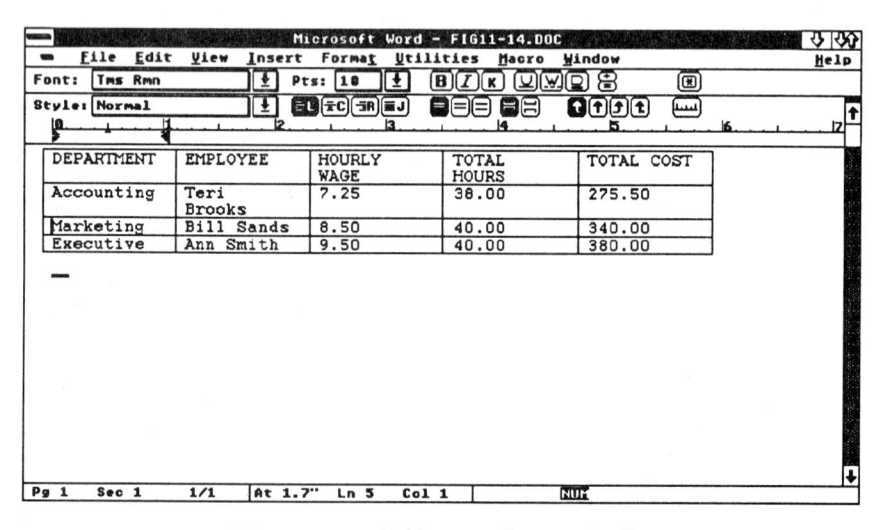

Figure 11.16 Table sorted numerically.

You will find that you can use Word's sorting capabilities in a variety of ways for rearranging the order of your documents. The Sort command is particularly useful for creating a form-letter mailing. In Chapter 16, for example, you will learn to create a data document file using Word's tables feature to store the addresses of your mailing. You can sort your addresses by zip code by selecting the zip code field. If you are familiar with bulk mail rules, you'll know that this feature is handy for separating your mailing by state.

Creating Side-by-Side Paragraphs

Creating side-by-side paragraphs in Word is a simple matter of creating a table with two or more columns. For example, consider the text in Figure 11.17. To create the appearance of side-by-side paragraphs, first create a table with two columns as follows:

1. Choose **Insert Table** or press **Alt,I,T**.
2. Enter the number of rows and columns that you want. For our example, choose **2** columns and **2** rows.
3. You can accept the default Auto for column width, or enter another value. We adjusted the column width after we adjusted the width of the columns using the Ruler. You can adjust the appearance of your table as you wish.
4. Click **OK** or press **Enter**.
5. Enter the text in each cell of the table as it appears in Figure 11.17.
6. The last step is to adjust the width of each column and the distance between columns. To adjust the width of the columns, use the Ruler or the Format Table command. Adjusting the distance between columns is always completed with the Format Table command as previously discussed.

Doing Math

With Word's built-in *math* feature, you can add, subtract, multiply, and divide. You can even calculate percentages. To do all this, type in the numbers, along with the proper mathematical operators, select the numbers and operators, and choose the *Calculate* command from the Utilities menu or press Alt,U,C. The result of a math calculation is

Adding and Polishing Word

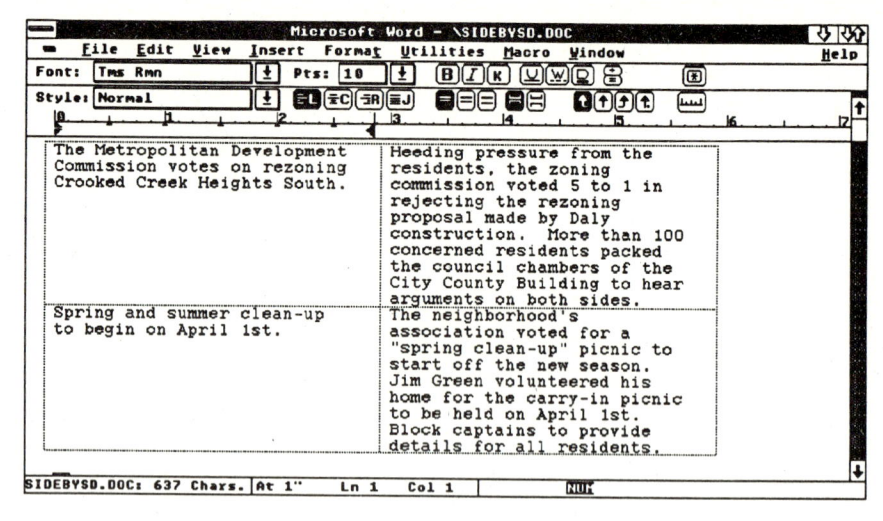

Figure 11.17 You create side-by-side paragraphs by placing the text in a table.

displayed in a status box in the lower left corner of the screen. Word automatically stores this result temporarily in the Clipboard so that with the Paste command you can insert it in your document. The operators that Word supports are listed in Table 11.3.

Table 11.3 Operators that Can Be Used in Math Calculations

+	Adds subtotal of numbers. Using the + sign is optional. Example: *4+2* or *4 2* yields the value 6.
−	Subtraction. Example: *7-5* yields 2.
*	Multiplication. Located at uppercase numeral 8. Example: *12*3* yields 36.
/	Division. This is the slash key. Example: *24/6* yields 4.
%	Calculates percentage. To calculate a percentage, type % sign after the number. Example: *10*40%* yields 4.

Doing Math in Columns

You can use the Calculate command to perform math operations in a table and then paste the results into your document. For example, to add the total numbers in the table illustrated in Figure 11-16, first select the column or group of cells that represent the numbers that you wish to add and then choose the Calculate command from the Utilities menu or press Alt,U,C. The result is displayed in the lower left corner of the status box as 995.5 (the status bar option found on the View menu must be on).

To add this value to your table, position the insertion point at the end of the last cell in the last row, press Tab to add another row, and type TOTAL in the first cell. Move the pointer to the last cell of the last row and choose the Edit Paste command or press Alt,E,P. Since Word stored the calculated value of the group of cells just performed, the result is now pasted into your document, as shown in Figure 11.18.

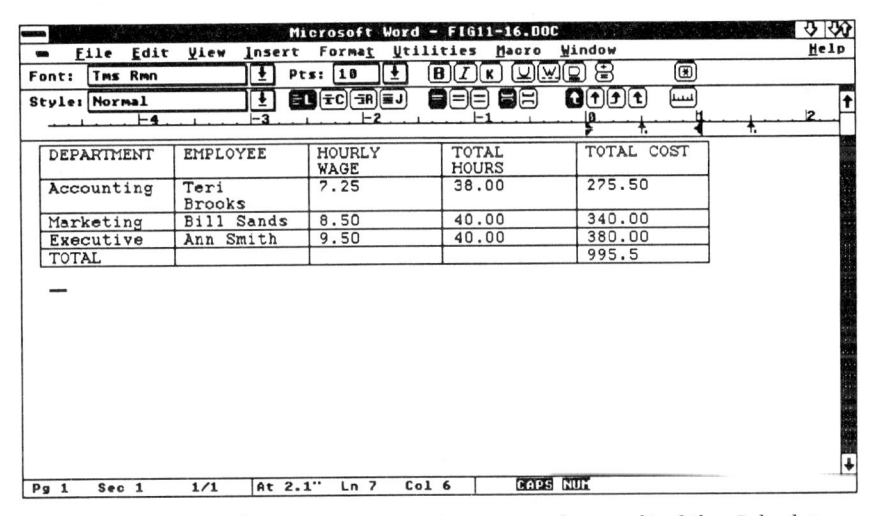

Figure 11.18 Use the Paste command to insert the result of the Calculate command into your table.

Setting Up a Spreadsheet in a Table

The table in Figure 11.18 is an example of manually using a columnar pad, similar to what accountants use, to list a series of values and then perform a mathematical calculation on those values. Instead of manually adding the values in a column, or even using the Calculate command and then pasting the results, you can use Word's table feature to simulate a simple electronic spreadsheet. The spreadsheet is an electronic version of the accountant's columnar pad that allows you to store values in the individual cells of a table. Since the cells of a table are made up of independent "fields," you can set up a table to actually refer to other cells. To refer to another cell, you must include a field, which is assigned a cell reference in the following form:

<RnCn>

where R refers to the row and C refers to the column. The n stands for the number of the row and column counted from the upper left corner of the table. Thus, the first cell in the first row is R1C1. The second cell in the first row is R1C2 and the third cell in the first row would be R1C3. As you move from left to right within a row in a table, only the number referring to the column will change. Now, suppose you had a table with two rows. The first cell in the second row would be R2C1. Figure 11.19 illustrates a table with 3 rows and 4 columns and their respective field "cell references."

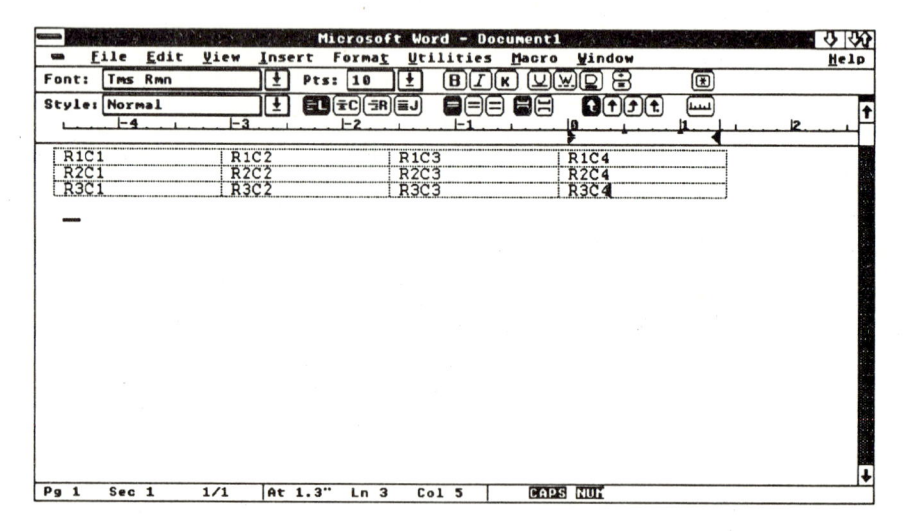

Figure 11.19 Each cell in a table has a unique cell reference.

Using Word's table, you can reference an individual cell or a group of cells. This is another key feature for creating an electronic spreadsheet. To refer to a group of cells, also called a range of cells, you separate the beginning cell reference and the ending cell reference with a colon. For example, to reference a rectangular group of six adjacent cells, such as R1C1, R1C2, R1C3, R2C1, R2C2, and R2C3, you would enter [R1C1:R2C3]. To refer to an entire row or column of cells, you need only enter the row or column reference. For example, to refer to the entire third row, enter [R3]. To reference the entire second column, enter [R2].

Now that you know how to reference different cell locations, Word lets you use "expressions" in fields to actually perform mathematical calculations automatically. In other words, a field allows you to insert special codes that instruct Word to insert specific information into a certain location. To illustrate, consider the following table:

Unit Sales of Gadgets

	1st Q	2nd Q	3rd Q	4th Q
Cam	100	124	99	186
Bill	85	90	100	140
Kate	110	115	102	175
Carey	90	95	101	123
Totals				

The table above contains five columns and six rows. Notice that the Totals for each quarter (1st Q, 2nd Q, etc.) are left empty. You can either select each column and use the Calculate and Paste commands to insert the total values, or you can insert a field that calculates the total automatically for you. The advantage of creating such a spreadsheet is that each time you change a value within any cell, the totals are automatically updated. For example, the field to calculate the sum of the second column would be in the following format:

$$\{=sum([R2C2:R6C2])\}$$

where the field characters {} must appear at the beginning and the end of the field. To insert the set of codes in the field, choose **Insert Field** or press **Alt,I,D** and then select the field type (see Figure 11.20). For this example, accept the default field type for expression and then move to the **Field Code** edit box or press **Alt+C**. Enter the instructions (as discussed above) for the field and then choose **OK** or press **Enter**. The Insert Field dialog box closes, inserts the field as specified and presents the calculated information for the field. Note: Since the Insert Field command automatically inserts field code characters (the braces), be careful not to type them in as a duplicate.

As a shortcut to choosing the Insert Field command, you can simply press the Insert Field Ctrl-function key combination: Ctrl+F9. Choosing this key will insert the field brace characters and place the insertion point inside. Then, simply type the coded instructions as before. Complete the table by inserting the field code instructions for the 3rd, 4th, and 5th columns using the **Ctrl+F9** method. The result should look something like Figure 11.21. Note that only the field code

Adding and Polishing Word

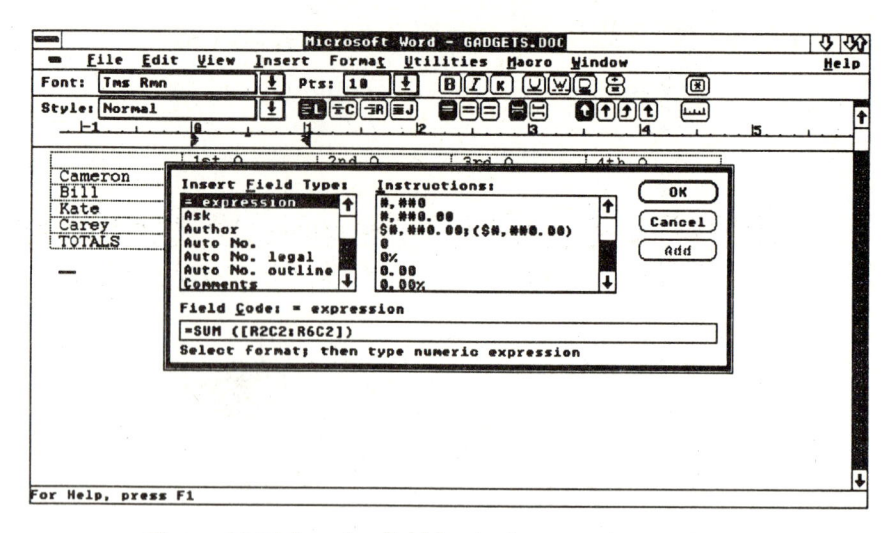

Figure 11.20 Insert a field by typing your instructions.

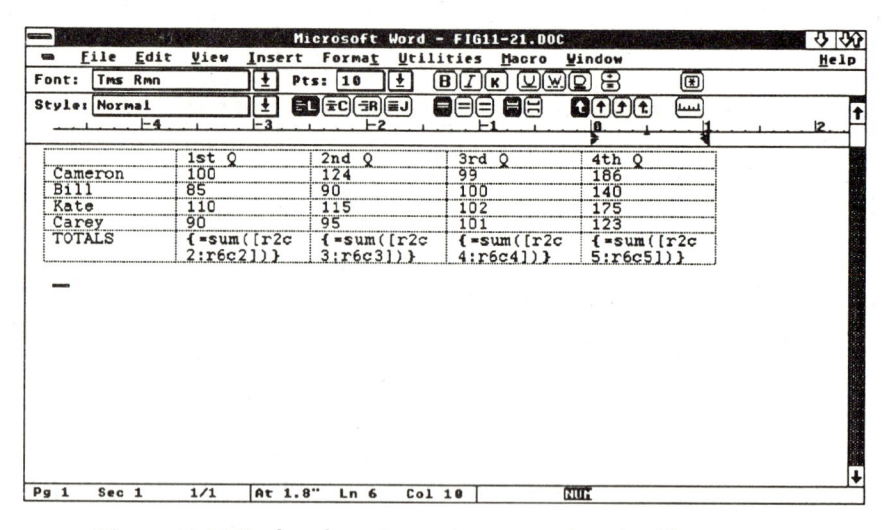

Figure 11.21 Each column's results are produced with appropriate field code instructions.

instructions will appear in the designated cells until we update them as we'll discuss next.

The last step is to ask Word to update the field. Updating a field means that you tell Word to follow the instructions placed in a field and show you the result. To do this, position the insertion point inside the cell containing the field in order to select it, and then press

356

11—Using Word's Tables and Math Features

the Update key, F9. If you attempt to select the cell by dragging with the mouse, when you press the Update key Word will only beep at you. If the field codes are not replaced with the results, check the instructions you entered in the field by placing the insertion point there and choosing View Field Codes (or Shift+F9 to toggle between seeing the field codes and the results). If the instructions are incorrect, you can make any necessary changes and then press F9 to update them again. For our example, position the insertion point inside a cell in which a field code resides, and press **F9**. Do this for each of the relevant cells. The results should look something like Figure 11.22.

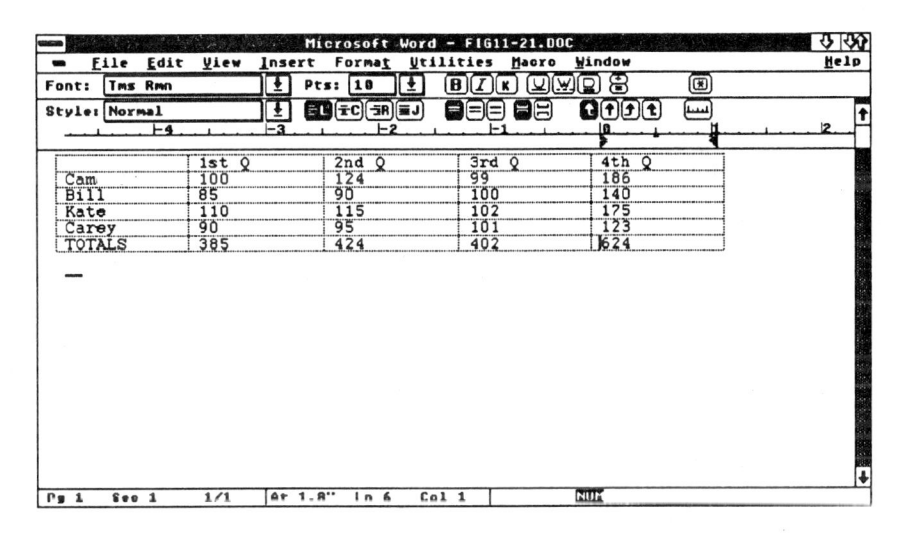

Figure 11.22 Choose F9 to update the results of your field codes.

Finally, you update the fields in a table too, using the method just described, or you'll see the instructions in a field, rather than the result you hoped for, whenever the document is printed. Using the Update Field key (F9) allows you to see the results prior to printing so that you can make any corrections. If you change any value within the table, simply press F9 to see the subsequent results.

Doing Mathematical Formulas

In short, creating a mathematical formula is combining mathematical statements and expressions. In Word you will insert formula codes using an EQ (for equation) field. To print formulas, however, requires one of the following three types of printers:

357

- HP LaserJet printer with at least 512K of memory
- A PostScript printer
- A printer with a PostScript compatible symbol font

When you create a formula, keep in mind that many codes have certain requirements. For example, every formula code following the EQ must be preceded by a backslash character (\). Further, some codes require that a list of elements be enclosed within a set of parentheses.

Creating formulas can seem confusing at first—perhaps at best. To illustrate, let's look at a simple example:

$$x = 1/3$$

To get the correct result in Word, you would enter:

$$\{eq = \backslash f(1,3)\}$$

where the entire formula is enclosed within a set of field characters (the friendly braces). On the left side of the formula is the equation identifiers, *eq,* a space, an equal sign, and another space. The right side of the equation is the interesting part. As stated, the formula code is preceded with a backslash. Then, you see the code option itself. In this case, an *f* for *fraction.* This code require two elements separated by a comma and enclosed within parentheses. The first element in the fraction is the numerator and the second the denominator. This example illustrates the special code for a formula (i.e., f for fraction). To use a special code in a formula result, it must be preceded by a backslash. For a complete review of the formula codes, refer to the *Microsoft User's Reference Manual.*

Inserting Formulas

To insert a formula into your document, you insert a field code that contains the field type and instructions for that field code. You can use either the Insert Field command (press Alt,I,D), or the Insert Field-key combination: Ctrl+F9. If you use the Insert Field-key combination, the field code characters will appear at the location of the insertion point with the insertion point blinking on the inside. To illustrate, let's enter our sample fraction formula.

1. Choose the **Field** command from the Insert menu or press **Alt,I,D**.   The Insert Field dialog box appears.

11—Using Word's Tables and Math Features

2. From the Insert Field Type, press **Alt+F** to select the **Formulas** option.

   Formulas is highlighted and EQ appears in the Field Code section.

3. Move to the Instructions edit window by pressing **Alt+I**, select **Fraction**, and then click the **Add** button or press **Alt+A**.

   The formula codes appear following the EQ in the Field Code section.

4. Press **Alt+C** or click on the **Field Code** edit box, and then enter the numerator and denominator. For our example, enter **1** and **3**, respectively.

   The formula code will now look like Figure 11.23 in the dialog window.

5. Choose **OK** or press **Enter**.

   The dialog box closes and Word displays the result of the formula at the location of the insertion point: The fraction 1/3.

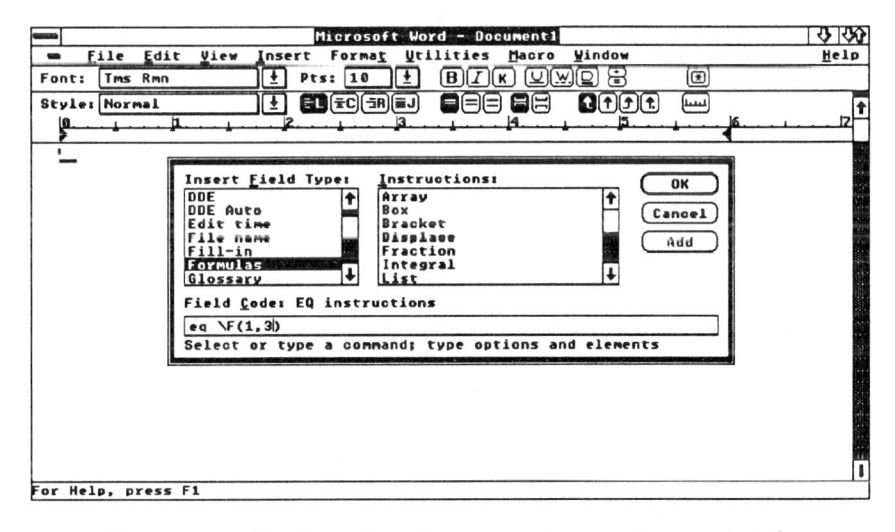

Figure 11.23 The formula code appears in your document at the insertion point.

Tip: Split the document window so that you can edit the formula codes in one pane and see the results immediately in the other pane.

Once the formula code is inserted into your document, you can select the field and press the Shift+F9 key combination to see the

359

result. If you followed the steps above, you noticed that the Instructions for the available types of formulas are easily added to the Field Code box by clicking the Add button. This is a convenience that Word provides so that you don't have to remember all the proper syntax for the formula codes. If you do remember the formula codes, you can just as easily use the Insert Field keys and type the formula code directly into your document.

Review

In this chapter you learned:

1. You can use Word's tables feature to create tables without using the Tab key and in a variety of other ways, including setting up a table of data as a data document file for a form-letter mailing.
2. A table created with Word's Insert Table command consists of a series of individual cells, similar to a spreadsheet which can contain text, numbers, and even pictures. Each cell can be formatted independently.
3. You can use Word's Utilities Sort command to sort financial data numerically or text material alphabetically. You can sort in ascending or descending order. In addition, you can sort tables, whole paragraphs, or items in a list.
4. Use Word's Utilities Calculate command to add, divide, subtract, or multiply. For more complex mathematics in tables, use Word's table feature to simulate a simple electronic spreadsheet.
5. To use the tables feature, position the insertion point where you want the table to appear and then choose the Insert Table command. It is easier to see the layout of your table if you first turn on the Table Gridlines option found on View Preferences.
6. You can determine the structure of your table by specifying the number of columns and rows it will have. You can add rows and columns to a table by using the Edit Table command.
7. To enter text in a table, move the insertion point and type the text just as in a document window. Each cell offers the word-wrap feature. You can also move from one cell to another by pressing the Tab key.
8. Word also lets you convert existing text to a table.
9. Before you can edit anything in a table, you must first select it.

10. You can change the sizes of rows, columns, and even individual cells in a table with the Table command from the Format menu.

11. Word enables you to add borders to dress up your tables. You can add a border around every cell, a single cell, or around a group of cells either vertically or horizontally.

12. A good use of Word's table feature is creating side-by-side paragraphs. This is a simple matter of creating a table with two or more columns.

TWELVE

Using Word's Glossary

In this chapter:

- Introducing Glossaries
- Creating and Inserting Glossary Entries
- Deleting Glossary Entries
- Printing the Glossary

This chapter introduces a tool that will help make your writing easier—Word's glossary. If you have to type repeatedly a section of text, such as a company letterhead or a long equation, you can use Word's glossary to simplify the task. You can use the glossary to store information temporarily, and, with a few clicks of the mouse or a few short keystrokes, insert that information anywhere in your document. This chapter discusses the procedures for understanding and using the Glossary command.

Introducing Glossaries

When many people think of a glossary, they are reminded of the listing of words and related definitions that appear at the end of a book. In fact, a dictionary like Webster's defines a glossary as a collection of specialized terms with their meanings. Although Word's glossary can be used to create such an animal, Microsoft has used the term *glossary* to define a more general function. You use the glossary to insert in your documents frequently used text or text you find too tedious to type or that is subject to typos. Each glossary entry can store any number of items, from a single character or word to several pages of text. You can even store graphics that you have created with another software package (such as a graph created in Microsoft Excel) and pasted into your documents. Before you learn the mechanics of using the glossary, you need to know a few key terms and functions that will help you understand how the glossary works.

Understanding How Word's Glossary Works

Word's Glossary is a storage area in RAM that opens automatically every time you fire up Word. You can store commonly used text (or graphics) so that it can be easily inserted into your working document. As an example, you might be required to enter a company name or address in several locations (other than within a header) within a document. Using Word's glossary, you enter information once, select it, assign a glossary name to that information via the Glossary command and then store it in the glossary "memory bin." Once the information is resident in the glossary, you use the Glossary command to paste a copy anywhere you specify in your document as many times as you like.

Exactly how the glossary works can seem a bit confusing. But it's important for you to learn the basics in order to use the feature properly. Each time you load Word, a little storage space is set aside in RAM. This storage space is called the glossary and it is just that: mostly empty space. But, as Word loads, a portion of that space is filled with a default normal glossary file. The contents of the glossary file are called *entries*. This file is empty until you begin to add entries to it. As you add entries to the glossary file, you have the option of making the entry available to all documents (Global) or to only those documents that have the same template as the active document (Template). When you quit Word, Word automatically provides you with the opportunity to save the entries added to the glossary file during the current work session (a message appears something like, "Save global glossary and command changes?"). If you elect to save those changes, the next time you start Word, the contents of the Glossary file will be available to you.

As you are reading about the glossary, you might be tempted to compare it to the Clipboard. In the Clipboard, though, new information replaces old information each time you execute a Cut or Copy command. It is only a temporary holding place that is available until you either replace its contents, or quit Word and turn off the computer. The glossary file, on the other hand, retains all the information you place in it for the current session (if you elect to save the changes you make to the glossary).

Creating and Inserting Glossary Entries

To access Word's glossary function for the first time, you must first define an entry. To do this, select the text you want to store as a glossary entry and then choose the Glossary command from the Edit menu. For example, this writer frequently types the name of the publishing company, Howard W. Sams & Company. The following steps show how to create this as an entry and add it to the glossary.

1. Select the text that you wish to store as a glossary entry. If necessary, type new text and then select it. For our example, select **Howard W. Sams & Company**.	The selected text appears highlighted.
2. Choose the **Glossary** command from the Edit menu or press **Alt,E,O**. If you didn't select any text in step 1 and there are no entries stored in the glossary file, the Glossary command will appear grey or dimmed. Select text first, and the command becomes available to you.	The Glossary dialog window appears.
3. The text that you selected prior to choosing the Glossary command now appears at the bottom of the window under the word, Selection (see Figure 12.1). To give this glossary entry a name, type something appropriate in the Glossary Name (access by pressing **Alt+N**) edit box. Glossary names may be up to 31 characters long, including	The abbreviation for Howard W. Sams & Company, or HWS, now appears in the Glossary Name edit window.

365

spaces. Probably the shorter you can make the name, the better, as long as you can recognize it later. Further, Word does not distinguish between upper- and lowercase characters. Word recognizes HWS, hws, and Hws as the same entry name. For our example, type **HWS**.

4. The next step is to tell Word whether this glossary entry should be available for all documents or just those documents based on the template of the active document. This step is called choosing the Context as Global or Template. Global (Alt+G) is selected by default. To change that, you'd click Template or type Alt+T.

    The context option is selected.

5. Choose **Define** or press **Alt+D**.

    Choosing Define stores the selected text as a glossary entry, closes the glossary window, and returns you to your document.

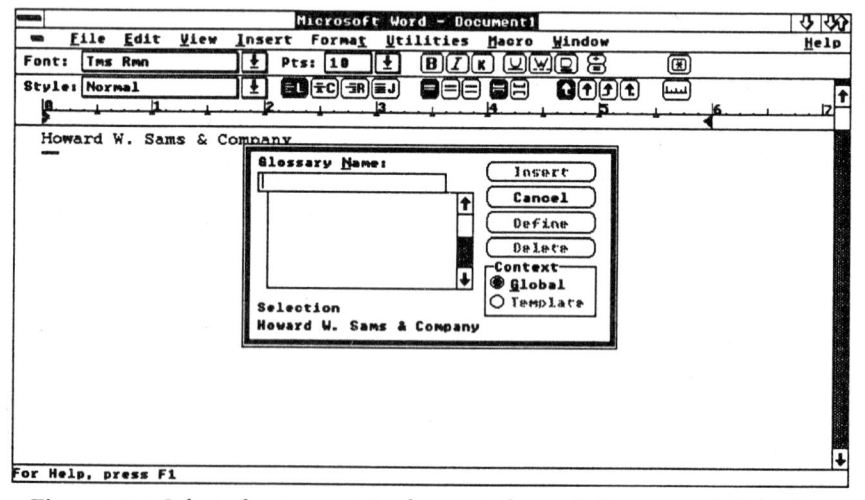

Figure 12.1 Selected entry text is shown in lower left corner of dialog box.

Once you have defined a new glossary entry, you can choose Edit Glossary without first selecting text. As the glossary window appears, you'll notice that each time you add an item to the glossary, it is added to the list box. The individual items in the list box, such as the HWS that we added in the exercise above, are *entry names*. These are abbreviations that represent the text stored in the glossary that you will insert into your documents. From now on, we call the text *entry text*. Together, the entry text and the entry name make up the entry. When you select one of these names from the list by clicking on it once (or pressing Alt+N and then using the arrow keys), the entry name is highlighted and listed in the Name edit box. At the same time, the entry text (or the first line of the entry text) is displayed in the area below Selection. For example, if you click on the entry name that we just created, HWS, the entry text will appear as expected, Howard W. Sams & Company.

If the entry text is too long to fit in the dialog box, Word will display a portion of the text followed by ellipses (...). To see the rest of the entry text, you must insert it into your document. You can then remove the entry text by choosing *Undo Insert Glossary Text* from the Edit menu, or you can use the Delete key to erase it.

When you create a glossary entry, it will contain any formatting, including character or paragraph formatting, the text has. When you create or select text from your document to add to the glossary, all formatting marks and options go along with it. If you prefer to select only the character formatting from text within a paragraph, be sure to omit the paragraph mark. Use the Paragraph option in View Preferences to highlight the paragraph mark so that you stop short of the mark when dragging through the text.

Inserting a Glossary Entry in Text

Now that you know how to create an entry, you can see that the value of the Glossary command is to save the time of entering text repeatedly. You can insert glossary entries with just a few clicks of the mouse or directly from the keyboard. The following steps highlight both methods.

1. The first step is to locate where in your document you want the glossary entry to appear. With the mouse or arrow keys move your insertion point to the desired location.

Adding and Polishing Word

2. Choose **Glossary** from the Edit menu or press **Alt,E,O**.	The Glossary dialog box appears.
3. From the list box, choose the entry name that you want to use. Scroll the box if necessary and then select the appropriate entry name. You can also type the name of the glossary entry that you wish to insert.	The selected entry name is highlighted in the Name edit box. The entry text appears at the bottom of the dialog box.
4. Click the **Insert** button or press **Alt+I**.	Clicking Insert closes the Glossary dialog and places the entry text at the insertion point within your document. Note that you can double-click the entry name from the list box to insert the entry text directly. You are soon returned to the document window with your inserted text safely in place.

If you change your mind after your glossary text is inserted in your document, and want to remove it, choose *Undo Expand Glossary Text* from the Edit menu or type Alt+Backspace. Like all Undo commands, though, you must execute it prior to giving another command or typing new text, and so on. If you forget, and the Undo option is dim and unavailable, you can erase the text with the Delete key or Cut command.

Inserting Entries with the Keyboard

Word enables you to insert glossary entries directly from the keyboard without resorting to the Glossary command. If you remember the exact entry name, you can use the Glossary key, F3, as shown in the following steps.

1. Using the arrow keys or the mouse, position the insertion point where you want the glossary entry to appear in your document.

368

2. Type the entry name. As an example, enter **HWS**.

3. Select the entry name.   The entry name appears highlighted.

4. Press the Glossary key, **F3**.   Word replaces the glossary name with the glossary entry text. If you entered an incorrect entry name, then Word will tell you that it's not in the glossary.

Deleting Glossary Entries

You cannot edit the components of a glossary entry. In other words, you cannot change the glossary name or replace the glossary text that corresponds to a glossary name. If you wish to change either of these components, you must simply delete the entry from the glossary and then define a new entry as desired. The steps to delete a glossary entry are:

1. Choose the **Glossary** command from the Edit menu or press **Alt,E,O**.   The glossary window appears.

2. Select the name of the glossary entry from the list box, or simply type the name of the glossary entry in the Name edit box.   The entry name appears highlighted.

3. Choose the **Delete** command button or press **Alt+L**.   The glossary entry is deleted.

4. Choosing one of the command buttons changes the Cancel button to Close. Choose **Close** to close the dialog box without further action.   Any changes made prior to choosing Close will still be in effect.

Printing the Glossary

If you wish, you can actually create a common book glossary with Word's glossary function. For example, you could enter the meanings to a variety of words as text entries and then assign the appropriate entry names to those meanings and store them in the glossary. When you have added all the glossary entries that you wish, you can print out the entire glossary alphabetically. The only drawback to this is that the entire contents will be printed, including any template glossary entries for the active document. To print the contents of your glossary, complete the following steps.

1. Choose **Print** from the File menu or press **Alt,F,P**.

    The Print dialog box appears.

2. Move to the **Print** box or press **Alt+P**.

3. Select **Glossary** from the list box or type glossary, if you wish.

4. Click **OK** or press **Enter**.

    In a moment the printing of your glossary begins. If any template glossary exists, it will print prior to the global glossary. A sample printout of a global glossary would look like Figure 12.2. This example illustrates the usefulness of using the glossary to store a variety of addresses that you might frequently use to insert into your documents quickly.

Review

In this chapter you learned:

1. Word's glossary is a storage area in memory that opens automatically every time you start Word. Use it to help you insert frequently used text into your document.

```
Global Glossaries
    Address
11711 North College Avenue, Suite 141, Carmel, Indiana
46032
    Crafts R US
Mrs. Janet Swadley, Owner
CRAFTS R US
222 79th Street
Indianapolis, IN  46268
    Dr-Blue
Dr. Edward Blue
The Blue Dental Clinic
505 Blackhawk Road
Hatchet Hill, ND 90012
    HWS
Howard W. Sams & Co.
```

Figure 12.2 A sample glossary.

2. Each time you load Word, the space allotted in memory to the glossary is filled with the contents of the default normal glossary file. The glossary file is empty until you add entries to it. You have the option of making entries available to all documents (global), or only to those whose templates are the same as that of the active document.

3. When you quit Word, it will give you the option of saving the entries that you added to the glossary file during the current work session. If you choose to do so, these entries will be available the next time you start Word.

4. To access Word's glossary function for the first time, you first must define an entry. Select the text that you want to store as a glossary entry, and then choose the Edit Glossary command. If you don't select text, the command will appear dim.

5. The real value of the Glossary command is to save the time you'd ordinarily spend entering text repeatedly. Use the Insert command button on the Edit Glossary dialog box to insert selected entries. Remember, the entry will be inserted at the location of the insertion point.

6. If you remember the exact name of the glossary entry, you can quickly insert it into your document by using the Glossary key, F3.

7. You cannot change the glossary name or replace the glossary text that corresponds to a glossary name.

8. To delete a glossary entry, choose the Edit Glossary command, select the entry from the list box, and choose the Delete command button.

9. To print the contents of the Glossary, choose the Glossary print option found on the File Print dialog box, and then choose OK. The entire glossary will print alphabetically.

THIRTEEN

Using Style Sheets

In this chapter:

- Introducing Style Sheets
- Using and Applying Styles
- Editing Styles
- Printing Style Sheets

Microsoft included a host of features in Word to make your work easier, and many consider the style sheet one of the most significant. Introduced in DOS based Word, the style sheet is one of the most powerful, and probably the most complex, tool that you can use. Once you master how to use the style sheet, it's not likely that you will ever want to work without it. This chapter introduces the concept of style sheets and helps you understand how to use them in your daily chores.

Introducing Style Sheets

Style sheets are one of the big added attractions of word processing packages today. Microsoft Word was the first to make these little time savers popular. At the time of this writing, you can't find a worthy substitute for Word when it comes to the variety of features offered.

The subject of style sheets can seem very complex. Their strong suit is that they enable you to save a tremendous amount of formatting time. Remember the writing process? Create the text. Edit the text. Format the text. Print the text. For many a productive writer, the formatting stage slows the writing process way down. With style sheets, you create a "blueprint" of how your document should look, either before or after you create and edit, and then let Word format your text automatically.

A style is just a way of naming the paragraph and character formatting.

Think of your document as a collection of individual paragraphs (and most are just that). Word will treat a single line or a heading as a paragraph if you press the Enter key after entering the text. Each paragraph within your document contains a set of character and paragraph formatting instructions, which may or may not be alike. This group of format instructions applied to a paragraph is called a *style,* and is identified by a unique name. The collection of styles for your entire document represents a *style sheet.*

If at all possible, you want to avoid repeating the same procedures over and over again. Up to now, any formatting that you have done manually has been done in this fashion: For each paragraph, you have carefully selected all the character and paragraph formatting elements including the font and font size, line spacing, alignment, and indents. By creating a style that represents all the repeating elements of a paragraph, such as headings, the body text, headers, or tables, you can apply the style once and the remainder of your paragraphs will follow suit. If you don't like a particular style's appearance, just modify the style, and every paragraph assigned to that style will be changed automatically. Of course, you can still assign different paragraphs to different styles, but, for consistency, it's best not to do so.

Once you collect all the styles for a particular document, you can store those styles in a style sheet that you can easily transfer from one document to another. This option prevents the need for repeating the same keystrokes and formatting decisions and lets Word remember where to place tab stops, which type of border to use, and whether the text is double spaced or single spaced, while you concentrate on the writing.

You can even copy style sheets from one document to another. If the destination document already has styles on its style sheet, then the two style sheets are merged. If any of the styles of the receiving document have the same style names as that of the merging document, then the receiving document's styles will be replaced by those of the incoming document.

Still not quite convinced style sheets are for you? Suppose you print a document with normal headings, left-justified in 10-point Times Roman type, and then discover later that you intended to use centered headings in a boldface Palatino font? Instead of searching through your entire document, changing the headings one-by-one manually, simply change the style for the headings element. Print the document first with one style and then the second. You decide. Manual formatting is easy, but quite time-consuming and not very flexible.

Before you can get a handle on style sheets, you must learn some of the basics of style sheets and their components, the styles. The sections that follow provide these basics.

Understanding the Basics

Although the concept of a style sheet may seem a bit intimidating, you have already been exposed to the style sheet. Every time Word loads and opens a document, it opens a default style sheet for that document. A style sheet may contain as many as 221 styles, but Word assigns 33 of these styles automatically. The default Normal style initially contains only these basic formatting elements:

- 10-point Times Roman type
- Single-spaced copy with no indents
- Left-aligned paragraph format

Once you add any new formatting style, such as a header, to your document, Word formats that element and adds the style to the default style sheet. You can add, delete, or modify styles within a style sheet. To view the contents of the default style sheet, choose either the *Styles* command (or press Alt,T,Y) or the *Define Styles* command (or press Alt,T,F) from the Format menu (see Figure 13.1). If you wish to view the alphabetical list of all the automatic styles Word applies to your document's elements, press Ctrl+A while either the Styles or Define Styles dialog box appears on your screen. Figure 13.2 shows a portion of that list. To see the remaining styles, scroll the list window.

Naming Styles

When you choose the Styles command, Word lists the styles available to you in a list box, as you saw from Figure 13.1. Notice that the Normal style is selected by default and highlighted, indicating that style of formatting is currently assigned to the paragraph where the insertion point resides. The format options representing the *definition* of the style are listed in the space below the list box. The style name and its corresponding definition make up the two parts of the style.

The first rule of thumb for naming a style is to choose a name that is descriptive of the document element. For example, you might name the title of a book Title; the main heading of text, Heading 1;

375

Adding and Polishing Word

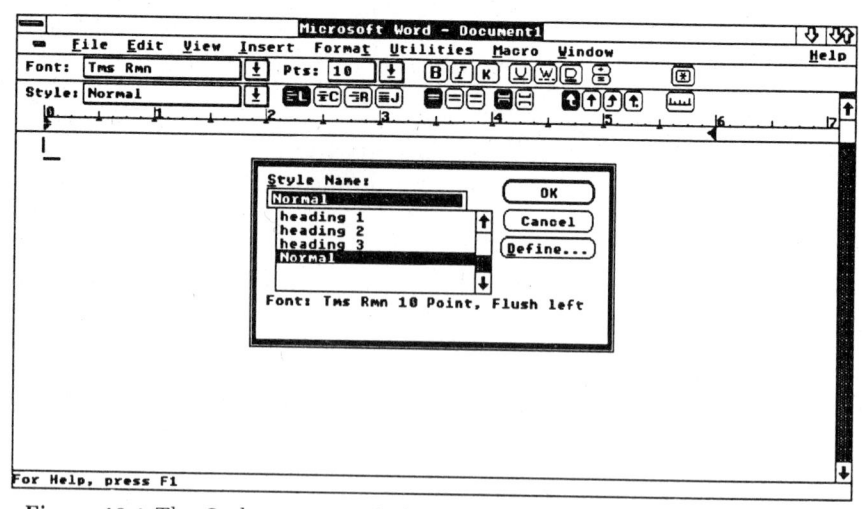

Figure 13.1 The Styles command shows the default Normal style applied to a new document.

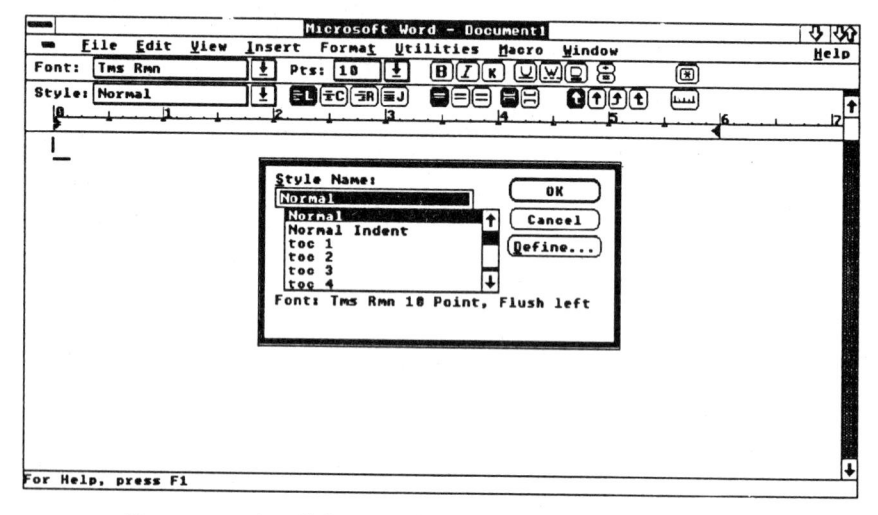

Figure 13.2 Scroll list window to view all automatic styles.

the second level of text, Heading 2; the body of text, BODY. Word will identify upper- and lowercase characters as names of different styles (e.g., Title is different from TITLE). Further, the style name is considered unique; if you try to name a style using a name that already exists, Word will ask you if you want to replace the old style name to match the existing definition (choose OK or Cancel).

Finally, you can assign a name up to twenty-two characters long, including spaces. You can also simply use the automatic style names by selecting them from the list box or by typing the automatic style name in the Style Name edit box. Since we have mentioned automatic style names more than once, let's discuss them next.

Automatic Styles

An automatic style is a predefined style that you can use to format common elements of a document. Examples of automatic styles include headers, footers, and subheadings. All automatic styles are based on the Normal style and are linked to the global document template (NORMAL.DOT) as well as any new document templates. You'll notice in Figure 13.2 that several automatic styles appear in the list box along with the Normal style. To see the definition assigned to a style name, scroll the list box to find the style, and then click on its name to select it (from the keyboard, activate the Name edit box with Alt+S and then use the up and down arrow keys). The resulting format definition will appear beneath it.

A great advantage to working with style sheets is that once you save your document, any styles that you have added to the document are saved automatically. Since the style sheet is opened automatically with your document, it is an integral part of that document and once the document is saved, the style sheet attached to that document is saved. This feature allows you to copy a style sheet representing one document and apply it to another document.

Using the Automatic Styles

There are three primary methods used to apply styles to your document text:

- Using the Mouse and the style box on the Ruler
- Using the Styles command dialog box
- Using the shortcut Styles key (Ctrl+S)

The easiest and fastest way to apply styles is with the style box located on the Ruler. Once you master the use of styles, you'll probably find the Ruler option to be the most effective. It's the best way to learn the basics as well. As an example, clear your screen by selecting New from the File menu, and then enter the sample text from Figure 13.3.

Once the text is entered, notice that it has not been formatted manually. Don't worry about typos; this is simply to illustrate Word's default automatic styles options. The key is to learn how to work with the styles box on the Ruler. To do this, complete the next set of steps.

Adding and Polishing Word

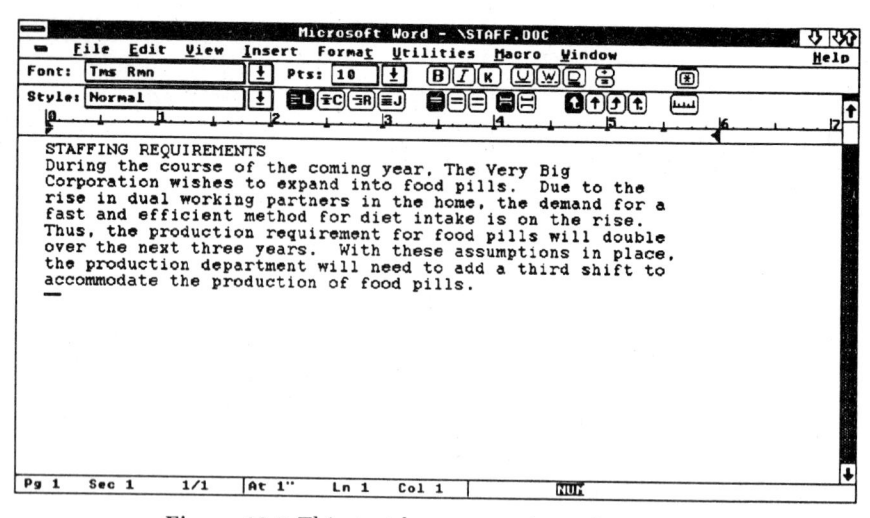

```
┌─────────────────────────────────────────────────────────────┐
│  ─              Microsoft Word - \STAFF.DOC            ↕ ▓▓│
│  ─   File  Edit  View  Insert  Format  Utilities  Macro  Window    Help│
│ Font: Tms Rmn      ↕  Pts: 10  ↕   B I k U W R ≡         ▨ │
│ Style: Normal      ↕   ≡L ≡C ≡R ≡J  ≡≡≡ ≡≡  ↕↑↑↑  ···     │
│ |0......|1......|2......|3......|4......|5......|6....|2↑│
│  STAFFING REQUIREMENTS                                      │
│  During the course of the coming year, The Very Big         │
│  Corporation wishes to expand into food pills.  Due to the  │
│  rise in dual working partners in the home, the demand for a│
│  fast and efficient method for diet intake is on the rise.  │
│  Thus, the production requirement for food pills will double│
│  over the next three years.  With these assumptions in place,│
│  the production department will need to add a third shift to│
│  accommodate the production of food pills.                  │
│  ▬                                                          │
│                                                             │
│                                                             │
│                                                             │
│                                                             │
│  Pg 1   Sec 1    1/1   At 1"   Ln 1  Col 1      NUM       ↓│
└─────────────────────────────────────────────────────────────┘
```

Figure 13.3 This text has not yet been formatted.

1. Select the first line of the text in Figure 13.3. You'll format this line as a heading. You could, of course, place the insertion point anywhere on the line if you had pressed Enter at the end of the line to depict it as an individual paragraph.

    The first line of text is highlighted.

2. Choose **Ruler** from the View menu in Full menus or press **Alt,V,R**.

    The Ruler appears.

3. Find the Normal style selection box in the lower left corner of the Ruler. Click the **Normal** window box open to display the automatic formatting style options.

    The Normal automatic style is highlighted.

4. The arrow at the top of the window is for scrolling the available selections. Since you want to format the first line as a heading, select the **heading 1** option.

    The moment that you click or double-click with the mouse, your selected text appears underlined, as shown in Figure 13.4. The style box on the Ruler displays the heading 1 formatting option.

378

5. If later you wanted to change the formatting of this paragraph, or any other paragraph, you would place the insertion point anywhere inside the paragraph, and then choose the Normal style from the style box on the Ruler. This option would return your paragraph to the default settings of the Normal style.

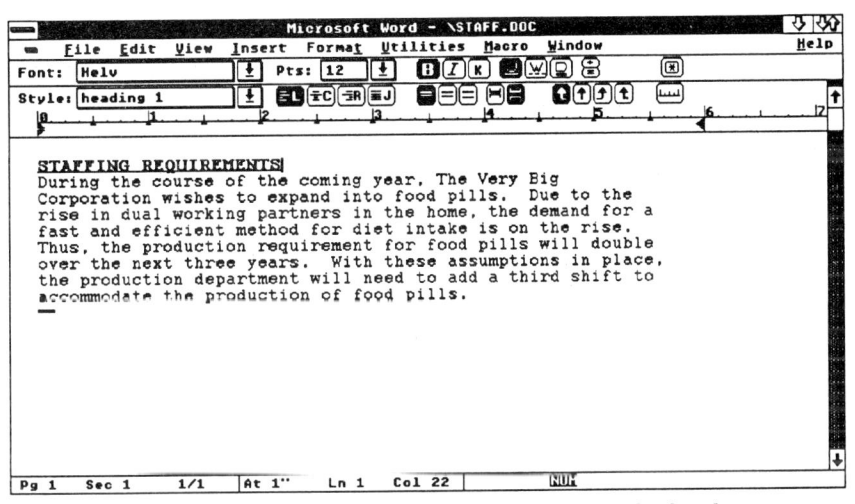

Figure 13.4 The first line is now formatted with the heading 1 automatic style.

Defining Styles

The character format of a paragraph is determined by the formatting of the majority of the characters in the selected paragraph. In other words, if over half of the selected text is italic, then the whole paragraph will be formatted as italic.

Using Word's default styles will probably satisfy your needs for a while, but sooner or later, you will want to customize your style sheet by adding new styles. You use one of three common methods to add the styles, called *defining styles*. One method uses the Define Styles command before you select any text and the other two define a style on a previous sample of formatted text. The sections that follow describe all three methods.

Defining a Style Before Applying It

The first method of defining a style is to open a new document (or an existing document based on the Normal style) and choose the formatting commands that define a style. With this method you use the Define Styles command located on the Format menu. This method also provides all style definition options and allows you to create multiple styles without first formatting your text.

You use the Define Styles command, located on the Format menu, to create, modify, add, delete, or combine styles to selected paragraphs. As with the Styles command, choosing the Define Styles command will display a dialog box that lists the default Normal styles alphabetically in a list box. If you want to view all of Word's automatic styles as well, press Ctrl+A while the dialog window, shown in Figure 13.5, is in view.

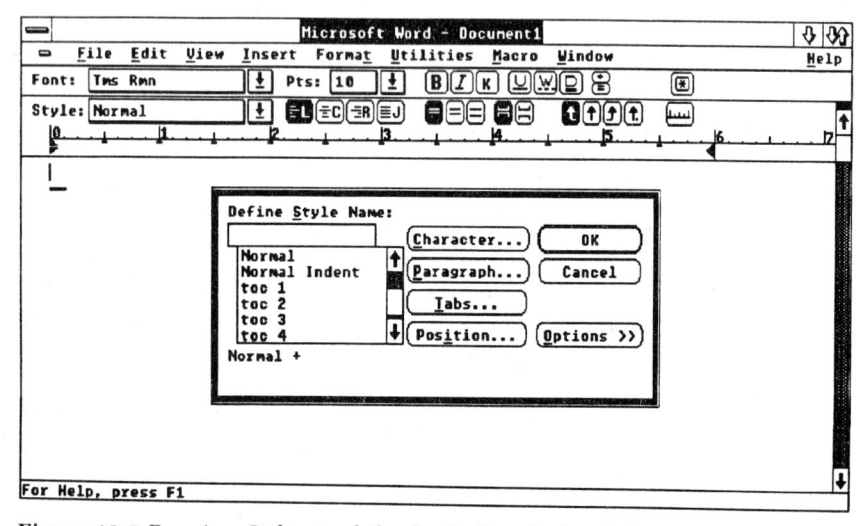

Figure 13.5 Pressing Ctrl+A while the Define Styles dialog window is open shows Word's automatic style offerings.

Unless you want to use the Normal styles (including all the automatic styles) offered by Word, your first step in creating a new style sheet is to define the styles themselves. The following steps highlight this method prior to selecting any text.

13—Using Style Sheets

1. Choose **Define Styles** from the Format menu or press **Alt,T̄,F**.

   The dialog box opens. Notice that the default Normal style is highlighted. If you have already selected another style for the current paragraph, that style will be highlighted in the Style Name list box.

2. Type a name that will represent your new style. Remember, the style name can be up to twenty-two characters and include spaces. You must complete this step for Word to establish your new style. Note that you can also select an automatic style from the list box by first pressing **Ctrl+A** to display the available options.

   As you type the name of the new style, it appears in the Style Name list box. Notice that the space below the list box now displays that the new style is based on the Normal style followed by the plus sign. The plus indicates that you are adding new formats to the Normal style.

As a shortcut to choosing formatting options from the Paragraph or Character dialog windows, press simultaneously Ctrl and the letter representing a formatting option (e.g., Ctrl+C adds centering to the style definition).

3. Choose the formatting options for the style by selecting either the **Character** command or pressing **Alt+C** or the **Paragraph** command or pressing **Alt+P**. Pressing one of these options produces the appropriate formatting dialog box as before. Choose your options from the dialog box, close it, and return to the Define Styles dialog box. Note that you can also choose the **Tabs** (**Alt+T**) or **Position** (**Alt+I**) buttons to make similar formatting selections as well. From a formatting dialog window, click **OK** or press **Enter** to

   As you add options using any of the methods, the options will appear below the status box. For example, if you choose a 12-pt Courier font with italics from the Character dialog box, and double spacing and centered from the Paragraph dialog box, Word will add these to the Normal setting for the style named in step 2, as shown in Figure 13.6.

381

Adding and Polishing Word

return to the Define Styles dialog box. Basically, you can choose format options the same way you do when formatting the document manually.

4. Choose **Options** or press **Alt+O**. You could also choose the Based On option or press Alt+B to base the style on a different style. Or you could choose Next Style or press Alt+N to select a style that you want for the paragraph following the current paragraph being defined. To add the formatting changes to the style definition made in step 3, click **Define** or press **Alt+D**, which serve to define the style without applying it to any text.

   The Cancel button changes to Close.

5. Choose **Close** or press **Alt+C** to close the dialog box without applying it to the current paragraph.

   This does not mean you've changed your mind, since the defined style will be retained.

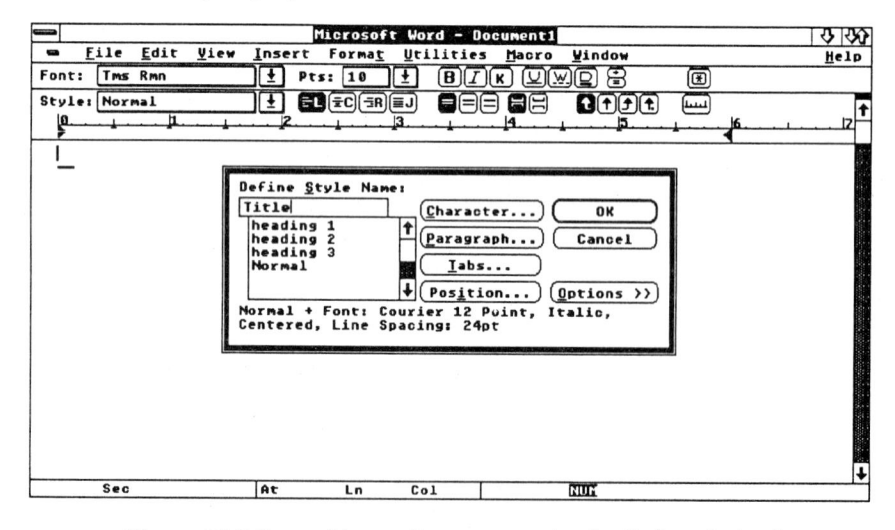

Figure 13.6 Formatting options appear in the Define Styles box.

382

You can use these steps to apply a new style to selected text. You can also add the defined style to both the active document and to its template. To do this, select from the Define Styles window the **Add to Template** option or press **Alt+A**. With the option off—the default position—the selected style will only be added to the style definition for the active document (available once you've selected Define). When the new style is defined, its name will appear in the list box when you click on the styles box on the Ruler. (It will also appear in the Define Styles list box.) You can then use this option like any other automatic style.

Creating A Style By Example

The next set of steps shows how to define a style based on the formatting of an existing paragraph. You can do this by using either the Style key (Ctrl+S) or by the Format Styles command. For example, consider the following text:

BUSINESS PLAN FOR STORE EXPANSION

Now suppose you wish to use this text as a main title with the following formatting options: 18-pt Times Roman font, centered text. You could format this paragraph manually (remember that a single line is a paragraph if you press Enter at the end of the line), or you can apply a style by first defining it with the following steps.

1. Select the paragraph that has the formatting you wish to define as a style. In this example, select **BUSINESS PLAN FOR STORE EXPANSION**.

   The text is highlighted.

2. You can define the style for the text with either the Style key or the Format Styles command. For the Style key, press Ctrl+S. Or, you could choose Styles from the Format menu or press Alt+Y to display the familiar Styles dialog window. The easier method is to use the **Style** key with the Ruler option on, and it's also a nice change of pace.

   The Ruler appears at the top of your screen with the style box selected. If the Ruler is off, the status bar at the bottom of the screen prompts you with the message, "What Style?"

383

3. With the style box selected, type in the style name that you want to appear as your newly defined style: **Business Plan**. Remember the style-name rules. You can enter more characters than the style box can hold up to the standard limit.

   As you type, the Normal title is replaced by the new name.

4. Press **Enter** or click anywhere outside the style box.

   Word presents an alert box with the message, "Define style 'Business Plan' based on selection?" The "style" is the name that you gave it in step 3. If you are using the Format Styles command, type the style name and choose OK.

5. Click **Yes** or press **Alt+Y**. Choosing Yes applies the new style and closes the alert box. Click **No** or press **Alt+N** if you change your mind.

   Your new style name appears in the style box representing the paragraph where the insertion point resides.

Basing A Style On Another Style

Using the Define Styles command you have learned how to create new styles not based on sample text. One option, though, called Based On, allows you to base the definition of one style on another style so that two styles, or paragraphs, have similar formatting. After you have based a style's definition on another style, any changes made to the original style will be reflected. For example, suppose all the headings in a document use a standard Roman font. If you change the font for the first heading style to Helvetica, then all the headings based on the first style will change to Helvetica as well.

Using and Applying Styles

You now know how to use the automatic styles from the Normal style and how to create new styles. The trick, of course, is to apply those style options to your paragraphs. If you have been practicing the steps, you'll have a good idea how to do this, but, for your convenience, this section highlights the method.

When you think of using styles, it's helpful to break the process down to a series of steps.

1. *Create and enter the text.* This step is the most important. Time savers like the glossary are beneficial for entering commonly used text.

2. *Edit the text.* Clean up your documents using any of Word's editing tools, including the Cut, Copy, and Paste commands; the Delete key; and the spelling checker.

3. *Create your style sheet.* This is the formatting step. Instead of manually formatting your text, you can now use the style sheet. This step might entail using Word's Normal styles, including any automatic styles; redefining existing styles (see the "Editing Styles" section later in this chapter); or creating new styles that fit your document's needs. Once all the key elements of the document (headers, titles, levels of headings, body of text area, addresses, footers, closings, etc.) have been defined by a style, you need to apply those styles to your unformatted text. Remember, as you create styles, you will use the Character and Paragraph commands, the Tabs and Position commands, and the shortcut keyboard commands. Keep in mind that you can give certain document formatting commands, such as margin settings, before or after your document is created.

4. *Apply the styles to your document's elements.* To apply styles to selected text areas, you use the Format Styles command, the Style key (Ctrl+S), and the Styles status box on the Ruler with a mouse.

Word follows some basic rules when applying styles. First, it only applies a style to individual paragraphs (you can select more than one at a time, even an entire document, if you wish). As you'll recall, an individual paragraph may be a single line if you've added a paragraph symbol at the end of the line by pressing the Enter key. If you want to include several individual lines in the same paragraph, use the Newline keypress (hold down Shift while pressing Enter). Of course, until you press Enter, all lines in a document wrap around and make up a single paragraph. When you create new paragraphs, the style of the next paragraph is attached, or linked, to the style of the current paragraph. Likewise, the style of the preceding paragraph is the same as that of the current paragraph. Sounds just like the basic formatting rules, doesn't it? Further, Word only allows you to have, at most, nine levels of directly linked styles. Finally, when you are applying a style to a portion of a paragraph, Word applies the style to the entire paragraph, regardless of how much of the paragraph you select. If this is not satisfactory for your purpose, you must use the manual formatting methods.

If you understand the rules, a quick review of style-setting methods is in order.

- Use the style box on the Ruler. This requires a mouse, but it is best for beginners.
- Use the Styles command on the Format menu. You can also use the Define Styles command if you are just now creating the styles as described in previous steps. In general, use the Define Styles for creating styles and the Styles command for applying them.
- Use the Style key. This is best left for experienced users. You must remember the exact name of the styles to use this one. If not, you can press the Style key (Ctrl+S) a second time to bring up the Format Styles dialog box.

Using the Ruler to apply a style to selected paragraph(s) is the easiest and quickest method for beginners and experienced users alike.

The Ruler method is preferable. It's quick and painless and it doesn't require that you remember too much (as the keyboard method does, for instance). Using a menu just seems natural and requires less time. Regardless of which method you use, the first step is always the same: *Select the paragraph(s) to which you want to apply the style.* Don't forget this step, or you'll waste a lot of time. You can select the paragraph or paragraphs (even an entire document) or you can place the insertion point anywhere inside a particular paragraph. Of course, unless you simply want to add a Normal default style to your text, you should create a set of style options that represents all elements of your document. Ready to go? Use any of the following methods, the choice is yours.

Method 1—Using the Ruler and Mouse to Apply a Style

1. Select the paragraph(s) to which you want to apply the style by dragging across the paragraph or positioning the insertion point in that paragraph.

13—Using Style Sheets

2. Choose **Ruler** from the View menu if you haven't already.

   The Ruler appears.

3. Click on the **down arrow** to open the style box window.

   Notice that the style for the current text is selected and highlighted. If you haven't chosen a style for this paragraph selection, the default Normal style will be selected for you.

4. Select the style from the list window that you wish to apply to your selected paragraph(s) by clicking or double-clicking with the mouse.

   The selected paragraph(s) are instantly formatted according to the style format definition that you selected.

Method 2—Using the Format Styles Command to Apply Styles

1. Select the paragraph(s) as usual.

2. Choose **Styles** from the Format menu or press **Alt+T+Y**. If you press Ctrl+A while the styles window is open you can view all the default styles as well.

   The list box depicts the available styles. If you want to create a new style, use the Define Styles command.

3. Select the desired style from the list box or type the name of the style.

   The formatting options available with each style are listed below the list box as you select the individual style name.

4. Click **OK** or press **Enter**.

   Word applies the style to the selected paragraph(s) immediately.

Note: Change your mind about the new format? To go back to the default Normal style, press Ctrl+Spacebar and the paragraph where the insertion point resides (the selected paragraph[s]) will revert to Normal.

Method 3—Using the Style Key to Apply a Style

1. Once again, select your paragraph(s).

2. Press the Style key, **Ctrl+S**.   The status box in the lower left of the screen now changes to a style status box and produces the message, "Which Style?"

3. Type the exact name of the style. If you forget the name of the style, press Ctrl+S again to retrieve the Styles dialog box.   As you type the name, it appears in the style status box.

4. Press **Enter**.   If the name that you entered was not listed in the Styles dialog box, the name is wrong and Word will give you the chance to correct it until you get it right.

That's all there is to applying styles. You now know how to create styles and an entire style sheet, if you like. The style sheet is attached to your document when you save it. Similar to any other file, you can alter the name of the style sheet or the contents defined by a style name.

Editing Styles

In this section, you'll learn how to delete a style (other than the automatic style), change a style name, and change the formatting instructions assigned to a style name. When you edit a style, any styles based on that style will also change.

Deleting a Style

Like most information that you collect, there comes a time when you no longer need a style. To delete a style from a style sheet, you choose the Define Styles command from the Format menu and use the Delete command from the expanded dialog window (choose Options to expand the window). The following steps highlight this procedure:

1. Choose **Define Styles** or press **Alt,T,F**.

    The dialog box appears.

2. Choose **Options** or press **Alt+O**.

    The dialog window expands.

3. Select the style that you wish to delete from the list box. Click it once to select it.

    The selected style is highlighted. Note that you cannot delete the Normal or any of the automatic default styles using this method, so don't select them.

4. Choose **Delete** or press **Alt+D**.

    Word displays an alert box asking you to confirm the deletion.

5. Choose **Yes** to confirm the deletion.

Caution: If the deleted style is applied to any paragraphs in the document, those paragraphs will lose their formatting.

Changing a Style Name

You cannot rename or delete any automatic styles provided by Word.

You can change a style's name that you've created if it is no longer distinct enough from other style names. You might, for example, have a style for the opening of standard business letters and another style for the opening of legal letters. One might be named Letter and the other named Legal-letter, with the formatting instruction changed slightly. The following steps show you how to change a name to avoid confusion.

1. Choose **Define Styles** from the Format menu or press **Alt,T,F**.

    The Define Styles dialog box appears.

389

2. Choose **Options** or press Alt+O to expand the dialog window.

3. From the style list, select the style that you wish to change. If you have a mouse, click it once to select it; otherwise, use the arrow keys.

    The style is highlighted and the insertion point moves to the style box.

4. From the bottom of the expanded dialog box, select the **Rename** command button or press Alt+R.

    The Rename Styles dialog box appears.

5. Type the new name. Remember, you can create a new name up to twenty-two characters and include spaces.

    If you enter the name of an existing style, Word tells you so and you can enter a new name.

6. Click **OK** or press **Enter**.

    Word returns to the Define Styles dialog box. Choose **Close** to close the window and return to the document.

Note that you cannot rename the automatic styles, but you can add new names that are based on the automatic styles. You can add an abbreviation to an automatic style name, for example.

Changing the Formatting of the Style

From time to time, you may decide that you need to modify the formatting instructions associated with a style name. If so, do remember that if you change the formatting instruction assigned to a style, all the paragraphs associated with that style will change. Similar to creating a new style, you can also "redefine" an existing style. To do this, either format a paragraph first and use the Style key (Ctrl+S) or the Format Styles command. If you wish to redefine a style that's not based on an example, simply choose the Define Styles command on the Format menu. The procedures for redefining an existing style are just like those for creating a new style, which we just discussed. The primary difference is that Word asks you if you want to change the existing style definition instead of defining it for the first time. For example, if you decide that the style for our previous Address example should be Left-Justified instead of Centered, select the style

13—Using Style Sheets

from the Defines Styles list box, choose the appropriate paragraph formatting option (e.g, press Ctrl+L), and then choose OK to redefine the style and close the window. If you wish to change an existing paragraph, select it first, format it, and then press Ctrl+S or choose Format Styles. Type the style's name and choose OK. Word asks if you want to change the style, so choose Yes to do so.

Use the following steps to guide you through the procedure for redefining a style using the Define Styles command with no example:

1. Choose **Define Styles** from the Format menu or press **Alt,T,F**.

    The Define Styles dialog window appears.

2. From the style list, select the style that you wish to edit.

    The selected style is highlighted. All the formatting instructions associated with the selected style appear below the list window.

3. Choose any of the formatting commands from the Character, Paragraph, Position, or Tab dialog boxes or use the keyboard shortcut commands by entering them along with the Ctrl key.

    Your modifications are reflected below the list window.

4. Choose **Options** or press **Alt+O** to expand the dialog window.

5. Click **Define** or press **Alt+D**.

    The formatting changes are integrated according to your selections made in step 3.

Merging Styles

Word also provides the convenience of merging styles from other documents with the styles of the active document. You can even merge from a document template or to a document template from the active document. The key is that once you define a style in one document, you can easily use it over and over again without the need to recreate it. The one rule to remember is that when you merge two style sheets, the incoming styles replace any existing styles that happen to use the same style name. To use Word's merge feature, refer to the following sets of steps.

1. Choose the **Define Styles** command from the Format menu or press **Alt,T,F**.

   The Define Styles dialog window appears.

2. Select **Options** or press **Alt+O** to expand the dialog box.

   The dialog box expands to display the Merge command button.

3. Choose **Merge** or press **Alt+M**.

   The Word Files and directories are listed in a window.

4. If you are merging styles to or from a template, choose the appropriate start button—**Alt+R** or **Alt+T**—and your task is complete. If you are merging styles from another document, select the appropriate document name from the list box. If necessary, select the directory that contains the document that you are merging or press **Alt+D**.

5. Choose **OK** or press **Enter**.

Printing Style Sheets

For a comparison of all your style sheets, you need to open each document in turn and print out the style sheet. To print the styles of a single style sheet, complete the following steps.

1. Choose **Print** from the File menu or press **Alt,F,P**.

   The Print dialog box appears.

2. Select **Styles** from the Print box or press **Alt+down arrow**.

   The Styles option is highlighted.

3. Choose **OK** or press **Enter**. The style sheet will begin to print. Each style name will be printed in boldface in the default font. The formatting instructions for that style appear indented to the right below the name.

Review

In this chapter you learned:

1. A group of formatting instructions applied to a paragraph and associated with a single name is called a style. A collection of styles for the entire document is called a style sheet. You can use a style sheet as a "blueprint" to format your documents automatically instead of manually.
2. Every time Word opens a new document, it opens a default style sheet for that document, called Normal. The default style sheet initially contains the Normal style: 10-pt Times Roman font, single spaced with no indents, and left-aligned paragraphs.
3. A style sheet may contain as many as 221 different styles, but Word assigns 33 of these styles automatically.
4. You can apply styles to your document text with the Styles commands, with the style box found on the Ruler, and by the keyboard method (using the Styles key, Ctrl+S).
5. To create or modify a style sheet, choose the Define Styles command from the Format menu. You can also use the style selection box at the left side of the Ruler to create and change styles.
6. The quickest and easiest method for applying styles is to use the style box on the Ruler.
7. To delete a style from your style sheet, choose the Define Styles command, choose Options, select the style from the list box, choose Delete, and then choose Close.

8. You can change a style name or the formatting instructions assigned to a style.

9. You can merge styles from another document or from a document template into the active document. When you merge styles, the incoming styles replace the existing styles of the same names.

10. You can print a style sheet by choosing the Styles option located on the File Print dialog box. To compare all style sheets, you must open each document and repeat the procedure.

F O U R T E E N

Chapter

Using Annotations and Revisions

In this chapter:

- Creating and Using Annotations
- Navigating Between Annotations Marks
- Editing Annotations
- Locking and Unlocking Documents
- Printing Annotations
- Creating and Using Revision Marks
- Searching for, Accepting, and Removing Revision Marks
- Comparing Two Different Versions of a Document

This chapter shows you how to use Word's annotations feature and how to mark revisions of your documents. These tools are useful for reviewing your documents. Annotations, for example, let you, or others who may read your documents, add comments that are attached to the documents themselves. The comments can be added to the documents or simply deleted. Revision marking, on the other hand, is a tool that you and others can use to see the changes that a document has undergone during its development. Both of these features help you review and polish your documents.

Creating and Using Annotations

Your annotation can be as long as you need to make your message clear.

Making annotations is a way that you can review and edit your documents on the screen. The original author of the document, or other reviewers, can attach, and initial, their comments on the document. You can even "lock" your documents so that only you can read the comments, a process we'll look at in a later section.

To create annotations, you insert an *annotation mark* at the location of the insertion point. When you create the annotation mark, it will enclose in brackets your initials and the sequential number of the annotation (e.g., [RKS1]). The annotation mark is formatted as hidden text, but it will appear under two conditions:

1. When you insert an annotation mark, an annotation pane opens in the lower left portion of the active window. It becomes the active pane regardless of whether other panes are open. The annotation mark will appear in the upper left corner of the annotation pane following a page/section number field. The page-number field is inserted by Word to help you jump from one annotation location to another across several pages or even jump to specific sections of your document. The page-number field is only visible if the View Fields option is selected. The annotation mark always appears here while the annotation pane is open, even if the Hidden Text option on View Preferences is turned off.

2. When you turn on the Hidden Text option located on the View Preferences dialog box, the annotation mark will be visible.

To enter annotations, complete the following steps:

1. Position the insertion point where you want to enter the annotation. As an example, consider the short memo shown in Figure 14.1. The insertion point is inserted just before the word Tuesday in the second line.

2. Choose the **Annotation** command from the Insert menu or press **Alt,I,A**.

The annotation pane appears at the bottom of the active window as shown in Figure

14—Using Annotations and Revisions

14.2. Note the annotation mark appears as formatted hidden text in both the document and in the annotation pane. In the annotation pane, the mark follows the page number field.

3. Type the annotation at the insertion point (it will appear to the right of the bracketed initials and annotation number). The comment can be any length and formatted using any of Word's tools.

4. Repeat steps 1 through 3 for all additional annotations. Figure 14.3 is an example of the same memo with three annotations.

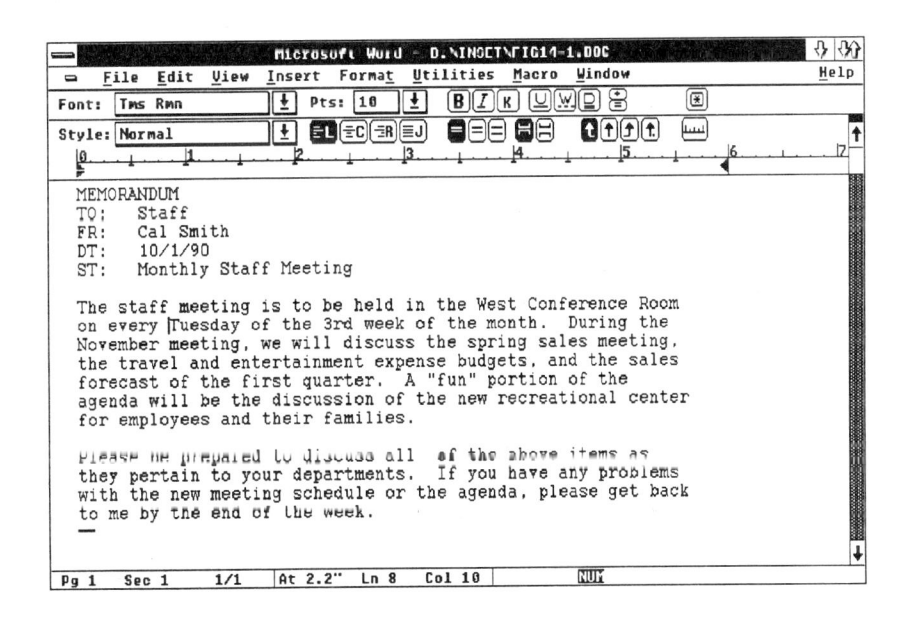

Figure 14.1 Position the insertion point where you want to insert an annotation.

Adding and Polishing Word

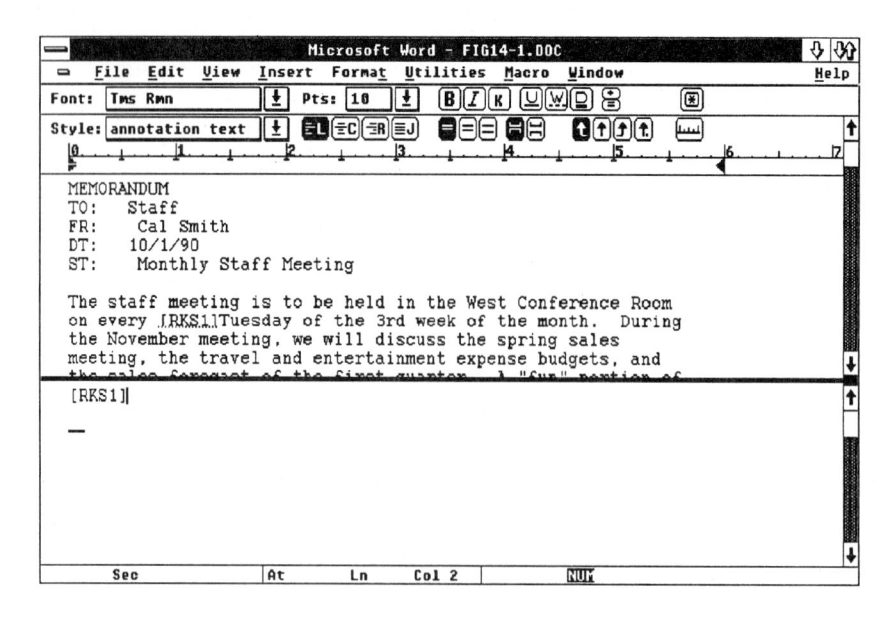

Figure 14.2 An annotation pane appears at the bottom of the active document window.

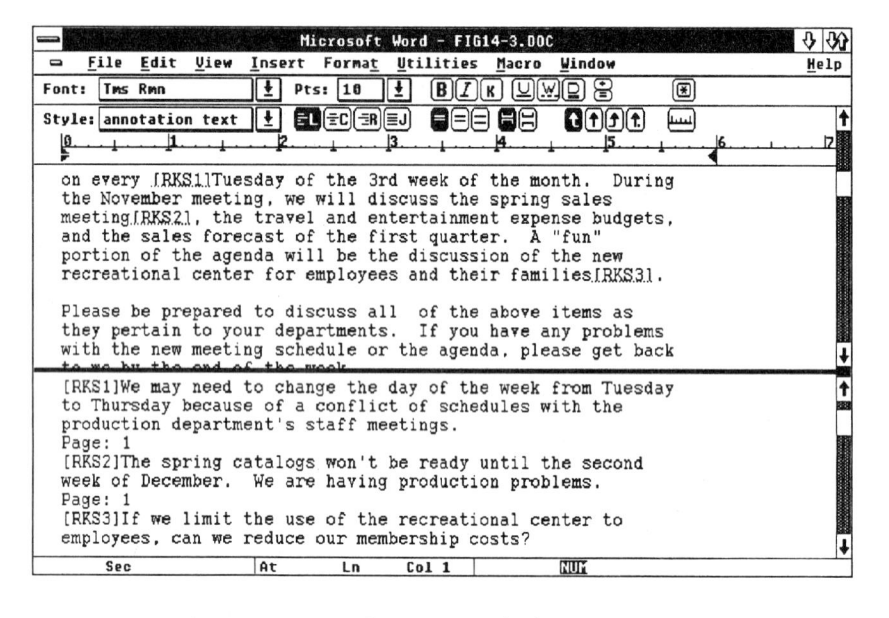

Figure 14.3 Sample memo with three annotations.

Opening and Closing Annotation Panes

Once you have created your annotations using the steps in the previous section, you should also know how to close or open the annotation panes themselves. Both opening and closing an annotation pane is accomplished using the *Annotations* command selected from the View menu or by pressing Alt,V,A. This command acts as a toggle for an open or closed annotations pane. For example, if you just inserted an annotation mark, Word will automatically open the annotation pane at the bottom of the active window. Once you type your annotations, you can close this pane by choosing the View Annotation command. Notice that when the annotation pane is open, a check mark appears next to the Annotation command in the View menu. Simply choosing this command again will close the annotation pane and remove the check mark. In general, there are three ways to open an annotation pane:

- Choose View Annotations or type Alt,V,A.
- Choose Insert Annotations or type Alt,I,A. This will insert a new annotation mark at the insertion point and open the annotation pane at the same time.
- Hold down the Ctrl key while you click on the split bar (located at the top of the vertical scroll bar), and then drag the split bar down the scroll bar to open the pane. This method requires that you have a mouse installed on your system.

To close an annotation pane, choose the View Annotations command a second time.

Tip: You can also close an annotation pane quickly if you double-click the split bar. You can't open an annotation pane using this method, because double-clicking the split bar opens a standard document pane.

Navigating Between Annotations Marks

There are two modes of navigation when working with annotations:

- Jumping from one annotation mark to another
- Moving between the annotation mark and the annotation text

To jump to an annotation mark, you use the following steps:

1. Choose the **Go To** command from the Edit menu or type **Alt,E,G**.

   The Go To dialog box appears.

2. Type the letter **a** for the "next annotation" and press **Enter**. You can also type the location of the specific annotation. For example, if you type a 3 and press Enter, Word will jump to the third annotation. For a complete listing of the possible destinations, refer to Table 14.1.

An alternate method for jumping to an annotation is to use F5, the Go To key. Pressing **F5** places a message, "Go To" in the status bar at the bottom of the screen. Either type **a** for the next annotation, or type the specific destination as listed in Table 14.1 and then press **Enter**. Using this method seems faster than opening the Go To command dialog box.

Table 14.1 Annotation Listing Destinations

If You Type:	You Will Jump to:
a	The next annotation mark.
a*number* (e.g, a5)	The annotation mark represented by the number. In this case, the fifth annotation mark.
a+*number* (e.g., a+2)	The *number* annotation mark after the insertion point. In this case, the second annotation mark after the insertion point.
a−*number* (e.g., a-4)	The *number* annotation mark before the insertion point. In this case, the fourth mark prior to the insertion point.

14—Using Annotations and Revisions

If You Type:	You Will Jump to:
a*number*p*number* (e.g., a2p3)	The *number* annotation mark on a specific page. In this case, the second mark on the third page. You can also reverse the listing as p3a2.
a*number*s*number* (e.g., a3s2)	The *number* annotation mark on a specific section. In this case, the third mark on the second section. You can also reverse the listing as s2a3.
a*number*s*number*p*number* (e.g., a1s2p3).	Any combination of specific annotation marks within a specific section of a specific page. This case illustrates the first mark within the second section of the third page of the document. You can use any combination of these listings (e.g., p3s2a1, s2p3a1, etc.).

Moving Between Annotation Marks and Annotation Panes

There are two situations in which you will need to navigate between the annotation mark and the text within the annotation pane. The first is from the document pane and the second from within the annotation pane. For example, suppose you wish to review the comments made on the third annotation of the second page of a document. If you are currently working inside the document pane, you would do the following:

1. Jump to the specific annotation mark. Choose either the **Go To** command, or press **Alt,E,G** or press **F5**, the Go To key.	Either the Go To dialog box appears or the Go To query in the status bar appears, depending upon which method you chose.

401

2. Type **a** for the next annotation or type the specific annotation location (see Table 4.1). For our example, you would type **P2A3** to jump to the second page and the third annotation (you could also type A3P2).

3. Press **Enter** to jump to the desired annotation mark.

4. To see the comments in the annotation pane, choose the **Annotation** command from the View menu or type **Alt,V,A**.

   The annotation pane appears at the bottom of the active document window.

5. If you wish to move from the document pane to the annotation pane, press **F6** or click inside the annotation pane with the mouse (if you have one).

Reading Annotations

Since annotations can be of any length, you can use the scroll bar on the annotation pane to scroll through the annotation text just like any document. If the annotation pane is not open, choose the **View Annotation** command to open the pane, and then scroll the pane to read the full annotation. If the document contains more than one annotation on more than a single page or section, you can use the **Go To** command or the Go To key (**F5**) to jump to a specific annotation location, and then read the text in the open annotation pane.

Now that your insertion point is located inside an active annotation pane, you may wish to jump to the next annotation mark. If all annotation marks are on the same document page, the annotation text will appear in the one pane. If the next or additional annotation marks appear on subsequent pages of your document, however, choose the **Go To** command, type **a** or the specific annotation mark location, and then press **Enter**. Remember, to save time, you can press the Go To key, **F5**, to display the Go To request at the bottom of the screen in the status bar. As before, type either **a** or the annotation mark location and then press **Enter** to jump to that location.

Editing Annotations

You can use all of Word's editing tools with annotation text.

Editing or formatting annotations is accomplished just like in any other document. First choose a specific annotation mark (see steps above to jump to an annotation), open the annotation pane by choosing **View Annotations** if the pane is not open, and then move to the annotation pane (if needed) by clicking inside the pane itself or pressing **F6**. Once inside the annotation pane, you can edit or format the text just like any other document text.

Moving Annotation Text

Remember, as a shortcut alternative to using Cut and Paste, you can use the Shift+Del and Shift+Ins commands, respectively.

You can move annotation text from the annotation pane to your document, an efficient way to revise and edit your documents based on input from reviewers. You can use either of two methods. Since the annotation text behaves just like any text, you'd use the Cut and Paste commands on the Edit menu to move the text from the annotation pane into the document. To do this, select the text while in the annotation pane, choose the **Cut** command or press **Alt,E,T**, and then move to the document pane by pointing and clicking with the mouse or pressing **F6**. Once you have positioned the insertion point where you want the text to appear, choose the **Paste** command or press **Alt,E,P**. An alternative to using the Cut and Paste commands is to use the Move to command. You will recall from Chapter 3 that you can move text by first selecting it, pressing **F2**, and then pressing **F6** to move from the annotation pane to the document pane as before. Position the insertion point and press **Enter** to move the selected text.

Deleting Annotations

To delete an annotation, you must delete the annotation mark from the document itself; you can't delete an annotation by selecting the annotation mark from within the annotation pane or by erasing the annotation text. To delete an annotation, complete the following steps:

1. Jump to the annotation mark that you wish to delete. Remember, this is the mark within the document pane. If no annotation pane is open, you'll need to turn on the

Hidden Text option found on View Preferences in order to see the annotation marks.

2. Select the **entire mark**: brackets, initials, number, and all.

   The selected annotation mark will be highlighted.

3. Delete the annotation mark by pressing the **Delete** key or choosing the **Cut** command from the Edit menu (press **Alt,E,T**).

   The annotation (text and mark) is deleted.

Locking and Unlocking Documents

As a limitation to adding annotations (as well as other changes) to documents, Word provides the ability of "locking" your documents. A document can only be locked, and subsequently unlocked, by the author of the document. When a document is locked, many commands on the menu bar are unavailable to reviewers and appear grey or dim while the insertion point resides within the document pane itself. (Some commands will also appear grey while the insertion point resides within the annotation pane.) To lock or unlock your document, first use the File **Save As** command. From there, click the **Options** command button (or press **Alt+O**) to display the expanded dialog box. Then choose **Lock for Annotations** or press **Alt+L** and press **OK** or press **Enter**. To unlock your document, simply turn off the **Lock for Annotations** by selecting it a second time (the option is not blackened when it's turned off).

Printing Annotations

In order to review your annotations, you may wish to print them out on your printer. This feature allows you to collect all the annotations in one place for a quick and easy review. Word provides the option of printing just the annotations attached to your document or of printing the entire document as well as the annotations. When you choose to print both the document text and the annotations, the annotations will be printed on a separate page following the document itself. As a handy reference, Word will print a page number at the beginning of each annotation that indicates where the annotation appears within

14—Using Annotations and Revisions

the document. If you decide to print only a portion of the document, then only those annotations that appear within that portion of the document will also be printed. The steps to print your annotations are:

1. Choose the **Print** command from the F̲ile menu or press **Alt,F,P**.

   The Print dialog box appears.

2. To print only the annotations, choose the **Annotations** option in the Print box. To print both the document and the annotations, select **Document** in the Print box and then turn on the **Annotations** option found under the expanded dialog box. You get the expanded box by choosing **O̲ptions** or pressing **Alt+O** and then **Annotations** or pressing **Alt+N̄**.

   The selected options are highlighted.

3. Choose **OK** or press **Enter**.

   Shortly, printing begins as you have specified. Figure 14.4 depicts the three annotations from our sample memo. Since all three annotations are on the same page, the page-number reference is to page 1.

Creating and Using Revision Marks

It is likely that you have edited some of your documents several times, creating several versions of the same document. To help you keep track of these different versions before you print out the final document, it is useful to mark in some way the changes made during the course of the editing process. Using Word's revision-marks feature on the Utilities menu, you can easily mark the areas that have been changed. The advantage to marking your document is that you can evaluate the changes made, determine if the meaning of the text is properly communicated or has been altered, and present the docu-

105

Adding and Polishing Word

```
MEMORANDUM
TO:     Staff
FR:     Cal Smith
DT:     10/1/90
ST:     Monthly Staff Meeting

The staff meeting is to be held in the West Conference Room
on every [RKS1]Tuesday of the 3rd week of the month.  During
the November meeting, we will discuss the spring sales
meeting[RKS2], the travel and entertainment expense budgets,
and the sales forecast of the first quarter.  A "fun"
portion of the agenda will be the discussion of the new
recreational center for employees and their families[RKS3].

Please be prepared to discuss all  of the above items as
they pertain to your departments.  If you have any problems
with the new meeting schedule or the agenda, please get back
to me by the end of the week.
```

```
Page: 1
[RKS1]We may need to change the day of the week from Tuesday
to Thursday because of a conflict of schedules with the
production department's staff meetings.
Page: 1
[RKS2]The spring catalogs won't be ready until the second
week of December.  We are having production problems.
Page: 1
[RKS3]If we limit the use of the recreational center to
employees, can we reduce our membership costs?
```

Figure 14.4 You can print all your annotations along with the document text.

ment to reviewers so that they can see the difference between the previous document(s) and the new one.

Word provides two general methods of marking the revisions of your document:

- You can tell Word to indicate the changes to the document as you make them.
- You can ask Word to identify the changes made by comparing the current version of the document with a previous one.

Regardless of which general method you choose, you also have several ways to indicate the changes themselves. For example, you can choose to insert change bars beside the altered text in the left or right margin. Or, you may wish to tell Word to enter the new text with bold, italic, or underlined text characters. You even have the option of displaying and printing new text double underlined. In the legal profession for example, it is common to draw lines through text that you are deleting and to underline text that you are adding. Drawing lines through text in Word is called *strikethrough* formatting (or *redlining*). Therefore, when you turn on the revision-marking feature of Word, you will accomplish the following:

- New text is marked in a format that you specify. The options to mark the new text include: Bold, Italic, Underline, and Double Underline. If you don't wish to mark new text in a specific character format (it will not stand out from the standard character format that you are using), choose Nothing. Choosing Nothing will not affect the printing of revision bars (see below).
- Deleted text will appear with strikethrough or redlined format.
- Vertical revision bars are inserted next to the text that has changed. This option does not affect any new text that you have chosen to be shown in a specific format. You can choose None to turn off revision bars, Left or Right to print revision bars in the left or right margins, or Outside to print revision bars in the left margin on even-numbered pages and right margin on odd-numbered pages of facing pages in bound documents. The revision bars will always appear on the left side of the screen when you select this option, but they will indeed print properly.

Now that we have defined the options for using the revision-marking feature of Word, let's list the steps necessary to turn on revision-marking:

1. Choose the **Revision Marks** command from the Utilities menu or press **Alt,U,M**.

    The Mark Revisions dialog box appears, as shown in Figure 14.5.

2. Choose the **Mark Revisions** option by clicking with the mouse or pressing **Alt+M**.

    The option is selected with an X.

3. From the Mark New Text With window, choose the option that determines how you want new text to appear when typed or inserted: Nothing, Bold, Italic,

    The selected option is blackened.

Adding and Polishing Word

Underline, or Double Underline.

4. From the Revision Bars window, select, if any, a revision bar to appear next to the changed text: None, Left, Right, or Outside.

   The selected option appears blackened.

5. Choose **OK** or press **Enter**.

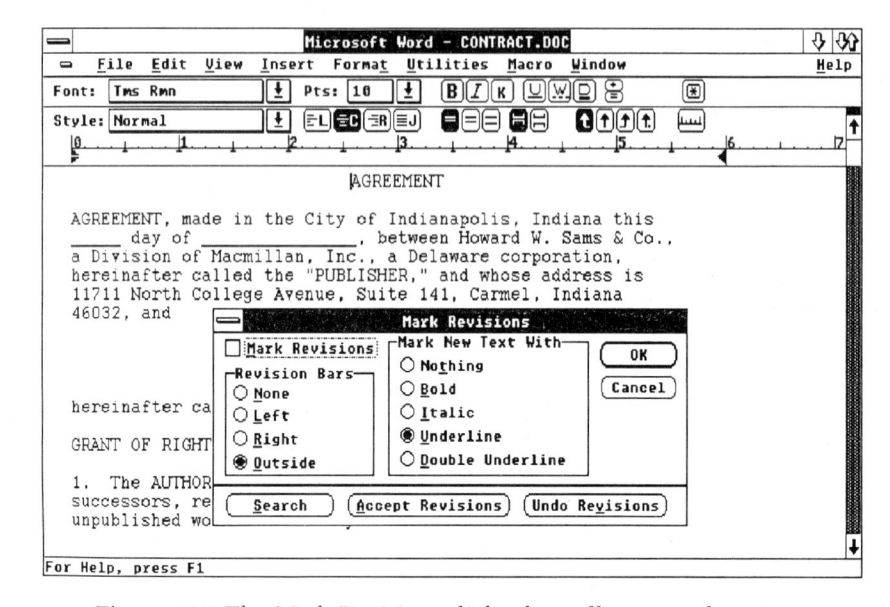

Figure 14.5 The Mark Revisions dialog box offers several options.

After you have turned on revision-marking, Word will mark the edits of your document based on the selections you made in the steps above. An example of revision-marking of bold for new text, strike-through for deleted text, along with left-sided revision bars is illustrated in Figure 14.6.

Turning Off Revision-Marking

To turn off revision-marking, simply choose the **Revision Marks** command or press **Alt,U,M** to display the dialog box again. Choose the **Mark Revisions** option or press **Alt+M** and then choose **OK** or press **Enter**. Turned off, the option appears empty and your document returns to its previous mode of operation.

14—Using Annotations and Revisions

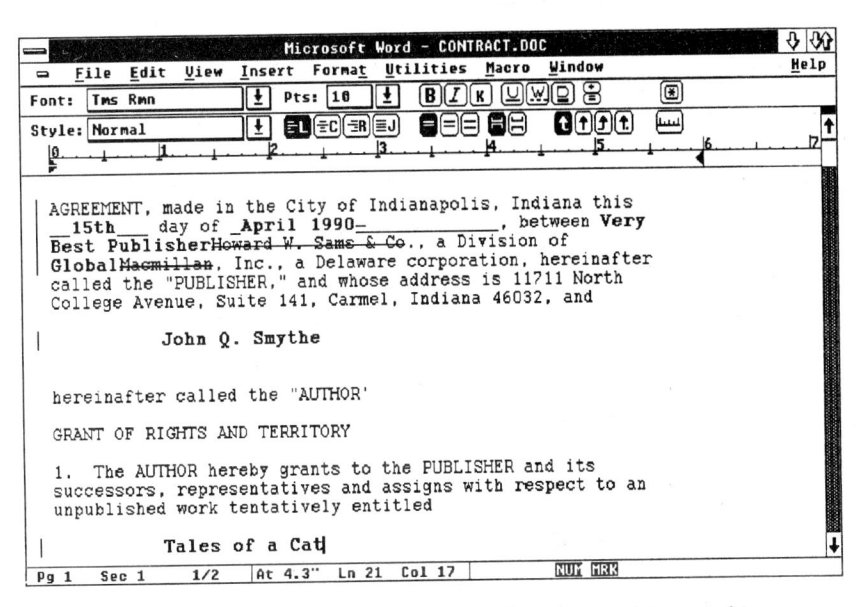

Figure 14.6 A sample legal contract showing revision-marking.

Searching for, Accepting, and Removing Revision Marks

Not all changes to a document are final. This is a key feature of the Revision Marks utility. Indeed, you have the option of approving some of the changes marked as revisions, or all of the changes, or of rejecting them all. When you wish to approve some of the changes, you do so individually using the Search button on the Revision Marks command. Using the Search button, you can search for the next text that has been changed and select it automatically. Then, you have the option of:

- Accepting the revision change by clicking the **Accept Revisions** button or pressing **Alt+A**. Choosing this option removes the special new text-marking and deletes the text highlighted by strikethrough and/or revision bars.

- Removing any of the revision changes that you made to the selection, including newly typed text.

- Skipping the current selection, going on to the next text that has revision-marking, and selecting it.

409

Of course, the revision-marking feature must still be turned on to allow this flexibility. One point to keep in mind: If you don't select any text and choose either the Accept Revisions or Undo Revisions command buttons, the commands will be carried out through the entire document. To approve the changes made to a document while revision-marking is on, complete the following steps.

1. Select the text where you want to review the revision marks. If you wish to review and approve the entire document, do not select just a portion.

    The selected text (or entire document) is highlighted.

2. Choose the **Revision Marks** command or press **Alt,U,M**.

    The Revision Marks dialog appears.

3. Choose the **Search** command button or press **Alt+S**.

    Word finds the next text that has revision-marking and selects it (see Figure 14.7). If you don't select a portion of the text, Word will search through the end of the document and then ask if you wish to search from the beginning. If you do, click **Yes**. If Word doesn't find any text with revision marks, it will tell you so.

4. To determine what to do with the selected text, choose from one of these three choices:

    • Choose **Accept Revisions** to accept the new text and to remove revision marks and the deleted text. If you don't select text, Word will ask if you wish to accept all changes. Choose **Yes** if you wish to do so.

    • To keep the text identified for deletion, choose **Undo Revisions**, which will remove any deletion marks, newly typed text, and revision bars. If you don't select text, Word will ask if you wish to change all revision changes. If you wish to do so, select **Yes**. This option is handy if you accidentally deleted text.

- Choose the **Search** button again to go on to the next text with revision-marking.

5. Repeat steps 2 through 4 until you have found the specific revision-marking that you are looking for or until you have reviewed all the marked revisions of the selection or document.

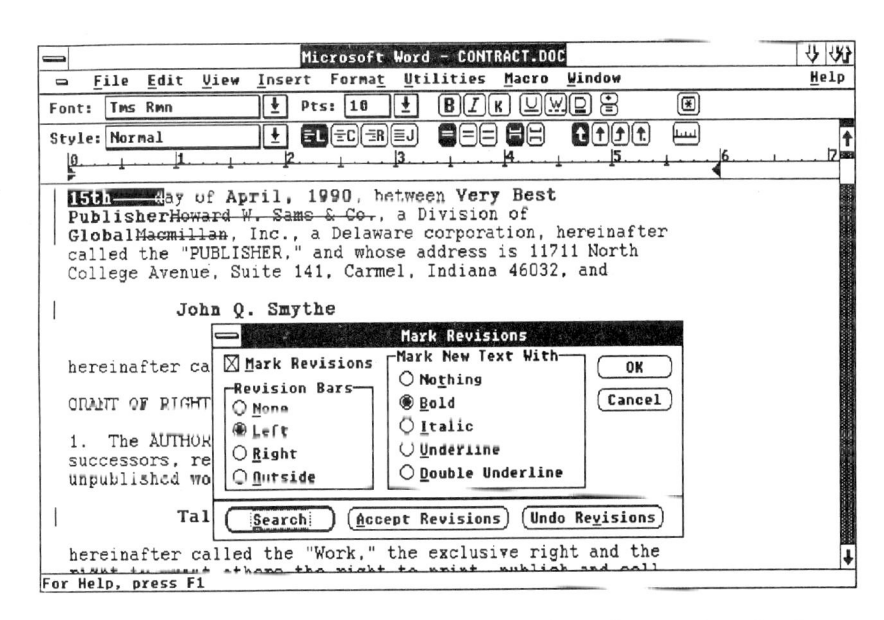

Figure 14.7 The Search button finds and selects the next text that has revision-marking.

Comparing Two Different Versions of a Document

Reviewing all the changes of a document one-by-one may seem a little tedious. Word provides an alternative to help you compare two versions of the same document by using the Compare Versions command on the Utilities menu. The Compare Versions command will compare a document stored on a disk (or in a directory in your hard disk) with the active document that appears on your screen. During the comparison process, Word will add revision bars next to the paragraphs of the active document that differ from the document stored on the disk (Word also identifies new text following the format currently selected on the Revision Marks dialog box). The revision bars will then identify any text that you wish to review. To compare two versions of the same document, simply complete the following steps:

1. First, open the document that you wish to check and make it active.

   The active document appears in the active window on your screen.

2. Choose the **Compare Versions** command from the Utilities menu or press **Alt,U,V**.

   The Compare Versions dialog appears.

3. Type the name of the document that you wish to compare with the active document. You can also select that document from a specific directory and/or drive from the Directories list window. If the document name doesn't exist in the current directory, Word will tell you so.

   The selected or typed name appears in the Compare File Name box.

4. Choose **OK** or press **Enter**.

   Word adds revision bars next to the paragraphs of the active document that differ from the text stored on the disk. Word also adds and formats new text using the format currently selected for new text within the Revision Marks dialog box.

Review

In this chapter you learned:

1. Annotations is a way that you can review and edit your documents on the screen by attaching initialed comments.
2. Annotations can be entered by the author or by outside reviewers who read the documents. The author, however, can lock the document so that no annotations can be added.
3. To insert an annotation mark, position the insertion point and then choose the Insert Annotation command.
4. When you insert an annotation mark, an annotation pane opens in the lower left portion of the active window. The annotation mark itself is formatted as hidden text but will appear when you first insert the annotation mark or if you have turned on the Hidden Text option located on View Preferences.
5. There are three ways to open an annotation pane: choose View Annotations, choose Insert Annotations, or hold down the Ctrl key while you click on the split bar and drag it down the scroll bar.
6. To close an annotation pane, choose the View Annotation command a second time or double-click the split bar.
7. There are two modes of navigation when working with annotations: jumping from one annotation mark to another or moving between the annotation mark and the annotation text
8. To jump to an annotation, choose Edit Go To and type a or a specific annotation location (e.g., a4 to go to the fourth annotation). You can also use F5, the Go To key. You can actually jump to a specific location via a section, a page, or any combination of annotations on a section or page.
9. Annotations can be of any length. Open a specific annotation pane with View Annotation and, if necessary, use the scroll bar to read the full annotation.
10. Once inside an annotation pane, you can edit or format it just like any standard text. You can also use the Cut, Copy, and Paste commands from the Edit menu to move any annotation text from the annotation pane to the document itself.
11. To delete an annotation you must delete the annotation mark itself. You cannot delete an annotation simply by erasing the annotation text.

12. Use the File Print command to print only the annotations themselves or to print the document in addition to the annotations.
13. To help you keep track of different versions of a document, you can use the revision marks feature. Revision-marking highlights the areas of the document that have been changed, enabling you to evaluate those changes before you print the document.
14. You can tell Word to indicate the changes to the document as you make them, or you can ask Word afterward to identify changes made by comparing the current version with a previous one. Use the Utilities Compare command to effect the latter option.

F I F T E E N

Working with Files

In this chapter:

- File Handling and Management
- Introducing Document Retrieval
- Searching for Documents
- Loading a Document
- Opening and Printing Multiple Documents
- Deleting Documents
- Using Document Templates

You have already used some of Word's file management features to save, retrieve, and print document files. However, we have just touched the surface of the full power of Word's electronic filing system. In this chapter we'll review a powerful operation of Word called the document retrieval feature. The document retrieval feature uses the *Find* command from the File menu to help you easily locate specific documents, open and print multiple documents, and to delete unwanted document files. In addition to exploring the Find command, we will examine another method for saving you lots of time—the document template.

File Handling and Management

This chapter is about managing and finding information or data. As we discussed in Chapter 2, programs and documents are stored on computer diskettes or hard disks as files. A file is generally one of two types; a program file or a data file. A *program file* contains the instructions of the program (e.g., Word for Windows) and tells the computer what to do. A *data file* contains data created by a program file or similar program. The focus of this book has been on creating such data files in the form of letters, memos, résumés, reports, etc. In Word, we call these data files, *document files*.

File name limitations are imposed by DOS. For a quick review of file-naming conventions, refer to Chapter 2.

In order to open a word processing file in Word (created either in Word for Windows or some other word processor), you must rename the file and provide it with the .DOC extension.

Using the operating system (DOS) and Windows (if you have it installed), along with key commands (such as Find), you have the tools to locate document files and access their contents. Since, over time, you will create many document files, you need to have a place to store them. You have two general choices: the floppy disk (5 1/4" or 3 1/2" micro) and a hard disk. Each file on the disk contains a series of computer bytes of data with a specific name assigned to it. You might even think of a byte as an individual character. The file name consists of two parts—a base name of no more than eight characters and an optional extension. The extension always follows the base name and a period, and it contains as many as three additional characters. File names must follow certain conventions; for example, they cannot include blank spaces. As a rule of thumb, you should always use a base file name that has some meaning in relation to the content of the data file. The file name extension can be used to describe the type of information in the file itself (e.g., .DOC for a document and .DAT for numerical data). For example, here are some examples of acceptable file names: NEWSLTR.DOC, SALES.DAT, 1QTR.DAT, LEGAL.DOC.

The floppy disk may contain several files. The number of files depends on the type of storage capacity of the disk and, of course, the size of the files placed on the disk. The most common types of diskettes available today are the 720K (generally DS/DD, or double-sided, double-density) and 1.4M (or high-density) models. The type of diskette that you should use depends on the type of disk drive installed on your computer system. If you have an 80286- or 80386-microprocessor-based computer, then you will likely have a 1.4M disk drive. Due to the size of storage space on the high-density disk, you will be able to store several files on such a disk without worry.

If you plan on storing several hundred, or even thousands of files, then you should look to divide such a large number between the floppy disks and a hard disk. A hard disk's storage capacity will also vary depending upon its size. However, a typical hard disk has the capacity to store tens of times the number of files a diskette is capable of storing.

Using a Hard Disk

A hard disk has a tremendous amount of room for storing your document files. Using DOS or Windows, you divide your hard disk into *directories,* each containing their own related set of files. You can liken the hard disk to a standard metal filing cabinet, where each drawer represents a different directory. Within each directory is a set of its own files, much like the manila folder variety stored in those dusty filing cabinets (see Figure 15.1). Soon you'll begin to accumulate several files, all equally important in their own right. Some files may be of a personal nature. Some files will be business letters, memos, reports, etc. With so many files scattered and stored on your hard disk, you'll soon need to organize them so they're not difficult to locate. The best way to organize all those files is to create a filing system that contains several directories, each one containing a similar type of document. For example, one directory named MTHYRPTS could contain all monthly sales reports from January to December. All personal letters could be in a directory named PERSONAL, and so on. Setting up such a filing system would lend itself to good file management. It is clearly easier to locate and retrieve a document when you have a general idea where to look.

If you have need of more than one filing cabinet (and most of us do!), you can have more than one hard disk drive designation. It is common for many large hard disks to be partitioned into more than one designated drive, such as the C drive and the D drive. Within each drive is a set of directories and related files.

Directories can be further divided into *subdirectories,* where the structure of such a beast is called a directory tree. Using our metal filing cabinet analogy, the subdirectories would be the individual manila folders contained within each metal drawer. The individual pieces of paper within each folder represent individual document files. Thus, a directory in a tree structure is simply a directory containing subordinate directories.

At the top of the directory tree, you will find the initial directory, or *root directory* (see Figure 15.2). Sometimes called the main directory, the root directory always has the name of the active drive followed by the backslash character (\). Like file names, directory or subdirectory names can only contain eight characters. Although you can add the optional file name extension as well, most people do not. When a directory is displayed from DOS (using the *DIR* command), you will see the file name followed by the familiar <DIR> symbol.

Adding and Polishing Word

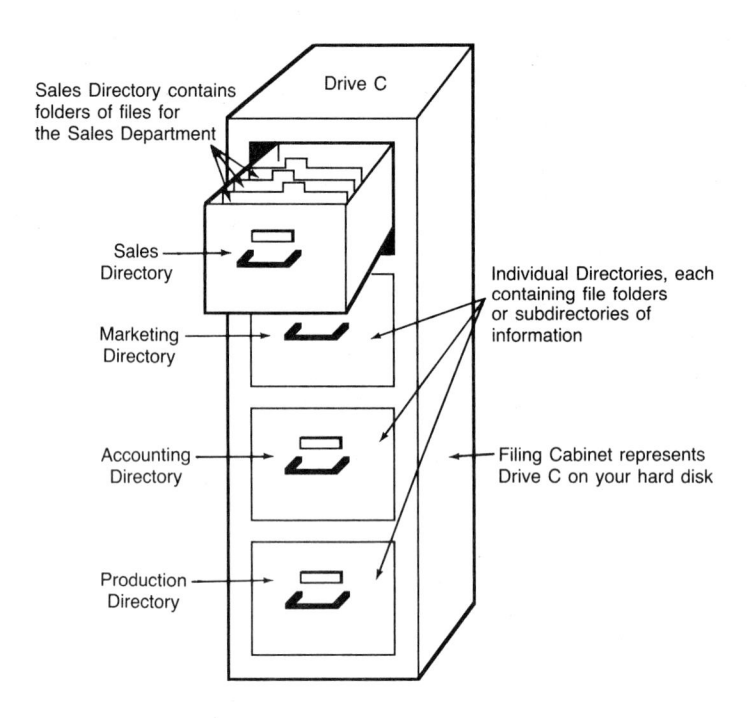

Figure 15.1 Storing files on a hard disk is similar to storing files in a standard filing cabinet.

Within Windows, you'll find that the directories appear emboldened on the MS-DOS Executive screen.

As a focus of this chapter, you find that navigating through the available directories is a matter of taking certain simple steps. First you activate the correct disk drive (select the correct filing cabinet). Next, you open the appropriate directory (the correct cabinet drawer). If necessary, you select the correct subdirectory (the manila folder). And finally, you choose from the available document files (the paper files within the manila folders). On the surface, these steps might seem a little complicated considering the near limitless number of directories and subdirectories that you could create. It is the job of Word's document retrieval feature, however, to make the task of locating document files a snap—and your life easier.

Introducing Document Retrieval

Word's document retrieval feature is a handy way to keep track of all your document files. The command used to access this feature is

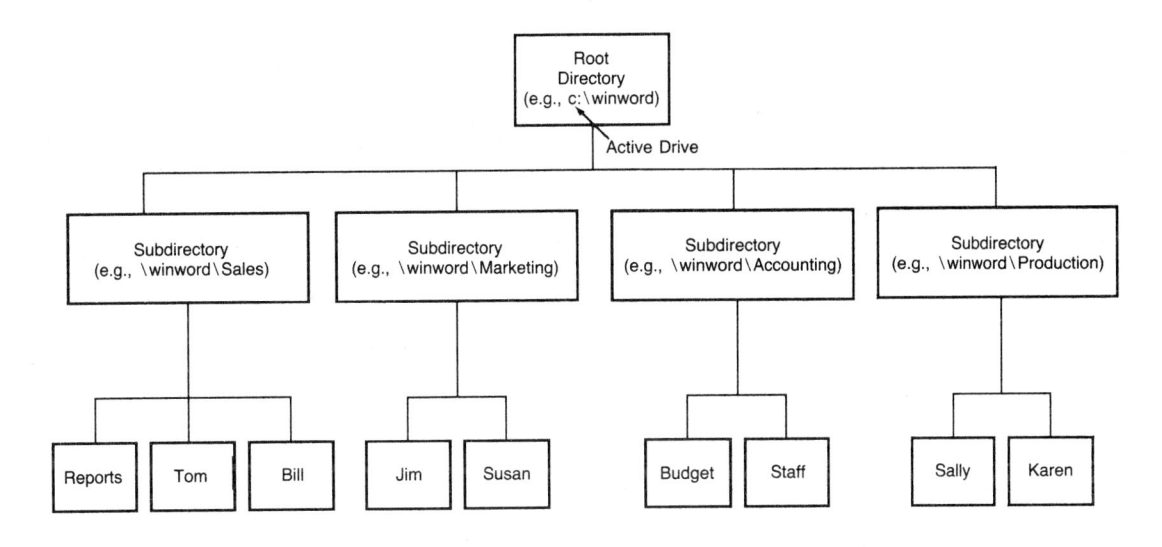

Figure 15.2 A directory tree may further divide the hard disk into subdirectories.

You can also access the Find command by choosing this command button on the standard Open dialog box from the File menu. Choosing either the Find command from the Open dialog box or directly from the File menu will allow you to search for documents that you are interested in.

called Find and is located on the File menu. At the heart of the document retrieval feature is the *summary information sheet,* "summary sheet" for short, that you attach (at your option) to the document at the time the document is saved. As you recall from Chapter 2, the Summary Sheet dialog box appears the first time you save a document (see Figure 15.3). The Summary Sheet dialog box will not appear if you already filled in the information for an existing document. In addition, you can elect to turn off the Summary Sheet dialog box option through the Customize command on the Utilities menu. However, if you don't fill in the information for the summary sheet, you will not be able to exploit all the features of Word's document retrieval system. For example, you may wish to search for a list of documents that address a particular individual. You can edit the information in any of the fields of the summary sheet at any time. By completing the summary sheets thoroughly, you have the flexibility of searching for documents in a variety of ways.

Searching for documents with the Find command is a simple but powerful process. As you learned in Chapter 2, you can save your files and store them in a variety of ways. You can save them in a particular directory on your hard disk, or you can save them to a floppy diskette that you can carry with you. With Find, you can search through particular directories on your hard disk or even through individual disk drives to seek out the desired document file stored on an external disk or hard disk. You can complete the search for a particular document by selecting specific fields of information that are

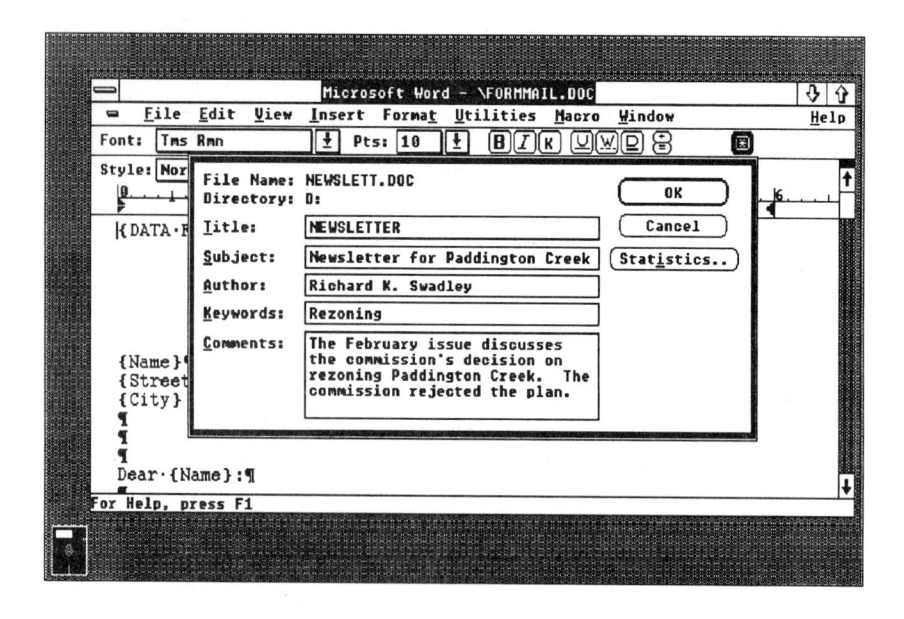

Figure 15.3 The summary information sheet is used extensively by Word's document retrieval feature.

stored on your summary sheets, including the title, subject or description of the document, the author who created it, a few keywords (e.g., a customer or product name), or comments that further describe the document.

To help facilitate your search for a document, the Find command enables you to list all available document files, and to sort them in a variety of ways: by name, author, creation date (including last time saved and by whom), and size. You can even choose to delete selected files.

As you would also expect, you can choose to print any of the documents that you locate with File Find. However, you might be surprised to know that this powerful command also has the ability to open multiple documents and/or to print them in succession.

Finally, the Find command provides access to any summary information sheet for any document that you wish to locate. This feature allows you to review and edit the summary sheet so that you can take full advantage of the document retrieval system. We'll discuss all of these features in the next few pages.

Using and Updating the Summary Sheet

The first step to maximizing the effect of Word's document retrieval feature is to complete the summary sheet the first time you save a document. Taking the time to complete the summary sheet completely will help you identify the document in order to retrieve it in a variety of ways. For a complete review of all the options on completing the summary sheet, refer to Table 2.3.

Word doesn't display the summary sheet information each time you revise and save a file. You'll find, though, that much of the information is updated automatically. For example, when you save your revision, the Date Last Saved, Last Saved By, and Revision Number fields are updated. If you print the document, Word will update the number of pages, words, and character counts as well. If you don't wish to print your document and you still want to update this information, choose the **Statistics** button on the Summary Information dialog box and then select the **Update** button.

From time to time, you may wish to see the summary information for a document, either to update it or simply to review its contents. To do this, complete the following steps:

Note that the Statistics panel is the only window that you cannot edit. To do this, you must return to the Summary Info dialog box.

1. Choose the **Find** command from the File menu or press **Alt,F,F**.

   The Find dialog box appears as shown in Figure 15.4.

2. In the File list box, select the document file whose summary information you wish to review. Note that the first time you use Find, Word will list all files with the .DOC extension in all directories in the current active drive. Once you have executed a search (discussed shortly), the File window will list the document files found during the previous search.

   The selected file will be highlighted.

3. To view the summary information for the selected file, press **Alt+M**.

   The summary information is displayed in a window like that we saw in Figure 15.3.

421

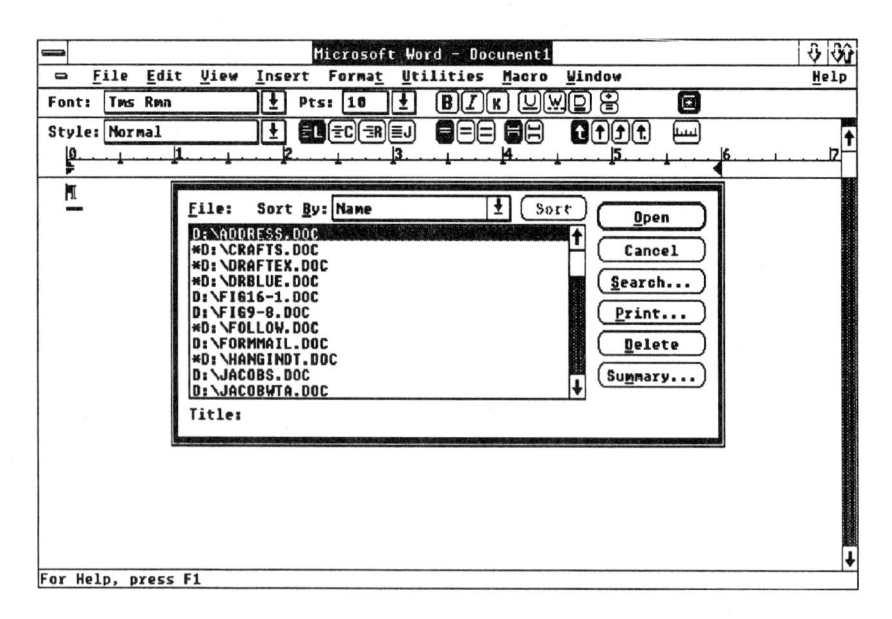

Figure 15.4 The Find dialog box.

Once the summary information appears on your screen, you can update any of its field boxes, except Statistics. Use either the mouse to click inside the box or press the Tab key to move the insertion point to the box that you wish to edit. Then edit the information contained in the box using the methods you use to edit standard document text. If you wish to edit the comment box, press Ctrl+Home and Ctrl+End to go to the beginning or end of the comment, respectively. To start a new line, use the Newline keypress, or Shift+Enter. If you wish to check—but not edit—the vital statistics of the document (number of words, revision number, etc.), choose the Statistics button or press Alt+I. Remember, though, you cannot edit any of the boxes in the Statistics box. To do that, return to the summary information window and edit the contents there.

Searching for Documents

Searching for documents, whether single documents or a list of documents, is the strong suit of the Find command. The secret is to specify the key fields or summary information boxes from which to pinpoint the desired file or files. For example, you may wish to search for all documents created by a specific author on a certain

If the files that you wish to search for are located on a different drive (e.g., on a diskette in Drive A instead of on the hard disk or C drive), it's sometimes easier to choose the File Open command, select the appropriate drive and directory where the files are located, and then choose the Find command button.

date. In this case, you would enter that information in the Author and Date Created boxes. To complete a search for documents, do the following:

1. Choose the **Find** command from the File menu or press **Alt,F,F**.

    The Find command, shown in Figure 15.4, appears.

2. Choose the **Search** command button or press **Alt+S**.

    The Search List dialog box appears, as shown in Figure 15.5.

3. In the Search list box, type one or more directories to search, separated by commas or semicolons. For example, you might type:

    \Winword\Letters

    or

    \Winword\Reports;\Excel

    where the first example indicates that two directories will be searched. The second example contains the subdirectory named Reports in a directory named Winword and a second directory named Excel. All directories named must be available on the current active drive.

    An example of listed path names is shown in Figure 15.6.

4. This step utilizes the full power of the Find command. The more summary information boxes you can complete, the easier Word can isolate the file(s) during the search. Information from these boxes is combined to narrow the search and pinpoint the desired document(s). For further information, use Table 15.1 as your guide.

423

5. Choose **OK** or press **Enter**.

Word compiles a list of documents based on the search criteria you specified in the boxes and lists them in the Find list window.

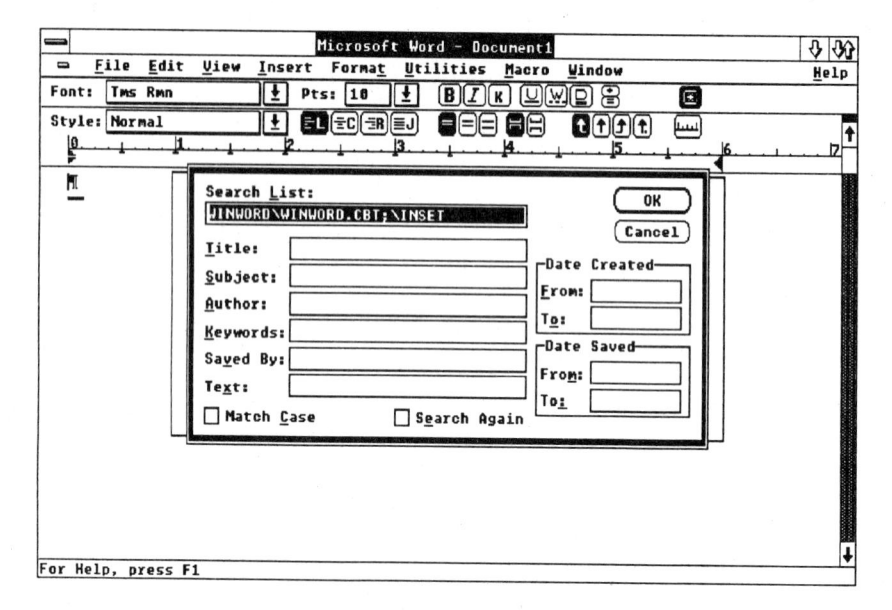

Figure 15.5 The Search list dialog box.

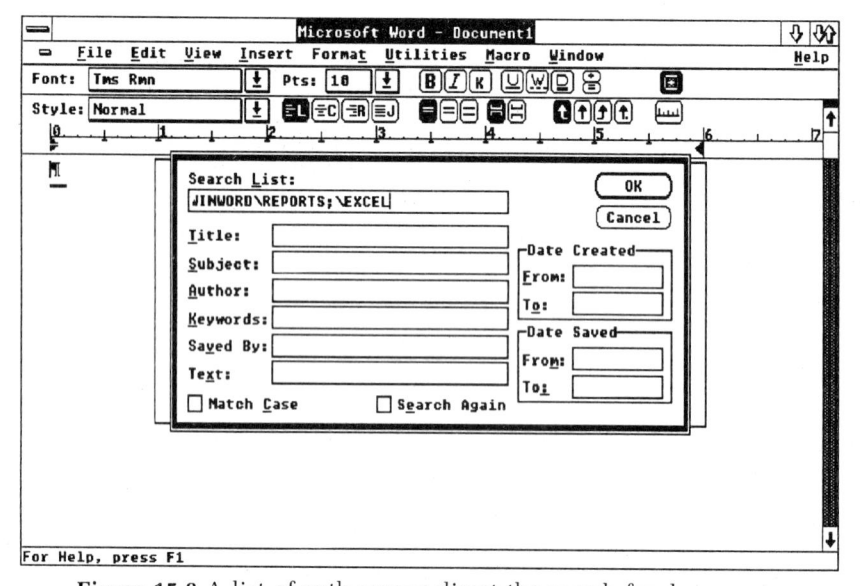

Figure 15.6 A list of path names direct the search for documents.

Table 15.1 Search List Boxes and Criteria

List Box	Type
Title	Enter the text that will appear in the Title box of the Summary Information dialog box. The title should be a more descriptive name for the document and can be up to 255 characters long.
Subject	Enter the text that will appear in the Subject box of the Summary Information dialog box. The subject should be a more detailed description of the document's contents but it cannot exceed 255 characters.
Author	Type the name of the person who created the current document. The name can be different from the author name inserted automatically by Word (inserted from the Your Name text box in the Customize window). This feature is useful if the author of the new document is different from the original document.
Keywords	Type the text that appears in the Keyword box of the Summary Information dialog box. Your keywords can be anything, but they are generally the names of topic areas covered in the document to be searched for. Keywords may be up to 255 characters in length, including spaces.
Saved By	Enter the author name that will appear in the Last Saved By box of the Summary Information dialog box.
Text	Enter any text that you want Word to search for in the document files. For example, if you want to search for "the fiscal year ending March 1991," enter those exact words, including spaces between words.

(continued)

Adding and Polishing Word

Table 15.1 *(continued)*

List Box	Type
Match Case	Turn this on if you want to search for text with the exact upper- and lowercase letters as the text you typed in the Text box.
Search Again	Choose OK if you want Word to only search through the list of document files listed in the Find list window. The search will be conducted using the previously set search options.
Date Created: From	Type the date from which to begin the search. The date must match the format specified in the summary information sheet (see Statistics). If you leave the From box blank, Word will search for all the documents created prior to the To date.
Date Created: To	Type the most recent date to include in the search. If the date in the To box is the same as in the From box, Word will search for all documents created on that single day. If you leave the To box blank, Word will search for all the documents created after the From date.
Date Saved: From	Type the date from which to begin the search. The date must match the format specified in the summary information sheet (see Statistics). If you leave the From box blank, Word will search for all the documents prior to the To date.
Date Saved: To:	Type the most recent date to include in the search. If the date in the To box is the same as in the From box, then Word will search for all documents created on that single day. If you leave the To box blank, Word will search for all the documents saved after the From date.

To search for more than one date, enter the dates separated by a comma. For example, 5/15/91,5/18/91 means search for documents on the 15th or 18th of May.

15—Working with Files

Caution: Word may not be able to find text that has been saved using the Fast Save option. A file saved with the Fast Save option on appears in the File list window with an asterisk before the file name.

You can also use some standard wildcard extensions to facilitate the search for documents. For example, you can use the question mark (?) to match any single character and the asterisk (*) to match any number of characters. You might enter Book? in the Title box to find any title that might be named Book1, Book2, Book3, and so on. If you enter sales*, Word would find words like salesperson and salesmanship. If you wish to search for a special character, precede that character with the caret (^) symbol. For example, to search for a question mark, type ^? in the Text box. Other wildcard characters allow you to search for more than one item in a key field at a time, such as an author or keyword. Such characters include the logical operators: comma (,) for a logical OR, ampersand (&) for a logical AND, tilde (~) for a logical NOT. A logical AND searches documents for both items in a field box. For example, you can search for documents that contain both of the following text items: Sales Quotas & Profit. If you enter: Sales Quotas, Profit in the Text box, Word would search for documents that contain either Sales Quotas or Profit in the Text box of the Summary Information dialog box. The NOT logical operator means search for anything but this item. For example, *edit~editor* tells Word to search for edit, not oditor.

To open a selected file and close the dialog box, choose the Open command button or double-click on the name of the file with the mouse.

Once you have completed your search, you can select a document to open, print, delete, edit, or review the summary information. These operations are all completed by choosing the appropriate command button from the right side of the Find dialog window. As a handy feature, at the top of the Find dialog window, you can choose to use the Sort button to sort all the document files listed in the window in one of six ways:

- Name—Selected by default, this option sorts alphabetically from A–Z.
- Author—Also alphabetically from A–Z.
- Creation Date—Chronologically.
- Last Saved Date—Chronologically.
- Last Saved By—Alphabetically from A–Z by name.
- Size—The smallest to the largest document.

If your list of available documents is longer than the list window, use the scroll bar on the right side of the window to scroll the files or use the up and down arrow keys. Either way, using the Sort button can shorten the time it takes to find a specific file.

Loading a Document

You can load any document that you find with Word's document retrieval feature. Loading a document in Word is called "opening" the document file. Once you have found the document through a search, highlight that document file by clicking on it with the mouse or by using the up and down arrow keys to move the highlight through the File list window. The name of the document will appear in the window along with the pathname and the drive name (e.g., C:\Winword\Letters\Legal). Then, to load the document, choose the **Open** command button or press **Alt+O**, press the **Enter** key, or double-click directly on the selected file name with the mouse. Note: If necessary, Word will display a dialog box that allows you to "convert" the selected file to a file format that Word can read. For example, if the selected file contained in Drive C is a WordPerfect file, Word provides the option of converting that document file to a Word for Windows document file. Of course, this option is only available to you if you installed the conversion options when you installed Word for Windows on your hard disk.

Opening and Printing Multiple Documents

Sometimes it is desirable to open or print several documents in succession. With the Find command, you can search for any number of documents and display them in the File window using the Search button as we discussed. If you wish, use the Sort command button to display the files in the order defined by the Sort By box. Once you have determined that the files that you wish to open are available in the Files window, use the following steps to open them:

1. Choose the **Find** command from the File menu or press **Alt,F,F**. If the File Find dialog box is already on your screen, go on to the next step.

   The File Find dialog box appears on your screen. The File window will list all the document files found during the previous search. Keep in mind that Word will list all the files with a .DOC extension from all available directories of the active drive if you haven't used File Find during the current work session.

2. From the File list window, select the documents that you wish to open. If you have a mouse, hold down the **Shift** key while clicking the file name of each file that you wish to open. If you don't have a mouse, hold down the **Shift** key while you press the up or down arrow keys. Pressing the arrow keys in this way will select a block of files, but you can press the Spacebar to exclude a file, and then press the Spacebar a second time to continue highlighting files.

   All selected files will appear highlighted.

3. Choose the **Open** command button (**Alt+O**) or simply press **Enter** since this button is highlighted.

   The files that you selected in step 2 will be opened in succession, from the top of the list to the bottom, in different windows. Word will also display a Convert From dialog box to allow you to convert the selected files from a format other than Word for Windows. To turn off this dialog option, choose the "Confirm Conversion" message at the bottom of the screen. Once all the files that you selected have opened, the last file selected is on top of a stack of windows and is the active window.

The number of files that you can open is limited to the amount of available memory of your computer and whether your computer is configured to use an extended memory manager (EMM). Otherwise, the maximum number of open windows available to Word is nine.

Printing multiple documents involves the same general steps as opening them. The first step is to select the files that you wish to open from the File Find list window, and then choose the **Print** command button or press **Alt+P**. The Print command dialog box will

429

appear. Choose your printing options from the Print dialog box and then choose **OK** or press **Enter** to begin the printing. Keep in mind that any print options that you choose will apply to all the documents that you have selected to print. For example, if you choose to print only the first page of document 1, then only the first page of any successive document will be printed as well. Printing multiple documents will begin with the first selected document and continue until all selected documents are printed in succession.

Tip: You can also select and print multiple documents directly from the MS-DOS Executive screen if you have the full version of Windows installed. To do this, select the files using the Shift+Click method as before, and then choose the Print option from the File menu.

Deleting Documents

If you have created a large number of files and they begin to accumulate, you can easily remove them from your system with the Delete command button. You can either remove one file at a time or several at once. To delete documents from the Find dialog box:

1. From the File list window, select the name or names of the document files that you wish to remove. To select more than one file name at a time, hold down the **Shift** key and click with the mouse or use the up and down arrow keys.

   The selected files are highlighted.

2. Choose the **Delete** command button or press **Alt+D**.

   Word asks you if you really want to delete the selected files.

3. Choose **Yes** or press **Enter** to erase the files.

   Word erases the selected files and removes them from the File list window.

Using Document Templates

Another time-saving tool of Word is the document template. A document template is simply a document based on the format of another document. In other words, any text, formats, styles, or structure that are the same for every document, can be saved as a "working template" from which to customize new versions of documents. The advantage of a document template is that any work that you have done to get the format "just right" does not need to be recreated. As you'll discover in Chapter 19, you can customize Word to work specifically with different types of documents. For example, you might create a document template that sets up the structure and format for a legal document. You'll also learn to customize Word so that only the menu commands and key assignments are available when the active document based on such a template is active. Even macros, or programs that you use to automate editing and formatting changes to your documents, can be available when you are working on a document template.

Document templates can contain all the elements of a standard document. You enter and format text the same way. You create styles and glossary entries as you would for a standard document. Note: When creating styles and glossary entries, choose the Template Context instead of the Global Context so that the items created will only work with an active document based on the template. File operations with document templates work the same as with standard document files. You open a document template with the File Open command and select its name from the File list. Microsoft even provides the *Sampler*, a variety of sample documents, each of which is based on a different document template. You can use these documents and others of your own making to build subsequent documents.

Creating Document Templates

If you're creating a template based on an existing document or template and want to retain the original document or template, use the Save As command on the File menu instead of the Save command.

Word provides five simple methods for creating document templates. Each method requires that you save the template once it's created.

- From scratch with the New Template option
- Based on an existing document
- Based on an existing template
- Based on modifying an existing document
- Based on modifying an existing template

Regardless of which of these methods you use to create your template, the key is to select and save the document using the New Template option instead of New Document. Remember to save any changes made to the document template (use Save for new templates and Save As when modifying existing documents or templates) and to type a descriptive template name for later reference.

431

Since creating document templates is rather intuitive and similar to creating a new document, we will only review the steps for the first two methods listed above. If you want to use any of the other methods, simply open the existing document file or document template with File Open, modify it as desired, and then save the template with the Save or Save As command. Remember to always select the New Template option instead of the New Document option when saving a file as a template. The steps necessary to create a document template from scratch are summarized below. The second set of steps detail how to create a template based on an existing document.

Creating a Template from Scratch

1. Choose the File **New** option or press **Alt,F,N** just like you were creating a standard new document.

    The File New dialog box opens.

2. Instead of accepting the default New Document selection, choose the **New Template** option or press **Alt+T** and then **OK** or **Enter**.

    Word will open your document template and it will look just like a standard document in the active window.

3. Use any of Word's editing and formatting tools for inserting text, creating styles, inserting glossary entries, and so on, just as you would for a standard new document. Choose **Template** over Global for the Context option, which tells Word to use only the styles and glossary entries for the active document based on this template.

4. Once you're satisfied with the template, choose the **Save** command or press **Alt+S**. Enter a name for the template, fill in the summary information if so desired, and then choose **OK** or press **Enter**.

    Your template is safely stored and ready for use the next time you wish to create another document based on this template.

Creating a Template Based on an Existing Document

1. Choose the **New** command from the **F**i**le** menu or press **Alt,F,N**.

    The File New dialog box appears.

2. Select **New Template** or press **Alt+T** instead of the default New Document. Don't choose OK just yet!

    New Template is darkened.

3. In the Use Template box, type the name of the existing document (include the extension) that you want to base the new template on. Now, choose **OK** or press **Enter**.

    The existing document appears in the active window.

4. Modify the template as you please. Then choose the File **Save** command or press **Alt+F+S** to replace the document file and save it as a document template. (If you use the Save As command, the existing document file will remain intact.)

    The Save dialog box (or Save As dialog box if you selected it instead) appears.

5. Enter a name for the template, fill in the summary information if so desired, and then choose **OK** or press **Enter**.

    Your template is safely stored and ready for use the next time you wish to create another document based on this template.

Editing in a Template

Remember to type or select the name of the template, not a document file name, when opening a document template.

Editing a template is the same as editing a standard document. You use the File Open command (and Search option if necessary) to locate and load the template.

Once the template appears in the active window, you can add new text, styles, and so on. When you have made all your changes, choose the Save command to retain those changes. The changes made to the template will appear in the next new document based on this template.

Changing Styles in a Template

Another editing change you can make to a template is to change styles, just as you can with a standard document file. However, if you do change the styles of a template, and subsequently save those style changes, existing documents based on that template are not automatically updated. To update the styles of existing documents, you are required to merge the styles from the template into the document. Merging styles from the active template into the active document is accomplished by the following steps:

1. With the existing document in the active window, choose the **Define Styles** command from the Format menu or press **Alt,T,F**.

    The Define Styles dialog box appears.

2. Expand the Define Styles dialog box by selecting **Options** or pressing **Alt+O**.

    The dialog box is expanded.

3. Choose the **Merge** button or press **Alt+M**. Select the template from which to merge the styles into the active document, and then choose **OK**. As a shortcut, you can also choose the **From Template** option to merge the template styles into the active document or the **To Template** to do the reverse.

    Once you choose OK, Word will ask if you wish to replace existing styles with the new styles. Since you do, choose **Yes** or press **Enter**.

Customizing Keys and Menus

In Chapter 19 we'll explore how to customize Word menus and commands given to key assignments. One feature of customizing Word is that you can create a customized version of Word to work with specific types of documents. For example, you might have one set of menus and commands (assigned to specific keys) to help you draft legal documents; another set for business reports; and another for sales literature. The idea promotes productivity. If you only need certain commands to get a particular job done, create a Word screen that will maximize this effort and minimize options that don't aid the effort. To do this, you'll have to create documents based on templates (although you'll learn to assign macros to menus without creating templates first). Word can then enable you to modify keys and menus to work with documents based on those templates. In this fashion, the original default settings for keys in particular remain safely stored on your hard disk. You use two commands on the Macro menu to accomplish this: the Assign to Key and the Assign to Menu. See Chapter 19 for details.

Review

In this chapter, you learned:

1. You can store documents in directories or create a tree structure and store your documents in subdirectories.
2. You can access Word's document retrieval feature with the Find command, which can be accessed directly from the File menu or from the Open dialog box.
3. To realize the full power of the document retrieval feature, you should complete the summary information sheet attached to every document.
4. You can search for a document by pinpointing specific fields of information on the summary information sheet. For example, you can search by author, title, text, keywords, name, a range of dates, or a specific date of being created or saved.
5. To search for a document(s), choose the Find command, select the Search button, enter the pathname of the directories to search, fill in the appropriate summary information boxes, and choose OK to compile the list of documents.
6. You can use the Find command to display the summary information sheet of any document and edit its contents.
7. Once a list of document files appears in the Find list window, you can use the Sort command button to list the documents according to a specific sort order (designated by Sort By). You can sort your documents by Name, Author, Creation Date, Last Saved Date, Last Saved By, or Size.
8. Loading a document in Word is called opening a file. Once you have found the document that you wish to load via the Find command, select the name of the file and then choose the Open command button.

9. Word allows you to open and print multiple files at one time. The number of files that you can open in a single sequence depends upon the memory configuration of your computer. The files will be opened in individual windows on your screen, beginning with the first selected file to the last. Thus the last file in the selected list will appear as the active window. The remaining files will be stacked, one upon another, in inactive windows. Windows only allows a maximum of nine windows to be open at one time.

10. You can also print multiple document files by selecting them with Shift+Click or Shift+Arrow in the Find dialog box. Word will print the first selected document and continue printing all selected files in succession. You can also choose to print only a range of pages instead of an entire document. Any specified range will apply to each selected document.

11. To delete an unwanted file, select it from the Find dialog box and then choose the Delete button. Word gives you one last chance to change your mind before deleting the selected file.

12. Word provides five methods for creating document templates. Once a template is created, you must save it to retain the template in memory. Basically, you either create a new document template from scratch or you base it on an existing document template.

13. To create a document template from scratch, choose the New command on the File menu, and then select New Template instead of the default New Document. Choosing OK will display the document template in an active window just like a standard document.

14. Document templates can contain all the same elements of a standard document. The advantage of templates is that you can save time and effort by creating a document that serves as boilerplate for similar documents.

15. Word also allows you to customize Word itself to work with a particular type of document. To customize Word, you create a document template and then use the Macro Assign To Key and Assign to Menu commands.

PART THREE

Advanced Word

S I X T E E N

chapter

Using Form Letters

In this chapter:

- Introducing Form Letters
- Preparing Documents for Merging
- Printing Form Letters
- Fill-In Form Letters
- Creating Mailing Labels

If you ever had to type the same letter over and over with only the names and addresses differing from one letter to the next, you'll like this chapter. This chapter discusses the art of the form letter.

Microsoft Word refers to the creation of a form letter as "merging documents together and then printing," or *print merging*. You'll learn about the components of form letters, how to create them, and how to use the *Print Merge* command in short order.

Introducing Form Letters

Many businesses today send the same document to hundreds, maybe even thousands, of people on a routine basis. Often the only differences in the documents are the names and addresses—the bulk of the document remains the same. In earlier days, this was a repetitive and boring process. If you address and send several Christmas cards each year, you know just how repetitive and boring.

Advanced Word

Place your variable information in the data document.

Most word processing packages, like Word for Windows, feature merge printing that lets you combine the contents of two files to create a form letter, slightly customized for each recipient. The concept is to create one file that contains the basic information—or form letter—that doesn't change, and a second file that contains the variable information—such as names and addresses—which does change. Word refers to the document file that doesn't change as the *main document,* and the file containing the variable information as the *data document.* When you use Word's Print Merge command, the variable information is inserted into the basic document at specified locations. The result is that Word will print multiple versions of your document, one for each of the specified names in your data document.

Using Word's print merge facility, you can customize your documents in a variety of ways. You are not limited to merely changing names and addresses for form letters; you can customize any portion of the main document. To create a billing letter, for example, you might specify the account balance of a customer within the body of a document. Some letters might be printed only if the customer's balance met certain conditions, such as the amount of days past due. Likewise, you would need to create a mailing label for the document. The sections that follow will get you up and running with the print merge facility. It's obvious that print merge isn't for creating form letters alone, but since that is the most common merge usage, the examples will illustrate this feature.

There are three steps to creating a form-letter mailing. The first step is to create the document files: the main document and the data document. The second step is to use the Print Merge command to combine the main document and data document into a single document and to print the resulting form letters. The last step is to print the mailing labels associated with the form letter mailing. All of these procedures are discussed in the sections that follow.

Preparing Documents for Merging

The first step of using the Print Merge command is to create a main document, which represents the bulk of your form letter.

Creating the Main Document

Before you try the steps for creating a main document file, you should know how Word uses the Print Merge command to merge your documents. This information will help you map out your main document.

16—Using Form Letters

When you create your main document, you enter the text as you do with any document, except you enter the information that you know will change with a "field code name" or *bookmark,* and enclose it in a set of characters that look just like braces ({}). The set of brace-like symbols (called *field characters*) refers to a place in your document called a *field*. Each field holds an item of information, such as a part of an individual's address: first name, last name, street address, and so on. This information is given a bookmark, such as {LAST NAME}, that represents that field position in your document. A bookmark name may contain 20 characters, but short names are recommended for simplicity. Word allows you to include up to 256 fields in a single document as long as each field matches the bookmark name in the data file. You can include fields anywhere in your document. To illustrate, consider the following as an address and salutation for a sample letter. Notice the number of fields.

{FIRST NAME} {LAST NAME}
{ADDRESS}
{CITY} {STATE} {ZIP}
Dear {FIRST NAME}:

When you create your data document (as you will in the next section), you create a list of all the variable bookmark name positions. Each position corresponds to an individual field of information. The set of fields for each document (e.g., a person's name and address for a letter) make up a *record.*

Your bookmark names must match, respectively, from main document to data document.

Now you know what is contained in the main document and data document files. What happens when you execute Print Merge? Choosing Print Merge from the File menu while the main document is active automatically opens the data file. The next step is a matter of substitution. Word will substitute the information contained in the fields from the data file to the corresponding locations in the main document file as specified by the bookmark positions. Of course, the bookmark names that you specify in the main document file and the bookmark names in the first paragraph of the data file must match.

Before you create a form letter, look at these few rules for naming fields. If you follow the rules, you'll save yourself time trying to figure out what went wrong.

- Bookmark names are unique.
- Remember to enclose each bookmark name on the main document within a set of field code characters ({}).
- Blank spaces can be used in bookmark names, but they can cause headaches. Remember that the bookmark names must

Advanced Word

match in both the main document and the first record (also called the header record) of the data file. The bookmark names may be in any order, but the order of the names will determine the structure of the data records.

*The quickest method for entering the field code character symbols into your documents is to press **Ctrl+F9**, the Insert Field key, at the location of the insertion point.*

Now you are going to create a main document file that could be used for a form mailing. In more complex documents, it's a good idea to map out the variable components before you go blazing away at the keyboard. This example is simple, so just enter the text from Figure 16.1 as you would any other text. To enter the field code characters ({}), press **Ctrl+F9**, the Insert Field key. It's important to note that the main document file and data document each must be given a file name that lets Word know which data document is to be used with which main document file during the substitution process. To do this, you must begin each main document file with DATA followed by the name of the data file. For example, a main document file might begin with {DATA-REJECTION LETTER} while the corresponding data document file is named Rejection-Letter. Use the following set of steps to create your main document file.

1. Save any work that you want to retain. If you haven't already, clear your screen by choosing **New** from the File menu and then **OK** or pressing **Alt,F,N** and then **Enter**. Select **Document** by pressing **Alt+D** and **OK** again to get a new document page (Options is selected by default).

2. Enter the field code characters by pressing **Ctrl+F9**. The insertion point will automatically be placed inside the field code characters. Type the word **DATA** followed by the name of the data document that will be merged later. For this example, your screen should look like:

   {DATA FOLLOW}

The data document will be created in the next set of steps. The DATA instruction tells Word which data document contains the field information that you want to merge with this main document file.

442

16—Using Form Letters

```
{DATA Follow}         Eddy's World of Appliances
                             12 Main Street
                         Indianapolis, IN 46268


{Name}
{Street}
{City} {State} {Zip}


Dear {Name}:

Thank you for your recent purchase of the XJ 6 super model
refrigerator.  During the month of June only, we will offer
a 25% discount on all models of washers and dryers in stock.
Just bring this letter in and get your discount on many of
the leading brands, including Maytag, Whirlpool, and General
Electric.

If you have any questions, please call Monday through Friday
during the hours of 9 to 5 at (317) 872-7222.

Kind regards,



John Eddy
President, Eddy's Appliances


P.S.  We offer free delivery within a 30-mile radius
```

Figure 16.1 Sample form letter created as a main document file.

3. Press the **End** key to move the insertion point outside the field code character set, or simply use the mouse or arrow keys. Enter the rest of the document as shown in Figure 16.1. Remember to enclose the bookmarks with the field code characters to denote the location of the individual fields. Use the End key every time you need to move outside a field quickly.

4. The formatting applied to the bookmark names will be applied to the data when

443

Advanced Word

      merged into this main
      document file. If you wanted
      any special formatting, such
      as italics or boldfacing, you
      would call for it now. For
      this example, it's not
      necessary.

5. Choose **Save** from the File menu or press **Alt,F,S**. Enter an appropriate file name (**FormMail** for this example) in the File Name box and click **OK** or press **Enter**.
    "Document1" is replaced with the new file name in the window title bar.

Now that your main document file is set, you need to create the data document. Keep the names of the bookmarks in mind so that you can create a compatible data file. If you need to, use the Print command to get a copy of the main document file or resize the windows so you can see both documents at once.

Creating the Data Document

Now that your form letter or main document file is created, the next step is to create your data document. This simple example involves the creation of these bookmark names to identify the fields (see Figure 16.2): Name, Street, City, State, Zip, and Salutation.

Of course, you could create a main document that requires a larger number of fields but the principles are the same. Keep in mind that each set of information for an individual recipient of your form letter is called a record. Your data document may contain several records. Three sample records are shown in Figure 16.2. It should be apparent what a field and a record may consist of, but there are a few additional rules that you must follow when creating a data document. A data file comprises two components.

- The *header record* is always the first line in your data document file. This record lists the names of the bookmarks exactly as they appear in your main document file. The bookmark names may be in any order, but keep in mind that the order of the names determines the structure of the data records themselves. The bookmark names are separated by commas or tabs (see Figure 16.2). You can include a space between bookmark names but Word drops the spaces between

16—Using Form Letters

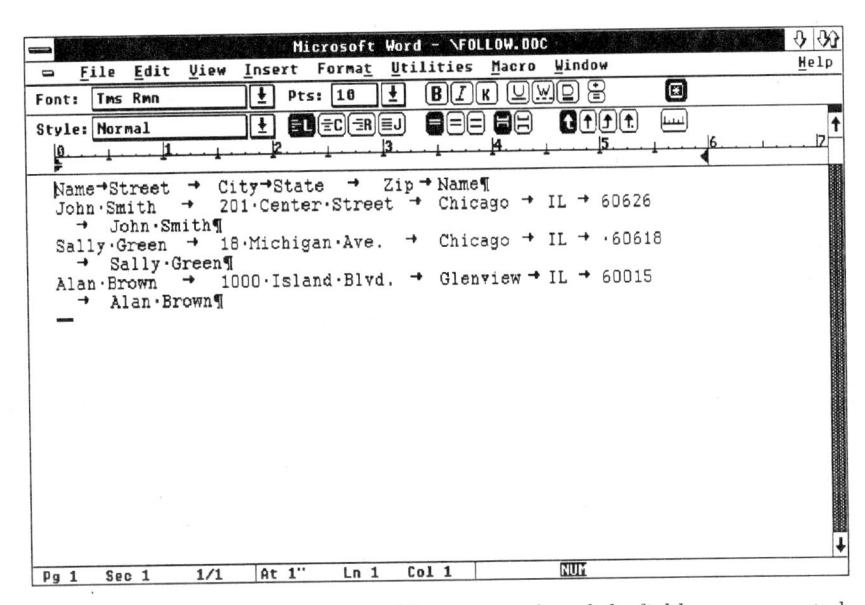

```
┌──────────────────────────────────────────────────────────┐
│              Microsoft Word - \FOLLOW.DOC        ↓ ↕    │
│   File  Edit  View  Insert  Format  Utilities  Macro  Window    Help │
│ Font: Tms Rmn    ↓  Pts: 10 ↓   B I K U W D          │
│ Style: Normal    ↓   ≡L ≡C ≡R ≡J  ≡ ≡ ≡ ≡  ↑ ↑ ↑ ↑    │
│ 0......1......2......3......4......5......6....17      │
│ Name→Street  →  City→State  →  Zip→Name¶                │
│ John·Smith   →  201·Center·Street → Chicago → IL → 60626│
│   → John·Smith¶                                          │
│ Sally·Green  →  18·Michigan·Ave.  → Chicago → IL → 60618│
│   → Sally·Green¶                                         │
│ Alan·Brown   →  1000·Island·Blvd. → Glenview → IL → 60015│
│   → Alan·Brown¶                                          │
│                                                          │
│                                                          │
│                                                          │
│                                                          │
│ Pg 1  Sec 1   1/1  At 1"  Ln 1  Col 1        NUM         │
└──────────────────────────────────────────────────────────┘
```

Figure 16.2 Records are separated by paragraphs while fields are separated by tabs in this sample data document.

the comma and the first character of the bookmark name. You can include 127 fields in a single header record. Without the header record, Word would not be able to link the data document to your main document file. You can store a header record in a separate file from the data document.

- The *individual records* contain the information that Word substitutes into the individual fields as identified by the bookmark names in your main document file. The order of the fields within each record is important. If you enter the fourth field where the third field should go, the result will not be what you expect. All the fields in one paragraph represent a single record. You use a paragraph mark to highlight the end of one record and thus the beginning of another (see Figure 16.2). Further, all fields must be in the same order for each record. Remember that there must be the same number of fields per record (i.e., per paragraph) in the data document file as there is in the header record.

The data document file is now defined, so it's time to create a data document to merge with the sample main document from Figure 16.1. The steps that follow can be used to create any new data document.

445

Advanced Word

If you want to include a separator, such as a comma, in a field, enclose the entire field in quotation marks (e.g., "101 Summit Ave, Apt. 2"). However, if you use tabs to delimit your records, you can have a comma within a field without the quotation marks. Tabs would be a preferred delimiter.

1. If you haven't already, choose **New** from the File menu or press **Alt,F,N** and then **OK** or **Enter** to get a clean document page.

2. Enter the data document's header record. Type the bookmark names, separated by commas or tabs, for each corresponding field in your document. Tabs are recommended. As a tip, use Word's table feature to quickly set up a data file or press **Alt,I,T**. Only press **Enter** when you have reached the end of a record. It's OK if the record wraps around to the next line. For this example, see Figure 16.2 as reference. Notice that the tabs used to separate fields line the fields up in relative columns.

   The header record must be the first line in your data document file. The paragraph symbol marks the end of the header record.

3. Now type the individual records, one by one, separating them by commas or tabs depending on which method you used to create your header record. You can use one or the other, but you can't mix them. At the end of each record, press **Enter** to insert the paragraph symbol and to mark the end of the record.

   This simple example shows three records, each containing 6 fields. You could have 127 fields in a single record. If you wish to include a blank field in a record, include two extra commas or tabs as a substitute.

4. Choose **Save** from the File menu to save the data document or press **Alt,F,S**. In the File Name box, enter the file name you gave the DATA instruction in the main document file. For this example, enter **Follow**.

   The file name appears in the File Name edit box as you type.

446

16—Using Form Letters

5. Choose **OK** or press **Enter**. If you wish, enter summary information and then choose OK or Enter again.

   The dialog box is closed and you are returned to the data document file window.

6. Choose **Close** from the File menu or press **Alt,F,C**.

Tip: Store both your main document file and the data document file on the same disk and in the same directory or Word won't be able to merge the documents together. The next step to creating a form-letter mailing is to print the letters. Also, when working with form letters, keep two windows open: One for the form and one for the data.

Printing Form Letters

You're now ready to use the Print Merge command to print out your form letters. You begin by using the two files just created in the previous two exercises. Print three letters, one for each record stored on the data document file. If you haven't created these files yet, do so now before continuing.

1. **Open** the main document file to make it active. If another Word document is active, **Close** it and use the **Open** command to choose from the list window the file named: DATA Follow.

   The main document file appears on your screen as the active window. The data document is opened automatically when you choose Print Merge, so you don't need to open it manually.

2. Choose **Print Merge** from the File menu or press **Alt,F,M**.

   Print Merge produces a dialog box like that in Figure 16.3.

3. Printing All letters or records is the default selection. Leave it that way and click **Print** or press **Alt+P** and then **Enter**.

   Word produces the print dialog box.

4. Make any selections from the Print dialog box that you need to, and then choose **OK**.

   Your form letters in the order of the records on your data document soon begin printing. Figure 16.4 shows the resulting documents.

447

Advanced Word

```
┌─────────────────── Microsoft Word - \FORMMAIL.DOC ──────────────┬─┬─┐
│   File  Edit  View  Insert  Format  Utilities  Macro  Window           Help │
│ Font: Tms Rmn     ↓  Pts: 10  ↓   B I K U W □  □         □              │
│ Style: Normal     ↓    ≡L ≡C ≡R ≡J  ≡ ≡ ≡ ≡  □↑↑↑  ⌐⌐                  │
│ 0........1........2........3........4........5........6........7         │
│ {{DATA·Follow}¶                                                          │
│                    Eddy's·World·of·Appliances¶                           │
│                         12·Main·Street¶                                  │
│                    ┌─Merge Records──────────────────┐                    │
│                    │ ● All           ┌─Print...───┐ │                    │
│ {Name}¶            │ ○ From:         │New Document│ │                    │
│ {Street}¶          │     To:         │  Cancel    │ │                    │
│ {City} {State} {Zip}¶                └────────────┘ │                    │
│ ¶                  └──────────────────────────────┘                      │
│ ¶                                                                        │
│ ¶                                                                        │
│ Dear·{Name}:¶                                                            │
│ ¶                                                                        │
│ Thank·you·for·your·recent·purchase·of·the·XJ·6·super·model·              │
│ refrigerator.··During·the·month·of·June·only,·we·will·offer·             │
│ a·25%·discount·on·all·models·of·washers·and·dryers·in·stock.··           │
│ Just·bring·this·letter·in·and·get·your·discount·on·many·of·              │
│ the·leading·brands,·including·Maytag,·Whirlpool,·and·General·            │
│ Electric.                                                                │
│ For Help, press F1                                                       │
└──────────────────────────────────────────────────────────────────────────┘
```

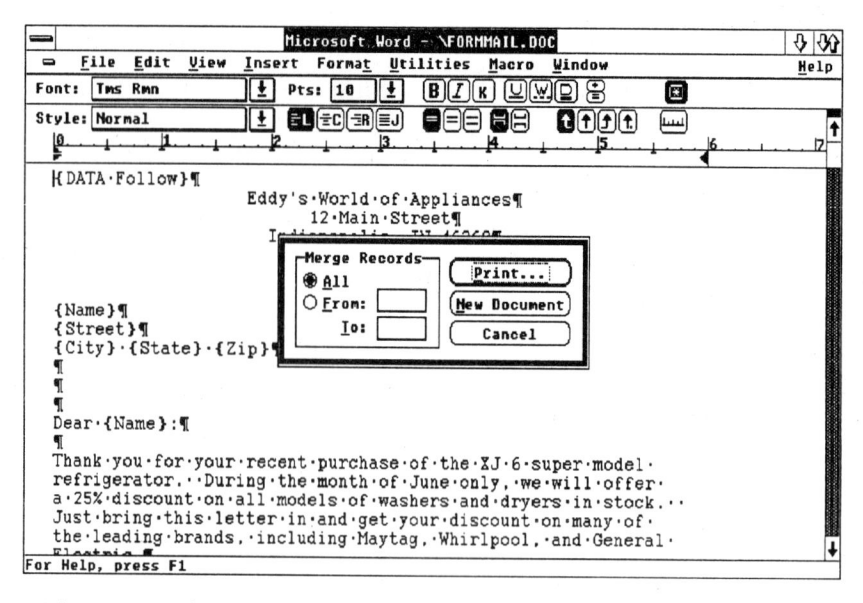

Figure 16.3 The Print Merge dialog box allows you to print form letters immediately or store them in a new document for printing later.

            Eddy's World of Appliances
                  12 Main Street
               Indianapolis, IN 46268

    John Smith
    201 Center Street
    Chicago IL 60626

    Dear John Smith:

    Thank you for your recent purchase of the XJ 6 super model
    refrigerator. During the month of June only, we will offer
    a 25% discount on all models of washers and dryers in stock.
    Just bring this letter in and get your discount on many of
    the leading brands, including Maytag, Whirlpool, and General
    Electric.

    If you have any questions, please call Monday through Friday
    during the hours of 9 to 5 at (317) 872-7222.

    Kind regards,

    John Eddy
    President, Eddy's Appliances

    P.S.   We offer free delivery within a 30-mile radius

16—Using Form Letters

```
        Eddy's World of Appliances
             12 Main Street
          Indianapolis, IN 46268



Sally Green
18 Michigan Ave.
Chicago IL 60618



Dear Sally Green:

Thank you for your recent purchase of the XJ 6 super model
refrigerator.  During the month of June only, we will offer
a 25% discount on all models of washers and dryers in stock.
Just bring this letter in and get your discount on many of
the leading brands, including Maytag, Whirlpool, and General
Electric.

If you have any questions, please call Monday through Friday
during the hours of 9 to 5 at (317) 872-7222.

Kind regards,
```

```
        Eddy's World of Appliances
             12 Main Street
          Indianapolis, IN 46268



Alan Brown
1000 Island Blvd.
Glenview IL 60015



Dear Alan Brown:

Thank you for your recent purchase of the XJ 6 super model
refrigerator.  During the month of June only, we will offer
a 25% discount on all models of washers and dryers in stock.
Just bring this letter in and get your discount on many of
the leading brands, including Maytag, Whirlpool, and General
Electric.

If you have any questions, please call Monday through Friday
during the hours of 9 to 5 at (317) 872-7222.

Kind regards,
```

Figure 16.4 The Print Merge command prints these sample form letters.

Choosing Print Merge tells Word to begin looking for the data document to merge with the main document file. If you didn't store your main document and the data document on the same disk and in the same directory, Word would ask you to find the data file before merge printing could occur.

Fill-In Form Letters

The form letter you just created is an example of a simple form letter whose contents doesn't change. However, there are other ways to use the Print Merge command to create form letters with more flexibility. One such method is to use the *ASK* instruction, which prompts Word to pause and ask for information in a dialog box during the Merge process. The advantage of using the ASK instruction is that you can put different types of information into fields immediately before printing a form letter. For example, if your company wishes to send a form letter announcing a sale on a specific product, you can insert a field that prompts you for text that describes that product. Although it's possible to create a new data document each time you wish to announce the sale of a different product, you could simply use this type of fill-in form letter to change the text describing the product in the field before you print the letter.

When you use an ASK instruction, the form letter will pause every time it's merged and prompt you for text to be assigned as a bookmark to each of the fields where an ASK instruction exists. ASK fields are not allowed in headers or footers, footnotes, annotations, or macros. The basic form of an ASK instruction is:

{ASK BOOKMARK "TEXT ASSIGNED TO B}}OOKMARK"}

where the entire instruction—you can use up to 255 characters—is enclosed within a set of field characters. ASK is the field code instruction that you insert into your main document, whereas bookmark is the name assigned to the text that is available to any other field that refers to this bookmark name. The text within the set of quotation marks is the prompt that you wish to appear as a message in a dialog box prior to printing the document. You can include any character as a part of the prompt text, including a question mark, to help clarify the purpose of the dialog message.

You can place ASK instructions anywhere in your document. If you have more than one ASK instruction inserted, the dialog prompts will appear in the order in which the ASK instructions are encountered. To illustrate the value of the ASK instruction, we can modify our main document file shown in Figure 16.1 to include two field prompts as depicted in Figure 16.5. To insert the ASK instruction fields, use the Insert Field command, select the ASK instruction from the field list, and then type the bookmark name followed by the text. Use the following steps to guide you through this procedure:

```
{DATA Follow}        Eddy's World of Appliances
                            12 Main Street
                        Indianapolis, IN 46268


{Name}
{Street}
{City} {State} {Zip}


Dear {Name}:

Thank you for your recent purchase of the XJ 6 super model
refrigerator.  During the month of {ask salemonth "which
month?"} only, we will offer a 25% discount on all models of
{ask product "which product for sale this month?"} in stock.
Just bring this letter in and get your discount on many of
the leading brands, including Maytag, Whirlpool, and General
Electric.

If you have any questions, please call Monday through Friday
during the hours of 9 to 5 at (317) 872-7222.

Kind regards,



John Eddy
President, Eddy's Appliances



P.S.   We offer free delivery within a 30-mile radius
```

Figure 16.5 Sample fill-in form letter

1. Position the insertion point where you wish to insert the ASK field instruction. For our example, we want to replace the specific month (June) in the second line and insert an ASK instruction that requests the user to type

   The Insert Field dialog box appears.

Advanced Word

the correct month. Thus delete "June," and select the **Field** command from the Insert menu or press **Alt,I,D**.

2. From the list of field types, select the **Ask** instruction.

   The ask instruction is placed in the Field Code box.

3. Move via mouse to the Field Code box or press **Alt+C** and enter a space, the bookmark name, space, and then the bookmark text surrounded by quotation marks. For our example, type:

   The result should look something like Figure 16.6.

   `salemonth "which month?"`

4. Choose **OK** to insert the field at the location of the insertion point.

   A dialog box appears asking you to respond to the prompt that you have just inserted.

5. Enter **June** and choose **OK**.

6. Repeat steps 1–5 to insert any additional ASK instruction fields. For our example, delete "washers and

   As before, a dialog box appears requesting that you respond to the new prompt.

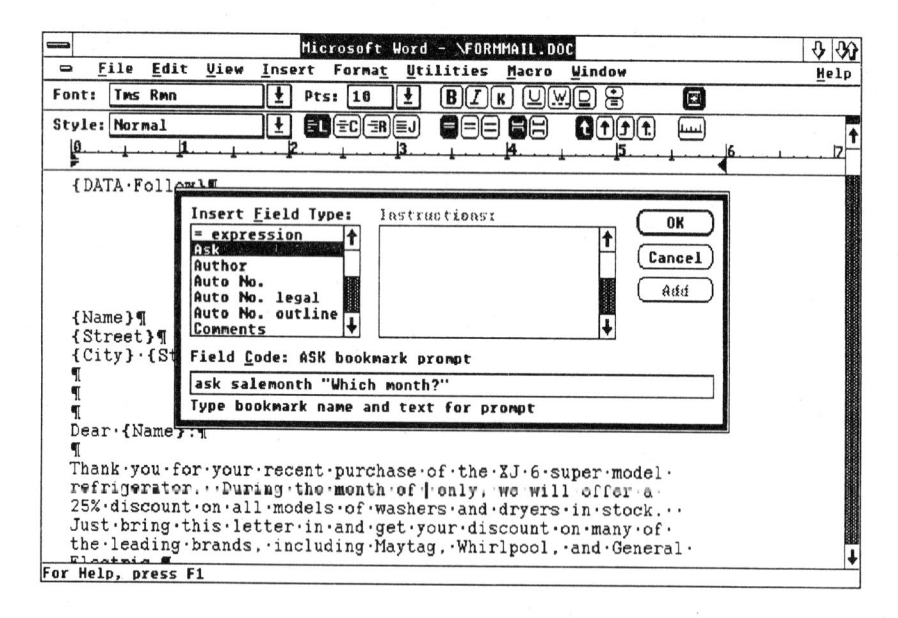

Figure 16.6 Enter the bookmark and bookmark text in a set of quotation marks.

16 — Using Form Letters

dryers" and position the insertion point to insert a second ASK field. Choose **Insert Field** as before, select **Ask** as the field type, and then type:

product "which product for sale this month?"

Choose **OK** to insert the field.

7. Enter **washers & dryers** and choose **OK** or press **Enter**.

Your document will now look like Figure 16.5.

The ASK instructions are now set up for your document. It is not necessary to save the document before choosing the PrintMerge command. When the Print Merge begins, Word will encounter the first ASK instruction and display a dialog box with the message text as shown in Figure 16.7. Enter the appropriate response (i.e., a specific month) and choose OK. Word will continue to the next ASK instruction and display the second dialog box, following the order that they appear in the document. Once the last ASK instruction prompt is satisfied, Word will merge the instructions for the first form letter and print it. Once the first document is completed, Word will immediately begin the second copy, stopping at the first ASK instruction as before. You can continue in this fashion until either all the records in the data document have been completed or until you choose to Cancel or stop the merging.

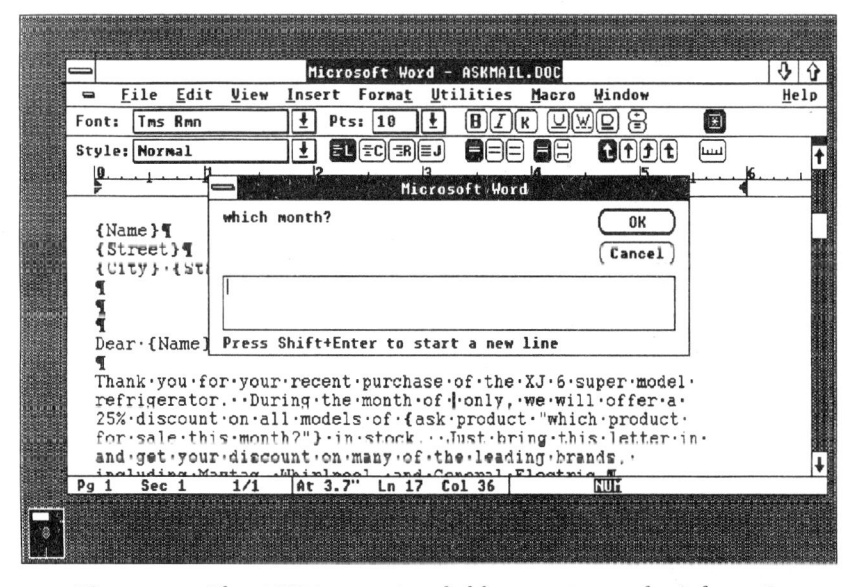

Figure 16.7 The ASK instruction field prompts you for information.

Our example of the ASK instruction is just one way to modify your form-letter mailings. You can actually use any of Word's field code instructions to add spice and flexibility to your form letters. For more information on fields, see the Fields section of your user's manual.

Creating Mailing Labels

Generally, the final step in creating a form-letter mailing is to let Word help you create the mailing labels. Of course, you could take the time to address all those letters manually, but you probably have better things to do with your time: like reading Howard W. Sams books.

Word allows you to create mailing labels to print directly on envelopes or on labels in a single- or multiple-column format. Since creating the proper positioning of text on a mailing label is so time-consuming, Microsoft has conveniently provided label templates to do this for you. You can, of course, create your own label templates or even customize existing ones.

Although Word provides the label templates to print your mailing labels, you still must create an address file that contains the specific mailing address information. Creating mailing labels is similar to creating the form letters just discussed. You first create a main document and data document file and then use the Print Merge command. In this case, the main document file is the selection of label templates provided by Word (or customized by you), while the data document file is the address file. Thus, the first step to creating mailing labels is to create the address file.

Creating the Data Document for Mailing Labels

The next step is to create the data document. For the exercise, use the names and addresses shown in Figure 16.8. Enter the appropriate header record and each of the records, separating each field with a tab or comma (you can also use a table), and pressing Enter at the end of each record. Complete the next set of steps using Figure 16.8 as your guide.

1. If you haven't already, **Open** a new document that you will create for the data document or press **Alt,F,N**.

   Your empty document window should be active.

As a tip, you can leave the main document open, shrink it, and then activate the new document. This method allows you to easily enter the exact field names into your data document, discussed in the next step.

2. Enter the header record in the first line as you would with any data document. The header record should contain the exact bookmark labels, separated by commas or tabs, just as they appear in the main document. For this example, enter **Name, Street, City, State, ZIP**. Press **Enter** at the end of the header record.

3. Enter each of the individual records, one for each address. The number of bookmark labels in each of your records must match the number contained in your main document. Remember to press **Enter** after the last field of each record. This example has three records with five fields in each record.

   If you use commas to delimit your fields and a field has a comma in it, remember to enclose the entire field in quotation marks (e.g., "University Park, Bldg. 2"). If you use tabs, it's not necessary to use quotation marks. Your document file should look something like Figure 16.8.

4. Choose the **Save** command from the File menu or press **Alt,F,S**. Save the document file with the same name that appears in the DATA instruction in the main document file. For this example, enter **Address** in the File Name edit box and then choose **OK**.

   As you enter the file name it appears in the File Name edit box. If you decide to customize or use your own address label template, you will need to save this data document file with the same name that follows the DATA instruction in the address (main document) file. This feature allows you to have more than one data document as long as each one has a

455

Advanced Word

different file name. In order to print the correct addresses from a specific data document file, the file name must match that of the label template.

5. Choose the File **Close** command (**Alt,F,C**). You are now ready to use the Print Merge command to print your mailing labels.

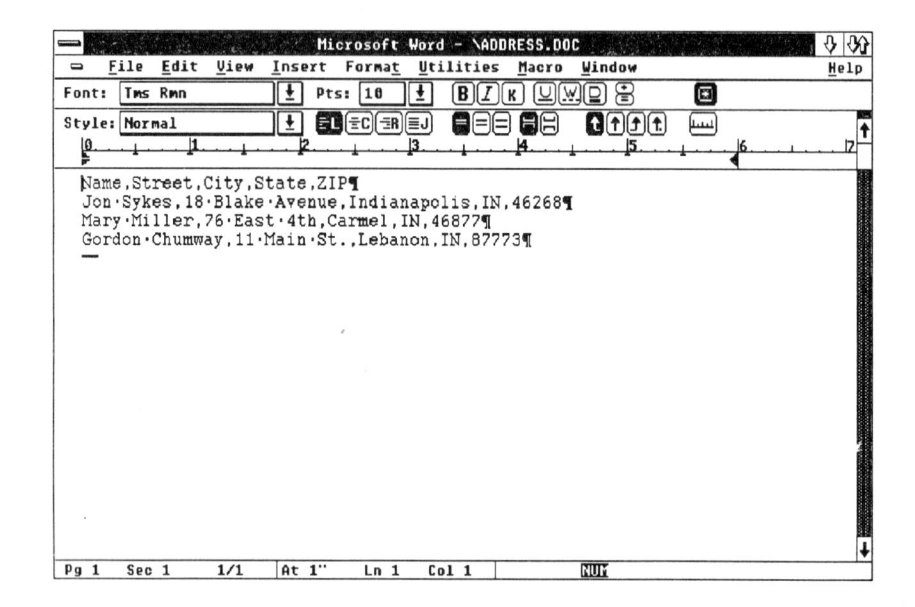

```
======================= Microsoft Word - \ADDRESS.DOC =======================
  File  Edit  View  Insert  Format  Utilities  Macro  Window          Help
Font: Tms Rmn      Pts: 10    B I K U W D
Style: Normal
 0        1         2         3         4         5         6        7
 Name,Street,City,State,ZIP¶
 Jon·Sykes,18·Blake·Avenue,Indianapolis,IN,46268¶
 Mary·Miller,76·East·4th,Carmel,IN,46877¶
 Gordon·Chumway,11·Main·St.,Lebanon,IN,87773¶




 Pg 1    Sec 1    1/1    At 1"    Ln 1    Col 1            NUM
```

Figure 16.8 Sample data document for printing mailing labels.

Once you have created your data document file that contains all the specific mailing addresses, you can either create your own main document file, or you can use the convenience of Word's label templates. The next section reviews how to save valuable time with the latter option.

Using Label Templates for Printing

Word provides special mailing label templates for both sheet-feed and continuous-feed printers. For sheet-feed printers, Word includes 1"

456

Word's label templates are a labor (yours)-saving tool.

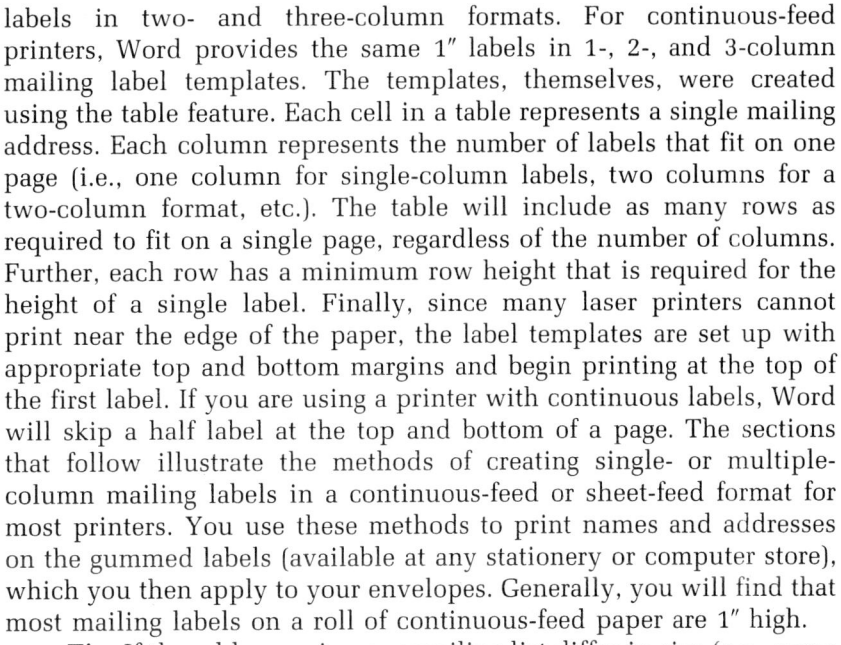

labels in two- and three-column formats. For continuous-feed printers, Word provides the same 1" labels in 1-, 2-, and 3-column mailing label templates. The templates, themselves, were created using the table feature. Each cell in a table represents a single mailing address. Each column represents the number of labels that fit on one page (i.e., one column for single-column labels, two columns for a two-column format, etc.). The table will include as many rows as required to fit on a single page, regardless of the number of columns. Further, each row has a minimum row height that is required for the height of a single label. Finally, since many laser printers cannot print near the edge of the paper, the label templates are set up with appropriate top and bottom margins and begin printing at the top of the first label. If you are using a printer with continuous labels, Word will skip a half label at the top and bottom of a page. The sections that follow illustrate the methods of creating single- or multiple-column mailing labels in a continuous-feed or sheet-feed format for most printers. You use these methods to print names and addresses on the gummed labels (available at any stationery or computer store), which you then apply to your envelopes. Generally, you will find that most mailing labels on a roll of continuous-feed paper are 1" high.

Tip: If the addresses in your mailing list differ in size (e.g., some have three lines, some have four lines), you can still use Word to print the mailing labels for you. You have to assign the entire name and address to a single field, such as {ADDRESS}. The trick is to use a Shift+Enter in the data document file to add a Newline character at the end of each line, instead of pressing Enter, which enters a paragraph symbol. Then, enclose the entire field in a set of quotation marks, since one of the addresses might contain a comma. Note, though, that this method only works for printers that support custom paper sizes. Otherwise, you must format your main document with the number of labels that will print per page (i.e., use one of the multiple-column label templates).

OK, if you've got your blank mailing labels (the continuous-feed variety in either single or multiple columns) loaded into your printer (Figure 16.9), and the data document file set as in the instructions above, then you're ready to print them. The first set of steps will print address labels in a single column using continuous feed. The second set of steps highlights the same procedure for multiple-column labels (e.g., 3 labels across). Remember, these examples are for use with Word's template label formats. We used a standard Laser printer (Laserjet Series II) that starts printing at the top of the first label. You should always consult your printer's user's manual for any special instructions when printing mailing labels.

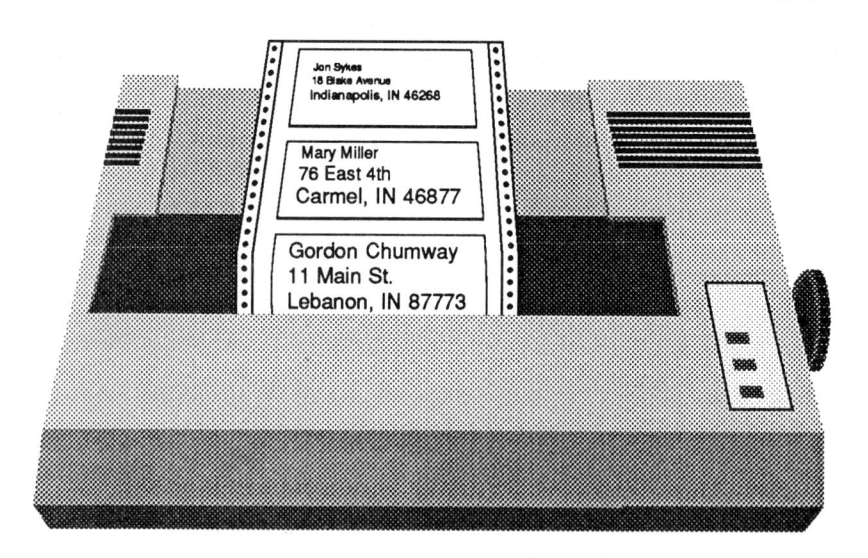

Figure 16.9 Continuous-feed mailing labels ready for printing data document file.

1. As usual, the first step is to **Open** the main document that you wish to insert information and make it active. For this example, you'll use one of the single-column templates provided by Word, so choose **New** from the File menu (**Alt,F,N**) and select the **Template** option (**Alt+T**). Then, move to **Use Template** or press **Alt+U**.

    The label templates are listed in a window with names such as LBL1COLT.DOT, which means 1" labels in a single-column continuous-feed. (LBL2COL.DOT means 1" labels in two columns using the sheet-fed option—the lack of a T following COL represents a sheet-fed option, while the number indicates the number of columns across.)

2. Choose from the label templates appropriate for the type of labels that you wish to print. For our example, use the arrow keys or the mouse to select **LBL1COLT.DOT**. Then, choose **OK**.

3. Choose **Print Merge** from the File menu or press **Alt,F,M**. Be sure that your printer is

    The Print Merge dialog box appears (see Figure 16.10).

properly loaded with the continuous-feed mailing label paper. The print head should be aligned with the first line of the first label. (Remember, laser printers will begin printing on the first line but at both the top and bottom of the page will skip half a label when using continuous labels.)

4. Click the **Print** button or press **Alt+P** to accept the default setting for printing all the mailing labels. If you wish to print only a portion of the labels, enter the number of the first address in the From box and the last address in the To box. If you wish to print a copy of the mailing labels to a new document file, first click **New Document** or press **Alt+N** instead of Print. Doing so lets you use Print Preview to see how the labels will appear before you print.

   The Print dialog box appears. If your data document contained a large number of addresses, it will take a while for Word to merge the information into the template label file.

5. When the standard Print dialog box appears, select any additional printing options and then click **OK** or press **Enter**.

   Shortly, your mailing labels begin to print.

Printing Multiple-Column Labels with Templates

The previous steps were designed for printing mailing labels in single columns on continuous paper. When you shop for mailing labels, you may find that you can purchase continuous-feed paper that prints labels in more than one column across the page. The process for creating multiple-column labels is generally the same as with single columns. Your label template will look slightly different, though, to accommodate the columns. You accomplish this with the *NEXT* field instruction.

Advanced Word

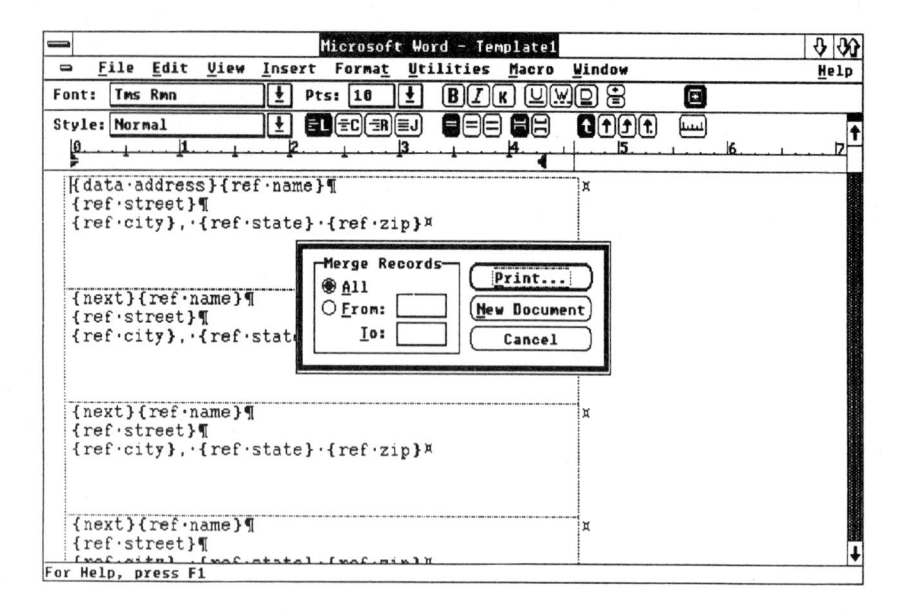

Figure 16.10 Use the Print Merge command to insert addresses from the data file into the label template.

Word uses the NEXT field instruction to create complete sets of mailing label instructions, one set for each record in the main document. In other words, if you want to print three columns of labels, you use three sets of instructions. When Word sees the NEXT field, it knows to read the next data from the next record in the data document.

Printing multiple columns of mailing labels is just as easy as printing them in a single column. The next set of steps accomplishes this task by printing our previous labels three across instead of in a single column. You could actually create your own main document file using the NEXT instruction, but since Word has provided some convenient templates, why bother? The multiple-column templates are ready and available in 2- and 3-column format for both continuous- and sheet-fed mailing labels. Remember to prepare your data document as before. If you decide to slightly change the format of the label templates, save the format using a new DATA instruction name and save the data document file with the same name. Once the data document file has been created and saved, complete the following steps:

1. Choose **New** from the File menu or press **Alt,F,N**. Then, move to **Use Template** (**Alt+U**).

   The label templates are listed in a window.

460

2. Choose from the label templates appropriate for the type of labels that you wish to print. For our example, select **LBL3COLT.DOT** to print labels three across with continuous-fed mailing labels. Then, choose **OK** or press **Enter**.

3. Choose **Print Merge** from the File menu or press **Alt,F,M**. Be sure that your printer is properly loaded with the continuous-feed mailing label paper. The print head should be aligned with the first line of the first label. (Remember, laser printers will begin printing on the first line but at both the top and bottom of the page will skip half a label when using continuous labels.)

   The Print Merge dialog box appears (see Figure 16.10).

4. Click the **Print** button or press **Alt+P** to accept the default setting for printing all the mailing labels. If you wish to print only a portion of the labels, enter the number of the first address in the From box and the last address in the To box. If you wish to print a copy of the mailing labels to a new document file, first click **New Document** or press **Alt+N** instead of Print. Doing so lets you use Print Preview to see how the labels will appear before you print.

   The Print dialog box appears. If your data document contained a large number of addresses, it will take a while for Word to merge the information into the template label file.

5. When the standard Print dialog box appears, select any additional printing options and then click **OK** or press **Enter**.

   Shortly, your mailing labels begin to print.

Advanced Word

Tip: You should provide descriptive names for your templates so you will know which template to apply to which type of label.

Review

In this chapter you learned:

1. To create a form letter mailing, use the Print Merge feature of Word.
2. Print Merge combines the contents of two document files: one file that contains the basic information that doesn't change, such as the form letter itself, and one file that contains the variable information, such as the names and addresses. These two files are called the main document file and the data document file, respectively.
3. The variable information is represented in your main document file by individual fields. Each field is surrounded by a pair of field characters that look just like braces.
4. Each field or placeholder position is given a field code name, called a bookmark. A bookmark name may contain 65 characters, but short names are recommended.
5. You can include fields anywhere in your document. The fields must match field names in the data document file. A document may contain up to 256 fields in a single document.
6. When you give the Print Merge command, the information stored in the data document file is inserted into the bookmark positions of the main document file. The sets of fields for a single document or label make up a record.
7. The quickest way to enter a set of field characters is to press Ctrl+F9, the Insert Field key. The field code characters are inserted on either side of the location of the insertion point.
8. The main document file must begin with the DATA instruction, which includes the name of the data document file. This is how the Print Merge command can link the two documents together.
9. The data document can contain several different records, one for each recipient of your form letter. The first line in the data document file is called the header record, and it lists the names of the bookmarks exactly as they appear in your main document file. You can include 127 fields in a single record. Each record is ended by a paragraph symbol (¶).

10. Field names in a data document file must be separated by commas or tabs. To create a data document file easily, use Word's table feature, as discussed in Chapter 11.

11. To begin printing your form letters, open the main document file and then choose the Print Merge command.

12. You add some flexibility to your form letters by including some of Word's field instructions in your main documents. The ASK instruction will prompt the user for information prior to printing out the document.

13. You can also create mailing labels in single- or multiple-columns to use with your form letters. Microsoft has conveniently provided label templates to prevent the necessity of creating your own.

SEVENTEEN

Chapter

Using the Outlining Feature

In this chapter:

- Introducing the Outline View
- Creating an Outline
- Collapsing and Expanding the Outline
- Reorganizing Your Outline
- Numbering and Renumbering Your Outline
- Printing Outlines

This chapter introduces Word's *outlining* feature, another of Word's tools for helping you organize your thoughts and create an outline for your documents. Once you master this chapter, you may find it's easier to organize long and complex documents.

Introducing the Outline View

Outline View is the third "view" or mode (fourth or fifth if you consider Print Preview and the default Normal Editing View) of creating and developing your documents. By now, you are familiar with the advantages of using the default Normal Editing View, Draft View (for faster execution), and Page View modes. Many people prefer to begin a writing project by organizing their thoughts, however, before plunging in and whacking away at the keyboard. The features of Outline View are designed just for those folks.

If you ever have to tackle a complex task, such as writing a long business plan, a thesis, a research report, or even a book, one approach you can take is to first develop an outline of all the main topics to be discussed, including any related items of information about each topic.

Creating an outline is a hierarchical approach to organizing a topic in which general statements are presented first, followed by increasingly less general and more specific ideas concerning the general topic (see Figure 17.1). As you proceed from general to specific, you develop a framework of detailed levels. Using Word's Outline View, this task is made simple. For example, you might write all your thoughts concerning the topic and its subtopics in a sort of outline. This outline would serve to form the structure of your document and illustrate how you think each topic relates to the others. Often, the outline that you create serves as the table of contents for the document. Chapter 18 discusses in detail just how to do this, but for now, you need to know about the Outline View and key elements of the *outline window*.

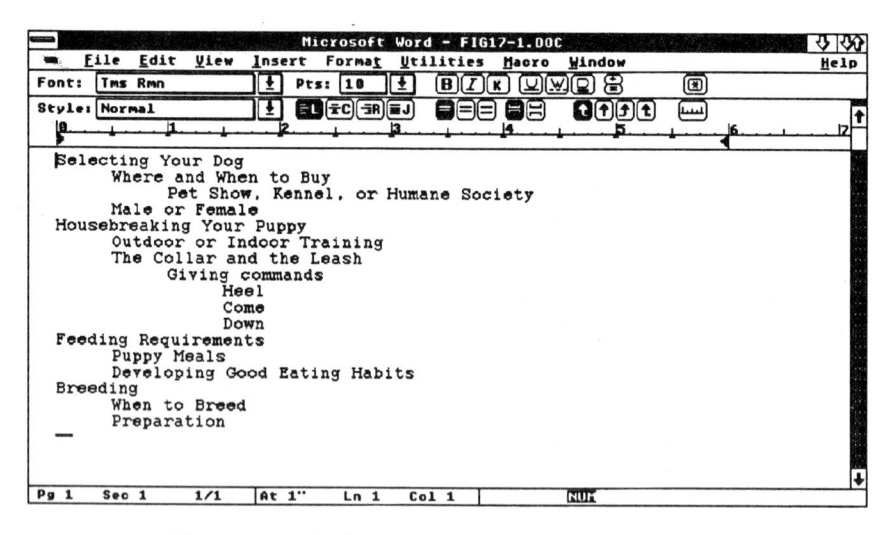

```
                  Microsoft Word - FIG17-1.DOC
   File  Edit  View  Insert  Format  Utilities  Macro  Window          Help
Font: Tms Rmn         Pts: 10        B I K
Style: Normal

Selecting Your Dog
     Where and When to Buy
          Pet Show, Kennel, or Humane Society
     Male or Female
Housebreaking Your Puppy
     Outdoor or Indoor Training
     The Collar and the Leash
          Giving commands
               Heel
               Come
               Down
Feeding Requirements
     Puppy Meals
     Developing Good Eating Habits
Breeding
     When to Breed
     Preparation

Pg 1   Sec 1    1/1   At 1"   Ln 1  Col 1            NUM
```

Figure 17.1 Outlines present a hierarchy of topics.

To access Outline View, choose the **Outlining** command from the View menu or type **Alt,V,O**. Your screen should look something like Figure 17.2. As with Page View, you can toggle between the previous view and Outline View by choosing the Outlining command a second time. Notice that once you select Outline View a check mark will appear next to the Outlining command the next time you pull down the View menu.

17—Using the Outlining Feature

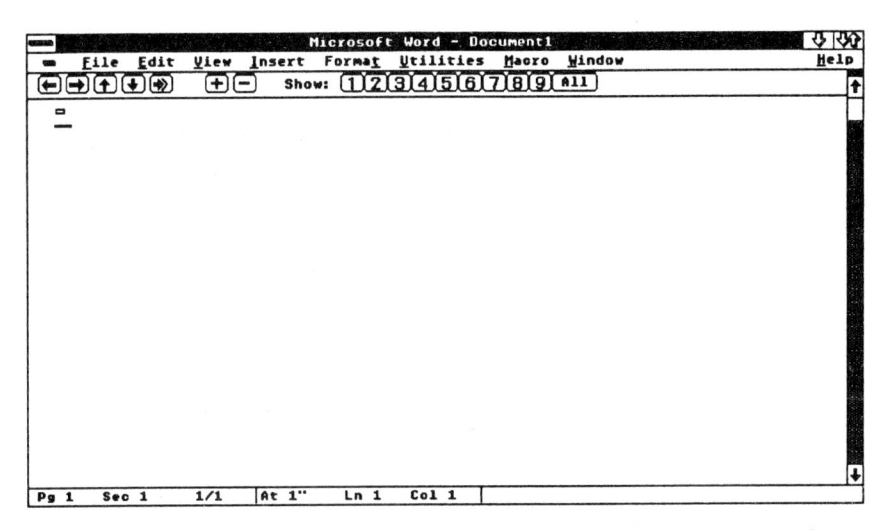

Figure 17.2 Choosing the Outlining command displays a window with a new set of icons across the top.

In Figure 17.2, you'll notice a new set of commands on the Ruler: the Outline *icon bar*. In fact, the old Ruler and any paragraph formatting options you have previously selected will no longer apply to the text that you see on your screen in Outline View (note, though, that character formats remain). That earlier formatting is not lost, however. Reading the icon bar shown in Figure 17.2 from left to right, the commands are:

For those without a mouse, you can use the combination keypress, Alt + Shift + arrow key, to select the corresponding commands chosen from the Outline icon bar. In other words, press Alt + Shift + left arrow to select the promote heading level icon.

- Left, right, up, and down arrow icons—The left and right arrows are used to raise and lower the level of headings. For example, if you select a first-level head, and then choose the right arrow, the heading will be lowered to a second-level head. Clicking the left arrow will raise the selected heading back to a first-level head. When you raise or lower a heading, you change its style as well as the amount of indent applied to that heading.

The up and down arrow icons are used to rearrange blocks of text. Instead of using the Cut and Paste commands from the Edit menu, in Outlining View you can use the up and down arrow icons to move selected text up or down one line at a time. Continue clicking the up or down icons until the selected text is moved to the desired location in the outline window. If you change the order of a heading, its subordinate text will move with it. Note that the heading levels themselves aren't changed, only the order of the paragraphs.

467

Advanced Word

- Body text icon—The fifth icon from the right (it looks like two arrows pointing to the right) is called the *body text icon.* It is used to "demote" a selected heading to body text. Any attached subordinate text (down to the next heading of any level) as well as the demoted heading becomes a part of the subordinate text of the preceding heading. You can also use this icon to insert body text into your outline, a use demonstrated in the first set of steps on creating an outline.

- Plus and minus icons—These are used to "expand" and "collapse" selected headings and their corresponding body text beneath higher-level headings. They're handy, for example, if you want to view only the main headings of a section of your outline. In that case, click the minus sign on the heading(s). The lower-level headings will be removed from view, but not deleted. Clicking the plus sign will expand your selected heading and display the lower-level headings once again.

- Show levels icon—The numbers 1 through 9 correspond to the levels of headings, with 1 the highest. Clicking these icons will display all corresponding level headings and collapse all subordinate levels for the entire outline.

- Show All icon—This icon is a "show toggle switch." Simply put, this icon shows or hides body text. Clicking Show All (it's just All on the Icon Bar) will either display your entire outline or display the outline with all headings except the body text. It does not erase the body text, only hides it.

Although not one of the options on the icon bar, Word does provide two additional options for viewing your text in Outline View:

- The Alt+Shift+F option—Pressing these keys alternates between displaying all the body text or displaying only the first line of body text in Outline View. When an outline is collapsed using this command, the first line will be followed by ellipses (...) to indicate more body text exists.

- *View Draft* command—Choosing this command will hide any character formatting that you have applied to headings. Any default character formatting will also be removed. If you wish to show the character formatting, simply turn off View Draft by selecting it a second time.

Before you learn how to use the commands in Outline View, there are some important points to keep in mind. First, when you choose Outline View, you are not creating any new documents. You are simply asking Word to give you another look at the current document already created in Normal Editing View or Page View. In Outline View, you can create an outline of your document, and then fill in the individual parts of the outline with text. Choose Normal Editing View (by selecting the Outlining command a second time) and take a look at how your document will appear as a standard document. Choose Page View to see how your final document will look before you print it. Outline View is a way to review how your document is organized (it's actually a fast method for reviewing or reorganizing pages).

One of the advantages of using the Outline View is that you can easily change the structure of your documents by rearranging the order of topics. Rather than retyping all the different levels of information, you can move entire sections of related text with a few keystrokes and mouse clicks. Where you could easily get lost within the global picture of the entire document, all you need to do is to move a particular topic or heading, and all the related text within that topic is moved as well. This feature is useful for writers who don't know exactly where a topic best fits within the structure of their document. They know the information is relevant to their project, so they include it and then worry about the organization later. Word's outlining feature is one more tool that you can use to help you write it now and "organize it later."

Word's outliner provides two general categories: headings and body text. Each heading has a level, such as level 1, level 2, and so on. Word allows you to have up to nine levels but your documents can become too complex if you try to use all nine levels. Most books, for instance, get along nicely with three or four levels. The body text is just like any regular text that you create within a paragraph in Normal Editing View. Body text doesn't have levels. At first, you will probably create the outline for your documents in Outline View and then go back and fill in the body text.

As you create your outline, Word will indent the levels of your headings to help you visualize the document's structure. The indentation is set according to the tab stop default measurements set in the Document dialog box. For example, when you first load Word, tab stops are set every 1/2". The level 1 headings represent a main topic or general idea and begin flush left. As you progress to more detailed topics, the subheadings will be indented at 1/2" intervals. Three levels of headings provide a good beginning for most documents. Although body text doesn't have levels, the body text will be indented 1/4" from the head that precedes it.

The format of your body text in Outline View will appear in the default Normal style. This is true even if you first create the document in Normal Editing View, format the text with character and paragraph formatting, and then choose Outline View. Your paragraph formatting is not lost in Outline View (character formatting remains), however. Choose Normal Editing View or Page View and the paragraph formatting reappears.

Character formatting can be applied in Outline View because you can easily choose the Ribbon and add such formatting just as you would in Normal Editing View or Page View. Paragraph formatting can't be applied in Outline View at all. However, Word does offer some "style." Each one of the heading levels is automatically assigned a style according to the default Heading styles available with Word. Chapter 13 gives more information on styles.

This introduces Outline View, but the easiest way to learn about it is to jump right in and create your first outline. The next section helps you do just that.

Creating an Outline

Some people do indeed plan their writing by writing all the main topics of a document and then rearranging the order until the document logically meets their approval. They then insert second, third, or further levels as they begin to develop the outline. Not all writers think this way, however. Some people write their best thoughts in no particular order and then expect later to mold these ideas into a logical structure. With Word's outliner, you can make both approaches work for you.

To create an outline, you can enter the new text in Normal Editing View, Draft View, or Page View and switch to Outline View, or you can simply begin in Outline View. For now, try beginning outlines directly in Outline View. Use the following steps to create the outline in Figure 17.1. If you prefer to first create your main topics, or level 1 headings, and then go back and fill in the subordinate levels of headings and body text, that's OK too (and often recommended for planning large complex documents). Once you see how easy it is to use the outliner, you'll probably use the mouse to relocate the insertion point to add lower-level headings.

If you don't want to view your outline with the default character formatting, choose View Draft.

1. Get a clean document page by choosing **New** from the File menu or typing **Alt,F,N**. Then, choose **OK** or press **Enter**.

   You should be working in the default Normal Editing View.

2. Choose **Outlining** from the View menu or press **Alt,V,O**.

   The screen appears in Outline mode and displays the icon bar across the top of the window.

3. Type your first-level head. For this example, type

   Selecting Your Dog

   and then press **Enter**.

   Word assumes that you want to begin with the first level. If you turn on the Ribbon option, you'll notice that Word begins with a default 12-pt Helvetica font and underlines the first-level headings. Pressing Enter tells Word that you have finished a first-level head and are ready for the next first-level head. Note that Word will apply the first-level head style as defined by the automatic styles.

4. The next step is to type the second-level head. First click the **right arrow icon** in the icon bar to move the line to the first tab stop or press **Alt+Shift+right arrow**. Then type the second line

   Where and When to Buy

   and then press **Enter**.

   Word indents according to the default tab settings to indicate that this heading is a second-level head. Pressing Enter always places the insertion point at the same level as the previous heading level. Use the left or right arrow icons to promote or demote the insertion point prior to typing the next heading. If the heading is to be at the same level, continue typing.

5. Continue clicking the arrow icons (or use Alt+Shift+arrow keypresses) and typing the subordinate headings until you are ready to type the next first-level heading. Click the right arrow icon again to enter the third-

   The indentation reflects the heading levels.

level heading and then type

Pet Show, Kennel, or Humane Society

Remember to press **Enter** after you've entered each heading.

6. For this example, type all four main (first-level) headings and the subordinate headings (remember to use the right arrow icon or the left arrow icon to specify the level before typing a heading).

When complete, your document should look like Figure 17.1, except in Outline View.

7. As you create outlines, you will soon want to add body text to your outlines as well as the headings. The last step then is to practice entering some body text. First, position the insertion point where you want to enter body text and then click the body text icon. For this example, place the insertion point after the heading, Housebreaking Your Puppy; press **Enter** to add a new line; and then click the **body text icon** to demote the heading to body text. Then, type

Housebreaking your puppy should be your first training concern. Puppies should be taken outdoors after meals and after a period of aggressive play.

With body text added to your outline, the document will look like Figure 17.3. You can easily add body text anywhere in your outline by first positioning the insertion point, clicking the body text icon, and then typing the desired text.

8. After you have finished typing your body text, press **Enter** and then click the **left arrow icon** to promote the insertion point to entering another heading.

17—Using the Outlining Feature

Caution: There is a bug in Word for Windows. If you click the body text icon and then select the Edit menu, it will crash.

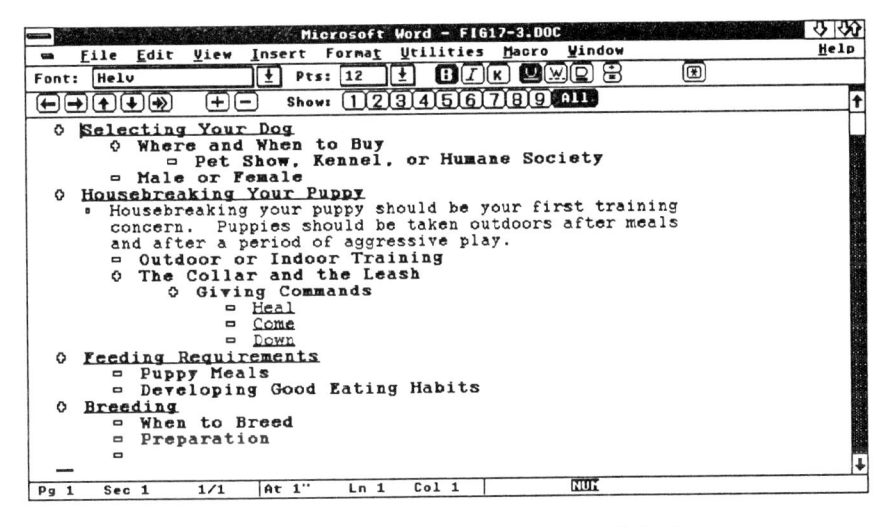

Figure 17.3 A sample outline, complete with body text.

The best way to learn how to create outlines is to jump right in and practice. Once your outline is created, you should test all the commands on the Outline icon bar. These commands are discussed more in the sections that follow.

Collapsing and Expanding the Outline

If you wish to hide all but the first line of headings, you use the Alt+Shift+I keypress.

Sometimes you will want to view all the details in your outlines, including subordinate levels of headings and related body text; at other times, as your outlines grow, you may find viewing all the detail too cumbersome. Recognizing this, Word offers several methods for collapsing your outline so that the screen only displays the levels of heads that you wish to view, giving an overview of the structure of your document. Another option you have is to display all the headings, but to hide either all of any related body text or all but the first line (Alt+Shift+F).

In looking at the Outline icon bar in the first section, you were introduced to all the commands necessary for collapsing and expanding outlines. You can, for example, collapse all material beneath a heading by selecting the heading first and then clicking the minus sign icon on the bar or pressing Alt+Shift+minus. You can also

473

select a particular level of head that you want to display and click the corresponding number on the icon bar to collapse all subordinate text. For example, to display only first-level headings, click the number 1 icon (see Figure 17.4). To expand material that you have collapsed, select the entire heading, and then click the plus icon or press Alt+Shift+Plus.

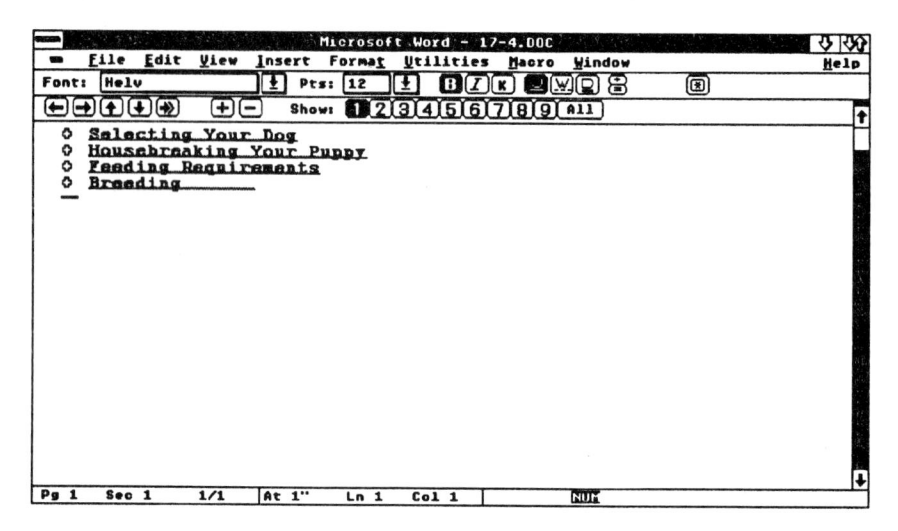

Figure 17.4 A collapsed view of sample outline showing level 1 heads only.

To collapse selected text to first level headings only, you can position the pointer over the heading level icon (it changes to a cross-hair) and double-click with the mouse. Double-click a second time, and the outline is returned to show all previous levels.

Continue to practice using the − and + icons to collapse and expand the outline you created with the previous steps. Try other exercises with the Show All text icon. Click the All icon to toggle between hiding body text and displaying your entire outline. When body text or subordinate levels are collapsed, a squiggly line appears under the preceding heading that the text is attached to (see Figure 17.4). Likewise, select the text and press Alt+Shift+F or click the All icon to toggle between showing all body text and displaying just the first line of body text followed by ellipses (see Figure 17.5). Use the Show All and First Line Only commands to collapse your outline in order to simplify your viewing.

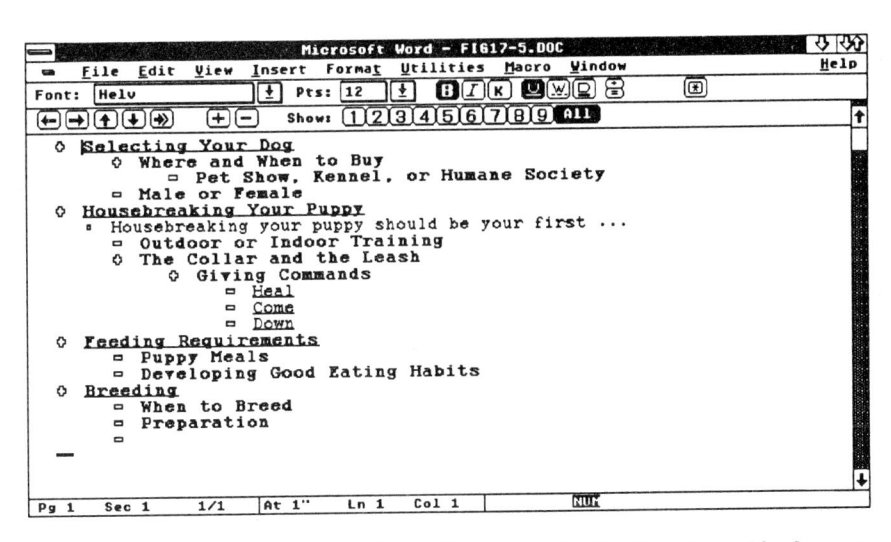

Figure 17.5 Choosing Alt+Shift+F displays only the first line of body text followed by ellipses.

Reorganizing Your Outline

When you select a heading level by clicking the level icon to the left of the text, all subordinate text for that level is selected as well. To select and subsequently move a single line, click in the selection bar or drag across the text with the mouse.

Word allows you to edit and reorganize your outlines like any other document. Word provides an easier method for moving blocks of outline text, however, than cutting and pasting text with the Clipboard. You can still use the Clipboard method if you want, by positioning the insertion point, selecting text, and cutting and pasting it just as you have earlier. For this exercise, you'll use the up and down arrow icons to move an entire section of text easily and quickly. It's important to remember that once you move text, the change will be reflected in your standard document as well. To get some practice, use the following steps to reorganize your sample outline, transposing the second main-level heading (Housebreaking Your Puppy) with the third main-level heading (Feeding Requirements).

1. When you move a heading, it is likely that you will want to move all its subordinate headings and body text along with it. Place the insertion point over the beginning of the heading until the pointer changes to a cross-hair and then click the mouse to select it. In this example, place the pointer over the heading icon in the line, **Housebreaking Your Puppy,** until it turns to a cross-hair and then click the mouse once to select it.

   The heading and all related subordinate text are highlighted, as in Figure 17.6.

2. To move the selected text down one line in the outline, click the down arrow icon once. If you want to move the text up one line, click the up arrow icon. For this example, click the **down arrow** *three* times to rearrange the entire paragraph of text in the outline.

   The selected text moves down in the outline one line at a time. After three clicks, the outline will look like that in Figure 17.7.

Tip: You can use the mouse or the keys to select and move text in Outline View. For example, to select text you can use the F8, or Extend Selection, option. To do this, first position the insertion point in front of the text that you wish to select, press F8 to turn on the Extend Selection mode, and then use the arrow keys to extend the selection of text. When finished selecting text, press the Esc key to turn off the extend selection mode. Then to move text within the outline, press Alt+Shift+up arrow to move text up or Alt+Shift+down arrow to move text down. For more keyboard methods, see Appendix B.

17—Using the Outlining Feature

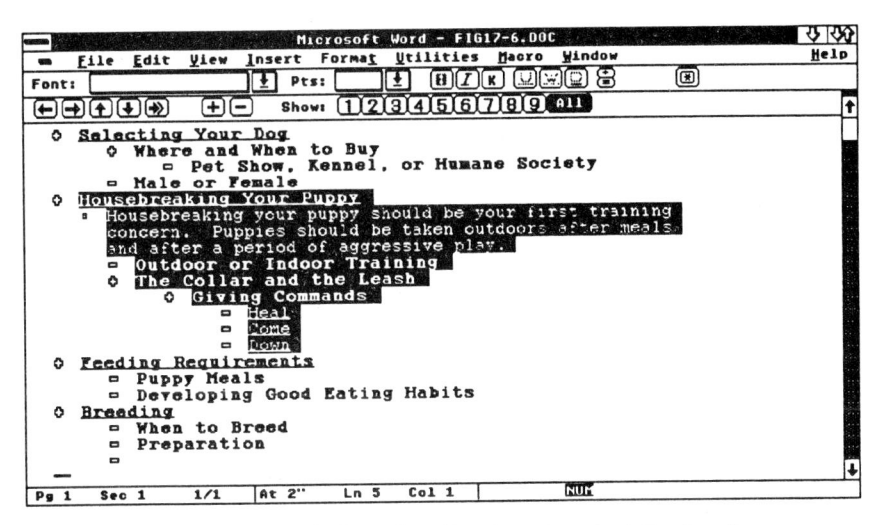

Figure 17.6 Click on heading icon to select the heading and its subordinate text.

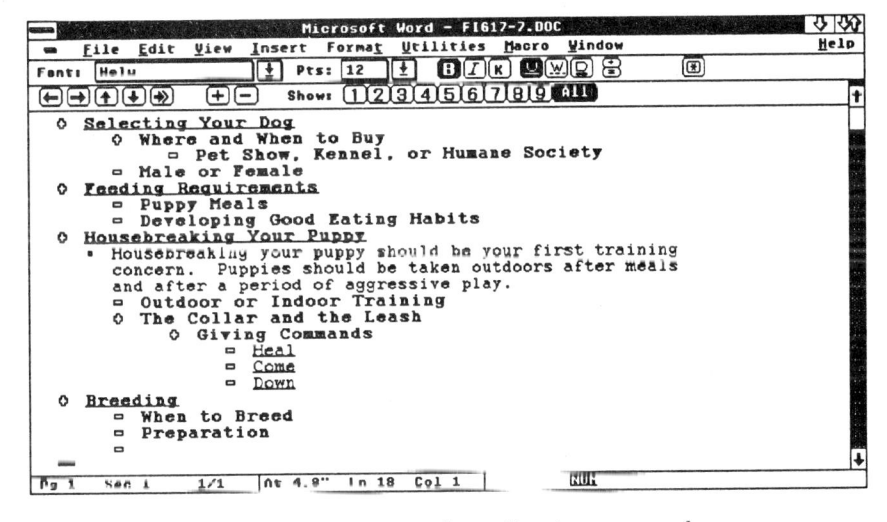

Figure 17.7 Your sample outline is rearranged.

477

Numbering and Renumbering Your Outlines

If you want to number only a portion of your outline, select the text and then choose the Renumber command. If you have inserted a heading above your outline (as body text), click the show all icon to collapse body text first.

So far, the sample outline has not displayed the numbers or letters that are common to outlines. You can use the *Renumber* command on the Utilities menu to number or renumber your outlines up to nine levels. Just like numbering any document, you can use automatic or manual numbering for selected portions of text or the entire document. Automatic and manual numbering are summarized in the following sections.

Automatic Numbering

To print your outlines with numbers automatically, first select all or part of the outline text, and then choose the **Renumber** command from the Utilities menu or press **Alt,U,R**. Choosing the **Automatic** option (see Figure 17.8) and then **OK** will insert one of three types of automatic numbering fields in front of the selected paragraphs. The three types of automatic fields are summarized as:

- LEGAL—The option inserts a field listed as AUTONUMLGL. The legal option automatically activates all nine levels and numbers the headings in legal format: e.g., 1.1, 1.1.1, 1.1.1.1.
- OUTLINE—This option inserts a field with the bookmark name as AUTONUMOUT. The outline option numbers the outline format according the *Chicago Manual of Style*: e.g., I.A.1.a)(1)(a)(i). Body text is numbered according to Sequence format as defined next.
- SEQUENCE—The Sequence option numbers the outline in standard arabic numerals format: e.g., 1.,2.,3.

The advantage of Word's automatic numbering option is that every time you rearrange, add, or delete headings, the numbers are automatically updated and produce a properly sequenced numbering scheme for your outline. Keep in mind, though, that when you execute the Automatic numbering option, all paragraphs created by pressing Enter (including blank lines) will be counted. If you renumber a second time with the Numbered Only option selected, then only the paragraphs with numbers are shown after renumbering. To remove numbers from blank paragraphs, you can select those paragraphs one at a time and then choose the Remove option from the Renumber dialog box.

17—Using the Outlining Feature

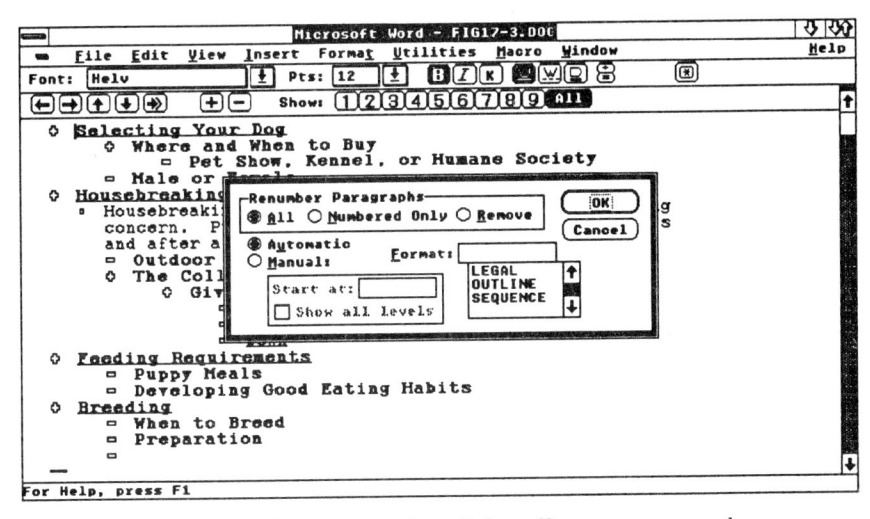

Figure 17.8 The Utilities Renumber dialog allows you to number your outlines automatically or manually.

Use the following steps to choose automatic numbering for your outlines.

1. Select the text that you wish to number or renumber. If you don't select any text, the entire outline will be renumbered.

    The selected text is highlighted.

2. From the Utilities menu, select **Renumber** or press **Alt,U,R**.

    The Renumber dialog box appears (see Figure 17.8).

3. Choose the **Automatic** Renumbering option or press **Alt+U**. Choose any other options from the Renumber Paragraph section. The default All numbers all selected paragraphs whether they have numbers or not. The Numbered Only option will renumber only those paragraphs that already have a number. The Remove option will remove numbers from selected paragraphs.

    All selected options are highlighted with a black dot.

479

4. From the Format list window, select the type of automatic numbering field you want. Choose from LEGAL, OUTLINE, or SEQUENCE.

5. Choose **OK** or press **Enter**.

The outline appears in the sequence format specified. Note: If the View Field Codes option is turned on, then the outline will appear with automatic numbering fields in front of selected paragraphs instead. However, when the document is printed, the correct numbering sequence will be printed instead of the fields.

Manual Numbering

Manual numbering works much the same way as automatic numbering as discussed above. The first step is to select the text that you wish to number or renumber. If no text is selected, the Utilities Renumber command will apply the numbering scheme to the entire outline. As with automatic numbering, you can choose to renumber all the paragraphs or the numbered paragraphs only or to remove the numbering from selected paragraphs. The numbering format for the Manual option, likewise, includes the LEGAL, OUTLINE, and SEQUENCE formats (see descriptions above). Choosing the Manual option, however, also adds the format called Learn to the list window. This option takes the first number from each level in the selection as the numbering format. The advantages of the manual option are that you can enter your own starting number sequence as long as it matches the format selected or typed in the Format box, and you can also enter your own specific format sequence. For example, you may wish to specify a numbering scheme with uppercase or lowercase roman numerals, uppercase or lowercase letters, or some combination of these. You can even type a format that includes periods or similar characters. If the first number in a selected portion of the outline is not to be 1, then enter that new starting value in the Start At box. Follow these steps for practice using the manual option to number our sample outline.

17—Using the Outlining Feature

1. Select the outline or the portion of the outline that you wish to number or renumber. If you don't select a portion of the outline, Word will automatically number the entire outline.

2. Choose **Renumber** from the Utilities menu or press **Alt,U,R**.

   The Renumber dialog box appears.

3. Click in the **Format** box or press **Alt+F**. Enter the numbering sequence that you want your outline to follow. For this example, select the OUTLINE option.

   Your new sequence appears in the Format box.

4. If you wish to start the numbering sequence with something other than the default value 1, move to the Start at box or press Alt+S and type the desired number. If not, leave the 1 as default as for this example. Note that the period serves to separate levels of heads when you insert your own start number.

5. Click **OK** or press **Enter**.

   Your new numbered outline now should look something like Figure 17.9.

OK, now you know how to create and number your outlines, but suppose you change your mind about wanting to number or you reorganize the order of the topics. To delete the numbering from an outline, choose the **Renumber** command from the Utilities menu a second time, and click the **Remove** button and choose **OK** or press **Enter**. In a few seconds, the numbering will disappear from your outline. Or, you can easily renumber any portion of your outline by selecting the appropriate text and then using the Renumber command again.

Now that you know how to create your outlines, it would be a good idea to put them to use while you are working on completing

Advanced Word

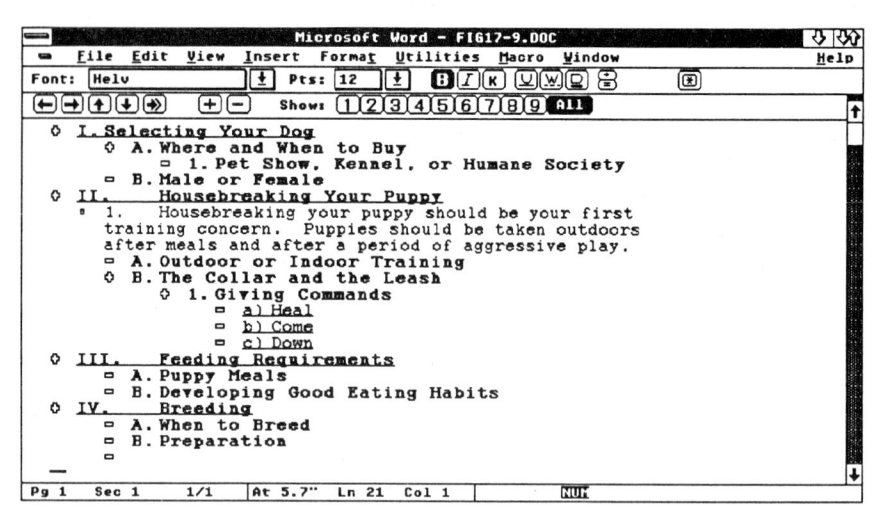

Figure 17.9 The sample outline is numbered with uppercase letters and arabic numerals.

the final document. The next section discusses how to print your outlines for this purpose.

Printing Outlines

You can print your outlines in order to use them while you're working in Normal Editing View, Draft View, or Page View. Word prints only the outlines appearing on the screen and not any collapsed text. This is a handy feature if, for example, you want to print an overview of the outline by printing only first-level headings. To do this, you'd collapse all subtext by choosing the number 1 icon on the Outline icon bar. Then you would choose the Print command from the File menu and press Enter.

Review

In this chapter you learned:

1. Outline View is an optional mode (others include Draft, Normal Editing View, and Page View) for looking at your documents via the View menu. For organizing long and complex documents, you can use Outline View to create a

hierarchical outline of topics, from the general to the more specific. As you proceed from the general or main topics to the more specific, you develop a framework of detail levels.

2. To access Outline View, choose the Outline command from the View menu, or type Alt,V,O. Word provides an icon bar from which to choose outlining options. You can use either the mouse to select options by pointing and clicking, or you can use the keyboard. To select commands from the Outline icon bar with the keys, press Alt+Shift+arrow key; the arrow key represents a corresponding command on the icon bar.

3. In Outline View, you can collapse or expand an outline to provide either a detailed or a more global look at the structure of your document. This feature is handy when your outlines begin to grow beyond a single screen.

4. Word's outliner consists of two general categories: headings and body text. You can have up to nine levels of headings and an unlimited amount of body text which you can fill in at any time. Body text is generally descriptive material that you don't want to forget to add to your document. It is formatted with the Normal style.

5. As you create your outline, Word will indent the different levels of headings to help you visualize the document's structure. The first subordinate heading is indented 1/2" from the main topic. Successive levels are indented in 1/2" increments. These indent levels are based on the default tab stop settings which you can change via the Format Document dialog box.

6. To create an outline, you can either begin typing in Outline View or you can begin in Normal Editing View, Draft View, or Page View and switch to Outline View. Beginners should start new outlines in Outline View.

7. Word enables you to reorganize your outline with the up and down icons. To move a heading, select it and then choose the appropriate up or down icon on the bar. When you select a heading icon, all the subordinate headings and text are moved along with the selected heading.

8. You may wish to view all the details in your outline, including subordinate levels and related body text; at other times, you may wish to collapse your outline to provide only an overview of the document. To help, Word provides several options for collapsing and subsequently expanding the outline to show its complete structure. For example, you can select a specific level of head to show and then hide all remaining levels.

9. You can number or renumber your outlines using the Renumber command on the Utilities menu. As with numbering any document, you can use automatic or manual numbering for selected portions of text or the entire document.

10. The advantage of automatic numbering is that every time you rearrange, add, or delete headings, the numbers are automatically updated to produce the proper numbering sequence.

11. The options for numbering outlines include LEGAL, OUTLINE, and SEQUENCE formats. If you select Manual numbering, then Word also adds a fourth format option called Learn. The advantage of the Manual numbering option is that you can select your own starting sequence number as long as it matches the format in the Format box.

12. You can print outlines (either an expanded or collapsed version) just as you would if you were working in Normal Editing, Draft, or Page View. Word prints outlines just as they appear on the screen. Word will not print any collapsed headings or subtext.

EIGHTEEN

chapter

Adding Tables of Contents, Indexes, or Footnotes

In this chapter:

- Adding Tables of Contents
- Creating Indexes
- Creating Footnotes
- Using Bookmarks

Word is truly a flexible word processor whose features seem to be limitless. This chapter takes you on a brief tour of several features and tools that you might use as you develop your documents. Two commands from the Insert menu, Table of Contents and Index, and one from the Format Document menu, Footnotes, will help with your editorial work.

Adding Tables of Contents

As you begin to create long, complex documents, you will find a need to create tables of contents and indexes that help the reader navigate through your work. Creating these elements of a document is generally a task that is left as "clean-up work," and is typically one that is tedious and sometimes may be poorly done. Often the mark of a well-done document is how easy it is to use as a reference. Can you find the information that you need quickly without endlessly searching through its pages? Two components that help a document achieve this effect are the table of contents and index.

If you have ever created a table of contents or index by hand, you are well aware of the frustration of redoing the work when changes to your document result in repagination. With Word's help, you only have to do the work once; Word accounts for any last-minute changes you make to the document.

The initial setups for tables of contents and indexes are similar. You use Word to enter fields into your document to mark the entries that you want to include in a table of contents or index. Each field contains instructions that tell Word to insert text or graphics into a document and to provide a specific page number. You can also use this "field method" for other types of information, such as lists, illustrations, and tables. Since both the Table of Contents and Index themselves are considered fields, you simply select the appropriate command from the Insert menu, and then Word compiles and creates the table of contents or index and places it at the field's location. If you edit or change your document, simply select the TOC or Index field and tell Word to update it (i.e., press F9, the Update key).

Creating Tables of Contents

Most tables of contents introduce the reader to the document's contents and provide a "roadmap" to the location of key topics. Some tables of contents only include the main topics or chapter titles as an overview. Others provide a more detailed look at the document, from main headings to subtopics, offering a detailed look at the structure of the document.

A table of contents is one of the first elements that you find when you open a book. Tables of contents are not reserved for books, however. Many long documents, such as business plans or research papers require a table of contents. Any document that is ten or more pages long should probably have a table of contents. Smaller documents generally do not need a table of contents.

Word offers two methods to create a table of contents: One is to use the outliner as introduced in Chapter 17, and the other is to insert the TOC Entry (TC) field that identifies the text as an entry and provides the necessary information for inserting that entry into a table of contents. The easier method, though, is to use the outliner to set up headings and then to collect those headings into a table of contents. This method is discussed next.

The Table of Contents from the Outline Method

If you haven't read Chapter 17 yet, it would be a good idea to do so before completing the next set of steps.

An outline organizes a list of topics from the general to the detailed. In Word, the main topics are formatted as level 1 headings, and the subtopics can be formatted in levels 2 through 9, depending on the complexity of the document. In Word's automatic styles list, you'll find a toc, or table of contents, style corresponding to the number of heading levels you create in the outline mode. For example, all level 1 headings are formatted with the corresponding toc 1 style, level 2 headings as toc 2 style, and so on. When you choose the Table of Contents command from the Insert menu (and then the Use Heading Paragraphs option), Word compiles a table based on the headings in your document. The style of table, including page number references, is formatted according to the default automatic toc styles provided by Word.

Since Word automatically compiles the table of contents based on the current headings of your outline, each time that you modify your outline, or add or delete text, the pagination may change and your outline will be updated but the numbers in the toc will not be updated. (To prevent having to reprint your table of contents, it might be a good idea to wait until your document is in final form before printing the final toc.)

Word cannot compile your table of contents until you give it heading styles.

Finally, if you haven't applied any heading styles to your document, generating the table of contents will simply produce an error message saying that no entries exist. You can avoid this by selecting the headings from your text, and then choosing the appropriate heading style (Heading 1 through Heading 9) with the style box on the Ruler.

Once the document has an outline structure and/or the appropriate heading styles have been applied, use your outline to create a table of contents by following these steps:

1. Create an outline using the methods discussed in Chapter 17. (Enter the outline in OUTLINE mode.) If no outline structure exists for your document, you can still compile a table of contents by applying the default heading styles from the style box on the Ruler.

Advanced Word

2. If your document contains any hidden text, turn off the Hidden Text option on the View Preferences dialog box. You don't want Word compiling page breaks based on hidden text that you may not print later.

3. Next, position the insertion point where you want the table of contents to appear in your document. At the beginning is a good choice. Then, choose the **Table of Contents** command from the Insert menu or press **Alt,I,C**.

   The Table of Contents dialog box appears as in Figure 18.1.

4. Accept the default **Use Heading Paragraphs** option or if it's not selected, choose it by pressing **Alt+H**. Also, select the **All** option unless you wish to print only selected heading levels. To print only selected heading levels, move to the From box (**Alt+F**) and enter the desired levels in it and the To box (e.g., enter from 1 to 1 for level 1 only).

5. Click **OK** or press **Enter**.

   Word compiles the table of contents, including page numbers, and inserts the TOC field at the location of the insertion point. (Now turn on the Hidden Text option in View Preferences if you want to see the fields). If your screen shows field codes instead of the actual table of contents, be sure to turn off

18—Adding Tables of Contents, Indexes, or Footnotes

the Field Codes option or press Alt,V,C. Finally, note that Word adds dot leaders to separate the headings from the page numbers. See Figure 18.2 as an illustration. Since our example used an outline that fit on a single page, all of the numbers reflect page 1.

Tip: To get a "structure peek" at how your table of contents will appear when the document is printed, choose the Print Preview command from the File menu.

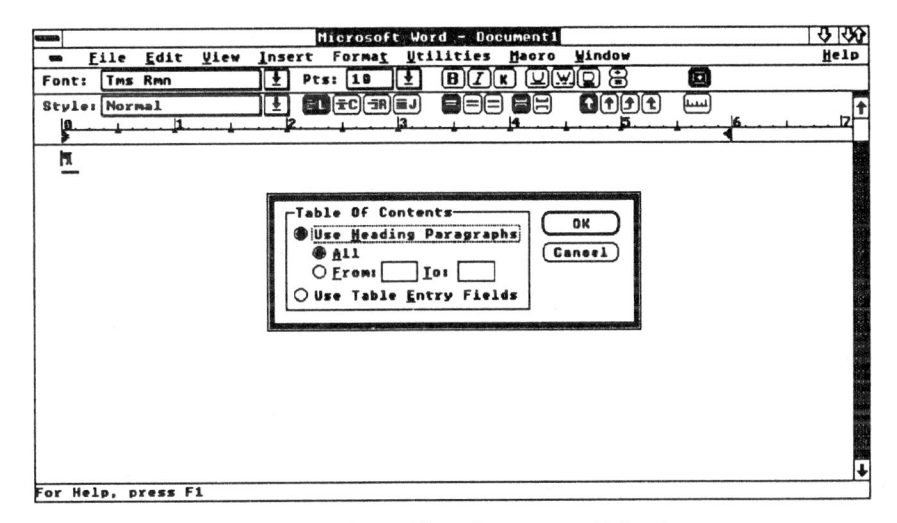

Figure 18.1 The Table Of Contents dialog box.

Once Word creates your table of contents, it inserts the table of contents at the insertion point within your standard document. If you want to erase the table, select it and delete it with the Cut command from the Edit menu or press the Delete key. Like all changes made to a document, you must save it prior to closing the document in order to retain the table of contents.

```
     Selecting Your Dog .......................................... 1
         Where and When to Buy ................................ 1
         Pet Show, Kennel, or Humane Society .................. 1
         Male or Female ....................................... 1
     Housebreaking Your Puppy .................................... 1
         Outdoor or Indoor Training ........................... 1
         The Collar and the Leash ............................. 1
               Giving commands ................................ 1
                  Heel ........................................ 1
                  Come ........................................ 1
                  Down ........................................ 1
     Feeding Requirements ........................................ 1
         Puppy Meals .......................................... 1
         Developing Good Eating Habits ........................ 1
     Breeding .................................................... 1
         When to Breed ........................................ 1
         Preparation .......................................... 1

     Selecting Your Dog
     Where and When to Buy
     Pet Show, Kennel, or Humane Society
     Male or Female

     Housebreaking Your Puppy
     Outdoor or Indoor Training
     The Collar and the Leash
        Giving commands
        Heel
        Come
        Down

     Feeding Requirements
     Puppy Meals
     Developing Good Eating Habits

     Breeding
     When to Breed
     Preparation
```

Figure 18.2 A sample table of contents created from an outline.

The Table of Contents from the Fields Method

If you have already completed your document, but did not set it up in OUTLINE mode first, you can either select each heading and then apply an appropriate heading style or you can use the Insert Field command to insert a field and identify a table of contents entry. With this alternate method, you place a hidden Table of Contents (TOC) entry field code (*tc*) in front of any text that you want to be a table entry. There is no limit to the number of entries that you can specify with the tc field format.

18—Adding Tables of Contents, Indexes, or Footnotes

The tc codes are automatically formatted as hidden text so they will not print in your final document. To insert a hidden tc code for a table entry, position the insertion point where the tc entry field code is to appear and choose the *Field* command from the Insert menu. Select tc from the Field Code box and then type the desired entry within a set of quotation marks. Repeat this procedure for all entries and then use the Insert Table of Contents command to compile the table of contents at the location of your insertion point. The following steps highlight this simple procedure.

1. Position the insertion point in front of the first table of contents entry. If you want to enter new text as a table entry, position the insertion point where you want the entry to be inserted.

2. From the Insert menu, select the **Field** command or press **Alt,I,D.**

   The Insert dialog box appears.

3. Either move to the Field Code box and type **tc**, or choose TC from the scroll window (see Figure 18.3) and then move to the Field Code box.

   The field code entry, tc, appears in the edit box.

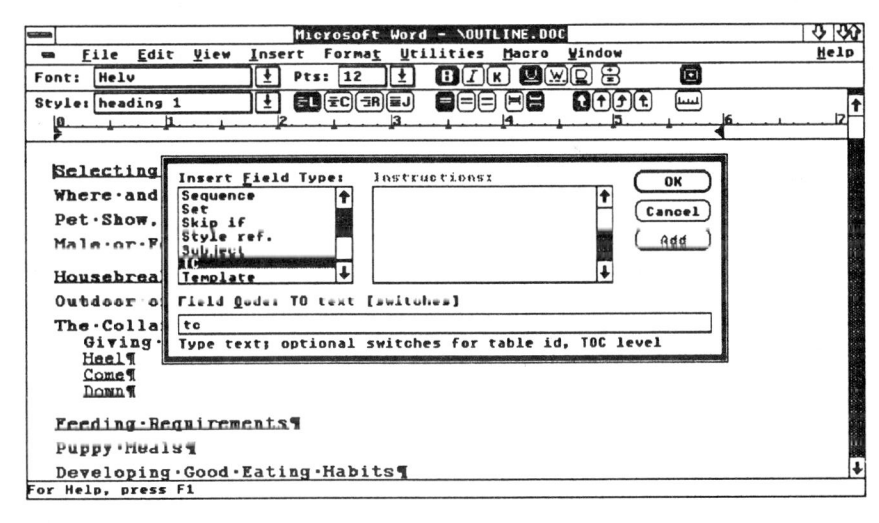

Figure 18.3 Either select or type TC in the Field Code edit box.

491

Advanced Word

4. If it's not there already, position the insertion point after the letters, tc, press the **Spacebar** once, and then type the text for the table of contents entry within quotation marks.

   The entry appears within quotation marks. See Figure 18.4.

5. Choose **OK** or press **Enter**.

   The text is assigned as a field code tc entry and you are returned to the main document window. The TOC entry appears in your document within a set of field code braces at the location of the insertion point. To view this, turn on the Hidden Text option on View Preferences.

6. For every table of contents entry, repeat steps 1 through 5.

7. Once you have assigned all the table of contents entries, the next step is to position the insertion point where you want the table of contents field itself to be compiled and printed. Then, choose the **Table of Contents** command from the Insert menu or press **Alt,I,C**.

   The Table of Contents dialog box appears.

8. To compile the table of contents, choose the **Use Table Entry Fields** option or press **Alt+E**, and then choose **OK** or press **Enter**.

   The table of contents is soon displayed on your screen at the location of the insertion point. Remember, make sure the Field Codes option is off or you will only see the field codes that Word inserts at the location of the insertion point (assuming the View Preferences Hidden Text option is on as well).

492

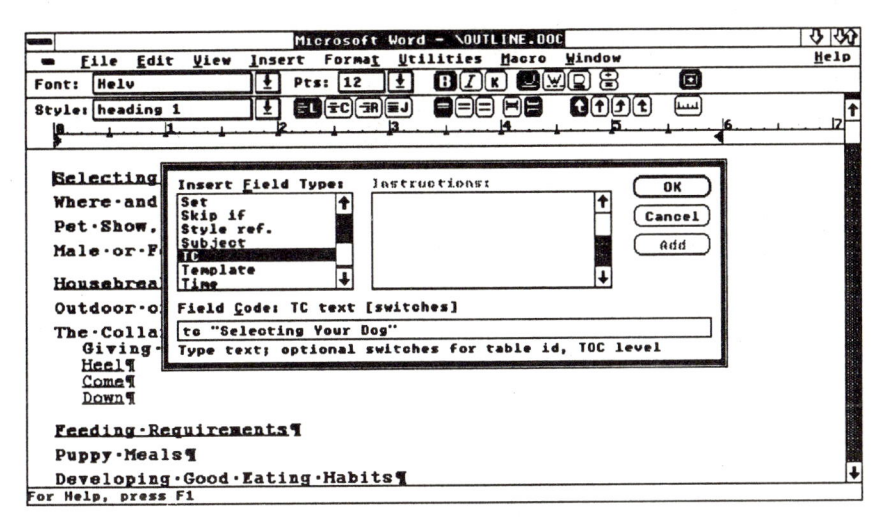

18—Adding Tables of Contents, Indexes, or Footnotes

Figure 18.4 A sample entry.

Word will format your table of contents according to the default toc automatic style codes regardless of which method you use to generate it. You can always reformat the table manually, however.

Creating Tables of Items

A list of tables is often useful in a reference document.

You've seen how to use Word's Table of Contents and Insert Field commands to compile and display a table of contents for your documents. Using the same procedures, you can also collect and compile a list of items that don't appear in a structured outline form. For example, you might wish to compile a list of figures, pictures, or tables that make up a chapter in a book. To do this, you have the option of applying style headings to selected text (either select it and apply the appropriate heading style or select it and demote it to an assigned heading level with Alt+Shift+right arrow). You can also insert a tc field code with the Insert Field command with a list identifier in much the same way as just discussed. Both procedures are detailed below.

Creating a Table of Items from an Outline

1. Select the text that you wish to collect into a list. For example, you might want to collect all tables. In this case, select an entire table.

   The selected text is highlighted.

493

Advanced Word

2. While the text is highlighted, either apply a heading style (use the style box on the Ruler) or demote the text to an assigned heading level. Microsoft suggests Heading 7 for figures, Heading 8 for tables, and Heading 9 for Photos.

3. Repeat steps 1 and 2 for all items that you wish to collect into a list.

4. Position the insertion point where you want the table of items to appear.

5. Select **Table of Contents** from the Insert menu or press **Alt,I,C**.

    The Table of Contents dialog box appears.

6. If it's not selected by default, choose **Use Heading Paragraphs (Alt+H)**.

7. In both the From and To boxes, type the number that represents the heading level that you wish to collect. For example, if you assigned all tables a heading level of 8, you'd type **8** in each.

8. Choose **OK** or press **Enter** to compile the list of items and display them at the location of the insertion point.

Creating a Table of Items Using Fields

1. Position the insertion point in front of the first table of items entry. If you want to enter new text as a table entry, position the insertion point where you want the entry to be inserted.

18—Adding Tables of Contents, Indexes, or Footnotes

2. From the Insert menu, select the **Field** command or press **Alt,I,D**.

   The Insert dialog box appears.

3. Either move to the Field Code box and type **tc**, or choose **TC** from the scroll window (see Figure 18.3) and then move to the Field Code box.

   The field code entry, tc, appears in the edit box.

4. If it's not there already, position the insertion point after the letters, tc, press the **Spacebar** once. Next, type the text for the list entry within quotation marks, press the **Spacebar**, type \f and press the **Spacebar** again, and then type a single text character that serves as a list identifier. For example, you might type f for figures, t for tables, p for photos, or c for contents (a Word default).

   The list entry might look something like Figure 18.5.

5. Choose **OK** or press **Enter**.

   The text is assigned as a field code tc entry and you are returned to the main document window.

6. For every item to be collected in the table, repeat steps 1 through 5.

7. Once you have assigned all the table entries, the next step is to position the insertion point where you want the table of items field itself to be compiled and printed. Then, choose the **Field** command from the Insert menu or press **Alt,I,D**.

   The Insert Field dialog box appears.

8. This time, choose or type the toc field code in the Field Code edit box.

495

Advanced Word

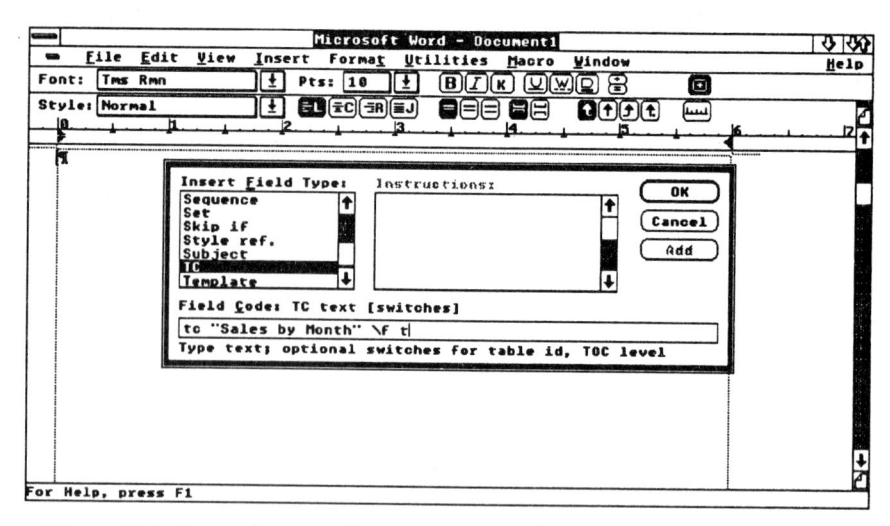

Figure 18.5 Correctly enter the text, spaces, and identifier in the edit box.

9. Position the insertion point after the letters toc, and type

   \f

   and press the **Spacebar**. Then, type the list identifier that matches the identifier in step 4. For example, if you entered t for table, type t to collect all tables with that identifier.

10. Choose **OK** or press **Enter**. Then, press F9, the Update Field key, to compile and create the table of items at the location of the insertion point.

Be sure to enter the proper spaces with the Spacebar. Your example will look something like this:

toc \f t

Creating Indexes

Making a useful index may be the most important task that you must do to complete a well-referenced document. It is also the most

496

tedious. Word helps, however, by providing the *Insert Index Entry* and *Index* commands. Similar to making a table of contents, you create an index in two steps:

1. Marking text as index entries by inserting Index Entry (XE) fields
2. Compiling the index entries and inserting the Index field itself with the Index command

Similar to the way you create a table of contents entry, you can create an index entry by inserting an index field code (XE) immediately *after* the text that you want to appear in the index. (You insert tc codes *in front of* table of contents entries.) Once you have identified all your index entries, position the insertion point where you want the Index field to be displayed and then choose the Insert Index command. The Index field is where all the Index entries will be compiled and listed. A handy feature of the Index field is that once you change, add, or delete index entries, you can use F9, the Update Field key, to provide an updated index.

Inserting Index Entries

Word provides more than one method to insert Index entries into your document. All methods generate a hidden index entry code (XE) that follows the text that you have identified as an index entry. The easiest method is to select the text in your document and then choose the **Index Entry** command from the Insert menu or type **Alt,I,E**. The selected text will appear in the Index Entry edit box, shown in Figure 18.6. To insert the index entry code, simply choose **OK**. To verify that the index entry is properly inserted, turn on the Hidden Text option found in View Preferences. Your index entry code would look something like Figure 18.7.

If you don't wish to first select the text, you can always choose the Insert Index command, type the text of the entry in the edit box, and then choose OK. It just seems easier to first select the text so that you get the spelling of the word correct.

Another method for inserting index entries is to first position the insertion point following the text for indexing and then choosing the **Insert Field** command or press **Alt,I,D**. As you discovered in creating tables of contents, you then scroll the list window to find the Index entry field code (XE), or type **XE** in the edit box, followed by a space and the entry text itself (see Figure 18.8). If the text is more than one word, enclose it within quotation marks.

Advanced Word

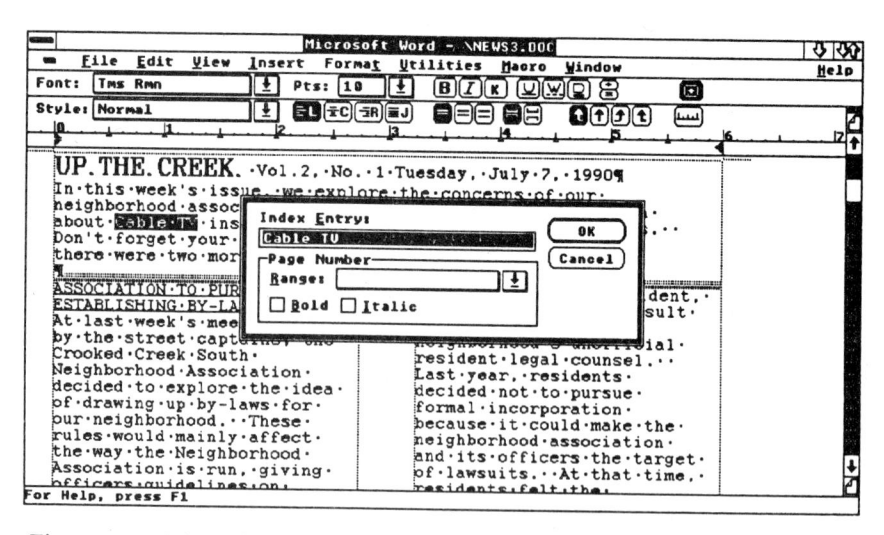

Figure 18.6 Selected text automatically appears in the Index Entry edit box.

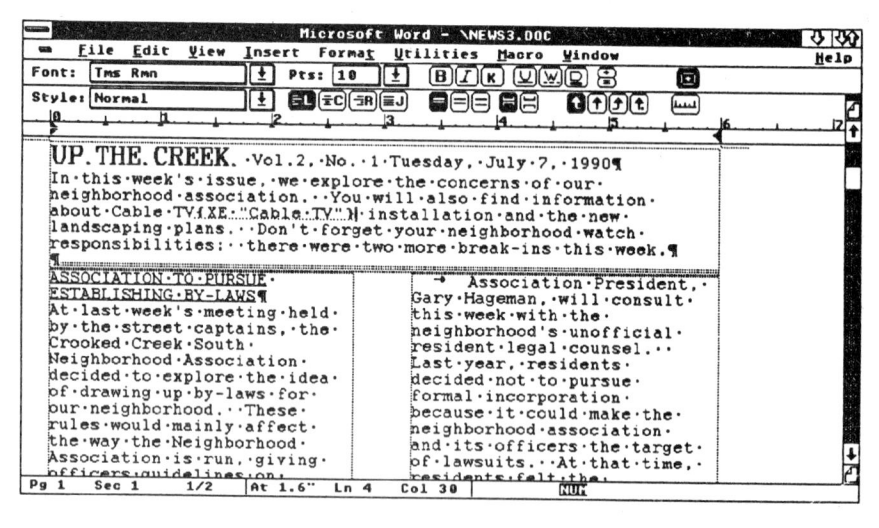

Figure 18.7 The Hidden Text option shows the index entry code in your document.

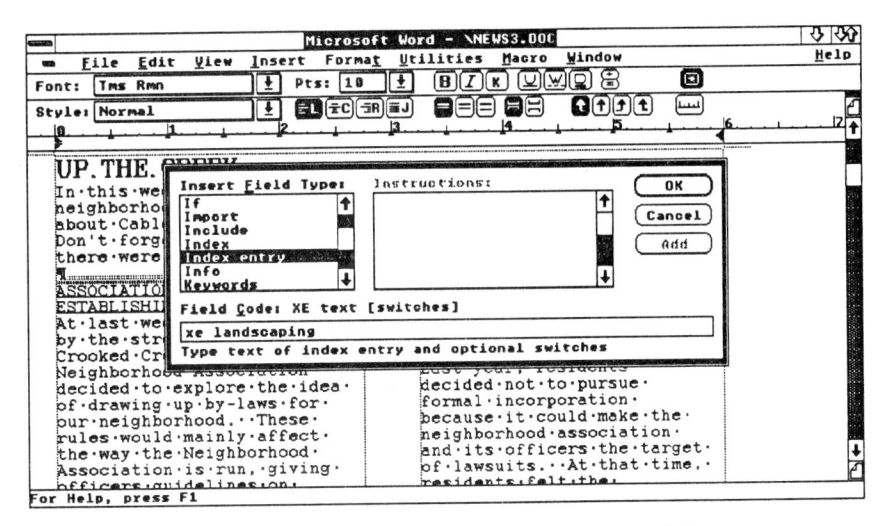

18—Adding Tables of Contents, Indexes, or Footnotes

Figure 18.8 Select or enter the field code (XE) and then type the index entry text.

Finally, you'd use **Ctrl+F9**, the Insert Field key combination, to insert the field delimiting brackets at the location of the insertion point. Remember to position the insertion point following the desired text for indexing. Pressing Ctrl+F9 produces the field code brackets with the insertion point on the inside. Type the index field code letters, **XE**, press the **Spacebar** once, and then type the entry text. If the text contains more than one word, enclose the text within quotation marks. For example, to index the phrase Blackberry Pie, type:

```
{XE "Blackberry Pie"}
```

Cross-References and Multiple-Level Index Entries

Word is quite a flexible tool for creating a variety of indexing possibilities. You can index all of your document, or just a portion of it. You can even index for a specific range of letters, such as from A to M or N to Z. Word also allows for more complex indexing. For example, you can cross-reference index entries by including a special switch (a back slash followed by a switch character) that separates the index entry and its cross-reference information. To illustrate, assume

499

Advanced Word

that you wish to index the word, Spaniel, and then cross-reference it with "house pet." To do this, you would take the following steps:

1. Position the insertion point after the indexed word: Spaniel.

   You might want to turn on the Hidden Text option in View Preferences so that you can see the effect of inserting your hidden index code when you have completed the task.

2. Press **Ctrl+F9**, the Insert Field key combination. You could also choose the **Insert Index** command and type **XE** in the Field Code edit box, but the first option is simpler.

   If the Hidden Text option is active, the field code character brackets appear.

3. Since the insertion point resides inside the field code characters (the brackets), simply type **XE**, a space, the entry text, a space, the text switch that tells Word to print the text instead of the page number, another space, and then the cross-reference text. If the text contains more than one word, enclose it within quotation marks. For this example, you'd type:

   {XE Spaniel \t "see House Pets"}

   where "see House Pets" is the cross-reference information that will print instead of the page number.

That's all there is to it. Now, suppose you wish to create a multiple-level index entry. For example, consider the following:

```
Spaniel
    Cocker,1
    OldEnglish,2
```

where Spaniel is the first level of indexing and both Cocker and Old English represent a second level of indexing. For this example, you would create the index entry as before but separate each level of entry with a colon (:). To accomplish this task, you would complete these steps:

1. Position the insertion point at the end of the text. In this example, at the end of Spaniel.

2. Select **Index Entry** from the Insert menu or press **Alt,I,E**.

   The Index Entry dialog appears.

3. Type the first level of the index entry, a colon, and the second level. You can continue indexing for additional levels by separating them with colons. For our example, you would type:

   Spaniel:Cocker

   and then choose **OK** or press **Enter**. For each second-level entry you would need to repeat these steps and enter the index entry separately.

The steps above show you how to insert multiple index entries and the steps previous to that highlighted the feature of including a field code separator switch in your entries. The switch options available to you include the \t switch for printing text in cross-referencing entries, \b for printing a boldface number, \; for printing an Italic number, and \bookmark to indicate a page range. You can also select these formatting options for printing your index by choosing the appropriate options in the Insert Index Entry dialog box (i.e., Bold, Italic, or a bookmark name in the Range edit box of the Page Number section). Now that you know how to insert index entries, you are ready to compile the index itself.

Compiling and Inserting the Index

Once you edit, add, or delete index entries, you can move the insertion point within the index itself, and then press F9, the Update Field key, to update the index.

Once you have identified and inserted all your index entries, you can use the Insert Index command to compile the Index and print it at the location of the insertion point. Thus, inserting the index is a simple process:

1. Position the insertion point.
2. Select **Index** from the Insert menu or press **Alt,I,I**.

   The Index dialog window appears as shown in Figure 18.9.

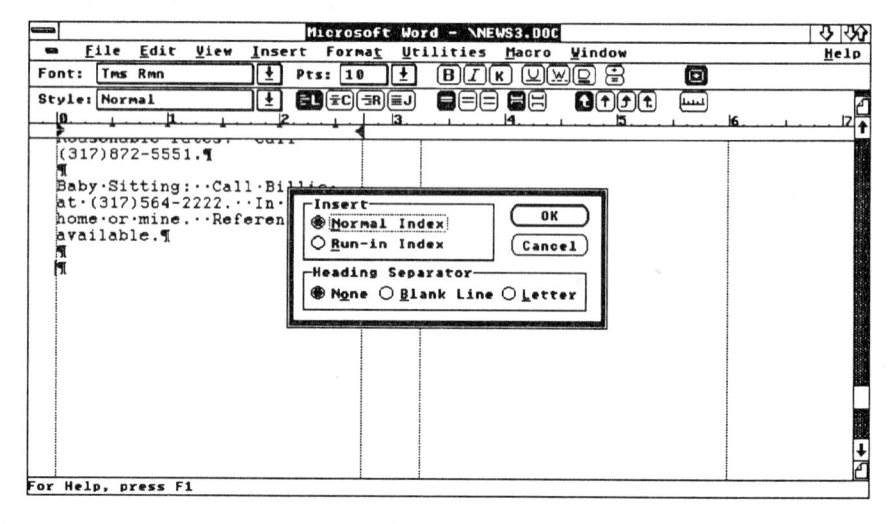

Figure 18.9 The Index dialog window.

3. Choose the format you prefer: either the default Normal style or the Run-In style.

   The Normal style, sometimes called *nested*, indicates that second-level index entries appear under the main entry. Run-in will show the second-level entries on the same line, wrapping to a new line when too long.

4. You also have the option of choosing a heading separator (None, Blank line, or Letter).

   Blank line places a blank line at the beginning of each letter section while the Letter option prints the letter of the following section, using the default Index Heading style.

5. Once you've made all your selections, choose **OK** or press **Enter**.

Soon your index is compiled; the index field itself is inserted and displayed at the location of the insertion point.

Deleting and Saving Indexes

To delete an index from your document, select the entire index field, and then use the **Cut** command from the Edit menu or press the **Delete** key. In other words, you can erase or edit the contents of the index just like any other portion of your document. If you wish to save the index, choose the **Save** command from the File menu to save the last changes that you made (i.e., the new index).

Creating Footnotes

If you've ever written a term paper, you know what a pain it is to incorporate footnotes into your document. Creating footnotes in Word is easy, however. Using the *Footnotes* command from the Insert menu (Alt,I,N), place the insertion point where you want the footnote reference marker to appear, choose the command, and then, while it is still fresh in your mind, type the footnote text in a footnote pane of the document window. Adding footnotes as you go prevents having to search for material to reference when you've finished the document. The best part is that Word keeps track of the footnotes by numbering them automatically and if you edit your text later, deleting or adding footnotes, Word will adjust the footnote numbers accordingly. When you're ready to print your document, you tell Word where to print them via the Footnotes section of the Document command dialog box.

Use the following set of steps as your guide to adding a footnote to your document.

1. Position the insertion point where you want the footnote reference mark to appear. You will have the option of choosing your own custom footnote reference mark in step 2.

2. Choose the **Footnotes** command from the Insert menu or press **Alt,I,N**.

   The Footnote dialog box appears (see Figure 18.10).

3. The Auto-numbered Reference box is checked by default. If you want your own reference marker, such as a special symbol or author name, enter the character(s) in the Footnote Reference Mark section. You can enter as many as ten characters in this section.

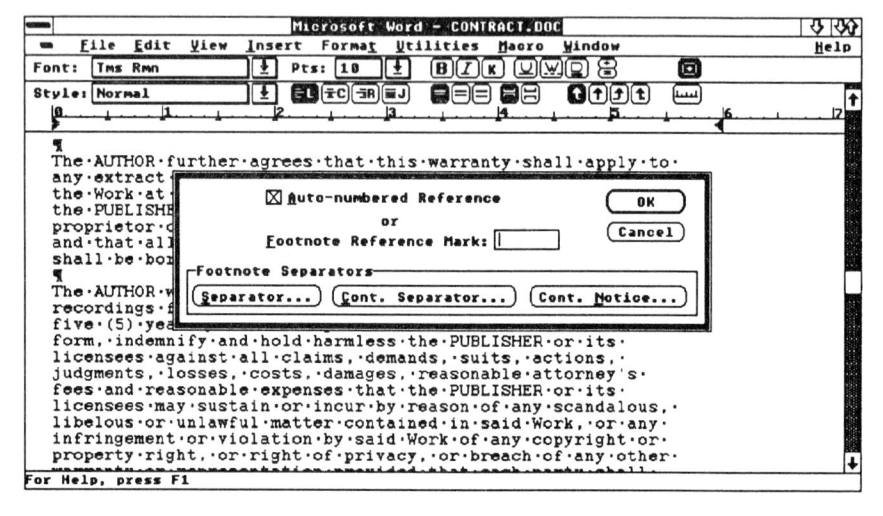

Figure 18.10 The Footnote dialog box automatically numbers your footnotes by default.

4. Click **OK** or press **Enter**.

   Word splits your document window into two parts at the location of the reference marker. The top part is the document window while the bottom half of the screen is the active footnote pane (see Figure 18.11). A footnote number will appear just to the right of the insertion point.

5. Enter the footnote text in the footnote pane.

Your text appears as you type.

6. When you have finished typing your footnote text, press **F6** to return to the document window. The footnote pane will remain open. If you wish to open or close the pane, choose the View **Footnotes** command or press **Alt,V,F**.

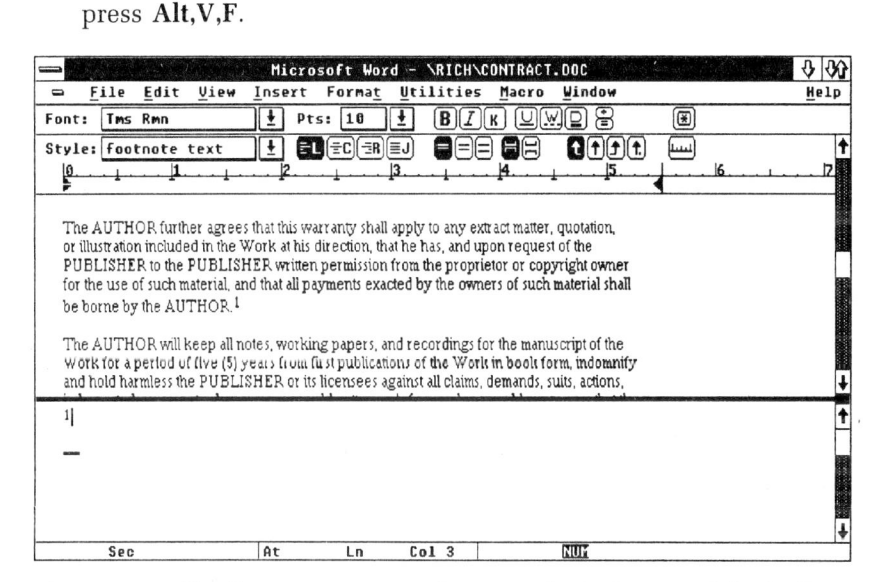

Figure 18.11 The Footnotes command opens a footnote pane at the bottom of the screen.

Editing Footnotes

You can edit or format text in a footnote pane just like any other text. To do this, choose the Footnotes command from the View menu and edit away. You can also access the footnote pane by choosing the Go To option (or pressing F5), typing f for footnote and then pressing Enter. Pressing Enter will jump your document from one footnote to another.

To close a footnote window, drag the split bar to the bottom of the window or double-click it. To open the footnote window again, double-click the reference mark or press Shift while dragging the split bar down the scroll bar.

Deleting Footnotes

To delete a footnote, select the reference mark in the document and choose the Cut command from the Edit menu. Simply deleting the text within a footnote pane will not delete the footnote itself. The footnote reference mark will remain in the footnote pane until it is deleted.

How and Where a Footnote Appears

Three separator options appear at the bottom of the Footnote dialog box (see Figure 18.10). These allow you to change the separator Word uses between the main text and the footnotes themselves. (The default setting is a 2″ line.) You use the Separator option to divide the main text and the footnotes at the bottom of the page where the reference mark appears. Use the Cont. Separator option to separate footnotes that carry over from one page to the next or to indicate that one or more footnotes will carry over to the next page; this option is blank by default.

The footnotes can appear at four different places in a document: at the bottom of the page, beneath text, or at the end of a section or the document. You can choose any of these four options in the Footnotes section of the Document dialog window in the Format menu (press Alt,T,D). In addition, you can even set the starting number for the first automatically numbered footnote reference. If your document contains more than one section, you can choose to restart the numbering sequence for each footnote with those individual sections.

Using Bookmarks

The bookmark concept was introduced in our discussion of the main document in creating form letters and the like in earlier chapters.

Even if you are just a casual reader, you've probably come across the term "bookmark." Similar to the tools that you may have used to mark positions in a book, you can use a Word bookmark to help you keep track of items or entire sections of text. A bookmark can contain anything, including text, tables, pictures, or several chapters in a book. In other words, you can use a bookmark as a name that you attach to selected text for many purposes, including:

- A "quick jump" reference for finding a particular place in your text. This feature utilizes the Go To command from the Edit menu or F5, the Go To key, that we introduced in Chapter 3.

- A label for specific text that you wish to perform a particular function with, including calculating (remember the table feature for setting up calculations like a spreadsheet), copying, moving, or cross-referencing. For example, you might wish to name a section in your business plan as "financial analysis."

Creating a Bookmark

Once you get a handle on creating and inserting bookmarks, you'll appreciate their many uses. Use the following steps to set a bookmark:

1. Select the text that you wish to name as a bookmark. Be sure to select all of the text, including pictures, captions, and tables. If you wish, you can simply select an insertion point.	The selected text appears highlighted.
2. Choose the **Bookmark** command from the Insert menu or press **Alt,I,M**.	The Insert Bookmark dialog box appears as shown in Figure 18.12.

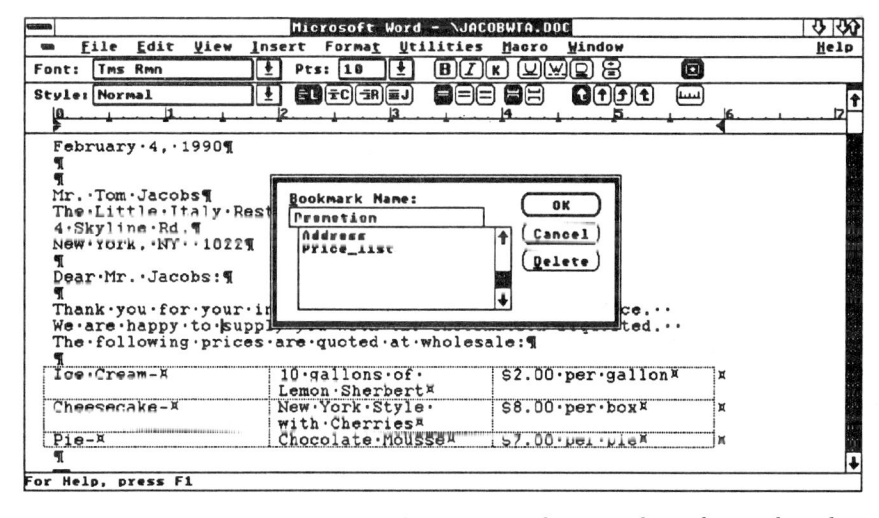

Figure 18.12 Type the bookmark name or select one from the Bookmark Name box to redefine it.

3. Type the name for your bookmark. The name can be from one to twenty characters long and must begin with a letter. It may include numbers and alphabetic and underline characters, but not spaces, colons, or any other characters. Each bookmark name must be unique within a document, but you can use the same name within different documents. Examples include: Schedule, Days-of-the-Week, Time-Study, Quarterly-Sales.

   The name that you enter appears in the Bookmark Name edit box.

4. Choose **OK** or press **Enter**.

   The bookmark is set.

Jumping to a Bookmark

There are two ways to jump to a bookmark, using the Go To command or F5, the Go To key. One command method is to choose the **Go To** command or press **Alt,E,G**; type or select the bookmark name from the Bookmark Name box; and then choose **OK** to jump. The second method is to first press the **F5** key, type the bookmark name in response to the prompt at the bottom of the screen, and then press **Enter**. If you don't remember a bookmark name you've used, press the F5 key a second time, which will list the bookmarks, and then select one from the list before choosing OK. Either way, Word will jump to and select the text represented by the bookmark.

Editing and Deleting Bookmarks

If you decide that the bookmark name represents the wrong selection of text, select the correct section of text, and then choose the **Bookmark** command from the Insert menu or press **Alt,I,M**. Type the existing bookmark name or select it from the Bookmark Name box. Choose **OK** or press **Enter** to redefine the bookmark.

If you wish to erase the bookmark, simply choose **Bookmark** (**Alt,I,M**), type the name of the bookmark or select it from the list box, and then choose the **Delete** button or press **Alt+D**. Choosing the

18—Adding Tables of Contents, Indexes, or Footnotes

Delete button removes the bookmark from the Bookmark Name list, but leaves the dialog box open. Choose **OK** or **Cancel** to close the dialog box. Remember, though, if you choose Cancel after you delete a bookmark, the bookmark remains deleted.

Review

In this chapter you learned:

1. To create a table of contents, use the outliner or the fields method. Both options use the Table of Contents command from the Insert menu.

2. To create a table of contents using Word's outliner, you must first apply heading styles to your document. Otherwise, Word will indicate that no entries exist.

3. When you create a table of contents, Word places the table (the field) at the location of the insertion point. To erase it, select the table and choose the Cut command or press Delete. Like all changes to a document, you must save a table of contents or it will be lost at the time you close the document file.

4. To use the field code method, you place a hidden TOC entry field code in front of the text where the entry field code is to appear and then select the Insert Field command. Select the tc code from the Field box and then type the desired text entry within quotation marks. Press OK and the text is assigned as a field code tc entry. The number of such entries in a document is unlimited.

5. To compile a table of contents based on entry field codes, you choose the Use Table Entry Fields option found on the Insert Table of Contents dialog box. The table of contents field is always set at the location of the insertion point.

6. Similar to creating a table of contents with the Insert Fields command, you can compile and display a list of items, such as figures, pictures, tables, and so on.

7. Word also enables you to compile an index. Similar to creating a table of contents, choose the Index Entry command from the Insert menu to mark text as an index entry, and then compile the index entries and insert the Index field itself with the Index command.

Advanced Word

8. To delete an index, select the entire index field and then choose Cut or press the Delete key.

9. To create a footnote, position the insertion point where you want the footnote marker to appear in your document, choose the Insert Footnote command to open a footnote pane, and then type the footnote text. To switch back and forth between an open footnote pane and the document pane, press F6.

10. To edit a footnote, choose the Footnotes command from the View menu or choose the Go To command or F5 key, and type f for footnote. Pressing Enter will jump your document from one footnote to another.

11. To close a footnote, double-click the split bar or drag it to the bottom of the document window. To open a footnote again, you can double-click the reference mark or press Shift while dragging the split bar. You can also choose the Footnotes command to act as a toggle between opening and closing a footnote pane.

12. To delete a footnote, select the reference mark in the document and then choose Cut. Deleting text from a footnote pane will not delete the footnote itself.

13. You can attach a bookmark to a selection of text for a quick-jump reference for finding a particular place in your document or as a text label.

14. To create a bookmark, select the text that you wish to name as a bookmark, choose the Bookmark command from the Insert menu, type the name of the bookmark, and press OK.

15. You can jump to a bookmark using the Go To command or F5, the shortcut Go To key. Either way, Word will jump to and select the text represented by the bookmark.

16. You can easily reassign bookmark text to a particular bookmark name or delete the bookmark using the Bookmark dialog box.

NINETEEN

Customizing Word and Using Macros

In this chapter:

- Preferences to Suit You
- Reviewing the Customize Command
- Introducing Macros
- Using and Running Word's Free Macros
- Creating New Macros
- Editing a Macro
- Customizing Existing Menus and Keys

In this chapter you'll learn about the many ways that you can customize Word to suit your needs. First, we'll look at how Word treats your documents by default and how to change those options. Then, we'll look at how Word appears on your screen and how you can make changes here too. A big part of this chapter, however, is learning how to use, create, and run macros to make your life easier. Finally, using commands on the Macro menu, you will learn how to customize the menus or commands given by specific keys so they work the way you work. We have a lot to cover in this chapter, so let's dig in.

Preferences to Suit You

If you have been reading this book cover to cover, you have learned a great deal about how Word works, and how it appears on your screen.

Advanced Word

You have also learned that the Preferences command found on the View menu provides several options that affect how your screen will appear as you work through your documents. Choosing Preferences or pressing Alt,V,E will provide a dialog box, shown in Figure 19.1, that you can use to adjust the screen. The default settings are marked with an X.

When you first turn Word on, the default selections that are turned on include: Vertical Scroll Bar, Display as Printed, and Picture Display. The remaining options are originally turned off. To turn them on, either click inside the box or press the Alt key followed by the underlined letter of the command. When you quit Word after making your choices, Word saves them and applies them automatically when you begin your next work session. The following is a summary of the options found in Preferences:

- Tabs—Displays the tab characters as a right arrow.
- Spaces—Displays spaces as dots between characters. Nonbreaking spaces will appear as degree symbols.
- Paragraph Marks—Displays the paragraph mark when you press Enter, and Newline characters when you press Shift+Enter. End-of-cell markers in tables are displayed as a sun-like character.
- Optional Hyphens—Normal hyphens appear as hyphens (-). Nonbreaking hyphens appear as double-long hyphens (—).
- Hidden Text—All hidden text appears with a dotted underline when this option is turned on.
- Show All—When you select this option, all the options in the left column, as well as Table Gridlines and Text Boundaries, are selected.
- Display as Printed—When this option is selected, you can see tabs, line breaks, and character formatting exactly as they will appear when printed. Of course, like a lot of formatting, some options are limited by the type of printer that you are using. If the option is turned off, your screen will allow you to see all formatting options that you might select, even if your printer cannot print it that way.
- Pictures—When this option is selected, pictures are visible. Turn it off and pictures will not appear, only an empty box frame.
- Text Boundaries—When this option is selected, you'll see the boundaries of such elements as margins, headers, and positioned objects while working in Page View.

- Horizontal and Vertical Scroll Bars—These are useful if you have a mouse to move around the scroll boxes. Use them to move left to right in a wide document or up and down in a long document.
- Table Gridlines—When using the Table command, this option allows you to see the invisible nonprinting lines between cells in a table.
- Style Area Width—A positive decimal measurement. If you enter a zero, the style area is closed.

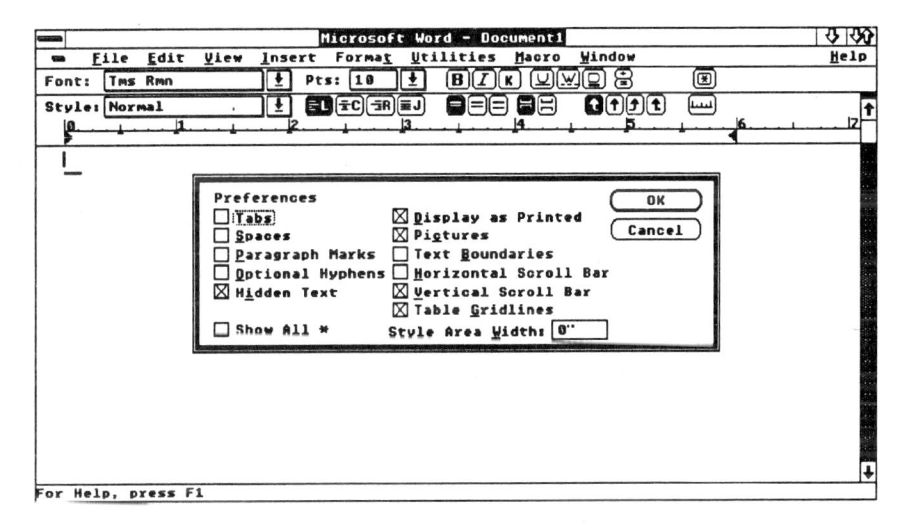

Figure 19.1 Use Preferences to change how your screen will appear.

Reviewing the Customize Command

Some additional general Word options are adjusted by making selections using the Customize command from the Utilities menu or pressing Alt,U,U (see Figure 19.2). To change from one of the default selections (those blackened or marked with an x), simply click inside the selection with the mouse, or press the Alt key followed by the underlined letter of the selection. The options are summarized here:

- Autosave Frequency—This Customize option enables you to tell Word to automatically prompt you at regular intervals for the purpose of saving your document. These intervals are at frequencies that you set (High, Low, Medium, and the default, Never). The ranges for these frequencies are set as follows:

Low frequency: 30–60 minutes

Medium frequency: 20–45 minutes

High frequency: 10–30 minutes

When you elect one of these frequencies, Word will automatically prompt you with the message shown in Figure 19.3. You can elect to save the changes made to the document at that time, or you can postpone saving it for a while by typing the amount of minutes in the Edit box and choosing OK. If you choose Cancel, the Autosave Frequency is reset and the countdown to the next message starts.

Note: The more editing you do in a document, the more often Word will display the Autosave prompt. The individual changes you make to a document are measured in kilobytes. When either 16 kilobytes (the maximum amount of changes) have been used, or the time interval that you set passes, Word will display the message.

- Units of Measure—This option allows you to change from the default Inches measurement to Centimeters, Points, or Picas. If you change the unit of measure here, however, Word assumes that all measurements are to be in your elected unit of measure, including the unit of measure illustrated by Word's Ruler. You can leave the default at inches and still specify an alternate unit of measure in a measurement field, when appropriate. As an example, you could type cm (for centimeter) after a number to change that number's measurement unit.
- Background Pagination—Instructs Word to automatically paginate your document as you add, delete, or modify text. This option is selected by default.
- Prompt for Summary Info—When this selection is on, the Summary Info dialog box will appear automatically when you save a new document. This option is also selected as a default option.
- Typing Replaces Selection—When this option is on, you can select text and then type any keystroke to delete the text and replace it with the new keystroke. If the option is off, then the new keystrokes are simply inserted into selected text at the beginning of the selection. The one exception to this is that pressing the Delete key will always erase the selection, regardless of whether the Typing Replaces Selection option is on or not.

19—Customizing Word and Using Macros

- **Your Name**—Use this box to enter your name in the Author box that appears in the Summary Info dialog box. If you don't want people to know you as the author, erase your name and leave this box blank.
- **Your Initials**—The initials in this box will appear in annotation marks.

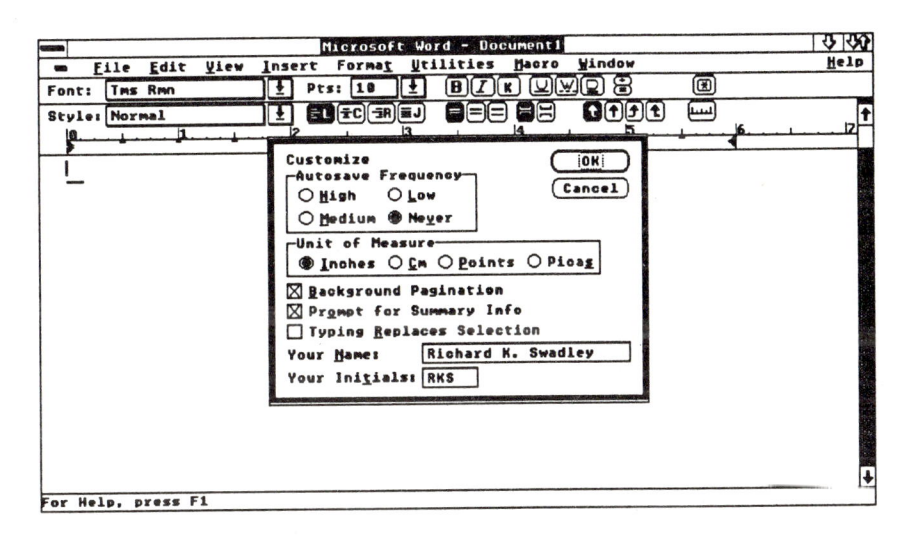

Figure 19.2 You can adjust some of Word's operations to work the way you do.

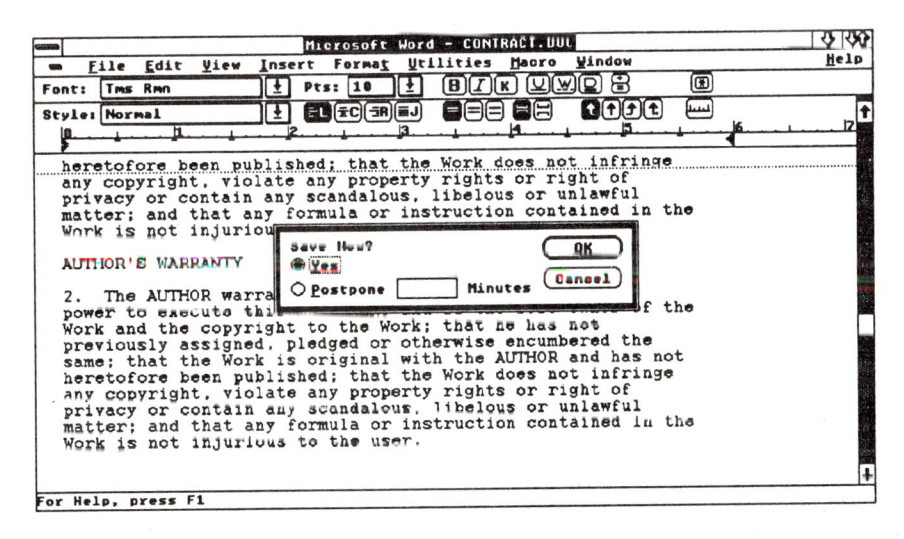

Figure 19.3 Word's Autosave feature prompts you to save your document.

515

Introducing Macros

Using macros simplifies your work sessions.

One of the best features of powerful word processing programs is to make complicated tasks simple. And, Word for Windows is no exception. In this section we will introduce the concept of a macro. By definition, a macro is a set of instructions that automate a more complex task. Generally, a macro defines a sequence of actions involving many keystrokes, such as selecting text, choosing commands from menus, setting formatting options in dialog boxes, typing, and so on. With a macro, you can record the sequence of actions and then perform the entire sequence by choosing a single command or pressing a key or two. Once the macro is created, you can use it as many times as you wish.

As you become a more advanced Word user, you'll learn all about Word's macro language as well as Word BASIC, the embedded programming language built into Word. We will not explore Word BASIC in this book, but you will find all the information you need in the reference section of Word's user's manual.

What we will cover here is how to create your own simple macros and how to use Word's supplied macros to do a variety of tasks. If you create your own macros, you can set them as global for use with all documents, or you can limit the macro for use on a specific type of document. The key point to using macros is that they are intended to enhance your productivity. Whether you find one of Word's free macros helpful, or you need to create your own, rest assured that the steps are simple to follow and easy to use.

Using and Running Word's Supplied Macros

Macros run without displaying all the menus and keystrokes that make up the macro itself (although you can program it to prompt you for information if you wish). In other words, a macro runs "behind the scenes" and simply accomplishes the task as you have defined it. You can select from a variety of macros that are supplied free with Word. You access these macros through the Run command found on the Macro menu. Use the following steps to run one of Word's supplied macros.

19—Customizing Word and Using Macros

It might be a good idea to save your document before you run a macro. That way, if you make a mistake and run the wrong macro, your original document remains safe.

1. Choose **Run** from the Macro menu or press **Alt,M,R**.

2. To see the list of macros supplied with Word, choose the **Show All** button (**Alt+A**).

3. Select a macro name from the list window (click with the mouse or press the up and down arrow keys to move through the list).

4. Once you select your macro, simply choose **OK** or press **Enter**.

The Macro Run command appears.

All macros as well as Word commands appear in a list window.

The selected macro's name appears in the Run Macro Name list box while a short description of the macro appears in the Description box. For example, if you select the first macro name, AppMaximize, the description tells you that running this macro will enlarge the application window to its full size (see Figure 19.4).

The macro runs "invisibly" and shortly the sequence of instructions assigned to the macro name are completed.

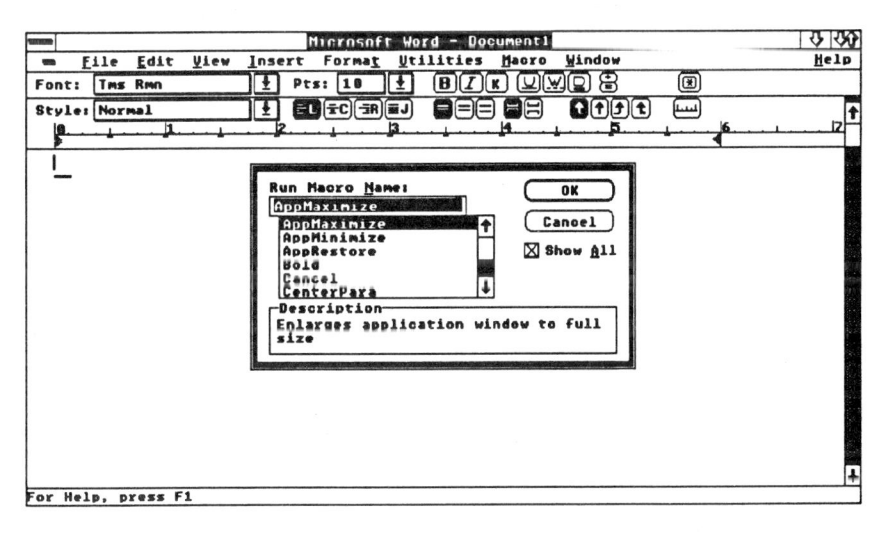

Figure 19.4 Access Word's supplied macros with the Macro Run command.

You will find that you can run any of Word's supplied macros or any new macros that you might create using these steps. Later, you will learn how to run macros by choosing them from a menu or pressing specific key combinations. But first, let's learn how to create macros customized to fit your needs.

Creating New Macros

Building your own macros is a four-step process.

As you begin to master Word, you'll find yourself performing many tasks repeatedly. Instead of reinventing the wheel every time, you can program these tasks into macros. Word provides two methods for creating macros. One method is to use the Assign to Key and Assign to Menu commands. Using these commands, you will type or choose representations for keystrokes and commands and assign them to a specific key combination or menu. This method is useful for creating simple macros, such as assigning keys to boldface text. For more complex macros, you use the *Macro Record* command to record a series of two or more keystrokes and commands. It is this latter method that we will discuss first. We'll discuss the Assign to Key and Assign to Menu commands at the end of this chapter.

The easiest way to understand how to create your own macros is to divide the process into the following steps:

1. Plan your macro. This step requires that you thoroughly map out what you want to accomplish. Sometimes it's handy to go through all the steps of choosing commands, performing the keystrokes manually, and writing them down on a piece of paper.
2. Record the macro. Once you have determined all the steps necessary to create the macro, choose the Macro Record command, name the macro, select its context (whether it's to be available for all documents or just the active document), perform the actions to record, and stop the recorder.
3. Run the macro to see if it works the way you intended.
4. Edit the macro. If the macro didn't perform the right way in step 3, or if you just wish to change it, you can use the *Macro Edit* command to change it. Then, run the macro to test the result.

Now that we have defined the steps for creating a macro, let's get some practice by working through a practical example. The next section guides you step by step.

Planning and Recording a Macro

Perhaps the best way to learn how to create a macro, is to just do it. For example, let's do a little planning. Suppose you find yourself creating the same general letter to many people. During the creation of such a letter, you make notes of the commands used to create specific elements as follows:

- You like to format your documents with 2" left and right margins. Choose the Format Document command to do so.
- You like the return address always centered and boldfaced. You also like the 13-pt Helvetica font. Other style choices you make include the center alignment icon from the Ruler and the boldface icon. Note: You could also choose the Paragraph and Character commands to select such options.
- You press Enter two times to separate the return address and the date of the letter.
- You choose to enter the rest of the letter in the default 10-pt Times Roman font using justified text alignment. Choose these options from the Ruler or the Paragraph and Character command dialog boxes.
- You choose one-and-a-half spacing with the Paragraph command.
- You set your tabs at 1" instead of the 1/2" default. Choose the Document command and type in the appropriate value.

Now that you have planned out your macro, complete the following steps to create it.

1. Choose the **Record** command from the Macro menu or press **Alt,M,C**.

   The Record dialog box appears, as shown in Figure 19.5.

2. Type a macro name in the Name edit box. Follow the same naming conventions as used with other files (i.e., eight characters). For our example, enter

   ltrsetup

3. Choose the context for the macro, either the default Global or Template. Global

   For our example, Global is left selected.

519

Advanced Word

allows you to use the macro with all documents while Template limits it to the document template of the active document. Note: The Template option will appear dim if your current document is not based on a document template. To use this option, you first need to create a document template.

4. As an option, you can type a short description for the macro that you are creating. In the Description edit window (**Alt+D**), type something like:

   Sets up page layout for general letter.

   Once the description is assigned to the macro, you must use the Macro Edit command to change it.

5. Choose **OK** or press **Enter**.

   The recorder is now on. Your screen appears empty just as if you were starting a new document.

6. The next step is to perform all the actions that you wish to record for this macro. For our example, complete the following actions. Remember, Word is recording all your actions.

   Choose **Format Document** or press **Alt,T,D**.

   Press **Alt+L** and type **1**.

   Press **Alt+R** and type **1**.

   Press **Alt+D** and type **1** (sets tab stops at 1").

   Choose **OK** to set the options and Close the Document dialog window.

520

Choose **Ribbon** and **Ruler** from the View menu, if necessary.

Choose **Roman**, 14-pt, from the Ribbon's style and size box (or choose from the Character command dialog box. Remember to close the dialog box if you use it.)

Choose **Bold** from the Ribbon.

Choose the **center** icon from the Ruler (or from the Paragraph command dialog box).

Type the return address. (Note that when you run this macro, you may need to format each line of the address separately. A possible solution is to use the Shift+Enter method to set the entire address as a single paragraph.)

James L. Bluebird Company
12 Feeder Avenue
Columbus, Ohio 11017
(512) 477-3000

Press **Enter** two times.

Choose **justified** alignment from the Ruler or Paragraph command.

Choose **Times Roman, 10-pt** font from the Ruler or Character command.

Choose **one-and-a-half spacing** from the Ruler or Paragraph command.

Turn off bold: A quick way is to type **Ctrl+B** to toggle off this option.

7. Once you have performed all the necessary setup actions in step 6, choose the **Stop Recorder** command from the Macro menu or press **Alt,M,C**.

That's all there is to it. You've created your first macro. Your screen will still show the results of the last actions you performed while creating the macro. Now you should close this document window and open a new document window.

Once you have created your macro, you're ready for the next step—running and testing your macro. Keep one point in mind: Though you have created the macro, it will remain safe and available to you only while you are still working in Word. The macro isn't saved just yet. When you exit Word, Word will ask: "Save global glossary and command changes?" Choose Yes to save the macro as a glossary file. Then the next time you start Word, the macro is available.

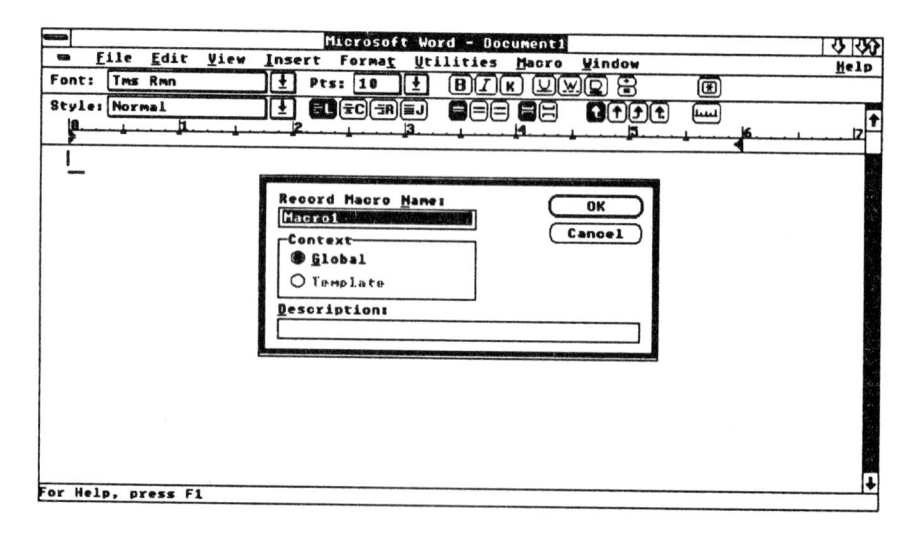

Figure 19.5 The Record dialog box.

19—Customizing Word and Using Macros

Running and Testing Your Macros

It's always a good idea to test your macro before you use it with an important document. Save any existing document, then test your new macro.

Now that you've created a macro, the next step is to run the macro to see if it meets your needs. To do this, begin with a new document window, and then complete the following steps:

1. Choose **Run** from the Macro menu or press **Alt,M,R**.

   The Run dialog box appears.

2. If necessary, choose the **Show All** (**Alt+A**) option to display all the available macros in the list window.

3. Scroll the Name list window and select the macro that you wish to run. For our example, select **ltrsetup**.

   The selected macro is highlighted (see Figure 19.6).

4. Choose **OK** or press **Enter**.

   Word soon builds your macro as you designed it. The result should look something like Figure 19.7.

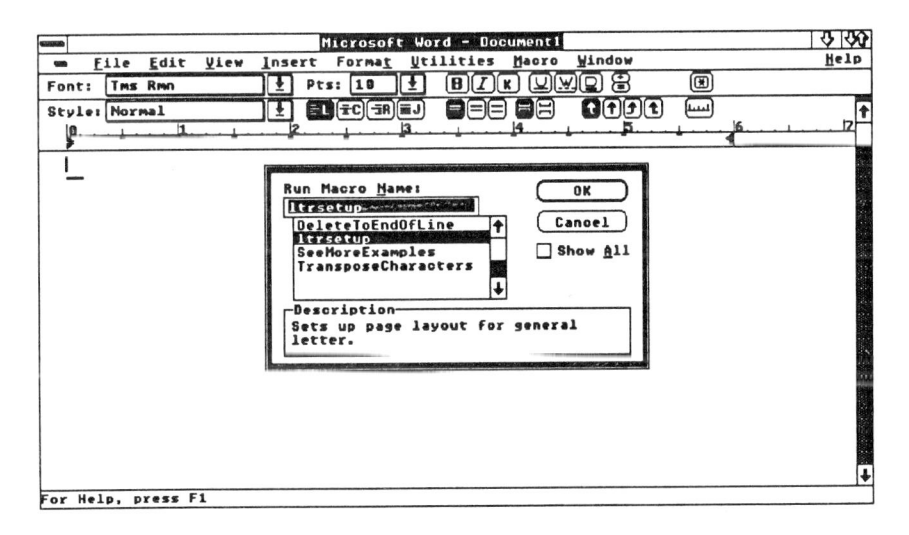

Figure 19.6 Select the macro name that you wish to run.

523

Advanced Word

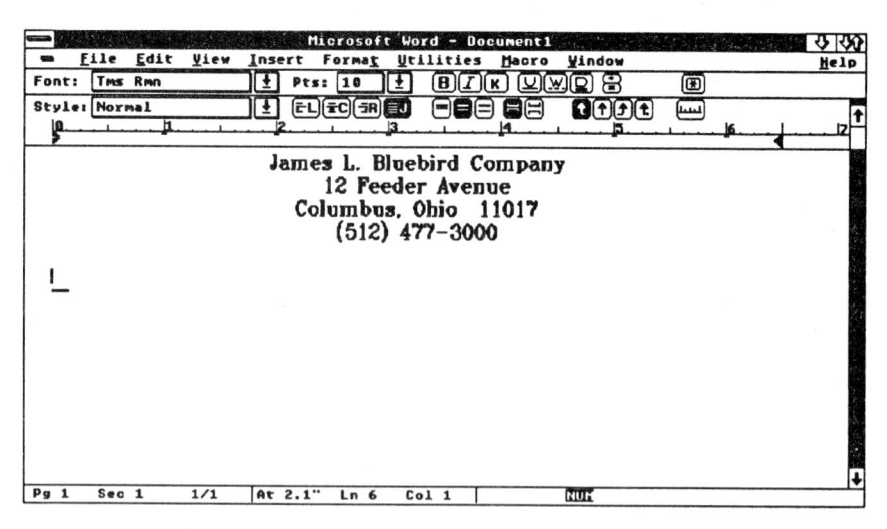

Figure 19.7 A successfully executed sample macro.

Editing a Macro

If you have created a short macro, and you decide it's not for you, the easiest method of changing it is to record it again. By choosing the Macro Record command and selecting the same name, Word will ask you if you want to "Replace existing macro?" Choose Yes to record or change the macro.

If your macro is long and complex, though, you may wish to use the Edit command on the Macro menu to decipher the macro language used to create the macro. To interpret all the macro programming language statements, you will need to refer to the "Macros" section of the *Microsoft Word for Windows Technical Reference* manual. The information in the manual is not too difficult to understand, but it does require some time and effort. Experience with BASIC programming is helpful. Once you have mastered the macro programming statements and functions, you can use the following steps to edit your macros:

1. Choose the **Edit** command from the Macro menu or press **Alt,M,E**.

    The Edit dialog box appears.

2. From the Macro Name list window, type or select the macro that you wish to edit. For example, choose the **ltrsetup** macro that we just created.

   The selected macro name is highlighted. If you type in a macro name not in the list, Word starts to create a new macro.

3. Choose **OK** or press **Enter**.

   The program representing the macro that you selected appears in a macro editing window. The macro program for ltrsetup appears in Figure 19.8.

4. Edit the macro using the *Technical Reference* as your guide. You can use many of the editing tools available in standard documents. As an exercise, for example, position the insertion point at the beginning of the fourth line where the definition of tabs is given (.DefTabs = "1"). Change the tab definition back to 1/2" by deleting the 1 and entering .5 instead. When you close the window in the next step, Word will give you the option of saving this change.

5. **Close** the macro editing window (**Alt,-,C**).

Renaming Your Macro

If you're not satisfied with the name given to a macro, you can easily rename it. To do this, complete the following:

1. Choose the **Edit** command from the Macro menu or press **Alt,M,E**.

   The Edit dialog box appears.

2. Select the macro name that you wish to rename.

   The macro name is highlighted.

Advanced Word

Figure 19.8 Your macro appears in a macro editing window.

3. Choose the **Rename** button.

   The Rename dialog box appears as shown in Figure 19.9.

4. Type the new name that you want to give the macro.

5. Choose **OK** or press **Enter**. Choose **Cancel** if you change your mind about renaming the macro.

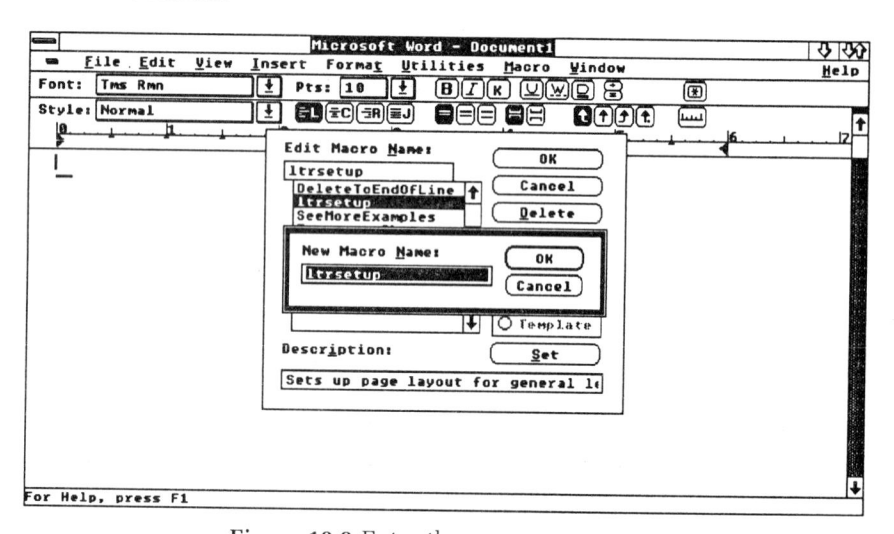

Figure 19.9 Enter the new macro name.

526

Assigning Your Macro to a Menu

Once you create a new macro, you will find it easier to access if you place it directly in the Macro menu itself. This feature allows you to choose the name of the macro from the menu and run it in a single step. Thus, you sidestep the need to choose the Macro Run command separately, and then search for a specific macro among a large list of available macros. This time-saving feature is accomplished with the following steps:

1. Choose the **Assign to Menu** command from the Macro menu or press **Alt,M,M**.

    The Assign to Menu dialog box appears, as shown in Figure 19.10.

2. From the Name box, select the macro name that you wish to assign. For our example, choose **ltrsetup**.

    The selected macro name is highlighted.

3. From the Menu box, select **&Macro**. (You will need to scroll down the list to find this option.)

    All selected options appear as shown in Figure 19.11.

4. Choose **Assign**.

    The ltrsetup macro name now appears in the Menu Text list window.

5. Choose **OK** to assign the macro name and close the dialog box.

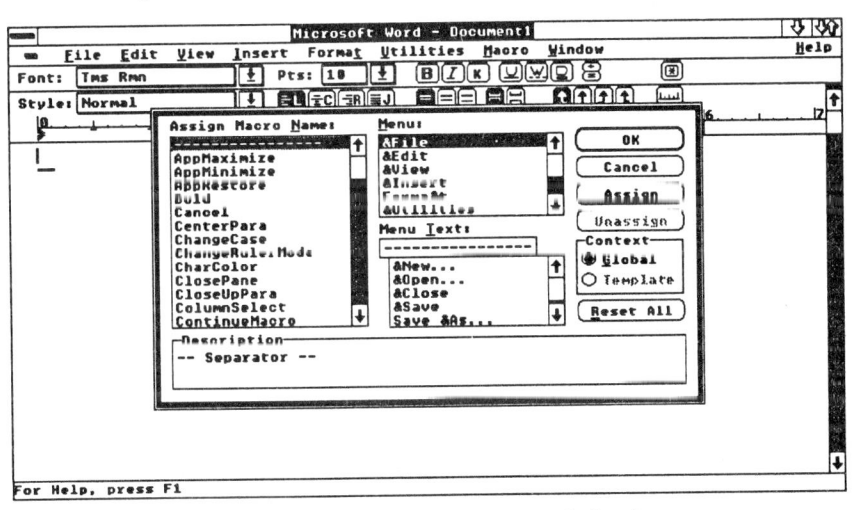

Figure 19.10 The Assign to Menu dialog box.

Advanced Word

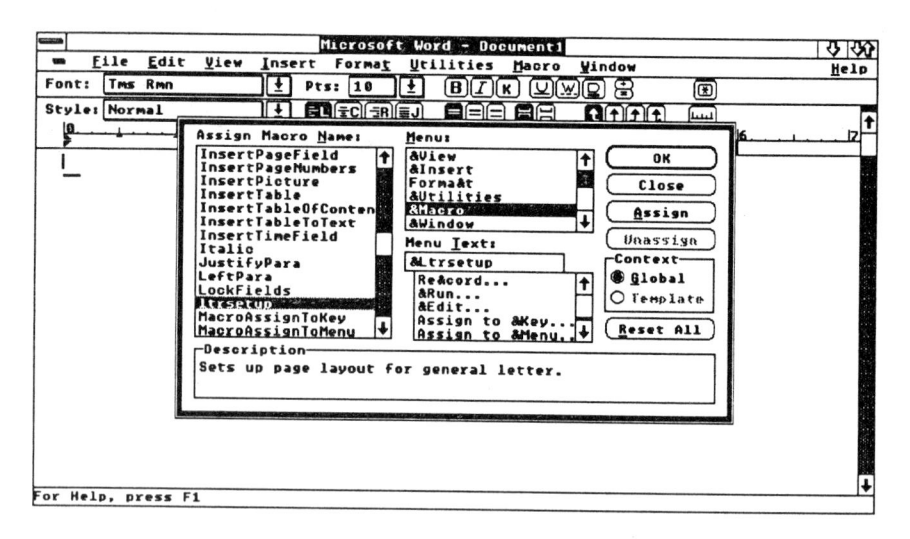

Figure 19.11 Scroll the Menu box to find the appropriate menu selection.

Once you assign a macro to the Macro menu, you can choose it directly to invoke the macro. Notice that Word will automatically identify the underlined letter to be used with the Alt key. If you wish to use a different key for choosing the macro command, type an ampersand (&) in front of that character as you type the new command name as you wish it to appear on the menu. For example, you can type &Setup in the Menu Text edit box to represent our sample ltrsetup macro, as shown in Figure 19.12. When you choose OK, the ltrsetup macro will be assigned to the Macro menu with the Setup command name, and the S will be underlined. S, then, will be the key that you press in combination with the Alt key. As you choose a specific command key, keep in mind those keys that are already assigned to a command. If you use the same key more than once, you will be required to press the key twice to access the specific macro.

When you have assigned a macro command to the menu, it will appear on the pull-down Macro menu just like Word's other macro commands. To remove it from the menu, simply select the Assign to Menu command again, select the macro name that you wish to remove (ltrsetup), and then choose the Unassign command button or press Alt+U. The Unassign command will not close the dialog window, but it will remove any command that you wish. To close the window, choose OK or Close.

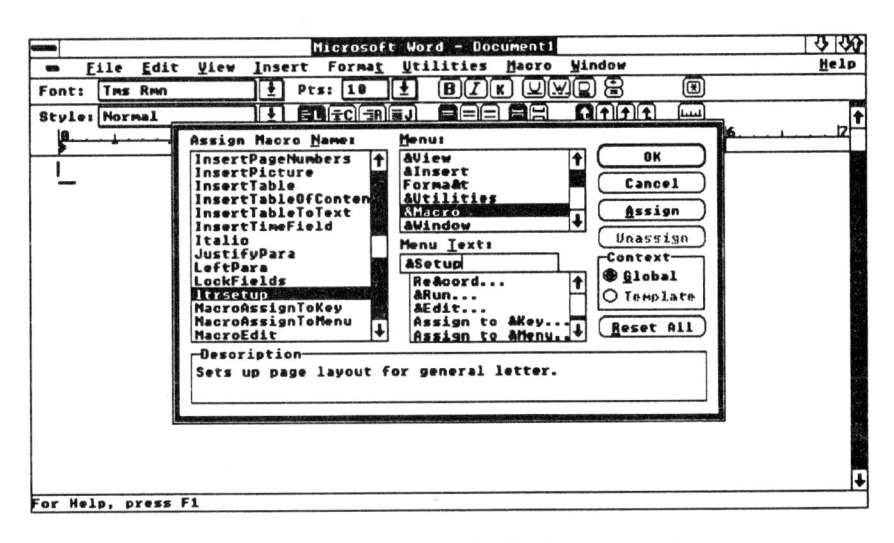

Figure 19.12 Enter any command title that you wish to appear in the Macro menu.

Deleting a Macro

To delete a macro altogether, you use the Macro **Edit** command or press **Alt,M,E**. From the Edit dialog box, select the macro name that you wish to delete from the Name list window, and then choose the **Delete** button or press **Alt+D**. (Note that you cannot delete a macro that you are presently editing.) If you have previously assigned the macro name to the Macro menu, you must choose the Assign to Menu command to remove it.

Customizing Existing Menus and Keys

A powerful feature of Word for Windows is the ability to customize any menu with any command. As you just learned, you can easily create a macro and add its command name to the Macro menu via the Assign to Menu command. You're not limited just to creating and adding macro commands, however. In Figure 19.11, you saw that the list window on the left contains all of Word's macros. This list also contains all of Word's menu commands, keyboard commands, and dialog options available for menus. This list, in fact, is Word's *command well*.

Adding an item from the command well to any menu is pretty straightforward. First select the command from the list, and then choose which menu you want it to appear on from the Menu list window in the upper middle of the dialog box. Then, simply choose the **Assign** button. If you wish to remove a command from a menu, complete the same process except choose the **Unassign** command button instead. You can see what command names are currently assigned to a particular menu by selecting that menu from the Menu list window and then scrolling the Menu Text list window just below it. The names in any of the list windows always appear in alphabetical order to help you search quickly.

That's about all there is to it. Word does provide some additional flexibility in the form of choice of "context," or when the command will appear on a particular menu, and the spelling of the command title itself. For example, Word will suggest a preset default Global Context selection that appears on the lower right of the dialog box. (Remember, the Template option is only available if the current active document is based on a template. Otherwise, the option will appear dim.) In other words, if you want the command always on the selected menu, then choose the Global option. If you want the command to appear on the menu only when you are working on a particular type of document, then choose Template. You'll recall that the choice of selecting the menu text was discussed in the previous sections. As a review, you simply need to type the title for the command (the command selected in the command well) in the Menu Text dialog box as you want it to appear in the menu; you need not type the same title as the name given to the command itself. For example, if you wish to give the Save command a name such as Store, simply enter the ampersand symbol (&) followed by the word Store. The Ampersand will tell Word to use the first letter following the ampersand, S, as the command key, and it will appear underlined in the menu. Of course, you must first select the command name as it appears in the command well list window. In this case, it appears as FileSave in the command well list window and &Save in the Menu Text list window. It is located in the File (listed as &File) menu by default.

The command buttons—Cancel, Close, and OK—are at the right side of the dialog box. If you choose the Cancel button, you close the Command dialog box without making any changes. When you choose the Assign or Unassign command buttons, Cancel changes to Close. Choosing Close will close the Command dialog box but does not negate the changes you have made; all your changes will be implemented. Choosing OK will assign a macro name and then close the dialog box.

19—Customizing Word and Using Macros

Create your document as a template in order to customize it for a particular use in the future.

At the bottom of the dialog window is the Description of the command or macro selected. You can't change the description here. To do this, you must use the Edit command on the Macro menu.

Finally, it is important to note that when you make a change with the Assign to Menu or Assign to Key (discussed next) commands, those changes are stored in a file referred to as a *configuration file*. The configuration file stores all other program defaults, such as Page Setup and Preferences and your style sheets. Word allows you to keep more than one configuration file at a time, so you can customize these (e.g., with different menu assignments and styles) to suit your needs. The point of this discussion is that you can easily create custom menus to fit a particular type of document, or simply customize your menus to reflect the way you like to work. For example, you might set up a selection of menus with commands to work only on legal documents. Choose the Template option and customize your menus accordingly. Once you have customized several configuration files, you can use the File Open command to access any file based on a specific document's configuration, and all the settings stored in that file will become current. When you quit Word, any changes you make to the menus, keystroke assignments, and so on, will not be saved automatically. To do this, you must respond Yes when Word asks "Save global glossary and command changes?"

The last option at the bottom of the dialog box is the Reset All button. Clicking it will cause the current configuration file to revert back to Word's original default menu settings when Word was shipped and cancels any menu or key changes made since you loaded Word. Of course, you must still save those global command changes when you quit Word.

The Assign to Key Command

Similar to customizing menus, you can use the Assign to Key command (found on the Macro menu) to add or delete key assignments, as long as you are working with a document template. You can also use the same procedures to assign a macro to a key or a combination of keys. Since Word uses many key combinations for commands by default, you might want to first refer to those key assignments (see Appendix B) prior to reassigning a key or macro name to a key. Further, to avoid duplicating any key assignment, Microsoft recommends that you use a prefix for custom key assignments. A common prefix is Ctrl+Shift followed by the command key that you designate. The trick is to assign custom keys with key combinations that you're unlikely to use otherwise, such as the End key on a numeric keypad. Of course, if you first delete a default key assignment, you free up a specific key combination for any command or macro name that you wish to assign.

Use the following steps to assign a macro name or a command to a specific key or combination of keys. To effect the change of key assignments, you must be working with a document template instead of a standard document.

1. Choose the **Assign to Key** command from the Macro menu or press **Alt,M,K**.

    The Assign to Key dialog box appears, as shown in Figure 19.13.

2. Select a macro name from the list window on the upper left corner of the dialog box. The keys currently assigned to the macro are listed below the window in the Current Keys window.

    The selected macro is highlighted. The description of the selected macro is displayed in the Description box at the bottom of the dialog box. The description provides information on the action performed by the selected macro. You can't edit the description here; to edit it, you must choose the Edit command.

3. Press the key or combination of keys that you want assigned to the macro that you selected in step 2. Remember, don't use a key assignment that you have already used (or that is assigned by Word by default) unless you first remove that assignment.

    The key or keys that you press will appear in the Key window box that appears to the right of the Current Keys box. The assigned macro will also appear here.

4. The next step is to choose the context for the key assignment. From the Context box, choose the default **Global** selection (**Alt + G**) if you want the key assignment available to all documents (i.e., based on the NORMAL.DOT document). If you want the macro assigned to be available only to those documents based on the

    The selected context option is blackened.

template as the active document, choose the **Template** option or press **Alt+T**. Of course, this option will appear dim if you are not working from within a document template.

5. Choose the **Assign** command button (press **Alt+A**) or press **OK**.

Pressing Assign will assign the selected macro to the key or key combination listed in the Key box, but does not close the dialog box. If you choose OK, then the macro is assigned to the designated key(s) and the dialog box is closed.

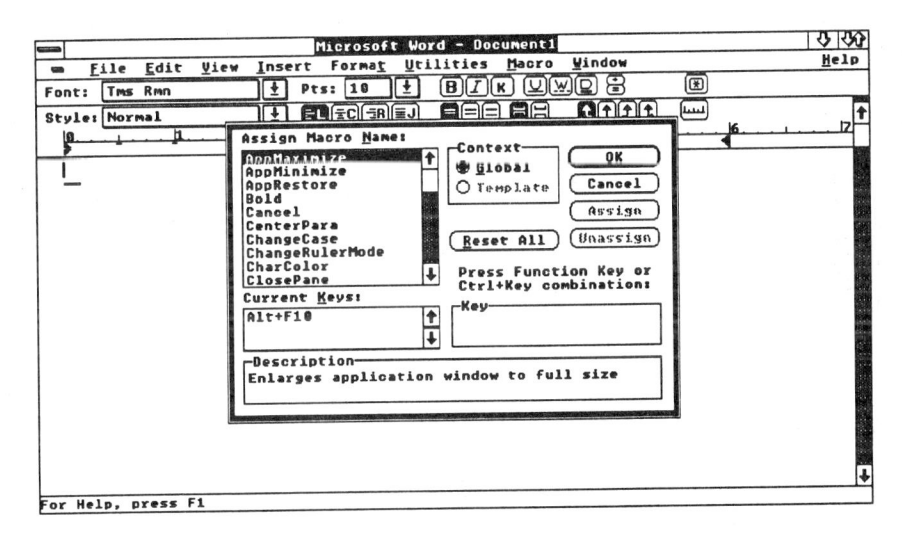

Figure 19.13 Use the Assign to Key to add or delete a key assignment to any key.

That's all there is to assigning macros to any key that you so designate. If you wish to remove a key assignment, simply choose the **Assign to Key** command to display the dialog box as before, select the macro name, press the key or keys assigned to that macro to highlight them in the Key box, and then choose the **Unassign** command button or press **Alt+U**. If you suddenly change your mind about removing a key assignment, Word has a safety net for you. Pressing Unassign changes this command button to **Reset** and pressing Reset will restore

Advanced Word

the key to its assignment when Word was first shipped. Pressing Reset All will reset all reassigned keys or key combinations to their original assignments when Word was shipped.

Review

In this chapter you learned:

1. Use the Preferences command on the View menu to affect how your screen will appear when working on documents. When you first start Word, the default selections include: Vertical Scroll Bar, Display As Printed, and Picture Display. To turn an option on, press the Alt key in combination with the underlined letter of the specific command option. When you quit Word and turn it on the next time, the settings that you selected in Preferences will be active as set during the previous work session.

2. The Customize command on the Utilities menu also includes some options that will affect the appearance of your screen and how Word works. The options include: Autosave Frequency, Units of Measure, Background Pagination, Prompt for Summary Info, Typing Replaces Selection, and Your Name and Initials as they will appear in the Summary Information box.

3. The default unit of measurement is inches. You can change this measurement to centimeters, points, or picas. If you do change this unit of measure, all measurements in this selection are affected, including those illustrated on the Ruler.

4. You can create a macro, which is a set of instructions that automates a more complex task. A macro records a sequence of actions that can be performed by choosing a single command or pressing a key or two.

5. You can create your own macros, or you can use Word's supplied macros, to complete many simple tasks. The result of using macros is greater productivity.

6. To use Word's supplied macros, choose the Macro Run command, select the name of the macro from the list window (choose Show All to display all available macros), and click OK.

7. The process of creating your own simple macros consists of these four steps: plan your macro; record the macro; run the macro; and edit the macro.

8. To begin creating your own macro, first choose the Macro Record command. Enter the name of the macro and choose its context (global for all documents or limited to the document template of the active document). Then, choose OK to start the recorder. Once the recorder has started, perform a sequence of actions that you wish to record as your macro. When finished, choose Stop Recorder and your macro is completed.

9. Always test your macros before using them in a document that you wish to save. In fact, remember to save your original document before using any newly created macro.

10. The simplest method for editing a macro that went wrong is to record the macro a second time, edit it, and save it using the same macro name. Word will ask if you wish to replace the existing macro. Respond yes to do so.

11. You can also choose to change your macros by using the Edit command from the Macro menu. Edit lists your macro using the macro programming language. This feature is useful for editing long and complex macros that you don't wish to record a second time. If you have some experience with the BASIC programming language, you will find that the embedded WordBASIC language that forms the foundation of the macro language is simple to master.

12. To change the name of a macro, choose the Edit command. From Edit, choose the macro name from the list window and then select the Rename command button. Type the new name for the macro and choose OK.

13. You can use the Assign to Menu command to assign a macro to the Macro menu. In fact, you can assign any macro to any menu using the Assign to Menu command.

14. To delete a macro, use the Edit command. You cannot, however, delete a macro that you are currently editing.

15. To customize Word to better fit your working methods, use the Assign to Menu and the Assign to Key commands. With Assign to Menu, you can reassign an existing command to any menu as well as change the name of the command or edit the menu text. If you wish to change the assignment of a menu to a key or combination of keys, use the Assign to Key command. For customizing your menus and key assignments to work with specific types of documents, you must first create your document as a document template. Such a procedure allows you to keep the standard menu and key assignments in place for documents while you customize those assignments for document templates.

TWENTY

Chapter

Working with Pictures

In this chapter:

- Working with Pictures
- Pasting and Inserting Pictures in Your Documents
- Changing the Size of a Picture
- Positioning Pictures
- Adding Captions
- Deleting Pictures
- Using Paste Link
- Linking with Spreadsheets

This last chapter is, well, fun. Word's documentation refers to any kind of graphic, such as drawings, charts, photographs, or other such visual elements as *pictures*. Word allows you to combine pictures and text in the same file and to manipulate the picture's size before you print the file as a single document. In this chapter, you'll learn to paste pictures or graphics created from other graphics programs into your documents, add borders, and to change the picture's size by cropping or scaling.

Working with Pictures

One of Word's best features is its ability to merge text and graphics in a single document. With Word for Windows, similar to desktop publishing programs, you can create professional-looking documents that use all of Word's features, including multicolumn text, tables, and various fonts. Finally, Word's ability to integrate pictures or graphics, created with other applications, in your documents is another tool that sets Word apart from most word processors today.

Pasting and Inserting Pictures in Your Documents

As you examine a document, you may decide that it could use a little "punch." The answer might just be a graphic or a piece of art. Remember the old saying, "a picture is worth a thousand words." For your documents, a thousand words might be an exaggeration but inserting graphics into your document can sometimes provide that extra visual aid that helps you make an important point. For example, a letter to the sales staff regarding its monthly quotas has more impact if you show a bar chart depicting sales levels. When explanations are not necessary, a graphic or art design can dress up your document just enough to get it the attention it deserves. Designing a letterhead? Try sprucing it up a bit with some art for a logo to replace the customary company name and address.

Microsoft coyly had this in mind by providing you with a source for creating pictures with the Windows Paint program. If you have a full-blown version of Windows as well as Word for Windows installed on your computer system, you have a dynamite package for creating stunning documents. With the Window's Paint manual, you can learn how to use that software application to create graphics and drawings independent from Word for Windows. Having learned how to create the graphics from that source, you can refer here for an introduction to importing your artwork into your documents. If you don't have a graphics software package, you can still read this chapter to learn the mechanics of pasting graphics into your Word documents. When you installed Word for Windows, the setup program offered several options for importing specific types of graphics files into your documents, such as Lotus PIC file format and HPGL plotter files. In general, you can always paste the following graphic file formats into your documents:

- Microsoft Windows Clipboard format with the Paste or Paste Link commands on the Edit menu (also requires DDE—see below).
- TIFF (Tagged Image File Format) files using the Picture command on the Insert menu.

- File formats that accept the DDE (Dynamic Data Exchange) format. A good example is the Microsoft Excel BIFF spreadsheet file. Note, the DDE is a means for passing information between Window's applications. For a complete review of DDE, see the *Technical Reference.*

To paste a picture into a Word document, you first create the picture with a commercial painting, drawing, or graphics program, such as Microsoft Paint. You can even paste charting information from a spreadsheet, such as Excel. Many of these programs have different methods for inserting graphics into Word, but the simplest method is cutting and pasting the desired picture using the Clipboard.

When you paste a picture into a Word document, Word treats that picture as a single text image, or character. Word places this picture character in a rectangular frame so that you can edit it as you do any other character. The picture inside the frame is invisible unless you turn on the Pictures option in Preferences from the View menu. When you select a picture (or click inside it with the mouse), the rectangular border displays eight black boxes, or sizing handles, that you can use to change the scale and size of the picture (see Figure 20.1). In addition, if you absolutely position the picture, Word lets you enter text that flows around the picture in order to make your documents look uniform. Even if you don't apply absolute position format to the picture, you can still add a descriptive caption above or below the picture.

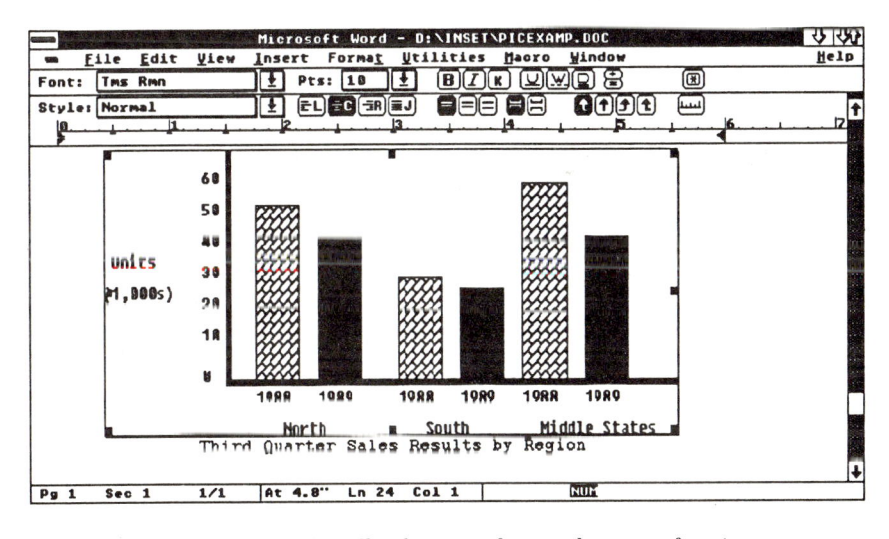

Figure 20.1 Sizing handles let you change the size of a picture.

You can use the Clipboard (Paste or Paste Link commands), Picture, or the DDE feature to paste pictures into your documents. To transfer a picture into a Word document with Paste, you create the picture with another Windows program, such as Windows Paint; copy the picture to the Clipboard; quit the application without quitting Windows; open Word; and paste the graphic into your document at the location of the insertion point. When you paste the picture in your document, it is surrounded by the rectangular frame and recognized as a single character. To illustrate, consider the document in Figure 20.2. Type the document as it appears and save it under the file name Graphics. Then complete these steps to insert the picture.

```
                    DOVER BOOK PUBLISHING COMPANY
                            12 Park Place
                          New York, NY  10022

MEMORANDUM
TO:   Regional Sales Managers
FR:   Samual Grimes, Publisher
DT:   January 7, 1990
ST:   4th Quarter Sales Results

The Sales figures for the third quarter of  fiscal 1989 have
just arrived, and I am terribly disappointed with the
results.  It appears that the current year has fallen
significantly below the previous year's sales levels, with
the exception of the middle states region.

At next Monday's staff meeting, I want each of you to
provide a detailed report concerning the sales activities of
the first three quarters.  Your analysis should include
market trends, budgeted cost expenditures, and new sales
promotions planned for bringing your region back on-line
with the sales plan.

If you need help in preparing for this meeting, please
contact me immediately.
```

Figure 20.2 Sample document memo lacking graphics.

1. For this example, we used Windows Paint to create the bar graph from Figure 20.1. Refer to your Paint user's manual for the necessary instructions.

2. Select the picture with the selection net and copy it to the Clipboard with the Copy command. Review the manual for the best methods of selecting a picture.

3. Quit the graphics program, but don't quit Windows or you will lose the contents of the Clipboard.

4. Open Word and retrieve the Graphics file, where you want the picture to appear.

5. Place the insertion point where you want the picture to appear. For this example, center it in your document following the second paragraph.

The document is ready for you to insert the picture. See Figure 20.3.

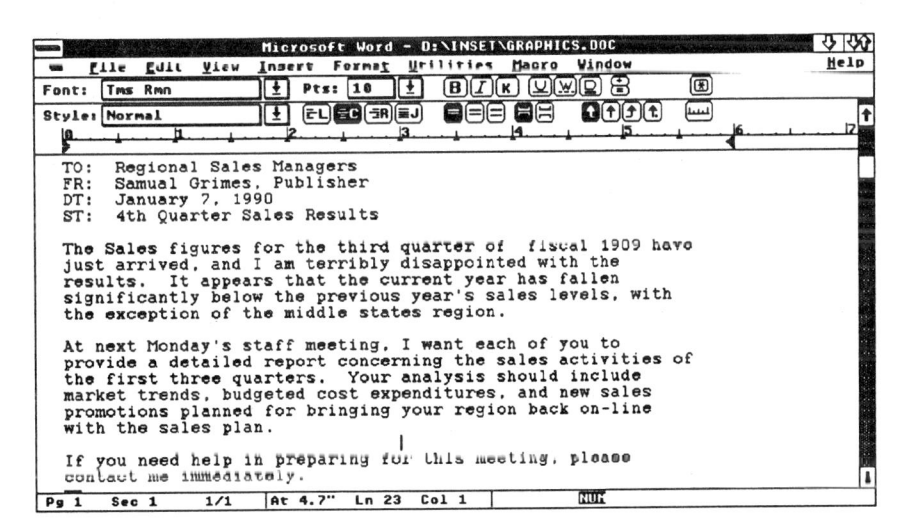

Figure 20.3 Position the insertion point where you want the picture to appear.

6. Choose **Paste** from the Edit menu or press **Alt,E,P**.

The picture stored in the Clipboard is inserted into your document at the location of the insertion point, as in Figure 20.4.

541

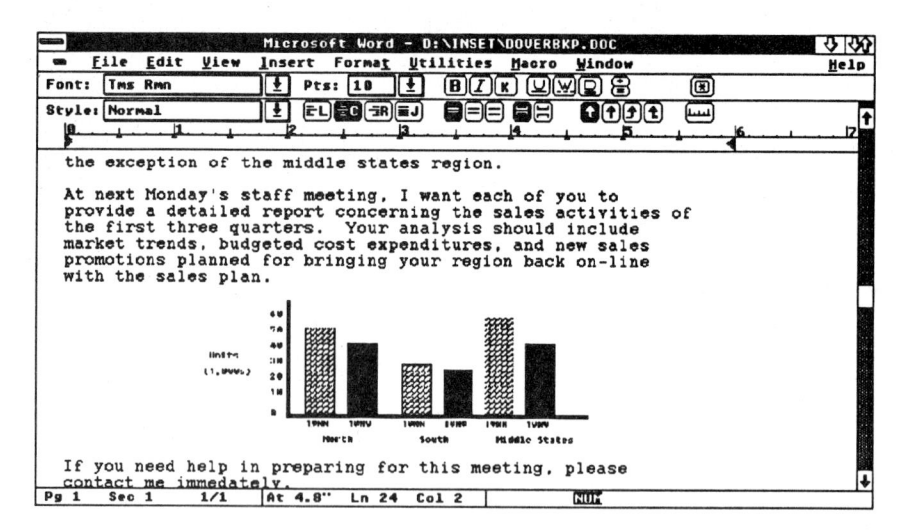

Figure 20.4 A document with a picture pasted from the Clipboard.

7. If you didn't use the selection net to select the picture from Windows Paint, you may have copied some extra white space. Use the mouse and the Enter key to add or remove extra blank lines above or below the picture. Remember, the picture is treated as a single character.

Inserting Blank Picture Frames or TIFF Graphic Files

Pasting pictures into your documents is one option available to you for mixing a picture file and a document file into a single file. You can also insert either a blank picture frame or a TIFF graphic file created with some other commercial graphics program. If you enter a blank picture frame, Word will insert a 1" square with a single-line border into your document at the location of the insertion point. You cannot paste a picture from the Clipboard into a blank picture frame. You can, however, change the size and scale of this empty picture frame any way you like. Once the empty frame is inserted into your document, Word treats the frame as a single character within a paragraph and reserves the space as if it were occupied by characters that you could see. With Picture from the Insert menu, you can insert an empty frame as a "placeholder" into which you can manually paste art at a later time. For example, you may wish to paste in a specific company logo as a letterhead. To insert a blank picture frame, complete the following three steps:

1. First, position the insertion point where you want the blank picture frame to appear. Remember, Word will adjust existing text to flow around the picture frame.

2. Next, choose the **Picture** command from the Insert menu or press **Alt,I,P**.

   The Insert Picture dialog box will appear, as shown in Figure 20.5.

3. Choose the **New Picture** command button (**Alt+N**) or simply press **Enter**.

   The dialog box closes, and the blank picture frame is inserted into your document at the location of the insertion point.

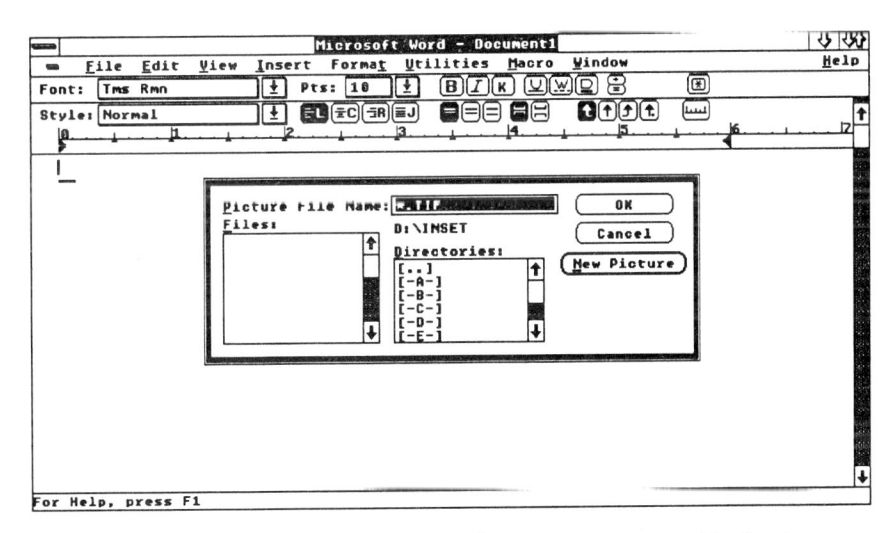

Figure 20.5 The Picture dialog box allows you to insert a blank picture frame or a TIFF file.

OK, you've now seen the Picture dialog box as shown in Figure 20.5. Can you guess how to insert a TIFF file located on a different disk or directory? It's simple. Instead of choosing New Picture in step 3 above, either type the name of the TIFF file in the Picture File

Name box or select the name of the TIFF file from the Files list window by pressing Alt+F. If necessary, you can switch to the Directories list box (click or press Alt+D) to select the specific drive and directory where the TIFF file is stored. For example, if you have a file stored on a diskette in drive A, select A as the drive, press Enter to list the TIFF files stored on that diskette in the Files window, select the appropriate file, and then click OK. Regardless of where the file is stored, once you have selected the appropriate file, press Enter to insert the TIFF file into your document at the location of the insertion point.

Changing the Size of a Picture

The maximum size of a picture that can be inserted into your document is about 22". Depending upon the limitations of your printer, a picture larger than this size may print on successive pages or not at all.

Once you insert a picture into your document, Word surrounds the picture with a frame. (Note that the picture frame is only visible if you turn on the Picture Border option in Format Picture.) The picture frame will often appear empty as you type or scroll the document. However, if you turn on the Picture option in Preferences, Word will fill in the picture frame when the screen is at a standstill. Viewing the contents of a picture frame is not the subject of this section, however. The purpose here is to learn how to change the size of the picture itself. You can change the size of the picture as long as it's selected. However, it does make the task easier if you can see the picture and the result of the change on your screen at the same time. To change the size of a picture, you'll either crop the picture or scale it. Cropping and scaling can be accomplished with either the mouse or the Format Picture dialog box.

Cropping and Scaling a Picture with a Mouse

Before you can change the size of a picture, you must first select the picture. Select the picture by moving the insertion point to the paragraph mark that represents the picture (press the down or up arrow key as necessary). If you have a mouse, you can simply click anywhere on the picture itself. When you do, the eight sizing handles appear on the picture frame as illustrated in Figure 20.6. The sizing handles are for cropping or scaling the size of the picture with the mouse. You drag the sizing handles in and out to change the size of the frame around the picture. Resizing the picture frame is called *cropping* the picture. By cropping, you can eliminate some of the edges (in this case, white space) of the graphic. If you hold down the Shift key while dragging, the picture will also be *scaled* as the size of

20—Working with Pictures

the picture frame changes (Figure 20.7). If you just want to resize the picture frame, move the handles without pressing the Shift key.

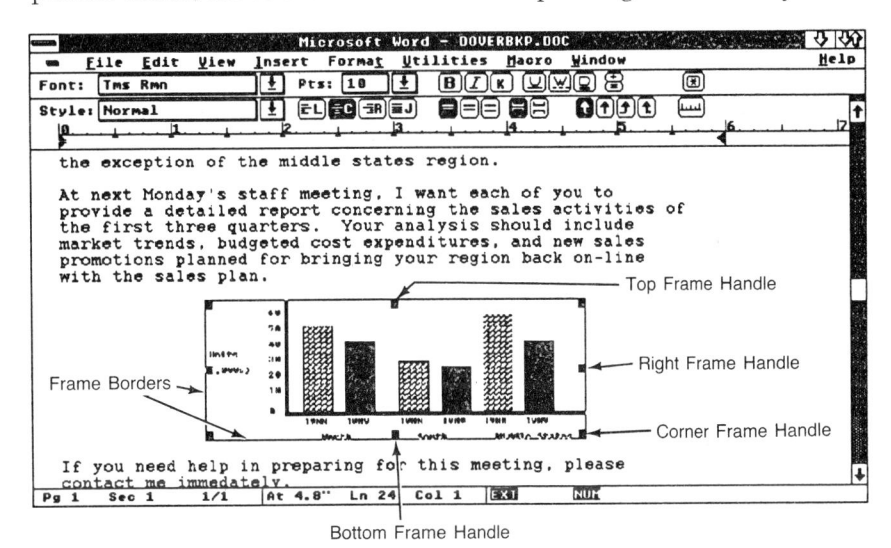

Figure 20.6 Use the sizing handles to crop your picture with a mouse.

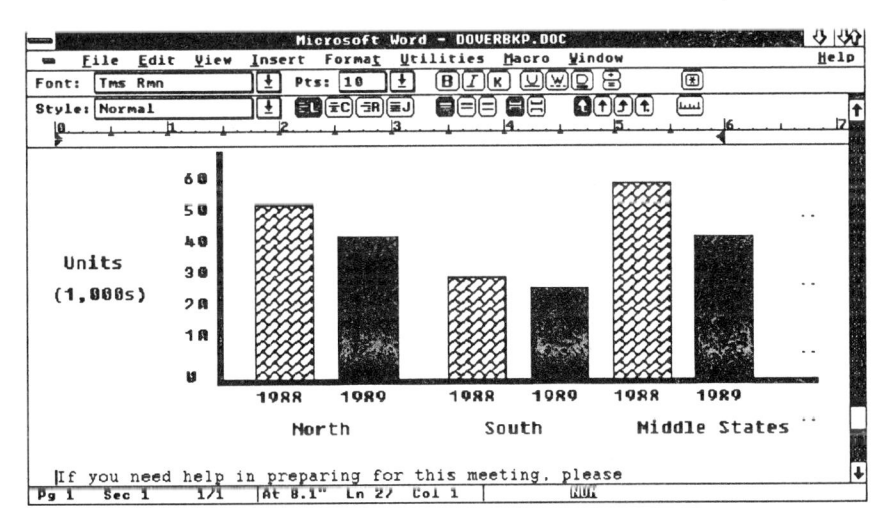

Figure 20.7 Holding down the Shift key as you drag the picture frame handle scales the graphic while you resize the frame.

If you drag the frame without scaling the graphic, Word will not center the graphic inside the frame. If you scale (Shift+drag) the graphic, however, the graphic is always centered in the frame. Dragging the top or bottom handles changes the depth of the frame, while dragging the left or right handles changes the width of the frame. As you drag, the lower left corner of the window shows the length or width of the frame. If you drag the corner frame, the frame moves diagonally only.

When you drag a sizing handle to crop a picture, the status bar at the bottom of the screen will show the measurements in the default unit of measurement set in Customize. If you Shift + drag to scale a picture, you will see the frame's percentage of change from the original picture. Once you shrink the picture frame, you can restore it to its original size by double-clicking inside the frame.

Using Format Picture to Crop or Scale

You can crop or scale a picture with the mouse as just discussed, or you can use the more precise method of using the Format Picture command. The first step to using the Format Picture command is the same as using the mouse: you select the picture that you wish to change. Here's something to keep in mind: The display monitor and the printer selected for your system will affect the picture sizes that you see in the Format Picture dialog box. The reason is that picture sizes are based on pixel sizes associated with your printer and its printing resolution. If you change printers, change display types, or turn off the Display as Printed option in the Preferences dialog box, Word will assume that pixels are display pixels instead of printer pixels and some distortion may result in the displayed picture. In part, this distortion could be due to a difference between the screen pixels of your display and that of your printer and its printing resolution.

As a helpful reminder, Word displays the original size of the picture in the Original Size area at the bottom of the Format Picture dialog box (see Figure 20.8).

To illustrate how to use the Format Picture command, let's change the size of the original picture that we pasted in Figure 20.4 by scaling it. Remember, when you scale a picture you simply change its size (either bigger or smaller than the original) while maintaining the same proportions. Cropping, on the other hand, is a method of reducing the amount of white space from the edge of the scaled picture to the cropping square. In other words, you change the size of the frame around a picture. (You can use cropping to "cut off" a part of a picture by reducing the frame.) To scale our picture from Figure 20.4 complete the following steps:

1. Select the picture by clicking on it with the mouse or place the insertion point just after the picture's paragraph marker.

    The selected picture appears in a frame with sizing handles visible.

2. Choose the **Picture** command from the Format menu or press **Alt,T,R**. If the Picture command appears dim, you didn't select the picture first.

3. To scale the picture, enter the current height and width of the picture as a percentage of the original picture. For our example, in the Height % box enter **200** and in the Width % box enter **150**. These values will make the picture twice its original height and 1 1/2 times its original width. If you enter values that are less than 100%, you would scale the picture to a smaller size than its original size. Remember, when scaling to a larger size, the maximum size for a picture in Word is approximately 22 inches.

The Format Picture dialog box appears as shown in Figure 20.8.

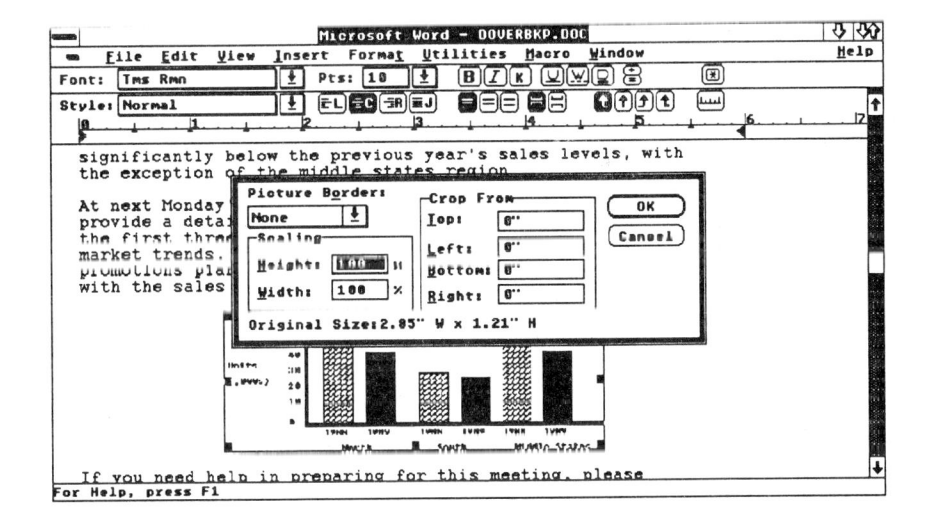

Figure 20.8 The Format Picture dialog box allows you to scale or crop a picture.

Advanced Word

4. Choose **OK** or press **Enter**.

The dialog box closes, and the selected picture is scaled up in size as shown in Figure 20.9.

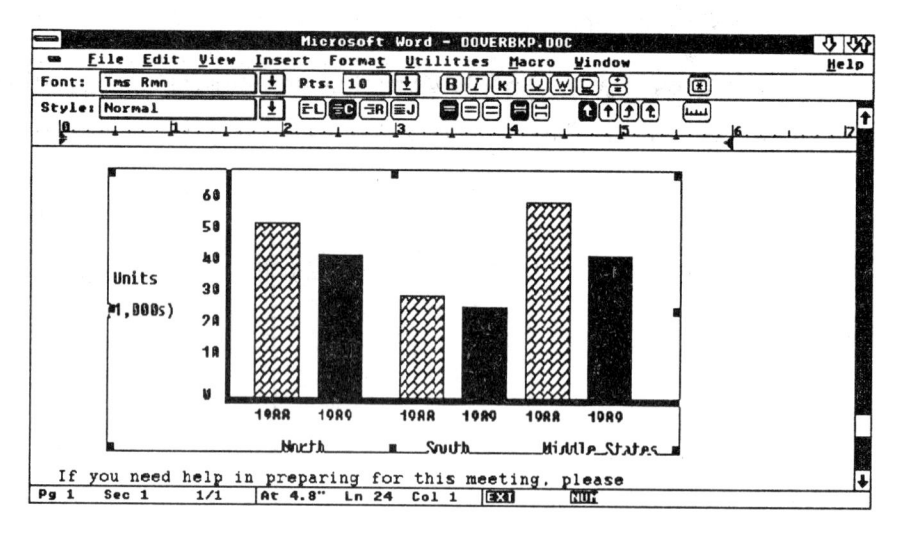

Figure 20.9 Our selected picture now appears twice as high and 1 1/2 times as wide as its original size.

Drawing Borders Around Your Pictures

Scaling or cropping your pictures is not the only formatting option available to you. If you wish to draw a border around selected pictures, this too is accomplished with the Format Picture command. Please note that the picture border that appears around an inserted picture frame on your screen is not printed with your document. If you wish to print a border, you should place one using the steps that follow. You could also select the picture as a paragraph and use the border option on the Format Paragraph dialog box, but that method places too much white space around the picture (from the left to right margins). The Format Picture option places the border just around the cropping square area. To illustrate, let's draw a border around our sample picture as follows:

1. Select the picture. Turn on the Picture Border option on the Format Picture dialog box, if necessary.

The selected picture is highlighted with picture frame and sizing handles visible.

2. Choose the **Format Picture** command or press **Alt,T,R**.
3. From Picture Borders (**Alt+O**), select the type of picture border (single, thick, double, shadow, or the default, none). For our example, select Shadow (press the **down arrow** 4 times).
4. Click **OK** or press **Enter**. The dialog box closes and the picture appears with the new border box as shown in Figure 20.10.

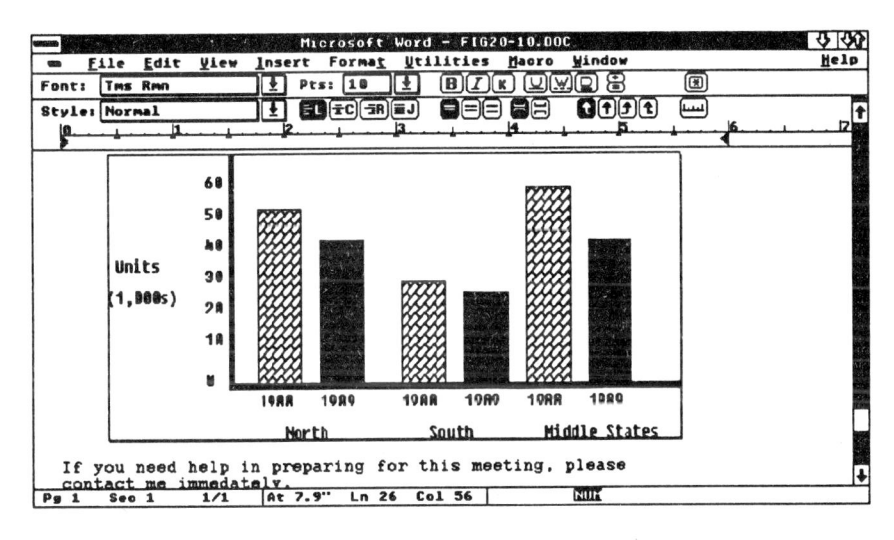

Figure 20.10 A shadow border box is added to the picture.

Positioning Pictures

Since Word treats your picture like a single character, you can use the Cut, Copy, and Paste commands in order to select the picture and move it to another location in your document. You can even format the picture with absolute formatting to move the picture in Print Pro view as an object. The advantage of applying absolute positioning to a picture is that you can reposition the picture anywhere on your document's page and, if necessary, flow text around the picture. This fea-

549

Advanced Word

ture of positioning pictures is just one more tool of flexibility that you can use for creating complex documents.

Applying absolute position formatting to a picture is just like applying it to any standard paragraph. You select the text and then choose the Format Position command. For a review of positioning paragraphs, see Chapter 7. However, to illustrate, let's change the position of our picture from the previous example so that it will now follow the first paragraph instead of the second. To do this:

1. Select the picture by clicking on it with the mouse or using the down arrow key to move just past its paragraph marker. You can also use any of the keyboard methods for selecting text including using F8, the Extend Selection key.

   The selected picture will appear with frame and visible sizing handles. You only want the sizing handles to appear. Do not drag across the picture with the mouse to highlight the picture in reverse text.

2. Choose the **Position** command from the Format menu or press **Alt,T,O**.

   The Position dialog box appears.

3. In the Horizontal box, choose **Centered** relative to the Page. In the Vertical box, type in the measurement, 3.88 in, and select **Relative** to the page as well. Note: The vertical measurement for this example is only relevant to this particular picture size. You can get a better feel for positioning objects by moving them in Print Preview.

4. Choose **OK** or press **Enter**.

   The dialog box closes, and the picture now appears in its new location. To see exactly how the document will look when printed, switch to Page View.

OK, now that you have formatted the picture as an absolutely positioned object, you can further change its location by changing the values in the Format Position dialog box, or better yet, you can choose the Print Preview command and move the boundaries of the object. For example, choose **Print Preview** from the File menu or

20—Working with Pictures

press **Alt,F,V** and then choose the **Boundaries** command option by pressing **B**. The boundaries of the elements of the document, including those of the picture, are shown in Figure 20.11. To move the picture, simply select it and drag it to its new location. Once satisfied, click outside the document page and the picture moves as you wanted.

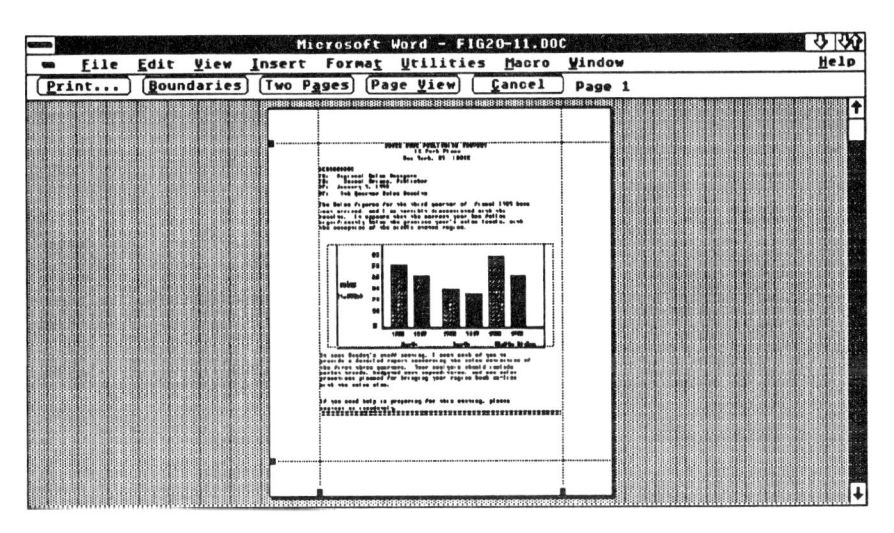

Figure 20.11 Use Print Preview to move absolutely positioned pictures.

Adding Captions

You can add a caption to a picture, either above or below the picture. To do this, position the insertion point as if you were creating a new paragraph above or below the picture, and then type the title or description of the picture. The caption is just like any other text paragraph so you can format it using the Character and Paragraph commands.

Some pictures, however, will be absolutely positioned; for those, you must apply the position formatting to the caption too. When both the caption and the picture are absolutely positioned, Word will keep them together and print them in the order that they appear in the document. In other words, if you position the caption above the picture, then the caption will be displayed and printed before the picture. To add a caption to a positioned picture, complete the following steps, using our sample graph.

Tip: To be sure to select caption text and picture accurately, select the paragraph marker that follows both elements.

551

Advanced Word

1. Position the insertion point either above or below the picture just as if you were beginning a new paragraph. For this example, position the insertion point after the picture, press Enter once and center the insertion point.

   The insertion point appears below the picture and centered.

2. Type the text for the caption. For our example, type:

   3RD QUARTER SALES RESULTS BY REGION

3. Next, select both the picture and the caption. Do not select text above or below the picture and caption or you will produce the wrong result when you position the selection.

   The selected picture and caption appear highlighted.

4. Choose the **Position** command from the Format menu or press **Alt,T,O**.

   The Position dialog box appears.

5. Type or select the position that you want for the picture in the Horizontal and Vertical boxes. For our example, choose **Centered** Relative to the Page for Horizontal, and enter **3.88"** Relative to the Page for the Vertical measurement.

6. Choose **OK** or press **Enter**.

   The caption will appear positioned just after the picture. Figure 20.12 shows the result of all the formatting options applied to our sample document.

Deleting Pictures

Deleting a picture in Word is just as easy as deleting any character or paragraph. To delete a picture, simply select it and then press the

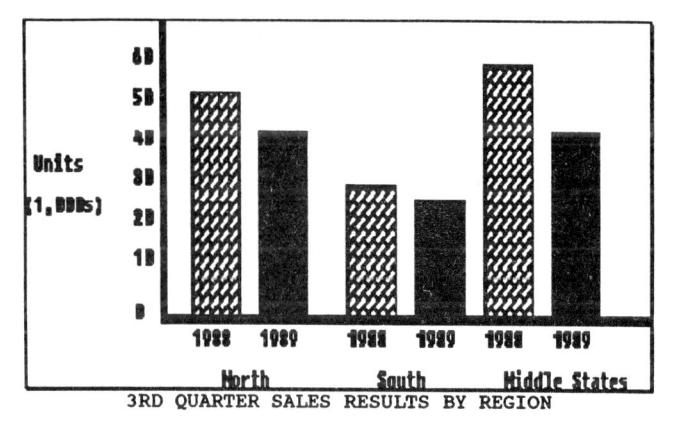

Figure 20.12 Adding a caption to your absolutely positioned picture.

Delete key. You can also use the **Cut** command to remove the picture from the document and place it in the Clipboard.

Using Paste Link

The Paste Link command found on the Edit menu allows you to set up a "link" between the source graphics program and your Word document. Paste Link works much the same way as the Paste command (also found on the Edit menu) except Word also inserts a DDE field into your document. It is the field that is the key because when you update the graphic in the source program, all you have to do is update the field in your Word document to update the graphic or picture as well (press F9 to update a field or to insert an automatic DDE field, called DDEAUTO). This saves time because you don't have to recapture the updated picture from the graphics program and then paste it into your document every time you update the original picture.

To use the Paste Link command, you must have Microsoft Windows installed on your hard disk. Likewise, you can only set up a link between programs that support the DDE format.

There are two requirements for the Paste Link command to work properly. First, the graphics package where you create the original picture must support DDE; and second, you must have both the graphics package and Word running at the same time for the DDE link to work. Depending on the amount of memory your computer has installed on it, this latter requirement may prevent your system from working. This author has found that your computer should have at least 2 megabytes of RAM available to run both Word for Windows and most graphics packages at the same time.

The following are sample steps to use to set up a link between your Microsoft Paint and Word. You can use these steps to use the Paste Link command with most other graphics packages, too.

1. You must have Microsoft Windows installed and running. Create the picture with a graphics program that supports DDE, such as Microsoft Paint. Then, save the document in Paint under a descriptive file name. This is important because if you try to link to an untitled Paint document, you'll get an error message.

2. Select the picture using a method such as the selection net in Paint.

20—Working with Pictures

3. Choose **Copy** from the Edit menu or press **Alt+E+C** to save the picture from its source program (Paint) to the Clipboard.

4. Switch to the MS-DOS Executive screen by pressing **Alt+Esc**. You don't want to quit running the graphics program. If necessary, start the Word for Windows program and open the document file where you want to insert the picture. Now, both the source graphics program (Paint) and Word for Windows should be running at the same time.

5. Place the insertion point where you want the picture to appear and then choose **Paste Link** from the Edit menu or press **Alt,E,L**.

    The Paste Link dialog box appears.

6. If you wish to create an automatic DDE link to update the picture in your Word document every time the picture in the source graphic's program changes, turn on the **Auto Update** option or press **Alt+A**. If you wish to simply insert a standard DDE link, leave the option off. A standard DDE link requires that you select the field with the link (the picture) and then press **F9**, the Update Field key, to update the picture.

7. Choose **OK** or press **Enter**.

Tip: You can also insert a DDE field link between a source graphics program and Word by using the Insert Field command. To do this, choose the place where the picture is to be inserted (as before), but then choose the Insert Field command and type DDE or DDEAUTO as the field type, type the name of the source graphics program, and choose OK. Of course, the picture must still be in the Clipboard and the graphics source program must still be running.

Linking with Spreadsheets

When Word documents containing automatic DDE links are opened, Word asks if you wish to establish the link and update the fields. Choose Yes to do so, or No if you want to update them later manually, which you accomplish by selecting the field and pressing F9.

A key advantage Word for Windows offers is its ability to import information from a spreadsheet created with another program. If you have Windows installed, you can even set up a communication link between a DDE-compatible spreadsheet, such as Microsoft Excel, and your Word document. The process is similar to setting up a link between a graphics package and Word, as discussed above. The choices are the same: you can insert a DDE field that you update manually (DDE), or an automatic update link (AUTODDE) that updates the new information automatically as it becomes available. And just like the Paste Link procedures for transferring a picture to your Word document, the first step is to create the spreadsheet information (such as a table of data) with a program like Microsoft Excel, and then copy it to the Clipboard. Don't quit Excel, but rather, switch to the MS-DOS Executive screen by pressing **Alt + Esc** and load Word for Windows. Open the document file and place the insertion point where you want to insert the spreadsheet information. Next, choose **Paste Link** or press **Alt,E,L**. Decide whether you want to insert a standard DDE link or an automatic one with Auto Update (**Alt + A**) and choose **OK**. Once you have established a DDE link, you can manually update it by selecting the field or spreadsheet information and pressing **F9**, the Update Field key. If you establish an automatic link (AUTODDE), the information in the Word document will be updated as soon as it's available in the spreadsheet program.

Once you have established a DDE link between a source program and the field in the Word document, you can always break this link by first selecting the field and then pressing Ctrl + Shift + F9, the UNLINK Field key combination. Pressing UNLINK Field locks the current information into place.

Finally, if you wish to set up a link with other Windows applications, choose the Insert Field command or press Alt,I,D, enter the type of field code for the type of link (i.e., DDE or AUTODDE), and then type the application name of the source program followed by the name of the specific file. For example, the field codes for a link might be

{DDEAUTO EXCEL SALES.XLS}

where DDEAUTO represents an automatic link between a Word document and an Excel document file named SALES.XLS.

Review

In this chapter you learned:

1. Word offers the ability to merge text and pictures in a document. To insert a picture into a Word document, you must create the picture in another application, such as Microsoft Paint. Save the picture to the Clipboard, open your Word document without quitting Windows, position the insertion point, and then choose the Paste command to insert the picture.
2. Using DDE fields, you can also insert pictures created with other graphics packages, spreadsheet files, or TIFF files. All files must be compatible with the DDE format.
3. A picture that is pasted or inserted into a Word document is surrounded by a rectangular picture frame. The picture frame is only visible if you turn on the Picture Borders option located on the Picture dialog box on the Format menu. This frame will not print when the document is printed. To print a frame or border around a picture, select the picture and use the Picture Border option.
4. You can change the size of a picture pasted into Word using either a mouse or the Picture command. You can change the size of a picture by cropping the picture or scaling it.
5. To select a picture, use the mouse to click on the picture itself, or use the arrow keys to position the insertion point immediately after the paragraph mark attached to the picture. Don't drag across the picture as you would standard text to select it.
6. Once you paste a picture into a document and select it, eight sizing handles appear on the picture frame. These sizing handles are for use with a mouse when dragging to crop the picture, or you can press shift+drag to scale the picture.

7. You can also insert a blank picture frame or a TIFF file into your Word document by using the Insert Picture command. You cannot paste a picture from the Clipboard into a blank picture frame. Such a frame is for reserving space in a document and manually inserting a graphic into that space at a later time.

8. For more precise cropping and scaling of pictures, you should use the Picture command. To make a picture larger than its original size, enter a value greater than 100% in the Height % and/or Width % boxes. To make a picture smaller, enter a value less than 100%.

9. Pictures in Word are treated as a single character. You can move the picture around your screen with the Cut, Copy, and Paste commands. You can also apply absolute positioning format to the picture just like any other paragraph and reposition the picture with Print Preview.

10. You can add captions above or below a picture.

11. To delete a picture, simply select it just like any other paragraph and press the Delete key or choose Cut from the Edit menu. Choosing Cut will place the Picture into the Clipboard.

12. Use the Paste Link command on the Edit menu to set up a manual DDE link or an automatic link (AUTODDE) between a source program and the Word document file. You can use this command to link graphics packages, like Microsoft Paint, or spreadsheet programs, like Microsoft Excel. Regardless of which program you use, the source program must always be running under Windows at the same time as Word, and must be compatible with the DDE file format.

appendix A

Installing Word for Windows

This appendix discusses the installation of Word for Windows. Like all Microsoft products, the installation procedure itself is straightforward and simple to follow. In order to use Word for Windows, you must have a hard disk. We'll assume that you do, but not that you have Windows installed on your hard disk. Although the general procedure is the same, we'll list the additional steps required for installing Word without Windows.

First, before you install Word for Windows, you should make a backup copy of all the diskettes of the size appropriate for your computer. Microsoft will have provided both 5 1/4" and 3 1/2" diskettes.

Making Backups

When you purchase Word for Windows, you should immediately make copies, or "backups." Disks do eventually wear out and accidental erasures can occur, so having backups reduces the chance that you will lose a valuable program. Once you've made the duplicate, place the original in a safe place in case you need to make another copy.

What about a hard disk? Age and accidents can affect a hard disk as well. Why not make an extra copy of your software to play it safe? The cost of a set of blank disks is much less expensive than the cost of another original set of Word disks.

DISKCOPY makes an exact duplicate of a diskette. If the disk receiving the disk is not already formatted, DISK-COPY formats the disk automatically.

The first step to making backup copies of Word is to be sure that you have at least the same number (and type) of blank diskettes as original diskettes that you wish to copy. Next, determine the configuration of your computer. In other words, does your computer have two disk drives of the same type (i.e., two 5 1/4" or two 3 1/2" drives) or does it have one 5 1/4" drive and one 3 1/2" drive. Your system may also have one floppy disk drive (either a 5 1/4" or 3 1/2") and a hard drive. The setup of your system is important since you can't make a copy of a disk inserted into a 5 1/4" drive onto a disk inserted into a 3 1/2" drive (the configuration of the disks themselves are different). If you have one diskette drive or a system with two different diskette drives, type the following DOS system command at the C> prompt

DISKCOPY A: A:

where the DOS command (DISKCOPY) is followed by a space, the source drive (A), a colon, a space, the destination drive (A again), and another colon. You'll then see a message telling you to place the source diskette into drive A and press any key. Place any of the original Word disks into drive A. You will be told to swap the source disk (the Word disk) and the target (a blank disk) several times until the copy is complete. You will then be asked if you wish to copy another. Press **Y** and press **Enter**, until you have copied all the Word for Windows disks. Note: Before you give the DISKCOPY command, make sure that you are at the root level of your hard disk. The root level is where your DOS files are stored. In other words, if your system prompt reads D> instead of C>, you may need to change to the root drive by typing **C:** and pressing **Enter** at the system prompt.

Warning: Don't mix the source and target disks during the copy procedure. If you do, you may accidentally erase an original disk.

If you have two identical drives named A and B, you can type the following command instead:

DISKCOPY A: B:

In this case, when you press Enter, Word will tell you to place the source disk (one of the Word disks) into drive A and the target disk (one of the blank disks) into drive B, and then to press any key. As before, when the copy is complete, a message will appear asking if you wish to copy another disk. Press **Y** and press **Enter** to repeat the procedure until all disks have been successfully copied.

Installing Word to Your Hard Disk

Now that you have made the appropriate backups of your Word disks, it's a simple procedure to install Word for Windows on your hard drive. The first step is to make the selected drive the current drive. In other words, if you are going to install the Word disks from drive A, type

A:

and press **Enter**. (If you are using the B drive, type **B:** and press **Enter** instead.) Once the appropriate drive is the current drive, you're ready to install Word. The following are the steps defined by Word's Setup program. The first set of steps install Word if you already have Windows installed on your hard disk. The second set of steps detail the same procedure without Windows installed. (Setup actually installs a "run-time" version of Word for Windows.)

Installing Word with Windows with Windows Already Installed

1. Insert the Word disk labeled *Setup* into the current drive (the A drive if the A> prompt appears on your screen).

2. Type **setup** and press **Enter**. Soon the Word Setup opening screen appears. If it does not, you may not be working from the current drive. Check to see that the Word Setup disk is indeed in the current drive.

3. Read the opening screen and follow the instructions that appear. If you are using a network, the steps that follow will be slightly different. We will assume that you are not using a network. Once you have read the opening screen, press **Enter**.

4. The screen asks you to select one of the following:

   ```
   Install Word for Windows
   View the README file
   Exit Setup
   ```

   Make your selection by using the direction keys to highlight it and then pressing **Enter**. Choose **Install Word for Windows**.

5. The screen informs you that you need to know the following about the configuration of your computer:
   - What kind of graphics adapter (display) you have
   - What kind of mouse you have (Microsoft or other), if any
   - What kind of printer(s) you have, if any
   - Which port your printer is connected to

   If you don't know the answers to the above, don't worry, the setup program will automatically detect many of the components for you. Press the **Enter** key to continue with Setup.

6. Setup will now determine the makeup of your hard disk. Some hard disks are actually partitioned into more than one drive even though you may physically have only one hard drive. These partitions might be designated:

   Hard Drive C
   Hard Drive D
   Hard Drive E

   Setup will recommend that you install Word on the drive that has enough space by default. Use the direction keys to select the specific drive where you want Word installed and then press **Enter**.

7. Setup will now ask that you specify the directory where you want Word installed. Setup will propose a specific directory that is based on your hard drive selection:

   C:\WINWORD

   if you've chosen Hard Drive C in step 6. You have the option of using the Backspace key to erase the current selection and typing a different directory. When you're satisfied with the name of directory displayed, press **Enter**. A message will appear that Setup is now copying the Setup disk file names.

8. Setup instructs you to insert the disk labeled *Program* into drive A and then press **Enter**. (If you are using the B drive as the current drive, insert the disk into drive B.) Soon, the screen informs you that Setup is now copying the Program disk.

9. The next screen installs the conversion programs. If you intend to try and read a document file created with another word processor, such as WordPerfect or Word for DOS, it's a good idea to take advantage of this option. Each conversion option that you select will take up some space on your hard disk, but the flexibility of converting documents with other file formats

A—Installing Word for Windows

is worth it. Of course, if you never intend to import files created with other file formats, then you can elect not to install the conversions. Following the screen instructions, use the arrow keys to highlight your selection and then press Enter. Choosing the **Install conversions** option will take you to a screen listing all the file format conversion options. Each time you add a conversion option, you will be returned to the original screen. You can elect to add all the conversions if you wish. Once you are finished adding the conversion options that you like, choose **Continue Setup with current selection(s)** and then press **Enter** to continue with Setup.

10. Setup instructs you to insert the disk labeled *Conversions* into drive A (the current drive), and then press **Enter**. A message will appear that tells you Setup is copying the conversions that you selected. Of course, if you didn't elect any conversions, Setup will skip this step.

11. Setup now informs you that you can install a set of graphic filters. Similar to conversions, this option allows you to open graphic files created with other programs. Choose from

    Install graphic filters

    or

    Do not install graphic filters

    and press **Enter**. Just like choosing the conversions option earlier, a second screen will appear if you elect to install graphic filters. You can choose from such options as graphics created with Lotus 1-2-3 and AutoCAD. Make your selections and then continue with Setup. Setup will copy the necessary files from the Conversions disk.

12. Setup now instructs you to choose from installing the set of tutorial lessons that come with Word. The lessons take up about 1.2MB of disk space. You can install Word with or without these lessons. Beginners should take advantage of these lessons, and then once you've mastered the program, you can delete the directory that contains the lessons in order to increase your disk space. Choose **Install tutorial lessons** and then press **Enter**. You are instructed to insert the *Tutorial* disk into drive A and press Enter. Setup will tell you that it is now copying the Tutorial disk. To complete this process, you are instructed to insert the disk labeled *Proofing Tools* into drive A (the current drive) and then press Enter. A message appears that tells you that Setup is copying the Proofing Tools and the Help disk. At this juncture, if Windows is not already installed on your hard drive, skip steps 13–17 in this section, and follow step 13 in the next section.

13. Setup will now detect whether or not that you have Windows already installed on your hard disk, and, if so, in what version. If you have an older version of Windows installed, Setup will suggest that you update your version of Microsoft Windows. Although this suggestion indicates that if you do update, other Windows applications will not be affected, an update might not be appropriate for your system. To play it safe, elect not to update your Windows files. If you do and you run into trouble, you can always reinstall both Windows and Word for Windows. Make your selection and then press **Enter**.

14. Setup now instructs you to insert the disk labeled *Utilities 1* into drive A (the current drive) and press **Enter**. Do so, and a message appears that Setup is now copying the Utilities 1 disk.

15. Setup now lets you install printer drivers supported by Word for DOS but not by Windows. Since you are using Windows, it is likely that you won't need to install these drivers (the choice is up to you). Choose **Do not install printer drivers** to continue with Setup.

16. Setup will now determine which type of printer you have connected to your system. If you have a laser printer, Setup will give you the option of installing soft fonts which allow special characters to be printed. Make your selection and then press **Enter**. If you do elect to install soft fonts, Setup will instruct you to insert the Conversions disk into drive A and press Enter.

17. Setup gives you the option of running a program called MEMSET, which helps you to optimize Word's use of extended/expanded memory. Make your selection and press **Enter**. Soon Setup provides the message that Word for Windows has been successfully installed!

Installing Word for Windows (Run-time Version—Windows not previously installed)

Follow steps 1–12 above.

13. Setup will not find Microsoft Windows on your system. Insert the disk labeled *Run-time Windows* into drive A (the current drive). Choose

    ```
    Install run-time Windows files
    ```

    and press **Enter**.

A—Installing Word for Windows

14. Setup lists the computers on which you may set up Word. Use the direction keys to select the computer that most resembles the one that you have and then press **Enter**.

15. Setup will list the display adapter, keyboard, and mouse or pointing device that your system contains. Select **No Change** if the list is correct, or select any item that is incorrect and then press **Enter**.

16. Setup will determine if your system has extended memory or not. Follow the instructions on the screen and then press **Enter**. Setup will install the necessary files.

17. Setup will allow you to install a printer or plotter. Choose the type of output device that is connected to your computer and then press **Enter** as appropriate. Setup will detect where your printer is connected (i.e, which printer port, such as LPT1). If you wish to change this port selection, use the arrow keys and press **Enter**. Setup will allow you to install another printer to another port if you so desire. If you have a second port to activate, select it and press **Enter**.

18. Setup lists the option of choosing the appropriate country settings. United States is selected by default, so simply press **Enter**. A message appears telling you that Setup is installing the appropriate files. You are instructed to insert the *Utilities 1* disk into the current drive. Press **Enter** to continue the setup. Soon another message appears to instruct you to insert the *Utilities 2* disk into the current drive. Press **Enter** to continue the setup and copy the necessary files. Continue to insert the appropriate disks and follow the Setup instructions until all files are copied.

19. Setup informs you that it needs to modify the CONFIG.SYS file to install the driver, HIMEM.SYS. Following the screen instructions, choose **Update CONFIG.SYS** and press **Enter**. Soon a message appears that the run-time version of Windows has been successfully installed. Press **Enter** to continue.

20. Setup now lets you install printer drivers supported by Word for DOS but not by Windows. Since you are using a run-time version of Windows, it is likely that you won't need to install these drivers (the option is up to you). Choose **Do not install printer drivers** to continue with Setup.

21. Setup will now determine the type of printer you have connected to your system. If you have a laser printer, Setup will give you the option of installing soft fonts which allow special characters to be printed. Make your selection and then press **Enter**. If you do elect to install soft fonts, Setup will instruct you to insert the Conversions disk into drive A and press **Enter**.

22. Setup gives you the option of running a program called MEMSET, which helps you to optimize Word's use of extended/expanded memory. Make your selection and press **Enter**. Soon Setup provides the message the Word for Windows has been successfully installed!

Appendix B

Keyboard Commands

You can access nearly all Word commands directly through the keyboard. As you become a Word for Windows expert, you may find keystroke shortcuts using the function keys improve your productivity as well. The following is a list of all the key assignments that are standard with Word for Windows. Keep in mind that if you customize your key assignments based on a template (see Chapter 19), the tables that follow will differ. (Note: For keystroke combinations that use a letter, you can type it as either uppercase or lowercase.)

Alphanumeric Keys

The key assignments for the alphanumeric keys are listed in alphabetical order by action. In other words, to find the key-combination assignment to apply the bold character format to text, look up bold in the list.

For This Action	Press Key(s)
Assign color	Ctrl+V
Assign font	Ctrl+F
Assign point size	Ctrl+P
Assign style	Ctrl+S
Bold	Ctrl+B
Center paragraph	Ctrl+C

(continued)

For This Action	Press Key(s)
Close pane	Alt + Shift + C
Close space before paragraph	Ctrl + E
Collapse outline	Alt + Shift + -
Continue macro	Alt + Shift + O
Copy to Clipboard	Ctrl + Insert
Create new column break	Ctrl + Shift + Enter
Create new line	Shift + Enter
Create new page break	Ctrl + Enter
Create new paragraph	Enter
Cut to Clipboard	Shift + Delete
Delete character left	Backspace
Delete character right	Delete (Del)
Delete word left	Ctrl + Backspace
Delete word or selection	Ctrl + Delete
Double line spacing	Ctrl + 2
Double underline	Ctrl + D
Expand outline	Alt + Shift + =
Hanging indent	Ctrl + T
Hidden text	Ctrl + H
Hyphen	- (Hyphen)
Insert date field	Alt + Shift + D
Insert from Clipboard	Shift + Insert
Insert or overtype mode	Insert (Ins)
Insert page field	Alt + Shift + P
Insert tab in table	Ctrl + Tab
Insert tab or move to next cell in table	Tab
Insert time field	Alt + Shift + T
Italic	Ctrl + I
Justified alignment	Ctrl + J
Left alignment	Ctrl + L
Nest	Ctrl + N
Nonbreaking Hyphen	Ctrl + Shift + -
Nonbreaking space	Ctrl + Shift + Spacebar

For This Action	Press Key(s)
One-and-a-half line spacing	Ctrl+5
Open document control menu box	Alt+-
Open Edit menu	Alt,E
Open File menu	Alt,F
Open Format menu	Alt,T
Open Help menu	Alt,H
Open Insert menu	Alt,I
Open Macro menu	Alt,M
Open space before paragraph	Ctrl+O
Open Utilities menu	Alt,U
Open View menu	Alt,V
Open Window menu	Alt,W
Open Word Control Box menu	Alt,Spacebar
Optional Hyphen	Ctrl+-
Repeat last action	Alt+Enter
Reset characters to previous format	Ctrl+Spacebar
Reset paragraph to default style	Ctrl+X
Right alignment	Ctrl+R
Show all in Outline View	Alt+Shift+A
Show all levels in outline	Alt+Shift+*
Show all special characters	Ctrl+*
Show automatic styles in define styles	Ctrl+A
Show first line only (Outline View)	Alt+Shift+F
Show headings to 1 in Outline View	Alt+Shift+1
Show headings to 2 in Outline View	Alt+Shift+2
Show headings to 3 in Outline View	Alt+Shift+3
Show headings to 4 in Outline View	Alt+Shift+4
Show headings to 5 in Outline View	Alt+Shift+5
Show headings to 6 in Outline View	Alt+Shift+6
Show headings to 7 in Outline View	Alt+Shift+7
Show headings to 8 in Outline View	Alt+Shift+8
Show headings to 9 in Outline View	Alt+Shift+9
Show variables in macro	Alt+Shift+V
Single line spacing	Ctrl+1

(continued)

For This Action	Press Key(s)
Small capitals	Ctrl+K
Start macro	Alt+Shift+S
Step macro	Alt+Shift+E
Step SUBS in macro	Alt+Shift+U
Strikethrough (in search and replace only)	Ctrl+Z
Subscript	Ctrl+ = (equal sign)
Superscript	Ctrl+ + (plus sign)
Trace macro	Alt+Shift+R
Underline (continuous)	Ctrl+U
Undo command	Alt+Backspace
Unindent hanging indent	Ctrl+G
Unnest	Ctrl+M
Word underline	Ctrl+W

Function Keys

The key assignments for the twelve function keys are grouped in two ways. First, all the actions associated with a particular function key are listed for easy reference. The second listing regroups all the actions of the function keys alphabetically by action.

If you have a standard keyboard, you can still perform all actions calling for the F11 and F12 keys. Generally, you simply need to press one extra key.

Function Key Assignments by Key

For This Action	Press Key(s)
Help	F1
Help mouse pointer	Shift+F1
Next field (same as F11)	Alt+F1
Previous field (Same as Shift+F11)	Alt+Shift+F1

B—Keyboard Commands

For This Action	Press Key(s)
Move	F2
Copy	Shift+F2
Grow font	Ctrl+F2
Shrink font	Ctrl+Shift+F2
File save as (same as F12)	Alt+F2
File save (same as Shift+F12)	Alt+Shift+F2
Expand glossary name	F3
Toggle case	Shift+F3
Spike	Ctrl+F3
Unspike	Ctrl+Shift+F3
Repeat last editing or formatting action	F4
Repeat search or go to	Shift+F4
Close document window	Ctrl+F4
Close Word window	Alt+F4
Go to	F5
Go back to previous insertion point	Shift+F5
Restore document window	Ctrl+F5
Insert bookmark	Ctrl+Shift+F5
Restore Word window	Alt+F5
Next pane	F6
Previous pane	Shift+F6
Next document window	Ctrl+F6 or Alt+F6
Previous document window	Ctrl+Shift+F6 or Alt+Shift+F6
Spell check selection	F7
Thesaurus	Shift+F7
Move document window	Ctrl+F7
Update source for INCLUDE file	Ctrl+Shift+F7
Move Word window	Alt+F7
Extend selection	F8
Shrink selection	Shift+F8

(continued)

For This Action	Press Key(s)
Size document window	Ctrl + F8
Column selection	Ctrl + Shift + F8
Size Word window	Alt + F8
Update field	F9
Toggle field codes view	Shift + F9
Insert field	Ctrl + F9
Unlink field and replace with result	Ctrl + Shift + F9
Minimize Word window	Alt + F9
Do field click	Alt + Shift + F9
Menu	F10
Icon bar mode in Outline View	Shift + F10
Maximize document window	Ctrl + F10
Ruler mode	Ctrl + Shift + F10
Maximize Word window	Alt + F10
Next field	F11
Previous field	Shift + F11
Lock field	Ctrl + F11
Unlock field	Ctrl + Shift + F11
File save as	F12
File save	Shift + F12
File open	Ctrl + F12
File print	Ctrl + Shift + F12

Alphabetical Listing by Action

For This Action	Press Key(s)
Close document window	Ctrl + F4
Close Word window	Alt + F4
Column selection	Ctrl + Shift + F8
Copy	Shift + F2
Do field click	Alt + Shift + F9
Expand glossary name	F3
Extend selection	F8

B—Keyboard Commands

For This Action	Press Key(s)
File open	Ctrl+F12
File print	Ctrl+Shift+F12
File save	Shift+F12
File save (same as Shift+F12)	Alt+Shift+F2
File save as	F12
File save as (same as F12)	Alt+F2
Go back to previous insertion point	Shift+F5
Go to	F5
Grow font	Ctrl+F2
Help	F1
Help mouse pointer	Shift+F1
Icon bar mode in Outline View	Shift+F10
Insert bookmark	Ctrl+Shift+F5
Insert field	Ctrl+F9
Lock field	Ctrl+F11
Maximize document window	Ctrl+F10
Maximize Word window	Alt+F10
Menu	F10
Minimize Word window	Alt+F9
Move	F2
Move document window	Ctrl+F7
Move Word window	Alt+F7
Next document window	Ctrl+F6 or Alt+F6
Next field	F11
Next field (same as F11)	Alt+F1
Next pane	F6
Previous document window	Ctrl+Shift+F6 or Alt+Shift+F6
Previous field	Shift+F11
Previous Field (Same as Shift+F11)	Alt+Shift+F1
Previous pane	Shift+F6
Repeat last editing or formatting action	F4
Repeat search or go to	Shift+F4
Restore document window	Ctrl+F5

(continued)

The Best Book of Word for WINDOWS

For This Action	Press Key(s)
Restore Word window	Alt + F5
Ruler mode	Ctrl + Shift + F10
Shrink font	Ctrl + Shift + F2
Shrink selection	Shift + F8
Size document window	Ctrl + F8
Size Word window	Alt + F8
Spell check selection	F7
Spike	Ctrl + F3
Thesaurus	Shift + F7
Toggle case	Shift + F3
Toggle field codes view	Shift + F9
Unlink field and replace with result	Ctrl + Shift + F9
Unlock field	Ctrl + Shift + F11
Unspike	Ctrl + Shift + F3
Update field	F9
Update source for INCLUDE file	Ctrl + Shift + F7

Direction Keys

The actions of the direction keys are simply grouped together by function for each of the eight keys (left arrow, right arrow, up arrow, down arrow, Home, End, Page Up, and Page Down). These actions generally refer to the movement of the insertion point on your screen. The exceptions are those actions that refer to Outline View that offer some specific function. For example, Alt + Shift + Left will promote the current heading to the next highest level in the outline.

For This Action	Press Key(s)
Left one character	Left
Extend left one character	Shift + left
Extend left one word	Ctrl + left
Left one word	Alt + left
Promote heading in Outline View	Alt + Shift + left

B—Keyboard Commands

For This Action	Press Key(s)
Right one character	Right
Extend right one character	Shift+right
Right one word	Alt+right
Extend right one word	Ctrl+right
Demote heading in Outline View	Alt+Shift+right
Up one line	Up
Extend up one line	Shift+up
Up one paragraph	Ctrl+up
Extend up one paragraph	Ctrl+Shift+up
Previous region in Page View	Alt+up
Move paragraph up in Outline View	Alt+Shift+up
Down one line	Down
Extend down one line	Shift+down
Down one paragraph	Ctrl+down
Extend Down one paragraph	Ctrl+Shift+down
Next region in Page View	Alt+down
Move paragraph down in Outline View	Alt+Shift+down
Beginning of line	Home
Extend to beginning of line	Shift+Home
Beginning of document	Ctrl+Home
Extend to beginning of document	Ctrl+Shift+Home
Beginning of row in a table	Alt+Home
End of line	End
Extend to end of line	Shift+End
End of document	Ctrl+End
Extend to end of document	Ctrl+Shift+End
End of row in a table	Alt+End
Up one window	PgUp
Extend up one window	Shift+PgUp
Top of window	Ctrl+PgUp
Extend to top of window	Ctrl+Shift+PgUp
Top of column in a table	Alt+PgUp

(continued)

For This Action	Press Key(s)
Down one window	PgDn
Extend one window	Shift+PgDn
Bottom of window	Ctrl+PgDn
Extend to bottom of window	Ctrl+Shift+PgDn
Bottom of column in a table	Alt+PgDn

Numeric Keypad (Note: Num Lock mode can be either on or off)

For This Action	Press Key(s)
Select entire document	Ctrl+Numpad 5
Select entire table	Alt+Numpad 5
Apply Normal Style to paragraph	Alt+Shift+Numpad 5
Expand outline in Outline View	Numpad +
Collapse outline in Outline View	Numpad -
Show all levels in Outline View	Numpad *

Index

A

accepting revision marks, 409-411
activating windows, 41
adding borders to tables, 345-347
adding captions to pictures, 551-552
adding word to dictionary, 307
additional printers, 247-248
aligning tables, 348
alphabetizing tables, 348-351
Alt (menu) key, 28-29
Alt-5 (select entire table) key, 337
Alt-Backspace (undo command) key, 110-111, 570
Alt-C (columns) key, 330, 338-339
Alt-D (directory) key, 81-82
Alt-E (edit menu) key, 569
Alt-Enter (repeat last action) key, 569
Alt-F (file menu) key, 569
Alt-F1 (next field) key, 570, 573
Alt-F2 (shrink font) keys, 571, 573-574
Alt-F4 (close Word window) key, 29, 571-572
Alt-F5 (restore Word window) keys, 571, 574
Alt-F6 (next document window) key, 571, 573
Alt-F7 (move Word window) key, 571
Alt-F8 (size Word window) key, 572, 574
Alt-F9 (minimize Word window) keys, 572-573
Alt-F10 (maximize Word window) key, 572-573
Alt-H (Help menu) key, 45-46, 569

Alt-hyphen (open document control menu) key, 12, 31, 569
Alt-I (insert menu) key, 569
Alt-M (macro menu) key, 569
Alt-R (rows) key, 330, 338-339
Alt-Shift-* (show all levels in outline) key, 569
Alt-Shift-1 (show headings to 1 in Outline view) key, 569
Alt-Shift-2 (show headings to 2 in Outline view) key, 569
Alt-Shift-3 (show headings to 3 in Outline view) key, 569
Alt-Shift-4 (show headings to 4 in Outline view) key, 569
Alt-Shift-5 (show headings to 5 in Outline view) key, 569
Alt-Shift-6 (show headings to 6 in Outline view) key, 569
Alt-Shift-7 (show headings to 7 in Outline view) key, 569
Alt-Shift-8 (show headings to 8 in Outline view) key, 569
Alt-Shift-9 (show headings to 9 in Outline view) key, 569
Alt-Shift-= (expand outline) key, 568
Alt-Shift-A (show all in Outline line) key, 569
Alt-Shift-D (insert date field) key, 568
Alt-Shift-E (step macro) key, 570
Alt-Shift-F (show first line only in Outline view) key, 468, 473-474, 569

Alt-Shift-F1 (previous field) key, 570, 573
Alt-Shift-F2 (file save) keys, 571, 573
Alt-Shift-F6 (previous document window) key, 571, 573
Alt-Shift-F9 (do field click) key, 572
Alt-Shift-hyphen (collapse outline) key, 473-474, 568
Alt-Shift-O (continue macro) key, 568
Alt-Shift-P (insert page field) key, 568
Alt-Shift-R (trace macro) key, 570
Alt-Shift-S (start macro) key, 570
Alt-Shift-T (insert tab field), 568
Alt-Shift-U (step SUBS in macro) key, 570
Alt-Shift-V (show variable in macro) key, 569
Alt-Spacebar (open Word control menu) key, 12, 31, 569
Alt-T (format menu) key, 122-125, 569
Alt-U (utilities menu) key, 569
Alt-V (view menu) key, 569
Alt-W (window menu) key, 569
Annotation command, 396-399
annotations, 395
    annotation mark, 396
    annotation panes, 399-402
    creating, 396-399
    deleting, 403-404
    editing, 403-404
    Go To command, 400-402
    hidden text, 396-398
    moving, 403
    printing, 240, 404-405
    reading, 402
applying styles, 384-388
ASK instruction, 450-454
Assign to Key command, 518, 530-532
Assign to Menu command, 518
assigning macros to menus, 527-529
automatic hyphenation, 319-320
automatic numbering in outlines, 478-480
automatic styles, 377-379

B

backing up documents, 66, 72
Backspace key, 26, 93-94, 568
backups, 559-560
block editing, 100-110
bold, 200
bookmarks, 441-444, 506-508
    creating, 507-508
    deleting, 508
    editing, 508
borders
    adding to tables, 345-347
    drawing around pictures, 548-549

setting with Paragraph command, 182-183
bound documents, 228-230

C

Calculate command, 351-353
canceling printing, 252, 265-266
Caps Lock key, 24
captions, 551-552
cells, 328-329
    cell references, 354-356
    inserting text, 331-332
    minimum height, 343
    resizing in tables, 341-342
changing directories, 81-82
changing size of pictures, 544-546
changing style formatting, 390-391
changing style names, 389-390
changing styles in templates, 434
changing window size, 41-42
Character command, 194-203
character formatting, 131-132, 187-203
    bold, 200
    character spacing, 195
    color, 195, 201
    emphasis, 195
    face, 188
    fonts, 188-203
    Hidden Text option, 200
    italic, 200
    kerning, 189
    points, 188, 195
    Ribbon, 191-194
    search and replace, 119-121
    Small Kaps option, 200
    style, 189, 195
    subscripts, 201-202
    superscripts, 201-202
    underline, 200
    x-height, 188
choosing
    commands from menus, 13
    commands with keyboard, 28-29
    commands with mouse, 29
    fonts, 193-197
    menus, 14
    subcommands from dialog boxes, 30
clearing screen, 61-62
clicking with mouse, 27
Clipboard, 90, 95-96
    displaying, 95-96
    saving contents, 96
closing windows, 41
collapsing outlines, 473-474
color, 201

Index

columns
  deleting from tables, 339-340
  inserting in tables, 337-339
  resizing in tables, 341-342
  Section command, 210
  snaking, 215-222
command well, 529-530
commands
  Annotation, 396-399
  Assign to Key, 518, 530-532
  Assign to Menu, 518
  Calculate, 351-353
  Character, 194-203
  choosing from dialog boxes, 30
  choosing from menus, 13
  choosing with keyboard, 28-29
  choosing with mouse, 29
  Connections, 245-246
  Copy, 104-106, 340
  Copy To, 106-110
  Customize, 513-515
  Cut, 98-99, 102-104, 340, 403
  Define Styles, 375, 379-384, 389
  Delete Printer, 248
  Document, 139-143
  Field, 491
  Find, 258-259, 419-427
  Footnotes, 503-505
  Format Picture, 546-549
  Format Styles, 387-388
  Glossary, 297-298
  Go To, 60-61, 114, 506-508
  Hyphenate, 318-325
  Index, 497
  Insert Index Entry, 497
  Insert Page Numbers, 284-285
  Insert Table, 328-330, 334-335
  Macro Edit, 518
  Macro Record, 518-519
  Move To, 106-110
  Outlining, 466-468
  Paragraph, 164-165, 176
  Paste, 103-104, 340, 403
  Paste Link, 554-556
  Position, 225-230
  Preferences, 512-513
  Print, 252-255, 263-265
  Print Merge, 440, 447-449
  Printer Setup, 247-251
  Replace, 115-119
  Run, 517, 523
  Search, 111-113
  Section, 209-224
  Styles, 375
  Table, 341-342
  Tabs, 171-176
  Undo, 110-111

View Annotation, 402
View Draft, 468
comparing documents, 412
compiling indexes, 502-503
connecting printers, 245-246
Connections command, 245-246
Copy command, 104-106, 340
Copy To command, 106-110
copying text, 104-110, 340
correcting misspelled words, 307-310
creating
  annotations, 396-398
  bookmarks, 507-508
  document sections, 212-214
  documents, 54-55, 61-62
  footers, 276-277
  footnotes, 503-505
  glossary entries, 365-367
  headers, 276-278
  indexes, 496-501
  macros, 518-522
  mailing labels, 454-459
  outlines, 470-473
  paragraphs, 55-57
  revision marks, 405-408
  tables, 329-330
  tables from existing text, 332-335
  tables of contents, 486-496
  templates, 431-433
cropping pictures with Format Picture
  command, 546-548
cropping pictures with mouse, 544-546
cross-references, 499-501
Ctrl-* (show special characters) key, 569
Ctrl-+ (superscript) key, 570
Ctrl-1 (single line spacing) key, 153, 161, 569
Ctrl-2 (double line spacing) key, 153, 161, 568
Ctrl-5 (one-and-a-half line spacing) key, 153, 161, 569
Ctrl-= (subscript) key, 570
Ctrl-A (show automatic styles in define styles) key, 375, 569
Ctrl-B (bold) key, 567
Ctrl-Backspace (delete word left) key, 568
Ctrl-C (center) key, 153, 155, 567
Ctrl-D (double underline) key, 568
Ctrl-Delete (delete word or selection) key, 568
Ctrl-E (close space before paragraph) key, 154, 568
Ctrl-Enter (create new page break) key, 144, 568
Ctrl-F (assign font) key, 567
Ctrl-F2 (grow font) keys, 571, 573
Ctrl-F3 (spike) keys, 571, 574

579

Ctrl-F4 (close document window) key, 571-572
Ctrl-F5 (restore document window) keys, 571, 573
Ctrl-F6 (next document window) key, 41, 571, 573
Ctrl-F7 (move document window) key, 571, 573
Ctrl-F8 (size document window) key, 572, 574
Ctrl-F9 (insert field) keys, 442-444, 572-573
Ctrl-F10 (maximize document window) key, 572-573
Ctrl-F11 (lock field) key, 572-573
Ctrl-F12 (file open) key, 572-573
Ctrl-G (unindent hanging indent) key, 167, 570
Ctrl-H (hidden text) key, 568
Ctrl-hyphen (optional hyphen) key, 569
Ctrl-I (italic) key, 568
Ctrl-Insert (copy to Clipboard) key, 105-106, 568
Ctrl-J (justification) key, 153-155, 568
Ctrl-K (small capitals) key, 570
Ctrl-L (left alignment) key, 153-155, 568
Ctrl-M (unnest) key, 167, 570
Ctrl-N (nest) key, 167, 568
Ctrl-O (open space before paragraph) key, 154, 569
Ctrl-P (assign point size) key, 567
Ctrl-R (right alignment) key, 153-155, 569
Ctrl-S (assign style) key, 377, 383-388, 567
Ctrl-Shift-C (close pane) key, 568
Ctrl-Shift-Enter (create new column break) key, 568
Ctrl-Shift-F2 (shrink font) keys, 571, 574
Ctrl-Shift-F3 (unspike) keys, 571, 574
Ctrl-Shift-F5 (insert bookmark) keys, 571, 573
Ctrl-Shift-F6 (previous document window) key, 571, 573
Ctrl-Shift-F7 (update source for include file) key, 571, 574
Ctrl-Shift-F8 (column selection) key, 337, 572
Ctrl-Shift-F9 (unlink field and replace) keys, 572, 574
Ctrl-Shift-F10 (Ruler) key, 39, 151-154, 572, 574
Ctrl-Shift-F11 (unlock field) key, 572, 574
Ctrl-Shift-F12 (file print) key, 572-573
Ctrl-Shift-Hyphen (nonbreaking hyphen) key, 568
Ctrl-Shift-Spacebar (nonbreaking space) key, 568
Ctrl-Spacebar (reset to previous format) key, 569
Ctrl-T (hanging indent) key, 167, 568
Ctrl-Tab (insert tab in table) key, 568
Ctrl-U (underline) key, 570
Ctrl-V (assign color) key, 567
Ctrl-W (Word underline) key, 570
Ctrl-X (reset paragraph to default style) key, 569
Ctrl-Z (strikethru) key, 570
cursor movement keys, 59-60, 574-576
Customize command, 513-515
customizing menus, 529-530
customizing Word, 512-515
cut and paste text, 101-104
    tables, 340
Cut command, 98-99, 102-104, 340, 403
    annotations, 403
    deleting text, 98-99
    tables, 340

D

data files, 416
date headers, 282-284
DDE fields, 554-556
decimal tabs, 344-345
Define Styles command, 375, 379-384, 389
defining styles, 379-384
Delete key, 568
Delete Printer command, 248
deleting
    annotations, 403-404
    bookmarks, 508
    columns from tables, 339-340
    documents, 430
    footers, 296-297
    footnotes, 506
    glossary entries, 369
    headers, 296-297
    indexes, 503
    macros, 529
    page numbers, 287
    pictures, 552-553
    printers, 248
    rows from tables, 339-340
    styles, 389
    text, 93-94, 97-99
dictionaries, 301-307
    adding words, 307
    main, 302-305
    supplemental, 302, 312-314
    user, 301, 311-314
direction keys, 25-26, 574-576
directories, 81-82, 417-418
disks, 416-418

Index

displaying Clipboard, 95-96
Document command, 139-143
Document Control menu, 12-13, 31
document files, 416
document formatting, 130-135, 209-234
   document templates, 135
   footnotes, 134
   hard page breaks, 144
   line breaks, 143
   margins, 134-143
   page breaks, 143
   paper size, 134
   setting margins, 133
   soft page breaks, 144
   tab stops, 134
   widow control, 135, 144-145
document retrieval, 418-427
   Find command, 419-427
   loading documents, 428
   opening multiple documents, 428-430
   printing multiple documents, 428-430
   summary information sheet, 419-422
document window
   end-of-document mark, 11-12
   I-beam pointer, 8-9
   insertion point, 8
   Maximize arrow box, 12
   Minimize arrow box, 12
   scroll bar, 12
   title bar, 11-12
documents
   bound, 228-230
   comparing, 412
   creating, 54-55, 61-62
   creating sections, 212-214
   deleting, 430
   inserting pictures into, 538-544
   loading, 428
   locking, 404
   multicolumn text, 215-222
   opening, 78-80
   opening multiple, 428-430
   page numbers, 281-287
   printing, 85-86, 240, 256-265
   printing multiple, 428-430
   saving, 66-60, 71-77, 84-85
   saving automatically, 67, 72-73
   searching for, 422-427
   sections, 210-224, 290-292
   summary information, 68-70
   templates, 430-434
   unlocking, 404
double-clicking with mouse, 28
draft printing, 254
Draft view, 16-18
dragging with mouse, 27
drawing borders around pictures, 548-549

E

Edit menu, 32-34, 94-95
editing
   annotations, 403-404
   bookmarks, 508
   footnotes, 505-506
   macros, 524-525
   outlines, 475-477
   styles, 388-392
   tables, 336-340
   templates, 433
   text, 93-125
end-of-document mark, 11-12
Enter (create new paragraph) key, 23-24, 568
entering text, 54-55, 63-64
exiting Word, 46-47
expanding outlines, 473-474

F

F1 (help) key, 44-46, 570, 573
F2 (move) key, 107, 571, 573
F3 (expand glossary name) key, 571-572
F4 (repeat last action) key, 571, 573
F5 (go to) keys, 61, 114, 506-508, 571, 573
F6 (next pane) key, 571, 573
F7 (spell check) key, 571, 574
F8 (extend selection) key, 91, 571-572
F9 (update field) keys, 572, 574
F10 (menu) key, 572-573
F11 (next field) key, 572-573
F12 (file save as) key, 572-573
face, 188
facing page headers, 292-294
Fast Save option, 77
field characters {}, 441-444
Field command, 491
file formats, 75-76
files, 53, 64-65
   data, 416
   document, 416
   extensions, 65
   file names, 64-65
   program, 416
fill-in form letters, 450-454
Find command, 419-427
   printing, 258-259
First Page option, 294-296
floppy disks, 416
fonts, 188-189, 195-200
   bold, 200
   choosing, 196-197
   choosing from Ribbon, 193-194
   emphasis, 198-200

The Best Book of Word for Windows

Hidden Text option, 200
italic, 200
kerning, 202-203
monospace, 202-203
points, 197-198
proportional spacing, 202-203
size, 197-198
Small Kaps option, 200
spacing, 202-203
styles, 198-200
underline, 200
footers
    creating, 276-277
    deleting, 296-297
    deleting page numbers from, 287
    First Page option, 294-296
    formatting page numbers, 285-287
    Glossary command, 297-298
    Insert Page Number command, 284-285
    positioning, 287-289
    varying by section, 290-292
footnotes, 134
    creating, 503-505
    deleting, 506
    editing, 505-506
    Section command, 211
Footnotes command, 503-505
form letters, 439-449
    ASK instruction, 450-454
    bookmarks, 441-444
    data document, 444-447
    fields, 441-444
    fill-in, 450-454
    header record, 444-447
    individual records, 445-447
    main document, 440-444
    printing, 447-449
Format menu, 34, 131-134
Format Picture command, 546-549
Format Styles command, 387-388
formatting
    characters, 131-132, 187-203
    documents, 130-143, 209-234
    headers, 279-280
    page numbers, 285-287
    paragraphs, 132, 147-183
    sections, 132
    tables, 341-351
formulas, 356-358
    inserting in tables, 357-358
    printing, 356-357
Full menus, 30-31
function keys, 22-25
    Alt-F1 (next field), 570, 573
    Alt-F2 (shrink font), 571, 573-574

Alt-F4 (close Word window), 29, 571-572
Alt-F5 (restore Word window), 571, 574
Alt-F6 (next document window), 571, 573
Alt-F7 (move Word window), 571
Alt-F8 (size Word window), 572, 574
Alt-F9 (minimize Word window), 572-573
Alt-F10 (maximize Word window), 572-573
Alt-Shift-F1 (previous field), 570, 573
Alt-Shift-F2 (file save), 571, 573
Alt-Shift-F6 (previous document window), 571, 573
Alt-Shift-F9 (do field click), 572
Ctrl-F2 (grow font), 571, 573
Ctrl-F3 (spike), 571, 574
Ctrl-F4 (close document window), 571-572
Ctrl-F5 (restore document window), 571, 573
Ctrl-F6 (next document window), 41, 571, 573
Ctrl-F7 (move document window), 571, 573
Ctrl-F8 (size document window), 572, 574
Ctrl-F9 (insert field), 442-444, 572-573
Ctrl-F10 (maximize document window), 572-573
Ctrl-F11 (lock field), 572-573
Ctrl-F12 (file open), 572-573
Ctrl-Shift-F10 (Ruler), 39, 151-154, 572, 574
Ctrl-Shift-F11 (unlock field), 572, 574
Ctrl-Shift-F12 (file print), 572-573
Ctrl-Shift-F2 (shrink font), 571, 574
Ctrl-Shift-F3 (unspike), 571, 574
Ctrl-Shift-F5 (insert bookmark), 571, 573
Ctrl-Shift-F6 (previous document window), 571, 573
Ctrl-Shift-F7 (update source for include file), 571, 574
Ctrl-Shift-F8 (column select mode), 337
Ctrl-Shift-F8 (column selection), 572
Ctrl-Shift-F9 (unlink field and replace), 572, 574
F1 (help), 44-46, 570, 573
F2 (move), 107-108, 571, 573
F3 (expand glossary name), 571-572
F4 (repeat last action), 571, 573
F5 (Go To), 61, 506-508, 571, 573

582

Index

F6 (next pane), 571, 573
F7 (spell check), 571, 574
F8 (extend selection), 571-572
F9 (update field), 572, 574
F10 (menu), 572-573
F11 (next field), 572-573
F12 (file save as), 572-573
Shift-F1 (help mouse pointer), 44-46, 570, 573
Shift-F2 (copy), 109, 571-572
Shift-F3 (toggle case), 571, 574
Shift-F4 (repeat last search or go to), 571, 573
Shift-F5 (go to previous insertion point), 571, 573
Shift-F6 (previous pane), 571, 573
Shift-F7 (thesaurus), 315-316, 571, 574
Shift-F8 (shrink selection), 571, 574
Shift-F9 (toggle field codes view), 572, 574
Shift-F10 (icon bar in Outline view), 277-278, 281-284, 572
Shift-F11 (previous field), 572-573
Shift-F12 (file save), 66, 572-573

G

Galley view, 14-15
glossaries, 363-370
    creating entries, 365-367
    deleting, 369
    inserting entries, 365-367
    inserting entries from keyboard, 368-369
    inserting entries into text, 367-368
    printing, 240, 370
    structure, 364-365
Glossary command
    footers, 297-298
    headers, 297-298
Go To command, 60-61, 114, 506-508
    annotations, 400-402
graphics *See* pictures

H

hanging indents, 167-168
hard disks, 417-418
hard page breaks, 144
headers
    creating, 276-278
    date in, 282-284
    deleting, 296-297
    deleting page numbers, 287
    entering text, 278-279
    facing page, 292-294
    First Page option, 294-296

    formatting, 279-280
    formatting page numbers, 285-287
    formatting with Ribbon, 280
    formatting with Ruler, 280
    Glossary command, 297-298
    icon bar, 281-284
    Insert Page Number command, 284-285
    page numbers, 281-287
    positioning, 287-289
    positioning with Print Preview, 288-289
    time, 282-284
    varying by section, 290-292
help, 44-46
Help menu, 35-36, 45-46
hidden text
    annotations, 396-398
    printing, 240, 262-264
Hidden Text option, 200
Hyphenate command, 318-325
hyphenation, 301-302, 317-325
    automatic, 319-320
    hot zone, 321
    manual, 319-320
    nonbreaking, 320-322
    normal, 320-322
    optional, 320-322
    selected text, 318-320
    undoing, 324-325

I

I-beam pointer, 8-9
Include option, 264-265
indent markers, 151-152
indentation, 161-168
    hanging indents, 167-168
    setting with keyboard, 163-164
    setting with mouse, 162-163
    setting with Paragraph command, 164-165
Index command, 497
indexes, 495-500
    compiling, 502-503
    creating, 496-501
    cross-references, 499-501
    deleting, 503
    index entry field codes (xe), 497-501
    multiple level entries, 499-501
Insert Index Entry command, 497
Insert menu, 34
Insert Page Numbers command, 284-285
Insert Table command, 328-330, 334-335
inserting
    blank picture frames, 542-544
    columns in tables, 337-339

583

formulas in tables, 357-358
glossary entries, 365-369
pictures into documents, 538-544
rows in tables, 337-339
text, 97-98
text in tables, 331-332
insertion point, 8
installing additional printers, 247-248
installing printer drivers, 241-244
installing Word run-time version, 564-566
installing Word with Windows installed, 561-564
italic, 200

J-K

justifying paragraphs, 154-157
kerning, 189, 202-203
keyboards, 19-22
    choosing commands, 28-29
    function keys, 22-23
    scrolling text, 59-60
    selecting text, 91
    setting tab stops, 170-171
    special keys, 22-23
keys
    Alt (menu), 28-29
    Alt-5 (select entire table), 337
    Alt-Backspace (undo command), 110-111, 570
    Alt-C (columns), 330, 338-339
    Alt-D (directory), 81-82
    Alt-E (edit menu), 569
    Alt-Enter (repeat last action), 569
    Alt-F (file menu), 569
    Alt-F1 (next field), 570, 573
    Alt-F2 (shrink font), 571-574
    Alt-F4 (close Word window), 29, 571-572
    Alt-F5 (restore Word window), 571, 574
    Alt-F6 (next document window), 571, 573
    Alt-F7 (move Word window), 571
    Alt-F8 (size Word window), 572, 574
    Alt-F9 (minimize Word window), 572-573
    Alt-F10 (maximize Word window), 572-573
    Alt-H (Help menu), 45-46, 569
    Alt-hyphen (open document control menu), 12, 31, 569
    Alt-I (insert menu), 569
    Alt-M (macro menu), 569
    Alt-R (rows), 330, 338-339
    Alt-Shift-* (show all levels in outline), 569

Alt-Shift-1 (show headings to 1 in Outline view), 569
Alt-Shift-2 (show headings to 2 in Outline view), 569
Alt-Shift-3 (show headings to 3 in Outline view), 569
Alt-Shift-4 (show headings to 4 in Outline view), 569
Alt-Shift-5 (show headings to 5 in Outline view), 569
Alt-Shift-6 (show headings to 6 in Outline view), 569
Alt-Shift-7 (show headings to 7 in Outline view), 569
Alt-Shift-8 (show headings to 8 in Outline view), 569
Alt-Shift-9 (show headings to 9 in Outline view), 569
Alt-Shift-= (expand outline), 568
Alt-Shift-A (show all in Outline line), 569
Alt-Shift-D (insert date field), 568
Alt-Shift-E (step macro), 570
Alt-Shift-F (show first line only in Outline view), 569
Alt-Shift-F (show first line only), 468, 473-474
Alt-Shift-F1 (previous field), 570, 573
Alt-Shift-F2 (file save), 571, 573
Alt-Shift-F6 (previous document window), 571, 573
Alt-Shift-F9 (do field click), 572
Alt-Shift-hyphen (collapse outline), 473-474, 568
Alt-Shift-O (continue macro), 568
Alt-Shift-P (insert page field), 568
Alt-Shift-R (trace macro), 570
Alt-Shift-S (start macro), 570
Alt-Shift-T (insert tab field), 568
Alt-Shift-U (step SUBS in macro), 570
Alt-Shift-V (show variable in macro), 569
Alt-Spacebar (open Word control menu), 12, 31, 569
Alt-T (split window), 43-44, 122-125, 569
Alt-U (utilities menu), 569
Alt-V (view menu), 569
Alt-W (window menu), 569
Backspace, 26, 93-94, 568
Caps Lock, 24
Ctrl-* (show special characters), 569
Ctrl-+ (superscript), 570
Ctrl-1 (single line spacing), 153, 161, 569
Ctrl-2 (double line spacing), 153, 161, 568

Index

Ctrl-5 (one-and-a-half line spacing), 153, 161, 569
Ctrl-= (subscript), 570
Ctrl-A (show automatic styles in define styles), 375, 569
Ctrl-B (bold), 567
Ctrl-Backspace (delete word left), 568
Ctrl-C (center paragraph), 153, 155, 567
Ctrl-D (double underline), 568
Ctrl-Delete (delete word or selection), 568
Ctrl-E (close space before paragraph), 154, 568
Ctrl-Enter (create new page break), 114, 568
Ctrl-F (assign font), 567
Ctrl-F2 (grow font), 571, 573
Ctrl-F3 (spike), 571, 574
Ctrl-F4 (close document window), 571-572
Ctrl-F5 (restore document window), 571, 573
Ctrl-F6 (next document window), 41, 571, 573
Ctrl-F7 (move document window), 571, 573
Ctrl-F8 (size document window), 572, 574
Ctrl-F9 (insert field), 442-444, 572-573
Ctrl-F10 (maximize document window), 572-573
Ctrl-F11 (lock field), 572-573
Ctrl-F12 (file open), 572-573
Ctrl-G (unindent hanging indent), 167, 570
Ctrl-H (hidden text), 568
Ctrl-hyphen (optional hyphen), 569
Ctrl-I (italic), 568
Ctrl-Ins (copy), 105-106
Ctrl-Insert (copy to Clipboard), 568
Ctrl-J (justification), 153-155, 568
Ctrl-K (small capitals), 570
Ctrl-L (left alignment), 153, 155, 568
Ctrl-M (move left indent marker back), 167
Ctrl-M (unnest), 167, 570
Ctrl-N (nest), 568
Ctrl-O (open space before paragraph), 154, 569
Ctrl-P (assign point size), 567
Ctrl-R (right alignment), 153, 155, 569
Ctrl-S (assign style), 377, 383, 385, 388, 567
Ctrl-Shift-C (close pane), 568
Ctrl-Shift-Enter (create new column break), 568

Ctrl-Shift-F2 (shrink font), 571, 574
Ctrl-Shift-F3 (unspike), 571, 574
Ctrl-Shift-F5 (insert bookmark), 571, 573
Ctrl-Shift-F6 (previous document window), 571, 573
Ctrl-Shift-F7 (update source for include file), 571, 574
Ctrl-Shift-F8 (column selection), 337, 572
Ctrl-Shift-F9 (unlink field and replace), 572, 574
Ctrl-Shift-F10 (Ruler), 39, 151-154, 572, 574
Ctrl-Shift-F11 (unlock field), 572, 574
Ctrl-Shift-F12 (file print), 572-573
Ctrl-Shift-Hyphen (nonbreaking hyphen), 568
Ctrl-Shift-Spacebar (nonbreaking space), 568
Ctrl-Spacebar (reset to previous format), 569
Ctrl-T (hanging indent), 167, 568
Ctrl-Tab (insert tab in table), 568
Ctrl-U (underline), 570
Ctrl-V (assign color), 567
Ctrl-W (Word underline), 570
Ctrl-X (reset paragraph to default style), 569
Ctrl-Z (strikethru), 570
cursor movement, 59-60, 574-576
Delete, 568
Enter (create new paragraph), 23-24, 568
F1 (help), 44-46, 570, 573
F2 (move), 107-108, 571, 573
F3 (expand glossary name), 571-572
F4 (repeat last action), 571, 573
F5 (Go To), 61, 114, 506-508, 571, 573
F6 (next pane), 571, 573
F7 (spell check), 571, 574
F8 (expand selection), 91, 571-572
F9 (update field), 572, 574
F10 (menu), 572, 573
F11 (next field), 572-573
F12 (file save as), 572-573
function, 25
numeric keypad, 25-26
Shift, 25
Shift-Delete (cut to Clipboard), 99, 103-104, 568
Shift-Enter (create new line), 57, 143, 568
Shift-F1 (help mouse pointer), 44-46, 570, 573
Shift-F2 (copy), 109, 571-572
Shift-F3 (toggle case), 571, 574

Shift-F4 (repeat last search or go to), 113, 571, 573
Shift-F5 (go to previous insertion point), 571, 573
Shift-F6 (previous pane), 571, 573
Shift-F7 (Thesaurus), 315-316, 571, 573-574
Shift-F8 (shrink selection), 571, 574
Shift-F9 (toggle field codes view), 572, 574
Shift-F10 (icon bar in Outline view), 277-278, 281-284, 572
Shift-F11 (previous field), 572-573
Shift-F12 (file save), 66, 572-573
Shift-Insert (insert from Clipboard), 568
Shift-Insert (paste), 103-104
Spacebar, 24
Tab, 25

L–M

landscape orientation, 250-251
line breaks, 143
line numbers, 222-224
line spacing, 152, 157-161
loading documents, 428
Lock for Annotations option, 77
locking documents, 404
Macro Edit command, 518
Macro Record command, 518-519
macros, 516-517
    assigning to menus, 527-529
    creating, 518-522
    deleting, 529
    editing, 524-525
    recording, 518-522
    renaming, 525-526
    running, 516-517, 523
mailing labels, 454-459
    creating data document, 454-456
    multicolumn, 459-461
    templates, 456-459
main dictionary, 302-305
manual hyphenation, 319-320
manual numbering in outlines, 480-482
margins, 133-143
    Document command, 139-143
    Print Preview, 138-140
    Ruler, 136-137
math, 351-353
    columns, 352-353
    formulas, 356-358
    operators, 352
maximizing windows, 42-43
maximizing Word, 43
menu bar, 14

menus
    choosing, 14
    choosing commands, 13
    customizing, 529-530
    Document Control, 12-13, 31
    Edit, 32-34, 94-95
    File, 32
    Format, 34, 131-134
    Full, 30-31
    Help, 35-36, 45-46
    Insert, 34
    Macros, 35
    Short, 30-31
    Utilities, 34
    View, 36-40
    Window, 35
    Word Control, 12-13
merge printing, 440-449
merging styles, 391-392
Microsoft Paint, 554-556
minimizing windows, 42-43
minimizing Word, 42-43
monospace fonts, 202-203
mouse
    choosing commands, 29
    clicking, 27
    cropping pictures, 544-546
    double-clicking, 28
    dragging, 27
    pointers, 9-11
    pointing, 27
    scaling pictures, 544-546
    scrolling text, 58-59
    selecting text, 90
    setting tab stops, 170
Move To command, 106-110
moving annotations, 403
moving text, 101-110
multicolumn mailing labels, 459-461
multicolumn text, 215-222
multiple level index entries, 499-501

N

naming files, 64-65
naming styles, 375-377
newsletters, 220-222
nonbreaking hyphenation, 320-322
Normal Editing view, 14-17
normal hyphenation, 320-322
numeric keypad, 25-26

O

opening documents, 78-80
opening multiple documents, 428-430
optional hyphenation, 320-322

Index

orientation
   landscape, 250-251
   portrait, 250-251
outlines/Outline view, 16, 19, 465-482
   automatic numbering, 478-480
   collapsing, 473-474
   creating, 470-472
   creating tables of contents, 487-489
   creating outlines, 473
   expanding, 473-474
   icon bar, 467-468
   levels, 469
   manual numbering, 480-482
   printing, 482
   reorganizing, 475-477
   window, 466
Outlining command, 466-468

P

page breaks, 143
   hard, 144
   soft, 144
page numbers, 281-287
   deleting, 287
   formatting, 285-287
Page view, 15-17, 232-235
   editing text, 234-235
   screen elements, 233-234
   scrolling text, 235
   selecting text, 234-235
paper feed option, 263-264
paper size, 134
paragraph alignment, 152
Paragraph command, 164-165, 176-183
   aligning paragraphs, 180-182
   choosing styles, 177
   paragraph alignment, 176-177
   paragraph spacing, 178-180
   setting borders, 177, 182-183
   setting indents, 177
   setting spacing, 177
paragraph formatting, 132, 147-161
   hanging indents, 167-168
   indentation, 161-168
   justification, 154-157
   line spacing, 157-161
   Paragraph command, 164-165, 176-183
   Ruler, 147-164
   searching and replacing text, 119-121
   tab stops, 169-176
   Tabs command, 171-176
Paste command, 103-104
   annotations, 403
   tables, 340
Paste Link command, 554-556

pictures
   adding captions, 551-552
   borders, 548-549
   cropping with Format Picture command, 546-548
   cropping with mouse, 544-546
   DDE fields, 554-556
   deleting, 552-553
   inserting blank frames, 542-544
   inserting into documents, 538-544
   positioning, 549-551
   scaling with Format Picture command, 546-548
   scaling with mouse, 544-546
   TIFF graphic files, 542-544
pointing with mouse, 27
points, 188, 197-198
portrait orientation, 250-251
Position command, 225-230
positioning
   footers, 287-289
   headers, 287-289
   paragraphs, 225-228
   pictures, 549-551
   tables, 348
Preferences command, 512-513
Print command, 252-255, 263-265
   draft printing, 254
   hidden text option, 264
   Include option, 264-265
   options, 253-255
   paper feed option, 263-264
Print Merge command, 440, 447-449
Print Preview view, 15-18, 267-270
   Boundaries option, 268-269
   Cancel option, 270
   One Page/Two Page option, 270
   Page View option, 270
   positioning headers, 288-289
   Print option, 268
   setting margins, 138-140
print queue, 260-262
printer driver, 241-244
Printer Setup command, 247-251
   options, 248-251
   orientation, 250-251
printers
   connecting, 245-246
   deleting, 248
   installing, 241-244
   installing additional, 247-248
printing
   annotations, 240, 404-405
   canceling, 252, 265-266
   documents, 85-86, 240, 256-265
   draft, 254

597

field codes, 240
Find command, 258-259
form letters, 447-449
formulas, 356-357
glossaries, 240
glossary, 370
hidden text, 240, 262-264
installing printer driver, 241-244
key assignments, 240
merge printing, 440
multiple copies, 258
multiple documents, 428-430
options, 253-255
orientation, 250-251
outlines, 482
paper feed option, 263-264
Print Preview, 267-270
print queues, 260-262
selected pages, 257
selected text, 257-258
style sheets, 240, 392-393
summary information, 240
troubleshooting, 266-267
Windows spooler, 260-262
working document, 256
program files, 416
proportionally spaced fonts, 202-203

Q–R

quitting Word, 46-47
RAM (random access memory), 52
reading annotations, 402
recording macros, 518-522
redlined text, 407-408
removing revision marks, 409-411
renaming macros, 525-526
reorganizing outlines, 475-477
Replace command, 115-119
replacing text, 115-119
resizing cells in tables, 341-342
resizing columns in tables, 341-342
resizing rows in tables, 341-342
retrieving documents, 78-80
revisions/revision marks, 395, 405-411
　　accepting, 409-411
　　creating, 405-408
　　removing, 409-411
　　searching, 409-411
Ribbon, 39-40, 191-194
　　formatting headers, 280
　　icons, 192-194
root directory, 417
rows
　　deleting from tables, 339-340
　　inserting in tables, 337-339
　　resizing in tables, 341-342

Ruler, 38-39, 147-164
　　applying styles, 386-387
　　close and open space, 152
　　formatting headers, 280
　　indent markers, 151-152
　　keyboard commands, 153-154
　　line spacing, 152
　　paragraph alignment, 152
　　Ruler view, 153
　　setting margins, 136-137
　　styles, 377-379
　　tab stop, 152
Run command, 517, 523
running macros, 516-517, 523

S

saving Clipboard contents, 96
saving documents, 66-67, 77, 84-85
　　as backup, 66, 72
　　automatically, 67, 72-73
　　Fast Save option, 77
　　Lock for Annotations option, 77
　　to different directory, 67, 73-74
　　to different file, 73-74
　　to different file format, 67-68, 75-76
　　to existing file, 66, 71
　　to second disk drive, 66-67, 73-74
scaling pictures with Format Picture command, 546-548
scaling pictures with mouse, 544-546
scroll bar, 12, 58-59
scrolling text with keyboard, 59-60
scrolling text with mouse, 58-59
Search command, 111-113
searching and replacing text, 111-122, 119-121
searching for documents, 422-427
searching for revision marks, 409-411
searching text with Go To command, 114
section break mark, 212-215
Section command, 209-224
　　Columns, 210
　　Footnotes, 211
　　Line Numbers, 211, 222-224
　　multicolumn text, 215-222
　　snaking columns, 215-222
　　Starting Sections, 211
　　Vertical Alignment, 212
section formatting, 132
selecting tables for editing, 336-337
selecting text, 92-93
selecting text
　　with keyboard, 91
　　with mouse, 90
　　with selection bar, 90
setting tab stops with keyboard, 170-171

Index

setting tab stops with mouse, 170
Shift key, 25
Shift-Delete (cut to Clipboard) key, 99, 103-104, 568
Shift-Enter (create new line) key, 57, 143, 568
Shift-F (help) key, 44-46
Shift-F1 (help mouse pointer) key, 570, 573
Shift-F2 (copy) keys, 109, 571-572
Shift-F3 (toggle case) keys, 571, 574
Shift-F4 (repeat last search or go to) key, 113, 571, 573
Shift-F5 (go to previous insertion point) keys, 571, 573
Shift-F6 (previous pane) key, 571, 573
Shift-F7 (Thesaurus) key, 315-316, 571, 573-574
Shift-F8 (shrink selection) key, 571, 574
Shift-F9 (toggle field codes view) keys, 572, 574
Shift-F10 (icon bar in Outline view) key, 277-278, 281-284, 572
Shift-F11 (previous field) key, 572-573
Shift-F12 (file save) key, 66, 572-573
Shift-Insert (insert from Clipboard) key, 103-104, 568
Short menus, 30-31
sizing pictures, 544-546
Small Kaps option, 200
snaking columns, 215-222
soft page breaks, 144
sorting tables, 348-351
Spacebar, 24
special keys, 22-23
spelling checker, 302-314
    checking single words, 311
    correcting misspelled words, 307-310
    repeated misspellings, 310
    stopping, 311
    suggested corrections, 310
splitting windows, 43-44, 122-125
spooler, 260-262
spreadsheets, 353-356
    cell references, 354-356
    linking with Word, 556-557
starting Word, 4-7
status bar, 36-38
stopping spelling check, 311
strikethru text, 407-408
style sheets *See Also* Styles
styles, 189, 374-393
    applying, 384-388
    automatic, 377-379
    changing formatting, 390-391
    changing name, 389-390
    defining, 379-384

    deleting, 389
    editing, 388-392
    merging, 391-392
    naming, 375-377
    printing style sheets, 240, 392-393
    Ruler, 377-379, 386-387
Styles command, 375
subdirectories, 417
subscripts, 201-202
summary information sheet, 68-70, 419-427
    printing, 240
    updating, 421-422
superscripts, 201-202
supplemental dictionaries, 302, 312-314

T

Tab key, 25
tab stops, 134, 152, 169-176
    setting with keyboard, 170-171
    setting with mouse, 170
    setting with Tabs command, 171-176
Table command, 341-342
tables, 327-359
    adding borders, 345-347
    aligning, 348
    cells, 328-329
    consistent height, 343
    Copy command, 340
    creating, 329-335
    Cut command, 340
    decimal tabs, 344-345
    deleting columns, 339-340
    deleting rows, 339-340
    editing, 336-340
    formatting, 341-351
    formulas, 356-358
    inserting columns, 337-339
    inserting formulas, 357-358
    inserting rows, 337-339
    inserting text, 331-332
    math, 351-353
    Paste command, 340
    resizing cells, 341-342
    resizing columns, 341-342
    resizing rows, 341-342
    selecting for editing, 336-337
    sorting, 348-351
    spreadsheets, 353-356
tables of contents, 485-486
    creating, 486-496
    entry field code (tc), 490-493
Tabs command, 171-176
templates, 135, 430-434
    changing styles, 434
    creating, 431-433

editing, 433
mailing labels, 456-459
multicolumn labels, 459-461
text
   color, 201
   copying, 104-110
   cut and paste, 101-104
   deleting, 93-94, 97-99
   editing, 93-125
   entering, 54-55, 63-64
   inserting, 97-98
   moving, 101-110
   multicolumn, 215-222
   scrolling with keyboard, 59-60
   scrolling with mouse, 58-59
   searching and replacing, 111-122
   searching with Go To command, 114
   selecting, 92-93
Thesaurus, 301, 315-316
TIFF graphic files, 542-544
time headers, 282-284
title bar, 11-12
troubleshooting printing, 266-267

U

underline, 200
Undo command, 110-111
undoing hyphenation, 324-325
unlocking documents, 404
updating summary information sheet, 421-422
user dictionaries, 301, 311-314
Utilities menu, 34

V

varying headers and footers by section, 290-292

View Annotation command, 402
View Draft command, 468
View menu, 36-40
views
   Draft, 16-18
   Galley, 14-15
   Normal Editing, 14-17
   Outline, 16-19, 465-489
   Page, 15-17, 232-235
   Print Preview, 15-18, 267-270

W-Z

widows and orphans, 135, 144-145
Windows, 40
   activating, 41
   changing size, 41-42
   closing, 41
   maximizing, 42-43
   minimizing, 42-43
   splitting, 43-44, 122-125
Windows spooler, 260-262
Word
   exiting, 46-47
   installing run-time version, 564-566
   installing with Windows installed, 561-564
   linking with Microsoft Paint, 554-557
   linking with spreadsheets, 556-557
   maximizing, 43
   minimizing, 42-43
Word Control menu, 12-13
word processing, 52-54
x-height, 188